CW01261516

Claude Debussy

Claude Debussy

A Critical Biography

François Lesure

English Translation and Revised Edition
by Marie Rolf

UNIVERSITY OF ROCHESTER PRESS

The University of Rochester Press gratefully acknowledges generous support from the Eastman School of Music, University of Rochester; and the James R. Anthony Endowment of the American Musicological Society, funded in part by the National Endowment for the Humanities and the Andrew W. Mellon Foundation.

Translation copyright © 2019 Marie Rolf

All rights reserved. Except as permitted under current legislation, no part of this work may be photocopied, stored in a retrieval system, published, performed in public, adapted, broadcast, transmitted, recorded, or reproduced in any form or by any means, without the prior permission of the copyright owner.

First published 2019

Original French-language edition: *Claude Debussy: Biographie critique* by François Lesure. World copyright © Librairie Artheme Fayard, 2003

University of Rochester Press
668 Mt. Hope Avenue, Rochester, NY 14620, USA
www.urpress.com
and Boydell & Brewer Limited
PO Box 9, Woodbridge, Suffolk IP12 3DF, UK
www.boydellandbrewer.com

ISBN-13: 978-1-58046-903-6
ISSN: 1071-9989

Library of Congress Cataloging-in-Publication Data

Names: Lesure, François. author.
Title: Claude Debussy : a critical biography / François Lesure ; English translation and revised edition by Marie Rolf.
Other titles: Eastman studies in music ; v. 159.
Description: Rochester : University of Rochester Press, 2019. | Series: Eastman studies in music ; v. 159 | Includes bibliographical references and index.
Identifiers: LCCN 2019005306 | ISBN 9781580469036 (hardcover : alk. paper)
Subjects: LCSH: Debussy, Claude, 1862–1918. | Composers—France—Biography.
Classification: LCC ML410.D28 L4313 2019 | DDC 780.92 [B] —dc23 LC record available at https://lccn.loc.gov/2019005306

This publication is printed on acid-free paper.
Printed in the United States of America.

Contents

	Preface to the Translation and Revised Edition	xi
	Introduction	1
1	An Unsettled Childhood: 1862–72	3
	The Parents	4
	Cannes	5
	The Commune	7
	Antoinette Mauté	9
	Genealogy	12
2	Failure of a Pianist: 1872–79	13
	A Ten-Year-Old Child at the Conservatoire	14
	Marmontel's Class	14
	First Concerts at Chauny	18
	A Second Prize in Piano	21
	Durand's Class	23
	First Friends at School	24
	Stay in Chenonceaux	26
3	Birth of a Composer: 1880–82	28
	First Prize in Accompanying	28
	The Villa Oppenheim in Florence	32
	Guiraud's Class	33
	Accompanist for Mme Moreau-Sainti	34
	Marie Vasnier	35
	First Visit to Russia	38
	Songs for Marie	40
4	The Path to the Prix de Rome: 1882–84	42
	Second Visit to Russia	43
	A Second Prize in the Prix de Rome	45
	The Concordia	47
	A Rebel at the Conservatoire	50
	L'enfant prodigue and the Prodigal Son	52
	Farewell to Marie	54

5	The Villa Medici: 1885–87	58
	Ernest and Gabrielle Hébert	60
	The "Begging Dog"	61
	Visitors at the Villa	64
	The Second Year	65
	The End of the Residency in Rome	67
6	Beginning of the Bohemian Period: 1887–89	71
	Achille and His Family	72
	Classmates and Friends	73
	The *Ariettes* and Bayreuth	74
	La damoiselle élue	75
	A Life in the Cafés	76
	The Pousset Tavern	78
	Chez Thommen	79
	From the *Ariettes* to the *Cinq poèmes*	80
	The 1889 World's Fair	82
	Conversations with Guiraud	84
7	From Baudelaire to Mallarmé: 1890–91	85
	The *Fantaisie* for Piano	86
	Rodrigue et Chimène	87
	Gaby Dupont	89
	The Librairie de l'art indépendant	90
	The Chat Noir	92
	Mallarmé	93
	Several Publications and a Commission	95
	Discovery of Maeterlinck	97
8	Esotericism and Symbolism: 1892	99
	Occultist Circles	100
	A Home: The Rue de Londres	103
	American Project	104
9	The Chausson Year: 1893	107
	Premiere of *La damoiselle élue*	108
	Performances of Wagner	108
	Visits to Luzancy	110
	Boris Godunov	112
	Pelléas at the Bouffes-Parisiens	113
	The Beginnings of Debussy's *Pelléas*	114
	The String Quartet	116

10	A "Fairy Tale" Gone Awry: 1894	118
	Bourgeois Interactions	118
	Concert in Brussels	120
	Engagement to Thérèse Roger	121
	The Breakup and Its Ripple Effects	123
	Return to *Pelléas* and the *Marche écossaise*	125
	Georges Hartmann	127
	Premiere of the *Prélude à l'après-midi d'un faune*	128
11	Pierre Louÿs; The Lean Years: 1895–96	130
	The Limits of a Friendship	131
	New Performance of the *Prélude*	133
	Collaborative Projects with Louÿs—*Œdipe à Colone*	135
	Cendrelune	135
	Daphnis et Chloë	136
	Aphrodite	137
	La saulaie	137
12	*Pelléas*—The Long Wait: 1895–98	140
	The Fontaines	140
	Life with Gaby	142
	Works in Progress	144
	A Plan to Get the Opera Performed (1895)	146
	Other Plans for *Pelléas*	148
13	From Bachelorhood to Marriage: 1897–99	150
	Some Publications	150
	Frères en art	152
	Nuits blanches	153
	A Year of Change: 1899	154
	Lilly Texier	155
	A Love Slowly Shared	157
	Marriage to Lilly	160
14	*Nocturnes*: 1900–1901	162
	Genesis of the *Nocturnes*	162
	Hope for *Pelléas*	163
	La damoiselle élue at the World's Fair	165
	Premiere of the First Two *Nocturnes*	166
	The Programming of *Pelléas*	167
	Premiere of the Three *Nocturnes*	168

15	The Composer as Critic: 1901–3	170
	Compositional Activities at the Beginning of 1901	170
	Critic at *La revue blanche*	171
	Monsieur Croche	173
	Critic for *Gil Blas*	175
	Emergence of the "National Tradition"	176
16	*Pelléas et Mélisande*: 1902	179
	Albert Carré and the Opéra-Comique	180
	Rehearsals for *Pelléas*	181
	Conflict with Maeterlinck	182
	The Birth of *Pelléas*	184
	Critical Reception of *Pelléas*	187
	The "Bataillon sacré"	188
	Visit to London	190
	A Summer in Bichain	191
	The Revival of *Pelléas*	192
17	From the *Fêtes galantes* to *La mer*: 1903	195
	First Consequences of Fame	195
	Concerts in Paris and in the Provinces	197
	New Works: The *Images*	199
	A Very Productive Summer: *La mer*	202
	Return to Paris and Initial Encounters with Emma Bardac	205
18	Debussyism; A New Life: 1904	207
	Debussy's Increasing Visibility and Influence	207
	The "Pelléastres"	210
	Emma Bardac	212
	The Lovers Escape to Jersey	215
	The Drama of the Breakup	218
19	*La mer*: 1905	221
	The Divorce and Its Consequences	221
	Concerts and Critics	224
	The Premiere of *La mer*	226
	Settling into the Avenue du Bois de Boulogne	229
20	Projects and Skirmishes: 1906–7	230
	New Relationships	230
	The Growing Fame of *Pelléas*	233
	New Controversies	235
	Debussy–Ravel	237
	The *Roman de Tristan*	239

21	Orchestra Conductor: 1908	241
	Taking the Plunge: Marrying Emma and Conducting *La mer*	241
	Pelléas Abroad	242
	Images for Piano (Second Series) and Further Dissemination of *Pelléas*	244
	Projects and Interviews	247
22	"The Procrastination Syndrome": 1909	250
	Concert in London	251
	Operatic Projects	252
	La chute de la maison Usher	255
	Laloy's Book and *Le cas Debussy*	256
	Works for Piano	258
23	Orchestral *Images* and Piano *Préludes*: 1910	260
	Premieres of "Ibéria" and "Rondes de printemps"	260
	Préludes, Book One, for Piano	262
	Foreign Composers in Paris	264
	Relationship with Emma in Crisis	266
	Maud Allan and *Khamma*	268
	Trip to Vienna and Budapest	269
	Proliferation of Concerts in Paris and Beyond	271
24	*Le martyre de saint Sébastien*: 1911	273
	Origins of *Le martyre*	273
	Concerts and Performers	275
	Rehearsals and the Premiere of *Le martyre*	277
	Trip to Turin	280
	Stay in Houlgate	281
25	The Year of the Ballets: 1912	284
	L'après-midi d'un faune	286
	Igor Stravinsky	288
	The Origins of *Jeux*	289
	Critic for the *S. I. M.* Journal	291
26	*Jeux*; Travel to Russia: 1913	294
	Completion and Premiere of the *Images* for Orchestra	295
	Préludes, Book Two, and *La boîte à joujoux*	297
	Premiere of *Jeux*	298
	Financial Distress	301
	Trip to Russia	304

27	The Final Trips: 1914	309
	From One Project to Another	309
	Trip to Rome	311
	Trip to the Netherlands	312
	Debussy the Pianist	314
	An American Interview	316
28	The War; Pourville: 1914–15	319
	Stay in Angers	319
	An Unexpectedly Productive Summer	322
	An Operation	324
29	"The Factories of Nothingness": 1916–18	327
	Visits and an Invalid's Torments	328
	Stay in Le Moulleau	330
	Satie: *Parade*	332
	The Chalet Habas	334
	The Last Months	335
	Postlude	338
Notes		341
Index of Works		507
Subject Index		511

Preface to the Translation and Revised Edition

François Lesure's legacy of Debussy scholarship is breathtaking in its scope and impact. His lifelong passion for Debussy's music and creative development manifested itself in numerous activities and publications, including his painstaking assemblage of thousands of letters written by and to the composer; his founding and oversight of a complete and critical edition of Debussy's works; his publication of Debussy's music criticism; his organization of exhibitions devoted to the composer; and his launch of the *Cahiers Debussy*, a journal devoted to Debussy scholarship.

Claude Debussy: A Critical Biography is Lesure's magnum opus. As director of the département de la Musique at the Bibliothèque nationale de France for nearly twenty years, he was in a unique position to study primary materials that were often unavailable to other scholars. Situated at the hub of Debussy research, he fostered and absorbed the pathbreaking work of many other experts in the field. His critical biography of Debussy thus consolidates sources and scholarship that advance our knowledge and understanding of the composer and his works far beyond any other biography to date. At last, the present English translation makes this seminal work accessible to the wide audience it deserves.

Lesure himself acknowledges his debt to earlier biographers of Debussy, including Léon Vallas, Marcel Dietschy, and Edward Lockspeiser. Nonetheless, his access to primary source materials—items such as the journals of Madame Hébert and Marguerite de Saint-Marceaux, and especially letters, such as those to and from Debussy's first wife Lilly as well as to his early publisher Georges Hartmann—that were unknown by these biographers enabled Lesure to explode a number of long-held beliefs and myths about the composer. The reader can almost imagine the author methodically working through Debussy's life experiences, day by day, following Debussy's copious correspondence. Unlike previous biographers, who tiptoed over some of the more unsavory aspects of Debussy's life, Lesure objectively chronicles the composer's activities and his opinions of other composers and performers. Lesure's account, like that of Vallas, documents the critical reception of Debussy's works, and, more than most biographies, fleshes out the cultural context in which the composer developed.

The present revised edition builds on the remarkable foundation established by Lesure. It includes new or updated information regarding, for example, the circumstances surrounding the composition of Debussy's *Marche écossaise* and *Suite bergamasque*, the completion of *L'isle joyeuse*, and his relationship with Alice Peter. It provides chronological details of the dissolution of his marriage to Lilly and his conflict with Maeterlinck over *Pelléas*, and newly discovered annotated sources for the text of *Crimen amoris*. Nearly 2,000 new endnotes furnish or complete bibliographic details and often provide crucial contextual information for readers beyond the French-speaking world, resulting in a book that is more than a third larger than Lesure's original French text. This work could not have been achieved without access to Lesure's personal research library and notes, kindly granted to me by Anik Devriès-Lesure, who donated them to the Centre de documentation Claude Debussy. While these documents are not yet catalogued, they are now conserved in the département de la Musique at the Bibliothèque nationale de France. The Dietschy materials are similarly housed in the same repository; also formerly among the holdings of the Centre de documentation Claude Debussy, they currently retain call numbers from the latter archive.

It has been a distinct honor for me to translate and revise Lesure's biography of Debussy, especially since I was privileged to work closely with him as a member of the editorial board for the *Œuvres complètes de Claude Debussy*. Over the nineteen years that I knew François Lesure, I grew to admire him as a musicologist who relentlessly pursued accurate and complete explanations (to the extent possible) for whatever musical issues or problems he was exploring. His insistence on backing up any point he made or any conclusion he drew with hard evidence and documentation (even though he did not always bother to note it down) reflected his consummate training and professionalism as a librarian. But such serious research was invariably carried out with his characteristic wit, humor, and frequent touches of irony—qualities, incidentally, that he shared with Debussy. And, again like our composer, while M. Lesure did not suffer fools gladly, once a fellow scholar earned his trust and respect by proving one's scholarly and musical abilities, he was exceedingly generous; in Lesure's case, that meant sharing his vast knowledge of source material, both primary and secondary, catalogued and uncatalogued. One small example of these qualities still brings a smile to my face: in the 1990s, as my editorial work on a volume for the critical edition was already well advanced, Lesure sent me a photocopy of some corrected proofs, a hitherto completely unknown source, for the work in question; knowing that this new source, while important and most welcome, would slow my progress on the edition, he attempted to soften the blow by adding a charming little poem, allegedly composed by "Claude Debussy":

PREFACE TO THE TRANSLATION AND REVISED EDITION   xiii

Pour Marie Rolf, petite mienne[1]
qui me corrige si bien
C. D.

I can only hope that M. Lesure would have been pleased with the additions and corrections that I have made to his own work in the present translation and revised edition.

Readers who study the table of contents in the present edition will notice some changes in the organization of the book. Lesure's original thirty chapters have been consolidated into twenty-nine; several chapters have been reordered and, in some cases, given new titles and/or subtitles of sections. The main reason for these changes is to preserve the chronological approach that Lesure himself established from the outset, but that he abandoned after his chapter 12 (covering 1897–98); at that point, he inserted a chapter on The Long Wait for *Pelléas*, then a chapter covering 1899–1900, followed by three chapters— on the topics of M. Croche, the *Frères en art* play, and *Pelléas*—before jumping to 1903 for his chapter 18. This chronological interruption in Lesure's book likely occurred because the first sixteen chapters were taken over from his first biography of Debussy, *Claude Debussy avant "Pelléas" ou les années symbolistes* (Klincksieck, 1992). Because Lesure's 1992 biography ended with the composition of *Pelléas*, his abandonment of a chronological approach was scarcely noticeable; however, it becomes an issue in his fully developed critical biography of 2003. In the present revised edition, chapters 12–17 (covering, with some overlap, the years from 1895 to 1903) are recast to follow a chronological order but also to limit the amount of switching back and forth from one topic to another that lends a disjunct quality to Lesure's original French edition. When appropriate, material in other chapters is reordered, usually reflecting newly ascribed dates for the letters cited (Lesure and Herlin's edition of Claude Debussy, *Correspondance, 1872–1918* [Paris: Gallimard, 2005] appeared after Lesure's 2003 biography of Debussy was published). Lastly, for reasons of space limitations, the final reflective sections in the original publication (titled "The Man in His Time" and "Conclusion") are omitted from the present volume; plans are underway to publish a translation of these sections separately. Similarly, the catalog of works is not included.

With respect to the translation, whenever possible I have tried to preserve Lesure's authorial voice, infused with its slightly ironic tone. His assumption that the reader would possess something equivalent to his own musical and historical knowledge often calls for expanded commentary, as does his laconic writing style. Indeed, some passages are so terse and obtuse that they might elude even a professional translator (which I make no claim to being) but that might well be surmised by a Debussy specialist who is intimately familiar with the topic. In addition, Lesure's tendency to pack multiple ideas within a single sentence necessitated some editorial license that involved breaking up long constructions and at times reordering the material to render the meaning more clearly. French institutions are referred to by their original names (such as the Conservatoire, the Académie des beaux-arts, the Institut de France, the Bibliothèque nationale de France, or the Théâtre des Champs-Élysées) rather than in translation. Similarly, titles of nobility are often kept in some French form (for example, the Princesse de Polignac or the Marquise de Clermont-Tonnerre), as are certain terms (such as the *concours* at the Conservatoire or the *envois* submitted by the winners of the Prix de Rome) because their usage is so common in both French and English. Titles of musical compositions and other works are generally given in their original language (e.g., *Das Rheingold* rather than *L'or du Rhin*) and French titles of works that are well known (e.g., *La mer*) are not translated into English.

The following editorial principles have been observed with respect to the text, the sources and their bibliographic references, as well as contextual information that is editorially added. Minimal editorial additions and emendations are made tacitly in Lesure's text, although major new sections are identified within brackets. In general, primary sources are privileged over the secondary literature, regardless of how they were cited in Lesure's original French edition. Whenever possible, updated sources are referenced; this principle applies most often to Debussy's complete correspondence, published after Lesure's death. While his 2003 biography (abbreviated as FL 2003 in the endnotes) cites many disparate sources in which Debussy's letters were formerly accessible, the present English translation and revised edition refers the reader to the comprehensive Claude Debussy *Correspondance, 1872–1918* (cited above), abbreviated as *C* throughout the endnotes. In instances where Lesure offers incomplete bibliographic information (e.g., lacking date, journal name, title, and/or author), I tacitly complete the citation. If Lesure gives no citation, I add one, signaling that the information is provided by "MR." When contextual or bibliographic information is editorially added either at the beginning or in the middle of an endnote, it is printed within square brackets. Similarly, square brackets are used for editorial additions within quoted passages. All bona fide ellipses, whether added editorially or in Lesure's original publication, are indicated by three spaced dots within square brackets: [. . .]. They are distinct from the French convention of suspension points, which do not indicate any missing material but rather a trailing off or a punctuation of the writer's thought. Suspension points appear in this book as three spaced dots without square brackets. Due to the enormous number of endnotes, many of which cite sources (such as reviews) only once, I give full references for the first mention of the source and shortened citations thereafter, within each chapter. Following this editorial procedure in lieu of adding a bibliography will limit the reader's need to flip through different sections of the book.

PREFACE TO THE TRANSLATION AND REVISED EDITION   XV

Rendering François Lesure's monumental biography of Claude Debussy into idiomatic English, updating its contents, and completing its bibliographic apparatus would not have been possible without the considerable cooperation and assistance of many individuals. Anik Devriès-Lesure, herself an accomplished musicologist, enthusiastically endorsed the project from its inception, not only giving me "carte blanche" in my work but also opening up François Lesure's research library to me. Anik personally spent a great deal of time assisting the librarians at the département de la Musique of the Bibliothèque nationale de France in identifying the documents within numerous boxes that comprise the Fonds Lesure.

Debussy colleagues around the world have generously proofread chapters, tweaking the translation and sharing their expertise on specific compositions or periods of Debussy's creative development. Denis Herlin took many hours and days out of his busy life to share his consummate bibliographic knowledge and to track down obscure sources that more often than not were available only in France. He also patiently clarified thorny passages in the translation, as did Mylène Dubiau, with whom I had many long and productive Skype sessions. Marianne Wheeldon graciously offered to read the chapters covering the last ten years of Debussy's life, and enthusiastically shared discoveries made when we were both working at the département de la Musique in summer 2018. David Grayson painstakingly sifted through the chapters surrounding *Pelléas*, with respect to both the translation and the accuracy of information conveyed, and helped identify obscure references. Helen Abbott, Jonathan Dunsby, Sylvia Kahan, and Richard Langham Smith each read specific chapters, offering alternative idiomatic translations for certain passages. And Peter Bloom fielded the occasional query from me, often sent late at night as I found myself stumped by a particular passage in French; invariably, a reply would be awaiting me by the next morning.

In similar fashion, many other colleagues responded to specific questions involving sources. I am grateful to John Clevenger, who reviewed the citations in the first four chapters that concerned documents in the Archives nationales, and to Jacek Blaszkiewicz, who ferreted out details of some of the reports made by Debussy's professors at the Conservatoire. Numerous other research questions were ably fielded by Myriam Chimènes, Chris Collins, Manuel Cornejo, Pauline Girard, D. Kern Holoman, Roy Howat, Barbara Kelly, François Le Roux, Kerry Murphy, Jean-Michel Nectoux, and Robert Orledge. Simon Morrison and Olga Shupyatskaya lent their expertise with respect to Russian translation and sources, especially concerning Debussy's experiences with Madame von Meck while a student at the Conservatoire and his trip to Saint Petersburg and Moscow in 1913.

At some point, every researcher experiences the sensation of looking for a needle in a haystack, and this project provided ample such episodes for me.

No reference was too daunting, however, for the professional librarians who assisted in my quest. I am indebted to Mathias Auclair, Benoit Cote-Colisson, Laurence Decobert, Séverine Forlani, Elizabeth Giuliani, and Catherine Vallet-Collot at the département de la Musique of the Bibliothèque nationale de France (Paris), Fran Barulich at the Morgan Library & Museum (New York), James Farrington and Robert Iannapollo at the Sibley Music Library (at the University of Rochester's Eastman School of Music, Rochester, New York), and Kimberly Tully at the Paley Library (Temple University, Philadelphia) for rising to every bibliographic challenge posed to them. Individual documents were located and shared or scanned by Thierry Bodin, Manuel Erviti, Simon Maguire, Jann Pasler, and Ross Wood; and Alexandra Laederich (former curator of the Centre de documentation Claude Debussy) facilitated introductions to the librarians who could help retrieve items from the Fonds Lesure for me.

A number of individuals helped bring this project from its inception to its final realization. Louise Goldberg (former managing editor for the University of Rochester Press) and Joan Campbell Huguet assisted with the translation through its early stages, Gilad Rabinovitch helped locate many sources, and Samuel Reenan provided both translation and research assistance throughout, in addition to proofreading the manuscript and indexing the volume. I am especially indebted to Ralph P. Locke, whose combined expertise as an editor, musicologist, and translator was perfectly pitched to this project. His constant (often daily) encouragement, enthusiasm, and objective assessment of my work sustained me over several years. Thanks also go to Sonia Kane and Julia Cook, editorial director and managing editor, respectively, at the University of Rochester Press, for their support and expert advice, and to Carrie Crompton, copyeditor extraordinaire.

Family and friends with French language fluency contributed much to this project as well. I am thankful to Karin Demorest, Alex Haas, Kate Lehman, and Phillip Lehman for helping to decode particularly difficult passages and for explaining various nuances of French language and culture. My husband Robin Lehman demonstrated his devotion and fortitude by listening to me read the entire book aloud, identifying awkward passages and suggesting improvements. No words can adequately express my immense gratitude to him and my profound joy in sharing our lives and work with each other. Each in their own way, our beloved children have also supported our various artistic endeavors, and continue to enrich our lives beyond measure.

Last but not least, the Eastman School of Music of the University of Rochester provided financial subventions for this publication. I am grateful for a Professional Development grant as well as Music Theory Research funds that have facilitated this project.

Marie Rolf

Introduction

Debussy's life was hardly the stuff of storybooks. Rather, it was the life of an artist who sacrificed nearly everything for his work. While it is commonly accepted that his compositions opened the path to the music of the twentieth century, Debussy's personality, as described in the writings that have been devoted to him, remains enshrouded in grey areas, due in particular to his relatively unstable private life.

Productive periods alternated with moments of uncontrolled uncertainty in his life, which can be understood only by establishing a rigorous chronology of the known facts. We have thus attempted to present Debussy on a day-by-day basis, somewhat in the style of a chronicle, based on his letters as well as on the catalog of his works. There is a great disparity between the years of his youth and those following *Pelléas*. During the former, although living a very difficult life, he continued to strive for a rigorous artistic ideal and fiercely sought the paths that would allow him to attain it. After 1904, he appears to be a victim of his success as well as of the new social status that was imposed upon him and that hindered his creative development. Most of his contemporaries thought that he was simply becoming gentrified and that he had opted for material ease and conjugal bliss. In reality, in spite of the satisfaction he felt in having successfully completed the *Images* for orchestra or the *Préludes* and the *Études* for piano, he often regretted not having maintained "that calm self-confidence, which is an admirable strength,"[1] and not having succeeded in eliminating, as he expressed it, "all that consumes the best parts of my thought."[2] If we add to this the slow progression of a terrible illness, his fate seems rather tragic, and we are not surprised to read, over the years, on his face as well as in his words, his sadness at no longer being able to satisfy a "desire always to go further, which took the place of bread and wine for me."[3]

No full-scale biography of Debussy has been attempted for more than thirty years. Since that time, scholarly studies have proliferated and numerous documents have come to light concerning the composer, his circle, and the context in which he developed artistically. Enough time has passed following his death that any reasons for discretion, which for too long have made it difficult to learn about important events in his life, no longer exist. At the same time, many oft-implied innuendos concerning the man can be cleared up, allowing us to understand better his complex and fragile nature. In this quest, the systematic expansion of his correspondence has proved to be fruitful, restoring many cuts in those letters already published and especially revealing new sources, such as his letters to the publisher Hartmann and to his first wife, to which his three primary biographers—Vallas, Lockspeiser, and Dietschy—could not have had access; even short notes he jotted down can prove to be valuable in confirming a contact or establishing a date.

In subtitling this book a "critical biography," we have endeavored to draw attention to this documentary effort and to emphasize that the firsthand evidence has been reexamined. Debussy's works, their genesis, and their dissemination are repositioned in the context of the composer's life, with special attention to the musicians who performed his works and to the inferences that can be made from how these compositions were interpreted, for better or worse. The numerous unfinished projects on which he worked have also been considered, so that we can better grasp the progression of his plans and hopes, as well as understand how these projects impeded his progress on other scores. In addition, we have considered the reception of his compositions, which allows us to follow the slow acceptance of his latest works and the reasons why they were rejected or misunderstood in much of the criticism published in France and abroad (at least, to the extent that we were able to ascertain). Our scrutiny of the press also enables us to give a sense of how involved Debussy was—voluntarily or not—in the artistic disputes of his time.

Our account most often focuses on the firsthand remarks of the persons concerned—remarks whose full meaning is revealed only when they are juxtaposed with intersecting events and opinions. To that end, this study includes numerous citations from Debussy's correspondence as well as his music criticism (*Monsieur Croche et autres écrits*).[4] The first twelve chapters of this book are essentially adapted from François Lesure, *Claude Debussy avant "Pelléas" ou les années symbolistes* (Klincksieck, 1992), with various additions and corrections (and with the omission of the text of the play *Frères en art*).[5]

Finally, after nearly thirty years of Debussy research, I am happy to remember the friendly working relationship that I shared with three of my predecessors: Stefan Jarociński, André Schaeffner, and Edward Lockspeiser. Although they are now deceased, I am indebted to each of them for various reasons.

François Lesure

Chapter One

An Unsettled Childhood

1862–72

For more than two centuries, many members of the Debussy—or de Bussy—clan lived within a rather narrow triangle of Burgundy, circumscribed by Benoisey, Semur, and Montbard. This was in the Auxois, a highly distinctive region of Burgundy, where the peasants had the reputation of being "reserved, stubborn, inherently individualistic, rather xenophobic," readily anticlerical while remaining attached to religious traditions, and having a proclivity for jokes and banter.[1] From the beginning of the seventeenth century, the Debussys had settled there, as farmers or winegrowers, but the farthest back we can trace the direct lineage of Achille-Claude is to Benoisey, that is, to the sixth generation (see the family tree on p. 12). The first family member to give up the plow was Pierre (identified as Pierre I on the family tree), who left his birthplace around 1760 to settle down as a farrier at Semur-en-Auxois.[2] Just before 1800, his son, who had the same first name, took the decisive step of leaving the Burgundian region and settling in Paris as a locksmith.

Claude-Alexandre, the grandfather of our composer, was born in 1812. He practiced his trade as a carpenter in the capital, after having been a wine merchant for a few years in Montrouge, where Manuel-Achille, who would become Claude's father, was born in 1836.[3] It is rather by chance that Achille-Claude Debussy was born in Saint-Germain-en-Laye. His parents had settled in that town shortly after they were wed on 30 November 1861, and they were to leave it two years later. Among such ancestors, the presence of a musician is difficult to explain.

There is no mystery about the family's origins. As they stemmed from the purest peasant stock, their becoming modest craftsmen or small shopkeepers could hardly be described as moving up in society. In any case, there was not even the faintest glimmer of a family member awakening to an artistic calling, even taking into account the fact that Manuel-Achille enjoyed going to see Ferdinand Herold's *Le pré aux clercs* or Gaetano Donizetti's *La fille du régiment* and that he had a "natural penchant" for music.[4] We should mention, however, that one of the paternal uncles of the composer, Jules-Alexandre (1849–1907), emigrated to England after the war of 1870 and practiced the profession of "artist musician" in Manchester.

The Parents

Hardly anxious to follow the traditional trade of his father's family, Manuel-Achille, at eighteen years of age, enlisted for seven years in the second infantry regiment of the marines. Only a marked taste for adventure could have set him on that path; he brought back many memories of an expedition "overseas," but we do not know precisely which faraway seas they were. In 1861, he returned to civilian life and reunited, at Levallois, with Victorine Manoury, the daughter of a wheelwright and a cook, whom he would marry several months later at Clichy.[5] Very soon thereafter, the young couple settled in Saint-Germain-en-Laye, at 38 rue au Pain, where they sold faience. There, on 22 August 1862 at 4:30 a.m., Achille-Claude was born. The father went out right away, at 11:00 a.m., to register his son at the town hall. As the couple had no actual relatives in town, Manuel asked two of the neighboring shopkeepers to serve as witnesses: André François Mallet, a carpenter, and Ambroise Fabre, an umbrella seller.[6] The mayor, J.-X. Saguez de Breuvery, declared in the register that "the infant was presented to us."[7]

Achille-Claude was baptized in Saint-Germain on 31 July 1864, nearly two years after his birth and even after the baptism of his sister Adèle, who was born eleven months after him. This oft-questioned delay can perhaps be explained by the couple's lack of religious convictions. They took care to correct this oversight at the insistence of the young child's aunt.[8]

In any event, this matter was the source of an unusual controversy. The baptismal certificate bears the name of Achille Arosa (thirty-five years old) as godfather and that of a certain Octavie de la Ferronnière as the godmother. The latter was none other than the child's aunt—Clémentine de Bussy, twenty-nine years of age, and a seamstress. If in this particular case she took a pseudonym, it was no doubt because the godfather did not wish to draw attention to the liaison that he had with her. From there it was only one step further to imagine that there was some secret surrounding the birth of the composer, that someone had wanted to hide the fact that Arosa was in fact his father. There is nothing to this hushed controversy, one that was somewhat encouraged by

Debussy's lifelong silence, with members of his circle, on the subject of his origins.[9]

Achille Arosa, whose father was Spanish, was an agent of transferable shares—called a *coulissier* (outside broker) at the time. He lived comfortably, in contrast to the very modest lifestyle of the Debussys. He surely helped them and offered his godchild presents that his parents were unable to give him— perhaps the tricycle, memorialized for us in a photograph, or the painter's palette that Debussy kept until his first marriage. Arosa possessed a taste for painting that led him to become a genuine collector. This inclination ran in the family: his older brother Gustave, a stockbroker, would assume the guardianship of Paul Gauguin in 1871. Be that as it may, the liaison between Arosa and Clémentine scarcely lasted beyond 1868—Debussy was, after all, only six years old at the time—because she soon became involved with a maître d'hôtel in Cannes, Alfred Roustan, whom she married two years later. Arosa's "education" of Achille, as well as the bourgeois and elegant atmosphere in which it would have unfolded, is therefore surely a myth, as is Achille's "discovery" of Arosa's collection of paintings at Saint-Cloud or in Cannes, where the latter never lived. In any case, Achille must not have heard anything further about his godfather, who, according to his son, was put off by Achille's "distant manner" and was said to have nicknamed him "*l'arsouille*" (the rascal).[10]

Business in Saint-Germain having proved to be mediocre at best, the Debussys gave their faience shop back to their predecessor at the end of 1864 and lodged with Madame Manoury in Clichy. We subsequently find them, on 19 September 1867, at 11 rue de Vintimille, where Emmanuel, their third child, was born.[11] Manuel then found employment as a salesman of kitchen supplies, while his wife worked as a seamstress just to make ends meet. Finally, in 1868 he began working at the print shop of Paul Dupont,[12] one of the first print shops in France to be conceived on a capitalist model and which had obtained a virtual monopoly for official publication. Manuel took up residence at 69 rue Saint-Honoré, not far from his place of work. This would be the highpoint of his "career," for it was the only stable job that he would have during his lifetime.

Cannes

Sometime before 1870, Victorine had entrusted her daughter Adèle to her sister-in-law Clémentine. No doubt, the latter had offered to help her out. Settled in Cannes, where she was already living with Alfred Roustan, Clémentine led a grander lifestyle than that of her Parisian family. In addition, she was generous by nature and loved children much more freely than did her sister-in-law Victorine, who kept Achille and Emmanuel (her favorite children) under her wing. At the very beginning of 1870, leaving her husband in Paris, Victorine departed with her children to join Clémentine on the French Riviera, where she brought into the world her fourth child, Alfred, on 16 February.

During this time, Manuel remained in Paris, where he had chosen to live with his father. The Franco-Prussian war broke out in July; soon thereafter, in September 1870, came the battle of Sedan,[13] the proclamation of the Republic, and the beginning of the siege of Paris. The Dupont print shop laid off its employees on 15 November. Finding himself without a job, Manuel accepted a modest post in the army, supplying provisions at the town hall of the first arrondissement, which would become one of the strongholds of the Commune.

Did Achille make one or two sojourns to Cannes during this period? Some have maintained that the absence of his signature at the bottom of his brother Alfred's baptismal certificate, dated 24 April 1870, implies that he had returned to Paris at that point in time.[14] This argument is not very convincing when we consider the following incontrovertible remark made by Debussy in 1909: "It was at the age of eight that I made my *first* and *only* visit to Cannes, in the South of France."[15] It is highly probable that, at this time when Manuel had almost no means of support, there was practically no other solution for the rest of the family but to remain in Cannes with the child's aunt, while, with the siege scarcely over, the Prussian army was preparing to occupy the capital.

Young Achille's most striking memories date from this visit. Forty years later, he mentioned them to his publisher Jacques Durand:

> I remember the railroad passing in front of the house and the sea on the distant horizon, which at times gave the impression that the railroad emerged from or entered into the sea (depending on your point of view).
>
> Then there was also the road to Antibes, with so many roses that, in my entire life, I've never seen so many of them at once—the fragrance along that road was always "intoxicating."
>
> [. . . And there was] a Norwegian carpenter who sang from evening till morning.[16]

Astonishing memories, in which one detects the sense of seeing, the sense of hearing, and the sense of smell all at the same time.

It was also Aunt Clémentine who sought out, if not discovered, Achille's musical aptitude.[17] While we do not know how this innate ability could have been detected in a rather sullen child, Achille himself memorialized the name of the unknown musician who had taught him the basic rudiments.

Around 1908, when Louis Laloy asked him several questions about his childhood years for the biography that he was preparing, Debussy remembered perfectly well an "old Italian teacher named Cerutti."[18] Jean Cerutti was in fact only forty-two years old; a violinist, he had married a young German woman and lived in Cannes in a house with a painter and two "artists."[19] This modest musician—still according to Debussy's confessions to Laloy—found "nothing remarkable" in the child.[20] This is hardly a surprise; though he had some musical facility, Achille was by no means a child prodigy, and his years at the Conservatoire would confirm this.[21] Other than pursuing a career as a sailor, essentially an extension of Manuel's youthful adventures, the only option for Debussy's life that suited both him and his parents was a career as a musician.[22] Later, he asserted that he regretted not having pursued painting.[23] To an interviewer from the *New York Times*, who in 1910 questioned him on his childhood, he replied: "I was quite an ordinary child in every way, very disobedient and very confident that my ideas were right."[24]

The Commune

In Paris, the situation had quickly become dangerous for Manuel. The insurrection of the Commune broke out several days after his boss at the town hall in the first arrondissement issued him a certificate, taking note "of his work, integrity, and productivity" on 15 March 1871 (referenced by Victorine Debussy in her letter to the military authorities, cited below). The former soldier joined the National Guard, at the very moment when Thiers[25] was trying to disarm it, thus triggering the outbreak of the Commune. Did Manuel act out of conviction, or was he simply taking a chance on finding a path to success? The former assumption seems more likely, in light of his swift promotion to second lieutenant and, on 3 May, to captain of the second company of the thirteenth federated battalion.

The newly appointed Captain Debussy very quickly found himself on the front line. On 8 May, he was sent to Issy with the battalion that received the order to occupy the fort. His commanding officer, Corcelle, who had been accidentally wounded, ordered Debussy to replace him at the head of the battalion. But scarcely had he approached the checkpoints at the Porte de Versailles when he was abandoned by his soldiers and arrested. Released two days later, he returned to Paris. On 22 May, MacMahon's troops having succeeded in penetrating the capital,[26] Manuel was taken prisoner at the fort at La Muette and soon ended up with thousands of other communards in the grim camp at Satory. It was not until August and September that he was subjected to two interrogations. Finally, on 11 December, he was tried and sentenced by the war council to four years in prison. After spending a long winter at Satory, he was issued a pardon on 11 May 1872. Victorine had inquired about the procedures for pleading extenuating circumstances, and had written the following letter to the military authorities on 8 June 1871:

> Commander, Sir,
>
> I am sending you herewith the documents that I think might be useful for M. Achille de Bussy, my husband, the ex-captain of the thirteenth battalion of the National Guard, who was taken prisoner at the fort at La Muette this past 22 May. I will add a few words to explain his participation in these recent events. Having lost his job last 15 November due to a downturn in business, as the postmark on the letter from M. Paul Dupont that I am sending to you shows, he was employed from 15 December to 15 March at the town hall in the first arrondissement, as the attached certificate also proves. (The head of food provisions certifies that M. Debussy was employed from 15 December to 15 March and congratulated him on his work, integrity, and productivity.)[27] Since that time, my husband has been unemployed, as have I since the beginning of the war. We have four children; the financial needs in our household have been enormous. In order to lessen them, my husband decided during the month of April to accept the position of captain in the National Guard so that his wife and children might be able to eat. That is the sole motive for his behavior. I dare to hope, Commander, Sir, that your big heart will acknowledge these extenuating circumstances, and that you will want to return my husband soon to the love of his children, for whom he is the sole provider.
>
> Kindly accept, Commander, Sir, my profound respect,
>
> Your humble servant
V. de Bussy[28]

This petition was not taken into account by the military authority, who believed that Manuel's acceptance of the rank of captain and his position at the head of his troops spoke for themselves. It was only after a year of actual incarceration that Manuel's sentence was converted to four years of suspension of his civil and family rights.[29] We can imagine his wife's distress, denied of all resources with her four children during this time and renting, perhaps thanks to Clémentine's financial assistance, a very modest two-room attic apartment on the rue Pigalle. The ten-year-old Achille must have vowed to get even with life some day!

Antoinette Mauté

These fateful events, however, would indirectly facilitate the beginning of Achille's musical career. In the Commune's jails, Manuel met another prisoner, Charles de Sivry, a self-taught and self-employed musician,[30] who persuaded him to seek advice from Charles's mother, Madame Mauté, about his son's musical gifts.

The police reports on Charles de Sivry and his mother Antoinette Mauté are available to us; they are difficult to decipher, as they were drafted in 1871, at the worst time of the anti-Communard reaction. Most troubling, in light of these extreme and partisan judgments, is the fact that the memoirs of Mathilde Verlaine (Antoinette's daughter) present an opposite perspective,[31] an almost too idyllic view of her family.[32] We can only try to read between the lines of these two sources, as we cannot reconcile them.

Antoinette-Flore Mauté (née Chariat) was forty-eight years old when she and Achille crossed paths. Widowed at age twenty-six, she was remarried to Théodore-Jean Mauté, the son of a grocer who had become independently wealthy. Already a fine pianist by the age of fifteen, she was said to have been a pupil of Frédéric Chopin. In any case, this is what she herself claimed, for Debussy recalled, at the end of his life, certain details that she had recounted about the Polish pianist's playing.[33] This is also what Mathilde wrote in her memoirs, where, however, she tended to embroider the facts. If there is one opinion of Madame Mauté that cannot be disputed, it is surely that of Verlaine himself: "She was a charming soul, an instinctive and talented artist, an excellent musician with exquisite taste, intelligent, and devoted to those whom she loved."[34] What a contrast to the police report, drawn up probably in June 1871, which offers an example of the hostility displayed by the Versailles powers with regard to artists or to people living on the margins and suspected of collusion with the Communards:

> Mme Mauté (de Fleurville)—whose last name, in her first marriage, was Sivry—is a woman of about 45 years of age, with loose morals, especially in the past, giving piano lessons, in spite of the 10,000–15,000 [franc] annual income of her husband. *Free thinker*, anti-religious, sometimes pretending to be a respectable woman when she is in the noble company that her piano connections procure for her. She is often friendly with the Rohans and the Beurges. A fervent apostle of Rochefort[35] and of the Hugos, she had hoped to marry her daughter to the former. A mediocre writer, she worked for music serial publications and wrote articles for *Le rappel*,[36] and regularly received all of her son's friends and also M. Henry de Rochefort in her home. She owns a small house at 14 rue Nicolet, in Montmartre, Chaussée Clignancourt.[37]

The report concerning Charles de Sivry is no more charitable, but its most serious allegations clearly could not be proved at the time of the trial, since the musician was acquitted:

> Charles-Erhard de Sivry, 22–23 years old, with virtually no money, is a distinguished musician, affiliated with all the secret societies in which he is something of an agitator. A bad poet, a member of the so-called Society of Parnassus. Formerly confined to or possibly a student at Mettray.[38] Assistant in a chemistry lab. As such, he has worked for at least two years on experiments with explosive materials and on weapons of destruction. He was very close to Rochefort, Vermorel,[39] and the main leaders of the Internationale,[40] for which he wrote some articles. It is with his music that he makes his living; *M. Mauté, his stepfather, considers him the worst sort of person.* He was secretary for several members of the Commune in succession, and for the Committee of Montmartre.[41] With his care and intelligence, which is great and dangerous, he helped to prepare for the burning of Paris. When the troops entered, he discreetly began to pack up and left toward the end of the week, taking quite a bit of money that he must have embezzled from several public funds. At the moment, he is an orchestra conductor in Néris, the place to which he escaped with a so-called lady to whom he says he's married, but who is believed to be an accomplice of the Commune. Among the other people who saw M. de Sivry most often is a certain woman of Callias,[42] at whose home Rochefort's portrait held the place of honor, surrounded by flowers. Ch. de Sivry is a very *dangerous* person.[43]

It is more likely that Manuel Debussy met Charles de Sivry in the camp at Satory than at the town hall, where they worked at the beginning of the Commune. Transferred from Néris, Sivry arrived at the camp on 20 July 1871. He did not stay there as long as Captain Debussy, and he was more fortunate than the captain: after two interrogations, he was dismissed on 18 October. However, during three months together at the camp, they had plenty of time to get to know each other and to exchange stories about their respective personal and professional problems. Sivry quickly persuaded Manuel to entrust his son to Antoinette Mauté, Sivry's mother, whom he knew to be a good teacher. "She looked out for me with the kindness of a grandmother," Debussy later recalled when Laloy questioned him about his childhood.[44] And to Victor Segalen he added: "My old piano teacher was a short and stout woman who pushed me into Bach and who played his music like no one does nowadays, bringing it to life."[45] We do not know if the lessons took place before or after Sivry's release, but what is certain is that Antoinette was quickly convinced of the child's musical gifts, that she took her work very much to heart, and that she generously offered him regular, high-quality lessons—enough that, after one year, he could conceivably be accepted into the Conservatoire.

At the time, the Debussy family was living on the rue Pigalle, not far from the rue Nicolet, where the Mautés resided; soon—at least beginning in September—they would be joined by Mathilde Mauté's husband, Paul Verlaine, who, while there, put the finishing touches to his one-act play in verse, *Les uns et les autres*.[46] One naturally wonders about the possible contacts between young Achille and the poet—even though after the birth of his son, the latter was often away from the house, to which he sometimes returned in a drunken state. And did Achille witness the chaos created by the presence of Arthur Rimbaud, which completely destroyed the fragile household?[47] Achille never alluded to whether he had known Verlaine or not.[48] On the other hand, when the composer was solicited in 1901 to participate in a festival devoted to Rimbaud, he replied enthusiastically, adding: "I like him much too much to have ever thought of the useless ornament my music would be to his text."[49]

It was a painful childhood, in which Achille, unlike his brothers and sister, did not attend school. During this time, his mother fanatically took it upon herself alone to teach him—an education whose inadequacy he would feel for a long time to come.[50]

Antoinette Mauté thus advised Achille's parents to apply for his admission to the Conservatoire. Manuel sought someone among his acquaintances who could support his son's application. We do not know how he succeeded in contacting Félicien David, who was not only a member of the Institut de France but also a member of the examination committees in voice, operatic declamation, and organ at the Conservatoire. Thus the former Saint-Simonian and renowned composer of *Le désert* was the person who in a sense carried Achille to the baptismal font of the institution, sending the following note to Charles Réty, the secretary of the Conservatoire:

> Dear Monsieur Réty, I am referring to you a child whose father would like to enroll him in piano study. The child has a good start. You will see for yourself; I would be pleased if you can admit him. Best wishes, Félicien David.[51]

On 22 October 1872, after auditioning with the opus 65 of Ignaz Moscheles, Achille was admitted to the Conservatoire, when only thirty-three of the 157 applicants had been accepted. It was an unexpected success for the parents, who really needed good fortune to smile on them at last!

Genealogy

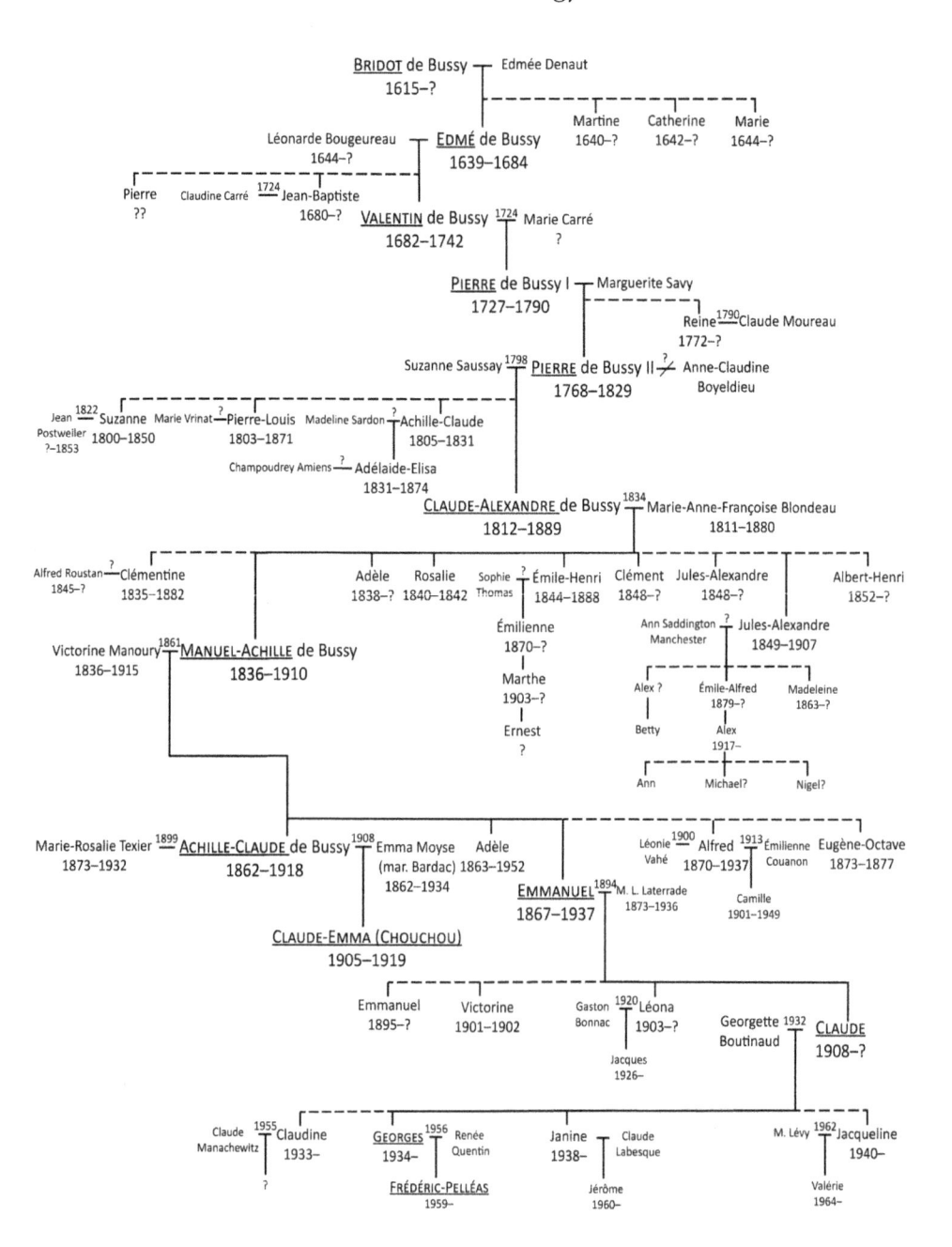

BRIDOT de Bussy — Edmée Denaut
1615–?

    Martine 1640–? Catherine 1642–? Marie 1644–?

Léonarde Bougeureau — **EDMÉ** de Bussy
1644–?   1639–1684

Pierre ?? Claudine Carré —1724— Jean-Baptiste 1680–? **VALENTIN** de Bussy —1724— Marie Carré ?
1682–1742

PIERRE de Bussy I — Marguerite Savy
1727–1790

Reine 1772–? —1790— Claude Moureau

Suzanne Saussay —1798— **PIERRE** de Bussy II —?— Anne-Claudine Boyeldieu
1768–1829

Jean Postweiler ?–1853 —1822— Suzanne 1800–1850 Marie Vrinat —?— Pierre-Louis 1803–1871 Madeline Sardon —?— Achille-Claude 1805–1831

Champoudrey Amiens —?— Adélaide-Elisa 1831–1874

CLAUDE-ALEXANDRE de Bussy —1834— Marie-Anne-Françoise Blondeau
1812–1889   1811–1880

Alfred Roustan 1845–? —?— Clémentine 1835–1882 Adèle 1838–? Rosalie 1840–1842 Sophie Thomas —?— Émile-Henri 1844–1888 Clément 1848–? Jules-Alexandre 1848–? Albert-Henri 1852–?

Victorine Manoury —1861— **MANUEL-ACHILLE** de Bussy
1836–1915   1836–1910

Émilienne 1870–?
Marthe 1903–?
Ernest ?

Ann Saddington Manchester —?— Jules-Alexandre 1849–1907

Alex ? Émile-Alfred 1879–? Madeleine 1863–?

Betty Alex 1917–

Ann Michael? Nigel?

Marie-Rosalie Texier —1899— **ACHILLE-CLAUDE** de Bussy —1908— Emma Moyse (mar. Bardac) 1862–1934 Adèle 1863–1952
1873–1932   1862–1918

EMMANUEL —1894— M. L. Laterrade
1867–1937   1873–1936

Léonie Vahé 1900 — Alfred 1870–1937 —1913— Émilienne Couanon Eugène-Octave 1873–1877

Camille 1901–1949

CLAUDE-EMMA (CHOUCHOU)
1905–1919

Emmanuel 1895–? Victorine 1901–1902 Gaston Bonnac —1920— Léona 1903–? Georgette Boutinaud —1932— **CLAUDE** 1908–?

Jacques 1926–

Claude Manachewitz —1955— Claudine 1933– **GEORGES** 1934– —1956— Renée Quentin Janine 1938– — Claude Labesque M. Lévy —1962— Jacqueline 1940–

?   **FRÉDÉRIC-PELLÉAS** 1959– Jérôme 1960– Valérie 1964–

Chapter Two

Failure of a Pianist

1872–79

"The Conservatoire is still that gloomy and dirty place that we knew in our day," wrote Debussy to André Caplet in 1909.[1] Although inaugurated in 1801,[2] it was not until 1881 that plans for the renovation of the building had begun,[3] and it would be thirty more years before the project was completed.[4] However, a ten-year-old boy would not initially notice these conditions; having had as yet no formal academic experience, he was certainly impressed by the high walls, the discipline, and the atmosphere of the historic institution on the rue Bergère. Achille would spend more than ten years of his life there—years that would strongly weigh on his development, no matter what he might say later. It thus behooves us to follow, year by year, not only the prizes he was awarded and the assessments he received from his teachers but also the friendships that were forged, and to attempt to reconstruct the context in which he lived.

In 1872, when Achille entered the Conservatoire, Ambroise Thomas had served as the director of the institution for only one year. After Daniel Auber's long reign, the building needed to be remodeled; a committee had been created in 1870, during the last year of the Second Empire, but its work had been interrupted by the Franco-Prussian War. Thomas limited himself to a few urgent measures, such as the elimination of the boarding component[5] and the establishment of courses in aesthetics (required for composition students) and in music history, as well as a vocal ensemble (for the best voice students)[6] and an orchestral ensemble;[7] these "exercises publics" had begun during the early years of the Conservatoire, but had been suspended for more than ten years. Lastly, Thomas changed several regulations dating from 1850 that concerned advisory committees on instruction, the admissions auditions, and the examination committees for the classes.[8]

A Ten-Year-Old Child at the Conservatoire

Achille's first teachers were Antoine Marmontel for piano and Albert Lavignac for solfège; he enrolled in their classes on 25 October and 7 November 1872, respectively. Various accounts agree on his lack of punctuality, due no doubt to his idling in front of shop windows or lingering over the books and magazines in the bookshops. He often arrived at the last minute or even after class had already begun, "with short and hurried steps" or "completely out of breath from having run," as Julien Tiersot recalled from 1876.[9] Camille Bellaigue also remembered the same tardiness, and Marmontel's tolerant welcome: "Finally, here you are, my child!"[10]

His mother was nevertheless strict with him; Achille later referred to the disciplinary slaps he received in those days. It was also expected that he would continue his general education at home before he sat down at the "old rosewood piano" that was available to him at 59bis rue Pigalle.[11] These youthful years were by no means happy ones, which the child, once he later became Claude (around 1890), seems to have erased from his memory. He was always dressed in "black velvet and with a collar of lace or white linen" (Lépine), "in a black jacket that was spiced up with a polka-dot tie and velvet trousers" (Pierné), "in a shirt cinched by a belt" (Bellaigue) or in "short breeches and a velvet shirt" (Bonheur). Among those who were struck by his physical appearance and have described their impressions, very few have dwelt on his body—"short, heavy-set, stocky" (Pierné)—but all of them emphasized his forehead, "bulging under his black hair" (Tiersot), "with the strength of a faun [. . .], protruding like a ship's prow" (Bonheur), "with a forehead like an Indochinese dog" (Léon Daudet); and some of them remember, in accordance with the period to which they were alluding, "his blazing eyes and the focused and wild expression on his face" (Vidal), and "his determined gaze, showing a tenacious personality" (Tiersot). This gave him, according to the Vasniers, the appearance of a Florentine from the Middle Ages; for a journalist in 1909, the look of a musketeer from the time of Louis XIII; or, according to Henri de Régnier, "the air of an Italian shepherd from Calabria."[12] Finally, for Raymond Bonheur, Achille seemed like a Titianesque character whom one could easily imagine in a Venetian palace. If we are to believe Gabriel Pierné, "his awkwardness and his clumsiness were extraordinary. He was also bashful and even uncouth."[13]

Marmontel's Class

The first assessment of Achille's early days with Marmontel came from Alphonse Duvernoy and was rather encouraging: "Toccata by Bach. Intelligent child. Nice sound" (January 1873), and then: "Moscheles, 1st Concerto. Some abilities, some future. Fair reading" (June).[14] In the following year, when Marmontel made his own overall evaluation of his pupil, he committed himself even further: "Charming child, true artistic temperament; will become a distinguished musician; promising future" (13 January 1874).[15] It was a prophetic opinion, if we note that Achille's teacher did not write that he would become a "distinguished pianist" but instead emphasized primarily his artistic temperament. Exactly the opposite appraisal was articulated by a less perceptive pupil in the class, Camille Bellaigue: "Nothing about him—neither his appearance, nor his comments, nor his performance—revealed an artist, present or future."[16]

Three times each week—Mondays, Wednesdays, and Fridays—Achille thus entered the courtyard on the faubourg Poissonnière side of the building and went up to the second floor where Marmontel's class took place. Each student sat down in turn beside the master, in front of the large Érard grand piano, and played the work that had been assigned to him. Marmontel's patience and kindness were proverbial, and he knew how to find the words to encourage the least gifted students. They never heard him play, except to illustrate a musical feature or a phrasing. Georges Bizet, Francis Planté, Louis-Joseph Diémer, and Isaac Albéniz had notably passed through his hands.[17] He was the great piano pedagogue, author of many works and exercises, and in the process of finishing *L'art classique et moderne du piano* (1876) and *Les pianistes célèbres* (1878). While Marmontel was not a pupil of Chopin, he had heard him on several occasions, and when the students whom he had chosen to compete in the *concours* came to work at his home on the rue Saint-Lazare, he could have them admire Eugène Delacroix's portrait of the Polish master, which his son would later bequeath to the Louvre. Perhaps Achille thus received some bits and pieces of Chopinian tradition that were more authentic than those he believed he had received from Mme Mauté.

About two weeks after his matriculation into the piano class, he was admitted to the class of "solfège for instrumentalists" taught by Lavignac, himself a former pupil of Marmontel. Achille was found to be far behind the faculty's expectations in music theory. After Marmontel was invited as a jury member for that class in January 1873, he noted bluntly: "Rather good dictation. No fundamentals. Rather well read."[18] Mme Mauté had been satisfied with imparting a cursory knowledge of solfège to Achille, while in the new class at the Conservatoire the teachers developed their students' aural facility with dictations, sight-reading in all the clefs, and transpositions at sight. After one year of work, Lavignac noted: "Reading is a little behind, but, as he is very gifted, I'm convinced that he will catch up quickly" (16 January 1874).[19] Marmontel, in the following June, was even more full of praise: "Very good: reading, dictation, and theory."[20]

Thus Achille's first two teachers were not put off by the child's rather withdrawn nature, and they knew almost immediately how to foster his natural gifts. Achille endeavored to do what was asked of him, and he was rewarded in the *concours* of 1874. Forgetting his initial reservations, on 11 June, Lavignac seemed completely won over: "Quite excellent student, intelligent, hard-working, and very well organized musically. I expect him to distinguish himself in the *concours*."[21] Meanwhile, in piano, Marmontel confirmed his first reactions on 23 June: "Charming musical nature; I very much want him to compete in the *concours*."[22] The results were a second honorable mention in piano, and a third medal in solfège.

Before a very impressive jury, which comprised notably Ernest Boulanger, François Bazin, Adolphe Danhauser, and Ambroise Thomas, the examination required a performance of Chopin's Concerto no. 2 in F Minor. Harsher than the piano jurists, the critic from *Le temps* wrote that an honorable mention had been given to Achille "because one must be much more lenient with the young!"[23]

The official awarding of the prizes took place in a traditional ceremony that Achille's parents surely attended. As a columnist wrote, "The distribution of prizes at the Conservatoire is above all a celebration for the parents."[24] M. de Cumont, the minister of public instruction, worship, and fine arts, was there, and he delivered a speech that seemed made to reassure Manuel and Victorine as well as Achille: "Work, work! It's all in that word: everything is possible through work. [. . .] Do you want to be great artists someday, to win fame, to find your fortune? [. . .] Don't complain about slow starts or lack of early opportunities; rest assured that it takes time to ripen talent just as it does to ripen fruits."[25] After this speech and before the concert, the winning students, who were waiting in the wings, were called upon, one by one, to fill the seats on the main floor of the concert hall that had been left empty for them. For the Debussys, it was a great beginning as well as a confirmation of the hopes they had placed in their eldest child and the reward for all their efforts. It had been less than two years since Manuel had been released from the prison at Satory, and he would have to wait two more years to regain his civil rights. He now had a job—as an assistant bookkeeper at the Compagnie Fives-Lille since 1873—and his son was beginning a career that was in accordance with his wishes. Finally, on 1 September, he settled his family, which included five children, into a two-room apartment with an anteroom at 13 rue Clapeyron.

The year 1875 was for Achille—or Chilo, as he was called by those close to him—a very good one of validation. At the age of thirteen, he was the youngest in the class of Lavignac, who continued to appear satisfied with him, though always with the same reservation: "Excellent reader, perfectly good ear; still a little behind in rudiments" (15 January).[26] Scholars have often ironically dwelled on this lack of progress, which, at Achille's tender age, could hardly be an act of passive resistance. What was most important, on the other hand, was the teacher's assessment of his good musical ear and his natural confidence, one of the most fundamental qualities for a future composer. On 9 June, Lavignac repeated: "Complete musical preparation and serious work" and added: "With Destefani, is at the head of the class."[27]

Marmontel expressed not even the slightest reservation. For the first end-of-term exam (22 January), which included Bach's Chromatic Fantasy, the teacher simply repeated his expression of "much future" and confirmed the candidate's intelligence and seriousness. Then on 22 June, he incorporated his wording from the previous year on Achille's "true temperament of an artist."[28] Lavignac's opinion proved correct: Achille was granted a second-place medal in solfège, while Destefani obtained the first prize.

In piano, the examination included Chopin's First Ballade. Out of fourteen candidates, the jury—in which Achille no doubt saw for the first time Jules Massenet, Ernest Guiraud, and also Jules Cohen, Henry Fissot, and Émile Paladilhe—decided not to award the first prize (a rather rare act at the Conservatoire) but instead to give two second prizes.[29] The first honorable mentions were shared between Léon-Lucien-Henri Lemoine, the grandson of the music publisher;[30] Eugène-Ferdinand Rabeau (who would die at age twenty-three); and, yes, Achille Debussy, whom the critic of *L'art musical* described as a "twelve-year-old child and a first-rate virtuoso of the future."[31]

The three years spent by Achille in this studious atmosphere had allowed him to bond with several classmates. While Bellaigue did not feel at all drawn to him, it was completely different with Pierné, to whom we owe precious memories: "That poor child, coming out of the most ordinary environment," he observed, "had aristocratic tastes in everything."[32] Raymond Bonheur expressed it even better: "Born poor, he entered into life with the tastes, needs, and nonchalance of a great lord."[33] Indeed, Achille had quickly adopted the habit of depending completely on the generosity of others (Arosa, Clémentine, etc.). We will see that—as soon as he was of age, so to speak—he borrowed money again and again from anyone who gave him the impression of having some. For the time being, it involved very modest gifts, like accepting a cup of chocolate at Prévost from Mme Pierné after class. At Bourbonneux,[34] another eatery, Pierné remembered Achille's preference for a tiny sandwich or a cup of macaroni rather than the large, filling cakes that his friends would generally choose.[35] This was his first contact with the comfortable middle-class world and a lifestyle that was different from his own.

Pierné also took him to his parents' home, where Achille leafed through a bound collection of *Le monde illustré*, the most opulent illustrated magazine of the day. There the young boy's shameless nature, as well as his profound attraction to pictures, appeared for the first time. Achille managed to persuade his friend, unbeknownst to his parents, to cut out some illustrations with beautiful borders—in particular, some reproductions of paintings or engravings, by

Meissonier[36]—and to steal them in order to decorate his meager room, leaving his friend to figure out how to explain this crime to his parents.

The year 1876 would not hold the promise of the preceding years, at least on the academic front. One might attribute this change to the child's awkward age, but it was due mainly to the fact that his personality was coming into its own.

First Concerts at Chauny

Marmontel was occasionally asked to identify accompanists to play for the opera class, which afforded his young pianists a new experience. In his memoirs, Camille Bellaigue told how he had held forth in the grand duet of the fourth act of *La favorite*.[37] Achille had an even more remarkable opportunity: in January, he was "lent" to the provinces to accompany a concert given by Léontine Mendès, a student in the voice classes.[38] The location was certainly not prestigious, it being in Chauny, a town in the department of Aisne, where a gala concert was organized by none other than the brass band of the glass-factory workers. But what an enjoyable experience it was for a boy of nearly fourteen, as it was his first public appearance, and in the company of a twenty-four-year-old singer, no less, "with a very high voice [. . .], a charming young person"[39] who seemed, in this respect, to foreshadow Mme Vasnier![40]

The first part of the concert on 16 January 1876 comprised eight compositions,[41] including some instrumental fantasies on *L'Africaine, Robert le diable*, and *La traviata*,[42] and it ended with a *chansonette*, "Le nid du berger," interpreted by M. Fleury, a "chanteur comique." "M. De Bussy, pianist" accompanied Léontine Mendès in an aria from Fromental Halévy's *La juive* and one from Gioachino Rossini's *Pie voleuse* (as *La gazza ladra* was known in French), and played a fantasy for cello and piano by Donizetti with Samary, "a cellist in the opera orchestra."[43] The second part of the concert included seven pieces; among these, Achille accompanied Léontine Mendès in an aria from *Mignon* by Ambroise Thomas, and the young pianist held his own, especially in a trio for piano, violin, and violoncello by Franz Joseph Haydn. For the conclusion, there was a "playful work" titled *Ous'qu'est mon vélocipède!*[44]

Thus the young Debussy was exposed to a musical genre typical of the nineteenth century: the full-length vocal and instrumental concert, consisting of a mélange of alternating opera excerpts and instrumental pieces. After the concert, he was again called upon (along with Messieurs Geffrin and Walberg, directors of the chorus and theater group, respectively) to play the piano in a performance of *La chanson de Fortunio*, an operetta by Jacques Offenbach that was given by the local theatrical company.

The public, by no means blasé, naturally celebrated these budding musicians who had come from Paris, and the local press erupted with eloquence and fervor in reporting the event:

> Mlle Mendès and M. Samary will come back to Chauny... De Bussy especially will return. De Bussy, who has so much energy in such a little body. What eloquence! What spirit! What genuine enthusiasm! We need not mention that the piano is a cold instrument, that there is such a wide gap between the striking finger and the resonating string, that life is lost on the way, and that the sound is dead! This budding little Mosart [sic] really plays up a storm. When he gets hold of the piano, his entire soul passes through the strings. It required the outstanding skill of Messieurs Mansart and Samary to keep up with him in the Haydn trio, where he was carried away in a charming frenzy: he is not even fourteen years old![45]

Similarly glowing, but more measured, was the review in *La défense nationale*:

> M. de Bussy, the accompanist of Mlle Mendès, is a very young pianist who has become proficient in his art to a degree that is quite remarkable. The public's impression regarding this young artist, before whom a brilliant career is opening, was what it should be, that is to say, excellent. It seems that this child—M. de Bussy is only fourteen years old [in fact, he was still thirteen]—has already taken second prize at the Conservatoire. This distinction, and the demonstrated skill that everyone noticed, leads us to believe that this young pianist will be a master in a few years. M. de Bussy also received his well-deserved share of bravos and curtain calls.[46]

Reading such spontaneous prose (copies of which Achille had brought back with him) certainly delighted father and mother Debussy. Even if the praise came from Chauny, back in Paris on the rue Clapeyron they could see it only as a happy omen for the career of a "virtuoso"—and all the more so when Achille was actually asked to return and made his way once again to the fair city of Chauny, on 18 March, for a concert given this time by the local band. He played two works similar in character to those of the first concert: a trio from *Guillaume Tell* and a *grande fantaisie* on themes from *Lucia de Lammermoor*. The critic of *La défense nationale*, while not wanting to repeat himself in his tribute, nevertheless issued a prophetic assessment: "In everyone's opinion, M. de Bussy is called to become a renowned artist and, with time and hard work, to move to the forefront of our musical celebrities."[47]

At the same moment, however, Achille's professors at the Conservatoire were clearly less enthusiastic. Three days after the January concert at Chauny, Lavignac wrote: "Remarkable intelligence; superbly gifted, but does not work enough and relies too much on his natural ability,"[48] while on 2 February, Marmontel agreed with his colleague, with only a few slight differences: "Good student, intelligent, studious, but a little disorganized and unfocused; he should put more care into his study."[49] This slackening was obviously due to the fact that Achille was taking his studies less seriously and that he was beginning to question their necessity and validity, especially as he felt more confident technically. Lavignac was not used to seeing a pupil challenge the sacrosanct rules of solfège; in particular, Achille wanted to know why ternary subdivisions of measures were called "compound," but he asked in vain. At times, however, Lavignac kept him after class; one winter evening, he introduced Achille to the overture from *Tannhäuser* and noticed such an impact on his pupil that he continued the tutorial and lost track of time. A guard—the forbidding Aubert Ternusse—had to admonish him and ask them to vacate the premises.[50] In the light of these personal contacts, one can read between the lines of Lavignac's judgment on 9 June: "Perfect for reading and dictation; still careless with respect to theory, although he understands it full well."[51] As for Marmontel, he predicted outright failure in his notes from 20 June 1876: "Not performing at all as I had hoped; unfocused, not punctual, he could do much better."[52]

Happily, a perfect dictation earned Achille the highest prize in solfège: the first-place medal. Two other examinees received the same result:[53] Henri-Joseph O'Kelly, who also studied with Lavignac and was destined to pursue a career as a choirmaster, and Anatole-Léon Grand-Jany, who would become an organist and professor at the Conservatoire.

For the piano *concours*, Marmontel's pessimistic premonitions were confirmed: no award for Achille. The examination seemed daunting to all of the students because it involved the first-movement Allegro of Ludwig van Beethoven's opus 111, "a very difficult composition and absolutely devoid of any sort of charm," as Henry Cohen commented blithely in *L'art musical.*[54] Camille Bellaigue described how the admirable Marmontel had patiently tried to help his students understand the work:

> As the *concours* drew near, more lessons were given at his home. Marmontel added run-throughs in the Salle Érard so that we could get used to playing in public. There our families and friends developed their predictions. Bets were taken, and favorites were chosen. At times, the first prize would be selected in advance by the public, and the jury, two or three days later, would merely ratify the people's opinion. This was the case for the exceedingly young Alphonse Thibaud, brother of Jacques, the great violinist. In him alone, and from the outset, after only one year of school, the formidable opus 111 seemed—even to us, his fellow students and competitors—to have found a worthy interpreter.[55]

On the jury were some old and some newer illustrious members: Henri Herz, Stephen Heller, Camille Saint-Saëns, Louis Diémer, Alexis-Henry Fissot, Jules Massenet, Théodore Ritter, and Auguste Wolff. The students' opinion was indeed ratified, and Thibaud thus began a brilliant career. As for Achille, he would keep his distance from Beethoven's music throughout his entire life.

Certain critics readily held Marmontel's teaching accountable for fostering a style of performance that was unsuitable for such repertoire: "Other than this brilliant and triumphant individual," wrote Octave Fouque, "we firmly believe that M. Marmontel's class has shown too little concern for the character and grand style of the required piece. [. . .] Less than ever did M. Marmontel's students escape the criticism, often levied against them, of their mannered style of playing."[56] If we are to believe Laloy, Marmontel had instilled in Achille a distaste for Beethoven; in order to intensify the expression in the "Pathétique" Sonata, he added some words to the melody of the finale: "Ô pauvre mère, douleur amère."[57]

A Second Prize in Piano

The academic year of 1876–77 was to have been a time for Debussy to focus on the piano. He took the class in "instrumental ensemble," normally a requirement for the students of all instruments (including piano) who had obtained a prize or a first honorable mention.[58] But the professor was a man in his sixties who had been teaching since 1848: René-Paul Baillot, the son of the great violinist.[59] Achille did not present himself for the exam in February; and the other students, among whom was Camille Chevillard, followed Achille's lead so well that only two of the unfortunate professor's students remained to compete in the next *concours*!

Without more solfège to work on and not yet enrolled in the harmony class, Achille would therefore have been focusing completely on improving his piano technique. We learn about his pianism from his professor as well as his friends, some of whom were struck by his unschooled manner of playing. The opinions of Pierné and Bellaigue agree fairly well on this point: "He amazed us with his bizarre performance," wrote the former. "Whether it was out of natural clumsiness or shyness, I don't know, but he literally charged at the piano and exaggerated all the effects. He seemed seized with rage toward the instrument, treating it brusquely with impulsive movements, and noisily huffing while performing difficult passages."[60] As for Camille Bellaigue, he remembered only his friend's "compulsion or tic—marking the strong beats of the measure with a sort of hiccup or snort."[61] Achille's professors were more tempered in their opinions. From 1873, Duvernoy acknowledged his "beautiful sound"—an expression taken up again by Henri Fissot in 1877; but the same Duvernoy, who would, over the years, acknowledge on three occasions Achille's "intelligent performance," indeed remarked in 1875 and 1876: "plays too fast" and "rushes too much."[62]

Paul Vidal made a technical comment: "He had trouble executing a trill, but on the other hand he had a facile left hand with an extraordinarily wide stretch."[63] Pierné added further: "His flaws would eventually fade away, and at times he obtained effects of surprisingly fluid sweetness."[64]

Marmontel's opinion that year followed suit: "I am much more pleased with this child, who was lulled by his first success" (31 January). Then he felt that Achille had "abandoned his lack of focus and taken a liking to work; I'm pleased with his progress and his musical intelligence" (21 June).[65] The *concours*, held *in camera*, ended on 17 July; twenty-one examinees played the first movement of Robert Schumann's Sonata in G Minor, op. 22. In addition to the director, Ambroise Thomas, the jury consisted of several pianists—including Alfred Jaëll, Henri Fissot, and Alphonse Duvernoy—as well as Ernest Guiraud, who was hearing Achille for the second time.

The criticism of Marmontel's pedagogy was clarified in the *Revue et gazette musicale*, where Charles Bannelier did not hesitate to explain his preferences: "It seems to us that Marmontel's class, with its tempo rubato and accents that are added or even contrary to those of the composer, and in spite of the brilliance of its execution and sonorous qualities, engaged with the spirit of the work less successfully than did M. Mathias's class, which played more straightforward rhythmically, more cleanly, and more accurately."[66] However, one of the three first prizes went to a Marmontel student—José Jimenez, a dark-skinned man from Trinidad—while two second prizes were awarded to Camille Bellaigue and Achille Debussy, who, as was observed in the same review, "are making normal progress."[67]

This success was at least as well received by Achille's parents—still suffering from the loss of their son Eugène, who had died of meningitis—as it was by the candidate himself. At the awards ceremony on 4 August, Manuel must have been proud to hear the voice of Lucien Guitry, who received a first honorable mention in tragedy that year, formally proclaim the name of his son among the prize winners.[68] A crowd was present and the minister of public instruction and fine arts showed up to personally distribute the awards. As for Achille, he must have saved his applause for a first honorable mention in voice that was awarded to Léontine Mendès, his "colleague" from the excursion to Chauny, who at the concert following the ceremony performed an excerpt from the second act of *Le songe d'une nuit d'été* (A Midsummer Night's Dream), composed by the venerable director Ambroise Thomas.[69]

Crowned with his second prize, Achille made his debut in an as-yet-unknown Parisian salon: that of Bizet's widow, Geneviève Halévy, who received the young prize winners from the Conservatoire in her home on the rue de Douai, where she had retired with her uncle, Léon Halévy. Not at all surprisingly, we find Achille's signature with the date of 1877 in the album of this attractive and witty woman, from whom Marcel Proust would draw his inspiration for the Duchesse de Guermantes.[70]

The beginning of the 1877–78 academic year brought a new development. Achille entered Émile Durand's harmony class on 24 November,[71] even though he could reasonably have imagined spending his last year with Marmontel in hopes of winning his first prize in piano, with its traditional reward—on top of everything else—of a grand piano offered by Érard.

Durand's Class

If Maurice Emmanuel is to be believed, Émile Durand was an unexceptional pedagogue who appeared to like neither his students nor music. It is true that he would hand in his resignation under curious circumstances in 1883, after an altercation with the brother of one of his students.[72] It seems that Achille did not like Durand any more than the latter did his pupil. After a few months, the professor noted on 19 January 1878: "Excellent musical setup, good aptitude for reading music, but very unfocused."[73] This lack of focus was the immediate result of the sixteen-year-old boy's skeptical attitude toward the discipline in question. We know what he later said about it: "I assure you that in the harmony class I didn't do much. In my time, the students were customarily drilled in a quite pointless little game that consisted of supplying the harmony intended by the professor," and, more explicitly: "The study of harmony, such as is practiced in the academy, is the most completely ridiculous way of combining sounds. Moreover, it has the serious shortcoming of standardizing the writing to such a degree that all musicians, with only a few exceptions, harmonize in the same way."[74] This critical attitude did not prevent Durand from appreciating Achille for his musical instinct and his "natural disposition as an accompanist and reader."[75] According to Antoine Banès, there were times when Durand would keep Achille after class: "Criticisms pelted the student's head and furious pencil marks riddled his ruled paper."[76] However, immediately following this first impulse, the teacher would collect himself, silently reread the pages so cruelly slashed by his pen, and conclude under his breath, with an enigmatic smile: "Of course, all this is hardly orthodox, but it's truly ingenious."[77] Since it was his duty to judge the work according to the requirements of academic exercises, the professor diplomatically put it this way on 19 June: "Debussy would be an excellent student if he were less disorganized, less careless."[78] In all likelihood, neither of them was surprised that no award was granted to Achille in this year of harmony study with Durand.

Marmontel's assessment was completely the opposite. Judging from his evaluations of the year, he had hoped to see Achille win the prize: "He is studying much better, less carried away than in the past; intelligent, will become an artist if he commits himself to deeper reflection."[79] But his doubt returned at the end of the year: "He has studied much better this year; he has performance abilities, but also substantial inconsistencies."[80]

The *concours* that year included the first-movement Allegro from Carl Maria von Weber's Sonata in A-flat Major, op. 39. There was only one first-prize winner among the men: Camille Bellaigue,[81] who, according to the critic of *L'art musical*, was "a skilled virtuoso" but lacked a "genuine [musical] temperament."[82] He would very quickly give up the piano in favor of a career as a music critic. Pierné received the second-place prize.[83] For Debussy there was nothing, and the critic from the same newspaper commented discreetly: "The second prize winner of 1877 failed [in his bid for a prize]. To award him one this year would be pointless; but it must be said that he did not distinguish himself in the *concours* and that the jury committee was harsh but fair."[84] In the notes taken by jury member Fissot, we find simply: "Not good enough for a second prize."[85] It was a dark year for Achille, who also had to face his father's disappointment.

The most unfavorable year in his long stay at the Conservatoire, however, would be the following one: 1878–79. Achille saw his three future companions in Rome pass ahead of him, applying themselves in their academic exercises more successfully than he: Georges Marty had obtained his first prize in harmony the preceding year, and Paul Vidal would get his within the year, while Pierné clinched his first prize in piano. The comparison of Debussy with the latter is all the more significant, as Pierné was almost exactly one year younger than Achille. But Pierné had musical parents who had enrolled him in the conservatory at Metz from the age of five, and, in addition, he benefited from the support of the director, who was also a native of Metz. Cheerful by nature, liked by his friends as well as his teachers, surrounded by a certain prestige as a precocious child, Pierné had everything that Debussy lacked, and Achille saw him as the embodiment of all the success that he himself had such trouble achieving.

First Friends at School

Fairly tight bonds of friendship had brought Achille closer to certain students in Marmontel's and Durand's classes. In the former, Paul Vidal explained simply: "I succeeded in winning him over and we quickly became great friends."[86] Then, in Durand's class, the circle widened: "We became quite close; with Pierné, we formed a trio that was nearly inseparable. Once a week, in good weather, we would go to do our counterpoint in the Parc Monceau, in front of the fountain, and Debussy was delighted by the frolics of the ducklings."[87]

Two other students found favor in Achille's eyes. The first was Raymond Bonheur, who had enrolled in a declamation class in 1878 and would even go on to compete for the *concours* in theater; he stayed with Durand for two years before withdrawing at the end of 1880.[88] Thanks to him, we have the finest portrait of Debussy at seventeen to eighteen years of age. The latter could scarcely have benefited from fruitful conversations in his family home; Victorine and Manuel had long ago taught him the little they knew. At the Conservatoire, most of his friends were focused on their technical progress and had no general knowledge. Bonheur was truly an exception. The way in which he grew closer to Achille is indicative: "We bonded rather quickly, over a book by Théodore de Banville—rather unexpected in that time and place—which I saw in his hands. [. . .] At the time, he seemed to me withdrawn and a little aloof, [. . .] in other respects strangely appealing, in spite of a certain brusqueness on first contact."[89] This new friendship would endure for many years, until Bonheur, after contracting typhoid in 1884, retreated to Magny-les-Hameaux in the Chevreuse valley, where he lived more and more like a hermit.

The second classmate with whom Achille became friends was René Chansarel, who was two years younger and who entered Marmontel's class in 1879. Chansarel had a refined sensibility, and he cherished modern literature; rather solitary, he was difficult to befriend. We will return to him a little later. This friendship, no doubt the least well known from Debussy's youth, lasted a good ten years.[90]

Marmontel still wanted to believe in Achille's success: his notes from the year were completely positive; he underscored Achille's progress, his aptitude, and his achievement, even adding that "his flighty nature has come to an end."[91] Émile Durand was a little more realistic, concluding on 20 June 1879: "Student is very gifted in harmony, but hopelessly unfocused."[92] Vidal and Bonheur were well placed to know what caused this carelessness. According to Vidal, "Instead of finding the harmonic realizations expected by the teacher, he [Achille] always went further, inventing solutions that were ingenious, elegant, and delightful, although by no means orthodox, and Émile Durand, who was a good but inflexible teacher, reproached him harshly."[93] Bonheur confirms Vidal's observation: "Whether it was a matter of [harmonizing] a melody or of [realizing] a given bass, it was rare that he would not bring in an ingenious realization, revealing the ordinary triteness of the given material by a subtle and unexpected harmony."[94]

A year was lost on the academic front: Achille received no awards, yet he had performed on piano not only Beethoven but also the *Allegro de concert*, op. 46, of Chopin. The critic of the *Revue et gazette musicale* wrote, cruelly, that the young composer seemed to be moving backward.[95] The atmosphere at rue Clapeyron had become loathsome, and Achille had to seriously question his future.

Stay in Chenonceaux

Fortunately, Marmontel found a diversion for his student after the end of the school year. Already in the preceding year, a chatelaine had asked Marmontel to send her a young pianist in order to provide entertainment for her soirees: at that time, he had chosen for her José Manuel Jimenez, the aforementioned student from the Caribbean, who had won his first prize in piano in 1877. The following year, he sent Achille to her, sensitively imagining that such a stay might not only ease the pain of his failure but also comfort his parents.

Marguerite Wilson had received the château of Chenonceaux as a wedding gift from her father Daniel Wilson, a Scottish engineer who had made his fortune by installing gas lighting in Paris. She had married an administrator in the young gas company, Eugène Pelouze, in 1857. "Very personable..., blond, and English to her fingertips"[96] and "sensual and intoxicating as a magnolia,"[97] she had a strong personality. She pushed her brother into politics—he would soon draw her into one of the biggest scandals of the Third Republic—and it was said that she was on very good terms with the president, Jules Grévy. She had three passions: Gustave Flaubert, Italian painting, and Richard Wagner. Very close to the self-taught painter Charles Toché, she had conceived with him a project for an extravagant "gallery" at Chenonceaux, composed of panels devoted to Spanish, Venetian, Chinese, and other art. Between the panels of Bartolomé Esteban Murillo and Louis XIV, the portrait of Richard Wagner (below the swan from *Parsifal*) took pride of place. Toché spent ten years working on all these frescoes.[98] Soon, he would add to this incredible mélange the portrait of the mistress of the house by Carolus-Duran.[99] He also had the idea of painting several regular houseguests in the orangery of the château, which is how it came about that Nicasio Jimenez, the young brother of José Manuel, appeared nude in one fresco.[100] José, a cellist, was part of the family trio, along with his father, and Marguerite Pelouze loved to see them dressed in white jabots, scarlet jackets, and plumed turbans. She had them play every evening, during meals, and also in the afternoon. Gustave Flaubert, who had been invited the previous summer, was disinclined toward music and had quickly become annoyed by these exotic musical productions; after about ten days, he had slipped away. Of course, he had met Toché, who became one of his admirers and began to want to illustrate Flaubert's *La tentation de saint Antoine*.[101]

One can easily imagine the wide-open eyes of the young seventeen-year-old Debussy, transported abruptly from the dark, two-room apartment of the rue Clapeyron to this fairytale castle. Here reigned an eccentric woman, a foreigner to boot, who was unlike anyone he had ever met.

Later on, this experience became part of the rich, secret garden of his youth. He alluded to it only once, when Laloy asked him in 1902 to find among his connections the name of a government official who might support his candidacy for the Légion d'honneur. Without mentioning the circumstances in which he had met Daniel Wilson (Marguerite's brother and the one responsible for the family's financial ruin), Debussy replied: "I have known only one politician in my lifetime: M. Wilson. He was, by the way, a charming man who truly detested music."[102]

Such was not the case for his sister: Marguerite was an especially ardent Wagnerian who, beginning in 1876 and 1877, had hosted at her home in Paris private evening soirees organized by the magistrate Antoine Lascoux—soirees that were called "little Bayreuth" and that had taken place from time to time in Charles Toché's studio. She was part of the small group of French pilgrims who were present at the famous opening of the theater at Bayreuth, in August 1876, along with Vincent d'Indy, Toché, Augusta Holmès, Camille Benoit, and Ernest Guiraud, and she would return to Bayreuth five times thereafter, even after having lost her fortune.[103]

We do not know if Mme Pelouze had invited other musicians to Chenonceaux in 1879, or what repertoire Achille was asked to play during those weeks. Paul Vidal was certain that it involved playing chamber music in particular and "also improvising a little."[104] But never had our young musician met as fanatical a supporter of Wagner, who was at the center of their conversations. Prior to Mme Pelouze, who could have spoken to him about the composer of the *Ring* cycle with the same enthusiastic passion? Certainly Lavignac, as we have seen, in some comments outside of class. Debussy might also have heard the overtures to *Tannhäuser* and *Der fliegende Holländer*, given by Jules Pasdeloup at the Cirque d'hiver in March 1879, and perhaps the first act of *Lohengrin*, which was performed in April 1879. It would have been easy for him to read the scores at the Conservatoire library.[105] But nothing indicates that his initial awareness of Wagner had taken place before his experience at Chenonceaux. This was the result—as were the allure of a grande dame and the discovery of a sumptuous way of life—of his unexpected stay in a royal castle. Just when all hope of pursuing a career as a pianist vanished, Achille was very determined to become a composer.

Chapter Three

Birth of a Composer

1880–82

Although no autograph musical manuscript by Achille is dated before 1880, it is clear that by then he had already tried his hand at composing some songs or little piano pieces. This means that the dates of 1876 or 1878, given for some songs in the catalogs based on the lists of works made by Jean-Aubry and Laloy,[1] have very little chance of being authentic. The fact that Debussy allowed these dates to be printed in the early catalogs proves nothing, since he gave unreliable dates to his youthful works in other instances, and he was not at all attentive to this sort of detail.[2]

His first compositional efforts most likely date from 1879. Furthermore, this is the year mentioned in the memoirs of Paul Vidal, who never tired of hearing particularly "Madrid, princesse des Espagnes" and the "Ballade à la lune."[3] Although the first of these songs, whose text is drawn from Alfred de Musset's *Contes d'Espagne et d'Italie*, has been rediscovered,[4] the second is unknown to us, as are other songs based on Musset poems that Vidal suggested were written under the influence of Edmond Missa, a fellow student in Massenet's class. With Pierné and Passérieu, Vidal heard Achille sing his own works, which "filled us with enthusiasm."[5] As Vidal pestered him to play some other songs, Achille played a trick on him by memorizing several of Émile Pessard's *Joyeusetés de bonne compagnie* and passing them off as his own.[6] The following year, when he arrived at Nadezhda von Meck's home, Achille surely had a number of his own compositions in his portfolio.

First Prize in Accompanying

In the meantime, the Chenonceaux dream had faded: Debussy had to come back to Paris and face family worries again, as well as to return—for the seventh year—to the Conservatoire. Since his previous failure barred him from enrolling in a composition class, he focused on the class in piano accompaniment that had been established the previous year by Auguste Bazille, an organist and former rehearsal coach for singers at the Opéra-Comique. A specialist in orchestral reductions at the piano, Bazille praised Léo Delibes's music because it was easy to reduce: "It's the kind of orchestral writing that falls naturally under the fingers,"[7] he used to say. Even if 1880 was not a momentous year academically for Debussy, it was a time of major developments in his personal life and in the direction of his career: his first real compositions date from that year.

The exercises assigned by the "conscientious and liberal" Bazille were described in detail by Maurice Emmanuel,[8] a classmate who entered the Conservatoire in 1881 and who recorded so many specific memories about Achille—sight-reading unknown pieces, transposing them to various keys, and spontaneously reducing orchestral scores at the piano—that at one point their veracity was questioned.[9] Where Achille introduced the most artfulness— or perverseness—was in figured-bass realization, to which he added his own passing tones, thus finding a way to break up the monotony of the harmonic progressions. Even more subtlety appeared in his harmonization of given melodies: "The good Bazille did not always approve of the underlying progressions invented by his pupil. But just as Marmontel could distinguish Debussy's impulsive temperament from his carelessness and his quirks, so Bazille listened, grumbled, and finally conceded. 'Conceded' is the word that Debussy himself used when recounting his exploits in the accompanying class."[10]

Bazille's report on 21 June 1880 stressed the virtues of his pupil more than the criticism he had meted out: "Great facility, good reader, very good fingers (could work more); good at harmony, a bit eccentric, much initiative and spirit."[11] His open-mindedness led him to privilege a solid technique over academic obedience. For once, the jury went along with him, granting the first prize to Debussy as well as to Henri-Charles Kaiser.[12] For Achille, this was the only first prize that he could list among his honors, after ten years of study.

However, it should not be forgotten that throughout the same year he still had to continue harmony lessons with Émile Durand, who clearly considered him a rebel. For example, Achille took mischievous delight in his cadential formulas, avoiding the $^6_4$ when moving from the dominant to the tonic. In addition, in his realization of the "given bass," the jury detected about half a dozen errors involving parallel fifths or octaves! Achille did not even meet the minimal requirements, and his name was expunged from the class list on 30 September. After three years of harmony, it was a stinging setback. However, in the process, the course of his career found essential clarity: he could give up working his fingers and appearing to embrace his father's pipe dream that he become a professional pianist, and hence embark on the path of musical composition.

A new diversion arose while he was in the middle of the *concours*.[13] Marmontel, kind as ever, had thought of him yet again when a Russian woman approached the Conservatoire, asking for a pianist to play music for her during the summer. Achille's parents—especially his father—were perhaps beginning to be reassured about their firstborn's future, noting that his talent was valued in well-to-do circles.

For the second summer, Achille found himself in close contact with an exceptional woman: Nadezhda Philaretovna von Meck. About fifty years of age and already widowed for four years, she had five boys and six girls; four of her children were already married. Her husband, Baron Karl von Meck, was said to have descended from the Teutonic knights of Riga; an engineer, he did not have much business sense but had amassed a fine fortune in a railroad company, thanks to the help of his spouse, assisted increasingly by their oldest son Vladimir. The Baron died of a heart attack upon learning of his wife's infidelity with his secretary.[14]

From that time on, Nadezhda traveled extensively, alternating between periods of elation and depression. Although she hated the world, she had an army of servants and tutors and was living in grand style, with a spacious mansion in Moscow and a dacha in the suburbs as well as an immense estate in Ukraine, at Brailov. After becoming a widow, she took refuge in music. A good pianist, she had known Anton Rubinstein and Franz Liszt. In August 1876, she was also at Bayreuth, whose local god did not succeed, as far as she was concerned, in dethroning her own idol. For she did have a god, as shown by her unquenchable passion for Pyotr Ilyich Tchaikovsky, to whom she paid a respectable monthly stipend of 1,500 to 2,000 rubles. For fourteen years, she wrote him ardent letters, although she had never come near him; only once did they catch sight of each other, during an evening at the theater, but they never spoke. In 1878, she rented a magnificent villa for him in Florence, the Villa Bonciani, contenting herself to pass by the house in a carriage and immediately writing to him: "Your neighborhood is such a delight."[15]

Each summer, she would choose a central location for her residence, from which she took side trips. In 1880, she opted to go to the mountains for her children, and it was at Interlaken, Switzerland, where Achille joined the von Meck family on 20 July. Nadezhda expected him to give piano lessons to her children, to accompany the singing of her daughter Julia (age twenty-seven), and to play four-hand piano duets with her. She was eager to play two- or four-hand scores, encouraging Tchaikovsky to make transcriptions of his works for piano, as needed.

"The day before yesterday," she wrote to Tchaikovsky, "a young pianist who has just won the first prize in M. Marmontel's class at the Conservatoire came to us from Paris. [. . .] This young man plays well; his technique is brilliant, but he lacks a personal involvement in what he plays. He has lived too little for that. He claims to be twenty, but looks no more than sixteen."[16] Achille evidently felt the need to improve his image and to endow himself with increased prestige, at the expense of the truth: he became older, claimed a first prize he had not won, and went on to say that he was a student of Massenet before even having matriculated in a composition class.[17]

From Interlaken, Nadezhda von Meck passed through the South of France to arrive, by the beginning of August, in Arcachon, where she took up residence at the Villa Marguerite. Thirteen years later, Debussy told Ernest Chausson about his memories of that place "among the pines."[18] It is very likely that he went on an excursion with Nadezhda from there to San Sebastián, where they attended a bullfight—which must have been the only sight of Spain that he would ever have.

They settled into a certain closeness, and several echoes of their conversations appear in Nadezhda's correspondence with Pyotr Ilyich. Of course, she spoke to Achille about her homeland, which he did not yet know, but most of all they discussed the musical values of their respective countries. Nadezhda learned that in Paris, Bizet and Massenet were regarded very highly, although she judged Russian pianists as far superior to their French colleagues; in addition, she did not believe in the *concours* system of the Conservatoire and confided to Tchaikovsky about Achille: "Now he is working toward the Prix de Rome. All these prizes are nonsense: they aren't worth a thing!"[19] Debussy pretended to show little interest in German music and was said to have declared: "Their temperament is not like ours; they're too heavy, not light."[20]

In matters of Russian music, Achille perhaps knew more than Nadezhda could have imagined. Even if he had not attended four concerts organized by Nicolas Rubinstein at the Trocadéro in 1878, he could have been at the Colonne concert on 25 January 1880, when Édouard Colonne had conducted Tchaikovsky's Fourth Symphony with great success. This was not the only opportunity during those years to hear the works of Tchaikovsky in Paris.[21]

Meanwhile, we might imagine that Nadezhda continued to nag her young pianist and to attempt to properly convert him to the music of her idol. On 19 August, she sat down at the piano with him to sight-read the Fourth Symphony (which had been dedicated to her) and, as early as the next day, informed the master of the result:

> Today my nerves are in a terrible state. When I play your Fourth Symphony, a fever penetrates every fiber of my being and it takes a full day for me to recover. My partner did not perform it well, although he sight-read it wonderfully. That is his only, yet great, strength. He reads a score, even yours, at sight. He has another virtue, which is that he is in awe of Your music. [. . .] I also played your *Suite* with him yesterday.[22] He was captivated by the fugue, saying: among modern fugues, I've never seen anything so beautiful. M. Massenet could never do anything like it.[23]

The Villa Oppenheim in Florence

Dissatisfied with the Villa Marguerite, Nadezhda soon left Arcachon with her entire retinue for a long journey, which took her first to Paris. It is not inconceivable that she had wanted to meet Achille's parents while there, since later, in a letter that we will soon read, she asked him to give them her regards. Then onward to Nice, two days in Genoa, and ten days in Naples, where she had hoped that Tchaikovsky would join her; finally to Florence, where she settled on 19 September at the Villa Oppenheim, a magnificent dwelling surrounded by terraces and gardens, on the hills near San Miniato. Music filled most of their time there as well: "I always play something new and, in any case, everything that I play is new for him," she wrote.[24] As for Achille, he took out of his portfolio his first compositional attempts, in particular a *Danse bohémienne* for piano, which she decided to submit to Tchaikovsky. "It's a lovely thing," replied the latter, "but too short, with themes that don't lead anywhere and a muddled form that lacks direction."[25] While there, Achille also wrote a Trio in G Major, intended for the small resident ensemble that Nadezhda had wanted to form: joining the pianist Debussy were the cellist Peter Danilchenko (called Petrouchka), who had just finished his studies at the Moscow Conservatory, and the violinist Ladislas Pachulsky, who occasionally served as house secretary and who had asked Tchaikovsky to guide him in his composition studies. This French-Russian trio, which played every evening, was even immortalized in a photograph; Achille hastened to send a print of it to his parents, entrusting it to a messenger, with this dedication: "I am sending this young man to bring you my kisses and all my best wishes. Your son Ach. Debussy."[26]

The photograph was also sent to Tchaikovsky, who decreed: "Bussy has something in his face and hands that vaguely resembles Anton Rubinstein in his youth. God grant that his destiny be as fortunate as that of the 'king of pianists'!"[27] And as Nadezhda, who agreed with him on the resemblance, complained that he had never written a trio, Tchaikovsky complied, even though he was not fond of that form; two years later, he dedicated his work to Nicolas Rubinstein, Anton's brother, who had just died. As for the trio by "Bussik," as he was affectionately called at the Villa Oppenheim, it could not be sent to Tchaikovsky because there was not enough time to prepare a copy of it.

Achille also had to satisfy his patroness's request to make a reduction for piano, four hands, of three dances from *Swan Lake*. It was not only completed but even published shortly thereafter by Jurgenson: "I ask you," Nadezhda cautioned, "not to reveal the name of M. de Bussy, because if Jules Massenet were to get wind of it, my young man might get into trouble."[28]

Obviously, she was becoming more and more attached to her "Bussik." A shadow in this family-like atmosphere was brought on by the influence of a pretentious tutor, but Nadezhda swiftly dispelled it:

My little Frenchman is leaving next week because I've kept him an extra two weeks. I'm sad that he's leaving because his music-making has given me great pleasure and, all in all, he is a good-hearted boy. But, as we should have foreseen, his friendship with our Russian tutor has had a bad influence on him. For some unknown reason, this tutor claims to be an aristocrat, and Bussy, who is still very childlike, imitated him and succeeded only in making us laugh at the airs he put on. The tutor left a month ago, and Bussy has changed completely.[29]

The musical activities at the villa intensified during his final days there: not only were trios performed, but also, in particular, Tchaikovsky's Waltz in F Minor, which Bussik "played very well,"[30] and his Piano Sonata. With Danilchenko, he played Bizet's "charming" suite from *L'Arlésienne* for four hands and some Glinka, which set Nadezhda's heart aflutter.[31] There was talk of giving the score of Tchaikovsky's *Maid of Orleans* to the young Frenchman, with the composer's consent, but Nadezhda changed her mind, fearing that Massenet, Delibes, Benjamin Godard, and others "would fill their pockets with ideas" from Tchaikovsky's last opera, as they had already done, she claimed, with his first symphony, which Achille also sight-read with her.[32]

Finally, shortly after 5 November, came the farewells: "Imagine, Pyotr Ilyich, that this boy wept bitterly when he left me. That naturally touched me deeply; he has such a big heart. He wouldn't have left had the administrators at the Conservatoire not objected to his desire to extend his stay."[33]

Guiraud's Class

Massenet was the most highly regarded professor of composition at the Conservatoire, even though he had held his position for only two years. When Achille told Nadezhda that he was Massenet's student, he may simply have been anticipating becoming one and may have genuinely intended to enroll in his class, as Marty, Vidal, and Bruneau had done.[34] However, he was directed to another teacher, one who had just been appointed: Ernest Guiraud, formerly a harmony professor, and, as of 1 December 1880, *titulaire* of a composition class. Perhaps the reason for this change of instructor was the late date of Achille's return to the Conservatoire; or perhaps Marmontel, who was a close friend of Guiraud, had advised Achille to approach the newcomer instead. Guiraud was certainly more an artist than a pedagogue, and his broad-mindedness might have been a better match for the youth's temperament. Besides, Guiraud had only three students during his first year. So Achille entered his class on 24 December—an odd time of year to start school.

His experience in César Franck's class also dates from that period of 1880–81. Although the Conservatoire archives are far less precise regarding the free auditors than they are for the regular students, Achille's name clearly appears there as such.[35] Vidal confirms that he attended the class "a few times" with Achille, and that both of them made fun of the teacher's idiosyncrasies.[36] We know that Franck favored improvisation over technique on the organ, an attitude for which he was criticized by some of his colleagues. His devotees have quoted the sort of remarks that accompanied his teaching: "Modulate. . . modulate. . . , far. . . far. . . Not too much. . . not too much. . ."![37] Achille would have been quickly bored by this little game—"this tiresome and persistent dreariness,"[38] as he would write later. Nevertheless, he liked the *Béatitudes*, and later, when he was renouncing Wagner, he would deem that Franck, judging by this work, was "allied with the great musicians for whom sounds in and of themselves have a precise meaning."[39]

A question that remains unanswered concerns Achille's participation in the music-history lectures of Louis-Albert Bourgault-Ducoudray, who since 1878 had taught the ancient modes and folk song. As a rule, the composition students were expected to attend these lectures, but no class roster remains in the institutional archives, and Bourgault's courses were of the "public lecture" type, intended for a broad audience, clearly showing that this discipline was regarded as somewhat marginal at the institution.[40]

We can verify, in spite of what has been said about it, that upon his return to Paris, Achille maintained excellent relations with all of his professors, even those for whom he had not excelled in his studies. One of his first gestures was to visit his former harmony teacher, Émile Durand, and present him with the manuscript of his Florentine trio, dedicated as follows: "Many notes accompanied by much affection" (Beaucoup de notes accompagnées de beaucoup d'amitiés).

He also had to think about making a little steady income and showing his parents that, even without being a virtuoso, a musician could survive. Lavignac remembered his perfectly infallible ear, as well as his family's limited resources, when the possibility arose of giving private lessons to a ten-year-old child, Georges Cuignache, who had just entered his class. The young boy thus became Debussy's first student. At the end of the year, Georges obtained a third medal in solfège; subsequently, it took him two more years to advance to the first medal![41]

Accompanist for Mme Moreau-Sainti

But Achille had increasing material needs: he was already collecting books, engravings, and curios. A more stable income was becoming essential. That is why, through the intervention of Paul Vidal and, it seems, with the recommendation of Charles Gounod, he became accompanist for the voice class of Mme Moreau-Sainti. For four years, he would fulfill this duty, which was rather thankless in general. Classes met twice a week—Tuesdays and Fridays at 3:00 p.m.—between November and June, first at 10 rue Taitbout, then at 7 rue Royale at the École internationale de musique.

Victorine Moreau-Sainti had taught in Paris since at least 1878; she was forty-one years old at the time. The daughter of a tenor who had enjoyed a brilliant career at the Opéra-Comique and who was a professor at the Conservatoire, she had been a student of Laure Cinti-Damoreau and had made her debut at the Opéra in 1856 in Giuseppe Verdi's *I vespri siciliani*. But seven years later, her marriage to the engineer Vital-Roux having interrupted her career, she found herself in Reims, where she modestly taught voice. After her husband's death in 1876, she returned to the capital and set up a voice class, which she taught according to the "Faure method" (developed by Jean-Baptiste Faure, the famous baritone), and coached a vocal ensemble; in November 1881, she partnered for some time with Peruzzi on a class of "vocal ensemble music" which brought together "society women" in the Flaxland salons.[42] She also held salons at her home on Sundays and sometimes took part in public concerts, as in 1878 with the performance of Henri Dallier's prize cantata at the Institut.

The repertoire chosen for the young society women who attended this class was rather eclectic. Some brief notices in the musical press give us a sense of the programming. Delibes was favored with excerpts from *Jean de Nivelle* and *Lakmé*, but also mentioned were an aria from Bizet's *Les pêcheurs de perles*, and the Gypsy song and the duet from *Aben-Hamet* by Théodore Dubois. Among the works for ensembles were a chorus by René Lenormand and some choruses from the Béarn region by Fernand de La Tombelle.[43] Achille would have chafed at most of this repertoire had there not been certain rewards that held his interest: the young singers whom he accompanied and who performed at times in class recitals or in afternoon student concerts. "Young upper-crust ladies" and "our most elegant society women" are some of the labels ascribed to them by the columnists. Already strongly attracted to women, Achille suddenly found himself like a kid in a candy shop and slightly besotted. Naturally, many of these ladies were older than the pianist who accompanied them. Such was the case with a beautiful redhead with green eyes, Marie Vasnier;[44] she was thirty-two years old and the mother of two children, ages ten and twelve.

Marie Vasnier

The portraits left to us by Paul Baudry (1885) and Jacques-Émile Blanche (1888) show Marie to be voluptuous—as Gaby and Lilly would also be—and having nothing of a Pre-Raphaelite look. Her husband, Henri-A. Vasnier,[45] who was said to have been an architect, was in fact a buildings registrar, which is to say that professionally he handled legal assessments in architectural matters.[46] This was how he made a living, but above all he was passionate about archaeology and Hellenism, as well as social issues. He became a member of several learned societies (the Association des études grecques, the Société d'archéologie française, the Société des antiquaires de France) and also of the Marmites, a club of anti-clerical Jacobins.

Eleven years younger than her husband, Marie found an avenue for personal growth through singing, which took place in the freedom of her home, whose atmosphere was more conducive to study than to sensuality. Achille's "blazing eyes" must have quickly perceived her desire to prolong a youthfulness which too early on had been devoted to raising her children.[47] At the age of nineteen, he was encountering a woman whose maturity could only boost his confidence, given his lack of experience, and whose amorous availability was placed at his disposal.

He did not delay in using a weapon that he had already mastered to some degree: he wrote some songs for her high soprano voice. A thorough study of the manuscripts from this period suggests that about ten of these songs were composed between the end of 1880 and the middle of 1881, that is to say very shortly after the beginning of his involvement with Mme Moreau-Sainti.[48] He chose poems by Théophile Gautier, Leconte de Lisle, and, in particular, Théodore de Banville. Some of these poems were daring, recalling or confirming André Suarès's suggestion that the youthful Debussy "must have switched from a timid disposition to cynical confessions."[49] The songs written for Marie were also love letters. To woo her, it was easier to take the mantle of Banville or Leconte de Lisle. In Banville's "Caprice"—the first song that he presented to her—the beloved woman, after having seemed to spurn her lover, tells him to come to her feet and to "adore her until death." In Leconte de Lisle's "Jane," the lover languishes because "two beautiful eyes" have "broken his heart," and in his "La fille aux cheveux de lin," he wants "to kiss the blond of your hair, to press the crimson of your lips" amidst the fields of alfalfa. Achille added dedications on the manuscripts that Marie could hardly have left out on her piano: "To Mme Vanier [sic], these songs, conceived in some way with you in mind, can belong only to you, as does the composer" (À Mme Vanier [sic], ces mélodies, conçues en quelque sorte par votre souvenir, ne peuvent que vous appartenir, comme vous appartient l'auteur); and "To Mme Vanier [sic], the only muse who has ever inspired in me something resembling a musical feeling (to mention only that one)" (À Mme Vanier [sic], la seule muse qui m'ait jamais inspiré quelque chose ressemblant à un sentiment musical [pour ne parler que de celui-là]). Finally, a more discreet confession convinces us that their relationship was not only literary and musical. It is found inside the score of *Hélène* (a cantata on a Banville text that he composed early in 1881), slipped in at the exact moment when the soprano solo enters: "Yes, you have said these words so sweet: I love you."

It is in this context that Achille continued to pursue his studies with Guiraud. The latter was not won over right away by his pupil; he noted simply: "Intelligent, promises to become a good composer" (31 January 1881) or just "intelligent, good student" (26 June).[50] At the beginning of May, however, Achille's passion for Marie was not yet strong enough to sway him from spending a summer far from Paris—as he had in the two preceding years. Purely material reasons also weighed heavily in his decision. The voice classes were on holiday break, and he had entrusted his pupil, the young Cuignache, to Vidal. He wrote to Nadezhda to offer his services to her once again. The positive reply reaches us, as usual, through her letter to Tchaikovsky: "My little Frenchman Bussik is very eager to come to me in Brailov. I shall not have the heart to refuse his request, although I already have a pianist, the elder Pachulsky."[51]

Meanwhile, Achille had saved a surprise for his Russian patroness: a Symphony in B Minor, the dedicated manuscript of which he had sent to her. Nadezhda replied to him in a most touching letter, written in French:

Brailov, 20 February 1881[52]

Dear Monsieur Debussy!

Although the pleasure of corresponding with friends is *forbidden fruit* for me (because of my nervous sufferings), in the present circumstances, I cannot deny myself the pleasure of writing these few words to you, to tell you how touched I am by the pleasant surprise that you have given me by sending your charming symphony.[53] I deeply regret not having you here to hear it performed for us; it would be a double pleasure for me, but alas, people are always slaves to someone or something, and it remains for me only to rest my hopes on the future and now to thank you very much, very deeply, dear Monsieur Debussy, and to wish you all the best, and above all the most brilliant progress in your wonderful career. Kindly accept my most affectionate regards.

Nadine de Meck

P.S. Please give a thousand warm regards to your dear parents on my behalf.

M. Anfray will deliver to you a small souvenir from me, which I hope, Monsieur, will *always* serve as a remembrance of me. It is an object, made in Moscow, which deals with a characteristically Russian subject: the scene portrays Vanya (the contralto role) from Glinka's opera, *A Life for the Tsar*.

Can you imagine that I have almost entirely given up music, first because I am really busy here, and second because my partner (Petrouchka) is so unpleasant in his role as pianist, that he is spoiling my appetite for music. My daughters send you their regards.[54]

First Visit to Russia

Nadezhda, who at first had thought of settling in Biarritz for the summer, was extremely busy with the sale of her estate in Brailov, so she remained in Moscow from mid-July until the end of September. Thanks to this change of plans, Achille would see Russia for the first time. He left Paris at the end of July. At the 27 June 1881 examination for the composition class,[55] he had presented a piece for chorus and orchestra, *Hélène*, on which Théodore Dubois, a member of the jury, had commented as follows: "Twisted, modulating too much, on the wrong track."[56]

Unfortunately, we have fewer details about the two months that Achille spent in Russia than we have about his stay during the previous year. Nadezhda's sons, Nicolas (called Kolia) and especially Alexander (who was Debussy's piano student), would certainly have shown him around Moscow and its attractions. And how we wish that the letters were preserved (those that at times he wrote to his mother) in which Achille described his exploration of that fascinating city with its multicolored architecture, which, Vidal claims, constituted "a major experience in his life!"[57] We learn from Nadezhda von Meck's correspondence with Tchaikovsky that, at least once, Achille left Moscow with Nicolas to go to the large country estate at Gourievo, about 120 kilometers south of Moscow, where Nadezhda's daughter, who had become Countess Alexandra Bennigsen, lived; there he played Tchaikovsky's Fourth Symphony again. Nadezhda finally gave him the *Maid of Orleans*, translating the words for him so that he could better understand the essence of the music, and also the overture to *Romeo and Juliet*, the score of which he had requested.[58] Perhaps he visited the theaters in Moscow, and when he later wrote in *Gil Blas*,[59] by way of an obituary for Robert Planquette, that he knew *Les cloches de Corneville* only in Russian,[60] that probably was no joke. He certainly did not fail to make use of Nadezhda's extensive music library every morning when he had free time.

On 2 October, Nadezhda von Meck left Moscow to return once again to Italy, passing through Vienna, Trieste, and Venice, with the intention of settling down in Florence. What a trip for Achille, who discovered the luxury of parlor cars as well as the landscapes of so many impressive cities along the way. After 12 October, they stayed in Rome, where Achille completed and dated "Triolet à Philis," based on a Banville text, and the *Ouverture Diane* (in the style of Tchaikovsky's "overture-fantasies," such as the aforementioned *Romeo and Juliet*) for piano, four hands, dated 27 November. Then they reached Florence, where Nadezhda's other children were going to join them for the Christmas holidays and where Achille put the final touches on "Souhait," also drawn from Banville's *Les Cariatides*.[61]

Achille's return to Paris thus took place in early December, even later than in the preceding year. If we are to believe Nicolas von Meck's memories, one of the family members was said to have pointed out the Villa Medici to Achille while they were walking in Rome, declaring: "This is your future home," and he reportedly cast a pensive glance at the building.[62] In any case, three years later, he told Paul Vidal, who was trying to be a good friend by convincing him to leave for Rome, that he already knew the city and loathed it.[63]

This visit, during which he had lived a most authentic Russian life and then discovered Rome, had still occasioned much music. It had also permitted a greater intimacy with the von Meck family—with Nicolas, who was nearly his contemporary; Julia, age twenty-eight; and Sonia, who was fourteen. He had Sonia sing "Ici-bas, tous les lilas meurent," passing this song off as one of his own compositions, even though it was by the Hillemacher brothers.[64] In the cabarets in Moscow or its vicinity, he had the opportunity to hear Gypsies, who gave him "the first example of music without rules"[65] and whom he would always remember.

Upon his return to Paris, Achille went to the Vasniers' home more often than he went to the Conservatoire. Each of these experiences, spent away from his family, served only to intensify his independent spirit. His parents saw their son drifting away completely from them—from his father, with whom he had "almost no ideas in common,"[66] and especially from his mother, who was overprotective and tended to smother him with her love. She was offended, and swiftly guessed that a woman was the reason for his indifferent attitude toward his parents. When she learned that this woman was married and the mother of a family, she was dismayed. She spoke about the situation with Vidal, who was a close friend of the family but no longer had any hold over her son. Achille's friends quickly learned about it, and some of them were in awe and astonished by the audacity—or the success—of their friend.

Whereas his best friends (especially Bonheur and Vidal) were in Massenet's studio, Achille kept in close contact with Guiraud's students, who were older and without much personality—which warranted the professor's opinion that he had a "sad class."[67] Among his students were Paul Jeannin and Florentin Piffaretti, called to become organists, and Mélanie Mel-Bonis,[68] who was soon married and would pursue a very modest career as a composer. As a way of seeking forgiveness for his tardiness, Achille dedicated his *Ouverture Diane*, for piano, four hands, to his professor—a gesture analogous to the one he had made to Émile Durand in the previous year. However, that did not prevent Guiraud from acknowledging, on 11 January 1882, that his pupil was not very diligent in his class: "Intelligent, but needs to be reined in. Returned rather late from his trip and has not yet been able to work much this year."[69] To his friends, Achille's increasingly independent character made him appear to be a leader, as on 6 March, when at the premiere of *Namouna*, Édouard Lalo's ballet, "the frenzy of his applause and his provocative attitude created such a scandal that, at the request of the subscribers, the box seats at the Conservatoire remained off-limits to the students of the composition classes for several months."[70]

Songs for Marie

In any case, Debussy's mind was elsewhere and he was once again seized with an insatiable desire for songs. A period of literary exploration at the end of 1881 led him to engage with new poets: Charles Cros, Louis Bouilhet, and Maurice Bouchor—attempts that remained in sketchbooks, such as a new Leconte de Lisle song, "Les elfes."[71] The most important event, in early 1882, was his discovery of Verlaine: on 8 January, he completed "Fantoches"—a song that he naturally dedicated to Marie, at whose home he had perhaps discovered and discussed the collection of *Fêtes galantes* poems, having spent his afternoons more often at her residence on the rue Constantinople than at the Conservatoire. There, in the small parlor on the sixth floor, he worked on the old, strangely shaped Blondel piano; and, in the evenings, Marie sang and he accompanied her.

The parlor functioned as a boudoir as well as a laboratory where new songs were immediately put to the test by the agile voice of his beloved. Achille and Marie went even further, performing in public, in the salons of the former publisher Flaxland (who had become a piano manufacturer on the rue des Mathurins), where "serious enthusiasts" were welcomed twice a week. That was how they lent their "gracious assistance"[72] during an evening performance given by the violinist Maurice Thieberg, on 12 May 1882. Achille first had to accompany the obscure musician in the Allegro of the Sonata in E-flat Major (op. 12, no. 3) by Beethoven, as well as in the *Pensées fugitives* by Stephen Heller and Heinrich Wilhelm Ernst, before performing his "Fête galante" and "Les roses" with Marie. The program did not even point out that it was a premiere of these songs, as it was for his *Nocturne et Scherzo*, which he played with Thieberg.[73] It was perhaps on this occasion that Achille discovered that the name of his interpreter was written Vasnier and not Vanier, as he had been spelling it in his dedications.

In another concert, of which no detailed program has been preserved, Achille accompanied Marie in the "Rondel chinois," a song on a poem by Marius Dillard that he had set to music during the previous year.[74] "To Mme Vanier [*sic*], the only one who can sing and make forgettable all that this music has that is unsingable and perplexing."[75] Another occasion reveals the young man growing bolder, carried away by his youthful passion: he published his first work, "Nuit d'étoiles," already two years old, which he dedicated this time to Mme Moreau-Sainti, as if he wanted to thank her for having allowed him to meet Marie. On 6 June, he sold the rights to it for fifty francs to Émile Bulla, a small Catalan publisher who was an acquaintance of his father.[76]

These three years, from 1880 to 1882, completely transformed Achille. He had almost forgotten his academic failures and he now composed music with ease. Even though he did not have his prize in piano, he had traveled more than any of his friends. The success that he had encountered with ladies in polite society had given him confidence, and now he was smitten by an exclusive love, which elated him and pushed him to compose. He was spreading his wings and was driven by an overwhelming desire to succeed. A sign of this awareness was the fact that he had calling cards printed with his name, "A. de Bussy."

Chapter Four

The Path to the Prix de Rome

1882–84

In spring 1882, Achille presented himself for the first time in the preliminary examination for the Prix de Rome.[1] The requirements included writing a four-voice fugue on a subject by Gounod, and then setting a text by Count Anatole de Ségur, "Salut printemps, jeune saison," for female chorus.[2] It is almost surprising to find in the notes of one jury member, Théodore Dubois, that Achille was described as "ingenious, progressing."[3] However, the student did not advance to the second round of the competition. Guiraud's opinion, on 26 June, suggests that their relationship had not yet blossomed into a friendship: "Some progress. Poorly balanced nature, but intelligent. Will get there, I believe."[4] This assessment was reserved, compared with that of Théodore Dubois!

It is unlikely that Achille showed his teacher everything he was writing at this time, including works such as "Flots, palmes, sables," a "Mélodie persane"[5] by Armand Renaud (2 June); a transcription for violoncello of his own *Nocturne et Scherzo* (14 June); a setting of *Hymnis*, a "comédie lyrique" by Théodore de Banville; *Le triomphe de Bacchus*, a suite for piano, four hands, whose title was also inspired by Banville;[6] and finally, *Daniel*, a cantata whose text came from an earlier Prix de Rome competition and which he set for three soloists and orchestra. He offered a copy of it to a classmate, Georges-Eugène Marquet (who had won a first honorable mention in comic opera in 1880).[7] This incessant production did not prevent him from writing an *Intermezzo* for orchestra (dated 21 June) for the examination that took place on 11 July, when he shared a second honorable mention with Edmond Missa.[8] Later, Debussy would criticize Missa in *Gil Blas*, while acknowledging that he had been "a kind and devoted friend."[9]

Second Visit to Russia

Now in his twentieth year, Achille felt much less urgency to join Mme von Meck for the summer. His love kept him back in Paris as long as the Vasnier family schedule could accommodate him. The beautiful weather lured them to Ville-d'Avray, where they rented a villa; Achille often went there for the day, returning in the evenings via the last train. In the country, he was more relaxed. Not far away was the home of Alfred Bruneau (the second-place winner in the Prix de Rome from the previous year), who was living there with his parents. On 14 July, a sad piece of news reminded Achille that he still had his own family: his beloved Aunt Clémentine, who had been the impetus behind his career, died in Suresnes without being able to share in the decisive success of a nephew for whom she had been the fairy godmother.

Marguerite Vasnier, Marie's daughter, remembered great croquet parties in the park at Saint-Cloud, or card games, when the weather was dreary; in both instances, Achille proved to be a sore loser. But he would quickly regain his good nature, striking a pose as a serenader while strumming his mallet like a guitar. "One day," Marguerite recounted, "some street singers stopped in front of the house; he began to sing along and to accompany them on the piano, then told them to enter and had them perform, while adding quips to make us all die of laughter."[10]

In this festive atmosphere, he waited until the end of August to request his passport for Moscow, which he obtained on the 31st. On 8 September, he arrived at Plesheyevo, a new residence—about fifty kilometers from Moscow, near Podolsk—that the von Mecks had just purchased. Nadezhda found Achille particularly cheerful: "He enlivens the whole house," she wrote to Tchaikovsky. "He's a real Parisian kid, witty as all get-out, and he excels at doing impressions. He imitates Gounod, Ambroise Thomas, and others to perfection. He's always in good spirits, always satisfied by everything, and makes everyone laugh hysterically."[11] Not only was Achille completely at ease in this family with whom he was living for the third time, but their mutual affection built up his self-confidence.

Musical pursuits were no longer as intense as in the preceding years: Nadezhda suffered from rheumatoid arthritis and could not play piano with him. Nevertheless, she steered her "Bussik" toward her latest discovery, Mily Balakirev's songs, which delighted her: "I find in them a picturesque character that speaks to the imagination. Not only is a melodic line heard, but it materializes from a sonorous background, as if emanating from one's imagination [. . .] and emerges as a misty tableau."[12] After this stay with Debussy at Plesheyevo, she went to Moscow and, on 3 October, left for Vienna; that year, due to her son Alexander's health, she had decided to make the Austrian capital the hub of her activities. This is how Achille came to spend nearly two months in Vienna. Did she take him to Paris, where she went on 26 October? This seems unlikely. On 19 November, she went back to Vienna, just in time to attend, with her family, a revival of *Carmen* with the great Pauline Lucca, and not, as has always been written, a performance of *Tristan* conducted by Hans Richter.[13]

So once again Debussy returned to Paris very belatedly, as far as the Conservatoire's rules were concerned. In his luggage, he brought back some new songs, "En sourdine" and "Mandoline" among them.[14] Thus ended for Achille this cycle of three summers spent in the company of an extravagant and passionate woman, in luxurious conditions—dwellings, grand hotels, and sleeping cars—for which he had developed a taste. Nadezhda von Meck was perfectly well aware of her personal role in the development of the young pianist, for when she learned, two years later, that he had won the Grand Prix de Rome, she wrote to Tchaikovsky, expressing an opinion that was quite apt: "I'm not surprised; he's a very precocious boy and his long visits with me allowed him to broaden his horizons and to refine his taste by his exposure to foreign musics."[15] It is true that, thanks to her, at age twenty he had already seen Rome, Florence, Moscow, and Vienna, and, while the prospect of returning to the two-room apartment on the rue Clapeyron weighed on him, he would, most importantly, be rejoining his muse, after three months of separation.

On New Year's Day 1883, he used the opening bars of "Mandoline" to offer his greetings to Marie, "I wish you a good and happy New Year," adding a brash dedication: "Among the wishes that are coming your way, allow me to express this one: that you might always be the person who gave the perfect shape—the dream of delirious composers—to the impoverished music of one who will always be your friend and devoted composer. Ach. Debussy."[16]

Ernest Guiraud still did not seem entirely won over by Achille when he saw his pupil again, following his delayed return from Russia. The teacher, who had gone to Bayreuth in July, reported his impressions of the place in his class. He was very irritated by the atmosphere in Bayreuth, created by the "musical dwarves, dimwits, and diehards from every country. [. . .] Here, one would be torn to pieces if one were foolish enough to venture the slightest criticism. Even mere enthusiasm is forbidden. [. . .] Only ecstasy is tolerated."[17] However, he was swayed by *Parsifal*, in which he found "beauties of the highest order that reveal the great musician [that Wagner was]."[18] Having to evaluate Achille on 9 January 1883, Guiraud expressed this rather ambivalent opinion: "Bizarre but intelligent nature. Writes music poorly. Has made some progress, however."[19] On the calendar for the month of February, two events affected Achille very differently: on the 2nd, he was permanently exempted from military service by a favorable lottery; and on the 13th, he learned about the death of Richard Wagner. But above all else, he continued to compose.

A Second Prize in the Prix de Rome

He decided to gather together the songs that he intended to give Marie into a volume,[20] and, shortly after his arrival in Paris, began to copy the five *Fêtes galantes* of Verlaine; on 31 March, he added "Coquetterie posthume" by Théophile Gautier, and, soon thereafter, the "Chanson espagnole" duet by Musset. Achille also indulged his taste for the picturesque Hispanic subjects that were in fashion by offering his beloved a "Séguidille,"[21] drawn from *España* by the same Gautier.

It was thus a period of very eclectic poetic choices, all the more so since around the same time Achille began to work on a more ambitious project, *Diane au bois* by Théodore de Banville. Using two scenes from that "heroic comedy," he attempted to work with a language that was more lyrical and of a more continuous dramatic flow, with harmonic boldness and some promising experiments in prosody. He showed these attempts to Guiraud, who advised him to keep them for later, because the preliminary examination for the Prix de Rome was drawing near.

Debussy claimed that he did not want to take the exam, but Vidal managed to persuade him, so that he might qualify for the second round of the *concours*. From 5 to 11 May, he was sequestered and expected to complete the following exercises: a vocal fugue (without piano), and a setting for chorus and orchestra of "Invocation," a text by Alphonse de Lamartine. The decision was announced on 23 June: Achille placed fourth, behind Vidal, Charles René, and Xavier Leroux, and ahead of Edmond Missa. All five candidates were then sequestered again, this time for twenty-five days, at the castle at Compiègne, as was the custom. They were provided with the text for the cantata *Le gladiateur* by Émile Moreau, a writer who specialized in texts of this sort. We can imagine Achille, steeped in Verlaine and Banville, being asked to respond to the entreaties of such a poem: "Death to the Romans!. . . Kill every last one of them!" We might add that *Le ménestrel* reported the facetious comments of the competitors, faced with these "harmonious lines [. . .] which have only one shortcoming: they could just as well do without music."[22]

This seclusion of more than three weeks, during which Achille was able to write the 118 pages of his cantata, would have been an ordeal without visitations from parents and friends, visits that were permitted in the evenings in a courtyard garden of the castle. The Vasniers did not fail to come and comfort their protégé, bringing their children along, and when Marguerite, Marie's daughter, asked why there were bars on the windows of the castle bedrooms, Achille explained: "It's because they doubtless consider us to be ferocious beasts."[23] Perhaps there was an opportunity, in the course of one of these evenings, for Debussy's parents to catch sight of that woman who had "captivated" their son.

On 23 June, the cantatas were performed at the Institut, presided over by Gounod. Debussy was fortunate to have some excellent performers, recruited no doubt by Guiraud: Alexandre Taskin, Antoine Muratet, and in particular Gabrielle Krauss, the great Viennese-born soprano. Vidal's cantata secured the first prize from the outset, but the struggle for second was fierce between Debussy and Charles René. After three ballots, the two candidates found themselves in a tie. Finally, on the fourth ballot, Debussy won the second prize, and was given the following evaluation: "Bountiful musical nature but passionate to the point of excess; some striking dramatic accents."[24] The critics praised the craft of the first-prize winner and the originality of the second. In the *Journal des débats*, Ernest Reyer identified in the latter "the temperament of a true musician" but stressed that his various skills needed to be "honed."[25] *L'art musical*, emphasizing his "highly original personality," deemed Debussy's setting of the scene "worthy of the top prize in every respect,"[26] while Edmond Stoullig thought that "the jury had acted wisely by requiring him to remain in school another year."[27] For that matter, it is possible that Achille felt the same way, knowing that a first prize would force him to move away from Paris, where he was held by ties much stronger than the desire for a brilliant career.

Far from bearing a grudge against the winner, Achille invited Vidal to a little party at his parents' home, where the latter was treated as "a child of the family."[28] Achille's professor Guiraud, who was beginning to envision a bright future for him, was also there.

Shortly afterward, the young composer found his real reward in joining Marie at Ville-d'Avray. Leafing through *Les aveux* by Paul Bourget, he chose the "Romance" to set for her, with the following text:

The ardent intoxication of life
Makes the enraptured lover swoon
And one hears the beating of only one heart.

And, at the beginning of autumn, he selected "Paysage sentimental," upon returning from a stroll in the park at Saint-Cloud:

. . . Ah! How your mouth gave itself up to mine
More tenderly than ever in that vast, silent woods
And in that languor of the death of the year.

Having savored Verlaine, Achille suddenly took an interest in this collection by Bourget, which had appeared during the previous year. While there is no doubt that the two men knew each other—the poet had sent his recent book to the composer in Rome—we do not know where they could have met. Achille knew him well enough to know that Bourget's muse, Minnie David,[29] had "such a delicious way of calling him Paul!"[30] In any case, prior to 1891 the composer would draw nine times from that collection of poems, in which Bourget displayed a mixture of trembling lyricism and dilettantism, inherited from a "modernity" that was dear to Charles Baudelaire.[31] No doubt Achille's choice to set Bourget's verses was made in the course of one of those "long discussions" on poetry to which Marguerite Vasnier alluded.[32] And he soon copied these two songs into the volume he was planning to give Marie.

In his final year of study at the Conservatoire, Debussy had become remarkably sure of himself, not only because he was an apparently fulfilled lover, but also because he was cognizant of having found, little by little, his path as a composer. Paul Vidal, having gone to the Villa Medici, wrote to Henriette Fuchs on 28 October, inquiring about his friend in telling language: "What do you make of Debussy? Has he come off his high horse?"[33]

The Concordia

Upon leaving for Rome, Paul Vidal once again proved to be a good friend: he passed on to Achille his job as accompanist with the Concordia, a choral society of amateurs. Following the society's general meeting on 25 November 1883, one could read in their report, at the end of the list of the board of directors: "Accompanist: M. Ach. de Bussy." His annual salary was 455 francs.

The Concordia had been founded in 1880 by an engineer from the École nationale supérieure des mines de Paris,[34] Edmond Fuchs, whose wife Henriette had sung for several years as a soloist in charity concerts and soirees. Its goal, according to the statutes, was "the study of choral music masterpieces and the public performance of this repertoire for the benefit of charitable works or for the common good."[35] The honorary president was Gounod, whose works were frequently performed by the society and who seemed to have taken a great liking to Achille.[36] Charles-Marie Widor was the group's orchestral and choral conductor.

The group's rehearsals were quite demanding. They would meet each Saturday at the Oratory chapel of the Louvre, "at 4:00 sharp for the Ladies, and at 4:30 for the Gentlemen,"[37] but much more frequently as the concerts drew near. During the previous season, the Concordia had performed *Athalie* by Felix Mendelssohn, and *Ulysse* and the *Rédemption* by Gounod.[38]

Henriette Fuchs was no Mme Pelouze nor Nadezhda von Meck. Far from having their independent spirit and their imagination, she had devoted her life to charitable works and had grown up in a very strict, morally principled environment. Achille had been able to hear in President Fuchs's speech that the Concordia, "in order to live up to its task, has the right and the duty to show itself to be increasingly rigorous in its choice of repertoire." Achille must not have felt very comfortable in that self-righteous, Protestant environment, from which professional choristers were excluded because they lived "at the altar in the mornings and at the theater in the evenings."[39] He did not take his job very seriously, and Mme Fuchs, the society's leading lady, quickly grew suspicious of him. From 30 November 1883 onward, Achille seems to have missed some rehearsals, and he apologized in a way that was not particularly credible to Henriette Fuchs:

> Madame,
>   As some family matters have forced me to leave on a trip, I found your message only today. As those same matters oblige me to leave again, I think I'll be back tomorrow morning, and allow me, Madame, to blame the circumstances ("hazard" [sic]) for managing things so poorly.
>   Again, a thousand pardons, and please accept my sincere regrets.[40]

A telegram, sent during the same period, attempted to explain another absence after the fact. Again, we leave Achille's original spelling:

> Madame,
>   A thousand pardons for not having been at the Concordia. All along I thought I'd be able to get up, but I was unable to ("je n'ai put" [sic]). I had a night of frightful sleep ("une nuit de lit affreuse" [sic]).
>   I will come on Thursday to beg your pardon, and to ask if you have been satisfied with me ("si vous avez été contente de moi jeudi" [sic]).
>   Affectionately yours.[41]

Such are the first two letters from Debussy that we have preserved today! In another missive, he anticipated that he "might not be at the afternoon rehearsal," because he was not feeling well.[42] Henriette Fuchs lost no time in complaining about her accompanist's cavalier attitude to Vidal, who tried to offer excuses for his classmate on 3 February 1884:

> What you tell me about Debussy only half surprises me. I've known him for a very long time, and one needs to make many allowances for him, because his upbringing is somewhat lacking, and he has experienced so few of life's lessons; if you can keep him, please do so, but I wouldn't want you to suffer on my account from whatever is going on. I've known from the start that if you dismiss him, it will be because you have no other choice, and I won't hold it against you.[43]

All the same, Debussy's role in four of the Concordia's concerts is documented. On 10 January 1884, the chorus performed substantial parts of Franz Liszt's *Die Legende von der heiligen Elisabeth* and J. S. Bach's *Actus tragicus* (*Gottes Zeit ist die allerbeste Zeit*, BWV 106), with some shorter works by Widor, Gounod, and Vidal (whose *Invocation* was given its premiere).[44] The concert on 1 March included excerpts from an opera by Charles Lenepveu, *Velléda* (whose subject was drawn from François-René de Chateaubriand's *Les martyrs*), and the choruses that W. A. Mozart wrote for *Thamos, König in Ägypten*, KV 345, specially translated into French for this occasion; these two works were interspersed with pieces by Anton Rubinstein, Chopin, Stephen Heller, Ambroise Thomas, Christoph Willibald Gluck, and Mendelssohn.[45] On 8 April, at the Salle Albert-le-Grand, the program comprised George Frideric Handel's *Ode for Saint Cecilia's Day* cantata and a repeat of the *Actus tragicus*, along with some works by Saint-Saëns, Rossini, Mendelssohn, and Giovanni Pierluigi da Palestrina (the "Kyrie" from the *Missa Papae Marcelli*).[46] Finally, the bulk of the concert on 21 May was devoted to the *Rédemption*, the sacred trilogy by Gounod.[47] The musical level of these amateurs was no more than average, but this repertoire, which introduced Achille to several choral works, was more rewarding to him than the operatic excerpts he had to accompany in Mme Moreau-Sainti's studio. He seemed to have shown a very special interest in Liszt's *Elisabeth* oratorio, as we learn from another letter sent to Henriette Fuchs:

Madame,
    I'd like to reply to you in person and to tell you how upset I am about everything that is happening, because I'd be very sorry were you to doubt the good will and the sincerity of the services that I'm permitted to give the Concordia.
    As for the scores of *Elisabeth*, I really don't have any of them. I'm astonished that you could even think that I had one. That is something I would not allow myself to do without asking your permission.
    Please allow me to come to talk to you about my troubles on Thursday morning, if that won't inconvenience you.

And the letter was signed: "Ach. Debussy, sick (but faithful) (no matter what anyone says) accompanist of the Concordia."[48]

We must not forget that, at the same time, Debussy had to fulfill his obligations for Mme Moreau-Sainti's lessons, which took place every Tuesday and Friday at 3:00 p.m. up to the month of June. It is clear that these obligations had become a pleasure and, at the beginning of February 1884, a student performance was deemed worthy of a small review by a columnist in the *Ménestrel*, who praised both Marie and Achille:

We recently attended a student recital given by the class of Mme Moreau-Sainti. There we heard a number of students, some of whom already deserve to be considered as artists. But what struck us in particular was how magnificently Mme Moreau-Sainti's method excelled in both applying itself to and asserting itself in the most varied styles. That is why Mme Vasnier vocalizes with a perfection that one does not often find in professional artists, one that Mlles de B. . . and F. . . display in grand style, showing very promising talents, and one that Mmes Duboc and Gentil convey remarkably in pieces of different genres such as *Lakmé* [by Delibes] and the song from *Die Walküre* by Wagner. M. Debussy is a highly skilled accompanist who should not be forgotten in this chorus of praise.[49]

After composing "Romance" ("Voici que le printemps") in January 1884 (celebrating springtime a bit early), Achille had written "La romance d'Ariel" for Marie in the following month. While these two songs confirm his commitment to Bourget's poetic collection of *Les aveux*, "Apparition" brought about his first contact with Stéphane Mallarmé. The periodical *Lutèce* had published this poem, presented in an almost Pre-Raphaelite style, at the end of November 1883. It may be a bit surprising to note that the song, completed on 8 February, was dated from Ville-d'Avray, where the Vasniers generally spent only the summer months.

A Rebel at the Conservatoire

Given this context, Achille was not very diligent in Guiraud's courses at the Conservatoire. He even declared to Vidal that under no circumstances would he go to Rome, that "this was completely out of the question for him."[50] He and Guiraud were becoming rather like cronies: in the evenings, they would meet in a small café on the rue La Bruyère, play billiards while smoking strong cigarettes until closing time, and then "walk each other, several times back and forth, to their respective homes."[51]

It was at the rue Blanche residence of Marmontel—who had harbored "a lingering memory" of Achille "that bordered on obsession"[52]—that the shameless pupil's exploits were described. There Debussy's reputation as a revolutionary was born and there the young Maurice Emmanuel—who was also in conflict with the official way of teaching—took some notes:

> One of [Marmontel's] greatest pleasures was to serve up some "new harmonies" to his guests that would jolt them all, except for Guiraud, who was teaching Debussy at the time and who would chuckle to himself. [Émile] Réty also recognized the source; several times he had scolded Émile Durand's undisciplined student. At the end of the session, Marmontel rendered unto Caesar that which was due him and identified the source: "My second prize winner in 1877!" he proclaimed. This took place in the years following 1880. It was at rue Blanche that I first got to know the harmonic improvisations with which Claude-Achille had regaled his piano professor; [Marmontel], finding indeed some pleasure in them, had mischievously stored those improvisations in his memory. I still hear the old master performing chord successions filled with augmented intervals, strings of "dominant ninths,"

and 6- and 7-note chords (for example: F, A, C, E, G, B, D), passages that astonished his adopted son Antonin and that produced various reactions among his guests. Guiraud smiled, utterly relaxed, a cigarette at his lips. Réty's pale face took on a sterner appearance. Reyer exclaimed, with exasperation: "I will never again dine with people who make music *like that!*. . ." One evening, in the company of these people, Théodore Dubois, who was a superb harmony teacher and not at all intolerant, although strictly faithful to the traditional system, found himself submitting to the test that Marmontel reserved for a few select friends: he was made to endure chords in the style of. . . Claude. Dubois's reply was unusual: "Everyone, come to my organ loft at the Madeleine for Vespers on Sunday, and I will take it upon myself, in the Magnificat, to produce some versets in that style, fashioning several of these chords for you *with one finger*. . ." A tempting, enigmatic proposal. On the day and at the appointed hour, the guests, who were punctual for the gathering, could hear two versets—which the organist made short so as not to disturb the faithful [worshippers] in any way—and which, in fact, looked odd: Théodore Dubois had drawn only the mutation stops, and had combined the *plein-jeu* with the *cornet*, *nazard*, and *tièrce*,[53] and while performing a purely melodic line, he produced chords, generated by the ranks of harmonic pipes whose contacts produced streams of parallel lines (embellished by jarring modulations created by the harmonics), recalling their unmistakable resemblance to some of the fanciful improvisations of the "second prize-winner of 1877!"[54]

This was also the period during which Achille indulged in his famous harmonic tricks in Léo Delibes's class, when the latter would go to chat with Émile Réty, the secretary at the Conservatoire. We owe these accounts yet again to Maurice Emmanuel:[55]

At the piano we used to hear some chromatic rumblings, imitating the bus that came down from the faubourg Poissonnière:[56] strings of consecutive fifths and octaves[; . . .] harmonies laden with sevenths that, far from "resolving downward," had the gall to "ascend" or not to resolve at all; brazen "false relations"; ninth chords *on every scale degree*, *eleventh* and *thirteenth* chords; *all the notes of the diatonic scale* played at once in unpredictable arrangements;[57] sparkling series of arpeggiations contrasted with two-handed trills played on three notes at once. For more than an hour, he held us under his spell around the piano, his tousled mop of hair constantly flouncing about while he played. Finally, the guard, Ternusse, alarmed by the strange noises that were echoing through the hallways, burst in to put an end to our "lesson." Debussy was a dangerous "fanatic," and we were asked to vacate the premises.[58]

Later, at the height of his fame, Debussy seems to have forgotten that he had indulged in these scenes, remembering instead a duplicitous existence, at least with respect to his professors. This is how he described this attitude to a journalist from the *New York Times* in 1910:

> For a long time, I did not want to study what I considered as foolishness. Then I realized that I must at least pretend to study in order to get through the Conservatoire. So I studied, but all the time I worked out my own little schemes. [. . .] Don't imagine for a moment that I ever told anyone of this. I kept it all to myself. Until I could give a proof of my ideas, I did not care to talk of them.[59]

L'enfant prodigue and the Prodigal Son

Having been lectured by both Vidal and Guiraud, Achille was sequestered from 10 to 16 May 1884 in the first round of the *concours*. The given text this time was *Le printemps*, by the illustrious librettist Jules Barbier. Achille was to compose a work for four-voice chorus and orchestra, for which he adopted a compositional style that was fairly learned but not free of technical errors.[60] The jury's decision was delivered on the 17th: as in the previous year, Debussy was ranked fourth, behind Xavier Leroux, Charles René, and Henri-Charles Kaiser. Once again, he had to leave for Compiègne, and, over the course of twenty-five days (from 24 May onward), was required to compose a cantata on Édouard Guinand's *L'enfant prodigue*, a text that had been commissioned by the Académie des beaux-arts.

At the Villa Medici, Vidal was worried about the turn of events:

> Debussy's advancement [to the second round of the *concours*] worries me a lot. The candidates have been given a cantata [text] that is not at all up his alley; alas, what will he do? It's true that Leroux hardly has what it takes to deal with that subject, but he has Massenet's support, and Debussy no longer has Mme Krauss to promote his cantata. [. . .] What can this *Enfant prodigue* be? From what angle is the subject taken? Is it dramatic? Pastoral?[61]

Guiraud advised his student as best he could with respect to the choice of soloists for his cantata: Rose Caron, who had begun a remarkable career and whose dramatic qualities Debussy's literary alter ego M. Croche would later praise; Ernest Van Dyck, little known as yet but destined to become one of the best Wagnerian tenors; and, finally, Alexandre Taskin, the baritone who had sung in *Le gladiateur*. Furthermore, fortunately for Debussy, Guiraud had been named as an additional jury member and thus was likely to take part in the deliberations. Chansarel would help his friend out by playing the orchestral reduction with him at the piano. Among the members of the audience was Jacques Durand (the son of the music publisher at the place de la Madeleine), who had just obtained a second honorable mention in harmony at the Conservatoire and who remembered long afterward those performances on 27 and 28 June for the Prix de Rome.[62]

The first reading of the work at the Conservatoire was for just the music division of the Académie, augmented by three supplemental jurors, among whom was Léo Delibes; Debussy's cantata was the fourth heard out of five. The next day, at the Institut, the final performance took place before the combined divisions of the Académie des beaux-arts. Jacques Durand reported that "It made a considerable impression. Debussy was at the piano, admittedly nervous although in control of himself; Chansarel, who played in the passages written for piano, four hands, seemed to show more emotion; Mme Caron was quite sensational in Lia's aria, Van Dyck in that of Azaël; then, after the final trio, I had the feeling that the battle had been won."[63]

Achille was on the Pont des Arts when it was announced that he had won the first prize, Charles René and Xavier Leroux having obtained the first and second "second prizes," respectively. Guiraud was elated. He let it be known that 22 out of the 28 votes had been obtained in the first round, thanks to the painters, but Gounod's support had played an even more decisive role. Delibes recorded his reactions in a notebook:[64] "Ambiguous tonality brimming with charm. [. . .] trying a bit too hard. Bizarre. Pretty sound. [. . .] tonality too wandering. [. . .] Lacks simplicity! Always over-the-top." And to conclude: "*Very interesting* in general, but *very intense* and *tormented*." While leaving the performance, Marmontel confided to Massenet and Delibes: "Oh, the little rascal! He still enjoyed Chopin's harmonies in my class! I'm really worried that he will no longer find them spicy enough."[65] The Académie explained its evaluation of Achille's score as follows: "Very marked poetic sense, brilliant and warm color, lively and dramatic music."[66] The critics were not in complete agreement. Arthur Pougin, translating the opinion of Ernest Reyer, wrote in *Le ménestrel* and *Le guide musical* that he preferred Charles René's cantata.[67] A. Héler[68] wrote in *L'art musical* that "in making an abstraction, so to speak, of the poetry that had been offered to him, he dared to emulate the color of the poetry. [. . .] Interesting music, rather disconnected, but expressive [. . .] which denotes a composer with a great future."[69] As for Charles Darcours (the brother of Charles Réty, the secretary of the Conservatoire), while he criticized the indecisive tonality in *Le Figaro*—the voices written with too little concern for tessitura and timbres, as well as a certain disorder in the music—he commended "a young composer with temperament, a pupil who has perhaps no more 'knowledge' than his fellow students, but who, from the first chords that he produced, shows that he is not 'like everyone else.'"[70] Later, André Suarès would describe the cantata as "intentionally caricaturing Gounod–Massenet."[71] The most unexpected comment, at least with respect to the information it offered, came from the *Progrès artistique*: "We can confirm that M. Paul Clèves, the savvy director of the Éden-Théâtre, was struck by the young composer's qualities when his cantata was performed, and has just commissioned him to write a ballet in three acts"![72]

Recalling the event twenty years later, Debussy admitted that "at first blush, one can't resist that little wisp of glory that the Prix de Rome temporarily brings."[73] If his excitement dwindled, it was because he suddenly realized the ominous consequences: at least two years of separation from Marie.[74]

Farewell to Marie

This victory temporarily reconciled Achille with his father and crowned him with the ultimate prestige with respect to his professors and his most skeptical friends. In any case, it released Vidal from the silence that he had imposed on himself concerning his classmate's private life. From Rome, on 12 July, Vidal literally exploded in a long letter to Henriette Fuchs, in which he revealed his true thoughts and which also sounds remorseful:

> So, our friend Achille has won the prize in spite of himself! Well, this dark, adulterous comedy has been going on for a long time. Already last year I had to persuade him to go into sequestration and do the second-round *concours*. He didn't want to. This winter, he told me that he wouldn't leave for Rome, even if he were to win the prize—that this was completely out of the question for him. Although it didn't surprise me at all, I was furious for a moment and I regretted having pushed him toward the Concordia. In the past, I saw his mother accusing me of being his accomplice in that saga; he made me serve as the pretext for all kinds of escapades. It was difficult to win back Mme Debussy's confidence, and the tears that I saw her shed over her son's misbehavior did little to remind me of the days when he was quite likeable. Everything that you could see me doing for him, I did for his mother, who is a good woman and who has treated me like a son. I don't know if he will get over his ego. He's incapable of any sacrifice whatsoever. Nothing has any hold over him. His parents are not wealthy. Instead of spending the money [he earns] from his lessons to ease their burden, he buys new books or knick-knacks, etchings, etc. for himself. His mother showed me drawers filled with them. His upbringing has been mishandled. His father wanted to exploit him, to make him a child prodigy, a little Dangremont,[75] and for a period of time he succeeded; but when the composer in him [Achille] was awakened, the piano and harmony studies went to hell, and from then on, he did only as he pleased, harboring a poorly disguised resentment of his father. It was only with the greatest difficulty that his father had forgiven him for abandoning his dream for his son—that of a lucrative life as a virtuoso; only recently has his father acknowledged him as a composer, and even so only from the time when he started winning medals for it. His mother loves him too much; she'd like to have him with her constantly, to see him work diligently, and that exas-

perates him. As a result, his parents have no power over him. That leaves Guiraud. He always treated him like a spoiled child, and Debussy repaid him with a lackadaisical attitude; I know something about this, since he would come to my place now and then during class time! Yet, if anyone can have an effect on him, it will be Guiraud.

His succubus preys on his every weakness. A pretty woman, she is much pursued by admirers, which stokes his narcissistic jealousy; a talented singer (so it seems—I've never heard her), she interprets his works exceptionally well, and everything that he writes is for her and sung by her. After that, how do you expect him to agree to go into exile for two years, to the Rome that he already knows and loathes? [. . .]

His moral sense is not developed; he's nothing but a hedonist. I'm furious. I've been a bloody fool. And yet, he has so much talent and temperament!

What would you have me write to him? Rome is unbearable, the stay at the Villa odious, nothing here instills a need to produce. . . He's not sociable by nature, and he won't know how to benefit from the few good boys who are here; really, I feel powerless. . . . To love an animal who doesn't love his own mother![76]

Indeed, Vidal had not yet spoken his last word. At Ville-d'Avray, where the lovers endlessly discussed his departure, Achille held onto one hope: every two years, the city of Paris organized a composition prize for a work with soloists, chorus, and orchestra that did not need to have a theatrical or religious context. The first-prize winner received a sum of 10,000 francs, and the second, 6,000 francs—relatively considerable amounts, when compared with the 4,010 francs that were allotted annually to the boarders of the Villa Medici and from which there remained only about 2,500 francs, once the directors deducted administrative expenses.[77] From his experience in several previous *concours*, Achille was well versed in that musical form. He even had in his portfolio a work that could be suitable, pending revisions: *Hélène*, a cantata for soprano, four-voice mixed chorus, and orchestra, on a poem by Leconte de Lisle.

But did he himself believe in it? The deadline for the submission of manuscripts was 29 September 1884, and he was not able to meet it.[78] At the beginning of October, he informed Gounod, who had become one of his strongest supporters and who began to *tutoie* him,[79] about an upcoming performance of his cantata at the solemn opening convocation of the school year at the Institut. He tried in vain to engage soloist Rose Caron, from the Théâtre de la Monnaie in Brussels, and wanted Gounod to intervene to get Gabrielle Krauss once again. "That will be difficult!. . ." Gounod replied to him. "Still, I'll ask; but I'm sure I'll have nothing to report, or rather I'll reply. . . in the negative!. . . So ask Carvalho to find someone."[80]

In the end, it was Mme Boidin-Puisais, who had sung the part of Brangäne for the performance of *Tristan* at the Château-d'Eau a few months before, who sang in *L'enfant prodigue* on 18 October with Taskin and Van Dyck. But at that same convocation at the Institut, Achille had to endure other official festivities, such as a eulogy for Victor Massé and another for Henri Reber, and especially a talk by Saint-Saëns on "the past, the present, and the future of music"[81]—the same Saint-Saëns to whom he sent, on 4 November 1884, a score of his *L'enfant prodigue* with his "very respectful admiration!"

A reception for the new Prix de Rome winners was also given by the permanent secretary of the Académie, Viscount Henri Delaborde, after which the same laureates went to a restaurant in the Bois de Boulogne to celebrate their success among themselves. It was a traditional schoolboy dinner, at the end of which the victors threw the dishes out the windows.[82]

Achille had just met an individual who for several years had served as a semi-official bridge between the Parisian artistic milieu and the Villa Medici: Count Giuseppe Primoli, called Gégé, the son of Charlotte Bonaparte and nephew of Princess Mathilde.[83] Nostalgic for the Second Empire, he split his time between his residence in Rome and that of the princess in Paris, where he had spent his youth and which continued to be home to a salon that was attended notably by the young Marcel Proust.[84] Not long after having met Primoli, Achille sent him the following letter, which shows his rather brusque manner, even at the age of twenty-two:

> My dear friend,
> I'm writing to ask a great favor of you. Perhaps you'll be surprised that I am approaching you, since I've known you for only a short time. But my antisocial behavior has made me few friends and that is why I'm contacting you, as I sense that you are kind and sympathetic to my problems.
> My parents are not wealthy and I cannot pay for my Prix de Rome dinner. I've tried in vain to sell some of my music. In short, everything has been against me. I've run up a few debts that I must pay before leaving, and I can't even buy flowers for her—*she who loves them so much*. So I'm asking you to lend me 500 francs.
> I'm very sorry to bother you about this; you've already done so much for my spiritual well-being. Now I have to trouble you with my material life; but, to repeat, I'm behaving this way because of the friendship that I believe you have for me. Anyway, my parents are desperately short of money and I don't want to be such a burden to them.[85]

Not having received a quick reply, Achille reiterated his request a few days later, in nearly the same terms.[86] In lieu of flowers, he had bound in supple morocco leather the collection of songs that he wanted to give to Marie as a token of his love. Even though he had just composed "L'ombre des arbres" on 6 January and "Chevaux de bois" (which he sent to his friend Alfred Bachelet) on 10 January, he added none of these future *Ariettes oubliées* to the thirteen pieces he had already copied out since February 1884. In addition to the *Fêtes galantes* by Verlaine, six songs on texts by Bourget were included in the volume because they had been particularly appreciated and sung by Marie, because they corresponded to a time of happiness in their relationship, and also perhaps because the last of the included texts, "Regret," had taken on a very real meaning. On the flyleaf, Achille inscribed the famous dedication: "To Madame Vasnier. These songs that have lived only through her and that will lose their charming gracefulness if they nevermore pass from her melodious fairy mouth. The eternally grateful author. CD." (a [sic] Madame Vasnier. Ces chansons qui n'ont jamais vécues [sic] que par elle, et qui perdront leur grace [sic] charmeresse si jamais plus elles ne passent par sa bouche de fée mélodieuse. L'auteur eternellement [sic] reconnaisant [sic]. CD.) The signature itself shows that he was at a turning point in his life: he replaced the convoluted Gothic initials that he had used for many years with a signature that was quite simple.

Lectured by Vidal, he had to pay a farewell visit to Henriette Fuchs. On 15 January 1885, he came, "a grave sinner, to beseech"[87] the director of the Concordia to pardon him, attempting to justify his numerous absences by his work for the *concours* of the City of Paris. He did not leave a very good impression, and Edmond Fuchs, when recounting the services rendered by the former accompanists in his 1887 speech to the general assembly of the society, thanked Vidal and Charles René, but did not mention "De Bussy" by name.[88]

As for Primoli, he did more than simply loan money to Debussy. He also introduced him to Claudius Popelin, an historical painter who became an enameller as well as a poet, and who experienced a difficult love life with Princess Mathilde, thanks to whom his son Gustave had won the Prix de Rome. Achille confided in Claudius, as to a guardian angel, and spoke to him about his passion for Marie and his anguish over his departure. Although poorly positioned to give fatherly advice, Popelin tried to reason with him and advised him to "turn this crazy love back into a lasting friendship."[89] On 28 January, Debussy took the train for Rome.

Chapter Five

The Villa Medici

1885–87

The first months spent at the Villa were almost as bleak as Debussy claimed in his letters to Henri Vasnier.[1] Nevertheless, five of his friends went to pick him up at Mount Rotondo, north of Rome. No doubt he found little comfort in the welcome given to him by the director, Louis Cabat, a landscape painter who had been running the institution for eight years and who was not involved with the boarders "except in an administrative way."[2] This second-rate artist, in fragile health, was at the end of his tenure and left a rather dilapidated Villa; there were scandals of mismanagement in addition to the well-known mediocrity of the boarders' work. As for Mme Cabat, she viewed the boarders as "excessively arrogant, ungrateful, unfair, and at times belligerent."[3] Achille was of nearly the same opinion: they were stiff, convinced of their own importance, self-centered, and exchanged only catty remarks, he wrote to Vasnier.[4]

One might at first suspect that, knowing Marie would also be reading his letters, Achille deliberately exaggerated his dark state of mind. But Vidal likewise denounced the "cliques that divide the boarders,"[5] and his first impression there had also been that of an "enormous sadness."[6] In a letter to Henriette Fuchs from 16 February, Vidal confirmed that, two weeks after arriving, Debussy "was terribly bored" and "dreamed only of returning to Paris,"[7] adding that "I'm as pleasant as my work and my taste for solitude permit me to be, but, in the end, I cannot interest myself much in such a self-absorbed person. [. . .] I don't refuse anything that he asks of me, but I don't go out of my way to create distractions in order to entertain him."[8]

To his "dear parents," Achille sent the family photo of the boarders, grouped around Cabat on the staircase that led to the Villa gardens. In this photo, Achille is seated at the top on a railing, near Marty and Vidal. He carefully marked the names of the residents and, under his own image, he wrote "the prodigal son."[9] In another photo (reproduced in the first edition of Vallas's book),[10] he is at the bottom of the staircase steps, and a friend is placing his hand casually on his shoulder. This friend was Gaston Redon (the brother of the painter Odilon), an architect, flutist, and music lover. Achille inaugurated his Roman concerts with his Prix de Rome cantata, performing it at the director's home on the very evening of his arrival on 30 January. It was apparently a success with "some people," but not with the composers.[11]

This was in fact the first time that Debussy found himself subject to the relative constraints of a communal life, which he was perhaps less ready than most to endure. Pierné remembered, thirty-five years later, that "there was no genuine closeness between him and his colleagues there. He kept very much to himself and would avoid our company. [. . .] We hardly saw him, except at mealtime."[12] But it was rather Pierné who was avoiding Debussy; Vidal, who stayed at the Villa one year longer, claimed that, on the contrary, Achille was close to him and to Xavier Leroux, that he was not "the solitary man whom he liked to portray in his letters,"[13] and that he knew how to be sociable on occasion. Scarcely a week after Achille's arrival, Vidal took his friend to a concert of the Società orchestrale romana, conducted by Ettore Pinelli (4 February), at which they both were "stirred with enthusiasm" for Beethoven's Second Symphony.[14] Around the same period, Debussy had the opportunity to hear *Lohengrin* for the first time, because Wagner's work (which had opened at the Apollo Theater on the preceding 27 December under the direction of Edoardo Mascheroni) was in production until at least 16 February, at which time there was a change in the cast.[15]

However, there is no doubt that during those first months, the young Prix de Rome winner thought only about the woman he had left in Paris, and he made no effort to adapt to this new life. He was unable to work; he had "a dead spirit" (*l'esprit mort*).[16]

When he wrote to Henri Vasnier in his first letter from Rome, in February 1885, Achille acted as if Vasnier suspected nothing, expressing his gratitude to him "for the place that you have been so willing to make for me in your family."[17] At the end of April, he could not hold himself back any longer and went to Paris for a few days; we do not know what subterfuge he used to receive his director's authorization to leave. In any case, it was no clandestine visit, for a few days after his return to Rome, in mid-May, he expressed his sorrow to Henri Vasnier for "having left you all."[18] Marcel Dietschy believed himself justified in dating this getaway to the following year, assuming an erroneous reading of a customs receipt by Vallas.[19] But we now know, thanks to the journal of Mme Hébert, the wife of the next Villa Medici director,[20] that it could not have taken place the following year.

Ernest and Gabrielle Hébert

June 1885 marked a big change in the life of the Villa and in the life of Debussy: Ernest Hébert, the new director, who received a six-year appointment on 1 January 1885, went to take up his position on 8 June. He had already led the institution for six years, from 1867 to 1873. He was now sixty-seven years old, and his German wife, née Gabrielle d'Uckermann, was thirty-six years his junior and said to be a good musician. As for Ernest, he was a painter but also an amateur violinist, and studied his instrument on a regular basis with Jean-Pierre Maurin; he had been friends with Gounod and Bizet, and had become acquainted in Rome with Giovanni Sgambati, Franz Liszt, and Princess Sayn-Wittgenstein, whose portrait he had painted in 1874. Even Debussy acknowledged that Hébert "loved music with a passion."[21]

The boarders, accompanied by Gégé Primoli, went to pick up Hébert at the train station.[22] On 9 June, the new director hosted a dinner for the residents and, to mark the change of leadership, required that they eat as a group from then on, while also allowing them to bring guests.[23] He hired a supposedly better cook—which did not prevent Achille from later recalling a dish, the "Roba dolce,"[24] which combined the smell of gasoline with that of curdled cream.

A decidedly more social life began for Debussy. Day after day, Gabrielle Hébert noted the detailed events of the Villa in her journal, thereby revealing to us the role that the composer played in them. On 11 June, after dinner in the evening, Vidal and Debussy played the overture of *Die Meistersinger* for piano, four hands. Did they do it in the hope of winning their director over to Wagnerian repertoire, which he did not like? In any event, the Héberts immediately grew very fond of Debussy: "Both of us sense the talent of this young boy," wrote Gabrielle. Meanwhile, they tried to have him near them often, as we can see by this calendar:

14 June: "Fireworks and music by the boarders until midnight."
20 June: "Gégé and Debussy go out with us by car: Borghese garden. [. . .] Debussy dines with us and plays his songs on Bourget's text."
24 June: "Alles[25] expounds on the beauty of the landscape at the Acqua acetosa[26] [. . .] the Tiber with its wonderful cluster of mountains. He tries to get Debussy to understand."
26 June: "Stroll with Debussy and Gégé at the Villa Pamphili."
27 June: "Long drive to Teverone with Princess Scilla[27] and Debussy. We go into Ste. Agnese. [. . .] A monk reminded [Hébert] of the church of Ste Constanze with some extraordinary mosaics on the ceiling. [. . .] Return. [. . .] Debussy plays some music. We go to bed at 1 a.m."
28 June: "Labatut, Naudé,[28] and Debussy for dinner with Princess Scilla."

30 June: "In the evening we go with Debussy to [the Basilica of] St. Paul Outside the Walls."

1 July: "Dinner with Mme Castellani and Deglane, Gégé, Barbotin,[29] and Debussy."

When Achille wrote to Vasnier, probably at the end of June, this is how he commented on this flood of invitations: "Concerning the Héberts, they are showing a rather tiresome interest in me. In their ploys to get me to like the Villa, they will make it a bit more odious for me. You will tell me that I haven't changed. But if they were in Paris, perhaps I'd like them a lot; here, they are only jailors to me and nothing more."[30] Among Debussy's duties was that of playing piano accompaniments for the director, a truly second-rate violinist who made him perform "all the Mozart sonatas," according to Laloy.[31]

From this same month of June—decidedly very full—date two gestures that were at the same time social and musical in nature. Achille notated the beginning of "Paysage sentimental" on a kakemono owned by Count Primoli.[32] This song, on a poem by Bourget, seemed to have enjoyed particular success among the residents at the Villa. Achille also wrote down the first measures of "Chevaux de bois" for an unknown recipient, without a dedication but dated "Rome, June 85," and with an unpublished tempo indication: "Mouvement de musique de Foire de St.-Cloud" (Tempo of the music at the fair at St.-Cloud).[33]

As for those whom he called his "jailors," Achille did not fail to take advantage of the good relationship he had established with them in order to obtain another leave of absence. Gabrielle Hébert's journal implies that, to that end, he fabricated some tale about an alleged illness. On 3 July, she noted: "Debussy is keeping me company; he no longer knows if he will be leaving. Received a letter from Dieppe, filled with concern.[34] [. . .] Debussy is having dinner with us." He dined with the Héberts again on 4 July and, on the 5th: "Debussy has just consulted with Alles regarding a more favorable letter that he received. Alles concluded that he will get his ticket and leave. Gégé [. . .] confided in me that he gave Debussy some money." He departed on 8 July: "Alles [. . .] is leaving at 6:30 with Debussy, who is dining with us, and Alles is spoiling him till the end."[35]

The "Begging Dog"

To communicate with Marie, Debussy enlisted an accomplice: a Villa Medici boarder who was in Paris at the time and who served as a courier for the lovers. Gustave Popelin was the son of Claudius, who himself had experienced a difficult love life with Princess Mathilde, as we have already seen. It was

62   CHAPTER FIVE

thanks to the princess's influence that Gustave had won his Prix de Rome. Hébert disliked him. Before leaving Rome, Achille sensed that he would need some help from the Popelins in Paris, and he wrote the following letter to the father:

> Dear M. Popelin,
>
> You will have heard from Gustave the good news about my leave. I need not tell you the utter joy I feel. I must also tell you that these two months have changed nothing in me, that they have only intensified some of my feelings. I have to acknowledge their strength, since without the person who is causing them, I cease to live, for it is surely "ceasing to live" when you see that you can no longer control your imagination. As I've told you, I have become too much accustomed to wishing and contemplating only *through her eyes*. I'm telling you this with some trepidation, as it's not at all what you had advised me to do—to try to turn this crazy love, which in its insanity keeps me from thinking straight, back into a lasting friendship. Thinking not only leads to deeper madness, but also inevitably to the realization that I have not done enough to further this love.
>
> I beg you, Sir, to forgive me. You know how much I value your friendship. It is to this friendship that I turn in asking for forgiveness. Please! Had I not had Gustave, whom I like so much and whose friendship I sorely miss right now, I very probably would have handed in my resignation. I've had such moments of despair that, I assure you, he needed to be there to cheer me up and help me regain my courage. Moreover, let me say that my only consolation is that this suffering has, in some way, allowed me to get to know both of you. I know full well that I have little right to tell you how fond I am of you, but never mind, I can't help myself.[36]

This second visit to Paris seems to have lasted nearly two months. Debussy rejoined Marie in Dieppe under difficult circumstances, since he was there unbeknownst to her husband; he lived "at the home of Monsieur Demailly, 16 rue des Bains," with people who "demand money from me every day."[37] He most probably exceeded the duration of the leave he had been granted, for when he came back to Rome on 2 September, Mme Hébert noted: "Debussy's arrival. Alles treats him a bit stiffly, but takes him out for the evening in his carriage." And he bestowed upon the young composer yet another favor, that of spending a few days alone in Fiumicino, at the seaside estate of Gégé Primoli, who was in Paris at the time: "Ah! I was able to satisfy my wild instincts as much as I wanted to," Debussy told Vasnier; "I did some work that was almost good, and I took walks, as if I'd always enjoyed them."[38]

The Héberts resumed their invitations for dinner as well as the strolls in the Roman countryside, during which the painter also took along his models— Nina or Amalia. But Achille was devoured by passion and jealousy. He sent a letter to Gustave Popelin that was more ardent than ever:

My dear Gustave,

If my letter gave you pleasure, how can I adequately express to you how much good yours did for me. You can well imagine my boredom. And *at this moment*, no one can pull me out of it, not even a little bit. I assure you that it's utterly excruciating. I have to say that Madame Hébert lavishes thoughtful attention on me. But it doesn't work; I can't cry out to her that I'm suffering, and deep down, all this attention is only a source of irritation for me.

Some problems are befalling me that (I fear) will considerably postpone my trip to Paris. So I wept while reading your sendoff "à bientôt" [see you soon], a phrase that gave me so much joy. That pleasure is over; *her last letter*, which I received the day before yesterday, scarcely concealed all the trouble that my presence there would make for her, telling me that it would be very imprudent for us to see each other. You understand that if I'm going to suffer anyway, I'd rather stay here than risk bursting into a blind fury, which would surely result from my being prevented to see her. Although I would be near her, that life would be unbearable, given the jealousy that I know is within me. To force her to do anything else would mean losing her; well, I'd much prefer even to lose her, while staying proud of my love, than to play the role of a begging dog who is inevitably left at the door. Besides, I told her that I wanted nothing to change and for her to be completely mine. Her response will show me if I've done the right thing. But this will show you how cowardly I am: I want to write to her that it's all the same to me, as long as I see her again, and yet I'm absolutely certain that that would lead to an irreparable break. Such is the life I lead. Ah! My former sufferings seem quite trivial compared with those I'm feeling now.[39]

In mid-September, the Héberts left for a vacation in France until the end of the year. There they did not completely forget their favorite boarder. While having lunch in Paris on 6 December with Paul Baudry, who was in the process of painting a portrait of Marie Vasnier,[40] they revealed to the painter the liaison between his model of the day and the composer—which Gabrielle expressed in her journal thus: "We revealed her 'affaire Debussy' to him."

[Word of the liaison between Achille and Marie likely reached her husband. In fact, according to Marcel Dietschy, he may have been turning a blind eye to his wife's relationship with the young composer for some time, but once it was clear that others (such as the Héberts and Baudry) knew about it, he became less tolerant.[41] By the end of the year,] M. Vasnier's letters to the young composer dwindled. In sending his wishes to the elder gentleman on 30 December, in rather clumsy terms, Debussy acted as if one of his letters might have offended him: "Allow me to ask you what, in my last letter, could have caused this great silence from you; I've sought in vain [for a reason], and assure you that I'm deeply saddened; I well know that my letters are full of troubles, but I can't do anything about that, and I don't want to believe that this is why you've abandoned me."[42]

During the three months while the Héberts were absent, Achille shut himself off, seeing very little of his colleagues, who accused him of wanting to draw attention to himself. In his letters, he continued to consider an imminent resignation. But he kept working. After having abandoned *Zuleima*,[43] a symphonic ode based on a text adapted by Georges Boyer from Heinrich Heine's *Almansor*, he again returned to *Diane au bois*, which had been left unfinished on Guiraud's advice and for which he suggested that Banville be asked to add a few choruses.[44] Achille also jotted down some ideas for a *Salammbô*, based on Flaubert, and finished a setting of a poem by Bourget.[45] At the end of September, a visit by Edmond Fuchs (from the Concordia!) gave rise to a "little celebration" with Vidal for a week.[46]

Hébert returned to the Villa, anxious to spend the New Year's festivities with the residents; but Gabrielle dubbed it "a tedious soiree," and even more tedious, no doubt, were the formal visits to the French embassy and to the Vatican that the director imposed on his boarders. For Twelfth Night, the director's wife bought them a cake and noted in her journal: "Debussy says that it's an *étouffe coquin*."[47] On 7 January, Hébert took Achille to the Apollo Theater to attend a performance of *Aida*.

Visitors at the Villa

In this same month of January 1886, a distinguished guest, Franz Liszt, appeared at the Villa, and the details of his visit, recorded in Gabrielle's journal, are particularly valuable here. On the 4th, Vidal chose for the master a piano, which arrived the following day. Princess Sayn-Wittgenstein "is dictating the menu for Liszt to us," wrote Gabrielle on the 6th.[48] On the 8th, the old man dined at the Héberts with Debussy, Vidal, and Redon—a dinner party during which he displayed "much congeniality." Debussy and Vidal played for him the *Faust Symphony* on two pianos, but the composer fell asleep while listening to his work! The following day, it was Vidal and Debussy's turn to go with their director to visit Liszt. It was most probably on this occasion that the two young musicians played Emmanuel Chabrier's *Valses romantiques* for him, as Vidal reported in his memoirs.[49] On 13 January, Liszt went up to the Villa again to have dinner. Afterward, for the assembled residents, he performed three pieces, among them *Au bord d'une source* and his transcription of Franz Schubert's *Ave Maria*. Mme Hébert noted that this performance took place "with everyone paying rapt attention." Debussy's knowledge of Liszt thus rested not on a fleeting contact but on three prolonged encounters, several months before the Hungarian composer's death in July of that year.[50]

A week later, the scene changed completely: some of Hébert's friends, the Hochons, arrived on 18 January and remained for a month. He was a professor, and she—Loulou, to those close to her—was something of a musician. A pretty woman, she was in search of adventure above all, and brought a breath of fresh air to the Villa—which did not prevent her from obtaining an audience with the Pope,[51] who granted her his apostolic blessing. On 21 January, Debussy and Vidal played on two pianos for the Hochons; this time, it was Alles who fell asleep while listening to excerpts from *Parsifal*. Social events continued throughout the following days, but on the 24th, according to Gabrielle Hébert's journal, the young architect Deglane remarked during dinner that "Debussy has become very unpleasant again since our arrival" (i.e., the return of the Héberts from their vacation). Gabrielle had another way of putting it; on 2 February, she wrote, "Debussy fait son Caro" (Debussy is flirting).

In other words, Loulou showed an interest in Achille, while the young composer seemed to be forgetting his devouring passion for Marie. People gossiped at the Villa, and Gabrielle was not the last to hear these rumors: Gégé Primoli—she wrote (in English!) on 9 February—"tells me that they have seen Loulou and Debussy kissing in the Villa."[52] On the 15th, Loulou was "lecturing Debussy," but about what we do not know.

In a letter to Henri Vasnier on 29 January, Achille described this period of his life as a boarder in the following rather elliptical terms: "The Villa Medici is very busy at the moment, Hébert having brought a lot of people with him. A Monsieur Hochon has also come. It seems they are high-society people; I don't know if you know them. I saw them once; they were asked to deliver kind regards from Guiraud. But all of this is neither here nor there and has certainly not made the Villa more pleasant for me."[53] Enough said! We will note, however, that the manuscript of "Green" (from his *Ariettes*, based on Verlaine) is dated precisely from this month of January and that it is tempting to think that the poetic lines describing "last kisses" and "this heart that beats only for you" perhaps no longer applied to the distant Parisian lady.

The Second Year

Moving away from these anecdotes, we may observe a significant change among the residents at the beginning of 1886: Marty and Pierné, having finished their terms, set out again for Paris, and Xavier Leroux arrived. For a year, Vidal and Debussy formed with the latter an "inseparable trio."[54] According to Vidal's memoirs, "the afternoons were spent sight-reading Bach's organ works—we each took a turn playing the pedal part. In the evenings, we would convene in Debussy's room, where we would recite from the plays of Shakespeare and Théodore de Banville. [. . .] We would also read the works of the Decadent poets, such as Adoré Floupette's *Les déliquescences*, which Debussy thoroughly enjoyed."⁵⁵ As for the songs that Achille sang in the evenings at the Héberts, Vidal remembered that "in particular 'Chevaux de bois,' 'Mandoline,' and 'Fantoches' were constantly requested."⁵⁶

After the Hochons left, life at the Villa resumed a more tranquil rhythm until 20 April, when Gabrielle Hébert's journal offers something of a revelation: "Alles loans the carriage to Vidal to pick up Mme Debussy." This shocking annotation surely was referencing a visit from the composer's mother to the Villa—an unexpected visit, to say the least, when one keeps in mind his family's modest means and limited lifestyle. We find confirmation of the event with Gabrielle's journal entry of 26 April: "The Debussys go out with Annibale." Clearly this was why Achille would not attend *Tannhäuser* at the Apollo Theater, while his colleagues went there and left him "saddled at home for the evening" on 25 April.

Among Hébert's invited guests around this time was the poet Maurice Vaucaire, who was on his honeymoon. Like the master of the house, he dabbled at the violin. A few of the boarders urged him on, making the conceited amateur look ridiculous while playing a sonata, accompanied by Debussy. This little conspiracy—reported by René Peter⁵⁷—had been staged by the young painter Alexis Axilette, on his way to taking his turn as the director's favorite. Vaucaire, however, did not hold it against his accompanist, to whom he was said to have proposed a musical setting of his adaptation of William Shakespeare's *As You Like It*. Debussy accepted in principle, but the project was never pursued. Another visitor, Alexis Rostand from Marseille (who hid behind the pseudonym of A. Montaux), remembered several years later the young winner of the Prix de Rome, "whose hair was cut *à la Britannicus*"⁵⁸ and whom he had met at the Hébert's home at the Villa:

> He was in that period of happy intoxication where one believes himself the consecrated recipient of genius. [. . .] D. complained about a persistent migraine and let slip some high-handed opinions from his lips. He would truly like *to think well of* Saint-Saëns and deemed that only one opera, *Tristan und Isolde*—which moreover he confessed to me he had never heard—was worth listening to. As for [Johannes] Brahms, of whom I spoke with admiration, he declared point-blank that he knew nothing about him. *O gioventù, fior della vita*! [O youth, flower of life!]⁵⁹

What took place in July and August, during the two months of leave in Paris? Marie probably returned to Dieppe, on holiday with her family. We cannot say whether the all-consuming passion of her young lover was becoming dulled or, more likely, the registrar (her husband Henri) had eventually lost patience and opened his eyes, as implied by the final awkward exchange between Henri and Achille at the end of 1885.

At the turn of the year, Achille wrote a touching letter to his former piano teacher, Antoine Marmontel:

Villa Medici

Dear Master,

I will begin my letter as very young children do: in sending you the best and most grateful wishes from one who hopes to see you in good health for many, many reasons, so precious . . . . . .

Forgive me for having waited for such a special day to write to you—and I will try to show you the extenuating circumstances that have caused my negligence. Upon arriving in Rome, I set about to write my *envoi*, having undertaken a work about which I'm a bit afraid (I'll tell you the details the next time I'm in Paris). It weighs too much on my thoughts. I live almost completely for it and have only very little time to do anything else, even though several other things would nevertheless be very pleasant; and my impressions of Rome might seem a bit like those of a recluse.

Moreover, my definitive impression is that, on the whole, we Parisians of 1887 will [always] be out of our element and deeply overwhelmed by the grandeur of Rome, in spite of everything.[60] Oh, if you only knew how bad our jackets and our hats make us look in the Sistine Chapel, not to mention the clothing of the English people still tainting that place. To be sure, I bow down with humility before these masterpieces; but I think we can draw from them only visual impressions and not spiritual ones—in other words, live with them.

I'm certain that those who shout their admiration from the rooftops are no more advanced than I, whose private passion has the courage to admit: you're too small, and don't try to climb this Jacob's ladder.

Another thing: if by chance you hear about a certain Monsieur Debussy who despondently plays the piano during the soirees at the Villa Medici, and if they speak badly of him, don't pay too much attention to it, knowing that he's doing what he can.

Permit me to finish by sending my respectful and devoted regards,

A. Debussy

The End of the Residency in Rome

During 1886, after his last letter to M. Vasnier, the only correspondence available to us is what Debussy addressed to the bookseller Émile Baron. The latter was in fact much more than a simple bookseller for Achille, who recalled dinner parties in the back of his shop on the rue de Rome, "where the body was so confined but the spirit so free."[61] Baron informed him of the latest publications that he so desired, and Achille ordered from him books by Jean Moréas, Joris-Karl Huysmans, Charles Morice, Charles Vignier, Henry Becque, and Jean Ajalbert, as well as a translation of Percy Bysshe Shelley, a play by Alexandre Dumas *fils*, and numerous periodicals.[62] Achille kept him posted, as he would a very close friend, on the progress of his "*envois*," and on his joys as well as his anxieties. It was likely in fall 1886 that he wrote this famous confession:[63]

I've had enough of this Eternal City; it seems to me that I've been here for an eternity, and that Paris, the people I love, and a certain shop on the rue de Rome which holds much of my affection—all of that seems to me no longer to exist.

I've had enough of music, of this same eternal landscape; I want to see some Manet and to hear some Offenbach! This seems like a paradox, but I assure you that breathing the air that comes out of this Spleen Factory gives you the most insanely fanciful ideas."[64]

Upon returning from his leave, which more or less coincided with the director's vacation, the waltz of invitations resumed and would not stop until the composer's departure. Let us open Gabrielle Hébert's journal once again:

7 November: "Ferrari [*sic*], Debussy, Axilette,[65] and the violinist Simonetti for dinner."
11 November: "Debussy and Redon for dinner."
26 November: "Debussy for dinner."
9 December: "Redon, Baschet, and Lombard[66] for dinner as well as Debussy. Music."
21 December: "Debussy [among others]."[67]
28 December: "Axilette and Debussy who makes us taste his cake."
31 December: "Go out with Debussy and Axi to buy a glazed chestnut cake."
6 January 1887: "Redon, Lombard, Baschet, Axi, Pinta,[68] and Barbotin and Debussy for dinner (for Twelfth Night). Redon is King."
10 January: "Redon, Lombard, and Debussy."
21 January: "Debussy [among others] in the evening."
29 January: "Debussy for dinner."
30 January: "Debussy [among many others] for dinner."
1 February: "Debussy dines with us."
11 February: "In the evening Debussy delights Mme de Pourtalès."[69]
14 February: "Debussy plays for us."
17 February: "Debussy and the Rostands for dinner."
23 February: "Gardet for dinner with d'Espouy,[70] Debussy."
25 February: "Performance of *Printemps* by Savard[71] and Debussy."
27 February: "Debussy [among others]. Beautiful evening."

To comply with the Institut's rules, in this same month of February, Achille hastily finished his second *envoi*, a symphonic suite for orchestra and chorus titled *Printemps*. It was said to have been inspired by a pictorial *envoi* by his colleague Marcel Baschet, which in turn had been based on Sandro Botticelli's *Primavera*. Because he did not actually complete it, he made up a story: his orchestral manuscript had been destroyed by a fire at the shop of the binder to whom he had entrusted the score. He could thus explain why he was able to send the Académie only an orchestral short score, "except for a few hastily reorchestrated pages."[72]

After a farewell dinner together on 1 March, the last mention of Achille in Gabrielle's journal, on 2 March, reveals a final disappointment: "Get supplies for Debussy. He is leaving in the evening. Alles gives him a small Virgin Mary with a dedication.[73] Debussy does not give me 'Paysage sentimental,' nor does he make good on his debts to anyone."

At the time of his departure from Rome, the entire city was bustling with preparations for the performance of Verdi's *Otello* by the artists from La Scala. About two weeks after his return to Paris, Achille sent the following fine letter to Hébert:

Thursday, 17.3.87

Dear Master,

First of all, forgive me for taking so long to give you some news from your poor little composer. The first reason for this delay is a bad cold, which started out Italian and then became French, in any case the cold to end all colds: Fever! Coughing! Exhaustion! The Whole Works! The second reason is that, since I have reentered the mainstream, my head is spinning a bit, or at least it was, because today, while I have genuine reasons to be happy, I feel very strongly that there are almost as many reasons for regret, my former life notwithstanding. Arriving in Paris made me feel like a very little boy (God forgive me, I was almost afraid of the carriages!) who comes timidly to try to make his way. Even my friends seemed to me like important figures: Vidal, very busy, barely granting me the favor of having lunch with him! Leroux according me an audience in the street, between two appointments! Pierné! Him I don't even dare approach.[74] Finally, all these people treat Paris as a conquered city! And you have to see how adaptable they are, how completely they've lost that beautiful sense of disgruntlement they once had with this place!

All this has upset me a bit! The last months that I spent in Rome also contributed to this state of mind; I lived a dream life during those months, completely immersed in my work, all my efforts straining toward a highly elevated artistic ideal, without concerning myself with what this or that person would think about it. Now, I wonder how I'll manage, with my excessively antisocial nature, to find my way and to struggle amidst this "Bazar au succès" [Success marketplace]. I predict countless problems and friction. Of course, I shall miss, with every fiber of my being, my very lovely room, your good friendship, dear Master, and your very warm encouragement. In the end, you see, one should make Art for five people at most, and five people whom one likes very much! But to try to get the respect of the Man about Town, worldly people, and other mindless idiots, my God that must be tiresome. Enough about me! I will end up by becoming tiresome myself!

My best day until now was Sunday at the Concert Lamoureux. The overture to [Ernest Reyer's opera] *Sigurd*: a little common, a bit of music for the opening of the Industrial Exposition, some vulgar brass riffraff, muted strings, an all-too-familiar mood of melancholy, threaded with the sound of the no less well-known "nasal bassoon." Excerpts from [Mendelssohn's] *A Midsummer Night's Dream*: proper music! At last! The first act of [Wagner's] *Tristan und Isolde*: it is definitely the most beautiful thing I know, with respect to its emotional depth, which embraces you like a caress and makes you suffer; in a word, we experience the same feelings as Tristan, without upsetting either our spirits or our hearts. Not very well sung but superbly carried out, at times even too planned out; one would like to see the music soaring more freely.[75] That is all the music I heard, the Opera having nothing that spoke to me. I went to see *Hamlet* again, in spite of what Coquelin thinks—that "the play is bad and Mounet-Sully is the first comic author of the Théâtre Français"—which would seem to insinuate that Coquelin is the first tragedian of it! Anyway, I found it rather beautiful, and Mounet devilishly evocative.[76]

I will end for now by asking you to express all my devoted friendship and my very considerable and very grateful regards to Madame Hébert. For you, my dear Master, I send you my warmest wishes.

Your boarder,

ADebussy[77]

How to explain that in such a short period time what Debussy had once called the "dreadful barracks" or the "spleen factory" had become—depending on his interlocutor—something of a Garden of Eden, conducive to creative endeavors? This is neither the first nor the last time that we will find apparent psychological contradictions within him.

Chapter Six

Beginning of the Bohemian Period

1887–89

The two years that followed Achille's return to Paris remain among the most difficult to retrace in his life. With practically no correspondence and very few accounts available to us, there is all the more reason to collate carefully what information we do have.

The reunions with Marie were happy at first, and Achille confessed in a letter to Hébert that he had "genuine reasons to be happy."[1] The lovers had no doubt found a meeting place, and he no longer felt the need to be the "begging dog," pleading for a tryst, as when he had come back in secret from Rome. But all this could not last very long. Marguerite Vasnier, Marie's daughter, declared that "the closeness we had in the past was no longer the same. We had moved, made new acquaintances. With his unsociable and moody nature, stuck in his ways, he no longer felt at ease."[2] Achille tried to resume the lessons that he had begun to give Marguerite, but this quickly failed because he was impatient and did not know how to meet his student at her level. As we have seen, since 1885 (when Achille departed for Rome), the Vasniers no longer maintained the same summer routines. That year, they spent their vacation in Dieppe (at Le Bas-Fort-Blanc)[3] at the chalet of the painter Armand Constant Mélicourt-Lefebvre. At that time, high-society Parisians often visited Dieppe; Countess Greffulhe owned a villa there, where Gabriel Fauré spent some time that same summer. And it was there that, one night, the painter Jacques-Émile Blanche was said to have seen Achille climbing a rope ladder, with Marie at the window![4] The following year, again at Dieppe, Gustave Popelin loaned his bachelor apartment to Achille, who lifted the bedroom curtain in order to see Marie arriving and later made some rather cynical comments about the scene.[5] The jealousy that had tormented the young composer so much in Rome had certainly dulled, and he had grown weary of taking precautions so as not to compromise his mistress. They were already old lovers, and Marie, herself now forty years old, had put on some weight and was much less attractive. When Achille dedicated his *Ariettes* to her in 1888, he wrote simply: "To Mme Vasnier, in grateful homage." And when in 1891 he went on to publish "Paysage sentimental," he would replace her name with that of Jeanne Andrée.[6]

Achille and His Family

In Achille's family, financial insecurity made a cruel reappearance when, on 12 April 1887, Manuel Debussy was laid off at the Compagnie Fives-Lille. In fact, he had been dealing with serious money problems for the previous two years: Achille had written to Claudius Popelin from Rome that his father was "worried"[7] and that, as his son, he was sorry not to be able to help him in some way. The relationship between the two had remained quite poor, and it is worth recalling that Achille had avoided seeing his father when he came covertly to Paris.

His bond with his brother Alfred was different.[8] Although only seventeen years old, Alfred showed uncommon literary gifts for a boy of his age. The upbringing that his aunt Clémentine had given him must have included training in English that was advanced enough to enable him to translate Dante Gabriel Rossetti's poem, "The Staff and Scrip"; his translation, "Le bourdon et la besace," was published in an issue of the *Revue indépendante* in November 1887. Furthermore, Alfred subscribed to the publication of Mallarmé's *Œuvres poétiques* and took an interest in the works of Villiers de l'Isle-Adam. In January 1888, he would ask Édouard Dujardin for information on the performances of the *Ring* in Karlsruhe, and shortly thereafter, Achille would join him in paying a visit to the director of the *Revue wagnérienne*. Alfred had a copy of the *Revue indépendante* sent to the address of Edmond Kelly, an American lawyer practicing in Paris who made use of the youth's talents as a translator.[9]

Since Alfred was already capable of earning something of a living at seventeen years of age, in the eyes of his parents, a comparison with their oldest son did not favor Achille, who was more or less living with a married woman and had a lifestyle that was far above his meager earnings as an accompanist or teacher. Manuel no doubt viewed the Prix de Rome as flattering, but would it pay the bills? To his son, he could point out plenty of examples from the newspapers of the already well-placed careers of his contemporaries: Alfred Bruneau, Gustave Charpentier, Charles René (who launched a career as a pianist and began to give composition lessons), and Gabriel Pierné (for whose works two publishers were already vying).

At least Achille was able to discuss his literary tastes, and especially *La damoiselle élue*, with someone at home. He had in fact decided to make Rossetti's poem the subject of his third *envoi* from Rome.[10]

The literary scene in Paris was much more likely to interest him than was the musical scene. Debussy came back home to find virtually the same concert programs as those he had known before leaving for Rome. Certainly, Massenet had been gaining more and more ground on the opera stage, while Wagner had not yet conquered all the opposition to his work. Although Wagnerian productions in Parisian theaters were almost nonexistent before 1891 (except for the premiere of *Tannhäuser* in 1861 and that of *Lohengrin* on 30 April 1887),[11] the composer could nevertheless be considered as solidly established in France after 1888. The *Revue wagnérienne* ceased its publication in that same year, considering its battle won: "Admiration of Wagner has become commonplace," wrote Alfred Ernst in Dujardin's periodical.[12] In the realm of symphonic music, Pasdeloup was toward the end of his career, leaving the field open for Colonne and Lamoureux, and, thanks to a minor rebellion within the organization, the "Franck group" had just taken control of the Société nationale de musique from Saint-Saëns and had begun to renew its mission. The literary world was in an even greater state of agitation, not so much because of Jean Moréas's 1886 manifesto, which called for "the recognition of Symbolism as the only movement capable of viably embodying the current proclivities of the creative spirit in art,"[13] but because of the new ideas that were circulating in several periodicals—which Debussy, as we have seen, avidly devoured—as well as the incessant quest for a slightly vague idealism, openly tinged with esotericism.

Classmates and Friends

Clearly Debussy felt a most profound need at this point in time to find his personal mode of expression, through means outside the realm of music. In 1887, he renewed his friendship with a young student at the Conservatoire who was three years his junior, Paul Dukas, primarily because both of them were able to discuss subjects other than just music: "We considered it genteel to speak as little as possible about music."[14] Dukas's father was a scholar who specialized in the Orient. The two young composers would celebrate their get-togethers by having lunch along the boulevards, at the "Dîner européen," and then walking together in the Bois de Boulogne, exchanging their ideals and aspirations.[15] On 25 May 1887, the day of the fire at the Opéra-Comique, Achille offered his friend a copy of the new publication of Mallarmé's *L'après-midi d'un faune*, with this dedication: "Friendships, esthetics. . . The whole gamut."[16] They also satisfied their musical curiosity by playing some Palestrina motets and masses together at the piano (reducing the full score for four hands!). Achille introduced Dukas to the songs of Alexander Borodin and Mily Balakirev that he had brought back from Russia, commenting on all of this repertoire with an "'It's great!' uttered in that distinctive tone which for him summed up admiration."[17]

He widened his circle of friends to include Michel Peter, the son of a renowned doctor, Charles-Félix-Michel Peter; Michel's brother René would become one of Achille's financial supporters. René reported on the "small dinner parties of young artists" organized by his father, which brought together the following: the playwright Georges Feydeau, who described Achille as a "sort of black-bearded hydrocephalic"; Léon Gandillot and Maurice Vaucaire, two authors whose work did not appeal to Achille; the painter Paul Jean Raphael Sinibaldi, one of the few students of Alfred Stevens; and especially Étienne Dupin, a financier, wealthy devotee of music, and "taciturn and charming being" who helped Achille out financially.[18] At the same time, the young composer came into contact with the Société nationale de musique, where his reputation as an avant-gardist had naturally brought him attention. There he met Ernest Chausson, whom he had perhaps already encountered at the Conservatoire and whose profile was quite different from those of the other single-minded musicians of that establishment. The son of a buildings and public-works contractor, Chausson first studied law before attending the Conservatoire, where he complemented Massenet's teaching with that of Franck. He was also passionate about painting. Sensitive and generous, having everything needed to lead the comfortable life of a dilettante, he devoted himself to composition, but was perpetually racked with self-doubt. Achille and Chausson were not close right away; their social status and other living habits at the time made their potential friendship difficult. At this point, Chausson still hesitated to invite the young Prix de Rome winner, with his bohemian appearance, to one of his splendid soirees in his town house on the boulevard de Courcelles.

The *Ariettes* and Bayreuth

The year 1888 was not marked by tangible career progress for the Prix de Rome winner, who cared little about finding a job and was dependent on the generosity of a few friends. His parents moved and settled into a more spacious apartment at 27 rue de Berlin, on the courtyard side of the fifth floor.[19] Nonetheless, Achille secured a publisher for his six *Ariettes*: the widow of Étienne Girod (on the boulevard Montmartre), who would release the songs in separate installments. He was probably referring to her in an undated letter to a friend when he mentioned a "compassionate and philanthropic publisher."[20] But he had another collection in progress, based on some poems from Baudelaire's *Les fleurs du mal*. Beginning in December 1887, he composed "La mort des amants"; in the following month, he wrote the second song, "Le balcon," the manuscript of which he gave to Paul Poujaud, a new friend and lawyer from the provinces who was a devotee of Vincent d'Indy's music in particular.

Achille's friendship with Étienne Dupin, nurtured by their similar literary tastes, provided the young composer with a trip that had long been in his dreams. Thanks to Dupin's generosity, he would finally get to take his turn as one of the French pilgrims to Bayreuth. The program for the year included *Parsifal* and *Die Meistersinger*, conducted by Hans Richter and Felix Mottl; in the role of Parsifal he reencountered Ernest Van Dyck, who had sung in his *L'enfant prodigue*. It was also an opportunity to mix with Pierre de Bréville, Charles Lamoureux, André Messager, Jules de Brayer, Maurice Bagès, Édouard Dujardin, Joséphin Péladan, and Robert Godet. Achille was surrounded by the primary leaders of the Société nationale de musique, to which he had been admitted on the previous 8 January;[21] among them were Bréville, Fauré, and Bagès, who made him promise in writing, in a polyglot letter that they sent to Vincent d'Indy from a restaurant in Bayreuth, to "produce an orchestral piece for the 1888–1889 season."[22]

However, he had not yet been released from his obligations to the Institut. Indeed, on 30 June 1887, he had agreed to accompany, together with René Chansarel, the cantata written by Bachelet for the Prix de Rome—which, one might add, received only a second prize. Achille fulfilled this particular task more to please Guiraud than la Coupole,[23] since Bachelet was a student of his former teacher. As for the Académie's evaluation following the delivery of his own (unfinished) score of *Printemps*, it ended a bit like the reports that had criticized Achille's first *envoi*: "We are waiting, and we hope for better in the future from a composer as highly gifted as M. Debussy." But it was preceded by a general assessment that is a little gem: "M. Debussy certainly does not fall into platitudes and banality; quite the opposite, he has a very pronounced tendency, even too pronounced, to search for the unusual. We recognize his feeling for musical color and for poetry, the exaggeration of which makes him easily forget the importance of precise design and clear form. He would do well to guard against this vague Impressionism, which is one of the most dangerous enemies of truth in works of art."[24] This label—"Impressionism"—continues to be connected with him until the present day!

La damoiselle élue

At the end of 1888, Achille completed his third *envoi*, *La damoiselle élue*, setting a text of Dante Gabriel Rossetti for female soloists and chorus with orchestra; he would later boast to Pierre Louÿs that in it he had "succeeded in not imitating *Parsifal*,"[25] although he had just returned from Bayreuth. It is almost surprising to note that this *envoi* was better received by the Académie than was the previous one. Here is the official report that was made public:

> A composition written on a rather obscure prose text, poetic music that is not devoid of charm, in which we find with regret the continual tendencies toward vagueness and opposition to a given form already observed in the composer's previous *envoi*, but this time more subdued and justified in some way by the nature of the subject.[26]

Debussy had used the two translations made by Gabriel Sarrazin: the incomplete version from *Poètes modernes de l'Angleterre* as well as the complete version, published in the *Revue contemporaine* in March 1885. This publication had impressed those in certain poetic circles, and, at the very moment when the composer was in the process of setting his text, Albert Samain endorsed the admiration that his friend Raymond Bonheur had shown for the "exquisitely pure inspiration" of this poem, with its "ideal and diaphanous atmosphere, where nearly disembodied visions, all floating, in lines, sway in a luminous music."[27]

After their return from Rome, it was customary for the prize winners to present an orchestral overture to the Académie, to be performed at its annual public concert. Achille did not want to be forced into this final academic requirement and took up his pen, at the beginning of September 1888, to inform the permanent secretary (as the latter reported) that he "is declining this honor because he is not in a position to have any work performed that would be worthy of the Institut."[28] The Académie could only take this ironic reply at face value, and charged Massenet to handle the matter. Since the latter made no further headway, the Académie was pleased to find a solution on 6 October, thanks to Georges Marty, who offered his *Ouverture de Balthazar* to fill the void left by Debussy.[29] Achille certainly did not want to identify himself with the Institut in his quest for fame. According to a letter from Delibes to Camille Erlanger concerning the performance of *La damoiselle élue*, the members of the Institut would have been "so divided among themselves" that no one would have accepted "the responsibility of taking a position on it."[30]

A Life in the Cafés

At the time, Parisian musical life seemed anything but vibrant, and Chabrier revealed its sad outlook in a letter to Ernest Van Dyck on 8 January 1889:

At the Opéra, Gounod and la Patti show off and bring in the money. Massenet is having *Esclarmonde* rehearsed at the Opéra-Comique, Saint-Saëns *Ascanio* at the Opéra; Godard tosses off a *Dante* [. . .] d'Indy works on a grand opus, but he has enough of them to last a couple of years! Lamoureux is doing nothing; the series is turning into family concerts—more choirs, and practically nothing for solo voice; he earns money, he does his job. I think he's tired; he is resting. He presented Chevillard to the orchestra, as if introducing his future successor. They're all getting fat. They no longer worry about anything; he quietly recycles his old programs—and the *bourgeois* people rush in to hear them. The time for serious pursuits has passed.[31]

Achille's circle of acquaintances gradually expanded during this, his so-called "bohemian" period. He effectively settled into life as a night owl. While many musicians sought their way into the salons, where their works so naturally found an outlet, Achille preferred—as did numerous literary men, journalists, and artists—to meet other creative individuals at the cafés, where friendships were formed, ideas were freely exchanged, and the most ephemeral of projects were hashed out. There he was able to broaden his intellectual development. We must therefore become acquainted with his new relationships as well as the places where they developed.

No doubt composers were a part of his sphere, but they were a very select group: Chansarel, Bonheur, Dukas, and Chausson. At the beginning of 1889, Achille made friends with Robert Godet, who, while a musician, had not made music his profession; at age 23, the young Swiss man was already a linguist, well on his way to acquiring something of an encyclopedic knowledge. The son of a clergyman from Neuchâtel and the half-brother of a theologian, he was a worrywart by nature, rather introverted, and he had just written an autobiographical novel, *Le mal d'aimer*.[32] He met Debussy within the circle of writers and artists that gathered around the poet and musician Maurice Bouchor,[33] thanks to Jules de Brayer, who seemed destined to serve as a connecting link and who at the time was the manager of the Lamoureux concerts. At one of these Sunday concerts, Debussy and Godet observed Mallarmé taking notes during the entire performance, and they may well have wished that they could steal his notebook from him! The two men would have a lifelong respect for each other without ever becoming close friends; Godet began by offering a copy of his *Le mal d'aimer* to Debussy, while the latter showed Godet the manuscript of *La damoiselle élue* and reserved a copy of the published score for him.[34] Godet soon learned about the *Ariettes*, thanks to Camille Benoit, their mutual friend. A student of Franck as well as a close friend of d'Indy, Benoit was a critic who translated Wagner's *Mein Leben* (under the title of *Souvenirs*) in 1884.[35]

The Pousset Tavern

Among the gathering places favored by Achille's acquaintances was a "Dutch" tavern—Chez Pousset (which insiders called "le petit Pousset"),[36] situated at the Châteaudun intersection—where theater people, painters, and journalists would come in the evenings to unwind and to exchange the latest gossip in their world until the wee hours of the morning. It was one of Achille's favorite meeting places. Several figures stand out from these café encounters, and it is no surprise that he instinctively gravitated toward the least conventional, the least rank-and-file among them, and, preferably, those who did not take themselves seriously. Among the most picturesque was a painter, Louis Welden Hawkins, an Englishman born in Germany who was as big as a giant. Having received some formal training from William Bouguereau and Gustave Boulanger, Hawkins cultivated a technique similar to that of the Pre-Raphaelites. Edmond de Goncourt depicted him as a character engaging in "a series of nightmarish, fantastic stories, with a sort of clownish delivery, mimicking an epileptic."[37] It is unfortunate that he did not carry out his plan to make a portrait of Achille.

Among the literary people who frequented the Pousset tavern was Villiers de l'Isle-Adam, a Wagnerian from early on and a friend of Baudelaire, whose "La mort des amants" he had set to music (and to which Charles de Sivry had added a piano accompaniment).[38] Achille was not able to know Villiers de l'Isle-Adam for long, because this "apprentice composer"[39] had been suffering from an illness since the beginning of 1889 and died on 19 August of that year.[40] Be that as it may, it was perhaps shortly thereafter that Debussy planned to set to music a scene from *Axël*, the drama on which Villiers had worked for nearly twenty years, which was published a few months after his death, and for which he had drawn inspiration largely from the symbolism of the *Ring*.[41] Alternatively, Debussy's project might have dated from 1894, when the play was performed at the Théâtre de la Gaîté on 26 February; Albert Samain told Raymond Bonheur that "the whole world of music was there" (toute la Lyre y était).[42]

Another regular customer, quite different in stature and more distinctly Parisian, was Catulle Mendès. This former Parnassian, well known in literary and journalistic circles, "held court"[43] at the Pousset tavern, where he would often arrive together with one or two women[44] or even "young men whom he believed to be his disciples."[45] To cite Goncourt once again, Mendès managed to juggle "nightlife, fornicating, and writing."[46] We will soon see how this "ruffian of letters"[47] tried to draw Achille into his wake, but first we should put to rest two stories that still persist in the Debussy literature.

The first concerns a "prophetic" article that Mendès published in the *Revue wagnérienne* in 1885, "Le jeune Prix de Rome et le vieux wagnériste" (The young Prix de Rome winner and the old Wagnerist), in which he seemed to predict a national reaction inspired by Wagnerian drama. Several biographers were quick to identify Achille as the young Prix de Rome winner in question. But we now know that this article was only a scarcely modified reprint of a text that had been published in the paper *Le gaulois* in 1876.[48]

The second story was reported by Alfred Cortot: Manuel, Achille's father, was said to have met Mendès by chance at the Café Napolitain, and the writer supposedly offered to help Manuel's son by using his influence at the Opéra and proposing a libretto, *Rodrigue et Chimène*, for him to set to music. This account is not very convincing, either, since it implies that Achille needed the help of his father to meet a man whom he could have approached more easily himself.[49]

But to get back to the Pousset tavern, it was also frequented by Raymond Bonheur and others connected to Achille. Among them are many whom we cannot leave unmentioned: the poet Raoul Ponchon, a friend of Chabrier and of Verlaine; the aforementioned Charles de Sivry, a marginal composer who survived the Commune and whom Achille had already met at a crucial time in his youth; a graduate of the École Niedermeyer, Alexandre Georges, to whose *Chansons de Miarka* he politely listened; a friend of Rimbaud, Henri Mercier, who was doggedly perfecting his translation of John Keats; Jules de Brayer, a modest organist who also went to the École Niedermeyer and was an unabashed Wagnerian, but also a proponent of Modest Mussorgsky's *Boris Godunov*; and a poet and writer on art, Gabriel Mourey, who found in Achille a conversationalist capable of discussing Jules Laforgue as well as the Pre-Raphaelites, Aubrey Beardsley, and Edgar Allan Poe (whose *Poésies complètes* Mourey had just translated). "They closed," remembers Bonheur, "and we proceeded along the deserted streets, filled with the charm of Parisian nights."[50]

Chez Thommen

On the left bank, another place—more along the lines of a "bistro" and less trendy than the Pousset tavern—attracted Achille at that same time: Chez Thommen, run by a respectable fellow from Baden and at times by his two beautiful daughters, Amélie and Louise.[51] Godet introduced Debussy to this establishment, where he met Adolphe Willette, who drew some Pierrot-like characters for the composer's song "Mandoline," and especially Georges Lorin. The latter, whose pseudonym was Cabriol, had been vice president of the Hydropaths, and was still friends with Charles de Sivry. Above all, Debussy worshipped Maurice Rollinat, more a poet than a musician,[52] praised to the hilt by some, but described by others as a ham and a conniver. Achille supposedly showed a polite tolerance for the "songs" that Lorin submitted to

Rollinat, which incidentally were harmonized by a first-prize winner from the Conservatoire, Jean-Louis Frédéric Lapuchin.[53]

Other characters frequented Chez Thommen. One was Camille de Sainte-Croix, a journalist and writer whose portrait was made by Louis Welden Hawkins and who was one of the first supporters of Gauguin; in 1888, Sainte-Croix wrote a pantomime for the Cercle funambulesque, for which Robert Godet wrote the music.[54] Others included Raphaël Collin and Jean Antoine Injalbert, with whom Achille discussed painting and sculpture. Jean Carriès was a sculptor turned pottery maker, one of whose vases Debussy owned. Charles Cros was a poet, whose "L'archet" (from his collection *Chansons perpetuelles*) Achille attempted to set to music.[55] As well, there were the poets Gabriel Vicaire, whose verses Achille described as "enchanting,"[56] and Louis Le Cardonnel, who was present at the Chat Noir as often as he was at Mallarmé's Tuesdays and who admired the Pre-Raphaelites. Le Cardonnel's "verbal music" captivated Achille.[57]

Still on the left bank, we should not forget the Vachette café, in the Latin quarter, where Achille sparred with Jean Moréas about Arthur Schopenhauer and Johann Wolfgang von Goethe's second *Faust*: "They egged each other on to such a degree that they ended up enjoying themselves, and to such an extent that, in the process of following the development of their shared hoax, it was no longer clear who was the doctrinarian and who the ironist."[58]

All of these artists and writers, whom posterity has by and large considered only second- or third-rate, were, for Debussy, if not the instigators, at least the creative spirits from whom he sought the "secret" for his own art. Much in the same way, Mallarmé sought to "find his own voice" through music.

From the *Ariettes* to the *Cinq poèmes*

For Achille, this café life was merely a backdrop on which his purely musical pursuits were grafted. On 2 February 1889, the first performance of his *Ariettes*, based on Verlaine poems, took place in a concert at the Société nationale de musique; also included on the program were Fauré's Second Piano Quartet as well as the incidental music written by Chausson for a marionette-theater production of Shakespeare's *The Tempest*. The amateur tenor Maurice Bagès, a friend of Pierre de Bréville, performed two of the *Ariettes*, accompanied by the composer at the piano. While Marcel Proust thought that Bagès had "a skillful and delightful charm,"[59] Mme de Saint-Marceaux, when she heard him in Fauré's songs, felt that he sang "with taste and without talent, as usual."[60] These songs passed unnoticed by the critics, except for Camille Bellaigue, Achille's former schoolmate in Marmontel's class, who pronounced in the *Revue des deux mondes* that these "laments" represented "the complete decadence, the total dissolution of music and of poetry."[61] It is quite probably this performance that led to César Franck's alleged comment that this was "music on needle tips" (de la musique sur pointes d'aiguilles).[62] Tiersot considered the *Ariettes* to be "of a very subtle artistic feeling, very desirable,"[63] while the critic from the *Guide musical* deemed that Achille Debussy was "a name to remember," and that he had a "refined, delicate artistic nature, seeking the original and avoiding banality. There are lovely pianistic sonorities in the accompaniment. At times, he has a slight tendency toward the cloying, toward the precious. But would one ever believe that M. Debussy went through the Conservatoire?"[64]

Several days later, Auguste Durand, who was already the publisher of *L'enfant prodigue*, brought out a *Petite suite* for piano, four hands, that Achille and Jacques Durand played together at the latter's home on 1 March.[65] It would be quite a few years before this work would become known. Achille was certainly satisfied with it; some months later, he paid a visit to Guiraud's class with Dukas (who was in military uniform at the time), and the two of them played the suite for the teacher's new pupils, among them Henri Busser.[66]

Convinced of Achille's innovative talent, Ernest Chausson sought to program one of his new works on the Société nationale's concerts. On 7 March, Achille replied that he could not give him *Printemps*, as he wanted to revise the orchestration, and it ran the risk of having too big a sound for the Salle Pleyel; the "gently subdued charms" of *La damoiselle élue*, he suggested, would perhaps be more suitable.[67] But it was still too soon for this work to be accepted by the public.

On the other hand, Achille was seeking to publish his *Cinq poèmes*. On 16 February 1889, when he had been asked to name his favorite poets, he had replied simply: Baudelaire. The day he had filled out this questionnaire, he claimed to have been "sad and searching" and was hoping to live "anywhere out of the world."[68] Even so, he confessed that he loved Russian cuisine and disclosed that he had just seen a pantomime at the Hippodrome about Mikhail Skobeleff, the Russian general who had just conquered Turkestan.[69]

In early April, Achille accepted an invitation from Michel Peter to spend several weeks by the sea at Saint-Énogat, near Saint-Lunaire. Their mutual love for *Parsifal* was not enough to compensate for a certain incompatibility of moods, and Achille accordingly complained to René Chansarel that he was surrounded by "lowlifes" and that his "morale" was in a state of "decline," of creative despondency.[70] In his replies and in a choice of words that all but parodied the most extreme Symbolism, Chansarel, citing Joris-Karl Huysmans and Verlaine, tried somewhat ironically to console him, asserting that he possessed more genius than the others and that his works would soon be understood by the elite.[71] These missives are obviously more truthful than the unreliable account written much later by René Peter, Michel's younger brother, who told the story of a turbulent boat trip to Cancale as well as a "getaway" for a few days of letting loose.[72] During these two months, Achille completed a chore for Durand, the transcription of Saint-Saëns's *Introduction et rondo capriccioso*, and was already working on his own *Fantaisie pour piano et orchestre* that was awaiting the "silky-smooth fingers" of his friend Chansarel.[73]

The 1889 World's Fair

Upon his return to Paris, Achille found the city in full swing due to the World's Fair,[74] which had officially opened its doors on 6 May and would continue through the end of September. There one could visit a Buddhist temple or the Chinese pavilion, and walk along the reconstructed "street in Cairo" or in the Moroccan souk. Music was heard everywhere, in multiple forms: Hungarian cimbaloms, Gypsy bands, Pahouin tribespeople from the Congo, Kanaka people from New Caledonia, and even, in the American pavilion, Thomas Edison's new and improved phonograph, which made it possible for everyone to hear Gounod sing the well-known song, "Il pleut, il pleut, bergère!"[75] However, not all of the pavilions were complete when the World's Fair began; in particular, the Vietnamese theater was not opened until 5 June. Achille lost no time in going there for "long afternoons"[76] with Raymond Bonheur, Paul Dukas, or Robert Godet, and most of his visits preceded his second trip to Bayreuth.

Precisely what was it, musically speaking, in those famous performances that fascinated the composer so much? At the Ngu-Hô Annamite theater, as it was called, the main show was a grand historical drama, *The King of the Duong*,[77] relating the story of a failed conspiracy against the king around 1,000 BCE, enlivened by war dances, battles, processions, and the like. Six musicians took part, some of whom played multiple instruments: two-stringed fiddles (*dàn nhị*), two oboes (*kèn bóp*), a transverse flute, and several percussion instruments—a suspended gong, two types of drum (battle and ceremonial *trồngs*) that were struck with sticks, and a large drum, the first group being reserved for the accompaniment of the dialogues.[78] What Achille called the "raging little clarinet that excites emotion," and that can be identified in an engraving in *L'illustration*, was in fact a type of oboe (*kèn*).[79] Altogether, the company, which came from Saigon and was directed by Nguyen Dông Tru, comprised about forty actors, three of whom were women.[80] Its repertoire was typical of that of the southern part of the country, of Chinese origin, without in any way being that "bad, decadent Chinese music,"[81] as Saint-Saëns, who had no competency in the matter, described it. In watching this show, Achille, according to Godet, could not help but make "irreverent comparisons with Bayreuth."[82]

A little further along the esplanade des Invalides was a Javanese village, the *kampong*, at the center of which was a bamboo-columned pavilion that accommodated performances. The show began with a procession by those playing the *angklung*, instruments with two or three bamboo sticks tuned in octaves, preceded by a *kendang*, a two-headed drum that was struck with the hands and whose player took the role of conductor. Then the gamelan orchestra chimed in, with its variety of percussion instruments and a single bowed instrument, the two-stringed *rebab*. Four *bedayas*, female dancers in the troupe of the ruler of Java (Mangko-Negoro, Prince of Solo) who were between the ages of twelve and sixteen, performed in their courtly dress; Vakiem, Sariem, Soekia, and Tanimah[83] captivated all of Paris with their sacred, nearly motionless, dances.[84] Which one of them took a cigarette from Achille's hands, drew a puff from it, and threw it away?[85] Beyond their indescribable charm, the composer remembered especially the "innumerable arabesques" of the gamelan and its polyphony.[86] It ended up influencing him even more than did the Annamite theater.

At the end of the month of June, on the 22nd and the 29th, two special concerts of Russian music led Debussy to rekindle, or rather to broaden, his acquaintance with that repertoire.[87] At the Trocadéro, Nicolai Rimsky-Korsakov conducted these symphony concerts, organized by the publisher Belaieff and featuring works largely by The Mighty Five, along with Alexander Glazunov and the pioneers Mikhail Glinka and Alexander Dargomyzhsky. Among the most notable works presented were Rimsky-Korsakov's *Antar*, *Capriccio espagnol*, and Concerto for Piano, op. 30, all conducted by the composer. Even though the modal writing and orchestral coloring of these Russian pieces were less novel than those elements in East Asian music, they still thoroughly captivated the young composer.

And yet, early in August he returned to Bayreuth, not for *Die Meistersinger* or *Parsifal*, but for *Tristan*, the score of which he knew by heart but which he had never heard performed.[88] That year, Étienne Destranges, a critic from Nantes, noted the presence of at least forty French citizens, while Lavignac listed 160 people, although they were not all at the same productions. Cosima Wagner received a few of these French attendees at Wahnfried, her villa; among those invited were Vincent d'Indy, Emmanuel Chabrier, Georges Hüe, Antoine Lascoux, Pierre de Bréville, Maurice Bagès, Paul Poujaud, Guy Ropartz, and André-Ferdinand Herold.[89] Of course, Achille was not among these privileged people, but neither were Godet, Chausson, Dupin, or Dukas, all of whom were part of the French contingent, as was Marguerite Pelouze, the doyenne from Chenonceaux![90]

This was the end of Achille's Wagnerian phase, even if his repudiation of that composer has often been exaggerated. A letter he wrote to Guiraud (and that survives only in a copy, presumably accurate) reveals the state of his soul upon returning from Bayreuth: "It saddens me to feel myself growing away from it."[91]

Conversations with Guiraud

On the whole, however, the year of 1889 had been ripe with new and fruitful contacts, and Achille's sonorous ideal was becoming noticeably crystallized. It was during this time that Maurice Emmanuel took the trouble to record in a small notebook the conversations that Achille had with Guiraud, during lunches at restaurants or at his home, which have been amply commented upon.[92] The young composer called for sonorous ambiguity, for chords that are incomplete—floating—or at least without resolution. He criticized Wagner—for not having gone far enough in his break with traditional opera, for including "too much singing,"[93] and for "outfitting"[94] his music in too ponderous a manner—though at the same time he praised *Tristan* for its themes that reflected the action. Finally, Achille iterated his personal quest for a subtle art and for "things half-said" in dramatic music.[95]

When these texts were discovered, some people believed them to be spurious because all they saw there was the aesthetic of *Pelléas*, already set out: "No time, no place. [. . .] No 'scene to set.' [. . .] Characters not communicating, but submitting to life and fate."[96] Yet, already in 1885, we find in his writing the rejection of an "overly rigid mold,"[97] striving (just like Baudelaire) toward "the long-sought-after expression of feelings of the soul,"[98] the "obligation to invent new forms,"[99] and his rebellion against traditional harmony—a rebellion that, as noted earlier, was common knowledge at the Conservatoire. The remarks in these notebooks, made prior to the time of *Pelléas*, are surprising only if we forget the slow maturation of the composer as he listened to the Symbolist poets and artists in search of a dream, of the imprecise, of freedom, and even of the esoteric.

The end of 1889 was gloomy. Achille contracted pneumonia during the month of December and, on the 6th, Adrien Dukas wrote to his brother Paul, who was in the military at the time, that he had run into Debussy, who was "racked by musical and financial problems."[100] On Christmas Day, the latter wrote to Godet (who had left for Switzerland) a long letter in which he spoke of "tendencies toward deep melancholy."[101]

No publisher seemed to want his *Cinq poèmes de Baudelaire*. However, the day after his visit to Bayreuth, Achille had gone back to composing the *Fantaisie pour piano et orchestre*, which was supposed to constitute his fourth *envoi* for his Prix de Rome. None of his other compositions was as strongly influenced by Javanese music; within the ostinato passage of the work's Finale, the Javanese influence is even more striking than that of d'Indy's *Symphonie cévenole* (Symphony on a French Mountain Air). Still, in order to make ends meet, Achille also had to take on some work for Durand and, in October, upon finishing an arrangement of the ballet music from Saint-Saëns's *Étienne Marcel*, he grumbled: "It's tough, earning one's daily bread!"[102]

Chapter Seven

From Baudelaire to Mallarmé

1890–91

At the beginning of 1890, an outward sign revealed Debussy's desire for a change: he abandoned his given first name, which he had never liked, for that of Claude-Achille; in addition, he adopted a new signature, with a very different style of handwriting. This was also the period when the *Cinq poèmes de Baudelaire* were finally published. René Chansarel had helped obtain permission from Baudelaire's publisher to use the poems. A subscription was organized by Gaston Choisnel, a cousin and future employee of Jacques Durand. The edition—whose presentation was typically Symbolist in character (featuring a large format, on simulated parchment with wide margins, and with titles printed in blue, golden yellow, and brown)—had a print run limited to 150 copies at a cost of 12 francs apiece. Debussy's score would appear in February 1890, with a dedication to Étienne Dupin, who had provided financial support.

This collection, which all commentators agree is deeply influenced by Wagner's work, was beyond the capability of amateur singers and was even likely to scare off some professionals. Several years later, its complexity had still not been processed by various critics, and Georges Servières, surveying all of the composer's songs in 1895, condemned the *Cinq poèmes* unequivocally: "Harmonic peculiarities and defects, constantly broken and disjointed rhythms, unsingable intervals, no concern for vocal registers. [. . .] The poetic lines are often poorly declaimed, the prosody violated, the meaning destroyed by the segmentation of the melody. Also, excessive chromaticism and grating modulations."[1]

For that matter, Claude-Achille would wait fifteen years before a public performance of the *Cinq poèmes* was given—an incomplete one, at that.[2] Nevertheless, we now know that private run-throughs took place at the homes of André-Ferdinand Herold and Ernest Chausson.[3] In neither case do we know the names of the performers, but it is likely that Claude-Achille himself would have been involved. Furthermore, the performance at the home of Chausson, with whom the young composer had not yet formed a close friendship but whom he used to meet at events of the Société nationale de musique, occurred during the very month in which the songs were published.[4]

Chausson had invited several close friends—in particular Vidal, who long afterward remembered having heard the first performance of the *Cinq poèmes* at Chausson's salon[5]—and also some important people who were influential in the artistic world of Paris. We have in fact two confirmations of this private event. When dedicating his recently published novel, *Méphistophéla*, to Debussy, Catulle Mendès added, "with hearty congratulations on his Baudelairean music and his lovely concert";[6] and on 9 March, Willy (Gauthier-Villars), in one of his *Lettres de l'ouvreuse*, made a similar allusion: "Debussy, who throws the fertilizer of his music on the *Flowers* of Baudelaire."[7] It was surely to thank Chausson that Debussy dedicated to him the first of his *Trois mélodies de Verlaine* in the following year. Considering the fact that the young composer would soon become acquainted with Mallarmé as a result of this concert, one could contend that the *Cinq poèmes* did more for his nascent reputation than did *La damoiselle élue* or the String Quartet.

The *Fantaisie* for Piano

By this point in time, Debussy's *Fantaisie pour piano et orchestre* had been completed, and the Société nationale de musique planned to perform the work on its concert of 21 April 1890. But the program was exceptionally full, comprising nine pieces: among them were César Franck's string quartet, Camille Benoit's *Les noces corinthiennes*, Fauré's *La passion*, some songs, and a prelude by Jacques Durand. As a result, at the last rehearsal in the Salle Érard, Vincent d'Indy, who was conducting, decided to perform only the first of the *Fantaisie*'s three movements.[8] Caught in a fait accompli, Claude-Achille silently removed the orchestral parts from the stands after the rehearsal was over, and sent a letter to d'Indy, explaining that he was distressed by this decision and that he would prefer an "adequate performance of the three movements to a satisfactory performance of only the first."[9] Publicly, the cancellation of the work was blamed on the pianist, Chansarel, who was declared ill. Three days later, on 24 April, Debussy sold the score to Choudens for 200 francs, probably thanks to the intervention of Catulle Mendès.[10]

Here a subtle chronological problem requires resolution. Mendès gave his support for the publication of the *Fantaisie* just before he began to pressure Debussy to write the music for *Rodrigue et Chimène*, an opera whose libretto he had penned. Godet is definite on this point, thus leading us to believe that these exchanges between the poet and the composer took place in March–April 1890. A telegram, sent after the performance of the *Cinq poèmes* and greeting its composer as the "master of the future," was followed by a visit from Mendès, for whom Debussy played his *Fantaisie*, and the poet's subsequent declaration of support to have it published. Mendès quickly "disclosed his intentions" by placing his *Rodrigue et Chimène* in Debussy's hands.[11] It thus seems clear that the date of "April 1890," placed on the first page of this score,[12] was intended to remind its dedicatee, Gaby Dupont, of the date on which the composition was begun—following a practice of dating after the fact that we have already noted in some of his earlier manuscripts.

Rodrigue et Chimène

In fact, Mendès had not written *Rodrigue et Chimène*, a libretto based on Pierre Corneille's tragedy *Le Cid*,[13] specifically for Debussy. From his files, he brought out an old "grand-opera poem" in four acts and five tableaux that he had completed in 1878 but that had never been set to music. While maintaining Corneille's structural framework, Mendès claimed to have gone back in time to the "primeval legends," so as to inject "a strange and warm local color, and all of the picturesque oddity of the old Castillian and Moorish mores."[14] In actual fact, he had taken elements of the first act and the beginning of the second act from Guilhen de Castro,[15] notably adopting the characters of the brothers Hernan and Bermudo. He had kept a small part of the first three acts and especially the denouement from Corneille's *Le Cid*, the choral parts being of his own invention. We do not know for which composer the poet intended his libretto; the press at the time mentioned that it was not yet possible to disclose a name, but that it involved "one of the most famous of the French school."[16] The names Gounod, Ambroise Thomas, or Saint-Saëns come to mind, but in June 1879 one periodical mentioned François-Auguste Gevaert.[17] The news had scarcely been made public, on 21 December 1878, when several librettists—Louis Gallet, Émile de La Rue, and Jules Barbier—claimed they had priority for this subject. Among the possible composers mentioned were Victor Massé, Aimé Maillard, and naturally Bizet, who had done a lot of work on a *Don Rodrigue* in 1873.[18] Ultimately, Massenet was the only composer in France to succeed in producing an opera on *Le Cid* (1885). In 1890, this whole uproar having been forgotten, Mendès could once again seek a way to get his libretto out, and instead of entrusting it to one of the musical "celebrities," he decided this time to enlist a rising star.

The pressures under which Claude-Achille agreed to write an opera based on a libretto whose aesthetic—with its traditional divisions and pompous verses—could only displease him are really no secret. First there was the financial difficulty in which he had found himself since his return from Rome. His bohemian and nocturnal life style created constant tensions with his parents, who continued to lead a bare-bones existence. His father, in particular, thought that it was time for his son, at age twenty-eight, to find a true profession in music, instead of keeping company with poets and artists who themselves were penniless. Catulle Mendès was an "established" figure. It had to be drummed into Debussy that this libretto would be his opportunity, that he should not let it pass, that thanks to Mendès he would finally go on to become famous. Did not Chabrier deem Mendès "the only man capable of laying his hands on a real opera,"[19] despite having found him worthy of a professorship in "trickery and extreme entanglement"[20] at the Collège de France? And had Chabrier not agreed to compose the music for his *Briséïs*?[21] Mendès provided the libretto for Messager's *Isoline*, and Pierné would soon take up his *Collier des saphirs*. Given these realities, Claude-Achille weakened and began to focus on composing this opera, despite his aesthetic discomfort with it. Had it not been already six years since he had won the Prix de Rome?

How are we to reconcile, however, the decisive statements made to Guiraud just the previous year with the return to a traditional style that *Rodrigue et Chimène* represented? Let us recall a few key phrases from those former discussions: "Music is made for the inexpressible; I would like it to appear to emerge from the shadows and at times to return to them; that it would always be unobtrusive."[22] And especially, concerning the poet who would be capable of writing a libretto that would echo his views: "He who, by leaving some things half-said, will allow me to graft my dream onto his; he who will create characters who come from no particular time or place; he who will not tyrannically force me to compose a big scene 'for effect,' and who will leave me free, here and there, to allow my art to take precedence over his and to complete his work."[23]

In accepting Mendès's offer, Debussy readopted a little of the mind-set he had had while composing his pieces for the Prix de Rome—a self-imposed discipline, counter to his most precious dreams. Now the essential difference was his greater maturity, which allowed him to make the best even of conventional scenes and to introduce experiments—as in act 2 of *Rodrigue et Chimène*—that almost take us into the world of *Pelléas*.

Debussy's personal and romantic life was filled with great uncertainty during this period. The names of several obscure women appear in the dedications of his works. Two piano pieces were notably dedicated to Mme Philippe Hottinguer: the *Ballade slave* and the *Tarentelle styrienne*—a curiously fanciful title, as the residents of Styria never danced the tarantella! Claude-Achille knew this woman through Chansarel, who was giving her piano and harmony lessons. Born Nelly de Wustemberg in 1821, into a family from Bordeaux, she was said to have worked with Clara Schumann and to have performed with Pauline Viardot. A widow since 1878, she had a reputation for helping young artists.[24]

Much younger was Rose Depecker, who was twenty-one years old when the *Valse romantique* was dedicated to her. Having entered the Conservatoire at the age of eight, she had obtained a first prize for accompanying in 1887 and a first prize for piano in the following year.[25] On 8 March 1890, she gave a recital before a "large audience of artists, professors, and distinguished amateurs."[26] It is quite possible that, among the "old and modern" works that she performed on this occasion, she may have programmed the *Valse* of a fellow Conservatoire alumnus with whom she had become friends. A charming individual, she had won the Popelin prize at the Conservatoire in 1888, but she also lived a difficult life, giving piano lessons as a substitute teacher for Mme Canivet.[27]

Gaby Dupont

Another woman appeared at the beginning of 1890, someone who would finally bring an element of emotional stability into Claude-Achille's life during this bohemian period. In April, he wrote her name in this somewhat formal manner on the first act of *Rodrigue*: "To Mademoiselle Gabrielle Dupont." This attractive young woman from Normandy, who was twenty-four years old, would become his companion for about eight years. Well-proportioned, she had light brown hair that she lightened further, a prominent chin, the blue-green eyes of a cat, and a dazzling complexion. She groomed herself very carefully and had "a way of carrying herself very erectly," with her head slightly tilted back.[28] The daughter of a humble factory worker and a dressmaker from Lisieux, Gabrielle was first employed at a local millinery, and then she tried her luck in Paris. When Debussy met her, she had just ended a brief liaison with a young aristocrat, Count Villeneuve.[29] For more than a year, Claude-Achille, who still lived with his family, saw her only on the sly, and he probably did not live with her before the summer of 1892.

Claude-Achille had become acquainted with a young painter, Léopold Stevens, who frequented the Café Napolitain and moved in the circle that included Dupin, Henri Mercier,[30] Jean Carriès, and Dr. Peter. Léopold was the son of Alfred Stevens, a Belgian painter who had had his moment of glory during the Second Empire.[31] If at times the latter has been called the "painter of love notes,"[32] it is because his life's work is filled with portraits of society ladies clutching songs or love letters that plunge them into ecstasy or despair. Of course, he was completely out of fashion at the height of the Symbolist era, and he began to suffer financial difficulties. However, Stevens fascinated Achille with his "outpouring of amusing anecdotes"[33] about the writers and painters he had known: Delacroix and Dumas *fils* had been witnesses at his wedding, he was friendly with Manet, and he viewed with sadness the budding success of the Impressionists.[34] Toward the end of his life, he was influenced by James Abbott McNeill Whistler and the Japanese; Baudelaire had read his own translations of

Edgar Allan Poe in Stevens's studio.[35] It is obvious that, his "porcine grunts"[36] notwithstanding, his conversation could only captivate the young composer. His wife was a good musician and his daughter Catherine, twenty-five years old and a goddaughter of Degas, not only performed but also enjoyed composing small works—on the poems of Musset, among others.

Léopold Stevens wanted to share his admiration for Debussy's music—especially for the *Cinq poèmes de Baudelaire*—with those close to him. He invited his composer friend to the family townhouse on the rue de Calais, which was something of a museum with Indian, Japanese, Flemish, and Italian objects.[37] Claude-Achille thus made a habit of visiting this welcoming family, where he was especially attracted to Catherine, that "pretty girl with gently wicked eyes,"[38] who evoked for Goncourt "the impression of an angel fallen from heaven."[39] But it was not love at first sight; in November 1890, Claude-Achille's dedication to her of a score of the *Cinq poèmes* was prudently worded: "To the sister of Léopold Stevens, Mlle Catherine Stevens."[40]

Relations between Claude-Achille and his parents had been rather tense, such that in October–November 1890 he moved in with his kindhearted friend Étienne Dupin at 76 boulevard Malesherbes; three letters dating from these months and addressed to Gustave Popelin and André-Ferdinand Herold give this address.[41] At any rate, it was a gloomy period in both his financial and romantic life. To which friend did he write, in pencil, this anxious missive: "Dear friend, forgive me, but can you loan me 20 francs until the end of the month—immediately, for my basic needs. I'm very ashamed to write to you, but I'm quite simply hungry"?[42]

The Librairie de l'art indépendant

It must have been still during 1890 that Debussy first came into contact with an unusual publisher whose shop, much like Mallarmé's salon and the informal cafés, would become a meeting place that played a part in Claude-Achille's development. Edmond Bailly (his real name was Henri-Edmond Limet)[43] had been an artilleryman for the Commune, so it was said, and boasted of having fired the last shot during the Père-Lachaise massacre.[44] He had enrolled at the Conservatoire at the end of 1877, and then again in 1886, without winning any prizes there.[45] In 1888, he was director of a small periodical titled *La musique populaire (Musique des familles): Journal hebdomadaire illustré; Théâtre; Beaux-arts; Littérature*, whose publication would soon cease. In October 1889, he set up business at 11 rue de la Chaussée d'Antin (the premises that had just been vacated by Édouard Dujardin and the *Revue indépendante*). Its rear courtyard connected to 14 rue Halévy,[46] where Bailly also had a shop, called "Comptoir d'édition," from which he sold "engravings, books, and music."[47]

There he published some of his own short compositions, which reveal only the modest talent of an amateur—*Chagrin d'amour, Mazoure* in F Major for piano (1887), and *Danse d'autrefois* for piano, op. 7 (1888)—before becoming emboldened in his more ambitious works—"Apparition" (an "adaptation" of Mallarmé's poem, 1894) and *Trois rondels de Charles d'Orléans* for voice and piano, op. 9 (1895).[48]

Within a few months, Bailly's Librairie de l'art indépendant succeeded in attracting some of the best Symbolist poets and writers, due in particular to a periodical managed by Viélé-Griffin, the *Entretiens politiques et littéraires*. Between 1890 and 1895, Bailly thus issued works by Villiers de l'Isle Adam, Henri de Régnier, André Gide, Jules Bois, André-Ferdinand Herold, Pierre Quillard, and soon Pierre Louÿs and Jean de Tinan. Victor-Émile Michelet recalled that Félicien Rops and, to a lesser extent, Odilon Redon were also regulars at the publishing house. Henri de Régnier, who had co-founded the *Entretiens politiques et littéraires* with Francis Viélé-Griffin, described the Librairie de l'art indépendant as follows:

> This shop on the Chaussée d'Antin was no ordinary place. Upon opening the door, one would find oneself in the presence of a stout woman with white hair and a small, bearded man with gold glasses: [. . .] Edmond Bailly himself. But Edmond Bailly, an odd character, was not only a publisher but also an occultist and a musician. [. . .] One would go to Bailly's to talk about literature. There, at times, one would call upon the spirits by means of a sort of wooden tripod by which one's hands would jerkily spell out alphabetical messages. Bailly led these experiences, all the while caressing his cat Aziza."[49]

A letter from Debussy to Chausson, written a little later in 1893, confirms these séances and the participants' state of mind: "I met Henri de Régnier at Bailly's, and he invited me to dinner; then we returned to Bailly's place and made the tables speak! In spite of the otherworldly interest of these revelations, I certainly would have preferred conversing with you."[50]

A moderate Wagnerian, Bailly was passionate about issues of synesthesia—the correspondences between music, writing, color, etc.; his esotericism was inspired by Emanuel Swedenborg in particular.[51] These occultist tendencies would culminate in 1893 with the publication of some issues of the periodical *La haute science*, "a journal documenting the esoteric tradition and religious symbolism."[52] In it Claude-Achille discovered a new world, far removed from the modest smattering of prosaic education that he had received from his mother or that had reappeared in conversations at the Conservatoire. That this environment could attract him is not surprising, especially as this trend was fashionable among many Symbolists. Already in Rome, in 1886, he had been keeping himself informed through his friend, the bookseller Baron, of a publication by Albert Jounet (*Rose Croix*) that dealt with the mysteries of the

Kabbalah.[53] Furthermore, Debussy thoroughly enjoyed *Les déliquescences d'Adoré Floupette*, which contained echoes of occultist themes.[54]

Writing to André Poniatowski, Claude-Achille praised Bailly in this way: "I recommend him to you, that fellow! If you only knew what that little man harbors within himself—eminent knowledge and really very artistic ideas; and he has a tenacity that at times makes mine pale in comparison."[55]

The first contact between the two men dates from the time when the edition of the *Cinq poèmes* was being sold at the Librairie de l'art indépendant; one hundred fifty copies were printed, fifty of which were on Holland paper. While Claude-Achille was not a regular visitor right away, the numerous "happy hours,"[56] to which he alluded in dedicating his manuscript of *La damoiselle élue* to Bailly, would certainly begin as early as the following year. According to Victor-Émile Michelet, the young composer gladly played his latest works on the excellent piano that was at the back of the shop: he "would arrive nearly every day at the end of the afternoon [. . .] either alone or with his faithful Erik Satie."[57]

The Chat Noir

Various reports exist of how Claude-Achille met Erik Satie. Their initial encounter has often been placed at the Auberge du Clou or at Bailly's; however, Vital Hocquet, a colleague at the Chat Noir, claimed that he had introduced the two men to each other.[58] In any event, that first contact had a rather electrifying effect on Satie, which one of his more recent biographers has readily attributed to a repressed homosexuality:[59] "From the moment I laid eyes on him," wrote Satie, "I was drawn to him and wanted to live constantly by his side. [. . .] We could read each other's minds, without the need for complicated explanations."[60] Henri Busser wrote that Claude-Achille had heartily recommended Satie to Ernest Guiraud, who at one point, in 1890, had accepted him as an auditor in his class at the Conservatoire. This apprentice composer, an unusual presence in that establishment, earned his living by playing piano at a cabaret in the evenings. Around 1888, he would become the pianist at the Chat Noir, where it is not inconceivable that he had met Debussy.[61]

At that time, the Chat Noir was no longer a simple café chantant. Located on the rue Victor-Massé since 1885, it presented, under the direction of Rodolphe Salis, more varied and ambitious shows; musical participants included Vincent Hyspa (whose "La belle au bois dormant" Debussy set in July 1890), Paul Delmet, and Jules Jouy. In the early 1890s, the cabaret was filled, with Fridays being a particularly chic day.[62] In January 1891, for example, *Phryné*, a Grecian scene performed as a shadow play with a set by Henri Rivière and music by Sivry, was a great success. In November, *Ailleurs*, a Symbolist revue in twenty tableaux by Maurice Donnay and with music again by Sivry, was performed.[63] Were Sivry and Debussy perhaps moved on that occasion to recall dark memories from 1871, when Debussy's father had met Sivry in prison? A full show alternated "poèmes mobiles,"[64] political satires, monologues, and mystery-plays, the Chinese shadow plays being the most artistic among them. The Chat Noir also went on tour to the provinces.

From 1890 on, Claude-Achille would go there to relax, but it was not he who was the pianist-accompanist, as has been claimed.[65] For him, as for many other artists or writers, the Chat Noir answered a need for "naughty intellectual pleasures" about which Goncourt spoke;[66] its shows were also reviewed, like those from the Opéra-Comique or the Éden, by the highbrow journals. In a letter from Camille Benoit to Paul Dukas on 24 May 1892, one finds the following observation: "Yesterday evening, passing by the rue de Laval at 8:20, I saw Debussy looking like quite the rascal and sitting at the table in front of Paul Robert, by the big open bay window of the Chat Noir."[67] Maurice Donnay also described one evening at the cabaret when Claude-Achille joyously conducted a "frenetic chorus" on a song from Ben-Tayoux titled "Le café."[68] He readily mixed with his easygoing friends and ended up serving as best man, along with the poet Maurice Vaucaire, at the wedding of Vital Hocquet (Narcisse Lebeau)—both of them regulars at the Chat Noir.

Like the Symbolists, Claude-Achille preferred an art that was elitist and disdainful of the public. Indeed, few of the other Prix de Rome winners were talked about so little or remained so off the radar. Debussy's artistic ideal was certainly represented in his *Cinq poèmes*, with its exclusive limited edition. But for a long time he failed to fulfill the dream expressed by Pierre Louÿs in 1890–91: to keep one's works "for oneself alone."[69] This was for severe financial reasons—unlike his future friend [Louÿs], Debussy did not have the means to provide for his daily living. In these difficult times, when he had no regular income, he was dependent on the generosity of Dupin, and perhaps on that of Chansarel, or Poniatowski, or Chausson, or Countess Greffuhle. Vital Hocquet talked about how, in order to clothe himself, Claude-Achille took advantage of the generosity of a tailor by the name of Hugo, who said to him: "You will settle all this with me when you become famous."[70]

Mallarmé

The autumn of 1890 was marked by an exceptionally significant contact. It all began when Claude-Achille was approached by the poet André-Ferdinand Herold, a former student at the École des Chartes, the grandson of the composer of *Le pré aux clercs*, and the son of a former Prefect of the Seine. Closely tied to the Symbolist movement, he proposed a meeting with Debussy at the

Pousset tavern. He had just revealed the *Cinq poèmes de Baudelaire* to Stéphane Mallarmé, who had been "very struck by the new beauty" of that music and was thinking of asking Debussy to collaborate on a production of *L'après-midi d'un faune* that he was planning with Paul Fort at the Théâtre d'Art.[71] Mallarmé, who diligently attended the Sunday Lamoureux concerts[72] and who sought in music a sustenance whose effect only he knew,[73] was hoping for "nothing more than a musical overture" for this performance.[74] As Herold wrote more directly: "He would be pleased if music were to be combined with the poem, and one evening, as I was arriving at the rue de Rome, he asked me: 'Do you think that your friend Debussy would write some music for *L'après-midi d'un faune*?' The following Tuesday, I brought Debussy to Mallarmé's home."[75] While this meeting probably took place in the fall of 1890, what is most surprising is the announcement, made a few months later, of a production envisioned for 27 February 1891: "*L'après-midi d'un faune*, 1 tableau in poetry by Stéphane Mallarmé, with music by Mr. de Bussy."[76] Fifteen days before the performance, Mallarmé asked if it could be delayed, but we do not know the reasons for that request.[77] Was the score not ready, on account of the romantic distress to which Claude-Achille alluded rather mysteriously when he wrote to Godet on 12 February?[78] Or else did the two men, in the course of their "long meditations,"[79] convince each other that the "gestation" of this project had to allow more time for further maturation? In any event, the anticipated production never took place.

The discovery of the Mallarmé–Debussy connection from the end of 1890 sheds new light not only on the genesis of the *Prélude* but also on the composer's aesthetic, at the very time when, paradoxically, he was working on Catulle Mendès's opera! It also clarifies the expansion of Claude-Achille's acquaintances from that period among the regular attendees at Mallarmé's Tuesday salons: Charles Morice, Henri de Régnier, Francis Viélé-Griffin, Georges Rodenbach, Marcel Schwob, Camille Mauclair, Pierre Louÿs, and perhaps Paul Gauguin, who was introduced to Mallarmé by Morice in December 1890 or January 1891. Should we take Louis Laloy's account literally when he reports: "It was there that he had seen Whistler grabbing a drawing by Odilon Redon and asking which way was up, and Verlaine sitting at the corner of the fireplace, tamping his pipe and asking Mlle Mallarmé for an absinthe *bien tassée*"?[80] In any event, there is no justification for Godet's or Mauclair's claim that Debussy "hardly ever" went to Mallarmé's home.[81] Even if he was not as devoted to the Tuesday salons as others were, he was there often enough to introduce Prince Poniatowski, an industrialist friend of Degas, to the poet, and to take both of them to the Saint-Gervais church to hear Palestrina, Tomás Luis de Victoria, and Josquin des Prez in April 1891.[82] Three days after Mallarmé's death, in a letter of condolence to his widow, Debussy was in a position to count himself among "those who knew the admirable being who was Stéphane Mallarmé."[83]

Several Publications and a Commission

Catulle Mendès's recommendation had introduced Debussy to the publisher Choudens. The composer profited from this relationship, even though the *Fantaisie* had not yet appeared, by ceding to Choudens not his large portfolio of songs written for Marie Vasnier, which he kept "for himself alone" (to cite again Louÿs's dictum), but rather some piano works that were more commercial in the eyes of the fortunate publisher of *Carmen* and *Faust*. Within several months, Debussy gave Choudens successively the *Marche écossaise* (15 January 1891); the *Ballade*, the *Valse*, and the *Tarentelle styrienne* for 200 francs (31 January);[84] and the first version of the *Suite bergamasque* for the same amount (21 February).[85] The *Rêverie* and the *Mazurka* were sold for 100 francs (14 March).[86] On 30 August, the composer convinced another publisher, Hamelle, to issue a more important group: three songs on poems by Verlaine and a fourth on a text by Bourget, to which he added the *Rêverie* and the *Mazurka*, "having forgotten" that he had already consigned them to Choudens five months earlier. He had to settle for 150 francs for the six pieces.[87] He knocked on the door of yet another publisher, the widow Girod, who accepted two songs. One of them, the early "Fleur des blés," was dedicated to Mme Deguingand, a former pupil of Mme Moreau-Sainti and the wife of a notary in Chatou. The other was a more recent song, "Beau soir," on a poem by Bourget. Claude-Achille was obviously in dire straits; his monetary needs must have been urgent for him to beg for such sums from publishers, and even to sell certain works twice.

[Providentially, the composer was commissioned at this time to write a work, the *Marche écossaise*, for General Meredith Read. An American whose ancestors hailed from Scotland, Ireland, England, and Wales, Read had served in the newly created position of US consul general to France and Algeria, and from 1869 to 1873 was stationed in Paris. Upon his retirement in 1880, he returned to the City of Light, living there until his death in 1896; it was during this time period that he met Debussy and asked him to compose a work using a Scottish piping tune that he believed had been passed down through his family, specifically the Ross clan. Claude-Achille thus wrote the *Marche des anciens comtes de Ross* for piano, four hands, based on the melody given to him by Read. The elaborate title page of the work—sold to Choudens on 15 January 1891 and published, with Read's permission, shortly thereafter—reflects information that Read himself provided to Debussy:[88] "The origin of the Earls of Ross, chief[s] of the Ross clan in Rosshire, Scotland, goes back to the most remote times. The earl was surrounded by a band of 'bagpipers' who used to play this march in front of their 'Lord' before and during battle, and also on festival days. The original march [melody] is the refrain of the current march."

In fact, Read's tune was not "The Earl of Ross March" as he had thought, but rather a piping tune titled "Meggerny Castle." Many other aspects of the story of how he met Debussy, a tale that has been told and retold by several biographers, are incorrect. One example involves the alleged assistance of Alphonse Allais, who supposedly served as a translator between Read and Debussy, at the Bar Austin, of all unlikely places. As a career diplomat, Read spoke and wrote perfect French, and he was more likely to be seen at the swanky Café des Ambassadeurs.][89]

It was also at Austin's—the bar dear to Baudelaire—where Debussy was said to have met Camille Claudel. We have only a single account of their relationship, that of Robert Godet, who was not as precise as we might wish.[90] Everything that has been written about a liaison between Claude-Achille and Camille is the product of conjecture.[91] Two years after having exhibited her work for the first time in 1883, the sculptress (sister of the poet Paul Claudel) entered the workshop of Rodin, whose model and mistress she became. Debussy presumably met her around 1891 and saw her, as did Goncourt later, "in a shawl embroidered with large Japanese flowers, with her childish head, her beautiful eyes, her quaint expressions, her provincial, clumsy way of speaking."[92] She had no natural inclination for music and even hated it, according to Jules Renard.[93] Yet, as Godet later recalled, she listened with increasing absorption to Claude-Achille as he played his works at his place or at Godet's,[94] while the composer watched her sculpt her "most perfect monuments of personal lyricism,"[95] or listened to her describe "the wonders of the spatial arrangement or the paradoxes of the perspectives" in Katsushika Hokusai's *Wave*.[96] Claude-Achille was particularly captivated by three of her sculptures: *La petite châtelaine*, the tremendous *Clotho*, and the *Valse*,[97] the last of which she gave to him (perhaps in 1892) and which remained in his study for the rest of his life. Among Camille's (and Rodin's) acquaintances was the Norwegian painter Frits Thaulow (who had arranged for Edvard Munch to come to France), some of whose paintings Claude-Achille also owned.[98] As for Godet, he had Camille's *Les causeuses* and *La petite châtelaine* at his home.[99]

That same year, Claude-Achille wrote two more piano pieces, the *Deux arabesques*, which he published this time with Durand, the firm run by the family of his former classmate. This was the first "pictorial" title that he had given to one of his works, and the word "arabesque" had perhaps been plucked from the mouth of Mallarmé during one of his Tuesday salons. None of Claude-Achille's piano works sparked any response in the press, and none of them was championed by any virtuoso during these years.

Thus it is understandable that, given the hardships in his life, Claude-Achille clung to the hope of fame that Mendès's notoriety could bring him. At the same time, however, he entertained the idea of pursuing some theatrical projects that would move him toward more personally satisfying horizons.

Discovery of Maeterlinck

At the very beginning of 1890, in a letter to Romain Rolland, André Suarès disclosed, without revealing his source, that Debussy was "working on a symphony on psychologically unfolding themes, inspired by the many tales of Poe, in particular "The Fall of the House of Usher."[100] Suarès noted that the composer had already sampled Symbolist texts with *La damoiselle* and the *Ariettes*, and that they were "full of ideas [. . . and displayed] a very subtle melodic style."[101] In the previous year, Claude-Achille had indicated in a questionnaire, without elaborating further, that Poe was, along with Flaubert, one of his two favorite prose writers.[102]

His first contact with Maurice Maeterlinck's work went back to the *Serres chaudes*, a collection published by Vanier in 1889; Godet tells us that "he [Debussy] had to breathe in the atmosphere" in order to familiarize himself with this new style of poetry.[103] Like most Parisians, Claude-Achille probably knew Maeterlinck's *La princesse Maleine* from a memorable article in *Le Figaro* in which Octave Mirbeau described the work as "the most brilliant of this era [. . . and] surpassing the most beautiful works of Shakespeare."[104] The character of this drama in a way foreshadows that of *Pelléas*, and it is not surprising that, in the following year, Debussy would seek authorization to set it to music. Maeterlinck's reply reached him through the intervention of journalist Jules Huret on 23 June 1891:[105]

> I've already been asked, quite often, for my permission to set *La princesse Maleine* to music. However, I believe it's not really suitable for that. Then again, I'm told by a mutual friend that Vincent d'Indy still has some interest in working with it himself someday,[106] and that is why I must withhold all permissions until he can reach a decision; I'm not sure if this would please M. Debussy.[107]

A third project grew out of a friendship that had been forged, as we have seen, with Gabriel Mourey (who translated Poe as well as A. C. Swinburne) at the Pousset tavern. Their mutual admiration for Laforgue, Verlaine, Mallarmé, and Rossetti created a certain closeness between them for two or three years, and Claude-Achille played the first act of *Rodrigue et Chimène* for his new friend. In 1891, Mourey announced the forthcoming publication of a set of prose poems, partially in dialogue form, which he called *L'embarquement pour ailleurs*, "with a symphonic gloss by C.-A. Debussy," which they both envisioned as a kind of frontispiece to the project.[108] Together, during the following year, they sketched out the basic elements of an opera "on the theme of *Being*," and Paul Adam, one of the former collaborators on the *Décadent* and then on the *Symboliste*, wrote to Mourey that he was delighted with this plan: "The first scene," he stated, "opened on a wild dance of monks and peasants in the cloister."[109] This is the way things often went in Symbolist circles, replete with projects such as journals that stopped publication after their second issue.[110]

At the end of 1891, Claude-Achille almost certainly went to hear *Lohengrin* at the Opéra, in order to compare the performance with the one that he had experienced in Rome. Pierre Louÿs, who was there, commented: "At last we will be able to go hear music without paying a thousand francs to travel to Bavaria!"[111] It was a success, in spite of demonstrations on the street and in the hall. Debussy also attended the Lamoureux concerts, and Willy noted his presence there, in a review published on 8 November, when Liszt's *Mephisto Waltz* and a concerto for violin by Max Bruch [presumably the oft-performed no. 1] were presented: "Debussy, reeling, more *fleur-du-mal* than ever," he wrote, "listened with disdainful pity."[112]

Finally, among his attempts to compose "for himself alone," he completed three songs on Verlaine's poems in December.[113] Much like the new versions of the *Fêtes galantes*, presented as a "first collection,"[114] these songs would have to wait several more years to be premiered or even published.

Chapter Eight

Esotericism and Symbolism

1892

In 1892 Claude-Achille's plans and contacts still far outnumbered any completed works that could have helped ease his financial situation. He gave no indication whatsoever of seeking public success, and even less of holding down a job—along the lines of, for example, Georges Marty, his former colleague from Rome, who was appointed professor of ensembles at the Conservatoire in February.[1] We could almost surmise that he had been blacklisted from the musical world, if we did not know how uncompromising he was. "He would sooner agree to forge counterfeit coins," observed Raymond Bonheur, "than to write three measures without feeling the urgent need to do so."[2] We learn from the news reports at the beginning of the year that, in January, *L'art musical* announced a series of afternoon concerts devoted to young composers, to be presented by "eminent literary figures": two performances focused on Gabriel Pierné (introduced by Georges Boyer), two on Georges Marty (introduced by Paul Milliet), and two on Charles René (introduced by Arthur Pougin),[3] who had won second prize in the Prix de Rome the same year in which Debussy had won first prize. But Claude-Achille was completely left out, and he certainly would not have lacked for writers to introduce his music!

The composer often went to hear new works by his contemporaries—as he did on 18 May for *La vie du poète*, one of Gustave Charpentier's *envois* from Rome, performed first at the Conservatoire and then again at the Théâtre du Châtelet on 29 January 1893 with considerable success. Debussy was particularly annoyed by this work, and he wrote that the future composer of *Louise* was "bound for glory that would be rewarding but hardly aesthetic. [. . .] It [*Louise*] is, as one might say, the triumph of the brasserie. It smells of tobacco, and the music is sleazy. [. . .] There is even a prostitute who moans in fake orgasms."[4] One of the most irritating reports for him and his friends appeared, a few months thereafter, in *Le ménestrel*:

We merely wish to point out how the sudden appearance of this fresh and luminous score conveniently comes to show the way for many of our young composers who, in so-called national societies or other groups, dwell on searching for an ideal of obscurity and gloom, completely contrary to the straightforwardness of French genius. The peculiar forms and the pathological quests in which they delight, at the expense of pure and healthy thought, can momentarily amuse those who are inquisitive about art; but after all these painful struggles to comprehend the incomprehensible, there is only emptiness and sterility.[5]

In this, his thirtieth year, Debussy was in a state of uncertainty: "My life is sadly feverish," he wrote to Godet on 30 January, "because of this opera; everything about it is wrong for me."[6] He had completed two acts of *Rodrigue et Chimène*, and all year long he would devote precious time to it, torn between the desire to shelve a work that went against his nature and a resignation to follow reasonable advice. This was perhaps the period in his life when he seemed the most uncertain about which way to turn. When his teacher Guiraud died suddenly in May, Debussy was getting ready to go to the funeral, even though he had the flu, but then he changed his mind, annoyed by his mother's admonition that he must "be seen there"![7]

Occultist Circles

Claude-Achille spent more time than ever at the Chat Noir and in his favorite cafés, but also at the Saint-Gervais church, where Amédée Gastoué observed him, "pencil in hand, jotting down in his notebook the melodic figures that he had found most striking in Gregorian chants and Palestrina motets."[8] At the Art indépendant, he had met Jules Bois, a very young writer from Marseille who was Catulle Mendès's secretary. Bailly had just published Bois's initiation poem, and the latter asked Debussy to write a "musical part" for his esoteric, one-act play, *Les noces de Sathan* (Satan's wedding). Paul Fort, who managed the Théâtre d'Art, announced its performance, with the composer's involvement, for the second half of March.[9] Debussy read through the text, which was worlds apart from that of *La damoiselle élue*. Represented within Bois's work—in an atmosphere of vague mysticism, lilies, purple, and "drifting darkness"—were Psyche, Hermes (as spokesman), Adam and Eve, Mephistopheles, etc., and an androgynous Satan![10] But it was really too difficult for Debussy to conceive of music that could portray curiosities about which he knew so little. Shortly before the performance, he declined the invitation, for musical as well as ethical reasons:

> I must say, my dear Bois, even though it may cost me our friendship, that I lack the necessary confidence to compose the music I promised for *Les noces de Sathan*. I can't envision the orchestra except on a scrap of paper. As for the

names of the players and where they come from, it's impossible to figure this out, except for Monsieur Burger who keeps being mentioned, but who however can't do everything. Forgive me, and above all don't think that I bear you any ill will. It's just that this whole thing dwells too much in the Unknown and is a bit of a "Bad Venture."[11]

This stance illustrates perfectly the limits of Debussy's loyalty to occultist circles: beginning with a genuine attraction, quickly followed by a rejection. It is clear that he was wary of any involvement. At the same time, he noticed how his new friend Satie was recruited by Sâr Péladan, who made headlines with the controversies surrounding the Rose+Croix—the excommunications and the fantastic trials. However, he was surely present, as were thousands of Parisians, including Verlaine and Émile Zola, at the first Salon de la Rose+Croix, opened by Péladan and Antoine de La Rochefoucauld with great success on 10 March at the Durand-Ruel gallery; there one saw most notably the paintings of Marcellin Desboutin, Fernand Khnopff, Carlos Schwabe, Félix Valloton, and Émile Bernard, and there Debussy could hear the *Sonneries* composed for the occasion by Satie. Later, on 19 March, after Palestrina's *Missa Papae Marcelli* was sung by forty choristers hidden behind a curtain, Satie's three *Préludes* for Péladan's *Le fils des étoiles* (subtitled as "pastorale" or "Chaldean Wagnerism"), were heard.[12]

It is easy to assume that this atmosphere of Wagnerian hysteria had especially irritated Claude-Achille, and his friendship for the composer of the Rose+Croix had to have been already very strong to withstand these outlandish displays, which were hardly in his nature. We have further evidence of this dynamic when, a little later (November 1892), Satie himself played the first version of his "Christian ballet" *Uspud* at the Auberge du Clou. While the listeners in the tavern guffawed at the quirkiness of what they were hearing, Debussy was the only one who remained unruffled.[13] His famous dedication, written on one of the printed copies of the *Cinq poèmes de Baudelaire*, dates from this period: "For Erik Satie—gentle and Medieval Composer—astray in this century, for the joy of his good friend Claude A Debussy" (pour Erik Satie Musicien Médiéval et doux, égaré dans ce siecle [*sic*], pour la joie de son bien amical Claude A Debussy)[14] to whom was echoed, on the same day of 27 October 1892, the dedication on the score of the *Sonneries de la Rose+Croix*: "To the good old chap, Claude A Debussy [. . .] His brother in Christ, Erik Satie" (Au bon vieux fils Claude A Debussy [. . .] Son frère en notre Seigneur, Erik Satie).[15]

We can point out some of Debussy's other reactions, which prove his reservation vis-à-vis this circle (too ostentatious, in his opinion), and, in any case, his refusal to see himself affiliated with any of these small groups. *L'initiation* was the official mouthpiece of the Kabbalistic order of the Rose+Croix of Papus and Guaïta,[16] from which Péladan broke away in order to create his Catholic Rose+Croix. Its June 1892 issue contained a review of a book by Édouard

Dubus, *Quand les violons sont partis*, into which a perfidious reference was slipped: "In these times of excess, stupidity, and astounding ignorance, in these times when the hoi polloi follow their noses toward the blather of Péladan, the painting of Henri des Groux [*sic*], and the music of Achille Debussy [. . .]"[17] Claude-Achille reacted immediately by writing a letter to Laurent Tailhade, the author of the article, assuring him of his personal admiration and playing off the misunderstanding: "Allow me to express surprise at your reference to me, and even more so since you speak of me probably without knowing my music. I might add that I've published too few things, and too little has been said about me to have been noticed by the humblest of common folk.[18] Your choice of names is unfortunate, as they are known only through a few individuals whom, I believe, you consider to be friends."[19] This retort was published in the following issue of *L'initiation*.[20]

The journalist was not so poorly informed, however, in associating the name of Debussy with that of the Belgian painter Henry de Groux. The latter was a capricious character whose *Le Christ aux outrages*, after having been sent back to the artist by King Léopold II of Belgium, had just been rejected by the Salon du Champ-de-Mars, in spite of support from the influential artist Puvis de Chavannes. The composer, accompanied by his friend Robert Godet, had gone to admire de Groux's painting "in something of a barn all the way down the rue Vaugirard," on the rue Alain Chartier (at the end of 1891), as he recalled to his friend twenty years later.[21]

It is undeniable that Claude-Achille, like many of the Symbolists, came under the influence of the occultists, but we cannot put any faith in the activist literature which claims that he could have been the thirty-third grand master of a Priory of Sion in the Rose+Croix order—following Victor Hugo and preceding Jean Cocteau! Furthermore, Debussy's membership supposedly went back to 1885, at which time he was at the Villa Medici. Of course, the sources corroborating these facts have mysteriously disappeared, and the writings that support them are more a matter of fabrication than of historical knowledge.[22] Some excellent studies have taken these texts seriously, attempting to find in them confirmation that the composer used the golden section and the Fibonacci and Lucas series in some of his compositions. Whether or not it was Debussy who introduced Satie to these proportional theories remains conjecture.[23]

Without claiming to make a comprehensive list of all of the encounters and fleeting friendships that Claude-Achille maintained during this bohemian period, one can point out those—at the Auberge du Clou or at the Nouvelle Athènes—with the following individuals:[24] besides Satie, there were the engineer Pierre-Joseph Ravel with his two "timid and silent" sons (one of whom was Maurice, the composer); Georges de Feure, an artist from Holland who made drawings and watercolors;[25] and Jules Dépaquit, who assumed the title of "annotator of consciences" and who "had proposed that Debussy become the blessed bard of a future and secret papacy, but the latter had declined that honor, for lack of confidence in his own abilities and for lack of courage to contend with such an important office."[26] Once again, the evidence points to initial sympathy on Achille's part, followed by evasion.

When not indulging in this playful and, in a way, stimulating company, he could be found at his desk, working on several projects that he enjoyed more than Mendès's accursed opera. He had the sheer pleasure of finally seeing *La damoiselle élue* published by Bailly, in a style that was as esoteric as the edition of the *Cinq poèmes* but conforming even more to his consummate taste; it had a run of 160 copies, with a cover illustration by Maurice Denis, whom Debussy thanked in June 1893 for his "unique and remarkable creation" (façon rare et précieuse).[27] The money from the subscriptions brought the composer immediate financial relief. For the same reason, he sold a short piano piece for 100 francs; this *Nocturne*, which he had initially titled *Interlude*, was issued simultaneously by the publisher Paul Dupont,[28] at whose firm his father was employed, and by *Le Figaro*.[29]

But he was working on more ambitious compositions as well. In Henri de Régnier's *Poèmes anciens et romanesques*, he had discovered a set of ten poems, *Scènes au crépuscule*, in which there were notable references to a chorus as well as some musical instruments—flutes and trumpets. Although we have no information about the three-part work that he was envisioning, inspired by these poems, it has long been considered to be a first draft of the *Nocturnes* for orchestra. However, the few fragments that are preserved under the original title in a sketchbook do not confirm this connection.

Another project was also linked to Régnier: a collection of songs for which Debussy decided to write the poems himself, the *Proses lyriques*. As early as 1892, he composed two of them, "De rêve" and "De grève," which he submitted to Régnier and whose texts he published separately in the periodical *Les entretiens politiques et littéraires*, led by Francis Vielé-Griffin.[30]

Finally, the composer had two works underway that would establish his early reputation: the String Quartet and the *Prélude, interlude et paraphrase finale sur l'après-midi d'un faune*. For the latter, the first draft of a symphonic triptych, he revisited the sketches written for Mallarmé's aborted production.

A Home: The Rue de Londres

In his personal life, around the middle of the year, an important event happened that Debussy had long been hoping for: he left his family home of the past thirty years and settled into a very modest, furnished apartment at 42 rue de Londres, near the corner of the rue d'Amsterdam, which he rented for 120 francs per annum. However, he would not stay there longer than a year. His life in general did not necessarily improve because of this change, but at last he was able to offer Gaby Dupont a less clandestine lifestyle, in keeping with their relationship as a couple.

It was there that Raymond Bonheur recalled, long afterward, having heard his friend play the *Prélude à l'après-midi d'un faune* "in its first state," which gave him a "dazzling feeling," at the end of a glorious summer day, with "the large window open, the setting sun streaming through to the far end of the room."[31] A more extraordinary visit would leave a very profound imprint on Debussy's memory: that of Mallarmé, whose reaction he wished to have even before putting the final touches on the score of the *Prélude*. Twenty years later, he recalled the physical surroundings of that visit as vividly as the poet's reaction to his work:

> At that time, I was living in a small, furnished apartment on the rue de Londres. The wallpaper depicted, oddly enough, a portrait of M. Carnot[32] surrounded by little birds! Can you imagine what looking at something like that might cause? A strong urge to avoid being home, for one thing.[33]
>
> Mallarmé came to my place, with a fateful expression and draped in a Scotch plaid shawl. After having listened, he remained silent for a long time, and then said to me: "I hadn't expected anything like that! This music prolongs the emotion of my poem and sets its scene more vividly than color could."[34]

This last sentence should suffice to repudiate the claims of those who have attempted to show that the composer wanted to convey many details of the poem in the order in which they appeared.[35]

American Project

In order to properly appreciate Debussy's progress in expressing his thoughts, there are no more eloquent documents than the long letters he sent to Prince André Poniatowski at the end of 1892 and the beginning of the following year. His first letters, written even before he came into contact with Pierre Louÿs, reveal everything that had brought about his Symbolist interactions.

Poniatowski was an "enlightened" industrialist. Both banker and gentleman farmer, he happily moved in literary and artistic circles, while criticizing their Parisian traits, and we have seen that Debussy had taken him to Mallarmé's home. In the middle of 1892, he was in the United States, where he was involved with railways. There he made connections with orchestra conductors Anton Seidl (who conducted the New York Philharmonic) and

Walter Damrosch (who would later follow in Seidl's footsteps), and hoped to convince Andrew Carnegie to help Debussy financially. It was in this context that in August he proposed to the composer a concert in New York that would be devoted to his works. Poniatowski's letters, sent to Bailly's bookshop, were delayed in reaching the musician, who was away from Paris. On 9 September, Debussy replied at length, mentioning the difficulty of communicating his "art, which is a little abstruse and requires that one be open to it,"[36] but declared himself ready to leave:

> Alongside the man who is accustomed to spending his days at a worktable, whose only joy comes from catching butterflies at the bottom of the inkwell, there is another one who is open to adventure, to turning his dreams into action! [...]
>
> Besides, it's thanks to my ability to see everything from an ideal perspective that I've not been overly taken in by the influences of the so-called artistic circles of Paris, circles about which you speak with an unfortunately very justifiable severity! But while I've been a part of it, it's only, one might say, from a position of insurmountable pride, which makes me find all those people more unfortunate than I, in spite of my genuine misery. And if you only knew how vain their conversations are; not only are they losers, they're drooling with envy!
>
> And it's precisely because of the various ways that constitute "having arrived!" here in Paris—by relying on everything that conceals mediocrity, nastiness, and shameful weakness—that I'm delighted to accept your proposal! if time has not run out.[37]

In order to "start with a bang" with the American public, Debussy suggested the following program: three *Scènes au crépuscule* that were "nearly finished" (a questionable claim), the *Fantaisie pour piano et orchestre*, and *La damoiselle élue*, "a little oratorio in a mystical and slightly pagan vein."[38] Note that he said not one word about the opera that he was on the verge of completing. Having waited a long time for a reply about launching this beautiful dream, he wrote again on 5 October, confiding in his friend and declaring his faith in his own artistic mission:

> In the end, whatever happens, I shall be forever grateful to you for remembering me, an act of imagination in an otherwise pragmatic country [the United States], and for helping me to escape the black hole which my life has so often become. Your act gives me the courage to continue, in spite of everything, in spite of the failures that overwhelm even the strongest people, in spite of the enemies that I have. [Speaking of which,] it's curious that, even though you've barely heard of me, you knew not to believe the throngs of people who detest me and talk about me in self-righteous circles, telling stories designed to shut doors irrevocably in the face of my music. So you

will understand easily enough how much I'd like, once and for all, to rid myself of all such people! To be able to satisfy my great ambition to run my own show in my own way, and to root out the imbecility in musical understanding that these last few years have implanted in the gentle listeners of our time.[39]

But the American dream did not come true.

Chapter Nine

The Chausson Year

1893

The year of 1893 began with two very different events for Debussy, as revealed in the much richer body of correspondence available to us from that year. The first was the premiere, at the Opéra-Comique on 16 January, of Massenet's *Werther*, which seemed to Debussy a model of nonsense and sentimentality.[1] The second was a "gilded visit" (*visite dorée*),[2] likely to guarantee an adequate material subsistence "for a year or two."[3] Poniatowski, seeing that his plans for concerts in New York were not going to come to fruition, felt himself "morally bound"[4] to send Debussy enough money to enable him to compose for some time without financial worries.[5] This assistance arrived at the perfect time since, following "several regrettable incidents," Claude-Achille had just burned his bridges with his family, who was waging a war "of needlings, some sentimental [. . .] and others unkind"[6] against him.

The subsequent months saw Claude-Achille growing very close especially to Ernest Chausson and his circle. Theirs was a rather complex friendship that calls for analysis. We have already pointed out the social gap that separated the two men, and we could add that their childhoods had differed: one had been gripped with poverty and anxiety for the morrow, while the other had been the object of attentive care and affection from a godmother and a tutor. However, Chausson's open-mindedness, his knowledge of literature as well as the visual arts, his natural and discreet generosity, in addition to his psychological vulnerability, in some ways minimized the distance created by such extremely different lifestyles. The first performance of *La damoiselle élue* at the Société nationale de musique gave them the opportunity to get to know each other better.

Premiere of *La damoiselle élue*

This event, held at the Salle Érard on 8 April 1893, took on something of the character of a family celebration. Claude had invited Godet and the Stevens family, and the program brought together several of his friends—Paul Dukas and Raymond Bonheur, each with an overture, and Chausson with the *Poème de l'amour et de la mer*. The orchestra and chorus were conducted by Gabriel Marie, and the soloists in *La damoiselle* were Julia Robert and Thérèse Roger, two singers who would soon reappear in Debussy's life.

The work met with only moderate success. A few critics reported on it, either to declare without much conviction that it consisted of "precise and delicate forms" and of a "subtle and rare art," but that "toward the end, the length of the solo voice had slightly weakened the good will of the public,"[7] or to lament that the composer "threw himself headlong into excessive chromaticism,"[8] or even to describe the work as "a very sensual composition, decadent, even slightly degenerate, but which has sparkling and exquisite passages."[9] In the eyes of Charles Darcours in *Le Figaro*, *La damoiselle* was far superior to the other works presented by that "mutual admiration society," by which he meant the Société nationale de musique: "They tell us that M. Debussy entered the Société nationale only quite by accident. However, this is the new blood that the venerable institution needed."[10] As for Willy, he scarcely committed himself when he wrote: "It goes up, it floats 'like a little feather.' I felt a couple of wings on my back."[11] Vincent d'Indy was one of those who congratulated Debussy in particular, but the composer drew the greatest pleasure from a gift by Odilon Redon of one of his lithographs.[12]

A few days later, Chausson took Debussy to his first meeting of the Société nationale. Each member gave his own opinion on the policies to adopt; Debussy suggested that the concerts be limited to one per month, but that the number of orchestral concerts be increased, and that works by foreign composers be allowed. On 23 April, the general meeting took place, where the committee members were elected: Fauré and d'Indy received the most votes (43). Behind them were Charles Bordes (42), Chausson and Chabrier (41), Camille Benoit (40), Pierre de Bréville and Paul Vidal (39), Debussy (28), and Dukas (5)![13] Now that he was joining a musical "institution" for the first time, would Claude-Achille change his attitude and follow the example of his colleagues who used such situations for self-promotion?

Performances of Wagner

Debussy had not yet abandoned *Rodrigue et Chimène*, which he promised to play for Chausson, and he even allowed himself to be persuaded by Catulle Mendès, his librettist, to participate in a lecture-recital on *Das Rheingold* and *Die Walküre*. This event was intended to explain Wagner's work to the public, and Debussy and Raoul Pugno were to play it on two pianos. On 16 April, Mendès wrote to the director of the Opéra, Eugène Bertrand, that he was getting ready to work with his performers: "I'm meeting Claude Debussy, the young Prix de Rome winner who has just had such a great success with his *Damoiselle élue* and who will hold forth at one of the pianos."[14] The performance, which took place on 6 May, was so favorably received by the public that it was repeated on 11 and 18 May. "It's ridiculous," Chausson told Eugène Ysaÿe, "but it is an enormous success. And as it brings in a little money for him [Debussy], he can't pass it up."[15] Even H. Moreno,[16] in the very anti-Wagnerian *Ménestrel*, noted that the two pianists had performed "the piano accompaniment with a feeling and depth of understanding of the work that one would not find among ordinary piano virtuosi."[17] Meanwhile, after three months of preparation, on 12 May, the Opéra had presented the first French production of *Die Walküre* in Victor Wilder's translation, featuring notably Lucienne Bréval (as Brunnhilde), Rose Caron (as Sieglinde), and Ernest Van Dyck (as Siegmund), under the direction of Colonne. For the first time, Wagner's success in Paris remained undisputed. In his journal, Henri de Régnier noted that as he was leaving the theater, he met d'Indy, Albéric Magnard, and Debussy, and that Mendès, Dujardin, and Jules Lemaitre were there as well.[18]

The day after Mendès's first lecture, Debussy had written to Chausson to express his regrets for having participated in that spectacle:

> Prodigious and quite inexplicable success; the impression was that *Wagner ought to be very grateful to Mendès*! for having brought back to the true religion so many souls who have gone astray! (It makes me gag!) Note that in his lecture he took great care to diminish the composer's role in order to glorify that of the poet. [. . .] If bolts from heaven, which may not happen very often, had fallen during that little family gathering, it would truly have been a once-in-a-lifetime event.
>
> I beg Wagner's forgiveness for having participated in all of that.[19]

Over several months, this new friendship with Chausson was expressed by Debussy in quite unusual terms, as shown by the almost excessive language in his letters:

> I may as well tell you that I'm really very fond of you, and that your intervention in my life is certainly one of the things that is most precious to me. And I think about this even more than I can say. (7 May 1893)[20]

> I'm incredibly bored without you here, and am like a poor little path that everyone has abandoned for the main road. I often indulge myself in the

melancholy illusion of going to your door, and it's sad to think that it won't be opening for a long time. (22 May)[21]

While I already liked you a lot, these several days spent near you have made me your very, very devoted friend forever. [. . .] How good it was to be a part of your life, to be in some way part of your family! But am I getting carried away, and aren't you going to find my friendship a bit bothersome? I want to please you so much that I often imagine perfectly crazy things. (4 June)[22]

Please continue to be completely open with me. I can promise you that I'm fully prepared to receive your friendship, almost to say, with kid gloves! [. . .] As you have to choose between so many lovely friendships, I'm really happy that you've included mine among them. (5 June)[23]

Now that you're no longer here, my heart weeps for the past, and I feel like I've lost all [emotional] support. (2 July)[24]

If I hadn't been able to get to know you and to experience your friendship, I'd complain very bitterly of the hardship that plagues me. (9 July)[25]

[. . .] my friendship, or to say it better, my affection for you, and that is not saying too much. (22 July)[26]

And more of the same in other letters.

Visits to Luzancy

These professions of friendship were doubtless sincere, considering the nature of Chausson's "intervention" (as Debussy put it) at that moment in his life. The two composers made a habit of seeing each other in Paris, but Chausson also invited Debussy twice to the house that he had rented in Luzancy, near La Ferté-sous-Jouarre, on the banks of the Marne River.

These visits took place between 30 May and 3 June, and in the middle of June. There Debussy found a very close-knit family hearth with four young children, in an atmosphere that was a bit novel for him. In addition to Raymond Bonheur, the painter Henry Lerolle (Chausson's brother-in-law) was also there with his family. They took many photographs, they played ball and billiards, and they went for boat rides—activities that were memorialized in lovely photos. They also sight-read some Mussorgsky and perhaps other Russian music,[27] which Chausson had asked Debussy to bring with him. Among the personal projects that were discussed was the *Marche écossaise*, which Debussy was in the process of orchestrating and which Chausson had suggested that Eugène Ysaÿe consider for a concert in Brussels. On 10 May, Chausson wrote to the Belgian violinist: "He has not yet finished (or even begun) the changes to be made in the finale of his march. To be absolutely certain that this will be done, I will put him up here for a few days, and I won't allow him to leave until everything is finished."[28] However, too many distractions during the visit prevented the work's completion, and Chausson offered to copy the orchestral parts himself; at the end of June he finally completed the task, with Bonheur and Lerolle, while his wife made a lovely binding for the score.[29]

Claude also tried to convince his friend to program some Satie works in the forthcoming concerts of the Société nationale. He showed him a *Gymnopédie*, a *Sarabande*, and a *Gnossienne*, which Chausson supposedly considered including on a concert the following winter[30]—an event that never came to pass. But Claude discussed in particular his own quartet, whose last movement he was having trouble completing, and he played the third *Prose lyrique*, "De fleurs," which pleased the mistress of the house so much that he dedicated it to her. As for Chausson, he was beginning to set Maeterlinck's *Serres chaudes* to music, while remaining extremely troubled by the completion of his opera, *Le roi Arthus*. Sometime in July, he left for Royan with his family, but kept in contact with the younger composer, whom he continued to call "dear friend"— almost never "my dear Claude" or "Claude-Achille." He sought ways to come to Claude's assistance, finding some underwriters for *La damoiselle élue*, suggesting it for some concerts at Angers or at the homes of "society ladies," and before long recommending him for a job as assistant conductor at the Casino in Royan—for Claude needed to be set up, Chausson thought, in a regular "job"![31] He also helped Claude in more tangible ways, writing to him in the middle of July, "Don't be sorry for those 'down-to-earth' details you tell me about. Perhaps we owe much of our friendship to them. [. . .] I'll see you tomorrow, we'll talk about your furnishings. [. . .] I'd also really like to be able to take away all the causes for your concern."[32]

Chausson was referring to the fact that, with the help of Étienne Dupin, Debussy was looking for an apartment for himself and Gaby, who had not been invited to Luzancy—unless he did not dare bring her along. Claude pointed out to his friend that "My girlfriend [p.a., abbreviation for *petite amie*] deserves all the thanks, for she really gets the short end of the stick in all this."[33]

At the same time, Chausson was playing the role of "adviser," as he himself explained, and at times this created tensions with Debussy. It is clear that Chausson stressed that the young composer sort out his personal life: "And your wedding?" he let slip.[34] Claude balked at least once. Could his friend be lacking confidence in him? Chausson replied quickly to Debussy's letter of 9 July:

> Perish the thought. Above all, you need to fully understand that I think only of your personal benefit in my relations with you, and that I act accordingly. [. . .] Also, rest assured that I have confidence in you; it's precisely because I

have confidence in you that [our] friendship has grown so quickly. Is that to say that I believe you should never refuse to get carried away? No; moreover, no one should, myself least of all. [. . .] Perhaps my words have gotten ahead of my thoughts. [. . .] I was pointing out a danger to you *that does not depend only on you.* That's all that I wanted to do.[35]

As for Debussy, he had not hesitated, in his previous letter, to share with Chausson his reflections on his social connections:

Let me tell you, since the opportunity presents itself and since I perhaps would not dare do it otherwise, that you are quite superior to the people who surround you, because of your qualities of sensitivity and artistic tact—qualities that the others seem to lack altogether. They go through the meadows of music, crushing bunches of little flowers under their disrespectful feet, without regard for [those flowers'] ability to affect us. [. . .]
I won't act like an inquisitive judge by citing names to you![36]

One final connection between the two composers is that Chausson asked for Debussy's opinion on his *Le roi Arthus* and played for him especially "Lyonnel's scene and the duet" from the first act. Chausson wrote about this scene to his wife, "There are a few places that he doesn't like, and many others that please him very much. . . There is one [passage] that you have always hated, and he does, as well: 'Je suis ta servante et ta femme' [I am your servant and your wife]. I shall see if I can find an alternative."[37]

Boris Godunov

This subtle psychological backdrop should not obscure the important musical discoveries of these months in 1893. Thus far we have mentioned only the name of Mussorgsky, who has, ever since, been at the center of a debate over which much ink has been spilled. At what point did Debussy fall under the influence of the Russian composer, and especially of *Boris Godunov*?

The figure who sparked this debate was a musician whom Debussy had met at the Pousset tavern: Jules de Brayer. At first a modest organist (following limited study at the École Niedermeyer), he had been part of the small French cohort that was present at the opening of Bayreuth in 1876, and had become the director of the Concerts Lamoureux. But, having discovered very early on a piano-vocal score of *Boris* at Saint-Saëns's home, he became a very active proponent of this work, although he was not successful in generating enthusiasm equal to his own. In 1889, Robert Godet—the only one to share his appreciation of the work—brought the score over to Debussy, who left it on his piano for a long time, apparently without showing much interest, except in the chorus of the young Polish maidens. As for the rest of it, he declared himself unable to make sense of the sung text, so Godet returned the score to Brayer.

André Schaeffner has thoroughly documented Debussy's knowledge, acquired from his youth, of Russian music in Paris; he attempted to show that Debussy's disinterest at that time was perhaps feigned, but, at the very least, hard to believe. Paul Dukas seems to agree with Schaeffner in claiming to have heard the coronation scene from *Boris* at the home of Debussy's parents on the rue de Berlin (which Claude left in the middle of 1892). However, a great deal of evidence leads us to believe that his true "discovery" of Mussorgsky took place during those weeks at Luzancy, in May–June 1893. Raymond Bonheur, who was present, claims that Chausson succeeded in procuring the score of *Boris*, which was sight-read "during entire evenings" by an "indefatigable" Debussy.[38] What is ultimately important for us to know is that he knew *Boris* well at the time when he began *Pelléas et Mélisande*.

Pelléas at the Bouffes-Parisiens

Between two of Mendès's last Wagnerian sessions and at a very busy time for Debussy, the composer had in fact attended the sole performance of Maeterlinck's *Pelléas et Mélisande* at the Bouffes-Parisiens theater on 17 May.[39] The previous year, he had purchased the publication of Maeterlinck's play at the Flammarion bookshop; his first reading of it had sparked his enthusiasm and, as he put it years later, "perhaps the secret thought of a potential musical setting."[40] However, we know nothing about his immediate reactions to the performance. Maeterlinck had merely supplied a few ideas for the costumes and had given no advice for the acting; he left its staging to Lugné-Poe, the director of the Théâtre de l'Œuvre, and especially to Camille Mauclair. Golaud was played by Lugné-Poe and Mélisande by Mlle Meuris, while the role of Pelléas was taken by a woman, Marie Aubry. The review, requested five days after *Die Walküre* was performed at the Opéra, was rather derogatory in general, noting a real monotony and scenes that were too cut up, with the curtain falling eighteen times.[41] In the audience were, among others,[42] Mallarmé, Whistler, Régnier, Louÿs, Léon Blum, Jacques-Émile Blanche, Henry Bauer, and Henry Lerolle, whom Debussy would soon meet again at Luzancy. Lerolle gave Chausson a nuanced opinion of the production: "Some very lovely things, not very well acted, with scenery that was either too spare or too much. [. . .] I prefer Ibsen."[43] It is surprising that in the extensive correspondence between Chausson, Debussy, and Lerolle a few days later, there is no mention of this *Pelléas*, but they definitely spoke about it when the three friends met again shortly thereafter in Luzancy. Debussy could not have known about Mallarmé's dismissive reaction to the notion of incorporating music within such a play since the latter wrote, in a passage in his *Divagations* that was not published until several years later: "In this art, where everything literally becomes music, the part of even a pensive instrument, [such as the] violin, would be pointlessly detrimental."[44]

Lugné-Poe's production certainly played a catalytic role in Debussy's decision, for the latter soon charged Henri de Régnier to sound out Maeterlinck for his authorization to set *Pelléas* to music. The reply, frank and warm, arrived on 8 August: "My dear poet, Please tell Monsieur Debussy that I wholeheartedly give him the full authorization necessary for *Pelléas et Mélisande*, and since you approve of what he has done, I thank him already for whatever he'd like to do."[45]

It was at this very time that Debussy made a courageous decision that finally led to the abandonment of *Rodrigue*, whose fourth act would remain without music.[46] On 10 August, he went to see Paul Dukas at Saint-Cloud and played for him the music he had completed for Mendès's opera, probably for the last time. Writing to d'Indy a few weeks later, Dukas declared himself surprised by "the sheer drama of certain scenes," while admitting that "the poem is, in fact, perfectly devoid of interest."[47] At the same time that he abandoned *Rodrigue*, Debussy temporarily shelved the *Fantaisie*,[48] so as to wipe out for good everything that called to mind his "compromise" with Mendès. The fundamental and aesthetic indecision that had characterized his attitude for the past two or three years was over. He even felt sure enough of himself to take up his pen publicly, with the intention of provoking, of drawing attention by going against the current of public taste and that of the Symbolists; he announced an article, "De l'inutilité du wagnérisme" (On the uselessness of Wagnerism), foreshadowing his literary propensities, but the article never went past the idea stage.[49]

The Beginnings of Debussy's *Pelléas*

In the following weeks, Debussy composed in true ecstasy, as shown by the cursory and hasty appearance of the first preserved sketches of *Pelléas*. He had already spoken to Chausson about his initial compositional attempts, and the latter wrote to him, on 28 August, that he hoped his health had improved and that he was able to "recommence" *Pelléas*.[50] Six days later, Debussy told him that he was completing Pelléas's death scene (act 4, scene 4),[51] but a month afterward he tore it up, conscious of still being under the influence of Wagner;[52] on 2 October, he claimed to have achieved something more personal, using silence as an "agent of expression,"[53] and he was satisfied enough with the scene to have Raymond Bonheur and Henry Lerolle hear it very soon thereafter.[54] From that moment on, he was firmly committed to seeing this work through to completion.

In that year, a turning point in his life, he grew closer to a poet who was eight years younger than he—Pierre Louÿs—whom he had probably met at the beginning of 1892 at Mallarmé's home.[55] In November, they went to Belgium together; Debussy first spent a few hours in Brussels at the home of Ysaÿe, for whom he played several of his works (among them, excerpts from *Pelléas*), and then went on to Maeterlinck's home in Ghent. He wrote to Chausson:

> I saw Maeterlinck, with whom I spent a day in Ghent; at first, he acted like a young girl being introduced to a future husband, but then he warmed up and turned on the charm. His speaking about the theater was absolutely remarkable. Concerning *Pélléas* [*sic*], he's giving me full authorization for some cuts and went so far as to point out some very important ones, *even some very useful ones*! Now as far as music is concerned, he says that he understands nothing about it, and he wanders into a Beethoven symphony like a blind man into a museum. But honestly, he's just great and speaks with an exquisite simplicity of spirit about his extraordinary discoveries. At one point, when I was thanking him for entrusting *Pélléas* [*sic*] to me, he did his best to convey that it was he who should be indebted to me for having wanted to set it to music at all! As I have a diametrically opposed opinion, I had to use all of what little diplomacy nature has granted me.[56]

Surrounded by the friendship of Chausson, of Lerolle, and soon of Louÿs, Debussy had now overcome the impasse in which he had been mired for too long, and from then on had access to a "libretto" that motivated him completely. His material life was also improving: in July 1893, not long before beginning *Pelléas*, he moved with Gaby into a three-room apartment at 10 rue Gustave Doré, on the courtyard side of the sixth floor. It was the beginning of a less bohemian lifestyle, to which Chausson generously contributed by offering him some furniture, while Lerolle gave him one of his paintings, which he hung above the piano. The critic Étienne Destranges would notice some "reproductions of Pre-Raphaelite paintings" there. A few weeks later, the poet Henri de Régnier visited him, noting in his journal that he lived "in a bright and sunny room. [. . .] The furniture includes a writing table, a bookcase, and a piano on which he play[ed] me his *Après-midi d'un faune* with a very personal, languorous passion."[57]

As Debussy wrote to Chausson, the initial period at the rue Gustave Doré gave "a new strength" to his antisocial tendencies. He thus declined an invitation from a salon host, Mme Sulzbach, who was hoping to introduce him to Gabriel Fauré: "I didn't consider it useful to accept that invitation. While I would perhaps lose out on, God only knows, the chance to hear a few eighteenth-century formulae, newly reworked by G. Fauré, I'm incapable of making nice with people who fundamentally mean nothing to me."[58]

Once again, he knocked on the doors of publishers, and on 21 September sold three old songs ("La belle aux bois dormant," "Romance," and "Paysage sentimental") to the publisher Paul Dupont, his father's employer, who would file them away for several years. The following month, Debussy brought to Durand his String Quartet, whose finale he had started over three times.[59] Those "barbarians at the place de la Madeleine,"[60] where his former friend from the Conservatoire was working, offered him a mere 250 francs for it.

He was certainly satisfied with the first parts of acts 4 and 1 of *Pelléas*, even if he claimed to be seized with anxiety when conveying the "nothingness" that defines Mélisande and the "otherworldliness" that is meant to characterize Arkel. Beginning in October–November, Debussy played some scenes for Henry Lerolle, Jules de Brayer, Raymond Bonheur, and Eugène Ysaÿe. The only one who was afraid to hear it was Chausson, who confided to Lerolle: "Even before hearing his music, I'm sure it will please me immensely, and I fear it will hamper the completion of my poor *Arthus*."[61] In contrast, it was Debussy who refused to play his sketches for Paul Dukas, whose opinion he feared: "Indeed, I'd prefer to wait to have an act or two finished for you, in order to give you a more or less complete impression of it."[62] The most enthusiastic was Lerolle, with whom Debussy established a more even-keeled friendship than with Lerolle's brother-in-law (Chausson), in spite of the fourteen years that separated the painter and the young composer. Lerolle—a friend of Albert Besnard, Alfred Lenoir, Louis-Henry Devillez, Edgar Degas, and Pierre-Auguste Renoir—had been one of the founders of the Société nationale des beaux-arts. He loved music and musicians, and himself played the violin as an amateur. It was he who had convinced the priest of Saint-Gervais (whose name was de Bussy!) to accept Charles Bordes as the kapellmeister there.[63] He had an utterly independent spirit, resistant to oppressive bourgeois conventions.

There was another attraction for Claude at Lerolle's home: his seventeen-year-old daughter Yvonne, whom Debussy had met the previous summer in Luzancy. Possessed with a grace and beauty that has been described as "unreal," she (with her sister Christine) went on to inspire the paintbrushes of Renoir and Maurice Denis.[64] Claude-Achille, who considered her to be like Mélisande's "little sister,"[65] would dedicate some piano works to her (three *Images* that he did not want to publish in that form). He also dedicated to her—in a very Mallarméan gesture—a beautiful Japanese fan on which he had sketched a few measures of *Pelléas*, in which the heroine appears, "her arms full of flowers."[66]

The String Quartet

Three days before the end of the year, the Ysaÿe Quartet came to the Société nationale to perform the premiere of Debussy's quartet. That concert of 29

December, said to have been preceded by numerous rehearsals, also included the Franck Sonata, played by Ysaÿe and d'Indy; the *Élégie* for violoncello by Fauré; and the String Quartet, op. 35, of d'Indy. In this context, Debussy's work was in no way an event, especially as the press was not readily present at the concerts of the Société. One of the rare critics to report on it, Guy Ropartz, detected the influence of "young Russia, with poetry of themes and rare sonorities,"[67] whereas Willy judged it to be "full of originality and charm"[68] but disconcerting. Octave Maus, who had come to support the Ysaÿe Quartet, wrote a favorable though very measured commentary in the Brussels periodical *L'art moderne* about that "extremely alluring art, at once simple and complex," whose scherzo seemed to him "delightful in its grace and ingenuity, in spite of subtleties behind which ideas are concealed."[69] When the score was published by Durand, Paul Dukas made a more careful and also more positive analysis, declaring his preference for the first movement and the Andante: "truly exquisite in its poetry and supreme delicacy of thought."[70] All told, these were meager reports, to which were added the serious reservations of his friend Chausson, who ultimately was not the dedicatee, but to whom Debussy would make a promise on the following 5 February, one that would not be fulfilled: "I will compose another quartet, which will be for you—and I mean, in all seriousness, for you—and I'll try to ennoble my forms."[71] Later, Albéric Magnard would say to Ropartz: "[The String Quartet] is barbaric, formless, but with wild rhythms and an admirable boldness of harmonies."[72]

Chapter Ten

A "Fairy Tale" Gone Awry

1894

Bourgeois Interactions

The intensive work that Debussy put into *Pelléas* did not prevent him from leading a life that bordered on the uncharacteristically sociable during the first months of 1894. In the absence of Chausson, who was spending time at Arcachon, Debussy was received by his mentor's mother-in-law, Mme Escudier, who had the idea to organize "ten Wagnerian gatherings" at her home at 77 rue du Monceau as a way of helping him. He was expected, playing alone at the piano and doing some singing, to render *Parsifal, Tristan, Die Meistersinger*, and excerpts from *Siegfried*. The performances were planned for Saturdays, from 4:00 to 6:00 p.m., beginning on 3 February.[1]

At the same time, he was introduced at the home of Mme de Saint-Marceaux, the commanding wife of a very influential sculptor who was not at all disposed toward Symbolist thought. Every Friday, at 100 boulevard Malesherbes, "Meg," as she was called by those close to her, organized musical soirees, for which Messager and Fauré became her closest advisers. In her salon, which was said to be the model for that of the Princesse de Polignac, one would encounter Massenet and Reynaldo Hahn as well as Chabrier and Chausson, and soon thereafter Willy, Jean de Tinan, and the young Marcel Proust. One such evening, in February 1894, after sight-reading *La damoiselle élue* with Debussy, Meg wrote in her journal: "There is no way he could demonstrate better what he wants or wanted to convey. He sings with a bad voice, to which we are becoming accustomed, since its expression is so convincing."[2] He returned the following day, to perform for her the *Proses lyriques* and especially "all that is completed" of *Pelléas*: "It's a revelation. Everything is new, the harmony, the writing—and it's all so musical."[3]

Debussy was aware of being at the center of a bourgeois circle, while speaking about it in his own ironic way to Chausson:

> I no longer recognize myself! *I can be found in the salons*, smiling away, or else conducting choruses at Countess Zamoïska's home! (yes sir!) and I bask in the beauty of the chorus of "Magnanarelles" [silkworm workers],[4] telling myself that to be flayed by fearless society ladies is the just reward for such dreary music. Then there's Mme de Saint-Marceaux, who has discovered that I'm a first-rate talent! It's enough to make you die laughing. But really, one would have to have a very weak character to fall for this nonsense. It's all so absurd![5]

Nevertheless, in the following weeks he would allow himself to be taken in by it all, to the point of completely compromising his reputation in circles that were willing to welcome him, provided that he adopt their conventions and rules.

With the first performance of two of the *Proses lyriques* at the Société nationale in mind, Debussy turned again to one of the two singers who had premiered *La damoiselle élue*: Thérèse Roger, the daughter of a music teacher who conducted a female vocal ensemble and who was a friend of the Chaussons.[6] The program of that concert on 17 February 1894 at the Salle Pleyel left the prime spot to the pianist Édouard Risler, who played a few of Chabrier's *Pièces pittoresques* and five pieces by Fauré. Claude-Achille accompanied Thérèse Roger in "De fleurs" (the *Prose lyrique* dedicated to Mme Chausson) and "De soir" (dedicated to Henry Lerolle). In *Le guide musical*, Guy Ropartz deemed them "absolutely exquisite."[7] Meanwhile, the critic of the *Progrès artistique* briefly mentioned those "curious but too contrived works, portraying in music what the decadent poets offer in their verse,"[8] and that of *L'art musical* underscored the difficulty of the accompaniment, concluding that the *Proses lyriques* had been a "great success among [musical] colleagues."[9]

When the collection was published in the following year, Georges Servières, that critic who was "always buttoned up in his Austrian officer's overcoat,"[10] trained his arrows on the poet: "Prose that is strongly inspired by Mallarmé, no doubt laden with symbolic meanings that are not easily revealed to the laity. What, for example, does the 'greenhouse of sorrow' mean, whose 'redeeming hands' must shatter 'the glass panes of evil'? Only the author could tell us."[11] Étienne Destranges demonstrated a much greater understanding of this collection, in which he preferred "De soir." While stating that these pieces were not easy to perform, he praised their originality and intensity of expression:

> M. Debussy's *Proses lyriques* are not, strictly speaking, songs. They can take a place next to certain pieces by the late Guillaume Lekeu and by M. Albéric Magnard. The vocal line, written on somewhat decadent and symbolic subjects, does not have the importance that it does in the average song. Here the accompaniment takes the primary role. In it, M. Debussy proves himself

a bold harmonist and skillful symphonist. Although written just for piano, all the accompaniments in this remarkable collection nevertheless suggest an orchestra.[12]

Concert in Brussels

In the following days, Debussy would take his music to foreign soil for the first time, responding to an invitation from the Libre Esthétique, a circle founded in Brussels by Octave Maus, a lawyer and connoisseur of art and music who was very close to Ysaÿe and d'Indy. The concerts took place in an art gallery that had opened on 17 February and that featured the artworks of Aubrey Beardsley, Eugène Carrière, Camille Pissarro, Pierre-Auguste Renoir, Paul Gauguin, and James Ensor, as well as those of Camille Claudel, Maurice Denis, Henry Lerolle, and Odilon Redon. After the first concert, on 23 February, in which d'Indy's String Quartet was performed, a program devoted entirely to Debussy's works was presented on 1 March.

The original program comprised not only the String Quartet and *La damoiselle élue* but also two of the *Cinq poèmes de Baudelaire* and *L'après-midi d'un faune*, based on Stéphane Mallarmé's poem. Changes in the program and the performers ensued when soprano Angéline Delhaye became hoarse. Thérèse Roger was frantically called upon to come from Paris; she sang *La damoiselle élue* as well as two of the *Proses lyriques* ("De fleurs" and "De soir").[13] However, *L'après-midi d'un faune* was withdrawn from the program, for unknown reasons; it would have been the true event of that concert, given that the orchestra comprised Ysaÿe's colleagues and pupils. Whatever the reasons for this change, the preliminary program reveals to us that the *Prélude* was virtually finished by that time.[14]

According to Debussy himself, the quartet was rendered "with a depth of feeling that it had lacked at the performance in Paris."[15] The musicians even began the first movement again, to allow the director of the Conservatoire (the venerable Gevaert, who had arrived late) to hear the work in its entirety;[16] for that matter, he would have understood nothing of that "harmonic cascade."[17] The local critics understood little more; Lucien Solvay declared the *Proses* "unsingable,"[18] and another journalist surprisingly detected in the quartet the influence of Alfred Bruneau and Borodin, "with hints of Grieg or reminiscences of Wagner."[19] Maurice Kufferath, who was the most prominent critic of the time, declared himself completely taken aback, commenting that Debussy was "an enthusiast of the new school of musical pointillism and of universal formlessness"; he launched into bold comparisons with "the rue du Caire at the 1889 World's Fair" and the gamelan, establishing a parallel between the quartet and the "neo-Japanese paintings of Montmartre and similar locales in Belgium."[20] In a more general way, the young Frenchman's music seemed to him "more contrived than inspired, more calculated than felt, [. . .] often more literary than truly musical and, on the whole, turning completely toward a purely external effect, even though it claims to be intimate and symbolic."[21] In his review published in *L'art moderne*, Octave Maus was naturally more complimentary, emphasizing for Debussy's disparagers that the quartet only appeared to be complicated and that it was, on the contrary, very classically constructed. He gave details that no other source corroborates—namely, that the composer was already working on another quartet, "whose third movement is finished."[22]

In the final days of February, even before his departure for Brussels, Debussy had written to Pierre de Bréville, announcing his engagement to Thérèse Roger.[23] What had happened so quickly with her upon his return?

Engagement to Thérèse Roger

Debussy was no doubt aware that his cohabitation with Gaby was hindering his social mobility. It is nevertheless difficult to explain how he allowed himself to become engaged within a few weeks' time to the salon singer, Thérèse Roger, who was physically unattractive. He was certainly pushed by Mme de Saint-Marceaux, who was a "matchmaker"; had she not already arranged Fauré's marriage? Lucien Daudet later compared Mme de Saint-Marceaux to Mme Verdurin: "pompous, know-it-all, informed, astute, at once casual and condescending, knowing a lot about everyone and not giving a fig about them."[24] Upon hearing the announcement of Debussy's engagement, Pierre Louÿs, immediately foreseeing that it would lead nowhere, was upset about it. He considered it a rash decision, whereas Chausson's circle rejoiced at the notion of seeing poor Claude finally "domesticated."

Even Chausson declared himself "literally dumbfounded" by the news, while predicting that "this marriage will be very happy, precisely because it is not one of those that has been meticulously thought through."[25] Lerolle, completely oblivious, idealized the scenario: "He's in seventh heaven. Thérèse is glowing, young and all. [. . .] He must earn some money and not live on Thérèse's means. [. . .] They've rented an apartment on the rue Vaneau, beginning 16 April. He's going to Thérèse's home every day and isn't working much."[26]

Claude's conversion to a bourgeois life seemed complete. He went with the flow, without knowing where he was headed, except perhaps toward a much-desired end to his financial troubles. On 8 March, he made a true confession to Chausson, expressing himself in some of the most disconcerting lines he would ever write:

For days and days, I've been meaning to write to you, but I'm so completely discombobulated, and my life is seeming to take on such new hues, that I must get a little used to all this. Anyway, I feel great joy mixed with quite a lot of confusion. Until now, I seem to have been sleepwalking, and I've unfortunately run into some nasty individuals along the way! Now that a sunny path is opening before me, I fear that I don't deserve so much happiness, and at the same time I'm fiercely determined to devote my entire life, all my strength, to protecting it! What you've told me about marriage has touched me very much, believe me, and it seems absolutely correct to me (novice that I am in such matters). It's certainly true that happiness is always to be found within ourselves, more so than in those who might appear to be the motivation behind it, and so, when we want another person to rejoice in our happiness, it's a subliminal feeling [within us]. But I feel so great to have offered my life, once and for all, and that from now on it will be lived for just one person!

I may have strayed into seedy places in the past! but my abhorrence for them will protect me for the rest of time, and I'm still young enough to be able to say that I bring a brand-new soul to a new life. Anyway, I have feelings that for good reason could never be expressed and that happily I've kept intact, always in the hope that one day I'd have the deep pleasure of seeing them blossom.[27]

In due course, he would come to recall with nostalgia those nasty individuals and those seedy places. As for marriage, he would remain single for many more years. The end of this letter was devoted to a subject in which Claude had more experience: it was a request for money, as if his admittance to the bourgeoisie called for payment in return! The explanation that he gave to Lerolle of this "unreal" event is very differently pitched, in a rather gauche tone with practically no discernible depth of feeling. Being on much more personal terms with him than with Chausson, Debussy asked the painter to vouch for his character with Mme Roger. In particular, he attempted to justify himself with respect to his financial position and announced some news, which we might add was false—that Gaby had just moved out:

I have something very crazy to tell you!
There's a plan for marriage between Mlle Thérèse Roger and Claude Debussy! It's completely unreal, but there you have it, and it's happened like a Fairy Tale! I might add that for a long time I've had a deep fondness for Mlle Roger, but this seemed so unacceptable to me that I didn't dare think about it! Please don't think ill of me. I've indeed told Madame Roger all about my [personal] situation, and that I'd like her daughter to remain completely *independent financially*!
As for me, I'll always manage. Now, Madame Roger would like to see you and to chat with you about me. I thought that that wouldn't be too unpleasant for you, and that you'd indeed be willing to do this small favor for me?

Incidentally, I'm *completely free*, since my last girlfriend left one morning in February—in order to improve her lot in life.

Be sure to tell Madame Roger about my great courage, and my great desire to be worthy of what she's done for me!

Next, *I'd ask you to keep all this between the two of us*! But really, I feel the irresistible need to dedicate my life to someone, and I think that Mademoiselle Roger is as worthy of it as anyone.

Anyway, come to chat with me. There are some things I really can't confide to a cold piece of paper.

Your true friend

Claude Debussy[28]

The Breakup and Its Ripple Effects

The scandal exploded within days. Some good souls as well as an anonymous letter reported that the betrothed had not broken up with his mistress and that she was still living with him; others did not hesitate to elaborate on the composer's former life and even on the couple's living situation, which moral codes would censure. On 15 March, Debussy received a letter from Chausson, who was still in Arcachon, asking for some explanation, especially concerning his debts. In his cryptic reply, Debussy renewed his intention to have "a life that is very straightforward, without mysterious undertones" and added, oddly: "This is actually a transformation that is as intellectual as it is moral."[29] But, at the same time, he asked Chausson for 1,500 more francs, in order to settle certain debts and to buy—amazingly enough—a dress for his mother. On 17 March, Mme de Saint-Marceaux wrote in her journal: "Debussy's marriage is off. There are dreadful secrets about his life. A butcher's cap would seem an appropriate headgear for his handsome Roman head.[30] It's a pity to think that such a good-natured artist leads such a depraved life."[31] On 19 March, Chausson confided to Lerolle that he was "sickened,"[32] and that he had decided to put an end to the Wagnerian gatherings at his mother-in-law's, only half of which had taken place.[33] On 20 March, Debussy went to Mme de Saint-Marceaux's home: "He came to justify himself," she wrote, "and to convince me that the rumors circulating about him are lies. He did not succeed. There must be two beings in him, each independent of the other. He has lost his moral compass."[34]

At this point, Pierre Louÿs came to his friend's defense. In a fine letter to Mme de Saint-Marceaux, from 22 March, he attempted to vindicate Debussy:

> I am aware that appearances have condemned Debussy, and I'm not surprised that people might be scandalized.
>
> Perhaps you'll permit me to add, however, that a young man can't dismiss like a chamber maid a mistress who has lived with him for two years, who has

shared his poverty without complaining, and who is without reproach, [for no reason] other than that he's bored with her and that he's getting married. Normally one escapes such a situation with a few bank-notes. [. . .] You know that Debussy wasn't even able to use that approach. He feels obliged to move. [. . .] If the announcement of his engagement hadn't been made so quickly, Debussy would have had the time to extricate himself completely. [. . .] He didn't do that, or rather, he didn't know to do that; he's been severely punished for this.

As for the rumors about his former life that have been reported to you, I guarantee that they constitute colossal slander. [. . .]

I know personally that Debussy is incapable of having lived like people say. I also know this from two individuals who have known Debussy for twelve years and who are as appalled as I am by the deplorable plot that is being played out around him. Moreover, I can name them: Messieurs Raymond Bonheur and Étienne Dupin. Monsieur Lerolle and Monsieur Chausson will tell you how reliable they are.

I write this in profound grief and with a vehemence that I beg you to forgive, Madame. I know nothing more painful than to see so disgraced within one week a man whom we love and esteem so much, who has been unlucky for fifteen years, and who finds all doors shut at the moment when people are beginning to discover his genius.[35]

But the breakup was already final, and its ripple effects heavily damaged Debussy's reputation, in spite of the courageous support of a few people close to him. At the beginning of April, Pauline Roger and her daughter Thérèse went to Arcachon to give Chausson a detailed report of the incident. The latter immediately shared his reactions with his brother-in-law, who continued his friendship with Debussy:

Mme Roger [. . .] was especially anxious to prove to me that she had not been as imprudent as one might generally think. And, in fact, if poor Debussy had replied honestly to all the questions that she had posed to him, this entire terrible ruckus would have been avoided. Truly, the more I learn, the less I understand. If I must, I can explain away the falsehoods, hollow excuses, and subterfuges—which are stupid and always useless—but to lie outright, with protestation and indignation, and about such serious things, that beats me. Dupin's last letter, which was shown to me, adds further to my bewilderment. That letter was written after the final breakup. Dupin declares on his honor that Debussy is innocent of everything (although in reality all the facts seem to prove him wrong) and that the truth will come out, etc. But God Almighty, if he can defend himself, which would thrill me, why doesn't he do so? And Dupin, why doesn't he write to you, or to Bonheur, or to me? As for Bonheur, he wrote to me, saying that Debussy should not be forced into being a family man. And that it's a matter of the qualities needed to be the father of a family. Would it were only that! When all is said and done, I just become enraged all over again.[36]

Debussy's previous biographers have not accorded enough attention to this episode, missing its most important points and thus contributing to the portrayal of the composer as amoral. On 11 May, Pierre Louÿs, after having battled on his behalf, concluded by wondering himself: "For two months, I've supported Debussy against twenty-five individuals; I'm convinced that I haven't made a mistake, but even so, I'd like to have proof of it."[37] And, on 13 March, Lerolle had written that "in Paris, this [gossip about Debussy's love life] is the only topic of discussion,"[38] especially within the circle of the Société nationale.

Return to *Pelléas* and the *Marche écossaise*

Fortunately, Claude had *Pelléas* to console him during all this ruckus, in which he had shown as much immaturity as he had indiscretion. Gaby generously forgave the unfaithful one, took up communal life with him again, and, as before, contributed to the modest household resources at the rue Gustave-Doré, working in fashion (especially making hats).[39]

Moreover, Debussy had kept some doors open. Certainly, his status with respect to the Société nationale was a bit uncertain. But he maintained very close relations with Lerolle, as with "a big brother whom one loves, even when he grumbles";[40] with the Arthur Fontaine family, whose little chorale he conducted; with Ysaÿe; and, we are not surprised to read at the end of a letter to Lerolle: "My kind regards to Chausson."[41] He dined from time to time at Jacques Durand's, where music was played. That is how, one evening when Paul Dukas was also there, they sight-read *Thaïs*, which had just appeared: "Debussy was not fond of that piece," wrote the publisher, adding that "he preferred other works by Massenet."[42]

But he also saw other friends, thanks chiefly to Pierre Louÿs. In March, the latter had invited Debussy along with two young friends, Jean de Tinan and André Lebey, regulars at the Art indépendant as well as at the brasseries in the Latin Quarter. Tinan, a broodingly handsome man, had just published *Un document sur l'impuissance d'aimer* (A document on the impotence of love) with Bailly; Lebey was still a lycée student but had already published some poems. The four of them, Tinan noted in his journal, talked about André Chénier, Hugo, and Baudelaire.[43] On 31 May, Louÿs invited some people to his place to hear the first act and a few other excerpts from *Pelléas*. They included the Natansons, from the *Revue blanche*; Paul Robert, a painter who was a great devotee of absinthe and who was known in the cafés as "the Don Juan of chez Maxim's";[44] and Henri de Régnier and Camille Mauclair. A little later, Debussy dined with Paul Valéry and André Gide, whom he described as "an old spinster, shyly courteous and polite, in the English manner."[45]

126   CHAPTER TEN

And he took refuge especially in his work. At this time, the performance of the yet-unpublished *Marche écossaise* raises a detail that until now has eluded the composer's biographers. The *Marche* was—as we have seen (see pp. 95–96)—the result of an unusual commission and, once orchestrated, had first been programmed for the concerts that Ysaÿe was organizing in Brussels. Remember that, in June 1893, Chausson made sure that the score and parts were ready, but the performance had been canceled for some unknown reason (see pp. 110–11). The project was taken up again by the Société des grandes auditions musicales de France, which Countess Greffulhe had overseen for the previous three years. On the organization's advisory committee were notably Chausson, Bréville, d'Indy, and Vidal, none of whom had any objection to proposing the *Marche* for a concert that took place on 29 May 1894. The program for the concert, conducted by Colonne at the Palmarium of the Jardin d'acclimatation, was substantial: besides Fauré, Magnard, and d'Indy, it included "Dansons la gigue" by Bordes, "La caravane" by Chausson, and the overture for *Polyeucte* by Dukas. Unfortunately, the score and orchestral parts for the *Marche écossaise* had been left at Ysaÿe's, and the work could not be performed.[46]

All summer long, Debussy toiled away, "like a horse pulling an omnibus,"[47] starting with the third act of *Pelléas*. He described several of its scenes to his dear Lerolle, with obvious satisfaction:

> The scene in the underground vaults is done, full of insidious and mysterious terror, enough to make the heads of the most hardened souls spin. And the scene depicting the climb up from those vaults is also done—full of sunshine, but of the sun bathed by our mother the sea; it will make, I hope, a lovely impression. [. . .] I've also finished the scene with the little sheep, into which I have tried to put something of the compassion of a child, to whom a sheep first seems like a toy that he's not allowed to touch, but it also evokes a sense of pity, no longer felt by those who worry about a comfortable life. Now I'm working on the scene of the father and son, and I'm afraid: I have to convey such profound and such elemental things! In this scene, there's a "petit père" that gives me nightmares.[48]

This was a very fertile time of creativity, for, in the same letter of 28 August, Debussy announced to his friend that he had just begun "some pieces for violin and orchestra that will be titled *Nocturnes*, in which I'll make use of separate groups of instruments"[49] and, in the following month, he explained to Ysaÿe, for whom he was composing the work, that "the first [nocturne] is represented by the strings; the second by three flutes, four horns, three trumpets, and two harps; and the third one brings these two groups together."[50] He added a very evocative comment about the influence of painting on his musical thought: "It is, in short, an investigation into the various permutations that a single color can give, as for example a study in gray would be in painting."[51] This conception of the *Nocturnes*, too Whistlerian in nature, would ultimately be abandoned.

Georges Hartmann

By September 1894, Debussy finalized the *Prélude à l'après-midi d'un faune*, which he sold to a publisher whom he had just met and who would play a providential role in his life: Georges Hartmann. Alfred Bruneau, who had worked as a proofreader at Hartmann's, described him with brutal honesty: "a fat guy with dirty blond hair, chubby-cheeked, conceited, with an imperious demeanor, and uncongenial."[52] But this Bavarian publisher's son, who occasionally wrote libretti, had had the reputation of supporting young French composers—Bizet, Saint-Saëns, Lalo, Franck, and especially Massenet—nearly all of whose lyric works he published. In order to disseminate these works more effectively, in 1873 he had founded the "Concert national," under the able direction of Colonne. But this activity led to financial difficulties, aggravated by Hartmann's passion for horse racing. His business was sold off in 1891, and he was barred from practicing the trade of publisher again. Nevertheless, he continued his publishing activity, thanks to a front man, Eugène Fromont.[53] He could thus sponsor, jointly with André Messager, Debussy's entrance into the Société des auteurs, compositeurs et éditeurs de musique (SACEM) on 10 January 1894, and then purchase his *Prélude* on 23 October for 200 francs—fifty francs less than the sum the composer had received from Durand for his String Quartet.[54]

Lerolle had the rather intriguing idea of organizing an evening concert at his home, during which Vincent d'Indy would present his *Fervaal* to several chosen friends, while Debussy would play some excerpts from *Pelléas*. He himself described this get-together in a letter to Chausson on 19 December. The Maurice Denis and Arthur Fontaine couples were there, as were Camille Benoit and Paul Poujaud, a lawyer from the provinces who was passionate about music. After the third act of *Fervaal*, which left Lerolle hungry for more, Debussy was prevailed upon to sit down at the piano, while d'Indy "grimace[d] with his moustache as he turn[ed] pages" and Poujaud "look[ed] quite amazed."[55] This is how the underground reputation of that score was spread, little by little, within musical circles, although it would not be heard by the public until more than seven years later.

The composer's fame also continued to grow, step by step, within the profession. In Massenet's class at the Conservatoire, there were already two "acolytes" of his music: Florent Schmitt and Ernest Le Grand. The latter had become friends with Debussy, who had asked him in June 1894 to help correct the proofs of his String Quartet. Charles Koechlin, who was also a member of the class, helps us fully understand why Debussy chose Le Grand, "the most gifted, the best composer, the most authentic *creator* of us all (and who since, by an inexplicable fate, has destroyed his compositions)."[56] Every Sunday, Le Grand would spend the afternoon at Debussy's home, playing J. S. Bach's organ works together on piano (four hands), but the composition of *Pelléas* was such a strain on Debussy that, one day, Le Grand opened Claude-Achille's door to see an individual with "a strange, transfigured air," who simply said to him: "No. . . not today!"[57]

A few of Massenet's pupils had works issued by Émile Baudoux, a publisher who, after having been employed by Hartmann, opened a firm at the beginning of 1894 that became something of a club for those faithful to the Société nationale, welcoming young composers in particular. Debussy himself frequented his shop on the boulevard Haussmann, no doubt because the Russian publications of Belaieff were available only there. Among Baudoux's shareholders was "an enlightened amateur, in the best sense of the word,"[58] Jean Bellon, who was a commanding presence and who invited Debussy to dine with a couple of these young musicians—Florent Schmitt and Charles Koechlin—at his home in Asnières. The latter recalled, "Debussy wanted very much to have us hear *La damoiselle élue*. But I was not put off by his opinions. He displayed a fierce hostility with regard to Saint-Saëns. [. . .] He treated Grieg very cavalierly. He criticized the opening of Franck's Sonata for Violin and Piano for its 'slightly easy-going sentimentality.'"[59] In the presence of such an audience, Claude-Achille maintained the same frank tone that he had had in his discussions with Guiraud five years earlier. He no longer tiptoed around the critics. On 16 December, while leaving the Cirque d'été, where Lamoureux had just presented Balakirev's *Thamar*, a journalist (whom he held in low esteem) confided to him: "You know, I don't like that music very much"—and Debussy retorted: "That, on top of everything else!"[60]

Premiere of the *Prélude à l'après-midi d'un faune*

On 22 December 1894, the premiere of the *Prélude à l'après-midi d'un faune* finally took place at the Société nationale. A few weeks earlier, the society had announced that it would be more open to the general public by organizing four orchestral concerts per year in the large Salle d'Harcourt, each preceded by a public dress rehearsal. Thus, on the program for the first of these concerts, given on 22 and 23 December, in addition to Debussy's *Prélude* were Alexander Glazounov's op. 19 fantasy, *La forêt* (first performance in Paris); Saint-Saëns's Third Concerto for violin (played by Mathieu Crickboom); and Franck's *Rédemption*. The young Swiss orchestra conductor, Gustave Doret, who had studied with Théodore Dubois and Massenet, described in a book of memoirs the close collaboration he had with Debussy on that occasion. He noted the concern for detail that the composer always brought to his score during the rehearsals; the flute solo, played by the very young Georges Barrère, was particularly satisfactory.[61] Debussy sent a note to Mallarmé, expressing himself in an elliptical fashion that attempted to emulate the master's style:

> Dear Master:
> I need not tell you how pleased I would be if you would be so kind as to honor with your presence the arabesques which a perhaps shameful pride has made me believe to have been dictated by the flute of your faun.[62]

We know that the work was repeated as an encore, no doubt on the evening of Saturday, 22 December. But the critical reception was, once again, barely competent. In the *Revue illustré*, Gustave Robert found in the *Prélude à l'après-midi d'un faune* "a slightly tiring bias toward originality."[63] Nearly a year later, after a performance of the work at the Concerts Colonne, Robert gave an analysis, pointing out the aural fatigue that resulted from the work's "incessantly elusive tonality," while at the same time acknowledging that the composer had created "a style all his own."[64] Charles Réty, under the pseudonym of Charles Darcours, saw in the work only an excessive pursuit of timbres, adding in a comical way that "Such pieces are fun to write, but never to hear,"[65] while Auguste Goullet, who was irritated because he considered it to be a success among the initiated, found it "indigestible"![66] Pierre Louÿs, the only one to criticize the performance, wrote in a letter: "I'll await the second performance of your piece, hoping they might play it a bit better. The horns were abominable, and the rest hardly any better."[67]

To Willy, who in the following year asked Debussy what relationship his composition had with the poem, he replied that "it is the general impression of the poem, for to follow it more closely, the music would lose momentum. [. . .] Just the same, it follows the ascending movement of the poem. [. . .] The end is the prolongation of the last line: 'Farewell to you both; I am going to see the shadow that you have become' (Couple adieu, je vais voir l'ombre que tu devins)."[68] And it was finally from Mallarmé himself that Debussy received the greatest tribute that he could ever imagine: a letter in which the poet declared that the composer's *Prélude* went "even further, truly, into nostalgia and light, with finesse, with malaise, with richesse."[69]

Chapter Eleven

Pierre Louÿs; The Lean Years

1895–96

In comparison with 1894, which had been a year full of promise, the subsequent years seemed empty and almost fruitless. Some projects, following the String Quartet and the *Prélude*, were too undeveloped to bring to fruition, and there were no premieres or even minor public attention in the offing. It seemed that the composer's fame was on the decline. This momentary lull affords us the opportunity to explore more closely his relationship with Pierre Louÿs, who played a key role at this time in Debussy's life. A considerable part of their correspondence has been published, and much has been written about their friendship from both sides. Surprisingly, the sustained exchange between writer and composer—each so creative, albeit in different ways—yielded virtually no fruit, even though they often dreamed of the two of them monopolizing the colonnes Morris.[1]

In November 1893, Pierre Louÿs wrote to his brother that for the past two months he had been seeing Debussy nonstop. They had even considered the crazy idea of living together in a large, eight-room house (one that could be divided) at the end of a path in Neuilly. They had met each other at Mallarmé's, then again at Bailly's; but Debussy's dedication of a copy of *La damoiselle élue* (in July 1893) was still rather impersonal, as he simply wrote: "With my deepest regards for Pierre Louÿs."[2] It was on the occasion of a trip to Brussels and Ghent that their friendship truly blossomed. On the following 1 January, Louÿs settled into a three-room apartment at 1 rue Grétry, where on Wednesdays he received his friends—Henri de Régnier, Pierre Quillard, Ferdinand Herold, Jean de Tinan, André Lebey, and Paul Valéry. Debussy was also one of the regulars at the house, and, when Louÿs left Paris, it was to Debussy that he gladly handed over the keys to his flat. It was also to him that Louÿs would propose, to no avail, a trip to Biskra in July 1894.[3] As the composer was very busy with *Pelléas*, and also perhaps because he did not want to desert Gaby, he thus missed sharing with his friend the charms of Meryem bent

Ali. Gide had said great things to him about that young woman, from Ouled Naïl (in Algeria), who had inspired the *Chansons de Bilitis*; in order to tempt his new friend, Louÿs compared her to a young Javanese girl. Finally, in 1894, Louÿs dedicated his booklet, *La maison sur le Nil ou les apparences de la vertu* (The house on the Nile or the appearance of virtue), which was published by the Librairie de l'art indépendant, to Debussy. This tale, written in a flippant style, relates the story of a young man—Biôn—who spurns a very young girl who offers herself to him.

The Limits of a Friendship

Louÿs was eight years younger than Debussy. It is not difficult to imagine the attraction he was able to exert on the latter, due not only to his cultivation and connections, but also to his free and independent lifestyle; he was prodigiously gifted, extravagantly generous, eccentric and complex, brilliant and impressionable, secretive and vulnerable. Although his complete works comprise thirteen volumes, he remains scarcely known to the public except for the *Bilitis* poems, *Aphrodite*, and *Le roi Pausole*, and he spent nearly as much time writing erotic works as he did literary ones. One often wonders which person is the real Louÿs—the friend of Gide, Wilde, and Valéry; the habitué of the ladies of the night in the Latin quarter; the erotomaniac photographer; the Hellenist; the bibliophile; or the author of light-hearted songs.[4]

His connections with music are not insignificant. He frequented the concert halls and the Opéra-Comique. While he valued Beethoven as much as he did Massenet and Ernest Reyer, he developed a passion for Wagner very early on, and went to Bayreuth twice, in 1891 and 1892. For him, *Tristan* was "the masterpiece of art," but *Parsifal* in particular was "the masterpiece of the soul"; he never lost his enthusiasm for the latter, which he heard seven times.[5] As late as 1897, he would confess that "literature is a much less powerful art compared with the greatness of music."[6] He claimed to have played the violin, viola, saxophone, bass clarinet, and piano. However, the instrument that was used most often in his home was the harmonium, as documented by some very lively photographs from this period.[7]

Through the approximately two hundred letters that the two artists exchanged, we can distinguish rather clearly what brought them together and what divided them. At first their relationship was relaxed, and, of the two, Louÿs was certainly more the prankster. The tone of their jokes, behind which they hid a certain sense of propriety, was much more ingrained in the writer, as was their aversion to taking themselves seriously. It seems to have been less natural for Debussy to follow suit. And they did not have very many mutual friends sharing in their camaraderie. Louÿs did not seem very eager to accompany his friend to see Raymond Bonheur, whom he perhaps considered a bit straitlaced, at his home in Magny. And Debussy participated only rarely in the antics of the trio of "little monkeys" (Jean de Tinan, André Lebey, and Louÿs), whose home base was in the Latin quarter. Nevertheless, thanks to Tinan's journal, we learn that Debussy went with them to a café-concert on 2 May 1895 along with two young prostitutes, Blanche-Marcelle and Dora; but at the end of the show, he took off with Louÿs for Montmartre. On 30 November, he went to the Parisiana with Louÿs,[8] along with two young girls who subsequently spent the night with Jean de Tinan.[9]

When Louÿs got involved in the launch of the *Centaure*, a periodical dedicated to literature and art, it did not even occur to him to encourage the literary tendencies of Debussy, though the composer had nothing but friends there—people such as Valéry, Lebey, and Tinan. In his memories of the very relaxed meetings that took place at the editorial office headquarters on the rue des Beaux-Arts, Léon-Paul Fargue recalled that, at times, Debussy would come "to make a little music, brought by Louÿs or arriving alone. [. . .] He would sit down silently at the piano in the small office-library and would start to improvise. [. . .] He would begin by brushing, by feeling, by passing over the keys, and then he would stroke them with his velvety touch, accompanying himself at times, his head down, with a lovely nasal voice, like a singing whisper."[10] In any case, Debussy was present—along with Alfred Jarry, Willy, Colette, Rachilde, Stuart Merrill, and Marcel Schwob—at the *Centaure* banquet, organized at the Salle d'Harcourt, on 18 May 1896.[11]

Louÿs was also Debussy's only close friend who paid any attention to Gaby. He dined regularly with the couple, and Gaby valued his company very much, asking Claude to embrace him or to send him "her nicest smile."[12] He was even thoughtful enough to send her some bananas from Algeria. One evening in 1897, when she had good reasons to be sad, she wrote him a simple and touching letter, which we still have today.[13]

More than once, the writer rescued his friend financially. Claude's urgent notes date from these years, when he was "in the worst mess," soliciting "a louis"[14] or 50 francs, or lamenting his lack of students. Once again, one wonders how he earned a living. At what point did Georges Hartmann start to grant him a monthly income of 500 francs? Probably around the middle of 1895, since in October the publisher wrote to SACEM:

> I completely forgot to ask you to have me registered as publisher of Debussy's *Prélude à l'après-midi d'un faune*, which Colonne is playing on Sunday at the Châtelet concerts, formerly the Concert National! I will try to promote this young artist (Debussy, not Colonne!) and to take on all of his works, which for the moment are all on deposit at Fromont. Keep an eye out![15]

The codes of friendship between Louÿs and Debussy were always honored when a serious moral crisis struck one or the other of them. We have already seen that Louÿs was practically the only person to rush to his friend's aid during the breakup of his unfortunate engagement with Thérèse Roger; he would be at his side again in April 1898 when Debussy would talk of suicide. Two years later, it was the composer who expressed his deep sympathy to Louÿs when the latter's wife fell seriously ill, following a miscarriage in Barcelona: "Naturally, fate would have you be far away, making it impossible for me to be useful to you, or even to offer a paltry handshake, by which I could express a bit of real affection."[16] Nevertheless, it seems that the writer's biographers may have too readily accepted the myth that Debussy, one day while in a state of distress, would have destroyed the manuscript of *Pelléas*, had Louÿs not intervened.[17]

New Performance of the *Prélude*

Late in 1895, the friendship between the two men was tested when the *Prélude à l'après-midi d'un faune* was heard on 13 October. One might think that this new performance, given at the Concerts Colonne and repeated the following Sunday, would attract more attention than did its premiere at the Société nationale. Colonne would have preferred to have been giving the premiere of the *Fantaisie* for piano and orchestra, a work that Hartmann had first suggested to him, but Debussy was unable to provide the changes he had requested on time.

Louÿs had been duly forewarned by his friend that his presence at this concert was very much desired; Gaby waited with a ticket for him in front of the Châtelet.[18] But, being in great distress and even on the brink of suicide, Louÿs did not show up, and chose to be frank with Debussy:

> My dear friend,
> Rarely have I been as tormented by indecision as I was this morning. On the one hand, your *first* performance before the general public; on the other hand, a demanding letter from Vallette[19] and the fact that I had twenty pages to write immediately today.
> I assure you that if it had been only a matter of my own pleasure... well, you know full well what it's like. But I didn't really have the right to leave my house today. I would've changed my mind only if you had had a financial interest in my being there, as for example on the evening that your quartet was performed. It's really awful not to be able to make a decision without choosing between these two alternatives: to upset my number-one friend or to harm a number-three friend. You won't be surprised that I chose the first alternative.[20]

A few days later, Louÿs received a letter in which Debussy expressed his disappointment "that it would be you of all people—among the *three thousand, six hundred individuals* who could not interest me but by their number—whom I missed that day!"[21]

The critical reviews were hardly more receptive than at the first performance of the *Prélude*: "Exquisite orchestral painting," wrote Willy, "dream music; here and there, charming innovations of instrumentation recall some page of a sublime Chabrier, but twenty times as refined. [. . .] Intoxicating charm of the imprecise! In its fluid uncertainty, an elegance dissipates, hesitant. . ."[22] From the outset, Victorin de Joncières stated that he understood "absolutely nothing of the poet's wild musings" and that Debussy was considered to be "a member of a small congregation of decadent composers who, they say, feign a profound disdain for everything that has been written before them"; he deigned to admit, in recalling the "odd flavor" of *La damoiselle élue,* that Debussy wrote better than "the so-called innovators" of the Société nationale, that he had the gift of color, and that he combined timbres with skill.[23] His only criticism of the *Prélude* was that Debussy "developed the middle part too much and needlessly prolonged the same sonorous effect which, charming though it may be, becomes monotonous in the long run."[24] In *Le Figaro,* Alfred Bruneau, a former classmate from the Conservatoire who had become a friend of Zola and an advocate of musical naturalism, clearly acknowledged in the composer a "rare and original" temperament and in the work "some patches of truly exquisite music," but concluded as follows: "I must honestly confess my preferences for a clearer, stronger, more virile art."[25] The specialized press was even more deaf: in *Le ménestrel,* Amédée Boutarel observed that the *Prélude* was based "on a theme, or rather a remnant of a chromatic theme,"[26] and Isidor Philipp sought "in vain a little heart, a little vigor"[27] in it. The harshest criticism was from Hugues Imbert, who lamented "the imitation of [. . .] Wagner"[28] in this "indecisive page of music."[29] Soon thereafter, Henry Eymieu saw it, similarly, as an "empty and pretentious page."[30] The only journalists to redeem somewhat the honor of their profession were Alfred Ernst, noting "the extreme novelty of the form,"[31] and the young poet Charles-Henry Hirsch, who had recently held forth at the *Mercure de France* and who wrote: "A truly great charm emanates from it, and one experiences a rare pleasure in following this [musical] description [of the poem], where, in the development of a motif, frequent events arise which animate the [poetic] scene in the most pleasing manner. And a close connection unites M. Debussy's composition with Mallarmé's magnificent poem."[32] Writing in his best prose, the composer thanked this critic for having been "one of the very rare individuals to 'understand' my modest attempt to illustrate this poem with corresponding arabesques."[33]

Collaborative Projects with Louÿs—*Œdipe à Colone*

For Louÿs, Claude was one friend among many others, someone he saw between his numerous trips to Algiers, Seville, and Egypt, or between his various girlfriends, Meryem, Zohra, and Marie de Régnier. Still, the two men always took so much pleasure in getting together and in endlessly discussing their collective projects. The first among these collaborations, dating from September 1894, has gone unnoticed until now. It concerned nothing less than an *Œdipe à Colone* (after the play by Sophocles), which Louÿs and Ferdinand Herold had intended to write together. In a letter from 8 September, Louÿs explained to Herold that he had already planned for Mounet-Sully to be the actor, and he seemed to want to run the show:

> Upon reflection, your idea of *Œdipe à Colone* seems perfect to me and very exciting, on the condition that it's written in verse. . . Would you like to do it together? I could do the first and the fifth acts. . . If you want to do it alone, *just ignore this letter*. . . Debussy is the only other person who is in on the secret of the project. He'd write the music, and he's thrilled with the idea.[34]

There are no more references to this project, which notably would have had Debussy confront the famous ode in which the nightingale and the chorus of muses sing continuously. It is surprising, however, that, while at the height of composing *Pelléas*, he could have contemplated setting Sophocles.

Cendrelune

The second project—which began as *Le roi des Aulnes* but turned into *Cendrelune*—was discussed for a longer time. Originally, it involved a commission that had come from Carvalho, the director of the Opéra-Comique, at the beginning of April 1895; it was to have been performed in his theater at Christmastime.

We have two versions of this Grimm-like children's story, each in two acts (although neither follows the lines of the traditional *Cinderella* story). The first is only a sketch, sent to Debussy in a letter from Pierre Louÿs on 19 April 1895: a little girl named Geneviève is raised by a wicked stepmother; on Christmas Day, she is lured and tempted by a queen of the Aulnes (i.e., elves, or Erls), whose favorite child is named Cendrelune; thanks to Saint Agnès and Saint Catherine, Geneviève resists this temptation and ultimately discovers that the queen is none other than her real mother.[35] In the more developed version, Cendrelune takes the place of Geneviève (from the earlier version), and the queen of the Aulnes (the Erlqueen) becomes a "Dame verte" (woodland sylph).[36]

Debussy sought from Georges Hartmann—himself a librettist—an agreement to publish the work. After having asked for some simplifications in the storyline, Hartmann agreed at the end of May. But, instead of working on it, Louÿs and Debussy continually proposed changes to each other. One night, Louÿs had the feeling that his script was just terrible and would not interest anyone. In the offhand manner that was natural to him, he suggested to Debussy that he might write a *Faust* or a *Psyché* instead, or, later on, a *Hamlet*. Another day, tired of Debussy's counter-proposals, he suggested that the composer write the story himself:

> Write *Cendrelune* yourself. You're perfectly capable of it. In the process of making changes in this little libretto, it's become completely foreign to me. As it stands, I wouldn't be able to develop it further. This religiosity, this triumph of the lily over the rose, of modesty over passion, it's Greek to me. [. . .] But when the day comes that I have the great joy of being set to music by my friend Claude, I'd like [the music] to be based on a [literary] masterpiece.[37]

Cendrelune would subsequently reappear in their correspondence from time to time, as if they still believed in it, but from then on it was Debussy who insisted that Louÿs work on it himself, rather than *vice versa*. The last time it was mentioned was in May 1898.[38] It is highly unlikely that even a single note of music was composed for this scenario, which from the start stemmed too much from a desire to put food on the table.

Daphnis et Chloë

A third joint project was even more short-lived. This time it concerned a ballet on a pastoral theme, *Daphnis et Chloë*, inspired by Longus. The idea originally came, in November 1895, from a director of light theatrical shows. As Claude apparently did not appreciate a proposal that gave him twelve days to write thirty minutes of music, Louÿs turned to, of all people, Massenet! Faced with the latter's refusal, he tried again and sent his script to Debussy two months later. In the writer's mind, it was another way for the composer to plug a few financial holes. Naïvely, Louÿs, who continued to believe that his friend could compose a score as quickly as he himself wrote prose, even suggested a few themes, the first among them being "constructed like the first phrase of *Parsifal*."[39] Even though Debussy wrote, "I'm working on *Daphnis*," on 8 May 1896,[40] it is doubtful that any of this work actually took place. After 1897, the two men no longer discussed it.[41]

Aphrodite

Their fourth project was *Aphrodite*. The success garnered by Louÿs's novel is well known, especially after François Coppée's unexpected praise in April 1896.[42] As for Debussy, he extolled "a prodigiously supple art" and "a notation of gestures" as well as "some romantic or colorful arabesques" in Louÿs's work, which delighted him; however, he did not hide his opinion that on that "fabulous foundation," Louÿs had developed "a texture that was too rich."[43] The writer was flooded by proposals to base an opera on his book from, among others, Isaac Albéniz, Henri Rabaud, and Ruggero Leoncavallo. In October 1896, he gave his provisional permission (very likely without informing Debussy about it) to the cabaret singer Yvette Guilbert, who offered to ask Saint-Saëns to write a comic opera on *Aphrodite* (with a libretto by Maurice Donnay) in which she herself—unlikely as it sounds—would sing the role of Chrysis.[44] As for Debussy, how could he have imagined devising music suitable for that hymn to sensuality? He was still too much a Symbolist to alter his palette so completely. Meanwhile, Louÿs gave no formal authorization to anyone as long as his friend Debussy had not yet relinquished his own plans for it.

In November 1897, the writer had the opportunity to have a ballet or a pantomime, based on his novel, performed at the Olympia theater. Debussy seemed reluctant to embrace the idea of suddenly becoming a music-hall composer. Always emphasizing the prospect of financial gain, Louÿs was slightly annoyed by the composer's reticence: "I believe," he wrote to him, "that your dignity, though severely compromised, would allow you to accept [this proposal], and the proof is that my own dignity has not been offended."[45] It goes without saying that the project fell through and Louÿs felt free to move on. It was Camille Erlanger who in 1906 had his music for *Aphrodite* performed on the stage of the Opéra-Comique, with Mary Garden as Chrysis. A little later, Debussy, who at that time was no longer seeing Louÿs, must have felt a little pang when reading his former friend's published remark that Debussy and Erlanger were the composers who had known how to express Louÿs's texts "superbly" well![46]

La saulaie

It is no accident that the last project between Louÿs and Debussy was the one in which the composer believed the most and which went the furthest. *La saulaie* is a poem by Dante Gabriel Rossetti that had been translated by Louÿs. It came from three sonnets included in the "Willowwood" section of the Pre-Raphaelite poet's collection, *The House of Life*.[47] Here Debussy felt much more at home than in the impromptu projects that had come previously, and in the month of May 1896, he asked his friend for the text.

Although we have recovered only short excerpts of this composition,[48] written for baritone voice and orchestra, Debussy had worked on it enough to announce to Ysaÿe, on 13 October, that he thought he would complete *La saulaie* by December.[49] He showed how important he thought it was by pointing out that one would find in it his "latest experiments in musical chemistry."[50] After the breakup with Ysaÿe, Hartmann referred the composer to Colonne, who hoped to program the work in January 1897. Debussy asked for an extension, but missed the new deadline. However, Hartmann did not give up on obtaining the score, for on 13 December 1899, Debussy wrote to him that he was working on it "in collaboration, one might say, with the good Lord,"[51] and in the Fromont catalogs from 1900, the work was announced as forthcoming. Lastly, on 5 January 1900, Debussy spoke about it to Godet, stating that "it's lovely, very much 'alive.'"[52]

This series of incomplete projects between Louÿs and Debussy is explained in part by the aesthetic differences that, despite their apparently deep friendship, separated them. Louÿs was much more eclectic than Debussy. While he valued Mallarmé, Rossetti, and Gustave Moreau, he remained "the Parnassian" in the eyes of some of his friends. "Louÿs is not at all a Symbolist," wrote Gide in 1892, "but still comes from the previous school of the Parnassians—from Gautier, Banville, Hugo, and Heredia."[53] In music, their mutual appreciation went no further than Offenbach's *Les brigands*, which they heard together at the Théâtre des Variétés. For example, Debussy was not as overtly enthusiastic about *Carmen* as was his friend,[54] and Wagner in particular was a subject of serious discord, at times leading them to heated verbal exchanges. In a long letter from 29 October 1896, written a week after one of these impassioned discussions, Louÿs attempted to explain why "Wagner was the greatest man ever to have existed" and to identify precisely which scenes in his operas "would never be equaled."[55]

As for Debussy's own music, it is clear that Louÿs was unable to perceive its utter novelty. His remark on the *Prélude à l'après-midi d'un faune* is rather perplexing: "It's always the wind in the leaves, and so varied, so changing"; and in *Pelléas* he saw only "a perpetual connection between the sense of the written phrase and the expression of the sung phrase."[56] In the already-cited letter concerning Wagner, we note some very vague proclamations, confirming that Louÿs did not go beyond the surface in his understanding: "Music, it's the breathing in and out of your faun's *Prélude*, it's the gust of air upon emerging from the underground vaults of *Pelléas*, it's the wind of the sea in the first act, it's the funereal monotony of the fifth act."[57]

This is the context from which emanated those rather absurd collaborative proposals that Louÿs reproached Debussy for not seizing more eagerly—as if he were addressing a composer who could adapt the style of his work to any subject whatsoever. One day in 1896, when he found himself in an especially appropriate place—the casino at Houlgate—Louÿs wrote a letter that was perhaps intended to tease the composer about his Symbolist beliefs, but that showed the degree to which he misunderstood the rigor of Debussy's artistic ideal:

> My dear Claude,
> Your error (if you've made one), is to believe that you are a composer who is accessible exclusively to the elite, even though you have what it takes to be the favorite composer in the public squares and the casinos.
> And so, don't get on your high horse because I'm telling you this. These days, Shakespeare and Hugo do the most for the French, and even surpass the earnings of M. Octave Feuillet.[58] That doesn't mean that they're idiots.
> Furthermore, you've got to convince yourself that there is no elite class and that Messieurs Ernest Chausson, Pierre Louÿs, Ferdinand Herold, and Raymond Bonheur do not constitute a public that is noticeably superior to Messieurs Émile Durand, Charles Martin, and Adalbert de la Roche-en-zinc, who occupy numbers 1, 3, 5, and 7 in the orchestra seats. One must write:
> First—for oneself
> Second—for people who have ordinary and honest emotions. (These people are worth more than the snobs.)
> I believe that the day when you write for both categories of the public (you and the others) at the same time, you'll be just that much more amazing to them. I'm telling you all this, by the way, because I'm sure that in your heart you agree with me, but perhaps you don't admit it to yourself. And I dare say that there will be a time when you will admit it.
> Your
>
> P. L.[59]

Debussy's reply was an invitation to lunch, followed simply by this postscript: "You'll explain to me a letter signed by P. Louÿs of which I understood nothing, so we really must find the man who presumes to use your signature without your ideas."[60]

How can one thus not agree with the commentator who concluded: "[There is] nothing comparable between Louÿs and Debussy; the two of them were superior in different domains. In their dealings with each other, they engaged only the least noble part of their nature, each one jealously reserving for himself—as a universe that was forbidden to the other—the devotion that each dedicated to his own art."[61]

Chapter Twelve

Pelléas—The Long Wait

1895–98

Besides his relationships with Louÿs and Hartmann, Debussy continued to foster friendships with, among others, Peter, Lerolle, Bonheur, Satie, and the Fontaines, a family with whom he had been in contact since 1893. Related by marriage to Chausson and to the Lerolles, the Fontaine family included four brothers who spent summers together at their estate in Mercin, in the department of Aisne. The eldest was Arthur, a chief engineer at the National Mining Services, who became a high government official as a director at the Ministry of Commerce; the three others, including Lucien, managed a large hardware business. Arthur in particular was an art lover; he supported Odilon Redon, Eugène Carrière, and Maurice Denis, and was friendly with Francis Jammes, Raymond Bonheur, and André Gide.[1]

The Fontaines

During the summer of 1894, Lucien came up with the idea of a small family choral group to be conducted by Debussy. We know that it began to meet in September, for at that time Debussy wrote that Lucien sang like "a sentimental bull."[2] The following year, the composer was received at Mercin "like the Prince of Wales."[3] No doubt the choral group met irregularly, but it was still extant in 1898, when it welcomed a new member, Mlle Worms de Romilly, who remembered being almost awestruck by it: "He [Debussy] was a wonderful choral conductor, with the patience of a saint, teaching each of us our different parts one by one, and he had succeeded in training a small ensemble, comprised of a handful of unreliable and ill-informed amateurs, that was musical and disciplined."[4] Of the repertoire they tackled, she remembered especially Chabrier's *Ode à la musique* and some Russian music. This young woman also asked Debussy for voice lessons and remembered the first day, when he arrived in a "small open carriage, called a 'tonneau,' pulled by a nervous pony and driven by M. Fontaine."[5] These sessions soon turned into piano lessons, and the teacher assigned her Schumann's *Kreisleriana* as a starting challenge. When she wanted to surprise Debussy by playing his *Arabesques*, he refused, saying: "Not those pieces, they're too awful!"[6] Besides some excerpts from *Tristan*, and occasionally works by Dukas or Chausson, they sight-read for four hands the works of The Russian Five (she adored Balakirev's *Islamey*); in particular, Debussy analyzed for her "one of his favorite pieces," Chopin's *Barcarolle*, a work that we might add she never did manage to play correctly.[7] "The poor great master," she added, "always kept an eye out for a little envelope, placed discreetly on the piano, that contained the payment for the lesson."[8] In April 1898, Lucien Fontaine would be the dedicatee of two *Chansons de Charles d'Orléans* that Debussy had written for the choral group, and, when the *Fêtes galantes* were published, the composer would dedicate one of them to Madame Lucien Fontaine (née Louise Desjardins) and the other to Madame Arthur Fontaine (née Marie Escudier).

It was at the home of Mlle Worms de Romilly, probably toward the end of 1898, that the first (private) performance of the "Prélude" from the suite *Pour le piano* (which had been dedicated to her) took place. She played it during an afternoon concert to which she had invited a few friends; the program included the duet from Édouard Lalo's *Le roi d'Ys* and some chamber music by Schumann. The performance of the *Chansons de Bilitis*, as yet unpublished, elicited abusive remarks from an elderly man from Argentina who was unaware that the composer was present![9]

In 1896, the need to keep food on the table led Debussy to offer again some Wagnerian presentations, similar to those organized by Mme Escudier, which had been discontinued two years earlier. In Mme Godard-Decrais's salon on the rue d'Aguessau, he gave a series of readings—each week, act by act—going from *Tannhäuser* to *Parsifal*, "with that rough voice, restrained, with bursts of gloom that were oddly effective, and with that pianistic sound, deep, velvety," which Gustave Samazeuilh, then an eighteen-year-old musician, remembered long afterward.[10] Since the small but socially prominent audience was so enthusiastic, Debussy even agreed to an additional gathering in 1897, where they heard *La damoiselle élue*, the transcription for two pianos of the *Prélude à l'après-midi d'un faune*, and a few excerpts from *Pelléas*.[11]

Debussy had not given up his habit of spending long evenings in the cafés, although the locations had changed somewhat. He regularly visited Reynold's, where Henri de Toulouse-Lautrec would often be seen and where the main attraction was Foottit—the prince of clowns, whose clacking tongue called to mind the whip of a postilion driver—as well as his inseparable Chocolat.[12] Above all, Debussy went to the Weber tavern on the rue Royale, "the first Weber at the time, which had only two small rooms."[13] There, he would join

Curnonsky and Jean de Tinan, with or without Louÿs, and a few artists such as Maxime Dethomas; Jean-Louis Forain, the caricaturist; Paul Robert, a "big mouth" and high-spirited guest, who left us a portrait of Claude; and, although more rarely, Léon Daudet, with whom he ended up going to the theater,[14] as well as Marcel Proust, for whom he never felt much sympathy and with whom he had, according to René Peter, "brief, but generally cordial interactions."[15]

Life with Gaby

Debussy's personal life during this period was only seemingly stable. He made three trips with Gaby: to Normandy, to Lisieux, and to her sister's home in Orbec, where her brother-in-law refused to receive him because he was living in sin. More often, however, Gaby would go to Orbec alone.[16] He continued to see sweet Catherine Stevens and to be taken in by her "wicked" eyes. But at her family home, the time was no longer filled with merry entertainment, as in the past, or with the singing of Offenbach, Hervé, or the light-hearted songs that Debussy accompanied at the piano. At the end of 1895 or the beginning of 1896, the Stevens family experienced great financial difficulties, which they tried to conceal from the aged and old-fashioned painter. One evening, noting Catherine's sadness, Claude proposed to marry her, suggesting that he would soon be comfortable enough because *Pelléas* was going to be produced. She kindly refused, telling him that they would speak about it again once *Pelléas* had been performed.[17]

Claude and Gaby's relationship had seriously deteriorated. On 9 August 1896, they canceled their plan for a day in the country with Pierre Louÿs before his departure for Spain because they were "too down in the dumps," and on 23 January 1897, Gaby wrote to Louÿs while Claude was away, playing Lekeu's Piano Quartet at the Société nationale, that she was "alone and sad, sadder than the weather."[18]

A few days later, drama exploded: Gaby found a letter in Claude's pocket that, as Debussy wrote, "left no doubt about the advanced state of a love affair that was salacious enough to stir the most hardened heart. With that!. . . drama. . . tears. . . a real revolver, and a story in the *Petit journal.*"[19] Nothing further is known about this suicide attempt at the very beginning of February, recounted so tersely to Louÿs, except what may be another of the stories that were fabricated about her: upon leaving the hospital, Gaby was supposedly taken in by Chausson and then by Ysaÿe.[20] These accounts are not convincing and are based on no reliable evidence. Gaby, who lost her father at roughly the same time (on 7 February), went to Orbec and Lisieux to be with her sister and her mother, and then quickly resumed communal life again; on 9 March Debussy wrote to Louÿs that she was sending him "her nicest smile."[21] But the scars left by that crisis were more serious for Gaby than the unfaithful one was willing to admit (Claude referred to them as "these insignificant little stories"),[22] and we can surmise that, from then on and for nearly two more years, the lovers lived a bit like strangers.[23]

In point of fact, the event took place in the context of even more profound distress. Louÿs was in Algiers at the time of the drama and did not come back to Paris until the end of April. Before leaving again for Egypt at the beginning of 1898, he tried to talk some sense into the composer, although he was hardly qualified for that task. At the time, Louÿs was the only friend with whom Debussy could share his pain, and Claude felt his absence all the more keenly because of this:

> I've been quite miserable since your departure, most passionately miserable, and I've cried a lot; such a simple act, which unites all of humanity, was the only thing left for me to do, given my state of anguish. I can't explain further, and, as my friend, you'll understand the rest.
>
> Naturally, I haven't been able to work much, music taking its just revenge for my having neglected it.[24]

In his reply, Louÿs was surprised by the seriousness of Debussy's condition: "Is this a complete secret?" he asked. "None of my friends mentioned it to me!"[25] A day later, he received an even more alarming letter in which Debussy called himself "alone and distraught" and spoke of suicide, "out of utter weariness from fighting against idiotic impossibilities."[26] This time Louÿs realized how desperate his friend was, and tried to show him the absurdity of his plan:

> You, my old friend, you don't have the slightest excuse to have these nightmares—because *you are a great man*; do you understand what that means? You've been told this; now, I'm telling you. And perhaps you'll believe me if I add that I've never said that to anyone. Whatever problems you have, you must hold on to this thought. You must continue your work, and you must make it known—two things which you must do in equal measure and which must be everything to you. It's not by giving music lessons that you will sustain yourself, but by doing everything possible to ensure that *Pelléas* is performed. You consider practical steps as beneath you, and perhaps you're mistaken; for it's most important that you're able to work, and you'll be able to work only if you have the essentials in your domestic life.
>
> Think about it. Everything that you tell me worries me deeply. If you think I might be helpful to you, tell me how. As for me, I'll do what I can without speaking to you about it.[27]

René Peter described this phase in Debussy's love life as being at a standstill, with the composer "temporarily unable to 'pull himself together.'"[28] However, he witnessed only one of Debussy's female acquaintances: an unexpected relationship with Alice Peter, who was the virtually separated wife of René's brother, Michel Peter, and a society lady to whom Debussy seemed to serve as a devoted admirer. Curiously enough, she was the dedicatee of "La chevelure," even though her "keen sense for practical life" made her quite unlike Bilitis or Mélisande.[29] Even more curiously, Debussy dedicated to her a newly modified version of "Clair de lune"—a song he seemed to have forgotten that he had already offered to Marie Vasnier and to Catherine Stevens, and that he ultimately dedicated to Mme Arthur Fontaine in the collection of *Fêtes galantes* that was published in 1903. Would any composer other than Debussy have dedicated the same work to four different women?

[Scholar Denis Herlin has documented a close relationship between Debussy and Alice Peter, positing that the composer had a secret liaison with her from sometime around the beginning of 1897 through June 1899.[30] In fact, it is likely that his affair with Alice was the cause of the crisis in his relationship with Gaby. They probably met through their mutual association with Étienne Dupin, who had underwritten Debussy's trip to Bayreuth, provided financial support for the publication of his *Cinq poèmes de Baudelaire*, and even put him up in his home for several months during fall 1890. In 1893, Dupin had married Alice's sister Marguerite Loewenstein. Witnesses at their wedding included Debussy's close friend Raymond Bonheur; Michel Peter (who married Alice presumably in 1894, but who was separated from her by 1896–97); and Jean-Baptiste Florimond Dansaert, who had married Alice's other sister Régina (called Régine) Loewenstein and who was Dupin's boss at the Dansaert-Loewenstein bank. Régine and her brother-in-law René Peter would collaborate on several theatrical projects, and René would attempt to involve Debussy in some of them. Thus, the Loewenstein-Dansaert-Peter families became a significant source of support for our composer, financially if not to a similar extent artistically, as were the Chausson-Lerolle-Fontaine families several years earlier. And all of these individuals witnessed the long gestation of *Pelléas*.]

Works in Progress

During the first months of 1895, some planned concerts had failed to materialize. In February, Debussy had received a friendly proposal from Vincent d'Indy, who was preparing to conduct some concerts in Barcelona and asked if he might have an orchestral work in his portfolio that could be included on his program. In his amusing reply, Debussy let d'Indy know that, short of replacing the harps with about a dozen guitars in the *Prélude à l'après-midi d'un faune*, he had no "transportable music," and that furthermore he reckoned that his *Marche écossaise* lacked "the special swagger of Spain."[31]

However, Hartmann pushed him to finish the works that were in progress, and to release even those with which he was not completely satisfied. As we have seen, this was the case with the *Fantaisie pour piano et orchestre*, for which the publisher had arranged a premiere by Raoul Pugno at the Concerts Colonne. Although Debussy claimed that he had worked on it "day and night" in September,[32] the already engraved proofs of the *Fantaisie* were covered with his corrections (which themselves were incomplete), and the work's performance was postponed once again. At the same time, he focused on a new project: he attempted to craft his own libretto from Balzac's *La grande bretèche*, out of which he was planning "to make something quite disturbing."[33] It was a venture (which picked up on the theme of a living person who is walled off from the world) that, although it never saw the light of day, was stored within his theatrical imagination.[34]

Between April and June 1895, Debussy wrote the fifth act of *Pelléas*, "trembling all the while,"[35] and then, in the following weeks, took up the second act. He wrote to Bonheur that he had believed it would be child's play: "But it's a torture from hell!"[36] Finally, on 17 August, he was able to announce to Lerolle that *Pelléas* was finished:

> It has not been without some blood, sweat, and tears—especially the scene between Golaud and Mélisande! For it is there where things begin to move toward the catastrophe; it is there where Mélisande begins to lie to Golaud and to realize her own motives, assisted in this by the said Golaud, who is a worthy man just the same; it also shows that one should not be absolutely frank, even with young girls. I believe that the grotto scene will please you; it tries to capture all the mystery of the night, where, among so much silence, a blade of grass, disturbed from its slumber, makes a completely unsettling noise. And then nearby is the sea, which airs its grievances to the moon, and then come Pélléas [*sic*] and Mélisande, who are a little afraid to speak amidst so much mystery.[37]

Debussy asked Bonheur and Dupin, the friends who had supported him the most, to listen to these scenes soon after they were written. Hartmann was also included, but as he was bound (in spite of himself) to the traditional values of opera, the composition's innovative qualities did not resonate much with him, and he even worried about the risk of staging a work that turned its back so decisively on convention. Debussy wrote,

> Now, all my anxiety begins; how will the world deal with these two poor little beings? [. . .] Take Hartmann, for example, who is certainly representative of an above-average intelligence. Well! Mélisande's death, as it stands at the moment, does not move him any more than it would move a small bench! It has no effect on him! Besides, in France, whenever a woman dies on stage, it has to be like the "Dame aux camélias," though one might replace the

camellias with other flowers and the Lady with an exotic princess! People can't acknowledge that one might die discreetly, like someone who has had enough of this planet Earth and who passes away to the place where serene flowers grow.[38]

A Plan to Get the Opera Performed (1895)

Debussy had hardly finished (for the time being) his score, when contacts were made to produce *Pelléas*. Although past Debussy biographers have briefly mentioned these negotiations, it is worth considering them more carefully, for they clarify in particular Maeterlinck's initial attitude toward the composer.

Paul Larochelle, a former colleague of the poet Paul Fort, had become the director of the Théâtre de la Rive Gauche, which took the name of the Théâtre Libre after André Antoine relinquished it in 1894. Larochelle was supported by Tola Dorian, the pseudonym of Princess Meshcherskaya. This literary woman, whom Albert Samain described as "a nutcase,"[39] was among the first to translate Swinburne into French. She had helped Paul Fort stage Villiers's *Axël* at the Théâtre de la Gaîté; on 26 February 1894, she attended this performance in her box, surrounded by her three former husbands. The previous year, she and Paul Fort had simultaneously taken an interest in *Pelléas*, but then in the end had left it up to Lugné-Poe and Camille Mauclair, in whom Maeterlinck had complete confidence. In August or September 1895, Larochelle and the Princess approached Debussy to convince him that they could be trusted with a score about which they knew nothing, and to set a date for its performance. In order to outdo Lugné-Poe and the Théâtre de l'Œuvre, they even announced in the 12 October issue of the *Écho de Paris* that *Pelléas et Mélisande*, a "play by Maeterlinck, [with] music by M. de Bussy," had gone into rehearsal at the Théâtre Libre.[40]

Debussy had not only alerted Hartmann, but had also informed Julia Robert, whom he no doubt had in mind for the role of Mélisande, for she was an exceptional pupil of Chabrier and one of the original performers of *La damoiselle élue*. He wrote to her about the plans for the Théâtre de l'Œuvre production: "It seems legitimate to me."[41] In any case, because Larochelle needed to have an idea of the music that would accompany the drama, a meeting with him and Hartmann was set up so that Debussy could play extensive excerpts of it for him. At first it was Hartmann who balked, and then Larochelle who withdrew from the project. Debussy grew all the more discouraged when this theatrical director was said to have declared "that he had no need to hear [the music for] *Pelléas*, since he knew nothing about it."[42]

In this matter, Maeterlinck's position was perfectly honest, both to Debussy and to Lugné-Poe, and he was quite dismayed by the scheming of Dorian and

Larochelle. On 17 October, he wrote to the composer in order to clarify his stance:

> My dear Debussy,
>   Poor Lugné had a close call and there he is, still quite panicked! Perhaps—unless he has some objections I don't know about—you could save him by authorizing him to deny the reports. That would be very valuable to him, it seems, at this time when most of the subscriptions are sold. You know that, deep down, I like Lugné very much; he has done some great things for me. Anyway, you'll make of this what you will, and I'm speaking to you about it only in the event that it wouldn't cause you any difficulty.
>   As for *Pelléas*, it goes without saying that it's all yours, and that you should have it played wherever and whenever you wish. I only confess to you that, personally, I'd be extremely averse to reestablishing connections with [Mme] Dorian, M. Antoine, or M. Larochelle, who is their representative. They did not treat me very well, and if the play were to be given in their theater, I'd prefer to stay completely out of it—provided, of course, that that would not be detrimental to you, for I put you well above all these petty things.[43]

And, a little later, Maeterlinck wrote to Lugné-Poe:

> Hôtel de la Paix
> Place de la Station – Ghent
>
> Dear old friend,
>   Here's what I know about the *Pelléas*-Debussy matter: two or three months ago, Mauclair wrote to me that the Dorian-Larochelle team was in the process of closing in on Debussy and was on the verge of securing *Pelléas* from him. He had told Debussy to be careful and had mentioned all of the problems we had endured. Debussy had seemed shaken. I then wrote a letter that Mauclair was to show him, in which I said that, since *Pelléas* as an *opera* belonged more to the composer than to the poet, I intended to leave total freedom to Debussy. However, should the work go to the Théâtre Libre, I'd withdraw completely, in order to put on record my absolute disgust at becoming involved again in that world I'd come to know. I refused to allow my name to be associated with whatever comes of the matter, or to appear on the poster or on the program, etc.; in a word, it should be the *Pelléas* of Debussy alone and not mine. I don't think I could express my disapproval more fully. What more could I do? Debussy is a man of very great talent, of genius, they say, whom I like and admire. This is why, if it happens anyway, I'll really have to bow out, for I don't want to prevent him, nor can I, from doing what he believes necessary for his work.
>   But is the news really true? I still don't believe it. We know that in that house the producers are better remunerated than the poets.
>   There it is, my poor old fellow. You surely see that I'm still faithful to you.
>   Yours truly,
>   M. Maeterlinck.[44]

The matter went no further. Perhaps the potential promoters of *Pelléas* realized that the finances required for the orchestra greatly surpassed their means, and that the orchestration of the work would have required a delay of several months.

Other Plans for *Pelléas*

A new project concerning *Pelléas* arose at the end of November 1895. Lugné-Poe had taken it upon himself to assemble some composers, seeking their advice on the role that music could play in theatrical performances, and more particularly in those at his Théâtre de l'Œuvre. Present, besides Debussy, were Vincent d'Indy, Ernest Chausson, Pierre de Bréville, and Sylvio Lazzari. In a letter to Hartmann, Debussy described the scene in his own way:

> Lugné-Poe took the floor and spoke directly, in a very American manner: "L'Œuvre wants to present some music and requests the contribution and support of young composers—they should put forward a work that will satisfy the guidelines requested." At this, the young composers turned to stone, and the audience squirmed. Finally, d'Indy broke the silence and uttered the name of *Pelléas*; several people seconded him, and fraternal warmth brought them nearly to tears! But an elderly gentleman stood up and said with a steady voice that belied his age: "L'Œuvre must put on a truly independent work, one that would be impossible at the Opéra or the Opéra-Comique! We have enough of their Wagnerian formulas and the pseudo-operas they have spawned."
>
> At that, everyone rose, speaking all at once, and it would have resembled a meeting of anarchists had Lugné-Poe not led the group to a little place where—of course—Norwegian drinks were imbibed. The result of all this is another letter from Lugné-Poe, received this morning, where he declares himself completely at my disposal: he believes he has 25,000 to 30,000 francs! and the support of Léon Jéhin![45]

That original meeting apparently led nowhere, and with it vanished the chances for *Pelléas* to see the light of day in the Symbolist atmosphere in which it was intrinsically conceived.[46]

Another opportunity to have *Pelléas* performed arose in 1896. Ever since Debussy had shown the score to Eugène Ysaÿe, the latter considered himself its godfather, and for that matter expected to be the dedicatee. But the violinist envisioned having only some excerpts from *Pelléas* performed in one of the subscription concerts that he was organizing with a newly created symphonic society in Brussels. He even took the liberty of announcing this truncated performance in his programs. Debussy reacted immediately, declining this offer and instead proposing *La saulaie* and his *Nocturnes* for violin and orchestra to him.[47] Not accepting defeat, Ysaÿe sent the composer a lengthy justification for his project four days later: in his opinion, a partial performance with carefully chosen soloists would be more valuable than a problematic performance of the whole. Besides, had not Wagner's works started off in France in the same way? He would have these excerpts performed in a concert that also included a cello concerto by a certain Joseph Jacob, an overture by Antonín Dvořák, and some "new" variations by d'Indy! As for the *Nocturnes*, it was impossible for him to play them himself, due to previous engagements.[48] Debussy's refusal closed the door on their collaboration once and for all: "Despite the joy I'd have in seeing you conduct this work, and the great passion you'd put into it, I don't think you should do it."[49]

The following episode would indeed position the work quite differently: in May 1898, the new director of the Opéra-Comique, Albert Carré (pressured by Messager, who had just been named the music director of that theater), promised, albeit informally, to produce *Pelléas* on his stage. In the following month, a new threat arose to unsettle their spirits: the performance, at the Wales Theatre in London, of a *Pelléas* in an English version, with incidental music by Gabriel Fauré. Georges Hartmann appeared quite annoyed by this news. Debussy, on the other hand, exhibited perfect composure in his reply on 9 August 1898.[50] While denouncing the behavior of Maeterlinck, who had not informed him of this event, he characterized the event as "purely anecdotal," adding with regard to Fauré: "To me, in all modesty, it seems unlikely that there would be grounds for confusion, if only from the fact that my score is much longer. Anyway, Fauré is the musical emissary of a group of snobs and imbeciles who will never see the other *Pélléas* [*sic*] nor have anything to do with it."[51]

Chapter Thirteen

From Bachelorhood to Marriage

1897–99

Some Publications

During the "Pierre Louÿs years"—which, throughout the correspondence between the two men, seemed so often carefree and slightly crazy—there was almost no mention of Debussy in the Parisian columns or in the press. The publications of the *Prélude à l'après-midi d'un faune,* based on Mallarmé (October 1895), the "Sarabande" for piano (February 1896), and "La chevelure" (October 1897) were not deemed newsworthy. In 1897, Debussy made a vague promise to the Société nationale committee (of which he was still a member) to write a new quartet and, astonishingly, a quintet with oboe![1] But plans outnumbered projects, and on the last day of that year, when the thirty-five-year-old composer sent his greetings to his generous publisher, he had to admit that he had accomplished next to none of his goals from the previous year.[2]

However, in Symbolist circles, whose vitality had largely dissipated, Debussy was still recognized as the musical representative. He was more than likely present—with Viélé-Griffin, Mallarmé, Jean de Tinan, and many others—at the one-year memorial mass in honor of Verlaine and at the Batignolles cemetery on 15 January 1897.[3] In any case, he attended the banquet for Mallarmé, on 2 February 1897, to celebrate the publication of the latter's *Divagations*—a get-together that incidentally caused ethical dilemmas for some people and the notable absence of Valéry and Gide.[4] Even if Debussy claimed to be bored at the banquet, at least he got to meet the Parnassian poet José-Maria de Heredia there. And, on 12 September 1898, he sent his condolences to Mallarmé's widow: "Permit me to express my genuine and deep sorrow along with all those who knew the admirable being who was Stéphane Mallarmé and who understand the loss that Art in all of its manifestations has just suffered!"[5]

The uncertain state in which Debussy found himself, creatively speaking, is confirmed by the number of projects that remained unrealized. Along these lines, Julia Robert proposed that he write incidental music for Verlaine's play, *Les uns et les autres*, chosen for the opening of the Théâtre Salon (the future Grand Guignol). Once again, he accepted but was not able to finish in time. When the Théâtre Salon opened in May 1896, Charles de Sivry, who was called upon to help, ultimately composed the score.

In the following year, the illustrator and caricaturist Jean-Louis Forain, whom Debussy had surely known at the Chat Noir or through Paul Robert, approached him to write music for *Le chevalier d'or*, a pantomime written by his wife: "It's not bad at all, even though it's not finished," Debussy told Louÿs.[6] The work was commissioned in February 1897, but seven months later, only its "musical outline" had been completed, and Debussy wrote that he needed two and a half months to bring it to fruition.[7] In the following months, despite his promises, and even though Mme Forain was pretty and witty, he was still struggling to finish it. No trace of this work has been found.

The year 1897 was not a complete loss, however. In an effort to help Satie become better known, Debussy had orchestrated the first and third of his *Gymnopédies* in February 1896. Their premiere was given on 20 February 1897 at the Salle Érard, under the auspices of the Société nationale and conducted by Gustave Doret. Above all, at the beginning of May, in response to a request from Floury (publisher of the periodical *L'image*), Debussy finally decided to turn his attention to the *Chansons de Bilitis*: "I want very much," he wrote to Louÿs, "to set one of the *Chansons de Bilitis*—number 20, among others. Would that please you and would you have any objection?"[8] "La flûte de Pan" was written quickly, then temporarily set aside. Louÿs then sent him the text of "La chevelure," as yet unpublished, which was to be inserted in the new edition of the *Chansons*. In sharing it with him, the writer was attempting to raise his friend's spirits:

> Here's the song.
> Try to set it just the same, my old fellow; you're not working because you have a hard life, and you have a hard life because you're not working. It's a vicious circle. But one must break the pattern immediately by going in a different direction, when trapped in this sort of situation. [. . .]
> Just promise me that you'll work four hours a day for one week. Make a solemn vow—in the name of Arkel—and you might see that your gray matter is only asking to be put to work.[9]

Frères en art

A curious literary essay, *Frères en art*, is also linked with this period. For a few years, Debussy had been friends with a "modest literary man,"[10] René Peter, whom he had met as a youth through René's father and older brother. From a well-to-do family, Peter was one of those to whom Claude appealed most frequently for financial support. Debussy helped him finalize his *Tragédie de la mort* by procuring (with much difficulty) a preface for it from Pierre Louÿs and by composing a "Berceuse on an old song from Poitou" for it in April 1899.[11] The play was published but never performed.[12] Together, Peter and Debussy planned several projects—fairy scenes, comedies, and farces—of which nothing remains but their picturesque and facetious titles: "Les mille et une nuits de n'importe où et d'ailleurs" (The thousand and one nights of anywhere and everywhere), "L'utile aventure" (The useful adventure), "L'herbe tendre" (The sweet grass), and "Esther et la maison des fous" (Esther and the nuthouse).[13] From 1898 onward, the two of them had undertaken, a little more seriously, a "dramatic satire" titled *Frères en art*, or *F. E. A.*[14] After having enthusiastically tossed off the first sketches with his friend, Debussy quickly became aware of the frivolousness of their improvisation and particularly the lack of definition of the characters. It would be "better to know the soul of all these people," he wrote to Régine Dansaert, around May or June 1898.[15] In fact, he decided to write the play by himself and no doubt did so in the following months.[16] That is how three scenes have reached us from his own hand, offering a unique glimpse into his imaginary theater.[17]

The *F. E. A.* scenes portray a fair number of characters, whose ages are meticulously indicated: about ten critics and artists (including a musician and general council member—Valady—who owns, amazingly enough, a château in the Vosges), and five women, who play no more than a secondary role. The primary characters are Durtel, of humble origin and a former insurance agent; the painters Maltravers, Talencet (who is successful), and Heldebrand (who is not); and Redburne, the English critic. The subject (as opposed to the action) centers on the creation of a mutual-aid society, of a brotherhood among artists, conceived rather cynically by Durtel. Edward Lockspeiser attempted to attribute real-life personas to these characters, suggesting that Redburne, for example, could be the Irish writer George Moore, a friend of Dujardin and Dukas, and that Heldebrand could be Adolf von Hildebrand, a sculptor and historian of German art.[18] As for Maltravers, who is "almost an anarchist" and whose works Mallarmé loved,[19] he occasionally sounds a bit like Debussy's alter ego, M. Croche, who would first appear in the *Revue blanche* in 1901. Maltravers has Debussy's artistic pride, the somewhat darker side of his early years, and his unconventional disdain for rules; it is impossible to confirm, however, that the composer had wanted to portray himself in the character. One might think of him when Maltravers claims that the truth "is not in books; it is rather in the form of a tree or the color of a sky,"[20] or that "art is freedom, but you make it a formula."[21] As for his friend Marie, she in no way reflects the Lilly whom we now know, though perhaps she represents the Lilly of Debussy's hopes and dreams.

The play, based entirely on the controversies surrounding the conception of art and on the clash of generations, is essentially centered on the painters' world; the tone is always close to irony, indeed sarcasm—in the style of Laforgue, as Lockspeiser points out—even when it concerns references to contemporaries like Ibsen, Rodin, Claude Monet, Rollinat, or "our dear and unforgettable Mallarmé."[22] While deriding snobbery and the wheeling and dealing of artistic circles, the author seems to want to denounce a quasi-conspiracy against young artists. Much more than a *pièce à clefs*,[23] the *F. E. A.* reveals to us Debussy's pessimistic view of the artist's condition, at a time when he might still have had misgivings about his own survival. In a way, it represents a farewell to his bohemian years.

Nuits blanches

On 14 July 1898, Debussy completed a song, "Nuit sans fin" (Endless night), based on his own text; it was the first of his *Nuits blanches*, a collection that he would soon regard as a second set of *Proses lyriques*.[24] This song reflects not only his state of mind at the time, but above all a dream that took a long time to blossom into reality:

> Endless night.
> Dreary sadness of the hours spent waiting!
> Broken heart,
> Fevered blood, beating out the sweet syllables of her name.
> Would that she—the too-much desired and too-much beloved one—come
> And surround me with her fragrance of a budding flower.
> Would that my lips nibble the fruit of her mouth,
> Until tasting her soul upon them.
> Thus have I wept in vain,
> Thus have I cried out in vain, to all that escapes me!
> Dreary sadness,
> Endless night!

Both this work and a second *Nuit blanche* dating from September 1898 were discovered nearly a hundred years later in a private collection.[25] The two songs were meant to be part of a set of five, whose publication was still being announced in 1900 in Fromont's catalogs. But throughout his life, Debussy kept them from being released, presumably because of the lyrics as much as the music. The heyday of Symbolism had passed, and this style of poetry could seem somewhat old-fashioned. His former friend from the Conservatoire, Camille Bellaigue, had just drawn attention to this issue when discussing the *Proses lyriques* in a mean-spirited article in the *Revue des deux mondes*: "Once again, I do not want to talk about the *Proses lyriques* at all, because I understand nothing about them, because in this work, the words and music demonstrate, for a weak mind, the beginning—or perhaps more than the beginning—of madness, in the way that the words and sounds are arranged. [. . .] Therefore, do not read them; they are ugly and they are dangerous."[26]

Since 1896, Debussy had clearly been pondering an orchestration of the *Proses lyriques*. It seems that he had not carried out this project completely, except for "De grève"—of which a partial manuscript has been found—and "De soir." Two years later, he apparently changed his mind, and peremptorily told Pierre de Bréville, the secretary of the Société nationale, that it appeared to him "quite pointless to amplify them with any sort of orchestral din."[27] At the beginning of 1901, the project was taken up again at the Société in a concert that was to have been conducted by Guy Ropartz. Here as well, Debussy seemed very hesitant, this time because of the personality of the conductor, who he believed would not have been "pleased" to conduct his work.[28] At the beginning of January 1901, Debussy wrote to Bréville that he did not have high hopes for a performance of the orchestral *Proses lyriques* "at this time."[29] Blanche Marot, who had recently sung his *Damoiselle élue*, had been engaged as a soloist, but on 12 April, Debussy scrapped the idea once and for all, writing to the singer with his reasons: there were only two rehearsals, and there were not enough strings in the orchestra.[30] Subsequently, a performance of the *Proses* was no longer an issue, as if Debussy had lost his appetite for songs that were too "dated."

A Year of Change: 1899

While offering his best wishes to Hartmann on New Year's Day 1899, Debussy suddenly announced two important changes in his life: "A lot of new events have taken place in my life. First, I moved; then, Mlle Dupont, *my secretary*, resigned her position. These things are very disturbing, and even if one is a musician, one is still a man."[31]

These two developments date from the preceding month, when Claude settled into a flat—on the sixth floor of a narrow apartment building at 58 rue Cardinet—consisting of two small rooms joined by a bay, from which one could catch sight of a little greenery. The furniture, the decor, and the pictures hanging on the walls were such that Pierre Louÿs promptly dubbed his apartment an "art-nouveauesque dive," while Ricardo Viñes noticed its "very 'modern style,' like that at Bing's."[32] Gaby was no longer there; she had chosen this moment to leave Claude for good. She had recently met a South American banker, Count de Balbiani, known in Parisian circles as "M. Victor," who soon would rent a lovely apartment for her on the avenue Niel.[33]

And yet, Debussy was not out of touch with the musical scene; on 5 March, when Chevillard gave the first performance of Rimsky-Korsakov's orchestral suite, *Scheherezade*, Claude showed that his interest in Russian music was by no means diminished. Colette met him there and described him at the end of the concert, at the home of Louis de Serres:

> Debussy couldn't get enough of Rimsky-Korsakov. He buzzed his lips, tried to recall—singing through his nose—an oboe motive, attempted to produce the low sound of the timpani on the lid of a baby grand piano. . . To imitate a pizzicato from the double basses, he stood up, seized a cork, and rubbed it against a window. . . Erect, a wild eye beneath twisted horns, the goat-hooved one thus pluck[ed] his favorite briar from the hedge. . .[34] To us, Debussy looked like a faun. I sang to him the phrase he was looking for, using the piano to help me, and his haunted eye became more human, seeming to notice me for the first time: "Good memory! Good memory," he exclaimed. Moved, what I heard was: "Good news! Good day!"[35]

That same day, he declined an invitation from Chausson to a dinner where Louÿs would be present and, albeit offering his "hope for a raincheck,"[36] he scarcely masked his aversion to rekindling a past—from nearly five years earlier—that still bothered him. Less than six weeks later, while Louÿs was on his honeymoon, Chausson was killed in a bicycle accident, and Louÿs solicited Debussy for his calling card to add to his own when paying his respects.[37]

Lilly Texier

Suffering from a lingering neuralgia, Debussy was still trying to finish the *Nocturnes*, and on 3 April 1899, he could finally confide to Hartmann that he had "regained a little moral peace."[38] In fact, he had just met up with Lilly Texier, whom he had seen briefly in the past but had hardly noticed, and for whom he suddenly felt an intense attraction.

Rosalie Texier, called Lilly or Lilo,[39] hailed from the department of Yonne, where her father was the telegraph official for the railroads at Montereau. Once established in Paris, she was hired as a model for the Callot sisters, who had set up their fashion house on the rue Taitbout around 1895. When Debussy met her, Lilly was twenty-five years old and the companion of a "pleasant fellow who dabbled in the financial market."[40] René Peter reported the circumstances under which they met: "Her first encounter with Debussy, arranged by some friends, myself included, elicited few outward signs of attraction on either side. Claude found her pretty enough, but 'silly'; at times, he even enjoyed imitating her small mannerisms, which she took very well, charming girl that she was. On the other hand, she and Gaby liked each other very much. Then the three of them lost touch with each other."[41]

Some eighteen months later, Lilly reappeared, and quickly became an important part of Debussy's life. For the first time, we have access to the direct and almost daily correspondence from the composer to the woman he was pursuing, during the first three months of their courtship.[42] The first two letters—from 21 and 24 April 1899—reveal the tone of that budding passion:

> My dear little Lili,
> Would you be so kind as to put on your pink petticoat and your black hat and come to say hello to me next Sunday around 2:30? We could chat and plan a few little parties with Georges.
> Your affectionately devoted
>
> Claude Debussy
> 58 rue Cardinet
> 6th floor
> (there is no elevator)
>
> If you can't, I'll cry; just let me know. (21 April 1899)[43]

> My dear little Lili,
> Claude has not yet recovered from the bites of your dear little mouth! And he can hardly do anything else but think about that evening when you gave him so much unexpected happiness in the nicest way, and with the most complete freedom in the world.
> You see, lovely Lili, there was between us, almost in spite of us, something ardently passionate that was burning in secret and just waiting for an opportunity to be expressed.
> And if you felt a joy as crazy, as intense as mine, you must admit that it would've been a shame if this evening hadn't happened, for us to show our feelings for each other.
> Accept my infinite thanks for all the love I have for you. Try to give me as much of your love as possible. . .
> Also, believe me when I say that this *Saturday*, when I'll see you again, seems terribly far off to me. . .
> Impatient for your mouth, for your body, and to love you.
> Your
>
> Claude (24 April 1899)[44]

Who was this Marie-Rosalie Texier? Born at Chalon-sur-Saône, she was ten years younger than Claude; she had spent her youth with the nuns in

Cannes and had unpleasant memories of that period. From her mother—an Italian from Nice—she acquired a southern French accent which Claude said was "yet another charm."[45] Her education was no more wide-ranging than Gaby's, and she sang, with an unassuming voice,[46] the popular tunes of the day, "those wonderful songs whose particular charm comes from their endlessness and that would associate 'the little birdie who comes from France'[47] with Mélisande's 'mes longs cheveux.'"[48] The tone of Claude's letters to her, sent while she was staying at her parents' home in Bichain (in Yonne), was a bit like that of a man writing to a little child or a shopgirl. Nevertheless, Lilly's "proud and independent nature"[49] would soon create clashes in the relationship.[50]

A Love Slowly Shared

Lilly knew who Claude was, more or less. Gaby had warned her,[51] and after love's first blush, there were plenty of ups and downs in their relationship before this sensible woman was convinced of the sincerity of his love.[52] For nearly two months, they met primarily on weekends, for Claude could not expect "to have her every day";[53] he promised never to restrict her freedom, but he "hungered and thirsted" for her, "to the exclusion of everything else."[54] Day after day, Claude's impassioned letters described minor episodes as great dramas that postponed the inevitable outcome; Lilly wrote to him at times with "smiles and tears,"[55] and he objected to a "nasty quarrel," or the "preposterous" ideas by which she expressed her doubts.[56]

At this point in time, Pierre Louÿs informed him of his marriage to Louise de Heredia, the daughter of the poet, and asked him to compose for the occasion "two hundred measures for two manuals and pedal [organ], in the bizarre march rhythm of $\frac{4}{4}$—a piece of pompous, lascivious, and ejaculatory character, as befits a wedding procession."[57] The news, which augured increasing loneliness in the future, could only have pushed Debussy to persuade Lilly to follow suit; but, while congratulating his friend the following day, instead of admitting that he himself was about to be married, Claude claimed that his "abiding bond with Music" prevented him from becoming "nuptial."[58] At any rate, on 21 May, Lilly left to spend two weeks at her parents' home in Tonnerre, where Claude wrote to her, virtually every day,[59] letters whose turns of phrase were reminiscent of *Pelléas*:

> Have you felt this marvelous light that surrounds us [even] when we must be separated from each other, and that our eyes seem riveted to each other? We whose love expresses itself through the eyes! Do you realize that this could create eternal bonds between us? It seems to me now and then that if you

were capable of being jealous, you could be jealous of my love for our love. . .
From the day I first met you again, life has passed by so quickly that I feel as
if I've hardly seen you.[60]

Lilly forgave him, and after a period of three days she finally replied that, if he wanted, she would be his, his possession, "a second self."[61] Claude continued to send her passionate missives, worded in similar fashion: "Today, in writing to you, I can hardly hold my pen. All of me would like to run to you, so that I may possess more quickly your lips and your eyes; I'd slit my wrists for no reason at all, so that my blood would flow and sing for joy at your return."[62] Some letters even contain direct quotes from *Pelléas*: "It feels like it's been a hundred years since I've seen you."[63] Yet, even while expressing such effusive feelings to Lilly, Claude was able, on 2 June, to send back the corrected proofs of the *Chansons de Bilitis* to Fromont, and to make an appointment with Hartmann.[64]

[That same day, Claude had received a letter from Lilly, sending him a "train of kisses."[65] She must have returned on 3 or 4 June, as his daily letters to her stopped and his next letter to her, written on 7 June, was sent to her home in Paris. Rather than drawing on phrases from *Pelléas*, he paraphrased Verlaine for his letter to her on 11 June: "Here are your fruits, and here is my heart that beats only for you."][66]

Scarcely had Lilly returned to Paris when she fell ill; "I spent two nights by her side," Claude wrote to Louÿs.[67] A new crisis arose in their relationship. No doubt stressed by her work at the sœurs Callot, she pondered her future, implying that she had other options. This is why, on 17 June, Claude tried to be more explicit:

> I'm no longer young, and I need to settle my life *once and for all*; I haven't done it until now because I haven't met anyone I truly love and in whom I have enough trust.
>
> And so I've met you again, and the secret love that I had for you in the past was able to develop with a passion that has quickly become exclusive and almost feral. I don't think I need to dwell on that matter.
>
> Now, just as you do, I want you to stop the work you're doing, and I had every intention of pulling you away from it as quickly as possible. The love I have for you cannot and will not be satisfied with our seeing each other only for fun; I'd like to be a complete part of your life and to try to make you happy, not only by my affection but by my devotion, which would surround every minute of your life.
>
> Presently, I'm earning my living, no more, and while I can offer, without fear, to share my life with you, obviously it won't be lavish!. . . and you'd have to love me enough to put up with a few meager months. . . Anyway, while I fully understand your fears for your future, why do I understand far less the fears you have about my love?. . . Some things do not lie, just the same, and

while you can truly say that you've been cheated on once, why doesn't your feminine intuition tell you that you can trust me, without dreading any kind of betrayal!? [. . .]

Instead of that, you write me a letter in which you seem to want to scare me, telling yourself that I wouldn't dare go against your resolve, and that what I could offer you would seem too pitiful in light of your other options?

You speak of an "enviable situation"!. . . I'm telling you that *you will be what you want in my life*; I agree in advance to everything that you can hope for and want.

Now, it would be ungracious of me to prevent you from being as happy as you think it possible to be, and if the situation you're being offered is so enviable, then all my love and devotion would go up in smoke!. . . It would be worth it even if it tore my heart out! One thing, though: you should think about this!. . . There are things in life as essential as bread and they can't be bought in a shop—like Happiness!. . . and it's only complete when one's material life is in harmony with one's emotional life.

I must add to what I was saying about "a few meager months." *Pélléas* [*sic*] *et Mélisande* will certainly be performed this winter, and after the month of September, my situation will improve considerably.

Frankly, in the end, I want to devote *my life* to you, in the most complete sense of these words. Now, do with me as you please. You hold my Happiness or my sorrow in your hands,

I remain forever
your

Claude[68]

Tension in their relationship was clearly mounting, likely due to Lilly's suspicion of Claude's infidelity. By 21 June, she decided "in no uncertain terms" to leave him.[69] Claude had a letter delivered to her, in which he admitted to having defended himself poorly, but recognized that he was "guilty only of fickleness," that in fact this was merely a matter "of trivial issues of wounded pride," of "unimportant things." It concluded in a desperate manner, unlike the tone of the rest of the letter:

> Upon reflection, all this lost happiness didn't take such a great toll on my life, and there's still a way to give it to you.
>
> I'll pack up all your belongings, which will be delivered to you in the morning of the day after tomorrow; I'm naturally keeping my ring, wanting to be buried with it.
>
> Just the same, receive my last and longest kiss
> He who was your
>
> Claude
>
> I'll wait until this evening for a word from you, and if I can hope for nothing more, just tell me that you forgive me. Your pride can surely make this sacrifice for someone who's going to die.[70]

160   CHAPTER THIRTEEN

Louÿs's wedding was approaching. The same day on which he penned this decisive letter, Debussy wrote to his friend that he had devised two versions of the march, "one that I've already written, and another that came to me last night."[71] He had been in touch with Eugène Bourdeau,[72] the organist at Saint-Philippe-du-Roule, where the ceremony took place on 24 June, but due to illness he himself could not be present at that very Parisian occasion. In fact, this marked the end of their friendship, for their respective marriages, neither of which would be happy, led to an irrevocable distance between them. As for Debussy's sole organ work, we have unfortunately lost all trace of it.[73]

Marriage to Lilly

Up until this time, Louÿs was the only person who had been informed of Claude's new love, with this remark: "It's interesting how blondes need gold for earthly sustenance!"[74] Then, in a letter to Hartmann: "I love with every fiber of my being[75] a young blonde (naturally) who has the most beautiful hair in the world and eyes that surpass the most extreme comparisons. . .[76] At last, she is to be married!" After 5 July, the correspondence between the two lovers stopped (until October). They were now confronted with other worries: Lilly was ill again, and on 4 September, Claude called to her bedside Dr. Abel Desjardins, a relative by marriage to the Fontaines and to Chausson. "Apart from the fact that she's adorable," Debussy wrote to Desjardins, "she's very courageous, and if her condition turns out to be serious, don't hesitate to tell her; please just bring her back safe and sound."[77]

The wedding was set for 19 October 1899. Was Debussy obliged to follow the custom of asking her parents for her hand in marriage? That is what Lilly is said to have confided, years later, to Jean Lépine, who added that the composer introduced his wife to his own parents only in the following year, during an arranged meeting at the World's Fair. Obviously not wanting a religious ceremony, the bridegroom claimed not to have been baptized. He humorously described the event to his pupil, Mlle Worms de Romilly, who wrote: "Debussy told us that the priest, with whom he spoke about officiating at the wedding, had requested eighty francs in payment; 'you'll understand that after that,' the master added indignantly, 'we just went to the town hall.'"[78] His witnesses were Pierre Louÿs, Erik Satie, and Lucien Fontaine, friends who were not used to being together and who constituted an odd assemblage: a writer at the forefront of the news, an obscure composer making his living as a pianist-accompanist in the Montmartre cabarets, and a businessman. Immediately after the ceremony at the town hall, Debussy left to give a lesson to his pupil so that he could pay for dinner at the Pousset tavern; Mlle Worms de Romilly recalled that "Lilo Debussy was seated on the bench at the foot of the stairwell of our apartment, waiting until the lesson was finished, so that she and her husband could embark on a honeymoon on the upper deck of an omnibus![79] They ended up at the Jardin des Plantes, through which the poor bridegroom, who loathed walking, trudged. [. . .] The banquet was funded by the payment for my lesson, and everyone went back on foot, for alas, not enough money was left to take the omnibus."[80] Clearly, the wedding—unlike that of Louÿs—was a quiet event, discussed only by those closest to him. As Arthur Fontaine announced to Francis Jammes, "Debussy was married. They say to a very pretty young face out of one of the most elegant couture houses in Paris."[81]

The young bride's health remained fragile and Claude still had "to buy all kinds of medicines" for her.[82] More than two years later, he would write to her from London: "The mysterious little being that you are has the unfortunate ability to acquire the most diverse and unexpected illnesses."[83] But in the period just after his wedding, he led a more regular existence and could get back to his "old" works, *La saulaie* and especially the *Nocturnes*. During the summer of 1898, he had declared to his publisher that he hoped these two works would be played before *Pelléas*, so as to prepare the public "for the *simplicity* of the latter."[84] For the time being, he confided to Godet: "I've begun to work again, an exercise to which my brain, clogged by thick and heavy problems, has become entirely unaccustomed."[85]

On 1 January 1901, Claude would give the short score of the *Nocturnes* to Lilly. He dedicated it to her with "the profound and passionate joy that I have in being her husband."[86]

Chapter Fourteen

Nocturnes

1900–1901

Genesis of the *Nocturnes*

The gestation of the *Nocturnes* is, of all of Debussy's works, the most difficult to reconstruct. The work's first iteration—that of the *Scènes au crépuscule*—was, as we have seen,[1] hypothetical to say the least. We know a bit more about his second idea, conceived for violin and orchestra, since the composer wrote to Lerolle on 28 August 1894 that he had begun three *Nocturnes* in which he intended to use "separate orchestral groups, in order to try to find nuances within these groups alone, because composers don't really risk enough in their music."[2] Whistler's influence is obvious here and indeed would have been perceived as such at the time when the work became known. The painter's biographer, Théodore Duret, would even attempt, as early as 1904, to compare the two art forms.[3] For various critics, Debussy would be the "Whistler of music."[4] We will recall that one month later, he outlined his plan to Ysaÿe, for whom the work was intended. On some undetermined date, perhaps near the beginning of 1894, Chausson wrote to Ysaÿe: "Debussy has already written the first part of your violin piece. I don't know it, and don't want to see it until my own piece is finished."[5] The composition of *Pelléas* subsequently delayed the continuation of Debussy's work, but he had scarcely completed his opera when he announced to Lerolle that he now wanted "to finish the three *Nocturnes*"[6]— his typical equivocal expression. In November 1896, everything changed when Ysaÿe let him know that he could not premiere his work. During the following year, the version for violin and orchestra was transformed into a symphonic version.

From the end of 1897 onward, the completion of these new *Nocturnes* became a leitmotif in Debussy's letters to Hartmann. On 25 June 1898, the composer reported for the first time that the score was finished,[7] but of course he was only talking about a rough draft, and the following months were spent orchestrating it. His correspondence shows how many other stages would still be needed: on 14 September, he declared that he had "reworked" two of the three *Nocturnes*,[8] and in early November he gave his publisher an "exuberant" performance of his composition;[9] then on 15 January 1899, he reported having started the orchestration all over again, and on the following 3 April, he mentioned having just rewritten the first movement.[10] Hartmann's patience was admirable, since on some ten occasions Debussy promised the score for the following week. Finally, in June 1899, he presented it to be bound but not engraved,[11] and it was only at the very end of the year that he could write: "Here are the 'Sirènes'!"[12] We can thus only believe the composer when he confessed that the *Nocturnes* "gave [him] more difficulty, the three of them, than the five acts of *Pelléas*!"[13]

Hope for *Pelléas*

André Messager, with whom Debussy had been somewhat acquainted since 1893, still had only scant experience as an orchestra conductor, but the success of Gustave Charpentier's *Louise*, which he had conducted, was also something of a credit to him. Georges Hartmann, one of the two librettists for his own opera *Madame Chrysanthème*, urged him to take a look at *Pelléas*. Debussy played some excerpts for him and, as the composer later explained to Maurice Emmanuel, at first Messager was surprised, then "sold."[14] The conductor broached the subject with Albert Carré, his colleague at the Opéra-Comique, and an audition took place around the middle of May 1898. "They must not have known the 'bear' for them to imagine that he would acquiesce to an audition," wrote Carré. "As it had to be completely private, I personally climbed up to the sixth floor of his little apartment on the rue Washington [*sic*].[15] Needless to say, I did not regret it."[16] The two men were won over by what they heard, and declared their intention to produce the work, but still unofficially, which was just as well, since the score was not yet finished.[17] Once Hartmann finally received the *Nocturnes*, he pressured Debussy into getting back to *Pelléas*, which the composer did around January 1900.[18] On 4 February, he wrote that he was in the process of "copying" it.[19] Accustomed to the delays of what he called this "incorrigible man,"[20] Hartmann set a nonnegotiable schedule for Debussy, as he was still anticipating a performance for the following winter:

> Yesterday I saw Messager. Carré is still quite amenable to performing *Pelléas* for next season. In every respect, it's important not to get on his bad side; *I therefore beg you* to give me *without fail* before 30 April, at the latest,[21] the *finished piano reduction* of *Pelléas*. I will really need all of *May and June* to have it engraved, July for the corrections, August to print it, and we *must* be able to give the parts to the artists by *September*. [. . .]

So, dear friend, don't *you yourself* be late; that's the advice I have to give you—and the favor I'd wish *for us*.[22] Unfortunately, I know what role the *financial side* plays in your impoverished life, and you must not allow yourself to be overwhelmed or controlled by events!

I may be rather verbose and preachy, but I assure you, I'm right about this and I have excellent reasons to caution you.[23]

But Debussy could not turn himself into a full-time copyist, especially because he made many corrections to his score along the way.

On 2 February, the production of Charpentier's *Louise* created a degree of attention that infuriated Debussy. He wrote at length to Louÿs and to Hartmann, expressing his disgust with this populist work, which he felt was based on "falseness" and "pomposity" and whose success shocked him. He concluded by declaring that "If it were possible to have *Pelléas* performed in Japan, I'd like that very much!"[24]

Yet during this period, he occasionally accepted invitations to the salons. Thus one Sunday, on 4 March 1900, he played Wagner's Prelude to *Tristan* at the home of the painter Édouard Dreyfus González. The audience included, notably, René Waldeck-Rousseau, the politician who guided the retrial and eventual pardon of Dreyfus, and Ricardo Viñes, a young Catalan pianist who noted the event in his journal but had not yet met his favorite composer, who (according to Viñes) quickly slipped away.[25]

Debussy's main concern, however, was the performance of his *Nocturnes*, the score of which had been published in February 1900. The initial plan was for it to be conducted by Colonne, who ultimately abandoned it: "The temporary death of my *Nocturnes*," Debussy wrote to Hartmann, "upsets me a lot. . . You know, all this is the fault of Wagner and his school."[26] The publisher then turned to Chevillard, who had recently taken charge of the Lamoureux concerts. Small consolations followed: on 10 March, the pianist Lucien Wurmser premiered Debussy's *Tarentelle styrienne* (a piece that had been composed about ten years earlier) at the Société nationale, and on 17 March, in the same venue, Debussy accompanied Blanche Marot, a singer friend of Hartmann, in the premiere of his *Chansons de Bilitis*. Once again, the response of the critics was inconsequential. In his review in *Le guide musical*, Hugues Imbert, who found the singer's tone "not very pleasant," penned only short, banal remarks on the subject of the "very odd and affected" works: "The composer," he added, "knew how to give a Grecian tinge to these rather licentious little poems!"[27]

Against this already gloomy backdrop arose an unexpected stroke of bad luck: Hartmann died suddenly, on 23 April. "This death truly saddens me," Debussy confided to Louÿs, "for this man was a providential being for me, and he brought to that role a good grace and a kind smile, qualities that are rather rare among art philanthropists."[28] This loss left the composer not only without a publisher but also virtually without financial support. He tried to restore

Lilly's confidence, evoking tears that, like rain, sometimes "fall almost happily because afterward the sun will shine... [...] However, we must struggle a little longer. And for that I'm counting on you, you who are my joy, my pleasure, my happiness, and also my highest and most beautiful hope."[29]

In the following months, the situation would become more tragic after Lilly became pregnant.[30] The young newlyweds could not possibly welcome a child into such lamentable conditions: Lilly underwent surgery and spent about ten days (14–23 August) in a clinic, at the maison Dubois.[31] Debussy again confided to Louÿs:

> But that's not all; it seems that her constitution is affected overall, and (just between us) she has signs of tuberculosis at the top of both lungs... We have to deal with this as quickly as possible by sending her to the Pyrénées for three to four months!... You can imagine what mental anguish this has caused, on top of our absolutely miserable financial state. You see the sum total of all the problems I've been experiencing for quite some time! I barely know which end is up after so many adverse events.[32]

La damoiselle élue at the World's Fair

The day after Lilly left the clinic, *La damoiselle élue* was performed as part of one of the concerts at the World's Fair. Debussy's potential inclusion on the program prompted a lively discussion within the selection committee. In the end, the Hayot Quartet played his String Quartet during the second official session, on 22 June, in the new Trocadéro palace, where the critics complained about hearing the "constant honking" of the streetcars and the "din of the crowd just outside."[33] *La damoiselle élue* was part of the seventh *grand concert* at the World's Fair. The performer was Blanche Marot, who had premiered the *Chansons de Bilitis* several months earlier, and whom Debussy thanked in a particularly warm letter: "The way in which you knew how to deliver 'all this is when he comes'[34] is one of the strongest musical emotions I've ever felt."[35]

Seven years after hearing *La damoiselle* at the Société nationale, certain critics still found it difficult to fully understand this already somewhat dated work. Adolphe Jullien saw in it only "floating visions, soft sighs of souls, vague calls of elves or of impalpable beings."[36] In his exploration of the work, Alfred Bruneau had a series of reservations, even while commending the "talent" of his former classmate from the Conservatoire: "The harmonic sophistication and the perpetual modulations relished by the composer diminish his work, rendering it both limp and bland. [...] Pre-Raphaelism, which is already sinking into oblivion, has been in fashion with us only fleetingly because it in no way aligns with our nature or our temperament."[37] Bruneau advised Debussy to write at last "music that suits the spirit and the genius of his race!"[38] On the contrary, Arthur Dandelot, the columnist of the *Monde musical*, had only praise to offer (apart from the orchestration, which he considered overdone) for a work of "exquisite poetic charm, like a pastel, or better, a stained glass of sounds that are deliberately softened and blurred."[39] The critic of the *Guide musical* found the instrumentation to be "delicate and refined," and in any case pointed out the public's favorable reception of *La damoiselle élue*.[40] Among the critics who had not yet weighed in on any of his works, one was of particular importance: Pierre Lalo,[41] the son of Édouard, who was becoming an arbiter of taste in *Le temps*. He wrote, "No composer, neither among the young nor the old, is endowed with a more appealing, more flexible, and more delicate melodic ingenuity, and in particular, no one is a more original, more refined, or more subtle harmonist."[42] In thanking him, Debussy paid special tribute to his father's memory, and he recalled having been thrown out of the Opéra for having applauded Édouard Lalo's *Namouna* too vigorously.[43]

Sometime in October, writing from Barcelona, where his wife was regaining her health, Louÿs suggested that Debussy compose incidental music to accompany the *Chansons de Bilitis* poems, which he intended to turn into *tableaux vivants*. Debussy accepted immediately, although he was very busy with rehearsals for the *Nocturnes* and dealing for the first time with Camille Chevillard, who was about "as pleasant as a bear cage."[44] The latter had agreed to conduct his symphonic triptych only if the third part—"Sirènes"—were removed, because the Nouveau Théâtre could not easily accommodate the placement of a chorus.

Premiere of the First Two *Nocturnes*

"Nuages" and "Fêtes" were thus premiered at the Lamoureux concerts, under the direction of Chevillard, on 9 December 1900. Maurice Ravel was present, as was Ricardo Viñes, who met Erik Satie there for the first time. "Divine, divine, divine," noted Viñes in his journal,[45] while Mme de Saint-Marceaux-Verdurin wrote: "Exquisite works of art. Music of dreams and impressions. [. . .] This music realizes all my artistic desires, it epitomizes my most intense feelings."[46]

A week later, Debussy confessed to Louÿs that he had been "reading the newspapers too much for the past few days."[47] He had found in them the same trite reservations that his works had always received—about his strangeness and his slightly morbid originality—but, for the first time, a certain understanding of the nature of his art also appeared. For Pierre de Bréville, his friend at the Société nationale, the score defied analysis, because its composer did "not ask of music all that it can give, but that which it alone is capable of suggesting."[48] Jean d'Udine, hardly given to easy praise, opined that Debussy's score "does not express itself in the sinuosity of defined melodic curves, but in its arrangements of timbres and chords—its harmony, as painters would say—maintaining at least something of a very strict homogeneity, which replaces the line with the equally supple beauty of sonorities that are knowingly arranged and logically sustained."[49] Alfred Bruneau, for once less reserved, stated: "There is nothing to the themes at all, in the traditional sense of the word, but the harmonies and rhythms suffice to convey the composer's thoughts in the most original and striking way."[50] And a newcomer, Gaston Carraud, a former pupil of Massenet, continued in the same vein by writing that "like a painter of prismatic colors, guided by a delicate and very sure taste, he knows how to combine harmonies and timbres, by means of infinitely evolving connections."[51] The anonymous critic of *La vie parisienne* preferred to list droll images that had come to mind: "Rustling pendants, chattering sistrums, dissipating fog at the edge of the bluish woods, flexible elegance of melodies in flight, pursued in vain, unraveled in the wind."[52]

Paul Dukas's article was the last to appear. In the *Revue hebdomadaire*, he declared his preference for "Nuages"; on the subject of "Fêtes," he posed a rather absurd question: had the music preceded the program or *vice versa*?[53] In thanking him, Debussy gently pointed out that the work was about "lingering impressions of a celebration in the Bois de Boulogne."[54] However, the composer tried to make Dukas understand that the essential issue was elsewhere, that he was "no longer, or almost no longer, thinking in musical terms,"[55] and that people should get away from their desks: "It's just useless to believe that music begets *thinking*! [. . .] It would suffice for music to force people to *listen*, in spite of themselves."[56]

The Programming of *Pelléas*

On 3 May 1901, great news arrived at Debussy's home on the rue Cardinet: a written promise from Albert Carré to produce *Pelléas* for the following season. Two days later, Debussy could not resist the pleasure of telling Pierre Louÿs.[57] The following Sunday, after a concert,[58] the writer arrived at Willy's home at 93 rue de Courcelles, and waved that letter in front of the guests: Colette immediately sent Vuillermoz, a young "ghostwriter" of Willy's at the time, to fetch some champagne to celebrate the event.[59] On 30 May, Maeterlinck traveled to Paris for a week and summoned Debussy: "Beginning tomorrow, I shall await you. I'll be pleased to see you again, to shake your hand, and to speak of our *Pelléas*."[60] At the playwright's insistent suggestion that Debussy entrust the role of Mélisande to his mistress, Georgette Leblanc, the composer replied evasively and attempted to object, claiming that the role was vocally minimal and demanded a great deal of flexibility. In point of fact, he felt that "not only does she sing out of tune, but she speaks out of tune."[61] Sometime thereafter, the singer, who had read through the score, replied to his objections:

> You could not possibly believe how impassioned I am by your work—it fulfills everything I've dreamed of. . . While your wishes are very clear, I don't find the singer's part to be minimal. . .
>
> Don't do me the injustice of continuing to believe that I perhaps wouldn't be "flexible"; on the contrary, I'm happy to yield to that which is true and beautiful. . .
>
> I sang a few of Mélisande's lines to Maurice, and he understood perfectly; he found the words "more beautiful thus." It's the triumph of your [compositional] logic. . .
>
> I remain so surprised, so delighted finally to find an operatic work that makes such perfect sense.[62]

On 6 August 1901, Claude left with Lilly for a full month in Bichain, where his father-in-law, now retired, had withdrawn. The day before his departure, Debussy was anxious to confirm the strength of his feelings to a new friend, Paul-Jean Toulet. This young writer had been introduced to him by Maurice Sailland, alias Curnonsky, who was working with him in "Willy's studio."[63] His lighthearted and refined imagination had immediately captivated the composer: "From the first day on," the writer had to confess, "we were bosom buddies."[64]

In Burgundy, Debussy wrote to Raoul Bardac that "the minutes pass without our knowing exactly how";[65] while nature remained beautiful, the "folk" of the region no longer stopped their work whenever the angelus tolled to strike "a solemn and chiseled pose"[66]—a turn of phrase that satisfied Debussy enough to reuse in his column in the 15 November issue of *La revue blanche*.[67] He wrote to Curnonsky that he was relaxing by reading Ponson du Terrail's adventures of Rocambole.[68] But he undoubtedly was working on the orchestration of *Pelléas* in particular. In a letter written in verse, Louÿs asked him already on 14 August 1900:

> Are you orchestrating *Pelléas*
> Beneath the flutes of Mélisande?[69]

Premiere of the Three *Nocturnes*

On 27 October 1901, Chevillard conducted the three *Nocturnes* at the Lamoureux concerts, with Beethoven's Ninth Symphony on the same program. This premiere of the complete *Nocturnes* sparked contradictory reactions from the audience: "Some people found an excuse to jeer vigorously, especially the third movement," wrote Debussy to Toulet,[70] and according to one critic, the wild applause from a small group was said to have provoked opposite reactions in another portion of the audience.[71]

Was the performance of this relatively new score completely satisfactory to its composer? That is unlikely, even if one questions the authenticity of the oft-reported dialogue between him and Chevillard during the final rehearsal, noted by Louis Laloy, a young musicologist and critic who would go on to become such a champion of Debussy: "I'd like that more blurred —Faster? —No, more blurred —Slower? —More blurred —I don't know what you mean to say. Gentlemen, let's resume!"[72] Laloy went on to claim that, "while pretending to have understood nothing of Debussy's remark, [Chevillard] had begun the passage again, while trying to comply with the composer's wishes."[73] The fact remains that Debussy, although a strong presence at the rehearsals, could not have prevented the female voices of the "Sirènes" from singing slightly out of tune, and that, besides, the conductor was naturally inclined toward more traditionally constructed works. Still, writing under the guise of M. Croche, Debussy made a point of thanking Chevillard for his "marvelous and comprehensive understanding of the music!"[74]

Curiously, the critics' response was somewhat less favorable for the entire work than it was for the partial performance. The same adjectives always appeared: "elusive and nearly imperceptible [. . . and] a little disconcerting,"[75] "never-ending chromaticism,"[76] and "arhythmic, imprecise, androgynous inspirations."[77] Attempting to analyze his "impression" after the event, Jean Marnold declared that "as poignant as it had been for us in its unexpected novelty, it would become dull in the long run."[78] In his regular column in *Le temps*, Pierre Lalo also spoke of his impression, especially with respect to the third movement of the work:

> One cannot imagine more supple intertwining of voices, more exquisite melodic contours, more graceful and more strange sonorities than those of the sirens' song. And its subtlety is so extreme that once again I feel myself seized by uneasiness when faced with M. Debussy's art; an anxiety mixes with the exquisite pleasure that it gives. This music is refined to such an extent that it ends up making people lose their taste for all other music; seasoned musicians as well as music lovers can no longer listen to anyone but Debussy.[79]

While thanking the critic, Debussy declared his surprise at Lalo's discomfort:

> I denounce deviancy! . . .
> In my opinion, a deviant art exists only very rarely or, if you will, suits only those people whose souls have become slightly tainted, and I would be sad if one fine day, my works could no longer be performed except "clandestinely."
> Please understand that I'm only trying—in short, and very tentatively—to extricate music from a legacy of heavy traditions, wrongly interpreted, and under which this art could well collapse, if we are not careful.[80]

Chapter Fifteen

The Composer as Critic

1901–3

Compositional Activities at the Beginning of 1901

At the beginning of 1901, a rather surprising event occurred: after so many aborted projects with Pierre Louÿs, the incidental music for the *Chansons de Bilitis* was finally performed in the reception room of the *Journal*, although it was not repeated at the Théâtre des Variétés, as had been originally discussed. "I'm spending every afternoon this week with nude women," Louÿs wrote to his brother.[1] The production consisted of short scenes depicting twelve of the songs, delivered by Mlle Milton, for which Debussy had written a "delicate mélange" for two harps, two flutes, and a Mustel celeste.[2] The performance took place on 7 February 1901 for an audience of three hundred people, who, according to the *Journal*'s cheeky columnist, "were able to feel themselves transported to the great epochs of pure nudity."[3] This work, which could hardly be described as Symbolist, was the last creation of its kind in which Debussy participated, and it contributed nothing to his reputation.

In order to take a break from the laborious task of correcting and copying *Pelléas*, the composer worked on two very different pieces for piano. Between January and April, he first composed a three-piece suite, titled simply *Pour le piano*, that would become commercially available in September; he offered the manuscript to a new pupil, Nicolas Coronio, who became something of a friend.[4] Even more surprising was the appearance in April of a piece for two pianos, written in a style that Debussy had long ago abandoned: *Lindaraja*, whose title came from one of the patios of the Alhambra in Grenada, an image that he had perhaps encountered in an illustrated periodical and kept in his portfolio.

He was also preoccupied with the two-piano reduction of his *Nocturnes*. Instead of calling upon experienced musicians, such as his friend Dukas, and even though he had undertaken this task himself for the *Prélude à l'après-midi d'un faune*, he decided to entrust the transcription to two young composers who were still at the Conservatoire: Maurice Ravel and Raoul Bardac. The latter, who since 1899 had also been his composition "pupil," was the son of a society lady, an amateur singer who had inspired Fauré's *La bonne chanson*. According to Roger Martin du Gard, who had been his classmate at the Lycée Condorcet, Raoul had an "artist's sensibility and a quick intelligence, supported by an incredible memory and exceptional intuitions."[5] On 8 April 1901, Ravel, who found him sensitive but a little aloof, described to Florent Schmitt the division of labor envisioned by Debussy: "Since I've shown some skill for this type of work, it fell on me alone to transcribe the third movement, 'Sirènes,' perhaps the most perfectly beautiful one and surely the most perilous, all the more since it hasn't been performed."[6] In the preceding months, Debussy had in fact made friends with a few of those who would go on to be called "the Apaches" and who admired his works: besides Ravel, and soon thereafter Viñes, there was Lucien Garban, who was also a student at the Conservatoire and to whom Debussy dedicated copies of *Pour le piano* and the *Trois mélodies* of Verlaine.[7] On 4 August, remarking on the fact that Ravel had won only second place in the Prix de Rome, Debussy wrote to Garban: "Ravel certainly should have won the prize straightaway, which first of all would have rid him of this slightly unfortunate honorific, which gives pleasure for only one day!. . . because it is, after all, nothing but an insufficiently gilded necklace that the Institut slips around your neck."[8]

Critic at *La revue blanche*

On 1 April 1901, Debussy became a critic, acquiring a musical platform in *La revue blanche*, one of the most esteemed journals in the literary and artistic world of Paris. This periodical had been published since 1891 under the direction of the Natanson brothers, who already knew Debussy because Pierre Louÿs had invited them to his home to hear the completed portions of *Pelléas* at the end of May 1894. Prior to Debussy's appointment, three music critics had written successively for the journal: the ultra-Wagnerian Alfred Ernst, a former student at the École polytechnique; then Gauthier-Villars (Willy); and, since 1898, André Corneau. In addition, Debussy had several friends among the regular contributors to the periodical: Ferdinand Herold, Pierre Quillard, André Gide, Henri de Régnier, and Maurice Denis.[9] The eclectic tone of *La revue blanche*, which often included both irony and humor, could only have pleased him. Whereas Louÿs distanced himself from the publication because of its pro-Dreyfus stance, Debussy's participation demonstrates his own impartial attitude on the issue.

Prior to this time, Debussy had been only vaguely inclined to write reviews. For several months, at the end of 1893 and the beginning of 1894, the periodical *L'idée libre* had announced the forthcoming publication of an article by him titled "De l'inutilité du wagnérisme" (On the uselessness of Wagnerism).[10] Perhaps Pierre Louÿs, his close friend at the time, dissuaded him from writing it. In any case, the study never appeared, and it is possible that not a single line of it was ever written. But its mere announcement was in itself intriguing. Paul Dukas wrote to Vincent d'Indy as follows: "I have no idea what it might be. But when it's published, I'll get a copy. It might well be profound, and, as the saying aptly goes: out of the mouths of babes comes the truth. The title is great, don't you think? You can sense the author's point of view."[11]

In accepting the job of critic, Debussy introduced an element of regularity into his life that was new to him: every two weeks, he had to choose noteworthy performances from the current musical events or, more precisely, those on which he had a personal point of view to express—"sincere and honestly felt impressions."[12] It was neither a matter of discussing "time-honored works"[13] nor of presenting analyses that dissected them "like curious watches,"[14] as he wrote from the outset in his first article.

The readers of *La revue blanche* had thus been duly warned, and for four months (except in the summer) they had indeed only a selective and very subjective picture of current musical events in Paris. On the Société nationale's concert of 20 March, for example, Debussy dwelt solely on Mussorgsky's song cycle *The Nursery*, deliberately omitting mention of his former fiancée, Thérèse Roger, who had sung some Chausson songs. He reported nothing on the 26 April concert of the same Société, where works by Chabrier, Bréville, and Séverac were performed, though he thought highly of them. He might have taken an interest in young Henri Busser's songs, performed at the Chevillard concerts—among them "L'archet," on a poem by Charles Cros that he had attempted to set to music himself a few years earlier.[15] He impulsively dashed off two pages when Paul Dukas's sonata was published,[16] but then he reported its premiere in two lines, failing to mention the name of the pianist, Édouard Risler.[17] As for Schubert's songs, we learn only that "their scent recalls the bottoms of the drawers that belong to some sweet provincial spinsters. . . ends of faded ribbons. . . pressed flowers."[18] As a critic, Debussy's lack of curiosity about operatic singing was such that he did not even bother to listen for voices that might be suitable for casting in *Pelléas*. He thus presumably did not attend a performance by Jean Périer, who on 6 July sang in Georges Pfeiffer's opera buffa, the *Légataire universel* (based on Regnard), because Debussy's alter ego M. Croche never mentioned it. In fact, Périer would go on to become the first Pelléas. But for choice in casting, the composer no doubt had confidence in Albert Carré, whose "wonders" he extolled.[19] Debussy would also try to be tactful in the praise he bestowed on Camille Chevillard,[20] about whom he would complain bitterly a few years later but who would then go on to conduct the *Nocturnes*. This was not the case, on the other hand, for Augustin Savard, his former colleague from the Villa Medici, whose work was hailed as follows: "Will more music perhaps follow this overture? One would really hope so."[21]

The overall tone of his eight columns for *La revue blanche* stood out completely from the style typical of all the other newspaper critics. Debussy did not aim to give his readers information; rather, he did his utmost to disseminate his own ideas on opera, on the symphony, and—suddenly and without reference to a particular event—on music played outdoors. Edmund Bailly had just published his pamphlet *Le son dans la nature* (1900),[22] in which, harkening back to the cosmogony of Edgar Allan Poe, he evoked "the music of plants," the "vegetative harmonies," or the "great symphony of the vegetal world."[23] The readers of *La revue blanche* were invited in turn to dream of "the beautiful lesson of freedom contained in the flowering of the trees"[24] or of "the mysterious collaboration of the air, the movement of the leaves, and the scent of the flowers with the music."[25]

Monsieur Croche

M. Croche, who claimed that his profession was that of an "antidilettante,"[26] finally made his appearance in the *Revue blanche* on 1 July 1901. Debussy used this appellation in only two articles—on 1 July and 15 November—and for very precise purposes: first, to criticize Pierre Lalo for having invoked Beethoven, Schumann, and Chopin regarding Dukas's sonata;[27] and second, to condemn the institution of the Prix de Rome[28] and to take Saint-Saëns and his *Barbares* to task.[29] As well, in a more general way, he advanced for the first time a few principles of his musical Credo.[30] While Edward Lockspeiser's claim—that the conversation with M. Croche constituted "the key to the thoughts of its author on music"[31]—might have been an overstatement, one must admit that assertions such as the following could only be entrusted to an alter ego: "I try to forget music [that I've heard] because it gets in my way when listening to music that is new today or that I will get to know tomorrow... [...] You are stuck in a rut because you know nothing outside of music and you agree to follow strange and barbarous rules."[32]

M. Croche had a very close precursor in M. Teste. Valéry's *La soirée avec M. Teste* (no doubt inspired by Degas)[33] had appeared in December 1896 in the second issue of the short-lived *Le centaure*, where Debussy had several friends, as we have seen.[34] The similarities between the two "chaps" have often been raised.[35] Valéry was naturally one of the first to be struck by the resemblance, while remaining a good sport regarding a composer with whom he had conversed on friendly terms five or six years earlier. He wrote to Pierre Louÿs:

I have the consolation of rereading my old works, now under the guise of music criticism. I have to tell you that I never would have dreamed this would happen. I don't know if you've read the *Entretien avec M. Croche*, but C. A. D. has certainly read *La soirée avec M. Teste*. I found it so comical—following the precedent of Leonardo da Vinci himself,[36] who made contributions in the musical domain (but of course he was multitalented, a true Renaissance man)—that I regretted not having written any more in order to provide longer passages for similar adaptation. Very curious and—all things considered—flattering, isn't it? Goodness![37]

Was it before or after the appearance of M. Croche that, one evening while talking with Debussy, Valéry thought to suggest that he write the music for a very original production, of which there is no trace in the composer's correspondence? His idea involved a ballet, but one without an actual program, based on the contrast between traditional dancers and female mimes, full of "gestures, smiles, and desirable anecdotes."[38] Valéry added in his letter: "Can't the music—yours, in this case—have a similarly dual nature, and be distinct in itself, despite the apparent unity of its sound [with the visual production], much as the facial expressions of the dancers are removed from the action of their *entrechats* [on stage]?"[39] At that time, Valéry was thinking about the Orpheus myth.[40]

The idea expressed in this letter from January 1901, even if it doubtless appeared a bit vague to Debussy, continued to take shape in the rich imagination of Valéry, who later recalled with greater precision the structural principles of his production:

I told Debussy that I envisioned an extravagant system based on an analysis of elements and on a rigorous (albeit arbitrary) set of principles by which I would assign a very clear and precise task to each of these elements.

Thus, the orchestra and the voice took on utterly distinct functions, and the dramatic action, mime, and dance were strictly separated and produced, each in its own time, for a specified duration. I went so far, I believe, as to divide the space of the stage into places, planes, and levels; these different areas, in each work, were to be assigned to this or that group of singers, dancers, or mimes, or even to a certain character, to the exclusion of all the others. My system gave a role to each part of the space as one would give to the actors. It was the same for time, divided and even... clocked. Moreover, the lighting and the scenery had to submit to no less rational conditions, and the total production would represent the most exacting system of constraints and division of labor that one could imagine.[41]

With performances of *Pelléas* approaching, Debussy was certainly not prepared to follow such systematic views, and Valéry concluded: "Debussy, naturally, viewed this apparently extremely complex idea, though very simple in principle, as quite unimportant; and since I saw it as merely a whim, the matter was not pursued."[42] It was not until 1929–31 that this failed *Orphée* would become Arthur Honegger's *Amphion*, in which Ida Rubinstein danced.[43]

But to return to *La revue blanche*, even if Debussy's few articles were far from being perfect in form, they had attracted attention to the composer's independent thought, and to his detachment from the "standard repertoire." However, this literary work, for which he was hardly prepared, did not flow easily from his pen, and the few manuscripts of articles that have reached us show numerous corrections and revisions. For the last of them, devoted to Massenet, Debussy asked the chief editor Félix Fénéon for some modifications late in the process,[44] and in December 1901, he finally relinquished his column, giving his reasons: "Overwork and aggravation from these last months are why I'm unable to write anything appropriate. At any rate, I tried. . . [This process] is relentlessly mindless!"[45]

At the end of 1902, Debussy felt the need to write criticism again, opening with views that might seem somewhat paradoxical. For the *Renaissance latine* monthly journal, he wrote an article titled "Considérations sur la musique en plein air" (Thoughts on open-air music), which advocated, with a humorous tone, for an expansion of the repertoire for barrel organ and for a music of "vocal and instrumental boldness" that would not feel confined.[46] Faced with this unexpected prose from the composer of *Pelléas*, the director of the journal simply inscribed "But, this is idiotic!" at the top of the proofs.[47] Hence Debussy promised to contribute to *Gil Blas* instead.

Critic for *Gil Blas*

He took on the fairly heavy responsibility of writing reviews for *Gil Blas* at the beginning of 1903. Although the tone of this daily was lighter and more "Parisian" than that of *La revue blanche* (which, incidentally, stopped publication in 1903), he had agreed to pen a weekly column. As a result, from January to June, he would write no fewer than twenty-five articles! Naturally, since he was not experienced in this literary practice, it took even more time away from his work as a composer, work that proceeded unabated. The paper envisioned giving equal weight to two rather differing opinions; for music, Debussy was thus paired with Colette, Willy's spouse and ghost writer, who offered a perspective on musical events that was less erudite but just as personal.[48]

The first article necessitated a trip to Brussels, since it was devoted to a work performed at the Théâtre de la Monnaie on 7 January: *L'étranger* by Vincent d'Indy. The two composers were not yet at loggerheads because of ideological differences, although the first part of d'Indy's *Cours de composition* had just appeared. Debussy expressed relative praise for *L'étranger*, as d'Indy had done for *Pelléas*. While he lamented its having "too much music" and its seeming to be "veiled," he dwelled at length on the libretto in order to speak less of the score, and he chose to write a bit hyperbolically in describing "the unforgettable beauty of so many pages in *L'étranger*."[49] D'Indy was so touched by this article that he took up his pen to tell its author, in an almost affectionate way: "What stands out for me at the moment is the joy of knowing that my work is cherished by the composer of *Pelléas*."[50] Another cause for his satisfaction—which would not last—was the warm description that Debussy gave of the school on the rue Saint-Jacques (the Schola Cantorum, which d'Indy had cofounded): a "little corner of Paris, where a love of music is everything."[51]

Emergence of the "National Tradition"

Some of the subsequent articles from *Gil Blas* confirm Debussy's conversion to an ideal of a national tradition, a notion to which he had already alluded in October 1902.[52] Contributing to this new focus were two events, the first of which was the performance of the first two acts of Rameau's *Castor et Pollux* at the Schola Cantorum, under the direction of Vincent d'Indy. On 2 February, Debussy wrote a positively enthusiastic article in which he repeated his definition of French music—"that clarity of expression, that precision, and that conciseness of form"[53]—and then declared that Rameau's work was "made of delicate and charming tenderness, of proper accents, of rigorous declamation in the recitatives, without that affectation of Germanic profundity."[54] For the first time, he named Gluck as the composer responsible for the wrong turn that French music had supposedly taken. On 23 February, Debussy's famous "Open letter to M. le Chevalier C. W. Gluck" was published on the occasion of the Opéra-Comique's revival of *Iphigénie en Tauride*, staged by Albert Carré. Debussy wrote about the work's poor prosody and its "almost uniformly pompous style,"[55] and he addressed Gluck directly in this paradoxical comparison: "Wagnerian formulae, in embryonic state, are already in your work"[56] and yet "Rameau was infinitely more Greek than you."[57]

One year later, he would repeat some of these declarations in an interview with Paul Landormy.[58] Once again, we find his definition of French music ("the clarity, the elegance, the simple and natural declamation"), the references to Rameau and Couperin, and the criticism of Gluck and Berlioz.[59] But this interview also contained an exaggerated opinion allegedly made by Debussy—"Massenet understood the true role of musical art"—accompanied by this remark: "One must rid music from all scientific methods. Music must humbly seek to give pleasure" (a rather empty formula that the official discourse on Debussy has continually rehashed).[60] Debussy reacted immediately to the outrageous remark that had been attributed to him, and confided to Louis Laloy: "It's extraordinary, how badly this so-called musician hears."[61]

It is important to try to understand why, through the success of *Pelléas*, Debussy suddenly appeared to be invested with a new role in the artistic arena of his country. His turn toward an aesthetic of national tradition is best explained by the ideas disseminated by writers who, at the time, were trying to find their way in discussing the legacy of Symbolism. The composer was always quite aware of the movements that bridged artistic and literary life. From 1890 on, had not Jean Moréas advocated for a "communion" with the poets of the Middle Ages and the Renaissance? Now, as an extension of his "Romanesque" school, there was something of a return to classical sources at this time, particularly among journals such as *L'ermitage* and *L'occident*. Some small groups agitated for this idea, among them the future music critic and historian Adolphe Boschot, who wrote in a letter about an ephemeral French school: "We are aware of being only one link in a great and glorious chain."[62] Did Debussy also find a reason for his rejection of Berlioz in Charles Maurras's criticism of Romanticism,[63] which held this movement responsible for the degradation of true beauty? Did he not already subscribe to the ideas of Adrien Mithouard,[64] who rejected cosmopolitanism? Besides, in this conceptual shift, he caught up with some of his former Symbolist associates, such as Viélé-Griffin, Maurice Denis, and Stuart Merrill, and he would soon favor, among poets, Charles d'Orléans and Tristan l'Hermite over Baudelaire and Verlaine.

Primarily from 1903 onward, this notion of neoclassicism became crystallized in the new generation of writers. During this time, it carried none of the backward-looking connotations that it would later have.[65]

In spite of the appearance of this "ideology," Debussy's columns in *Gil Blas*, on the whole, conveyed his general musical opinions. The first article certainly revived M. Croche, but it portrayed a slight warning against the terrible practices that can stem from tradition: "Saint-Saëns is by definition a traditional composer. He has accepted its conditions of dryness and forced submission."[66] Debussy considered him the "official head of the young French school," whereas he saw Vincent d'Indy as "the chosen head of a still younger group."[67] While Debussy excoriated his former colleagues Edmond Missa, Alfred Bachelet, and Alfred Bruneau in a rather fraternal tone, his friend Paul Dukas, who had just produced his *Variations, interlude et final sur un thème de Rameau*, was put in his place with this brutally honest comment: "I prefer my Dukas without Rameau."[68] In comparison, Massenet, "the musical historian of the feminine soul,"[69] was spared as one whose music could be loved "with an almost forbidden passion."[70] Going back in time, Debussy hardly referenced anyone except Berlioz, "the favorite composer of those who know little about music," who mistakenly took Gluck as a model, and whose influence "on modern music" was "practically nonexistent."[71] Finally, the only composers to receive emphatic praise—whatever reservations may have existed—remained the Germans: Wagner ("[The *Ring*] is as irresistible as the sea")[72] and Richard Strauss (who "is very close to being a genius").[73] This did not prevent our critic from concluding, "Let's stick with France."[74] But was Rameau really enough to represent a national tradition all by himself? Debussy's position on the matter appeared to be based on principle, although it was hardly consistent with his opinions on the whole.

Chapter Sixteen

Pelléas et Mélisande

1902

Debussy had decided at the end of 1901 to entrust the premiere of his new piano work, *Pour le piano*, to a young Catalan pianist, Ricardo Viñes, who had been living in Paris for roughly fifteen years. He was a good friend of Maurice Ravel and had earned his first prize in piano at the Conservatoire in 1894.[1] Enthusiastic by nature, his tastes in literature and painting—for Poe, Baudelaire, Huysmans, and Odilon Redon—could not have failed to appeal to Debussy. The composer had heard him play at the Société nationale and had confessed to Ravel that he liked his sound very much.[2] On 30 November 1901, Viñes came to the rue Cardinet to play Debussy's new suite by heart for both the composer and Ravel;[3] he then returned two more times, once in the presence of Lucien Garban, to perform the work for Debussy, who seemed very satisfied.[4] This was the beginning of a collaboration that would last for more than ten years. The first public hearing of the "Prelude"–"Sarabande"–"Toccata" took place on 11 January 1902 at the Société nationale, to which Debussy was ever faithful, and, as Viñes wrote in his diary: "It was such a phenomenal success [. . .] that I could have encored everything."[5] In fact, the only movement that was given an encore was the "Toccata," which at times reminded the critic for the *Guide musical* of "the good humor of Emmanuel Chabrier."[6]

In his column in *Le temps*, Pierre Lalo lavished high praise for the work, while repeating the remark he had already made concerning the *Nocturnes*: "We are most often swept away by its magic, but irritated at times by being subjected to its spell."[7] The other, more banal critics noticed the "harmonic rustlings" (Samazeuilh)[8] and the "colorful and picturesque pages" (Dandelot)[9] of a score that was the first of the masterpieces for piano from the composer's maturity.

Albert Carré and the Opéra-Comique

The plan of attack for the production of *Pelléas* was already underway. After the first contacts with Messager and Carré, in May 1898, Debussy had gradually given up his beautiful Symbolist dreams for an "exclusive" performance of his opera, and, under pressure from Hartmann, came around to the solution of having it produced at the Opéra-Comique. Moreover, on 14 July 1898, he asked his publisher to demand "an agreement so that they won't be able to drag this out for centuries,"[10] but it became clear to him the following year, from reading the theater program for the next season, that things were still in the same state. When Carré's written promise finally arrived, on 3 May 1901, Debussy resigned himself once and for all, knowing that there were no other options. But he was surely sincere when he wrote to Louÿs from Bichain, on 2 September 1901, that he feared he would again encounter in Paris "the apathy that the place called the Opéra-Comique epitomizes for me."[11] Even though we do not know the exact date of his letter to René Peter, in which he announced that he had just withdrawn his work from that theater, there is no doubt that the Opéra-Comique was the ultimate destination for the work.[12] Later accounts, at the time of the *Pelléas* revivals, would only confirm his state of mind, as in his comments to Jacques Durand in 1903.[13]

Most of the accounts concerning the premiere of *Pelléas* imply to the reader that this work was so highly anticipated that all forces, conscious of the event's importance, were mobilized in its favor, and that the entire traditional context of fashionable repertoire had receded into the background for its benefit. The reality, however, was quite different.

At the outset, Carré himself had been hesitant to list *Pelléas* among the many works on his theater's playbill. According to Messager, Carré was envisioning instead some "performances that were not part of the regular season, or some special matinees, intended for Sunday concert-goers."[14] It was Messager who supposedly convinced him not to appear to "emphasize the work's unique aspects."[15]

Activities at the Opéra-Comique unfolded at an impressive pace; the number of productions at the beginning of 1902 (including the matinees, of course) was 37 in January, 35 in February, and 36 in March! Charpentier's *Louise* (which had already surpassed 100 performances) and Massenet's *Grisélidis* alternated as the most frequently performed, more often than Gounod's *Mireille* and Massenet's *Manon*. This did not prevent the theater from also celebrating the 900th performance of Bizet's *Carmen*, all while beginning preparations for Georges Hüe's *Titania* almost simultaneously with those for *Pelléas*. Busser wrote, not without reason: "In this theater, one must really be able to be everywhere at once!"[16] This schedule makes one's head spin, considering what it meant for the staff as well as for those in charge of the music—that is to say,

André Messager for the orchestra, Henri Busser for the choruses, Louis Landry for the vocal rehearsals, and the director Albert Carré. One might also call into question the musical quality of productions that were given at such a frantic pace. During that time, most of the critical attention was directed toward the first Parisian performance of Wagner's *Götterdämmerung* at the Théâtre du Château d'Eau, under the patronage of the Grandes auditions musicales de France. It was in rehearsal under the baton of Alfred Cortot and, after having been announced for 5 May, was ultimately postponed until 17 May. That was the big event, much more so than Debussy's opera, and at the same time, the town council was preoccupied with naming a street in Paris after Richard Wagner![17]

Rehearsals for *Pelléas*

Pelléas thus found itself on the "production line" of a national theater for which it had certainly not been conceived and where professionalism was hardly separable from a certain routine. The casting was nothing less than exceptional. The press had begun to report on it at the beginning of December: *Le ménestrel* announced that Mary Garden would be Mélisande.[18] This Scottish soprano, a student of Lucien Fugère, was not an unknown quantity; she had attracted attention in April 1900 when, at the last minute, she replaced Marthe Rioton in *Louise*,[19] and she went on to sing the title role of Gabriel Pierné's *La fille de Tabarin* in February 1901, in a cast that also included Jean Périer. On 25 February, she was still singing in *Louise* (the 139th performance) while in the midst of rehearsals for *Pelléas*. At the end of 1901 and beginning of 1902, Périer (Pelléas), who had participated in the premiere of Messager's *Véronique* in 1898, was appearing in Daniel Auber's *Le domino noir* and Messager's *La basoche*, even while rehearsing Arthur Coquard's *La troupe Jolicœur*. Both Hector Dufranne (Golaud) and Félix Vieuille (Arkel) were also performing in Gustave Charpentier's *Louise* and in Édouard Lalo's *Le roi d'Ys*. These singers thus did not descend from the heavens, as one might infer when reading certain commentaries that arose from the legend of *Pelléas*; rather, they were resident performers, fully versed in the standard repertoire of the Opéra-Comique. The main set designer, Lucien Jusseaume, belonged to the naturalist tradition that was opposed to all things avant-garde; he was considered a specialist in landscapes and had been working continuously at the Opéra-Comique for four years.

Around April 1900, Debussy finalized his piano-vocal score of *Pelléas*, in anticipation of a performance that he was told had been set for the following season. The first three acts were probably entrusted to Fromont, the publisher who was Hartmann's successor, during summer 1901.[20] On 28

August 1901, Debussy wrote to him: "Talk to me about *Pelléas*," and then insisted, on 2 September: "You aren't giving me any news [. . .] that worries me. [. . .] There's not a day to lose."[21] Finally, the last two acts were delivered, probably in September. The time to engrave and correct the proofs of the five acts was very short, so much so that the singers had to work from proofs during the rehearsals. The piano-vocal score did not appear until the beginning of May 1902,[22] while the orchestral score would not see the light of day until 1904.

After the combined rehearsals had started, Messager opened them up to a few musicians and critics who were curious to be the first to hear this work. Debussy himself intervened so that Godet, who had assisted him at the last moment in correcting the orchestral parts, would be allowed entry; this same Godet, at the end of one rehearsal, took him to the Austin bar and introduced him to the eccentric Symbolist painter Henry de Groux. Paul Poujaud and André Hallays were also able to make their way into the hall. One newspaper, *Le monde artiste*, even published the reactions of one of the privileged listeners, who tried to give his readers a foretaste of the work's musical structure:

> The musicians who heard the score that M. Debussy has written on M. Maeterlinck's play agree that it is the most original music that has been composed since Wagner.
>
> This week one of them said to us: It's absolutely novel music, without a precise tonality, somewhat drifting but with an intense flavor, personality, and expression. No chord suggests dominance of this or that key. If, by chance, one encounters a major or minor triad, it quickly leads to something else that is vague. And the metric organization shares in this pursuit, this novelty. Many of the measures are in $\frac{6}{4}$ and $\frac{9}{4}$. Certainly, these sorts of time signatures are not new, but never have six beats been given such rhythms or been beaten in this way.
>
> As for the declamation, it is no less original. M. Debussy has devised a style of *parlando* whose origin one might recognize in Italian scores, but which he wrote and measured in his own way. [. . .] In addition, the vocal part is almost always written in the middle range of the voice. Mlle Garden has scarcely more than two or three high notes in her entire part.[23]

Conflict with Maeterlinck

As soon as Maeterlinck learned from the press that Mary Garden had been chosen for the role of Mélisande, he sent a letter to Carré (on 15 January). In it, he expressed his hope that the director would be civil enough to grant his "natural and legitimate desire" to assign the role to his mistress Georgette Leblanc, objecting that the registration form for *Pelléas* at the Société des auteurs was signed by Debussy alone and not by himself, and that it had been backdated to 3 May 1901 but not deposited until 30 December 1901.[24] By 27 January, Debussy believed that there was nothing more to fear, and announced his victory to Peter and Coronio: "With Maeterlinck, it's in the bag [. . .] Carré is cool as a cucumber. . ."[25]

Nevertheless, the playwright threatened to stand in the way of the performances, and discussions with him quickly became public. He decided to bring the dispute before the Société des auteurs, which took up the matter at its meeting on the following 7 February 1902: Maeterlinck tried to prove that his letter to Debussy of 19 October 1895 was by no means a general blank check, and that he believed his demands regarding the performers for the work were perfectly legitimate. The following week, on 14 February, the Société convened with Debussy and Maeterlinck, each of whom explained his point of view to the commission. But whereas the composer immediately agreed to arbitration, Maeterlinck asked for time to think it over, and on 21 February made it known that he would prefer to appeal to the courts, "keeping the advantage of two jurisdictions, which would not be available under the arbitration of the commission."[26] On 23 February, *Le monde artiste* made the dispute public, while seeking to minimize it:

> A slight disagreement has arisen between the poet and the director regarding the matter of casting the role of Mélisandre [*sic*], one of them endorsing Mme Georgette Leblanc, who currently is not a member of the artistic staff of the Opéra-Comique, and the other endorsing Mlle Garden, a resident performer of the theater who has been accepted by the composer to create the role. A small misunderstanding, in short, which will surely be smoothed over in the great collaborative effort that is being mounted to bring to light the name of the young composer Debussy, one of the musicians in whom the critics and the public are justifiably confident.[27]

But Maeterlinck was champing at the bit and plotting ways for revenge. For once, we are tempted here to rely on Georgette Leblanc, who gave the following account:

> Justifiably angry to find himself robbed in the eyes of the law, Maeterlinck brandished his cane and announced to me that he was going to give "Debussy a few whallops. . . to teach him a lesson. . ." [. . .]
> I waited in agony, convinced that a drama would break out. I could not picture Debussy, with his tragic expression, taking kindly to a reprimand!. . .
> I kept looking down the deserted street to see if Maeterlinck was returning.
> Finally, he appeared at the top of the hill, waving his cane heavenward with comical gestures.
> It was a pitiful story. As soon as he had entered the room he threatened Debussy, who was sitting calmly in an armchair, while a distraught Mme Debussy rushed toward her husband with a bottle of smelling salts.

She had begged the poet to go away, and, my goodness, there was nothing else to do.

Maeterlinck, who did not like musicians any more than he did music, kept saying as he laughed: "They are all deranged, sick, these musicians!"[28]

On 14 April, *Le Figaro* published Maeterlinck's famous letter condemning the new work and hoping for its failure.[29] In a telegram sent that very day, Debussy asked for Godet's help in replying to the letter,[30] while Carré simply issued the following note to the press: "M. Carré, who loathes the commotion that is made surrounding works before their appearance, will deliver his reply to M. Maeterlinck after the premiere of *Pelléas et Mélisande*."[31] In addition, certain newspapers took sides against the playwright, arguing that the matter concerned a purely musical choice, one that should be in the composer's hands; as it was expressed in *Le Monde artiste*, "Isn't he the best judge of the tessitura and quality of the voices?"[32]

The Birth of *Pelléas*

On 13 January, two days after the premiere of *Pour le piano*, the rehearsals for *Pelléas* began. They would continue for more than three months, a period of time that was not at all exceptional; rehearsals for Massenet's *Esclarmonde* had gone on for six months. Rather than giving a narrative account of the premiere of *Pelléas*, we offer here a calendar of events, documented from the Opéra-Comique's *livre de bord* (log),[33] some notes taken by Henri Busser in his appointment-book,[34] and a few letters available to us, as well as some announcements in the press.[35]

For sixty-five days, Debussy was virtually a constant presence at the Opéra-Comique—that is to say, he was there nearly every day in the early afternoon, except for Sundays, days off, and those days when the stagehands were the only ones working. For about two weeks, he worked alone with the singers and the chorus master Louis Landry, with whom he had rubbed shoulders while they were pursuing their studies at the Conservatoire;[36] then, starting on 27 January, Messager joined them. The most surprising revelation in the theater's "log" is Maeterlinck's presence, on 19 March, at a rehearsal of the third act with the orchestra. We know nothing of his demeanor on that occasion, but the encounter with Debussy and Messager was certainly chilly. What is most lacking in these sources is the element of the staging and the personal role of Albert Carré.[37] However, a few days before the performance, Debussy asked him for more lighting for each of the first three scenes and, thinking like a man of the theater, for some modifications in the fifth tableau (act 2, scene 3), writing: "We must not reinforce an inviting atmosphere for the cave, which has a particular character in *Pélléas* [*sic*]."[38]

13 January	Rehearsals begin for the singers, with Debussy and Louis Landry
27 January	Messager begins to attend rehearsals
7 February	Maeterlinck at the Société des auteurs et compositeurs dramatiques[39]
14 February	Confrontation at the Société des auteurs between statements made by Maeterlinck and Debussy[40]
21 February	Maeterlinck withdraws from the Société's arbitration process and prefers to appeal to the courts[41]
23 February	*Le monde artiste* makes public the dispute between Maurice Maeterlinck and Albert Carré
5 March	Little Blondin (Yniold) at the rehearsals for the first time
8 March	Orchestral readings begin, with Debussy and Messager
17 March	"In the little theater, the orchestra and singers are rehearsing the first three acts of this work. M. Messager wants these three acts completely learned before moving on to the two others"[42]
19 March	Maeterlinck attends a rehearsal with Debussy and Messager. "Albert Carré assures me that I will conduct *Pelléas* after Messager leaves in May" (Henri Busser)[43]
23 March	The premiere is set for some time between 10 and 15 April[44]
24 March	Rehearsal of the fourth and fifth acts[45]
1 April	"Messager [. . .] came to ask me for 75 measures of interlude music for the second act" (Debussy)[46]
2 April	Rehearsal of the third and fourth acts[47]
7 April	Orchestra, artists, choruses, and servants. "We're doing nearly the entire play" (Busser)[48]
7 and 9 April	"Carré asks Debussy to add some longer interludes" (Busser)[49]
10 April	Rehearsal of the set changes
11 April	In costume: artists, chorus, extras, sets
12 April	Massenet in attendance[50]
14 April	Dress rehearsal of the sets in correct sequence, changes of floor coverings, scrims, furniture, props, complete lighting, projections, front curtain and draw curtain
14 April	Maeterlinck publishes in *Le Figaro* a letter in which he wishes a "prompt and resounding failure" for *Pelléas*[51]
15 April	M. Carré announces that he will not respond to Maeterlinck until after the premiere[52]

17 April	"Messager bristles, dressing down the orchestra and poor Périer" (Busser)[53]
18 April	Debussy writes to Carré, asking for more light in the production as well as an additional rehearsal[54]
25 April	Final dress rehearsal for the house; Carré expresses his satisfaction[55]
27 April	After a rehearsal, Octave Mirbeau publishes an article in *Le journal* that is favorable of the new work[56]
28 April	At 1:15, public dress rehearsal: "First act surprises. Second also. A few protestations. The third, stirring after the scenes with the hair and the child. The fourth, success begins.[57] The fifth, great success. [...] Debussy is in Messager's office, where he receives visits and congratulations." (Busser)[58] Henry Roujon, the Undersecretary of State for Fine Arts, demands that act 3, scene 4 be suppressed. Debussy requests a rehearsal for the following day.[59]
29 April	Meeting for final wrap-up
30 April	First performance. "Two curtain calls after every act. Better impression than at the public dress rehearsal. A few small cuts. Always some who are resistant." (Busser)[60]

It is difficult to get a true measure of these events, given the quasi-mythological literature that combines singers' tainted memories with stories aimed at reclaiming a leading role after the fact. Among those we can be certain were present, and apart from the critics who in a few cases were also friends, were Godet, Satie, Louÿs,[61] Toulet, Curnonsky, Lebey, Fargue, Valéry, Régnier, and Mlle de Romilly. Marguerite de Saint-Marceaux was also there, and wrote in her diary: "The musical work is an absolute masterpiece. The public understands nothing of it."[62]

On the evening of the dress rehearsal, while Debussy was carrying out the adjustments necessitated by the request for a cut in the third act, Godet and Satie waited for him on the boulevard des Italiens. Then Satie, who was growing impatient, left, so Debussy met up with just Godet and proposed that they have tea and a tête-à-tête at his home on the rue Cardinet. It was there that, without making the least allusion to the performance that had just taken place, Debussy launched into a completely unexpected discourse on Carl Maria von Weber and the originality of his instrumentation; Godet later transcribed his comments, of whose spirit (if not the letter) we can be assured.[63]

After the premiere, Debussy went for a ride in the Bois de Boulogne "in a jalopy" with Peter, Lilly, and a female friend. There too, "he hardly spoke a word about *Pelléas*!"[64]

At the Opéra-Comique, Albert Carré, who was about to marry Marguerite Giraud, was proud of the season on the whole: premieres of Massenet's *Grisélidis* and Bruneau's *L'ouragan*, and revivals of Auber's *Le domino noir*, Lalo's *Le roi d'Ys*, Camille Erlanger's *Le juif polonais*, and even François-Adrien Boieldieu's *La dame blanche*! Finally, the preparations for Georges Hüe's *Titania* were well underway. As for Messager, he had left Paris, after the third performance of *Pelléas*, to conduct in London.

Critical Reception of *Pelléas*

The emergence of *Pelléas* as one of the major artistic events of the beginning of the twentieth century bears all the hallmarks of a myth. Awaited by a small circle of Parisian musicians for several years, the opera had synthesized overnight the aspirations of an entire generation, bathed in Symbolist dreams and ready to welcome the liberating work.

Weeks after the first performances of *Pelléas*, Debussy wrote that "eight months of fatigue and anxiety" had left him completely drained.[65] Nevertheless, he had faced all the hazards of newfound fame and could take stock of the "*Pelléas* effect." Some fifty reviews were scattered on his desk—those from the first wave (the dailies of 1 and 2 May), then the monthlies, whose publication extended into July.[66] Debussy himself critiqued the critics in an interview granted to Robert de Flers that appeared on 16 May;[67] he mentioned about a dozen of them, dwelling especially on the following three: Catulle Mendès, who reproached him for not rendering "the poetic essence of the drama";[68] Willy, who lamented that the melodic line was always in the orchestra and never in the voice;[69] and Eugène d'Harcourt, who accused him of having broken the rules of the musical Holy Trinity: melody, harmony, and rhythm.[70]

The surprise came from Vincent d'Indy, who had had a negative reaction during the public dress rehearsal, even if he did not actually utter the comment to Jean Huré that Vuillermoz claimed to have overheard: "This music will not survive because it has no *form*."[71] Revising his first impression, he ultimately wrote a much more nuanced opinion, setting aside his professorial proclivities and taking into account the opinions of Paul Dukas, Paul Poujaud, and André Messager. The article, which appeared in the journal *L'occident*, surprised many in its moderation; nevertheless, it contained, in the course of one sentence, this revealing comment: in this work, "most of the time the music plays only a secondary role"![72]

Debussy did not let the first reactions to his work go to his head, and he maintained a strong presence at the Opéra-Comique, putting all his energy into battling the slightest inattention to detail, especially since Henri Busser had replaced Messager on the podium. The performance of 10 May had "not gone very well" on account of "a lot of ridiculous little things," and on the 13th, *Pelléas* had been replaced by *Le roi d'Ys* because Périer had lost his voice.[73] Between these two dates, Debussy visited Paul Dukas in Éragny, where beautiful photos were taken which depicted the serious but relaxed hero of the day. The main purpose of their meeting was to convince the honored guest, Pierre Lalo, to write a favorable review in his very popular column in *Le temps*.[74] He more than fulfilled the expectations of the two friends, to the extent that Pierre Louÿs was almost taken aback by his article: "No composer has ever had any review like this during the fifteen years that I've been reading them. [. . .] It's very courageous. And terribly well written."[75]

The "Bataillon sacré"

Also in the theater, and more effective than the best critics, was the famous *bataillon sacré* (sacred battalion) of the third galleries.[76] Debussy did not seek contact with these ebullient admirers, but he obviously knew of their existence. Indeed, Pierre Louÿs wrote to him that he was going to the Opéra-Comique on 25 May: "They tell me that your friends are meeting on Sunday at your first matinee and that there still is interest in intimidating the idiots of this new audience."[77] One of Willy's "ghostwriters," Émile Vuillermoz, was among the ringleaders of the peanut gallery; he was still practically unknown in Parisian circles and was doubtless attributed too exclusive a role. Edmond Maurat, then a young student at the Conservatoire, wrote: "Upon arriving at the third galleries of the Opéra-Comique, I saw Vuillermoz in the first row, surrounded by a large retinue who proved themselves more and more imposing with each successive act," and he added this highly subjective remark: "Without the persistence of Vuillermoz and his friends, the work would probably have been taken off the playbill after a few performances."[78]

Among these proselytizers, Vuillermoz himself noted "that faithful circle of musicians, giddy with respectful delight, who met each other every evening in the same seats throughout the twenty performances."[79] Léon-Paul Fargue went so far as to claim that he missed "none of the first forty performances,"[80] and Désiré-Émile Inghelbrecht remarked that after the opera "they would get together at each other's homes and *would play the music again*, some at the piano, others singing."[81] And so it was around this love, experienced as a "hallucination" (still in the words of Vuillermoz),[82] that the informal group of those who would soon call themselves "the Apaches" was notably established.

Sitting farther down in the hall, the regular operagoers had differing attitudes: Paulus [Jean-Paul Habans], the popular singer, left the hall laughing,[83] while Jules Renard documented in his journal: "Gloomy tedium. [. . .] I await a rhyme that never comes. [. . .] I like the wind better than this. [. . .] I feel nothing. [. . .] It's a special audience of rich ladies who go only to the Opéra-Comique or to the Opéra."[84] Attentive to all Parisianisms, Willy characterized in his unique way the snobbish audience members who hailed from good neighborhoods:

> Lovely Suzanne de Lizery has not missed one performance of that delightful and fashionable masterpiece. When she runs out of things to talk about, she may well wind up hearing a few notes of it some day or other. Last Friday, the music-loving elite were better listeners (Count Perlino de Saussine, the Marquis de Gonet, etc.), as the poets Fernand Gregh and Amédée Rouquès in addition to the politicians Denys Cochin and Gustave Mesureur [. . .] and Mmes Raoul-Duval, Paul Lebaudy, and Pierre Girot adorned the hall.[85]

The summer vacation period was not enough to slow that craze, and a young pupil of Massenet, Henri Rabaud, described for his friend Max d'Ollone the ambiance of his seaside resort: "I have some neighbors who play *Pelléas* all day long, and the other day, on the cliff, I passed by a very elegant lady who was walking alone while singing: 'Mes longs cheveux descendent.'"[86]

The reactions of musicians will be of greater interest to us. Paul Locard describes with some precision the responses of those sitting near him during the performance on 28 May:

> The musicians had in a sense monopolized the hall, and demonstrated a degree of enthusiasm that froze the opposition. In the shadow of a box, M. [Alexandre] Guilmant muses and admires; the priests of the Schola—Messieurs d'Indy, de Bréville, and Bordes—approve, Charles Koechlin is moved, M. Colonne savors "this new theater," and next to me, a very interested M. [Léon] Jehin takes in the happy smiles of Albert Diot, seated on my other side.[87]

Shortly thereafter, while Gabriel Fauré confessed that *Pelléas* had given him "intense chills—true emotions—in more than one place," he remained no less "resistant to Debussy's compositional practices."[88] Certainly, although composers had been won over by the work's novelty, they remained bewildered with regard to their own creative inclinations. Déodat de Séverac asked himself: "Is it possible to discover more after *Pelléas*?"[89] and Erik Satie supposedly said: "I must seek something else, or I'm lost."[90] *Pelléas* had a decisive impact on some other musicians, such as the young Maurice Delage, who previously had hardly thought of composing and who, on account of his passion for the new work, made friends with Maurice Ravel. The latter, according to Koechlin, had been the first to utter the word "genius,"[91] and it was around this mutual enthusiasm that the "Apaches" group first bonded. Even in the provinces, the most curious individuals, like Georges Jean-Aubry from Le Havre, also sought out earlier works by the composer of *Pelléas* and delighted in them.[92]

CHAPTER SIXTEEN

Visit to London

In the weeks that followed, Debussy maintained close contact with Messager, not only because he was indebted to him but because he suddenly felt uncertain about the future. He wrote frequently to the conductor, who was in London, and he hastened to accept Messager's proposal that he join him there for a few days. In fact, Debussy stayed for a week, from 12 to 20 July; leaving Lilly in Paris, he sent her three letters, written in a childish tone that showed his passion had lost much of its intensity. In London, he had a "delightful room" on the Thames and once again met Mary Garden, who behaved "like a silly little fool" with Messager, "her director, her master."[93] Debussy strolled through the city, which he described in a nearly cinematographic way to Lilly: "It smells of tobacco and tar, and one sees some poor little creatures who sweat profusely, while large, apoplectic men move slowly, for fear of jiggling their old fat. The flower merchants have straw boaters or feathered hats which, obviously, come from the trash bin rather than from Virot![94] It's pitiful and pretentious."[95] But best of all, he went to see *Hamlet* at the Lyric Theatre, played "by a man who is quite simply a genius": Johnston Forbes Robertson.[96] Mary Garden remarked that she had never seen anyone "experience a play as intensely";[97] sitting next to her, Debussy was that much more taken by the acting because he could follow the text only from his memories of having read it. Claude also became acquainted with the world of Covent Garden, including the future director Percy Pitt[98] and the Italian baritone Antonio Scotti.[99] Debussy probably attended two "English" operas that were performed during his stay: certainly *Princess Osra*, by the obscure Herbert Bunning[100] (libretto by Maurice Bérenger, sung in French), since Mary Garden sang the title role; and Ethel Smyth's *Der Wald*, heavily influenced by the Germanic repertoire and, incidentally, sung in German.

For the first time in Debussy's life, he had no backlog; no works were in progress, except for the *Nuits blanches*, the cycle he apparently decided not to pursue.[101] He confessed frankly to Messager: "In order to do what I want, I must make a completely fresh start. To begin a new work seems to me a bit like a perilous leap where one risks breaking one's back."[102] Even before the *Pelléas* performances ended, however, he had returned to Baudelaire's translation of Edgar Allan Poe's tales, and thought no longer of "The Fall of the House of Usher," as in 1890, but of "The Devil in the Belfry": "There's something there that can be tapped, where reality mingles with the fantastic in happy proportions," he wrote to Messager on 9 June.[103]

But, at the same time, unexpected problems arose. Upon his return from London, he found Lilly seriously ill; the diagnosis was kidney stones. On top of that, the executor of Hartmann's will, General Bourgeat, who was eager to profit from the potential income from *Pelléas*, asked Debussy to reimburse him for the numerous advances that Hartmann had given him. Fortunately, a settlement was reached: Fromont, Hartmann's former "associate," agreed to repurchase from Bourgeat the *Tarentelle styrienne, Ballade,* and *Valse romantique* for piano; the *Rêverie, Mazurka,* and *Suite bergamasque* for piano and the *Marche ecossaise* for piano duet; as well as the *Fantaisie pour piano et orchestre.* This deal had been concluded on 5 July, a few days before Debussy's departure for London.[104]

A Summer in Bichain

Lilly's doctor had recommended that she leave Paris as soon as possible. Claude opted for the least costly solution—that of going to his in-laws' home in Bichain, in the department of Yonne. They would stay there for nearly two months, beginning on 24 July. While there, he hardly worked at all, feeling like a "squeezed lemon,"[105] cultivating "a vast field of laziness," and declaring that all of his projects had been "dashed on the banks of a charming little river."[106] However, he revised the orchestral score of *La damoiselle élue* for Durand,[107] who had already published a new edition of the *Cinq poèmes de Baudelaire* on the previous 21 June. He wanted to try to maintain ownership of the orchestral score of *Pelléas,* and planned with Fromont a subscription for which they calculated the sale price; first it was 100 francs, then 80, only to drop eventually to 20 francs.

He also focused on the revival of *Pelléas.* As Jean Périer had not been reengaged for the following season (he would go on to sing in a play, *Les aventures de Corcoran,* at the Châtelet),[108] Messager thought at first of Louis Delaquerrière, a "very good musician";[109] however, there were concerns that his voice was "completely worn out."[110] Albert Carré had the strange idea of converting Pelléas into a trouser role, and broached this subject with Jeanne Raunay,[111] the soprano who had not wanted to premiere the *Chansons de Bilitis* for moral reasons but who was taken, it seems, with *Pelléas.* Debussy seemed hesitant at first, even while acknowledging that the idea was not "absolutely absurd";[112] but hearing the singer just once convinced him that this solution was "idiotic."[113] Her Pelléas would have had "the voice of a slightly breathless and impassioned old man."[114] Carré had already announced the news to the press, which expressed its astonishment. It was Busser who suggested Lucien Rigaux—a young novice who had graduated from the Conservatoire[115] the previous year and who was "a tall, elegant, handsome boy, with a piercing voice"[116]—and he was hired. The scene with the little sheep was also to be restored. Debussy expressed his confidence in Messager, who, to his great satisfaction, took up the baton again.

Having returned to Paris on 15 September, the composer renewed contact with a few of his friends: Curnonsky, Toulet, and Peter. Pierre Louÿs let him know that his new home, on the rue de Boulainvilliers, was closer to Debussy's place, but for all that, their former intimacy did not return. Besides, the writer was already in decline, almost depressed. A few weeks earlier, the press had announced that he had just entrusted the adaptation of *Aphrodite*—their former joint project—to, of all people, Leoncavallo![117]

As the 30 October revival of *Pelléas* drew near, Debussy spent every afternoon at the Opéra-Comique. Upon the announcement of Toulet's departure for Tonkin,[118] they discussed the scenario for their *Comme il vous plaira*, based on Shakespeare's *As You Like It*. On 21 October, Debussy made a few suggestions. He wanted to introduce a chorus in the wings, "that would underscore several details of Orlando's struggle," and to entrust the different songs in the text to an ensemble: "The duke is rich enough to be able to summon the Chanteurs de Saint-Gervais and their director to the Ardennes forest."[119] He also specified a few days later that the songs were to be sung "in the old-fashioned way, that is to say, as part of the action."[120]

During this same month of October 1902, appearing in the first issue of the journal *Musica* was Debussy's response to a survey on the following topic: "Is it possible to predict what the music of the future will be?" This little commentary marks, above and beyond its slightly cavalier tone, an important shift in the composer's aesthetic position. Describing the "veneered style" that seemed to him quite common in the music of his time, Debussy took up the subject of opera: "As for contemporary dramatic music," he wrote, "it has gone from Wagnerian metaphysics to Italian banalities—not a particularly French orientation. Perhaps it will lead to clarity and conciseness in expression and form (fundamental qualities of the French genius). Will we rediscover the multifaceted fantasy of which that art alone is capable?"[121] This is a very new subject in Debussy's writing; prior to that time, he was far from endorsing an argument for a beneficent national tradition. Such language was rarely used by M. Croche. So what was happening here?

The success of *Pelléas* drew a great deal of attention to the composer. He was aware of having left the shadows and, from then on, playing a key role in the artistic world. Did this elevated status, which was also social in nature, impose some new obligations on him? Might he perhaps have felt the need to be less negative in his opinions, to adopt an aesthetic stance in which he would endorse a less isolated position? In any case, it was the beginning of his increasingly pronounced nationalism, to the point of disturbing those who wished that he would identify consistently with the avant-garde.

The Revival of *Pelléas*

He had to return, however, to the oppressive atmosphere of the theater. The Opéra-Comique continued to experience a period of healthy prosperity. During the summer hiatus, some work had been done to enlarge the stage and the wings in preparation for Edmond Missa's *Muguette* and Reynaldo Hahn's *La carmélite* (with its libretto by Catulle Mendès!). In addition, the tenor Albert Alvarez filled the hall in *Manon*, and the 150th performance of *Louise* was celebrated. Once again, Debussy attended all the rehearsals for *Pelléas*, especially since, apart from restoring the scene with the sheep, he had to guide the first steps of Lucien Rigaux, Suzanne Dumesnil (Yniold), and Jeanne Passama (Geneviève). The revival took place on 30 October; between then and 6 January 1903, the work was performed ten times. A few critics took up their pens again, generally to praise the new Yniold, who was more reliable than young Blondin and who gave the role "its fateful, instinctive, and tragic importance."[122] Rigaux was not judged as positively. He had more voice then Périer but "one hears it far less,"[123] and the fervor of his predecessor was missed; besides, he constantly had to make sure to control his voice in a register that was too high for him.[124] They no longer laughed in the hall, "but they are still talking."[125]

The hullaballoo surrounding Debussy began to foster new performances of his works in the Sunday concerts. But this ripple effect did not yet win over everyone. A few protestors came forward when Camille Chevillard conducted the *Prélude à l'après-midi d'un faune*, following Balakirev's *Thamar*, at the beginning of November. The critics described the work with the same adjectives as before. One commentator surpassed himself, however, in making a truly sensational discovery: "The entire end of the piece," wrote Jacques d'Offoël in *Le guide musical*, "is constructed on a theme by Verdi, that of the chorus of priestesses in *Aida*. This confluence is interesting to point out, since I doubt that M. Debussy sought in Verdi a model for his work."[126] Surely Debussy himself was the most surprised of all, despite his already extensive collection of critical howlers.

As for Colonne, he was hoping to perform *La damoiselle élue* on one of his December concerts. Although Debussy was sick with the flu, he received Colonne on 10 December in order to give him the new orchestral score.[127] Upon reading through the music, the conductor questioned his ability to conduct a work that contrasted sharply with the traditional repertoire of the Sunday concerts. He suggested that the composer conduct it himself, while at the same time declaring, "I see what has to be done, very innocent, very pure."[128] Despite this pressure, Debussy refused. At the last rehearsal (on 20 December), Louis Laloy, who had just met the composer following the publication of his article on *Pelléas* in *La revue musicale*, noticed an unexpected visitor, who was no friend of M. Croche:

> *La damoiselle élue* was about to begin when the door of the neighboring box opened and I saw Camille Saint-Saëns enter, accompanied by a young male friend closely shadowing him. Heavy and sullen, his sagging nose locked in the acrimonious crease of his lips, framed by his gray, lichened beard, he

listened without saying a word, in the darkest corner, and exited while berating his disciple, who did a poor job of helping him fit into the sleeve of his overcoat.[129]

This performance had the feel of a premiere, even though the work had been heard by audiences before,[130] since the principal soloist this time was the well-known star, Mary Garden. At the concert on 21 December, the program note itself set the tone for the critics, by reiterating such expressions as "a peculiar atmosphere," "its harmonies are like the wings of a butterfly," and "it's a sonorous dusting of sound."[131] For Jean d'Udine, "these saccharine and mystical refinements" were perhaps delicious, "but this is an art of luxury, an art of opulence."[132] Jacques d'Offoël, on the other hand, reported an opinion that was phrased in a novel way: "It is poetry saturated in music, according to M. de Régnier's description of *Pelléas*."[133] The combatants coming from the "battalion" were present in the hall, chanting "De-bus-sy! De-bus-sy!"—which strongly antagonized some of the critics.[134]

Chapter Seventeen

From the *Fêtes galantes* to *La mer*

1903

The year 1903 began with an official honor for Debussy, and the manner in which he was notified put the composer of *Pelléas* significantly further along the path of contemporary aesthetic recognition. On the first Sunday in January, the poet Fernand Gregh, Debussy's neighbor, knocked on the door of his home on the rue Cardinet and announced that the composer had become a chevalier of the Légion d'honneur.[1] The two men had met at the Pousset tavern, where, according to Gregh, Debussy was called "the hydrocephalic Christ."[2] Was it a coincidence that this young poet, who had praised the humanity of *Pelléas* in *La revue de Paris*, had just a few weeks earlier published an article in *Le Figaro* that had all the appearances of a manifesto, moving away from Symbolism and the dream in favor of a more humanistic art, and calling for a renewal that would not treat traditional values with disdain?[3]

First Consequences of Fame

The bestowal of this award was due to the initiative of the composer's new friend Louis Laloy, who had approached Jules Combarieu, then director of *La revue musicale* and head of the office of the minister of public instruction.[4] Debussy thanked him "for the joy you have given my aged parents and all those who love me."[5] Indeed, one can imagine the pride of the former communard, glimpsing the little piece of red ribbon on his son's jacket when the composer paid him a surprise visit; but this gesture also reveals the true self-satisfaction Claude felt upon finally entering into the world of social respectability, a form of revenge against a lot in life that had been adverse for far too long. Henriette Fuchs, setting aside her resentment of her former accompanist,[6] programmed *La damoiselle élue* on the Concordia concert in March, which Debussy left to Silvio Lazzari to conduct, feeling no need to attend the dress rehearsal himself.[7] Ernest Chausson's widow would also attempt a reconciliation with the person who had left her family with the memory of a scandal about ten years earlier.[8] In refusing her invitation, Debussy graciously recalled only the kind deeds from the 1890s: "I'm infinitely grateful to you for not having forgotten the already distant past, the memory of which will forever be a part of me, because there are some men [referring to Ernest Chausson] who are irreplaceable."[9] But he found it rather amusing to note that his recent celebrity was leading self-righteous ladies to forget the past.

In the final days of 1902, he belatedly recalled that Victor-Émile Michelet, a Symbolist writer with whom he had associated at Bailly's bookshop, had asked him to compose a few pages of music for his first play, *Le pèlerin d'amour*, a fantasy in one act whose premiere was set for 10 January at the Odéon.[10] Michelet let him know that Paul Ginisty, the director of the theater, could provide for only five musicians. Offended, Debussy replied, "We're not in a pub where five Gypsies fill the bill! We absolutely must have the following instruments: 2 violins, 1 viola, 1 cello, 1 double bass, 2 flutes, and 1 harp. Anything less would be absurd."[11] As this was a no-win situation, deep down he was relieved at having to abandon a project that had immersed him once again in the depressing atmosphere of life before *Pelléas*. "Since they have so much contempt for music in that place," he wrote to Michelet on 3 January, "it would be better to do without it altogether."[12]

His publisher, Eugène Fromont, who seemed disinclined to engrave the expensive orchestral score of *Pelléas*, sought instead to profit from its composer's recent fame by publishing or reissuing editions of Debussy's works for which he already had the rights. He issued a new printing of the *Marche écossaise* and a "deluxe edition" of three piano pieces that had been composed earlier (*Ballade, Danse,* and *Valse*).[13] As well, he published a revised edition of the *Ariettes oubliées*, songs he had acquired as part of veuve Girod's holdings, updating them with a beautiful dedication:[14] "To Miss Mary Garden, unforgettable Mélisande, this music (already a bit old) in affectionate and grateful homage" (À Miss Mary Garden, inoubliable Mélisande, cette musique [déjà un peu vielle] en affectueux et reconnaissant hommage). Above all, he had obtained from Debussy the first set of *Fêtes galantes*, containing some new versions of yet-unpublished Verlaine songs; here again, the composer had to sort out the dedications, leaving out Catherine Stevens, to whom he had presented "En sourdine," and Alice Peter, to whom he had dedicated "Clair de lune."[15] The new honorees were the wives of his three loyal friends: Robert Godet, and Lucien and Arthur Fontaine. Debussy was less happy about allowing Paul

Dupont, his father's former employer, to republish a mélange of *Trois mélodies* from his youth, which the critic Georges Servières deemed unworthy of the composer of *Pelléas*.[16]

Concerts in Paris and in the Provinces

Between writing articles for *Gil Blas*, Debussy had to deal with performances of his "old" works. These compositions were gradually entering the repertoire, thanks in particular to the Parent Quartet, which played his String Quartet no fewer than three times in the span of three months.[17]

On 27 March, at the Salle Érard, Debussy himself served as accompanist in the second performance of the *Chansons de Bilitis* by Lucienne Bréval, who had to repeat "La chevelure" as an encore.[18] For a composer as particular as he was in the realm of art song, it is amazing that he would choose a grand-opera singer to perform settings of such intimate poetry. A critic who heard her in the same work a few years later declared his surprise: "I had never heard a singer deliver 'La chevelure,' 'Le tombeau des naïades,' and 'La flûte de Pan' with such melodramatic gestures, which, by the way, did nothing to improve the vocal defects."[19] Vallas also bore witness to Lucienne Bréval's interpretation, describing it as "exciting, passionate, romantic, and theatrical."[20] Debussy, however, was sufficiently happy with her performance to repeat it the following month and even to offer the singer a beautiful working manuscript of *Pelléas*.[21]

The Schola Cantorum—where Debussy had never spent much time—organized three "concerts of French contemporary music," including works by Debussy, Chausson, and Fauré. The program of the first, performed on 21 April, included Debussy's String Quartet (by the Parent Quartet); the third of the *Proses lyriques* and the *Chansons de Bilitis* (by Lucienne Bréval); *Pour le piano* (by Ricardo Viñes, who had given its premiere the year before); and the transcription for two pianos of the *Nocturnes*, which, as we recall, had been prepared by Raoul Bardac, Lucien Garban, and Maurice Ravel.[22] Paul Landormy, who attended the concert, mentioned the odd experience of hearing the *Bilitis* songs performed in an abandoned chapel, and reported that Debussy, who was playing from memory, had made a mistake in the accompaniment of one of the songs and had to begin again, "with a hint of a smile at the corner of his lips."[23] The musicologist Michel Brenet pointed out that Lucienne Bréval, once again, had to repeat "La chevelure" as an encore; he observed that, despite a torrential rain, the audience was "large, elegant, and enthusiastic," but that the transcription of the *Nocturnes* had disappointed him.[24] As for the review by the Schola, it mentioned only the concert's great success, and a certain Jean de Muris went so far as to write in *La tribune de Saint-Gervais*: "M. Debussy knows that no one at the Schola is put off by his techniques and that we will happily follow him in all his daring innovations."[25] Among the published reports, one stands out for its excessive praise—praise such as the composer had never known. To be sure, Jean Morland, a.k.a. Jean Marnold, spoke and wrote incisively: "Each line," he wrote in the *Mercure de France*, "each measure is a stroke of genius, a conquest in sound. [. . .] In the future, even from today forward, we will characterize music as being before or after Claude Debussy. [. . .] Such a great leap in the art of music is a phenomenon without precedent."[26]

The French provinces were also waking up to the music of Claude Debussy. The Société des concerts in Marseille had performed the *Prélude à l'après-midi d'un faune* at the end of 1902, under the direction of Paul Viardot; some members of the audience thought the work was constructed with "wrong harmonies."[27] In Bordeaux, the performance of the *Nocturnes* went much worse: on 11 January 1903, the work was booed and the musicians in the orchestra—especially the violinists—were themselves participants in the slaughter. They "visibly laughed while playing their parts," causing "some unexpected dissonances," while "M. Pennequin conducted with gestures that were at once indignant and apologetic."[28] Nothing of the sort seemed to have happened in Pau, where Édouard Brunel conducted the first two movements of the *Nocturnes* in November 1902,[29] or in Monte-Carlo or Marseille, where Léon Jehin and Paul Viardot conducted, respectively, the *Prélude à l'après-midi d'un faune*.[30] A few months later, in August 1903, Jules Danbé also performed the *Nocturnes* in Vichy.[31]

A veritable Debussy Festival took place in Lyon on 10 December 1902, for an "elite gathering" at the home of Mme Mauvernay. A voice teacher at the local conservatory (Ninon Vallin would become her pupil), she did well in planning the event. She had asked Fernand Baldensperger, a professor at the University, to introduce the works:[32] the *Nocturnes* and the *Prélude à l'après-midi d'un faune* for two pianos (played by Joseph Jemain and Georges-Martin Witkowski), *Pour le piano*, an *Arabesque*, the *Proses lyriques* (sung by Victor Debay), and the first two *Chansons de Bilitis* (sung by Mme Mauvernay herself).[33] For the provinces, it was an important premiere, which Debussy could have attended, had he been more committed (as were many of his peers) to supporting the dissemination of his works. This experience was repeated on 20 February 1903, with a slightly different program and, again, "for a select audience"; in addition to the *Nocturnes* and the *Prélude à l'après-midi d'un faune* (both for two pianos, this time performed by M. Émile Herman and Joseph Jemain), as well as *Pour le piano* (played by Joseph Jemain), the *Proses lyriques* (sung by Victor Debay; "De grève" was repeated as an encore) and the *Poèmes de Baudelaire* (Debay sang, although we cannot confirm whether in full or in part) were presented. The performances of the last two works were essentially their premieres. Paul Landormy gave a pre-concert talk and Mlle Claude Ritter ended with a recitation of some poems by Leconte de Lisle and Sully-Prudhomme.[34]

To these initial proliferations of his works, Debussy was merely indifferent. When *Le monde musical* wanted to send a photographer to his home so they could feature him on the cover of their publication, he refused, writing to its manager Auguste Mangeot that "it's so easy to pass unnoticed in a crowd, and not be singled out."[35] Instead, the magazine reproduced the portrait of him that Jacques-Émile Blanche had just painted and that was then on display at the Société des beaux-arts.

Debussy spent the week from 26 April to 3 May 1903 in London, in order to report for *Gil Blas* on the entire *Ring* cycle, conducted at Covent Garden by Hans Richter, "the king of orchestral conductors."[36] There he got together with Messager, an encounter that was all the more pleasurable since it was the anniversary of *Pelléas*, and he also returned to the Cecil Hotel, where this time he had only a "small, dirty room that overlooked an even dirtier little courtyard."[37] To Lilly, who once again remained in Paris and was still slightly under the weather, he gave some news of his "tetralogical treatment":[38] *Das Rheingold* was less tedious than he would have thought,[39] but *Siegfried* was terribly boring.[40] The only evening he had free from the Wagner performances, he spent at the Empire Theatre, where the ballet and the "fiery waltzes" of Leopold de Wenzel reigned.[41] The most extraordinary moment of his stay was a visit to the Tate Gallery, to see the canvases of Joseph Mallord William Turner, a painter whom he had long admired; he lingered there for "a long time."[42] For economical reasons, and perhaps also because he lacked interest in the production, he did not stay in London to attend the performance of Messager's *Véronique*, which was given in English. He sent his apologies to Messager soon after having returned to Paris.[43]

New Works: The *Images*

Before the end of May, Claude was living alone at the rue Cardinet, Lilly having gone to stay at her parents' home in Bichain. He clearly needed this solitude, for he had now emerged from the state of creative lethargy in which *Pelléas* had left him. He applied himself in earnest to his work, like a bachelor in the apartment whose ambiance has been depicted with a certain finesse by one of his students who went there on a regular basis:

> The Debussys lived there, on the fifth floor of a narrow building [. . . in] a little flat that was meticulously clean and orderly. From the windows was a view of a bit of greenery, and that peaceful retreat was disturbed only at certain times of the day by the joyful cries of a group of children in a school courtyard.
> There one felt an atmosphere of intimacy, of peace, in two little rooms connected by a bay. One was the master's studio, where manuscripts, inks,

and pencils were lined up in perfect order on his desk. There were also a sofa, a few Oriental rugs, and, on the walls, paintings by Lerolle, Jacques Blanche, Thaulow, and some drawings portraying Lilo Debussy. [. . .]

In the other room were an upright piano, some books, some scores. [. . .]

Lilo respected his sleeping in, until late in the day (for he worked at night and stayed up until morning). [. . .]

The two cats, whom Debussy cherished, occupied a central place in the family; he catered to their every whim. Silent, like their master, they were allowed to lie solemnly on the desk and, if they wished, to scatter the pencils.[44]

The main excuse that Claude gave Lilly for being left alone for a few weeks was that he had to compose a *Rapsodie* for saxophone, which was called "Moorish" at the time.[45] It had been commissioned from him two years earlier by an American, Élise Hall, who was president of the Orchestral Club of Boston. The intermediary was a French oboist from the Boston Symphony Orchestra, Georges Longy, who had just arrived in Paris for the express purpose of collecting the score: "I have to get going on it," Debussy wrote to Messager on 8 June, "and here I am, desperately seeking out combinations that are the newest and most idiomatic to show off that aquatic instrument."[46] But for all that, he did not lose his zest for life; he invited Camille Mauclair and Alexandre Charpentier (a friend who was a sculptor) to have lunch,[47] and he went out with "the Indians" (as he referred to them for Lilly)—which is to say, Curnonsky and Toulet, who had returned from Tonkin.[48]

But he had more personal works in progress than that commission, which we might add he would never completely finish. He returned to piano repertoire and took up once again his *Suite bergamasque*, which had been sold to Choudens in 1891 and transferred to Fromont by General Bourgeat. However, the story of its contents poses a slight problem. In a catalog of Debussy's works that appeared on 1 March 1904, this *Suite* was announced with the following movements: "Masques," "Sarabande," "L'île joyeuse." Ricardo Viñes seemed to confirm these contents, at least in part, when he wrote in his journal in June 1903 that Debussy played two pieces from the *Suite bergamasque* for him, adding that "One of them, 'L'isle joyeuse,' is absolutely beautiful."[49] But how can these claims be true when we read in *Le courrier musical* from 1 May 1903 until 1904 that the *Suite* comprised the following pieces: "Prélude," "Menuet," "Promenade sentimentale," "Pavane"?[50] [Roy Howat has shown that the two advertised suites must have been separate projects, and he offers a compelling hypothesis—based on links of motivic material, tempo, and pitch/tonal centers—that the piece published as *D'un cahier d'esquisses* was intended as the middle movement between *Masques* and the piece that became *L'isle joyeuse*. He suggests further that circumstances involving Debussy's publishers as well as his personal life resulted in the separate publication of each of these three pieces, along with the enforced publication of the four-movement *Suite bergamasque* as we know it, an earlier suite originating from around 1890.][51]

At the same time, Debussy devised a large set of *Images*, which he had already begun in 1896. Instead of offering them to Fromont, he gave them to Jacques Durand, who gradually became his main publisher. The contract they signed on 8 July 1903 is the only document that reveals to us this original grand design, one that was never completely realized in this form:[52]

Images
Twelve pieces for piano, 2 hands
and for 2 pianos, 4 hands, or orchestra

Series I		Series II	
I. Reflets dans l'eau	⎫	I. Cloches à travers les feuilles	⎫
II. Hommage à Rameau	⎬ 2 hands	II. Et la lune descend	⎬ 2 hands
III. Mouvements	⎭	sur le temple qui fut	
		III. Poissons d'or	⎭
IV. Ibéria	⎫ 2 pianos	IV.	
V. Gigue triste	⎬ and [or]	V.	
VI. Rondes	⎭ orchestra	VI.	

In this initial plan, one immediately notices not only the two books of *Images* for piano, whose titles were already virtually in their final state,[53] but also the *Images* for orchestra, whose titles would be slightly modified at the time of their publication, no less than ten years later.[54]

A few days earlier, on 4 July, Debussy had once again received Ricardo Viñes, who reported a conversation relating to the composer's secret garden:

> Debussy played for me again his new piano pieces *Pour le piano*,[55] a copy of which he will be sending me at the end of the month. What a coincidence; I told him that these pieces made me think of Turner's paintings, and he replied that, in fact, he had spent a great deal of time in the Turner room in London before composing them![56]

Before leaving for Bichain, Debussy decided to give up *Gil Blas* and music criticism.[57] He had once again entered into an active phase of creation, and the job of critic absorbed entirely too much of his time. Nearly ten years would pass before he took up his pen again for a newspaper. In his last article, "Le bilan musical en 1903" (A musical assessment of the year 1903), he once again championed Rameau ("the perfect counterpart to Watteau"), whose *La guirlande* he had just admired at the Schola and which gave him a new opportunity to condemn the "heavily cosmopolitan traditions" that prevented French music "from developing freely."[58]

More surprising was his decision to attend the Prix de Rome performances, unless he was thinking about devoting a column to that event. Reporting on it to Messager, he again adopted his most passionate tone:

> You have no idea what goes on in that place. . . And how it breeds distaste for music. These gentlemen now devote themselves to bestowing the prize to cantatas that no longer even follow sacrosanct tradition, but to so-called "dramatic" music. And one has to listen to this. . . It makes one apoplectic! Monsieur Laparra, who won the prize this year, appears to be Leoncavallo's best pupil.[59] Oh, God! What music! What a delightful temperament, like that of a butcher![60]

The gentleman in question, Raoul Laparra, was in fact a student of Fauré as well as of Massenet and André Gedalge; meanwhile, Maurice Ravel had failed in his third bid for the Prix de Rome. Debussy was said to have appreciated the latter's quartet, which was already circulating among those close to him, whereas the composition's dedicatee—Fauré himself—thought that the finale did not work.[61]

A Very Productive Summer: *La mer*

Lilly always seemed to be slightly under the weather. While awaiting Claude in Bichain, she repainted the home of her parents, to whom he sent a langoustine from Chez Leprince to reward their patience for his absence.[62] Lilly and Claude were clearly becoming more distanced from each other, as reflected in the tone of his letters: "You know, you write letters that would have delighted Mme de Sévigné![63] Goodness! Madame! What eloquence. . . It's also clear that you're happy; I can see you from here, getting mother Texier all stirred up, wrapping father Texier around your little finger. Ah! Dear little Captain One-Two, do be gentle with that paintbrush in your hand."[64]

The composer arrived in Bichain around 10 July and would remain there until 1 October. Unlike the previous year, these two and a half months were devoted to intensive work. For several months, Debussy and Messager had been correcting the orchestral proofs of *Pelléas*[65]—a task that was all the more unwieldy because Debussy made many changes in the score, which sometimes confused Gulon, Fromont's engraver. The composer ordered a piano from Montereau because he was also putting the finishing touches on the *Estampes*, written for that instrument. Partial to the number three, he curiously combined the Orient ("Pagodes") with Spain ("La soirée dans Grenade") and France ("Jardins sous la pluie") in this set, and joked about the way in which this music came from his pen in the Yonne countryside: "When one can't afford to travel, one has to make up for it with the imagination."[66]

Finally, Debussy embarked on a new orchestral work, *La mer*, whose speedy conception was startling: it took him only a year and a half to compose *La mer*, whereas the saga of the *Nocturnes* had extended over more than five years, and he would need seven to complete the triptych of the orchestral *Images*! He saved his first mention of this new work as a surprise for his publisher Jacques Durand: "I'm working on *La Mer*. . . with God's good will, it will be well under way by the time I return."[67] On 12 September, during stormy weather, he pointed out that its general outline was already set, indicating its divisons: "*La Mer*, three symphonic sketches for orchestra: I. Mer belle aux Îles sanguinaires. II. Jeu de vagues. III. Le vent fait danser la mer." On the same day, he also confided in Messager, with remarks that are worth recalling:

> Perhaps you don't know that I was destined for the fine career of a sailor, and that only happenstance turned me in another direction. Nevertheless, I've retained a sincere passion for Her [the Sea]. You'll tell me that the Ocean does not exactly bathe the Burgundian hillsides. . . ! And that it could well look like landscapes that are painted in a studio! But I have innumerable memories; that's worth more, in my mind, than a reality whose charm generally weighs too heavily on one's thoughts.[68]

Just as some people have wanted, rather in vain, to correlate the third of the *Estampes* ("Jardins sous la pluie") with precise events, so too have they wondered about the origin of Debussy's projected title for the first movement of *La mer*. "Mer belle aux Îles sanguinaires." Might it have been inspired by the memory of a short story by Camille Mauclair, published in *L'écho de Paris littéraire illustré* in 1893, which guides the reader to the discovery of three islands inhabited by people who have never communicated among themselves and who represent a progression from youth and life toward old age and ruin?[69] Or, more prosaically, had Debussy appropriated a phrase about nature that would be the dream of any Parisian, a phrase that often recurred in the weather forecast published in the newspaper *Le temps*, concerning those islands situated at the mouth of the Bay of Ajaccio: "La mer est toujours belle aux Îles Sanguinaires" (The sea is always beautiful in the Sanguinary Islands)? The title, which ran the risk of eliciting some colorful commentary, would in any case be replaced by "De l'aube à midi sur la mer" (From dawn to noon on the sea).

In June, Pierre Louÿs sent Debussy *Sanguines*, his collection of tales and short stories, which Claude brought along on his walks in the countryside "filled with summer, with mosquitoes, and with an almost orphan silence."[70] And the composer sent his friend a copy of *Pelléas*, albeit a year after its publication! Debussy perhaps had no idea to what extent Louÿs had plunged into a state of psychological and creative turmoil. These few gestures were the only reminders of their past closeness, and no mention was made of their former collaborative projects. Some semblance of an explanation emerged during this same month, suggesting that Louÿs may have invoked Lilly as one of the pretexts for the unraveling of their friendship. But Claude persisted in questioning his friend's analysis of their relationship, writing on 19 June:

> Dear Pierre,
>   You don't understand because it's been too long since you've seen me. If not for that, you'd see how simple it is.
>   Among the things that have upset me, I'd point out, among others, a letter I wrote (last year) in which I asked to see you before leaving for the country, to which you responded with the vaguest hope. . . It seems to me that nothing's changed since then, has it?
>   I couldn't avoid finding out, because one always learns these things, that while your door was firmly closed to me, it was cordially opened to others. Don't worry, I won't mention those people by name.
>   The fact that we're both newly married neither could nor should alter our relationship. You were much too steadfast a friend for anyone in the world, even a woman, to be able to dream of ending it. I can even attest that my wife considers you every bit as much a friend as I do.
>   These are the fissures [between us]. . . I'm well aware of the ridiculous melodrama in all this. Call me a sentimental old fool and let's not speak of it again. . .
>   Let me hear back from you, or come to the house, and you'll see that nothing has changed for you. You'll see again that little winged figure of Isis, to whom I've addressed prayers about you quite often.[71]

While awaiting a reply, Debussy removed the name of Pierre Louÿs as dedicatee from the proofs of the second *Estampe* ("La soirée dans Grenade"), leaving only that of Jacques-Émile Blanche, the painter of his portrait, on the collection.

Another concern ultimately gave Debussy pause—namely, what he would do as a follow-up to *Pelléas*. After a work so long in the making, and at a period of time when the page had clearly been turned on the Symbolist movement, on what important operatic project would he now focus his efforts? He placed all of his hopes on Poe's tale, "The Devil in the Belfry," the libretto of which he had begun the previous summer. The manner in which the composer notified Messager of his project is indicative of the importance he attached to it:

> We shouldn't be too hasty in declaring the *Diable* "done". . . The storyline is more or less complete, and the musical colors I want to use are almost set. Before all this is over, there will be many sleepless nights and a great deal of hope.
>   As for the people who so kindly hope that I'll never be able to escape from [the style of] *Pelléas*, they are deliberately blinding themselves to reality. Clearly, they don't know that, were this to happen, I'd immediately turn to growing pineapples in my bedroom, as I believe that to "repeat oneself" is surely the most intolerable thing. Furthermore, it's likely that these same

people will find it scandalous for me to have abandoned Mélisande's shadow for the devil's ironic pirouette, which will be the pretext for accusing me once again of quirkiness.[72]

Debussy harbored few illusions regarding the ability of Paul-Jean Toulet (an opium addict) to finish *Comme il vous plaira*, for which he had begun to adapt a libretto from Shakespeare (*As You Like It*) and whose composition the press, at the beginning of July, had surprisingly announced as in progress and even nearing completion.[73] A rather cryptic letter addressed to Colonne on 30 September mentioned a "concerto with the form and special orchestra of those by Johann Sebastian Bach."[74] Debussy added that he had worked on it, but that "too many things" remained "to be finalized."[75]

The end of the very productive stay in Bichain was marked by a period of relaxation, which led Debussy to gaze at the area's "diverse species of trees" in particular, for he had "expected too much effort" from his "intellectual apparatus."[76] Perhaps to satisfy one of Lilly's yearnings, as she wished to have a home of her own, he briefly entertained the notion of owning property in the region. He told Jacques Durand, though, that he had to deal with "an old man who was ironically indecisive yet persistent, one day wanting to sell and the next day no longer wanting" to relinquish a plot of land for which he was asking 3,000 francs.[77] In fact, Debussy would never become a homeowner, and the near future did not make him regret it.

Return to Paris and Initial Encounters with Emma Bardac

In writing a friendly letter to his student Raoul Bardac, Debussy mentioned his pupil's "charming mother" Emma, to whom he sent his "deep devotion," at the same time conveying Lilly's "faithful remembrance" to her.[78] This thought must have been very much on his mind when he returned to Paris on 1 October. A few weeks later, he would reserve for Emma a copy of the *Estampes*,[79] with a slightly enigmatic dedication: "For Madame S. Bardac / and with regard to an inkwell. . . / her very devoted / Claude Debussy / November 03" (pour Madame S. Bardac / et a [*sic*] propos d'un encrier. . . / son tres [*sic*] dévoué / Claude Debussy / Novembre 03).[80]

He was once again consumed by rehearsals for the new revival of *Pelléas*, for twelve performances beginning on 30 October. "This theatrical life disgusts me as much as it numbs me," he reiterated to Jacques Durand.[81]

But first, he was determined to set a date with his publisher for *Le diable dans le beffroi*, which at the time he had intended for the Opéra-Comique. Even though at that point he had only produced some notes for the plot of the first two scenes, and although he seems to have sketched no more than three pages of music, he specified in the contract that it would concern a "musical fairy-tale in 2 acts and 3 scenes" and very optimistically promised the first act in a year and the second act before 15 May 1905![82]

On 15 November, a completely unprecedented confluence of events occurred: two organizations programmed the *Prélude à l'après-midi d'un faune* for the same day. Chevillard conducted it at the beginning of the Lamoureux concerts, and Gabriel Pierné, in his conducting debut, presented it at the Colonne concerts. At the latter, there was some opposition between the audience on the main floor of the Châtelet and those in the upper balconies, but in the end the work was encored.[83] On the following Sunday, Pierné performed the *Prélude* again, followed by another encore that was prompted, as one journalist described it, "by an assertive minority."[84] Ten days before the dual Parisian performances, Ferruccio Busoni made history by conducting the Berlin Philharmonic in the first German performance of the same work. The critic of the journal *Signale* spoke of "orchestral grimaces that appeal only to our external ears"![85]

One wonders who initiated the strange proposal that Debussy complete Chabrier's *Briséïs*, based on a libretto by Catulle Mendès. Only the first act had been finished by the composer and performed in concert, posthumously in 1897, because Vincent d'Indy had not been willing to fulfill Chabrier's dying wish—that he undertake the completion and orchestration of the two following acts. On 26 November, Debussy accepted in principle the publisher Enoch's proposition, on condition that the legal and financial issues would be settled according to his wishes. Did he want to curry favor with his former librettist (*Rodrique et Chimène*)? Not very likely. No doubt he had only a very vague knowledge of the state of Chabrier's manuscript. In any case, the project did not move forward.

Dating from the same period is a separate piece for piano, Spanish in character, in which Debussy, for the first time, notated the music on three staves: *D'un cahier d'esquisses*[86] was published at the beginning of the following year in one of those music albums that flourished at that time (*Paris illustré*), and then, several years later (in 1909 or 1910), by the Brussels publisher Schott. Because of this decision to place the work with a foreign publisher, several years passed before it was premiered.[87]

Chapter Eighteen

Debussyism; A New Life

1904

Debussy's Increasing Visibility and Influence

Among the signs that Debussy had emerged within the musical establishment, a modest one was his first role in an official organization. He was appointed as an alternate juror for the *concours* of the Ville de Paris—the same *concours* he had almost entered in 1884 (in order to avoid going to Rome), in which he would have competed with Vincent d'Indy.[1] On this jury, he would meet up with, of all people, his former Prix de Rome colleagues Vidal, Leroux, and Marty.

In the early months of 1904, Debussy would strike up a friendship with Louis Laloy, a man of about thirty whose background was different from that of his usual friends. A student at the École normale supérieure who had passed his aggregation exam, Laloy was about to defend his doctoral dissertation on an esoteric subject, Aristoxenus of Taranto. He had also attended the Schola Cantorum and had devoted some articles to Debussy in *La revue musicale* that were quite different from what most critics had to say. He is the only person affiliated with a university ever to have become part of Debussy's entourage, as the composer had a certain distrust of people who were "too well informed." Laloy's interest in Rameau and his curiosity about East Asian music, which impressed Debussy more than did Edmond Bailly's dabbling in the subject, certainly helped to bring them together. This friendship, while not compensating emotionally for the estrangement from Pierre Louÿs, would be important to Debussy from this point forward.

The first weeks of the year would be filled with two premieres, which drew limited audiences, as in the past. On 9 January, under the auspices of the Société nationale, Ricardo Viñes premiered the *Estampes*, a set of three pieces that Durand had just published. On the whole, the critics preferred "Pagodes," whereas the audience demanded an encore of "Jardins sous la pluie." As for

"La soirée dans Grenade," it elicited a comical comparison similar to others already seen issuing from the critics' pens: "We could not help but recall Liszt's *La clochette*, and at every turn, the composer of the *Rapsodies* showed off. . . his fingerwork."[2] Marnold, who proved to be more measured than usual, asserted that "among the chiaroscuro shadings, and beneath the shimmer of expressive energy, there lurks more than just the picturesque."[3] Unlike many of Debussy's previous works, the first performance of this composition would not be its last: Joseph Édouard Barat programmed the *Estampes* on one of his concerts (9 February),[4] and Viñes would play them again in Brussels and in the Parent concerts (March–April).[5] On 16 January, Laloy introduced this composition at the home of a grande dame from Gotha, the Princesse de Cystria, as part of "an hour of music devoted to the works of Claude Debussy."[6] On this occasion, Blanche Selva played the *Estampes* and the Zeitlin Quartet performed the String Quartet, while Debussy assumed his former role as vocal accompanist: to Marthe Legrand in two of the *Trois mélodies de Verlaine*—"La mer est plus belle" and "Le son du cor s'afflige" (probably its premiere)—and to Maurice Bagès, who sang two *Proses lyriques* and even "Mandoline," "with an extreme and amusing tempo," as noted by Mme de Saint-Marceaux.[7] She added, "Debussy is here, with his head of 'the thinker' and his deep-set, Roman eyes. I'm trying to bring him back to my place, which will be difficult."[8] Mme de Saint-Marceaux indeed represented a decisively closed chapter in the life of Debussy, the erstwhile fiancé of Thérèse Roger.[9]

It was also Laloy who urged the composer to work with the Compagnie française du Gramophone, recording with Mary Garden the *Ariettes oubliées* and Mélisande's hair scene ("Mes longs cheveux") from *Pelléas* in February.[10] Debussy even agreed to endorse the gramophone, writing at the request of Alfred Clark, the company's founder, that it "guarantees the music complete and accurate immortality."[11]

More and more performers programmed his works: Clotilde Kleeberg-Samuel played the *Danse (Tarentelle styrienne)* in Brussels, Berlin, and London;[12] the Parent,[13] Enesco,[14] and Sechiari[15] quartets familiarized audiences with the String Quartet; and pianist René Billa played works ranging from the *Arabesques* to the *Estampes* (Aeolian Hall, 8 March).[16] *La damoiselle élue*, which Messager presented on 4 February at the Opéra-Comique (with Mary Garden),[17] was conducted in Marseille by Gabriel Marie with Marie de la Rouvière[18] (from the Schola). Édouard Brahy presented the *Prélude à l'après-midi d'un faune*[19] to an unresponsive audience in Angers, while in April, under the baton of Nava, the work "captivate[d]" the audience of the Société musicale de Constantinople![20] The *Nocturnes*, which Jean d'Udine complained were no longer played,[21] were conducted by Ysaÿe in Brussels in January, as a farewell to the composer.[22] Debussy wrote on 30 December 1903, perhaps to one of the violinist's assistants, informing him that his corrected score was being sent. Alerted to the frequently flawed performances of "Sirènes," he offered the following advice: "Please make sure that the choristers are placed within the orchestra and not in front of it; otherwise, the effect is the exact opposite of what I wanted. This group of voices must not sound more strongly than any other section of the orchestra; in short, it must not 'stand out' but 'blend.'"[23] Two years later, when Johan Halvorsen conducted these *Nocturnes* in Oslo, Grieg would start the applause that led to an encore of "Fêtes." He bore no grudge against Debussy for the latter's sarcastic article about him in *Gil Blas*.[24]

The most convincing confirmation that Debussyism had taken hold is found in the acknowledgement, or, more often, the denunciation, of certain composers' imitation of the master's compositional procedures. Reporting in May 1902 on Déodat de Séverac's *Nymphes au crépuscule*, Victor Debay deemed that "one senses too much imitation of M. Claude Debussy's *L'après-midi d'un faune*, with less originality."[25] And the obscure Henri Mulet found himself accused of using some "orchestral sonorities *à la* Debussy."[26] Even foreign equivalents to the composer were revealed: Hans Pfitzner was hailed as the "Debussy of Germany"[27] after the performance of his fairy-tale opera, *Die Rose vom Liebesgarten*.

The most unusual connections and the most unexpected comparisons soon spread, in an attempt to situate Debussy's art. Although no one at the time saw a possible influence of Maurice Ravel's *Jeux d'eau* on the *Estampes*, Auguste Mangeot, the director of *Le monde musical*, believed he had discovered, on the occasion of a concert by Risler dedicated to Gabriel Fauré's music, one of the sources of the latter's musical language. Mangeot wrote: "In the 6th Nocturne and in the 3rd Impromptu, one finds harmonies that were *invented* by the composer of *Pelléas*."[28]

Laloy, on the other hand, had the idea to try to link Debussy and Schumann in a concert. In an introductory talk, he portrayed both composers as intuitive artists; as he declared on 10 May in the Salle des Mathurins, they "do not consciously *will* the music they write, but simply *feel* it."[29] In demonstration of his rather questionable observations, Mme Camille Fourrier, accompanied by Blanche Selva, notably sang the *Ariettes* and one of the *Trois mélodies de Verlaine*. A few days later, the couple of Émile Engel and Jane Bathori[30] performed a more comprehensive selection in a matinee concert for "supporters of the young and daring composer" at the Bodinière;[31] their program included "Harmonie du soir," "Chevaux de bois" (which was encored), two *Fêtes galantes*, the "Flûte de Pan" (encored), two of the *Estampes*, and two scenes from *Pelléas* ("La chevelure" and "Le meurtre"). As was her custom, Bathori accompanied herself at the piano.[32] She would become one of the most faithful champions of Debussy's music.

With regard to the assessment of his compositions, one of the most careful studies was that of a young musicologist, Lionel de La Laurencie, who was equipped with a solid general and musical education. In his "Notes sur l'art de Claude Debussy" (Notes on the art of Claude Debussy), he reviewed the composer's harmonic innovations, melodic construction, and fresh perspective on opera.[33] Relying on Jean Marnold's analysis of the *Nocturnes* that had been published a few months earlier,[34] he asserted that never before had a composer applied cyclic principles so masterfully. More subtly, he revealed a "perpetual procreation of themes"[35] in the score and observed that the cells were "pregnant with possible transformations."[36] Finally, he took care to deny any break with the past and to link Debussy to tradition.

The "Pelléastres"

It would take less than two years after the first performances of *Pelléas* for the term "Debussyist" to become established in a polemical way. The attack came not from a music critic, but from a very turn-of-the-century gossip columnist. No one anticipated that it would come from a person who had a great deal in common with Debussy—with interests in the Pre-Raphaelites, Gustave Moreau, Odilon Redon, Charles Baudelaire—and who was a friend of Gabriel Mourey and Jules Bois. Poet, playwright, and novelist, Jean Lorrain had a reputation in Parisian circles as a "dandy specializing in the perverse"[37] or as a "salon adventurer";[38] he tended to model himself after the "downtrodden,"[39] and indeed, as he was pressed on every side to pay bills, he needed to produce articles daily in order to survive. In fact, in his article from 22 January 1904 in *Le journal*, he portrayed the audience, more than the composer, in a satirical way: those "Pelléastres," more elegant than the Wagnerians, younger and more handsome, "drinking in the gestures of Mlle Garden, the scenery of Jusseaume, and the lighting of Carré, archangels with the eyes of visionaries, and while feeling these impressions, whispering into each other's ear to the depths of the soul."[40] Debussy was nevertheless quite irritated by the beginning of the article, which took direct aim at his work:

> Faithful to every revival of *Pelléas et Mélisande*, this legendary audience for Lugné-Poe's premieres will be found again at the Salle Favart. Devotees of the nostalgic melodies with which Grieg underscored the text of *Peer Gynt*, those who also appreciated the skillful orchestration of *Fervaal*,[41] these people have all unanimously embraced the music of M. Claude Debussy. Gripped with admiration for the sunny pizzicati of the little gem *L'après-midi d'un faune*, they consider it their ordained duty to swoon over the deliberate dissonances of the long recitatives in *Pelléas*. The tension of those sustained chords and those interminable beginnings, announced a hundred times over, of a phrase; that pleasure-seeking titillation, exasperating and ultimately cruel, imposed on the listener's ear through the building up,

interrupted a hundred times, of a theme that never ends; this whole work in limbo, of little tremors, *artistique*, so much, so quintessentially... no kidding! and unsettled... imagine! it could win the votes of an audience of snobs and poseurs. Thanks to these men and women, M. Claude Debussy became the leader of a new religion, and during each performance of *Pelléas*, the atmosphere in the Salle Favart was like that of a sanctuary. One no longer went there except with a contrite expression, with winks of complicity, and with knowing looks. After the preludes, listened to in devout silence, there were greetings in the aisles among the initiated, fingers on their lips, and strange handshakes quickly exchanged in the shadows of the boxes, with faces of agony and wide-open eyes as if returning from the world beyond.[42]

To whom did Debussy turn to confide his profound irritation and his urge to reply? To none other than Pierre Louÿs, despite the rift that had grown between them, because he was the only one of his friends who could advise him well in such matters. The writer's response was indeed full of common sense:

Without question, there's nothing to be done. [...]
    What is this article? A tale in two columns, which does not concern you, with a very offensive preface regarding a portion of your audience, and five or six harshly worded lines about your music. Nothing about you as a person. [...]
    As for replying to him, a hundred times no! Reply to music criticism if it's signed by Reyer or d'Indy. But don't argue with a journalist. No artist does that.[43]

This constant mention of "Debussyists" and "Pelléastres" in the general press perfectly illustrates the change of direction that was taking place at the beginning of 1904. From then on, Debussy's work was established as one of the mainstays of musical life: "It is the question heard at all hours of the day," observed Raymond Bouyer, "I notice it at the theater as well as at five-o'clock gatherings."[44] The split between those who appreciated and those who denigrated the composer's work would continue for a long time.

Amidst all this hubbub, was there much breathing space for Debussy to compose? It is striking that during all these months he does not allude at all to progress on *La mer* or to the operas based on Poe, but rather to less ambitious works, some of which were being completed and others that remained in the planning stages. The first in the latter category was the incidental music he had agreed to write for Shakespeare's *King Lear*, which André Antoine was producing, in Pierre Loti and Émile Vedel's translation. Called to task at the beginning of 1904, Debussy replied to Antoine that there "are two months left to write the incidental music... That's precious little time."[45] This did not deter the press from announcing that he had composed a "fairly extensive" score for the play.[46] He had also promised to write "something for the chromatic harp[, . . .] an instrument [that is] completely unknown to me," he confessed on 28 November 1903.[47] This harp without pedals had been designed by Gustave Lyon, the director of the Pleyel company, who was attempting to offer an improved alternative to the pedal harp and who had just received permission to create a special class for it at the Paris Conservatoire.

Debussy had been commissioned to write a work for chromatic harp with orchestral accompaniment for the *concours* at the Conservatoire in Brussels. He chose to compose two *Danses*, one sacred, the other secular, using for the former the theme of a "Danse du voile" that a Portuguese composer, Francisco de Lacerda, had just published in *La revue musicale*.[48] He struggled in April and May to deliver his manuscript to Durand on time. These *Danses* were published around the same time as the *Trois chansons de France* (settings of poems by Charles d'Orléans and Tristan l'Hermite), which he dedicated "to Madame S. Bardac."

Word of a final project became known in June. Debussy was said to have heard Marguerite Moreno read excerpts of Joachim Gasquet's *Dionysos*, a play on an ancient Greek subject that was going to be performed during the summer at the Théâtre d'Orange under the direction of Mme Caristie-Martel. According to one columnist, Debussy supposedly promised "his immediate collaboration," while another writer added that his work included an orchestral and choral part.[49] While his intentions may have been genuine, the work was never even begun.

There was yet another hazard of fame. On 10 April, it was announced again that Debussy had completed *Le diable dans le beffroi*, based on Edgar Allan Poe's story.[50] From then on, his every move, just like that of Massenet or Saint-Saëns, was scrutinized by the press. He would soon learn this the hard way.

Emma Bardac

Who was Emma Bardac? She was nearly the same age as Claude; their birthdays were only a few weeks apart. Born Emma-Léa Moyse, she was originally from Bordeaux, where her father, Jules-Isaac, had a small business. In 1879, at the age of seventeen, she married the banker Sigismond Bardac; this wealthy man was, according to Gustave Schlumberger, "a very great and very intelligent collector."[51] Less than two years later, the Bardacs had a son named Raoul. Although we do not know the details of Emma's musical education, we do know that she took voice lessons with Mme Édouard Colonne[52] and that from early on she associated with professional musicians. The available information about her background and the development of her personality is sparse and imprecise. Although Emma lived until 1934, one gets the feeling that those who knew her during her first forty years have deliberately buried information about her past, leaving behind nothing more than rumors.

It is clear that the most significant experience for Emma during the 1890s was her close relationship with Gabriel Fauré. In her salon on the rue de Berri, one would find the best students from the master's composition class: Charles Koechlin, Jean Roger-Ducasse, and Maurice Ravel.[53] In 1892–94, she inspired Fauré's *La bonne chanson* as well as the passion of its composer. He wrote his famous cycle on Verlaine's poems at Prunay, in the Seine valley near Bougival; there the Faurés had settled in the small house of his in-laws, the Fremiets, which was close to the Bardacs' large villa. "Every evening," wrote Roger-Ducasse, "Fauré went to the 'château' to show his day's work to its interpreter. And often, very often, [. . .] she would send him back to make corrections. [. . .] She had him rework entire measures."[54]

He dedicated another song, "Prison," to Emma in 1894, and again in the following year, a *Salve regina* for soprano and organ. Fauré was also fond of her toddler, Hélène (called Dolly), who was born in 1892 and for whom he wrote his celebrated *Dolly Suite* for piano duet in the following years. As for Emma's banker husband, who seemed only peripheral in all of this, he received, rather curiously, Fauré's dedication of a new printing of *La naissance de Vénus*, a lengthy "mythological scene" for soloists, chorus, and piano (or orchestra), written in 1882.

Emma was not usually keen on participating in private concerts such as those that were covered by the press.[55] Still, at the beginning of 1896, she sought to become acquainted with the poet Albert Samain, and urged Fauré to invite him to meet her. The poet described this occasion to his sister in the following way:

> That dear man M. Fauré just asked me if I might not be free this very evening, and if so, whether I'd want to dine at his place, where he was eager to have me hear a song that he had composed for a selection from *Au jardin de l'infante*,[56] and which would be sung by one of his friends, a young woman named Madame Bardac. He added that Mme Bardac, who had read my book and had been smitten with it, wanted very much to meet me.[57]

The dinner took place accordingly, and after the performance of Fauré's "Soir," drawn indeed from Samain's *Au jardin de l'infante*, the poet concluded that Emma had "a feeling for nuances and especially a purity of expression, altogether rare."[58]

She was already rather well known in society: in May 1896 and January 1898, Willy noted her presence at the Société nationale and at the Colonne concerts.[59] Her son Raoul, called Rara by his friends,[60] helped introduce her into other musical circles. As Roger Martin du Gard describes him, he was "a typically precocious little Jew";[61] at twelve years of age, he had already composed several works, one of which was a *Romance* for piano and violin that had been performed by Eugène Ysaÿe.[62] Raoul studied with Fauré and Gedalge. We have seen that, sometime around 1899, he asked Debussy for lessons, very probably influenced by his mother, who discovered the *Proses lyriques* and the *Cinq poèmes de Baudelaire*, which she sang, accompanied by Charles Koechlin.[63] During this period, Emma began to distance herself from Fauré and to associate with the group called the Apaches, which included Lucien Garban and Maurice Ravel. A rumor, enigmatically reported by Tristan Klingsor, could have referred to her: "A singer of great talent and cunning set her sights on [Ravel]. She courted him aggressively, without success. [. . .] She settled for another charming artist."[64] What is certain is that in 1903 Ravel dedicated to her "L'indifférent," the most puzzling of the three songs of *Schéhérazade*, in which Klingsor's poem seems to replicate a scene: "Your lips sing at my doorstep [. . .] But no, you pass on, and from my threshold, I watch you depart."[65]

Debussy's acquaintance with Emma also dates back to 1903. We have seen that before the end of that year, some form of complicity had been established between them, expressed by dedications and gifts of manuscripts. Petite, mischievous, coquettish, and charming, Emma had a very lively disposition—"a sensitive nature,"[66] as Claude would later say—in addition to a cultural refinement that contrasted sharply with the shallow knowledge of Lilly, the shopgirl. The first months of 1904 afforded them the opportunity to meet discreetly, which sealed their mutual attraction.

In June, Debussy's personal life changed radically. On the 6th, Emma sent him flowers after receiving a copy of the *Trois chansons de France*, which he had dedicated to her. In sending his thanks for this gesture (one that is ordinarily considered to be more masculine than feminine), this forty-two-year-old man showed a degree of passion that bordered on poetry, so different from that which he had expressed for another woman—Lilly—five years earlier:

> How kind of you. . . and what a wonderful fragrance!—But most of all, I'm profoundly happy for your thought, which enters into my heart and remains there; it's because of these things that you are unforgettable and adorable. . .
>
> Forgive me if I've kissed all these flowers as if they were a human mouth. Perhaps it's crazy? Just the same, you can't blame me—any more than you can blame a rustling of the wind.[67]

And on 9 June he took the final plunge, sending this letter to her via pneumatic post:

> "It's raining heavily on the city."[68] Would you be so kind as to grant me a few moments this afternoon? I'd like to have you "on your own" for once, without counterpoint or development.

If you'd like to come to my place, I'd be deliriously happy, but you should do as you please and I'll meet you wherever you want.

All this is not from a madman but out of a pure—and slightly anxious—desire![69]

Did Emma come to his home on the day when Claude begged Lilly to go to a neighboring friend's house, as he wrote to Pierre Louÿs on the 12th, to explain why Mme Louÿs missed seeing Lilly when she came to visit?[70] It does not matter, for the dedication of the *Fêtes galantes* is enough to convince us that their love was sealed during those days—"To thank the month of June 1904. A. l. p. M."[71] Debussy also placed these words on a page of sketches for *L'isle joyeuse* (measures 117–44): "The attached measures belong to Mme Bardac—p. m.—who dictated them to me one Tuesday in June 1904. The passionate gratitude of her Claude Debussy."[72]

Since the time of his relationship with Marie Vasnier, Debussy had not tended to associate the person he loved with his musical activities. The following month, in offering Emma a heavy package containing the corrected proofs for *Pelléas*, he tutoied her,[73] while still calling her by her married name: "To Mme Bardac. . . these four hundred and nine pages of varied timbres which are barely worthy of the shadow that your little hand makes on this enormous book."[74]

On 16 June, he participated in a soiree organized by Mme Colonne with an unusual program, one that juxtaposed his own works with compositions by Gustave Charpentier. He served as accompanist for the *Ariettes* and the *Fêtes galantes*. Emma was no doubt present, for, perhaps in order to soften the shock between the two parts of the program, two songs by Raoul Bardac had been slipped in as an interlude.[75]

The break with Lilly was not as abrupt as most reports have claimed. In mid-June, Claude and Emma escaped for a few days to the Chevreuse valley. From there, Debussy wrote to his publisher Durand on a postcard depicting the castle of Dampierre: "Excuse me for being here before having finished the *Danses*."[76] Yet only a few days later, on 22 June, Debussy still referred to Lilly in a letter to Laloy: "We're leaving for the country very soon,"[77] and on 2 July, the married couple hosted the same Laloy for lunch: "I was their only guest, and both of them had me happily admire their china plates, which they had put in the stove to crackle, in order to imitate artistic stoneware. [. . .] There was no hint of the storm to come."[78]

The Lovers Escape to Jersey

Writers have often accepted the scenario that Claude left his marital home on the evening of 14 July to rendezvous with Emma. What really happened was very different; some myths and guesswork may well be corrected by considering all the sources, including the letters that Debussy sent to Lilly.

On Friday, 15 July, Claude arranged for Lilly to go to Bichain. In his own words, he put her "unceremoniously into a carriage"[79] and the next day sent her an explanation that completely avoided facing up to the problem in their marriage:

> For reasons that I'll explain to you later, it was necessary. . . Also, I've got to find new things, at the risk of losing my momentum; for some time, I've been worried about going around in circles with the same ideas. Now I seem to have found a new path, from which I dare not stray, whatever the cost. It's also a matter of survival.[80]

Three days later, he sent her another letter, still not reporting the decision that he had made, but at least alluding to the deterioration of their relationship: "I sincerely believed that I could make you happy by asking you to entrust your life to me! Alas, sometimes I've had my doubts, as you so often told me things that drove me away from you. . . and my resulting anger was mostly filled with regret."[81] After calling her "a very spoiled little girl who doesn't allow anyone to question her whims or caprices," he offered a cheap philosophical remark: "Do you see, my poor dear, that an artist is, in short, an appalling man on the inside, and perhaps also a deplorable husband? What's more, conversely, a perfect husband often makes for a pitiful artist. . . It's a vicious circle."[82]

But he did not reveal any decision to her, and, although he curtly signed his name as "Debussy," he led her to believe that he would join her "around the 15th of August."[83] Very shortly thereafter, he treated her instead to a truly unexpected surprise: Lucien Fontaine took Claude and Abel Desjardins for a car ride, paying an impromptu visit to the Texier home in Bichain. Claude claimed that he might have been jealous of Lilly's joy in seeing these two friends, but all three men returned to Paris that evening, in the middle of a storm.[84]

Truth be told, Debussy was only buying some time, lacking the courage necessary to tell Lilly outright that he was intending to start a new life. On 30 July, he stated again that he would go to see her at the end of the following week.[85] Yet that ended up being the very time when he ran off to Jersey with Emma: a romantic escape—perhaps suggested by Emma—and one that has been compared to the departure for the fabled Greek island of Cythera.[86] Contrary to the oft-repeated claim, Debussy did not compose *L'isle joyeuse* there, inasmuch as this work had already been written a year earlier. From the Grand Hotel in Jersey, he wrote to his publisher Jacques Durand: "This countryside is delightful. I'm at peace here, which is even better, and I'm working in complete freedom, which hasn't happened to me for a long time. . . In short, if anyone wants to appoint me Constable of St.-Hélier—that's what they call the authorities in this region—I'm quite ready to serve."[87] And, in fact, he corrected the proofs of *Masques* and the second series of *Fêtes galantes*. Two items of note from that (undated) letter are a bit mysterious, but revealing. Claude borrowed from his dear Jules Laforgue the affectionate term with which, as we have already observed, he referred to Emma—"À la petite Mienne," which would appear in the dedication of the *Fêtes galantes*.[88] In addition, he implored Durand to help him by keeping his location confidential: "Do not divulge my address to *anyone*, including my charming family."[89] It may also have been in Jersey that he purchased a Blüthner piano, a baby grand called an "Aliquotflügel," which he later showed with some pride, at his home, to the pianist Maurice Dumesnil: each note in the treble had an extra, fourth string that was not struck by a hammer but resonated sympathetically, producing harmonics and enriching the sonority of the instrument.[90]

After Jersey, the lovers settled in Pourville, where they photographed each other on the hotel balcony in a state of relaxation, with the Norman countryside in the background. Now and then, Claude hopped over to Dieppe—the town that must have brought back memories of Marie Vasnier—to pick up his "poste restante" mail, and to keep the exact location of their hideaway secret. On 11 August, he finally decided to share his intentions with Lilly, but without revealing anything about the underlying reason for the break—his liaison with Emma:

> My dear little Lilly, [. . .] Forgive me for what follows. Maybe I should have told you at the time of my trip to Bichain; I couldn't find the right moment, nor perhaps the necessary courage. . .
>
> First, let me tell you that I have the greatest possible fondness for you, and this only makes more painful what I honestly feel I must tell you today.
>
> After these days spent away from you, when for the first time I could reflect dispassionately on our life, I'm very clearly convinced that, while having loved you very much, I've never been able to make you happy, as was fitting. . . I also remembered those angry moments when you asked me *to give you back your freedom*. . .
>
> Why I now realize that you were right, I can't say! There are many infinitely sad reasons for it, the details of which I'll spare us. Please note that I'm admitting in this matter all the times that I could have been wrong; however, I often tried to put on a brave face in the midst of a bad situation, but one word from you would shatter everything, rendering the illusion impossible. Besides, you're still too young and pretty for me to prevent you from finding the happiness you deserve. . . We're no longer children; so let's try to pull ourselves out of this situation, without a fuss and without involving other people. Moreover, all this does not mean that we should become enemies. And if I feel the undeniable need to be alone, it's because—you need to understand this—I keep coming up against things about you that distress me, and I couldn't work anymore as I'd like to, with this nerve-racking anxiety of

not knowing where I was headed; once again, in spite of this, I won't forget my devotion to you as always. As for the rest and for all the material things, I leave them for you to sort out at your convenience. Whatever you ask of me will be fine. Most of all, don't let your pride get in the way of this matter; between us, that would be ridiculous.

Obviously, this letter will cause you grief, if I can guess by what it has cost me to write it. But why ruin everything by allowing something that was beautiful and that perhaps could have been even more beautiful to continue any further? One final thing I ask of you is to take care to preserve the memory of our relationship, without involving the narrow and ridiculous opinions of people who've known neither love nor devotion.

In understanding me, you'll forgive me for having hurt you a little, and you'll believe that I remain dearly devoted to you.

Claude Debussy[91]

The Drama of the Breakup

The stay in Pourville was not all passion and relaxation, since André Antoine was urgently demanding the incidental music for *King Lear*. Debussy also revised *L'isle joyeuse*, corrected the proofs for the piano reduction of the String Quartet, and tried in vain to "finish *La mer*."[92]

On 22 August, Debussy was in Paris, but probably for only a short time.[93] Lilly returned to the rue Cardinet, probably on 13 September.[94] Husband and wife must have met, because, the following day, Claude wrote to Lilly from Dieppe that he had "returned tired, broken, and no longer knowing very well either what to do or what to think. [. . .] More than ever, I need peace, to the point of wanting to die, seeing that, whatever I do, I'll certainly hurt someone."[95] Shortly after 20 September, he returned for good to Paris with Emma and, three days later, gave an address to André Antoine that appears in no other source: "in care of M. Chauviré, 23 rue Pierre Charron."[96] Finally, shortly before 30 September, he took up residence at 10 avenue Alphand.[97] He sent Lilly some terse notes, mostly to postpone visits. On four occasions she threatened to kill herself,[98] and, on 13 October, she shot herself in the stomach with a revolver; the bullet lodged within a vertebra.[99] She was taken to the clinic on the rue Blomet, where Abel Desjardins operated on her.

Who at that time was told about this drama? In musical circles, the rumor of a divorce had already spread, but not the suicide attempt; on 26 October, Ricardo Viñes noted in his journal that at the home of the Benedictus family, "they were talking about the divorce of Mme Bardac, who wants to marry Debussy."[100] At the time, it seems that Debussy had turned to his father for help.[101] On 4 November, the press got wind of the incident:

It has been announced that the young wife of a distinguished composer—considered to be the leader of the young school, as evidenced by a recent work that was highly acclaimed in a national theater, although very controversial at first—attempted to kill herself a few days ago.

This young woman, well known in the artistic world, where her dark-haired beauty was noticed,[102] was in despair upon learning of her husband's infidelity. She tried to starve herself, refusing all food, gripped by heartbreak.[103] She then wanted to hasten the end and grabbed a revolver. Wounded by two bullets, she was transported to a hospital on the rue Bizet.[104]

Today her condition is fairly reassuring. But a divorce is imminent: the husband has not reconsidered his original decision, and the wished-for reconciliation has not taken place.

The composer in question will then marry the young divorcée of an art-collecting financier who is equally known in Paris.[105]

Pierre Louÿs gave his version of the drama to his brother:

> My outing yesterday was to see poor Mme Debussy, who shot herself in the chest on 13 October, after having been abandoned by her husband. The bullet went all the way through her stomach. [. . .] However, the operation was very successful and the unfortunate woman appears to be out of danger, but she will remain without a penny and without shelter. . . The husband has left with a Jewess in her forties, Mme E[mma] Bardac. I believe that you know Bardac, or at least that he has come into your office on business. Quite accustomed to his wife's running off, he replies with a smile to those who ask him about her: "She just took up with the latest fashionable composer, but it is I who have the money. She'll come back to me." [. . .] I wrote to Louise to ask if she'd be willing to take the poor woman into our home, at least for a few weeks.[106]

Other than Louÿs, to whom Debussy had written one last time on 12 June, many of his acquaintances were shocked by the news, and his student Nico Coronio began to collect donations on Lilly's behalf. Pierre Louÿs was said to have donated, on condition that his name not be disclosed. Mary Garden visited Lilly at the rue Blomet, as did René Peter, who wrote that "Lilly never knew she had so many friends."[107] Henri Busser met her at Mary Garden's home on the day she left the clinic, and he found her "unrecognizable."[108] A room in the Hôtel Américain, at 19 avenue de Friedland, was rented for her before she moved to the avenue de Villiers. And soon, the composer, who during those tragic weeks wrote to practically no one and remained in hiding, could count on one hand the individuals who remained loyal to him.

Did he attend the Colonne concert on 6 November, only two days after the papers had made Lilly's suicide attempt public, and, if so, with whom did he shake hands? His *Deux danses* were being premiered there, with Mme

Wurmser-Delcourt appearing as soloist.[109] Certain critics had not come, preferring to hear Albéric Magnard's Third Symphony, which received its first performance on the same day. Regarding Debussy's work, the critic for *La quinzaine musicale* revealed his equivocal feelings: "I do everything I can to dislike it. It is not possible [. . .] an irresistible attraction [. . .] of alluring whole-tone scales."[110] Hugues Imbert, attempting to describe an art that he considered unhealthy, evoked "the footsteps of Salammbô as she makes her appearance on the terrace of the Hamilcar palace."[111] He offered, as did others, a comparison to the visual arts: "His musical framework has no architecture, so to speak; [. . .] If one wanted to look for a point of comparison in Impressionist painting, one might point to certain canvases by M. Carrière, in which images are barely visible, immersed in a hazy atmosphere."[112] A little earlier, Lionel de La Laurencie, soon followed by Camille Mauclair, had evoked the painter Henri Le Sidaner.[113] As for Gabriel Fauré, he simply denied any originality in the *Danses*: "One finds in them an abundance of the same peculiar harmonies, curious and seductive at times, and at times also simply disagreeable."[114]

Around 5 December 1904, a long letter that Debussy addressed to Paul Robert shows how he tried to justify his position with respect to his friends, who were subjected to Lilly's "duplicity" (*double jeu*).[115] He was aware of the rumors being circulated about his integrity: "My 'friends,'" he wrote, "gathered at my wife's bedside, conferring on the most sure-fire ways to bring me down";[116] he knew that Messager and Mary Garden were among them, and it pained him to note that Raymond Bonheur was "offering no help" to him.[117] As for the composer, he remained "poorer than Job" and had no intention of accepting any money from "Mme B."[118] He claimed to be someone "who is not as bad as he's cracked up to be, and who loves independence above everything, even above the laws and his own peace of mind."[119]

Chapter Nineteen

La mer

1905

The Divorce and Its Consequences

As far as Parisian society was concerned, Debussy had left his wife to live with a wealthy woman. That "prudish public indignation," as Laloy described it,[1] led to many of his friends deserting him and to a loneliness that was much more acute than what he had endured during the mini-scandal of 1894. In addition, as he was living in an upscale neighborhood of Paris, all appearances were against him. He would be the object of people's gossip and increasingly malicious criticism.

The divorce negotiations with Lilly were "something of a nightmare"[2] that lasted until August 1905. On 3 January, *Le Figaro* had published the false news of a second suicide attempt by Lilly.[3] Debussy had written to Durand that he was "working relentlessly," but that he was "annoyingly harassed by the press campaign that Mme Debussy has really wanted to organize against me. It seems that I can't get divorced like the rest of the world. . ."[4] and, on 27 February, he confessed to Fromont: "I'm sorry you haven't heard more from me; my grief and problems are overwhelming."[5] At the end of March, Lilly still did not seem resigned to the divorce, and she even proposed that they live together again on a trial basis. On the 22nd, Claude rejected the idea of any further meeting and made a concrete offer to her: a monthly allowance of 300 francs and a sum of 10,000 francs, admitting his fault in the matter. Shortly thereafter, negotiations were initiated in earnest with lawyers as intermediaries. (During this time, Debussy sold the orchestral score of *Pelléas* to Jacques Durand for 25,000 francs.[6] Maeterlinck had likewise agreed to sign over his rights, which also applied to "all the changes that might subsequently be introduced by those producing the work.")[7] On 20 May, the composer again lamented:

"I'm inundated with meetings and discussions, and so far, nothing is working out."[8] Emma, who was several months pregnant, had succeeded in obtaining her own no-fault divorce on 4 May, for while her liaison with Debussy had, for Sigismond Bardac, an "offensive character," the latter himself was also guilty of some "publicly flaunted relationships with several actresses." A month later, Emma received a small gift from Claude for her birthday which showed his pleasure in sharing some purely musical references with her; it concerned a short piano piece with the following comments: "The seventh chords send their apologies!!! But fortunately here are the ninth chords, armed with all their harmonics, that send the hapless sevenths packing and that borrow some godlike glimmers from the color of the sky in order to celebrate the precious birthday of my little darling."[9]

On 17 July, Debussy was ordered by a ruling of irreconcilable differences to pay Lilly a monthly pension of 400 francs. To guarantee payment of this alimony, should he predecease her, he had to take out a life annuity from the Nationale insurance company; as the beneficiary, she would receive 3,600 francs per year.[10] On 2 August, the Civil Court of the Seine upheld these provisions in finally granting the divorce. The press announced the news the very next day. At the time, the only letter Debussy was obligated to write was a reply to greetings from Jacques Durand, who had proposed that he become the exclusive publisher of the composer's future works. This contract with Durand was finalized on 17 July, the same day of the first court order.[11] Circumstances thus drove Debussy to give up his independence as a composer.

Throughout 1905 and 1906, there is a sense that Laloy and Durand were the only friends with whom Debussy remained in close contact. On 14 April 1905, the manner in which he thanked Laloy (who had shown his sympathy by writing to the composer) is indicative:

> My dear friend...
>   I want above all to tell you that you have never ceased to be a friend! And that this friendship is becoming even more dear to me by the simple gesture—but so rare—that you just made by writing to me as you just did, with a perceptive sympathy, one that prevents you from callously tromping through life. Anyway, I've seen so many desertions taking place around me...! enough to make me forever sickened by all mankind. [...]
>   I won't tell you here what I've been through! It's nasty and tragic, and sometimes it ironically resembles a trashy novel... Anyway, I've suffered a lot emotionally. Did I need to repay some forgotten debt in life? I have no idea... but I've often had to smile so no one would suspect that I was about to weep.[12]

In Debussy's correspondence during the following years, there is no further trace of Peter, Dukas, Fontaine, or Curnonsky,[13] and Godet seemed to be distancing himself from the composer after 1902.[14] It took some time even for Raymond Bonheur to speak to him again.[15] On 19 September 1904, before the drama exploded, Debussy had written to Messager one last time, declaring that he would have "some discomfort" in describing to him the "singularly odd" life that he had led in recent months.[16] A page in his life had truly turned.

While all this was going on, he was not completely away from his work desk. In his little personal notebook, Debussy had clearly blamed Lilly for the gap in his "productivity of these last four years," on account of the "daily tyranny" she had supposedly exerted on his thoughts and relationships.[17] Nevertheless, he had just published *Masques*, *L'isle joyeuse*, and the second series of *Fêtes galantes*. The *Danses* had been produced and he had continued the orchestration of *La mer*; its *particelle* is dated from 5 March 1905,[18] but on 13 January of that year he confessed that he had "reworked the end of 'Jeu de vagues,'"[19] and was discussing with Jacques Durand the possibility of entrusting the premiere to Colonne or Chevillard.[20]

Debussy was likely unaware, for the most part, of the fate of his works abroad. In July 1904, Vincent d'Indy had conducted the *Prélude à l'après-midi d'un faune* in Russia, at Pavlovsk, a vacation spot for people from Saint Petersburg. The work was poorly received, although this did not prevent a second performance from occurring a week later, one that elicited the same response. Rimsky-Korsakov's opinion of this work was emphatic; he confided to Aloÿs Mooser that it was nothing more than "rubbish."[21] In Berlin, on 1 December, a performance of two of the *Nocturnes* was secured, thanks to the initiative taken by Ferruccio Busoni, and in Vienna, the *Prélude* would also be heard. But the Germans were still much less open than the French to accepting Debussy's music. At the same time, the renowned violinist Joseph Joachim (who, though born in Hungary, settled in Germany by the time he was twelve years old) expressed his opinion that *Pelléas* was "a huge mess."[22]

At the beginning of 1905, when Debussy learned that Ricardo Viñes would give the premieres of *Masques* and *L'isle joyeuse* in the Parent concert series,[23] he summoned the pianist, who came twice to play these particularly difficult pieces for him by heart. The second time, Viñes declared that the composer was "very pleased," but during the first performance, at the Salle Aeolian on 10 February, the pianist admitted that he had "not played them very well."[24] Eight days later, he performed them again on a Société nationale concert at the Salle Pleyel, to greater audience approval. "A triumph," wrote Julien Torchet, who confessed that even he was beginning to love—"like a kind of prohibited pleasure, almost of perverted enjoyment"—this music, which "consisted this time of two very rhythmic pieces, full of character."[25] One might consider his assessment trivial, but it is almost glowing in comparison to that of Jean Chantavoine, who described these pieces as simple "scribbles."[26] Some works that Torchet considered to be "products of his school" appeared on the same program; among them were excerpts from *En Languedoc* by Séverac and two songs by Maurice Ravel.[27]

The revival of *Pelléas* at the end of March brought Debussy back to the Opéra-Comique, his presence being all the more necessary since Albert Carré was away for reasons of health and Alexandre Luigini had replaced Messager as the orchestra conductor. After the dress rehearsal on 3 April, Debussy wrote to thank those performers from the premiere who were still there—Périer, Vieuille, and Dufranne[28]—and wrote to Carré that he regretted his absence, reminding him in measured terms that "you brought out that share of tangible beauty in the work that made it able to live."[29]

Concerts and Critics

During 1905, Debussy's music was increasingly performed, but it also provoked more discussion. The String Quartet was played quite frequently by several ensembles: the Luquin Quartet (18 January),[30] the Paris Quartet (8 February),[31] and the Parent Quartet (10 February).[32] The latter group would offer it again at the Salon d'Automne in November.[33] While Ricardo Viñes continued to play *L'isle joyeuse* (April)[34] after its premiere, other pianists followed suit and often programmed "Jardins sous la pluie" (David Blitz,[35] Auguste Pierret,[36] Jeanne d'Herbécourt[37]) and the *Arabesques* (Mlles Clémence Oberlé,[38] Magdeleine Boucherit[39]) on their concerts. In Grenoble, a small chamber-music society presented the first local performance of the *Estampes*, played by Edmond Arnaud, and "La soirée dans Grenade" was encored, even though the audience displayed their "utter bewilderment."[40]

The songs continued to be championed by the duo of Jane Bathori and Émile Engel (recital in Brussels, 1 February)[41] and Jeanne Raunay (December),[42] while Mme Camille Fourrier selected the Verlaine songs for a recital at the Schola Cantorum (8 February)[43] and premiered the first two *Chansons de France* at the Théâtre des Mathurins (15 May).[44] Most significant, no doubt, is the fact that these works were programmed in more popular venues, such as student performances (the *Petite suite* was performed by Marcel Chadeigne's students on 15 June at the Salle Pleyel)[45] and in the casinos (the *Prélude à l'après-midi d'un faune* was offered in September–October at the casinos in Biarritz and Vichy)![46]

More and more, the critics were inclined to reveal or to denounce Debussy's influence on the work of young composers. For example, works by Henry Woollett, Florent Schmitt, and Antony Lamotte at the Société nationale were deemed "very polished, [. . .] impressionist pictures free of design, always with a very interesting color";[47] likewise, Gabriel Grovlez was considered to be "under the obvious influence of M. Debussy."[48] The following year, Jean Huré would protest because some people accused Déodat de Séverac "of resembling

Debussy"[49] and others "shouted Debussyist" with regard to Florent Schmitt's *La procession dans la montagne*.[50] A German paper, the *Neue Zeitschrift*, did not hesitate to invent a "Debussy school,"[51] in which it grouped Déodat de Séverac, Rhené-Baton, and Eugène Lacroix. The critics took every opportunity to express their perplexity regarding the evolving musical language.

In 1905, several more specifically Parisian articles attempted to take a position regarding Debussyism, contributing toward further defining the factions. On 15 September, two articles that were very different from each other appeared simultaneously. One, "La Debussyte" by Camille Mauclair, was an amusing description of the musical disease of the time that brought up this confession: "I've heard that he [Debussy] was very annoyed by the zeal of these men."[52] The other article, "C'est du Debussy," was by Jean Huré, a young organist and composer. He endeavored to explain, with profuse musical examples, the origin of Debussy's harmonic innovations in the works of Chopin, Franck, and Chabrier, as well as those of Wagner and Liszt. What listeners discovered to be characteristic of Debussy's style, Huré wrote, was only the systematization of the dissonances practiced by these composers.[53]

Laloy really wanted to encourage Debussy to take up his pen again and to give his point of view in *Le mercure musical*, the new journal he had just launched with Jean Marnold. On 2 May 1905, the composer, apparently relenting, promised some "Interviews with Monsieur Croche" (Entretiens avec M. Croche);[54] then he changed his mind, after having read a few issues:

> Except for you, dear friend, the people at the *Mercure musical* are dreadful; above all, they're terribly full of information. I really don't see what poor M. Croche would do among so many unabashed specialists. [. . .]
> Don't hold it against me. . . I'd like you to succeed and I only fear that you're too sensitive or too well brought up for journalist types.[55]

And he wrote sarcastically about the "very charming stupidities" of Armande de Polignac, about "the Byzantine cabinetmaker" Marnold, and about Jean d'Udine—was he "a man or a limpet?"[56]

In response to the articles that came out in September, Émile Vuillermoz, who would soon hold a key position in music criticism, entered the fray with an article in the November issue of *Le mercure musical* that bore an innocuous title, "Une tasse de thé" (A cup of tea). In it, he settled his differences with Mauclair as well as with Laloy and Huré, refusing to distinguish between true or false Debussyists and maintaining that "the art of a composer like Debussy crystallizes a set of scattered tendencies that are floating in the musical atmosphere that we breathe, and in this way he has become truly representative. [. . .] Besides, it does not matter whether Debussy invented his unique harmonies or not. His originality lies not in them but rather in the novel proportions of his musical combinations and in what he has been able to elicit from them."[57]

The Premiere of *La mer*

Debussy's chief preoccupation was *La mer: Trois esquisses symphoniques*, his most important work since *Pelléas*. On 8 August, he first referred to correcting the proofs,[58] and a few days later, he shuddered at the thought of the clueless Chevillard having been called upon to conduct the work.[59] As he was continuing to proofread this complex score by himself, it is not surprising that he sent new corrections to Durand and his collaborator Choisnel at the beginning of September. The score of *La mer* was not commercially released until 15 November, and four years later it would be corrected again in a second edition.[60] Moreover, the rehearsals were tedious—as they were for *Pelléas*—due to the errors that remained in the orchestral parts.[61] Debussy attended the rehearsals, and once again recognized the conductor's inability to understand such a score:

> That man should have been a lion tamer, and while one must admire him when he works the orchestra, what a Caliban on the other hand!!![62] [. . .] "Jeux de vagues" still needs to be gone over in detail. The two other movements are almost ready; they need only final touch-ups. This is the moment I fear with Chevillard; he's clearly not much of an artist.[63]

La mer was performed at the Concerts Lamoureux on the following two Sundays. On 15 October, it was heard after Beethoven's Seventh Symphony and followed by Franck's fourth *Béatitude*, Vincent d'Indy's *Symphonie sur un thème montagnard*, and Berlioz's *Le carnaval romain* overture. And on 22 October, it was preceded by the overture to Lalo's *Le roi d'Ys*, Haydn's Symphony no. 2 in D Major, Saint-Saëns's symphonic poem titled *La jeunesse d'Hercule*, and an aria from Mozart's *Die Zauberflöte*, and followed by Franck's fourth *Béatitude* and Felix Weingartner's orchestration of Weber's *Invitation to the Dance*.

Some fifteen critics took it upon themselves to judge these symphonic sketches,[64] which resulted in a new anthology of journalistic blindness; they used phrases such as "cleverness,"[65] "incomprehensible and without grandeur,"[66] with a "strident and often disagreeable sound,"[67] a "rather weak imagination with respect to timbre,"[68] "some Debussy made for America,"[69] and so on. There is little need to rehash reviews by those who placed the work in the pictorial domain of a description of nature. Debussy took the trouble to reply to Pierre Lalo, who had written that he had neither seen nor felt the sea in this score, issuing the following remark: "You love and defend traditions that no longer exist for me."[70] Even the program note for a performance of *La mer* on 9 March 1910, written by Charles Malherbe, had given an example of anecdotal inspiration by curiously recalling the composer's stay in Jersey and by emphatically maintaining that these were musical "paintings" based on "nature";[71] he also pointed out that they were a product of "a sustained effort" over two years and "not an improvisation."[72] Meanwhile, several critics, such as Alfred Bruneau,[73] Louis Vernon,[74] and Jean d'Udine,[75] commented that *La mer* lacked the "seductiveness" of the *Nocturnes*. Finally, there were those who nonetheless tried to point out the originality of the work. For Calvocoressi, Debussy had "considerably condensed and clarified most of his innovations here."[76] Marnold discovered "the fabric of polyphony that is most noteworthy, with an eloquence and sparkling imagination that are unprecedented. There are pages where we feel ourselves at the edge of an abyss and can perceive its depths; there is an orchestra with unimaginable sounds."[77] Paul Dukas appeared to be singularly cautious in his praise, noting the composer's "technical virtuosity" and concluding simply that he was on the path to "renewal."[78]

The mediocrity of Chevillard's performance, pointed out by certain critics, is without doubt, but it explains only in part the very reserved reception in general that *La mer* received in Paris. The following 3 December, it was performed again in Brussels at the Concerts populaires. There, listeners were especially interested in comparing it to Belgian composer Paul Gilson's own *La mer*, described as his robust, "Flemish fresco."[79] The audience could only be disconcerted by what the critic of the *Guide musical* described as a "continual pursuit of elusive harmonies, [. . .] the equivalent of hazy colors and luminous transparencies."[80]

Perhaps no composition by Debussy has suffered as much as *La mer* from the gap between the originality of the musical ideas and the long delay in its acceptance. It may also be considered as the most secretive of his works, because the composer did not divulge details or refer to it, either in his letters or in his writings. It took several generations, during which time musical language evolved, for the particular nature of that score to become comprehensible, as it so greatly eludes the capacities of traditional analysis. In 1905, even for those listeners who were most attentive to innovations, *La mer* was a much more puzzling work than *Pelléas* had been; the changes in meter and tempo, the elliptical spirit in the unfolding of the motives, the "continuous vacillation," and the sudden dynamic outbursts as well as a new orchestral rhetoric were all experienced only with respect to their "kaleidoscopic" features, to borrow Jean Chantavoine's expression.[81]

It has been repeated again and again that the composer often reaffirmed his love for the sea, but it is quite futile to try to understand *La mer* apart from its intrinsically musical elements. The "network of pictorial, literary, and psychological associations" evoked by Edward Lockspeiser is not a sufficient explanation for the composition of *La mer*.[82] Certainly, Turner and Hokusai constituted part of Debussy's world, and it is obviously no accident that the composer wished to have Hokusai's "Wave" (one of the earliest images in his *Thirty-Six Views of Mount Fuji*) on the cover of his score. We should not overlook what Debussy stated in a letter written a few months after the premiere of *La mer*, recognizing that "music has this over painting: it can bring together variations of color and light within a single dimension."[83] But while he remained attracted to the notion of a correspondence between the arts, it amounted to only an influence, and certainly did not involve the means employed. Lockspeiser's demonstration that Debussy's score was "certainly the first great Impressionist work in music" or that "the spirit of Turner was still prominently in his mind" would come later.[84]

Since Lockspeiser's study, other analytical questions have been posed: for example, does the work follow the principles of the golden section? Can one demonstrate that it uses the Fibonacci series, as has been shown with respect to certain pieces by Schubert and Bartók? Without getting into the details, one might first wonder how Debussy, who seemed so removed from the mathematical world, could have consciously or unconsciously forced himself into such restrictive compositional practices. Roy Howat, who has supported this theory with brilliance tempered by caution,[85] was justified in invoking a few of Debussy's comments that might indicate his openness to this idea, especially regarding a measure that at one point was missing in "Jardins sous la pluie": "It's necessary for the sake of number," Debussy wrote, "the divine number, as Plato and Liane de Pougy would say."[86] Later, the composer would cite Plato again, this time with respect to Stravinsky's *Le roi des étoiles*, which for him suggested "the harmony of the eternal spheres."[87] In 1915, in *En blanc et noir*, he would restore four measures out of "concern for the proportions."[88] Finally, while critiquing the architecture of the new Opéra-Comique, Debussy wrote that he would have preferred the building to have been inspired by the "theory of light waves,[89] the mysterious harmonies that connect the various parts of an edifice."[90] In any case, the matter of proportions was obviously a major concern for Debussy, and Roy Howat admits that the composer's intuition played the greatest role, more so than all other theoretical modes of thinking. Howat's argument, which he attempted to prove with respect not only to *La mer* but also to *L'isle joyeuse*, involves considerable conjecture and implicit reasoning, more so than the manipulation of theoretical diagrams. Would this devotee of Edgar Allan Poe deliberately conceal every trace of calculations in his sketches and manuscripts, all the while considering the creation of a work (as did the hero of Poe's "The Philosophy of Composition") as a mathematical problem?[91]

With *La mer*, Debussy turned away from Symbolism once and for all. Did he feel less need to draw from the creative processes of the literary or plastic arts? In any case, he succeeded in mastering a personal style of writing, and his score marks a crucial stage in this progression by presenting problems of form, thematic material, and "development" in an entirely new way.[92] That is what he increasingly suggested when he spoke of his "chemistry."[93]

Settling into the Avenue du Bois de Boulogne

Even before his divorce was officially granted, Debussy took Emma to Eastbourne, on the English coast, at the end of July. Their departure resembled an escape, and it was followed by an "almost primal physical relaxation" on the little beach at the local Grand Hotel.[94] During a month's time, in addition to proofreading *La mer*, he put the final touches on the first series of the *Images* for piano, confiding to Durand: "I'm beginning to see my way clearly again in my creative projects, and my thinking machine (*machine à penser*) is gradually recovering."[95] Before returning to Paris, he spent a few days in London, "without much joy," in order to satisfy Emma's curiosity.[96]

At the beginning of September, with Emma's delivery of their child fast approaching, the selection of a new home became urgent. For a period of time, the couple moved to the Hôtel de la Feuilleraie in the quiet area of Bellevue, near Paris, and in October they moved to 64 avenue du Bois de Boulogne, in a "square filled with upscale residences."[97] There, on 30 October, fifteen days after the premiere of *La mer*, Claude-Emma Debussy was born. Soon called Chouchou, she was registered on 2 November "as having been born of unnamed parents."[98] Five days after Chouchou's birth, Debussy wrote to Laloy: "The joy of becoming a father has somewhat overwhelmed me and still frightens me."[99]

This year, loaded with personal and musical events, ended with two premieres: the third of the *Trois mélodies de Verlaine*, sung by Mme Camille Fourrier (6 December),[100] and the "Hommage à Rameau," played by Maurice Dumesnil (14 December),[101] the young pianist who had just won a first prize at the Conservatoire.[102] More significant and symbolically charged was the fact that Debussy's music was heard for the first time at the Conservatoire on the rue Bergère. On 17 December, Georges Marty, his former companion at the Villa Medici, conducted the *Prélude à l'après-midi d'un faune*: "And the walls have not collapsed," commented Jacques d'Offoël, who persisted in recognizing a theme from *Aida* in the work.[103] However, a "subscriber [. . .] blew a few shrill toots on a whistle. The audience flinched like an old English woman who had heard a 'shocking' or 'improper' word. But M. Marty [. . .] just kept smiling. Doesn't he know that, indeed, in some boxes (that shall remain unspecified) there still are listeners who suffer terribly from the prelude to *Tristan*?"[104] There is no doubt that this event had been made possible, thanks to the new director, Gabriel Fauré. Prodded by Emma, Debussy had congratulated him on his appointment, on 28 June: "If one decides to put 'the obvious choice' at the head of our Conservatoire, what will come to pass? And what old traditional dust will be shaken off!"[105]

Chapter Twenty

Projects and Skirmishes

1906–7

After his separation from Lilly, Debussy's relocation to a private mansion away from the center of Paris represented an abrupt change in his life—quite different from his former lifestyle. Emma was accustomed to living in comfort; the birth of Chouchou, in addition to the presence of Emma's daughter Dolly, led to the employment of a nurse and a housekeeper. While Debussy's copyright revenues had increased, and the income and the amounts stipulated in the contracts with Durand for each work were much more substantial than those the composer had received before 1905, his expenses had become onerous and would weigh more and more heavily on his daily life.

All of Debussy's biographers have reiterated that Emma had been expecting to inherit the fortune of her uncle, the financier Osiris, and that he likely disinherited her when she decided to begin a new life with the composer. A reading of the fourth and final will and testament of Daniel Iffla Osiris, drafted on 20 July 1906, provides a completely different view of the facts.[1] Given that the Pasteur Institute was the financier's chief beneficiary (for about forty million francs), Emma had no reason to hope that she would receive his entire inheritance. Among numerous private bequests, Osiris granted a yearly annuity of 3,000 francs to his nephew (the composer Raoul Bardac) and a sum of 100,000 francs to Dolly (Raoul's sister) which, however, she could not access until she turned twenty-one or married. "Mme Emma Moyse, divorced from M. Bardac," was to receive "an annual sum of no more than 5,000 francs."[2]

New Relationships

From then on, Debussy would lead a life of hard work, with little exposure to the outside world; he would sit at his desk, on which his favorite objects, such as the wooden toad he called Arkel, were placed. His parents now lived nearby, on the rue La Fontaine, and several photographs from 1906 (no doubt taken by Emma) show their happiness in visiting their son at his beautiful home. Manuel had just retired.

Among Debussy's new acquaintances was a young Portuguese composer, Francisco de Lacerda, who was born in the Azores. He had been a student of Vincent d'Indy at the Schola Cantorum, where he would later become a professor. In 1904, for his *Danse sacrée*, Debussy had borrowed the theme of Lacerda's "Danse du voile," which had been awarded a prize in a competition held by *Le Figaro*. At the beginning of 1906, Debussy befriended Lacerda, and recommended him to Alexandre Luigini[3] and Albert Carré, describing him as "a solid and proven composer who can be of real service with anything involving choruses, orchestra" and so on.[4] Debussy gave Lacerda the score of Jean-Philippe Rameau's *Fêtes de Polymnie*, which Durand had asked him to edit for Rameau's *Œuvres complètes* (even though Saint-Saëns was one of the editors-in-chief of the publication).[5] Debussy also wanted to help Lacerda publish, on a subscription basis, a collection of his country's folklore, suggesting the title of "Chants et danses d'un petit peuple oublié" (Songs and dances of a small forgotten community) and offering to write the preface for it.[6]

In April, a young writer named Victor Segalen paid Debussy a visit. Twenty-eight years old and a naval doctor, he had just spent two years in Oceania, from which he had brought back not only a love of Maori songs but also the material for his essay *Les immémoriaux* (The immemorials) and a Buddhist drama, *Siddartha*. A good pianist, he had been captivated by Debussy's music. As he had studied naval medicine in Bordeaux, he may have heard the *Nocturnes* there, during an unfortunate performance of the work in 1903, when the musicians were giggling while playing their parts and the audience was booing.[7] In any case, in April 1906 he asked Claude Farrère to put him in touch with Debussy, with whom "he want[ed] to try to tackle a Hindu subject."[8] Farrère, who found Segalen intelligent and likable but a little naïve, advised him to contact Pierre Louÿs, of all people. Finally, on 27 April, Segalen introduced himself directly to the composer and, rather than providing a completed libretto, outlined the topic of his proposed subject on the life of Buddha.[9] Debussy urged him to continue to develop the project. During their conversation, he showed interest in the music that Segalen had heard in Polynesia and strongly encouraged him to write an article based on the notes he had brought back. "Voix mortes: Musiques maori" (Dead voices: Maori music), edited by Laloy and dedicated to Debussy, was published in October 1907 in *Le mercure musical*.[10] This is how Debussy's interest in "other" musics—those he had heard in 1889 and those he had discussed with Bailly or Laloy—was rekindled.

An unexpected encounter with Paul-Jean Toulet showed how sensitive the composer was to the opinions of his former friends, since the turn of events that had preceded his new life. While visiting the Durand-Ruel gallery on 5

May, he had the impression that Toulet was avoiding him. That same evening, Debussy wrote to Toulet in order to express his surprise, adding: "I find it hard to believe that, given your usual outlook on life, you'd agree with the attitude of some of my so-called friends."[11] Toulet responded immediately that he had felt the same tension, reassuring the composer that this was not the case. Their relationship resumed, more closely than before, and the writer became a regular guest at Debussy's house on the avenue du Bois de Boulogne.[12]

Laloy remained the most frequent visitor to Debussy's home, as much on a social basis—dinners and bridge parties—as on a professional one. On 6 February, he gave a talk on "the works of Claude Debussy" at the beginning of a concert of songs and piano pieces at the Salle des Agriculteurs.[13] Mme Camille Fourrier, the wife of a doctor, had organized the concert, in which she herself sang five songs.[14] Lucienne Bréval sang the *Chansons de Bilitis*,[15] and Jean Périer sang the *Chansons de France*, the third of which was probably receiving its first performance.[16] In addition, Ricardo Viñes premiered the three *Images*, after having played them for the composer twice beforehand; he also performed "Pagodes," by his own admission "very badly," because he had not practiced sufficiently.[17] At the end of the program, Auguste Delacroix and Armand Petit played the third movement of *La mer* for piano, four hands, which no doubt convinced Debussy that this version was almost unplayable and persuaded him to favor a version for two pianos instead.[18]

On 24 February 1906, Debussy confessed to Raoul Bardac that he was writing "very little music,"[19] and then to Durand on 18 April that he "continue[d] to stagnate in the factories of Nothingness,"[20] and on 9 June that he was suffering from "a case of over-scrupulousness."[21] He nevertheless announced that he was "working to make up for a very bad period."[22] The only composition that he completed during these months was the "Serenade for the Doll" (by 8 March).[23] Octavie Carrier-Belleuse, a piano professor who had won her first prize at the Conservatoire in 1877,[24] had asked Debussy for a short piece for her *Méthode moderne de piano*.[25] Two years later, this "Sérénade" would be included in his *Children's Corner*, a work that bore witness to the central role his daughter played in his life. The *Méthode* did not appear, with the "Sérénade" included, until 1910.

In June and July, Debussy returned to two long-standing works in progress, "Ibéria" and *Le diable dans le beffroi*. But the family needed a change of atmosphere, and Chouchou was already old enough to enjoy the beach on the coast of Normandy. On 8 August, Debussy took his family to the Grand Hôtel du Puys, near Dieppe, where they stayed until 1 September. The hotel had few comforts, and the only place available for him to work was a small table, seventy-five centimeters long.[26] The little beach was "absurd," and there one regularly encountered some "really ugly" English people.[27] The hotel's cuisine was mediocre and even the sea seemed inadequate and resembled a "leaky bathtub."[28] At his little table, Debussy pondered "three different ways to finish 'Ibéria.' Should I flip a coin, or should I search for a fourth solution?"[29]

No sooner had he returned to Paris than he met up again with Paul Dukas, a friend with whom he had lost touch. Dukas wanted Debussy to hear his *Ariane et Barbe-bleu*, and left the score of the third act with him. The somewhat hollow praise that Debussy sent him on 19 September leads us to believe that he was not very enthusiastic about that opera,[30] an opinion that was verified later when he told Victor Segalen that he did not care for the character of Ariane, calling her a "freelance traveling salesman."[31]

The Growing Fame of *Pelléas*

The end of the year was particularly busy, with the Opéra-Comique's revival of *Pelléas*, now under the baton of Franz Ruhlmann. Debussy objected to a general carelessness that he perceived among the performers. He even apologized for his impatience during the rehearsals in a letter to Dufranne, adding: "Please exaggerate, if anything, the depressing and poignant sadness of Golaud... convey strongly all that he regrets not having said or done... and all the happiness that he now will never experience."[32] However, the fiftieth performance would be celebrated, and, following the custom of the time, Debussy contributed 100 francs to the theater's pension fund.[33] Sitting in the audience at this production was Giacomo Puccini, who was in Paris for rehearsals of *Madama Butterfly*[34] and who lamented—as did others—that the "irritating" Marguerite Carré was one of the performers in his opera.[35] Also in attendance was Pierre Louÿs, who had clearly written off his former friend but pestered Debussy to consider writing an opera on *Conchita*, an adaptation of *La femme et le pantin*. Puccini's opinion of *Pelléas* was not surprising: the work was "truly interesting, despite its dark color, as monochromatic as the habit worn by a Franciscan monk."[36]

The work continued to be successful, however, with the public. Jacques Rivière, a young writer impassioned by *Pelléas*, noted that year: "Two performances each week do not wear out its success. Every time, endless cheering erupts throughout the hall: everyone brings his score, even those seated on the main floor and in the boxes; gloved hands applaud wildly."[37] Pierre Lalo recorded that "the Debussyist religion has replaced the Wagnerian religion."[38]

On 25 March 1906, Debussy had lunch at Durand's office with Richard Strauss, who had expressed a desire to meet him.[39] But no real dialogue between the two composers took place because Strauss seemed preoccupied exclusively with copyright problems, about which his lunch partner maintained an "obstinate silence."[40] The following year, on 21 May, "the symphonic domestic," as Debussy called him,[41] was in Paris once again for the highly anticipated performances of *Salome*, and so was finally able to hear *Pelléas* at the Opéra-Comique. His assessment—quite characteristic of the incomprehension of a composer who was original in his own way but unreceptive to the subtleties of Symbolism—was meticulously reported by Romain Rolland, who was in the same box as Strauss that evening:

> After the first act (the first three scenes), he said to me: "Is it like this all the time?" —"Yes." —"Nothing more?. . . Nothing more. . . No music. . . Nothing connects. . . It doesn't hold together. . . No musical phrases. No development." [. . .] "Me, I'm a composer first and foremost. Whenever music is part of a work, I want it to be the focal point; I don't want it to be subordinate to anything else. This is too modest. [. . .] There's not enough music for me here. There are very delicate harmonies, very good orchestral effects, very tasteful; but this is nothing, nothing at all. I find that it's merely Maeterlinck's play, all alone, without music." [. . .] He was sure to mention every single Wagnerian imitation, and this was not intended as praise. "But this is all *Parsifal*," he told me of a passage. Yet, the hair scene ["Mes longs cheveux"], the prelude to the underground scene, and the following scene gave him a certain pleasure. Of course, these were his favorite scenes in the entire score. But he always returned to his slightly disdainful praise: "It's very refined."[42]

Romain Rolland, who had solicited a musical autograph from Debussy in 1905,[43] would devote an article to *Pelléas* in a Berlin journal (1907), which he reprinted in his collection *Musiciens d'aujourd'hui* (1908).[44] He began by declaring that the work "was one of the most significant accomplishments in the history of French music; [. . .] one of the three or four most important dates in our operatic theater," but, after having identified its original features, he expressed some reservations, deeming that *Pelléas* represented only one facet of the French genius,[45] and abruptly declaring in a footnote: "In fact, I'm not a Debussyist. My sympathies lie with a completely different art."[46]

The Opéra-Comique had become a required stop for every European composer visiting Paris, and sometimes journalists reported these composers' opinions as they left a production of *Pelléas*. Thus Rimsky-Korsakov, on 23 May 1907, declared that the work had no future, that it was very monotonous, and that he did not understand its "harmonic combinations," doubting that the composer himself understood them; Nikisch, on the contrary, was very favorable, with this criticism of the performance: "The orchestra generally played too loudly and too uniformly and did not enter into the music's intimacy."[47]

Yet again it was *Pelléas* that prompted Debussy to leave for Brussels on 27 December 1906. At the invitation of Maurice Kufferath and Guillaume Guidé, the directors of the Théâtre de la Monnaie, the composer spent fourteen days there—two weeks during which he sent depressing letters to Durand and Laloy that show him once again grappling with the disappointments of the theatrical experience:

> My nerves are shot from spending afternoons with an orchestra that lacks tact and taste. As for M. Sylvain Dupuis, he's more like an ox than an orchestra conductor. . . he has a special way of distorting the simplest of rhythms in a way that, I hope, belongs only to him.
> As for the singers, it's an odd mix. . . [Jean] Bourbon has a lovely voice but declaims like a house painter. M. [Henri] Artus is singing Arkel; he has neither the voice nor the body type for the role. He strips all nobility and emotion from the character; besides, he reeks of wine like a furniture mover. Mme [Jeanne] Bourgeois won't be bad in the role of Geneviève; Mlle [Marguerite] Das has a light voice and is slightly disconcerted by the lack of florid passages in the role of Yniold.[48] (to Durand, 3 January 1907)

> I had to reteach the orchestra, whose Flemish spirit is about as manageable as a 100-kilogram weight. . . the woodwinds, heavy and strident, and the brass, in contrast, sounding as if wrapped in absorbent cotton. . . add to that their annoying ability to warp the simplest rhythm. . . In short, a constant struggle—utterly exhausting—to end up with something more or less acceptable.[49] (to Laloy, 23 January 1907)

Debussy departed from Brussels before the premiere, which was a genuine success. Since he had left the impression that he was a particularly demanding composer, he charged Sylvain Dupuis with thanking the musicians in the orchestra "for their good will and patience."[50] According to some critics, "the staunchest Wagnerians" declared themselves captivated, and Paul Gilson, composer of the Flemish *La mer*, wrote that the orchestra of *Pelléas* was "expressive to the point of cruelty."[51] As for Debussy, he confided something in his thanks to Kufferath that cannot be found elsewhere: "Very simply, I admit that the five acts of *Pelléas* would have benefited from being condensed into just three acts."[52]

New Controversies

Back in Paris, Debussy was sought out by Colonne, who programmed the *Prélude à l'après-midi d'un faune* twice and continued to demand the music for *Le roi Lear*. Did Debussy orchestrate "Le jet d'eau," one of the *Poèmes de Baudelaire*, to please him or to satisfy Durand's editorial appetite? He always shied away from this sort of task. He was even more reticent after the unfavorable reception of this orchestrated song when it was performed by Hélène Demellier, one of Mme Colonne's best students, on 24 February 1907.[53] The most unexpected and most subtly worded attack did not come from one of the composer's usual opponents, but from Émile Vuillermoz, the mastermind of the "bataillon sacré" who had led the fight in favor of *Pelléas* and who wrote the following lines in the 3 March 1907 issue of *La nouvelle presse*:

> The genuine admirers of the composer of *Pelléas*—and they grow in number every day—have long deplored the silence observed by their favorite composer. Working hard, no doubt, during his retreat, M. Debussy has been disdainfully delivering nothing but revivals, reprints, and scraps from the bottom of the barrel.[54] Under other titles and in new arrangements, his former output is methodically reviewed with the greatest sorrow by avid lovers of musical first editions and unpublished works! This "Jet d'eau" (simply extracted from the *Cinq poèmes de Baudelaire*, which all Debussyists know by heart) is not able to quench their thirst for something new. With what contemptuous ease has the composer of the *Nocturnes* orchestrated this old song, his sole intention being to maintain a presence on Colonne's posters for the winter season. No fluidity, freshness, or sparkle is found in the instrumentation of this work. The beloved descriptive techniques of *Pelléas* recur at random, without any justification. One misses the piano accompaniment when faced with an orchestra that is devoid of cohesion or color, in which one does not find—either in the harps or in the inevitably muted trumpet—the exquisite vision of the "gerbe d'eau, qui berce ses mille fleurs que la lune traverse de ses pâleurs"![55]
>
> In his long idleness, will M. Debussy lose the prodigious skill and the instrumental touch that have made him unquestionably one of the most astonishing poets of the modern orchestra? In this case, I see only one remedy for this unfortunate situation: that the composer of *Pelléas* read the works of the young composers who are considered members of his school, and that he listen to this *small class* about which—a little too easily, one might add—contemporary critics get all worked up; there he will find very skillful realizations of all the sonorous discoveries that he seems to have forgotten. The master will learn a useful lesson from listening to his impudent disciples, and he will understand and be startled by the danger that is growing around him. If he does not renew his efforts to firmly regain the leadership of the contemporary musical movement, the composer of *Pelléas* will realize that the young parasitic generation developing around his work is altogether more successfully "Debussyan". . . than Debussy himself![56]

Even more than Pierre Lalo's diatribes, this prose must have affected Debussy at a moment when, while remaining above the fray, he admitted that he found himself in a "state of conflict between music and myself."[57] At the time, he often saw Laloy, and it was no doubt with his permission that the musicologist wrote a reply to Vuillermoz—without citing the latter's name but indicating Debussy as the composer—in an article titled "Les écoliers" (The schoolchildren).[58] In it, Laloy denigrated the attitude of the critics who demanded "a monthly ration of completely new harmonies," and he stooped almost to the point of obsequiousness in describing Debussy as the "purest composer to have appeared since Mozart."[59] The following passage probably flattered the composer the most:

> The role of forerunner would certainly not displease him; but the person who should succeed him and inherit his legacy has not yet been revealed. And Ravel, you might say? We must put an end to this ridiculous misunderstanding. Ravel is not Debussy's disciple, nor his heir, nor his rival. He is a composer of a completely different nature, suited for certain types of works that I have tried to describe, while acknowledging that such a young composer can still give us many surprises. But there is obviously nothing in common between Ravel and Debussy, except that they are living in the same period of time and that the younger of the two has inevitably utilized certain devices that the elder had introduced into the musical language. It is thus of little importance to us that a clumsy friend has attempted [to draw] impossible parallels. The works are there, and Maurice Ravel knows himself too well; I would even say that his self-respect is too strong for him to even want to try to "be Debussyan."[60]

Debussy–Ravel

Debussy's relationship with Ravel was initially cordial, but had become somewhat uneasy. At the Société nationale, Ravel's *Jeux d'eau* (1902), the String Quartet (1904), and *Miroirs* (1906) had been heard,[61] and the performance of the *Histoires naturelles* on 12 January 1907 had recently attracted some attention.[62] Works of the two composers were juxtaposed in certain concert programs, as on 10 February 1905, when Viñes played Ravel's *Jeux d'eau*, which was a "colossal success," followed by Debussy's *Masques* and *L'isle joyeuse*.[63] At a concert in which the Parent quartet had performed the quartets of the two composers, Raymond Bouyer wrote that they were both "musical equivalents of Whistler's nocturnes, though slightly decadent, or, when joyful, of Monticelli's colors."[64] While Calvocoressi found their works rather different,[65] Romain Rolland felt that Ravel was "more Debussyist than Debussy."[66]

The first clash between the two composers was caused by a critic's indiscretion. In the 9 April 1907 issue of *Le temps*, Pierre Lalo published the text of a letter that Ravel had sent him on 5 February 1906, in which the latter staked his claim to a technical innovation in writing for the piano:

> You dwell at some length on a rather special style of pianistic writing whose invention you attribute to Debussy. Yet *Jeux d'eau* appeared at the beginning of 1902, while the only [piano] works by Debussy that existed at the time were the three movements from *Pour le piano*—pieces which I need not tell you how passionately I admire, but which, from a purely pianistic point of view, produced nothing really new.[67]

A year later, Louis Laloy praised Ravel's *Histoires naturelles*, comparing them to Mussorgsky's *Nursery* cycle, "but united by such confidence of taste and such wonderful skill."[68] Debussy fired back a letter to his friend, revealing much about his attitude toward his younger colleague:

> I've received no. 2 of the *S. I. M.* . . . and am surprised to read in it that a man of your taste deliberately renounces the pure and instinctive masterpiece that is the *Nursery* for the contrived Americanism of M. Ravel's *Histoires naturelles*. In spite of the undeniable skill of the latter, these songs can only be music that is "out of place." So leave the task [of commenting on these songs] to Calvocoressi, the lackey![69]

Debussy appeared more measured when addressing Jacques Durand, who in the meantime had a score of the *Histoires naturelles* sent to him: "It's extremely odd! It's artificial and fanciful, a little like a sorcerer's house. But 'Le Cygne' is quite pretty music nonetheless."[70] Finally, he explained himself further to Laloy, denying the existence of "humoristic music":[71] "I agree with you in acknowledging that Ravel can't be more gifted, but what irritates me is his self-portrayal as a 'trickster,' or better yet, as a charming Fakir who makes flowers spring up around a chair. . . Unfortunately, a trick is always prepared, and it can astonish only once!"[72]

While these reactions remained unknown in the small musical world of Paris, the same was not true of the "'Habanera' affair," which we will briefly summarize here.[73] Ravel had apparently lent Debussy the manuscript of the second piece of his *Sites auriculaires* for two pianos, first performed (by Ricardo Viñes and Marthe Dron) in 1898. Debussy would have noticed the characteristic effect of an extended pedal, which he himself subsequently employed in "La soirée dans Grenade." Ravel complained about this, first to those around him,[74] then by inscribing the compositional date of 1895 in the orchestral version of the "Habanera," which he reworked in his *Rapsodie espagnole* of 1907. This little incident, as well as a joke that Ravel was said to have made concerning Debussy's remarriage, contributed to the increasing distance between the two composers.

At the end of this 1907 season, Debussy congratulated Gabriel Astruc, a music publisher and very dynamic impresario whom he already knew, on the five historic Russian Concerts that he had organized at the Opéra, and which Debussy found "admirable," although containing "peculiar oversights."[75] However, the composer declined an invitation to attend a banquet in honor of the Russian musicians, doubtless to avoid having to mingle with Fauré, d'Indy, Messager, and Ravel, since he was squabbling with all of them, each for quite different reasons.

The *Roman de Tristan*

Debussy continued to struggle with the *Images* for orchestra. He told Segalen, "I can't allow myself simply to dash them off. Until now, I've left nothing incomplete. I don't want to do that!"[76] But he was always on the lookout for a large-scale operatic project. In July 1907, just before leaving for the coast of the English Channel, he received a visit from Gabriel Mourey, who made a very tempting proposal, which the composer described to Victor Segalen:

> After I read Bédier's *Roman de Tristan* when it was first published,[77] I found it so beautiful that I immediately wanted to turn it into an opera. It struck me as essential to restore the legendary character of *Tristan*, so terribly deformed by Wagner and by [his] dubious philosophizing, which remains even more inexplicable in this work than anywhere else. . . Then I forgot about this project until recently, when Mourey, whom I had not seen for years, sought me out and told me about his plans for *Tristan*. My enthusiasm—badly dormant, I admit—awakened, and I accepted![78]

In the excitement of this new project, the Debussys left again for Pourville at the beginning of August, in spite of a "natural aversion to living in a hotel":[79] the Grand Hotel was "very nasty, with a casino, some games, some small horses, old bastards, and young hookers";[80] it's full of English people who "put on ceremonious outfits to eat revolting food."[81] Just the same, Debussy's old friend, Curnonsky, came to visit; but their former bond no longer existed, and the latter seemed to him like an "American 'businessman.'"[82]

During the first days there, he was gripped with "unbearable"[83] intestinal attacks and thought only of returning to Paris with its "circular railroad,[84] whose sound is more pleasant than that of the waves."[85] He slaved at his worktable, sketching a few themes for *Tristan*. He thought about reorchestrating *L'enfant prodigue*, which Durand wanted to republish, and took up the *Images* again, particularly "Rondes de printemps," in which he sought to render the music "incorporeal," confessing along the way a deeply felt thought: "I'm more and more convinced that music, by its very essence, is not something that can slip into a rigorous and traditional form. It is made of colors and of rhythmicized time."[86]

Since an indiscretion by Mourey had already given the press an opportunity to announce that *Tristan* would be scheduled for the following season at the Opéra-Comique,[87] Debussy decided to confess to Segalen that he was not able to start on *Siddartha*: "I know no music capable of penetrating that abyss!" he exclaimed.[88] He suggested that Segalen think about the Orpheus myth,[89] from which he believed "something admirable" might be made.[90] And, returning to Paris around 15 September, he noted bitterly that he had done "nothing of worth,"[91] that he had spent "a month of vacation, musically inert."[92]

Just after his return, he worked on *Tristan* with Gabriel Mourey for an entire day: "I think we're on the right track," he wrote to Durand on 25 September.[93] The refinement of the libretto continued well into November, but he confessed to Segalen that Mourey's prose did not strike him as "very operatic," and that many of the passages did not exactly "'call' for music."[94]

Since the end of the previous year, Debussy had been approached by a young critic from Le Havre, Georges Jean-Aubry, who had founded a "Cercle de l'art moderne" in his hometown. The composer agreed to become an honorary member of this organization, which proposed to disseminate contemporary French music in England. Another member of this circle was André Caplet, winner of the Prix de Rome in 1901, who visited Debussy in October 1907; recognizing that he could trust Caplet's taste, Debussy gave him carte blanche to organize a concert devoted to his works at Le Havre.[95] This was the beginning of a collaboration that would take on a great deal of importance in Debussy's life.

The only newsworthy event in which he was involved at the end of 1907 was the premiere of the *Petite suite*, orchestrated by Henri Busser, on 4 November. The composer attended rehearsals, as did Busser, who described an episode in which Debussy had asked for more flexibility and Chevillard supposedly retorted (while turning his back to the composer): "Flexibility, I don't know what that is! Faster or slower!"[96] This comment was nothing more than an almost literal repetition of the dialogue already described between the two men before the premiere of the *Nocturnes*.[97]

At the end of November, Debussy invited the Laloys and Ricardo Viñes to dinner, in order to have them hear the second book of *Images*, which he had just finished. The Catalan pianist described the scene in his journal as follows:

> Debussy played me three new pieces that will be published, and one of which is dedicated to me—the very first work that he's dedicated to me! All three are marvelous, and we played them twice. Mine bears the title "Poissons d'or"; it's extremely beautiful and very original. Then we asked him for the first three *Images* and he played them for us as well. We were there until one o'clock in the morning, talking almost the entire time about the Schola Cantorum and about the wrongs done to music by the second-rate musicians who lead that institution. Debussy's wife (the former Mme Bardac) is very likable, and she has a daughter of about fifteen, quite sweet.[98]

The romance with the Schola Cantorum had indeed passed. From then on, this institution considered itself a competitor of the Conservatoire and extended its influence over the Société nationale de musique. While Debussy himself preferred to steer clear of the conflict, which would continue until the war, the Debussyists—especially the critics—were among the most vitriolic with respect to the temple on the rue Saint-Jacques.[99]

Chapter Twenty-One

Orchestra Conductor

1908

Taking the Plunge: Marrying Emma and Conducting *La mer*

Claude and Emma had lived together for more than three years. The topic of marriage must have often strained their conversations. It has been said that Debussy was likely uncertain about this matter. He referred to it, in a slightly ambivalent way, in a letter to Laloy from 15 October 1907: "I work on important things, alternating between joy and sadness. . . in short, peace does not dwell in my soul! Is this because of the hectic environment in this part of Paris. . ? Am I truly not cut out for domestic life? So many questions, and I lack the strength to answer them."[1]

A few days before, he had announced to Victor Segalen: "I don't even talk about music with my wife. Unless it's about inconsequential music."[2] And yet, he gave in to Emma's pleas, under pressure from elsewhere: a law of 9 November 1907 regarding children born out of wedlock allowed them to legitimize Chouchou. So Claude married Emma on 20 January 1908 at the town hall of the 16th arrondissement. He was forty-five years old.[3]

The day before, he had taken another plunge by stepping up to the podium in a concert hall for the first time. Although he had considered conducting for some time,[4] the occasion was unplanned: Colonne was supposed to conduct *La mer* on 12 January; as the rehearsals proved to be "lamentable," Debussy told Segalen: "I was asked to conduct the performance."[5]

> It was not without a pounding heart that I mounted the podium yesterday morning for the first rehearsal. It's the first time in my life that I'm playing the role of conductor; rest assured that my genuine inexperience must disarm those curious beasts called "orchestral musicians," their goodwill notwithstanding.
>
> Other impressions. . . : one really feels the heart of one's own music. . . When it "sounds" quite well, it feels as if one has oneself become an

instrument issuing many different sonorities, unleashed merely by the movements of the little baton.[6]

And to Paul-Jean Toulet, he wrote on 22 January:

It's enjoyable as long as one is searching for orchestral color from the end of the little stick; but afterward, it feels like an exhibition where one's success seems to me not unlike that of a freak-show performer, or of an acrobat who successfully executes a dangerous leap.[7]

The audience reception for this new performance of *La mer* was much more spectacular than it had been when Chevillard premiered the work in 1905. Willy described the scene in this way:

For an indefinite period of time, there were howls of wild joy, barrages of clapping hands, curtain calls, and frenzied shouts. Ten times Debussy made his way through the forest of music stands to approach the prompt box, acknowledging his heartfelt gratitude; now and then, a sudden, strong, and piercing whistle—like a departure signal given by a train conductor—triggered the triumphal convoy again [. . .] rekindling the enthusiasm of aching biceps and stinging hands. In order to satisfy the delirious music lovers, the triumphant hero, who had rushed down a staircase, had to be brought back one last time, already clothed in his overcoat and donning his bowler hat, which, in our modern costume, substitutes for the ancient laurel wreath.[8]

The critics were once again divided between those who saw a "continual and vague flitting,"—prompting one listener to exclaim, "I am seasick!"[9]—and those who agreed with Laloy's highly developed and profound article. Laloy revealed the composer's new approach, "a tight style—established, assertive, full, in a word, classic";[10] a solid structure; a harmony that "spreads across the entire orchestra, passes from one group to the other, grows and deepens in turn, and above all manifests itself in vivid accents, in decisive motives, even in complete melodies, which bring these formerly immobile elements to life, divide them into successive planes, and give them fluidity.[11] [. . .] They [the movements] are truly dances [. . .] of intertwined rhythms which suddenly appear, call each other, organize themselves in gleaming circles, in disjunct and constantly reformed processions, and in harmonious uproars."[12]

Pelléas Abroad

Debussy traveled abroad only very rarely for performances of his compositions—even for *Pelléas*, which, thanks to Durand's impetus, continued to be successful. In letters to his publisher, Debussy at times gives hints of his preferences and opinions in favor of a particular conductor. For example, on 23 August 1907, he wrote: "For Munich, I'm delighted. . . I think Mottl might possibly give a more intense performance than Messager."[13] In Frankfurt (17 April 1907), Cologne (15 September 1908), Munich (9 October 1908), and then in Berlin (6 November 1908), *Pelléas* was given in Otto Neitzel's German translation, which Debussy had praised to Durand two years earlier. It is somewhat surprising that his lack of German did not prevent Debussy from expressing this opinion: "The translation is perfect, nearly all the accents are in place, and it is truly a tour de force. I might add that the German text is more poetic than the French. You must admit that one couldn't ask for more."[14] While its reception was relatively favorable in Frankfurt, the performances in Munich and Berlin were not at all successful, in spite of a few reviews that were more or less sympathetic. In his article reporting on the Frankfurt performance, Hugo Schlemüller went so far as to write that the score of *Pelléas* resembled a series of "harmonic abortions."[15] Felix Mottl, who had in his own country so happily defended Chabrier and on whom, as we have seen, Debussy's hopes were founded, had ultimately declined the offer for Munich.[16] In Berlin, Joaquin Nin claimed that the audience was "polite and very patient," the criticism "absurd, ridiculous, and naive," and that "the Berliners did not understand a single note of it!"[17]

In New York, *Pelléas* was performed in French seven times at the Manhattan Opera (beginning on 19 February 1908), with several of the singers from the Parisian premiere (Mary Garden, Jean Périer, and Hector Dufranne), under the direction of Cleofonte Campanini. The reception was very lukewarm. A few weeks later, on 2 April, the work survived the ultimate test at La Scala in Milan, where it was sung in Italian under the direction of Arturo Toscanini, who, convinced of the difficulty of his undertaking, decided to see his risky venture through to the end. It was a real battle. The dress rehearsal went relatively peacefully. At the premiere, the fracas was especially disruptive during the third act, making it nearly impossible to hear the second scene, but at the end of the fourth and fifth acts, applause prevailed. The seven performances were able to take place, just the same, thanks to a few avant-gardists and the students from the conservatory.[18] Among the critics, Ildebrando Pizzetti compared *Pelléas* to the first Italian operas by Peri and Caccini.[19]

Debussy once again made the trip to London, where, benefiting from his quite recent experience as an orchestra conductor, he conducted the *Prélude à l'après-midi d'un faune* and *La mer* on 1 February, for a particularly generous fee. When he was offered 100 guineas, he retorted: "And yet you pay Caruso 400 guineas?"[20] As a result, Sir Edgar Speyer, the sponsor, agreed to raise the sum to a full 200 guineas.[21] Make no mistake about it: Debussy's travels were mainly determined by the financial terms he was offered.

Henry Wood, the organizer of the Promenade Concerts at Queen's Hall, was struck by the composer's physical appearance:

> I recall most vividly my first impressions of that dark, bearded Frenchman: his deep, soulful eyes; his quiet and rather grating voice; and especially his enormous head. I have never seen such a head on a man of his stature; it reminded me of heads of the early Egyptians.
>
> Debussy seemed delighted—almost like a child—because he thought that we in London appreciated his music more than his own countrymen. [. . .]
>
> Not even Strauss had received a warmer welcome.[22]

Segalen had also come to London and attended the rehearsals. He described Debussy's irritation, when instead of the four rehearsals he had hoped for, he was offered only one with the full ensemble. The composer worked with the brass, woodwind, and percussion sections in the morning, and the strings in the afternoon. Segalen reported the following: "Always the same fragmentary feeling of abrupt, luxurious bursts quickly stopped by the conductor's cutoff, with corrections or directions. Three, four measures at a time."[23]

England was better prepared than other countries to understand Debussy's music, as its culture was still responsive to the Symbolist aesthetic.[24] He was "the Mallarmé of music" for the critic Arthur Symons, who was Verlaine's translator and who found in Debussy a resemblance to Rossetti's later portraits. And it was also in England that the first monographs devoted to the composer—by Louise Liebich (1907) and William H. Daly (1908)—appeared.[25]

Images for Piano (Second Series) and Further Dissemination of *Pelléas*

At the beginning of 1908, Parisians had their first opportunity to hear the second series of *Images* for piano. The movements were dedicated respectively to three men: Alexandre Charpentier, a sculptor who had become a regular visitor at the avenue du Bois de Boulogne;[26] Louis Laloy, to whom was dedicated a piece with a title "in the Chinese style" ("Et la lune descend sur le temple qui fut"); and lastly, Ricardo Viñes, who premiered the work on 21 February and who was the dedicatee of "Poissons d'or," which evoked a black, Chinese lacquer panel, depicting fish in mother-of-pearl and gold, that hung in Debussy's study. This matinee concert, at which Maggie Teyte—the future Mélisande—sang the *Fêtes galantes*, was held in the hall of the Société française de photographie and organized by Charles Domergue, a young violinist who, thanks to his wife's fortune, had financed a Cercle musical for the previous two years. This first performance of the *Images* was an "absolute fiasco," in the words of

Viñes.[27] The critical reception was trivial or negative. Along with Vuillermoz, it was Marnold—until this point an almost unconditional supporter—who deplored the evolution of Debussy's style, "which borders on evaporating into the abstract or on disintegrating into the exquisite. Its strength, or what gives the illusion of strength, appears to be chiefly intellectual, and cannot disguise the strong willfulness, if not the effort, that went into its making."[28] The performance of André Caplet's transcription of *La mer* for two pianos, six hands, also went unnoticed; it was played on 6 March at the same Cercle musical by Marcel Chadeigne, Auguste Delacroix, and Jean Roger-Ducasse (who would grow closer to the composer).

It was not until 1 April 1908 that *Pelléas* was produced in France outside of Paris—at the Grand Théâtre in Lyon, under the direction of Philippe Flon. For three evenings, the opera was performed with completely new singers in the cast; the halls were half empty, in spite of the active support of a few critics. The main critic and future biographer of the composer, Léon Vallas, had cause to lament: "Not even five hundred music lovers are capable of interest in a new work."[29] The composer, who had taken it upon himself to explain the composition at length to the orchestra conductor, was fortunately unruffled.

At the beginning of May, Debussy was pleased to go to the Opéra for one of the last rehearsals of Rameau's *Hippolyte et Aricie*. He even submitted an article to *Le Figaro* in which he reiterated his admiration for Rameau's "true and well-placed expressiveness,"[30] yet he feared that "our ears have lost the ability" to listen to it "with thoughtful sensitivity."[31] Indeed, while he valued the talent of the tenor Rodolphe Plamondon (Hippolyte), he criticized the conducting of his colleague Paul Vidal: "Poor interpretation at the Opéra. Not in the rhythm of the work. After all, one need only look at a portrait of Rameau to see all that is required in terms of precision and clarity. Anyway, it was not played in the style of that period, with that magical and suitably appropriate element."[32] All the same, he was moved by the fourth act: "On these simple words, 'Hippolyte is no longer,' Rameau focuses in on a single, admirable measure, without using thirty-six superimposed themes!"[33]

The Parisian musical landscape was becoming more rigid under the pressure—deliberate or not—of certain critics. At the end of 1907, Camille Mauclair had attempted to identify "the musical chapels in France."[34] With regard to the relationship between Debussy and Ravel, we have already noted the mayhem caused by some indiscretions. At the revival of *Ariane et Barbe-bleue* in March 1908, the critic Pierre Lalo seemed to want to add fuel to the fire by establishing a sort of moral and aesthetic barrier between those partial to *Pelléas*—who, compared with people of taste, consisted of "degenerate aesthetes"[35]—and those partial to Paul Dukas's opera. And Lalo went so far as to write: "On some days, the displeasure of finding ourselves aligned with them could make us think that *Pelléas*, in order to have such partisans, must have some flaws in it that we have not yet noticed."[36] Debussy immediately reacted to this outrageous remark with great intensity:

> What I find most painful in this affair is that the means employed are so base and that in the end the "good Jew" [Dukas] would be defended by the "bad Jesuit" [Lalo]... I do not deny for one second that the music of *Ariane et Barbe-bleue* is much more likely to satisfy these gentlemen's taste than the music of *Pelléas*. But why try to prevent the venerable "scoundrels" from preferring their "flaws" and eternal damnation?[37]

Truth be told, some critics, such as Jean Huré, expressed similar moral judgments; reporting on Dukas's *Variations* for piano, Huré did not hesitate to write: "We are very far from the delightful Debussyan seductions, which momentarily fascinate but quickly wear thin: the *true composer* enjoys these neither for a long time nor often, just as the *sane man* takes pleasure in his vices, even delicate and refined ones, for only a rather short time."[38] Fortunately, the friendship between the two composers subjected to such comparisons was strong enough to withstand these types of tests.

In June 1908, Sergei Diaghilev took a big risk in producing *Boris Godunov* at the Opéra; the leading role was sung by Feodor Chaliapin, whose performance had been the high point of the five historic Russian concerts the previous year. Lalo took advantage of the occasion to indulge in a comparison of the two operas: "*Pelléas* and *Boris* have several harmonic progressions and a few orchestral sonorities in common, nothing more."[39] Debussy's music "is ordered, with as many harmonic refinements as *Boris* is full of disorder and chaos."[40] Debussy, who had attended the second performance on 21 June with André Caplet, considered it his duty to thank the critic for setting the record straight: "To have provided some clarity regarding the *Boris–Pelléas* debate is a decent gesture on your part, all the more so since, a certain number of fools having participated in it,[41] this issue threatened to be blown all out of proportion."[42]

At the same time, Debussy was particularly worried about a revival of *Pelléas* at the Opéra-Comique on 13 June, with a new Mélisande who had been recommended by Jean de Reszke: Maggie Teyte, a twenty-year-old Englishwoman. "She has a charming voice and a true sense of Mélisande's character,"[43] the composer thought at first; but subsequently he was dissatisfied with rehearsals, so much so that he seemed to reject nearly the entire cast in a fit of pique four days before the performance: "Miss M. Teyte continues to have about as much emotion as a prison door; she is a more-than-distant princess... Périer admirably mimes the music; Dufrane [sic] bellows; only Vieuille remains the same—which is to say, very good."[44] In the end, Debussy would acknowledge that Maggie Teyte did "not fare too poorly" in comparison with Mary Garden.[45] However, *Pelléas* seemed to have lost its shock effect. Ravel noted on 19 June: "The day before yesterday, I saw Séverac at a performance of *Pelléas* (small audience—clearly, it's not going nearly as well this year)."[46]

Projects and Interviews

While everyone waited and seemed to clamor for major works from Debussy, ones that were likely to create a new sensation, he divided his time between the composition of *Children's Corner* and putting the final touches on three *a cappella* songs—the *Chansons de Charles d'Orléans*—which, following the *Chansons de France*, confirmed his support of the national tradition for which he had campaigned over the previous five years. He also went back to the libretto of Victor Segalen's *Orphée*, suggesting many modifications. But above all, this was the period during which he revisited Edgar Allan Poe's stories, focusing no longer on *Le diable dans le beffroi* (on which he tried to work right after *Pelléas*) but on *La chute de la maison Usher*—the tale whose character is the most musical, beginning with the strange, warped improvisations that Roderick plays on his guitar. In *La chute*, Debussy returned to a theme about which he had spoken to Godet nearly twenty years previously—namely, his slightly morbid fascination with women in the process of becoming disembodied: "There are times when I lose a clear sense of my surroundings; and if Roderick Usher's sister were to enter my house, I wouldn't be surprised at all";[47] and "the external world scarcely exists any longer for me."[48] He worked on *La chute* in this fashion during June and July, and even planned for its performance. On 5 July, he saw Giulio Gatti-Casazza, the former director of La Scala who went on to head the Metropolitan in New York and to whom he gave first rights for the two Poe dramas, *Le diable* and *La chute*, on condition that they be "always performed on the same evening."[49] At the end of the contract, he also gave priority to the Metropolitan for his "future works, and specifically for *La légende de Tristan*."[50] The sum of 10,000 francs, 2,000 of which were paid in cash, sealed this arrangement. Gatti-Casazza himself reported that Debussy had cynically admitted to him: "You're making a bad deal, and I even feel some remorse in taking these few dollars, because I'll probably never see any of these works to completion. I write for myself alone; the impatience of others is of no concern to me."[51]

This amount was not enough, however, to allow the Debussy family to spend a month by the English Channel, as they had in previous years, and the composer complained about his "dismal, dried-up" budget.[52] Instead, he had to settle for escaping a few times to Bois-le-Roi or to Avon, near Fontainebleau, to Bel Ébat, the splendid home of Jacques Durand.[53] Aside from this, he led "the life of a termite" and "devour[ed] about twenty pages of manuscript paper a day."[54]

He began to give in to requests for interviews. Early in the year, he had already replied to Maurice Leclerq's questions about the influence of Wagner, twenty-five years after the composer's death, and had told him that "there are no longer any leaders of compositional schools who are likely to influence the work of the following generation. Being the leader of a school presupposes [. . .] not only some techniques but a doctrine, one's own grammar," and that seemed to him applicable to all the arts.[55] In the following months, he received a visit from two American journalists, with whom he was a bit more forthcoming. To Emily Frances Bauer from *Harper's Weekly*, who was surprised to see him in his Parisian study in the middle of summer, he declared, still completely immersed in his dabblings with Poe: "I live in an imaginary world, driven by something suggested by my personal environment, rather than by external influences, which distract me without bringing anything to me. I feel exquisite pleasure in searching deeply within myself, and if something original is to come from me, it can only be through this process."[56] Then, he brought up again the wrongs done to French music by Germanic music and rather gratuitously broached the problem of American composers, who seemed to him "less Germanized" than those of many other countries, before concluding, in response to a question about *Le diable* and *La chute*, that these works would be completely different from his composition based on Maeterlinck's play. After having said that he was in no way a revolutionary, Debussy lamented to the second journalist, Charles Henry Meltzer, that the critics were "capable of perceiving the [music's] form but not its substance."[57] Finally, Debussy confided to him that he no longer had "much sympathy for long musical works. Given modern intellectual evolution, operas in five acts have become tedious. [. . .] At the moment, I'm interested in condensed forms of opera."[58]

Erik Satie reappears in Debussy's correspondence in 1908. Had the events of 1905—specifically Lilly's suicide attempt and Debussy's liaison with Emma—created a distance between them, as well, for some time? At forty years of age, Satie had enrolled at the Schola Cantorum, where he often saw Francisco de Lacerda in particular, before the latter's appointment as orchestra conductor in Montreux. "Your friend, E. Satie," wrote Debussy to Lacerda on 5 September 1908, "has just finished a fugue in which boredom hides behind wicked harmonies, and in which you will recognize the mark of that discipline which is so distinctive at the institution cited above."[59]

Other young composers came to see him. Edgard Varèse, who had just settled in Berlin after his studies with d'Indy, Roussel, and Widor, came in November 1908, in the hope of introducing his symphonic poem, *Bourgogne*, to Debussy.[60] Manuel de Falla, who had performed his *Danses sacrée et profane* the previous year in Madrid, also visited. Others certainly contacted Debussy, for, as he wrote to Piero Coppola on 12 June 1908, "I can't reply to all the letters, some of which are written only out of a feeling of morbid curiosity."[61]

He did not completely lose interest in the development of contemporary painting, but he was shocked by what he saw at the Salon d'Automne in October: Derain (*Les baigneuses*), Vlaminck (*Voiliers sur la Seine*), Bonnard (*Après le dîner*), Matisse, Rouault, and so on. These artists were lumped together in this decisive judgment: "Some people, who I want to believe are without malice, are taking pains to make everyone (and themselves included, one must hope) disgusted with painting."[62] This resolute condemnation of the "Fauves" included Maurice Denis, Debussy's former "collaborator" for *La damoiselle élue*, who presented decorative panels dealing with the adventures of Psyche and some illustrations for Dante Alighieri's *La vita nuova*; in Debussy's view, he was now bringing back "in pink, the worst style of M. Ingres."[63]

Children's Corner was premiered by Harold Bauer at the Cercle musical on 18 December,[64] immediately following a difficult revival (on 16 December) of *Pelléas*—with a new Golaud (George Alexis Bobeuf, called Ghasne) and a new Arkel (Louis Azéma), who together showed "a colossal lack of understanding that happens only in the world of opera."[65] We have seen that the first piece composed for the *Children's Corner*—"Serenade for the Doll"—had been intended for Octavie Carrier-Belleuse's method book (see p. 232); for "The Little Shepherd," Debussy was said to have used one of the motives that Lacerda had sent him on some postcards. The collection was dedicated, naturally, to Chouchou, who would soon practice the pieces herself at the piano. This anglomaniacal portrayal of a child's universe (the titles of the work and all its movements are in English) once again risked putting off his admirers as well as his detractors. At the premiere, Debussy remained outside the hall, waiting for his pianist to let him know if the work had "clicked" with the audience.[66] However, Léon Vallas, who apparently had attended the concert, noted that Harold Bauer played the work "in a slightly Romantic way, with what some people felt were unnecessary contrasts and affectations."[67]

Chapter Twenty-Two

"The Procrastination Syndrome"

1909

"Nothing very special has marked the beginning of 1909 for me," Debussy wrote to Gabriel Mourey on 6 January, "apart from a more pronounced case of procrastination. . . and this strange need to never finish, which does not jibe with the opposing need of my publisher."[1] For several years, Debussy had been working on the composition of the *Images* for orchestra (no longer for two pianos, as he had originally projected in 1903),[2] and at the beginning of 1909, a certain urgency can be detected in his production: the manuscript of "Ibéria" that was to be sent to the engraver is dated Christmas Day 1908, the short score of "Rondes de printemps" bears the date of 30 December 1908, and that of "Gigues" is dated 4 January 1909. While immersed in this work, Debussy gave a veritable course in orchestration to Segalen in their interview on 17 December 1908:

> "Composers no longer know how to deconstruct sound, how to keep it pure. In *Pelléas*, the sixth violin part is as necessary as the first. I strive to use each timbre in its pure state, like Mozart, for example. [. . .] We've learned too much about mixing colors, about having them emerge from the shadows or the masses. [. . .] Wagner went very far in this direction. For example, he arranges most of his instruments in groups of two or three. The height of this approach is found in Strauss, who messes everything up. [. . .] On the contrary, I strive to preserve the purity of each timbre, to put it in its true place. [. . .]"
>
> Debussy's concern: not enough percussion. [. . .]
>
> On the layout of the orchestra: "The strings should not be a barrier, but a circle, around the other instruments. Break up the woodwinds. Mix the bassoons with the violoncelli, and the clarinets and oboes with the violins, so they won't enter with a thud."[3]

At the beginning of February 1909, when Gabriel Fauré invited Debussy to become a member of the Conservatoire's Conseil supérieur (replacing Ernest Reyer!), he accepted. And this appointment was announced in the press as "a major artistic event. It has created a genuine sensation in the traditionalist circles of music instruction,"[4] wrote Maurice Leudet, a journalist for *Le Figaro*. He immediately came to interview Debussy, who criticized the way harmony was taught, the voice classes, and the Prix de Rome, but praised the quality of the instrumental classes: "They're perfect. French instrumentalists are unequaled throughout the world."[5] However, he claimed to be incapable of presenting these ideas to the committee: "It would require an authority that I lack, as well as public-speaking skills that I don't have. I might not be able to fight for my ideas."[6]

Concert in London

At the end of February, Debussy crossed the English Channel again to return to Queen's Hall, where he conducted the *Prélude à l'après-midi d'un faune* and the *Nocturnes* on the 27th; the performance was, in his own words, "stupendous."[7] The orchestra had been prepared by Henry Wood—the "wooden" conductor, as Debussy called him.[8] At a tempo change during the performance of "Fêtes," Debussy made a mistake and wanted to stop the orchestra; the musicians would not comply and continued to play. The audience, who no doubt noticed the incident, applauded, so as to prompt a repeat performance.[9] The version of events that Debussy gave to Durand contained a detail that was sadly more down-to-earth: "The concert went beautifully; 'Fêtes' was encored, and it was only at my insistence that we didn't do the same for the *Prélude*... But I couldn't stay standing any longer as I 'was marinating' in blood! A very difficult position in which to conduct anything."[10] Some years later, he had the opportunity to express his opinion of the British public: it "has a most remarkable capacity for attention and respect; it does not think itself compelled to noisily express dissatisfaction whenever it fails to grasp at first hearing the purport of a new work."[11]

Not only was Debussy ill, but so was Emma, who accompanied him. That same evening, he was unable to attend the entire reception given in his honor at the Music Club—a fashionable meeting place where his songs were performed, with an introductory speech given by the club's president, Alfred Kalisch. Moreover, Debussy had to cancel two other engagements, in Edinburgh and in Manchester, where he had been invited by Tony Jules Gueritte's French Concerts Society. For several months, he had complained of serious health problems. On 7 March, he mentioned "almost daily hemorrhaging" to Georges Jean-Aubry,[12] and, a few months later, he reported on a treatment that he had to follow every morning.[13] Although the doctors could not detect the nature of his disease at the time, it is clear that these were symptoms of an already developed cancer that would lead to his death ten years later.

Upon his return to Paris, Debussy elected to dine with Toulet on 11 March[14] rather than attend a concert given by the Engel–Bathori duo along with Viñes in the Salle de l'Université et des Arts.[15] At that event, the audience would hear no fewer than twenty-one of Debussy's songs—including the *Chansons de Charles d'Orléans*, the *Fêtes galantes*, the *Proses lyriques*, and the *Chansons de France*—as well as four piano pieces. Barely recovered from his exhaustion, the composer conducted the *Prélude à l'après-midi d'un faune* at the Concerts Sechiari on 25 March; as a critic from the *New York Times* observed, he was given a ten-minute ovation upon his arrival, followed by a protester's shout from the first balcony: "Down with the Debussy claque!"[16] The second performance of the *Chansons de Charles d'Orléans* was given at the Concerts Colonne on 9 April, likewise conducted by the composer; it was a complete success with the audience, to such an extent that he had to give an encore of the last two songs.[17] Once again, the critics—doubtless unaware that these works had been composed about ten years earlier—proved by and large hostile, accusing Debussy of pastiche[18] or finding nothing of substance in these "lightweight miniatures" (*œuvrettes*).[19] The *Revue musicale* considered these pieces to be the "subtle works of a goldsmith in the modern style."[20] Taking advantage of the fact that *La damoiselle élue* had been programmed on the same concert, another critic let his venom flow: "The beautiful little girl, whom we once loved, is today nothing more than a wrinkled, drab, dull, boring old maid; he who created her conducts *La damoiselle élue* with a weary arm."[21]

Operatic Projects

However, Debussy continued to spend time in search of new operatic projects. At the end of 1908, he had informed a journalist that he had written "only a few notes" for the Bédier–Mourey *Tristan*, but that he had not yet abandoned the idea.[22] Already a year and a half had passed since the press had announced this project as being near completion. But Joseph Bédier's cousin, Louis Artus, a successful author of light comedies and vaudevilles, asserted that he had received a right of first refusal to adapt the work; he even informed Debussy of this permission in March 1909, during a discussion at the Société des auteurs. Gabriel Mourey then suggested the idea of a *Psyché*, to which Debussy immediately replied: "Think what genius would be needed to rejuvenate that old myth, one already so exploited that the feathers of Amour's wings are completely plucked out. . . There are still beautiful stories that lie dormant in legends, perhaps even closer to our joys and sorrows than the mythological Elsa."[23] Encouraged by this response, the insistent Mourey went on to make some new suggestions to the composer—the most absurd being a chanson de geste[24] from the thirteenth century (titled *Huon de Bordeaux*) and a *Marchand de rêves*. Debussy dismissed the first, which would have had him fall back on a world of "characters in helmets and a ready-made legend," but suggested that Mourey adapt a tale from Perrault, *Le chat botté* (Puss in Boots).[25] Then, too, there was Segalen, who left two completed acts of *Orphée* for Debussy, with a third act well underway, before leaving for China; although he parted from the composer with "tears in his eyes,"[26] he never imagined that a new disappointment was awaiting him and that Debussy would soon thereafter want to revisit his beloved Poe-based dramas instead.[27]

One wonders what drove Debussy to cling in this way to so many theatrical projects. To Segalen, who asked him about this issue, he admitted: "It's a waste of time. One cannot summarily dismiss people," and he mentioned some other offers he had received, from Jean Aicard and Georges Cain.[28] Even while Debussy was discussing the projects just mentioned with Mourey, Segalen, and Diaghilev, he was unveiling yet another theatrical project to Laloy, in the hope of appeasing him after having abandoned the ballet script: "In a secret corner of my heart, I'm saving a plan to work with you on Aeschylus's *Oresteia*. . . In that project we will be absolute masters of our own destiny, with all the time we need."[29] Was Debussy slightly obsessed with searching for the "great libretto," so typical of a nineteenth-century composer's mindset?

In May, a new visit to London—his fifth—brought him satisfaction as well as frustration. The trip involved a new production of *Pelléas* at Covent Garden, with a pre-concert talk delivered by the critic Edwin Evans. In a beautifully written letter to Evans, Debussy took the trouble to explain the originality of his opera and, in short, dictated to the critic the basic structure of his speech: it should avoid a discussion about melody or operatic expression as much as possible, and instead emphasize the unconventional commentary of the symphonic writing, the role of motives attached to the characters (who are in no way slaves to the leitmotif tradition), and the "simplicity" of a score that focused on the very essence of the drama.[30] The directors of the theater, H. V. Higgins and Percy Pitt, welcomed him very cordially during at least ten days of rehearsals. Debussy was happy with Pelléas (sung by Edmond Warnery) and Golaud (Jean Bourbon);[31] a bit less so with Arkel (Vanni Marcoux), whom he asked to exaggerate the character's "great kindness";[32] and very annoyed by the director from Marseille, Fernand Almanz, whom he wanted to kill.[33] The most pleasant surprise came from the orchestra and its conductor, Cleofonte Campanini, who, in spite of distracting gestures ("resembling the operation of a hand pump"),[34] showed "a fairly accurate understanding of the work."[35] After a lackluster dress rehearsal, Debussy followed his usual practice of not attending the premiere (which took place on 21 May), preferring to remain at his hotel, where Emma was ill the entire time. The public reception was enthusiastic, "as we have rarely seen in England,"[36] Campanini assured him.

This was compensation, in a way, for the overwhelming failure that *Pelléas* had suffered in Rome two months earlier. There, the theater director Costanzi, who was obliged to postpone some performances of Amilcare Ponchielli's *La Gioconda* due to the whims of a prima donna, had decided at the last moment to produce *Pelléas*. It was a resounding disaster: the uproar of the audience, furious at being deprived of a voice they had eagerly awaited, was such that it was practically impossible to hear any scene of the opera under normal conditions.[37] Two hours later on the same day, at the Corea theater, Richard Strauss conducted *Till Eulenspiegel* and *Ein Heldenleben*, whose strength and boldness were hailed by the Roman public. The critics found an unexpected opportunity to compare two art forms (opera and symphonic music), generally condemning what was called Impressionism even in Italy.

In Paris, the Ballets Russes season dominated the news. For the first time, Diaghilev was offering an entire month of choreographed productions at the Théâtre du Châtelet, which had been renovated for the occasion. Debussy and his friends attended the performance of 11 June, when Chaliapin sang in Rimsky-Korsakov's *Ivan le terrible* (the title given at the time to the opera *The Maid of Pskov*); the event ended with a ballet, *Le festin*, a story pieced together by Diaghilev with music by various Russian composers, featuring the dancing of Vaslav Nijinsky and Tamara Karsavina. Debussy was far from being enthusiastic about the costumes by Bakst and Benois, commenting thus: "As for the ballet, I've probably lost my taste altogether for this sort of production, since I was bored by it. Even so, what an unusual way of clothing people! Don't we have better than that at the Folies-Bergères?"[38] There was not one word from him on the dancers, who were delighting all of Paris.

Diaghilev, who was trying to elevate the musical component in his ballets, came with Laloy to ask Debussy if he might agree to write a ballet score, preferably on a subject set in eighteenth-century Venice, for the coming season. A meeting at Durand's offices gave them an opportunity to outline the conditions of this project to some extent and, in a few days, the composer wrote the story line for *Masques et bergamasques*. He needed to do some explaining about this situation to Laloy, who had hoped to be its author: "I intend to enjoy myself writing this ballet," Debussy simply told him.[39] But soon, he announced to Laloy that he had completely given up on it, for that year at least.[40] The text is the only part of the project that remains; published by Durand the following year, this script shows, more than anything else, Debussy's familiarity with the world of the commedia dell'arte.[41]

La chute de la maison Usher

Instead of going to a seaside resort on the English Channel, as he had in previous summers, Debussy remained in Paris with his family. Busser, who visited him on 5 July at his house on the avenue du Bois de Boulogne, found him depressed: "He seems to be bored there," Busser noted in his journal.[42] At the Conservatoire, Debussy had participated in the juries for the female singers and then for the wind instruments, the latter of which gave him much pleasure ("velvety flutes, [. . .] wonderful bassoons");[43] in November, he had to return to the rue Bergère, this time for the piano *concours*, where he was captivated by the young Brazilian Guiomar Novaes, who had "eyes intoxicated with music."[44] At the time, he was working primarily on *La chute de la maison Usher*, finishing the second version of the libretto in three scenes, and was able to announce to his publisher that he had nearly completed Roderick's monologue, "mixing the low sounds of the oboe with the harmonics of the violins."[45] He would soon describe the story lines of his Poe-based projects to an Italian journalist who had come to interview him on his works in progress:

> The first works of his that we will hear are based on two short stories by Edgar Allan Poe: *La chute de la maison Usher* and *Le diable dans le beffroi*. The first is one of the most extraordinary short stories ever imagined by the troubled soul of the writer from overseas. [. . .]
>
> Roderick Usher, fearing that his sister Madeline might not really be dead, as the doctors claim, has her body taken down beneath the house, waiting for an opportunity to bury her. On a stormy night, during a tragic evening when the fury of the elements and the anguish of human beings come together, the young woman (who is not dead), after a desperate struggle to escape from the depths, comes to die beside her brother, who also passes away at that horrifying moment. And the entire house disappears, collapsing into a pond whose water laps against the walls.
>
> The second story is a fantasy in the style of Sterne.[46] One day, a mischievous devil hides inside the belfry of a peaceful little Dutch town, and instead of letting the clock strike at noon, he forces it to strike one o'clock, one hour later. This leads to a very amusing confusion among these good, fat Dutchmen.[47]

Debussy's work on the Poe operas is closely linked to gloomy bouts of depression, around the time when he was undergoing his first medical treatment. He told Caplet about "bad days," "dreams in a vast emptiness," "an obsessive idea (*idée fixe*)," and the like.[48] He admitted that at certain times this "tyranny" was "almost harrowing" and that because of it he was neglecting to correct the proofs of "Rondes de printemps," a job in which André Caplet was assisting him.[49] The bond between the two men had become very close during this year of 1909, for several reasons: Caplet had the "soul of an old, skeptical

Norman" which won Debussy over;[50] Caplet had been given an official warning by the Institut for not having respected the rules concerning the *envois* from Rome; he had drawn from Verlaine and Edgar Allan Poe for his own compositions; and he had also dreamed of working on a *Salammbô* himself. So many commonalities brought them together and told Debussy that Caplet had a "prodigious musical instinct."[51]

Laloy's Book and *Le cas Debussy*

At the beginning of September, the composer received a copy of the book Laloy had written about him. This work is often considered to be an "official" biography, all of the facts presumably having been approved by Debussy. Without a doubt, it is valuable because it records information from Laloy's conversations with him, but one might question some of the author's opinions, which the composer hardly could have endorsed in his heart of hearts, such as his "lifelong" disavowal of Wagner or this comment concerning Fauré: "The rebirth of our music began with him."[52] For that matter, it is hard to imagine Debussy demanding changes from this academic scholar, when, for example, Laloy wrote that "it is possible that [. . .] *Pelléas et Mélisande* is the masterpiece of Symbolism, and the *Nocturnes* that of Impressionism."[53] As for the advice that Laloy gave to performers of Debussy's music at the end of the volume, the composer commented: "I wouldn't change a thing. [. . .] One need only read and understand it,"[54] and when he had the book in hand (of which only 500 copies had been printed), he briefly thanked Laloy for "the meticulous and charming account" that he had written about him.[55]

In fact, Laloy could not claim to be the sole possessor of the key to the Debussyist message. A critic from the *Nouvelle revue française*—hearing one of Laloy's lectures delivered at the Salle Mors for the Société des dilettantes at the end of the year—was somewhat annoyed to hear him always extolling the composer's "pantheism" or "faith in nature": "Was it not more important to praise Debussy's lack of pedantry and vulgarity, his exquisite choice of means, and his carefully considered intent, without which emotion does not develop, completely and effectively, into art?"[56]

Laloy's monograph coincided with a new period of polemical unrest. The most intense attack came from a somewhat amateur philosopher, Raphaël Cor, who published a long article in the October issue of the *Revue du temps présent*, a mouthpiece of the young Catholic poets: "M. Claude Debussy et le snobisme contemporain" (Mr. Claude Debussy and contemporary snobbery).[57] There he offered some assertions that were more radical than those made by the composer's most persistent detractors, namely that Debussy was "perhaps the leader of the most uncompromising school that has ever been known in music,"[58] that he claimed "to treat any melodic element with disdain,"[59] and that he had nothing but contempt for the great composers; as for his music, it was "Lilliputian art, for the lowest form of humanity"[60] or "art of the miniaturist applied in the style of a mural."[61] In passing, Raphaël Cor curiously pointed out a few unfortunate composers who had not known how to resist Debussy's influence: Gabriel Grovlez (*La chambre blanche*), Gabriel Dupont (*La Cabrera*), and even Paul Dukas (in the second act of *Ariane et Barbe-bleue*). Of course, Cor scoffed at the composer's acolytes, especially Laloy, the author of the first French biography of Debussy, whose hyperbolic assessment of *La mer* was an easy target: "In my opinion, only M. Debussy's music and the spectacular sights of nature can cause such suffering by the power of joy and by the sheer excess of their beauty."[62]

Following this article, the editors of the *Revue du temps présent*, Charles Francis Caillard and José de Bérys, immediately seized the opportunity to drive home their point, and, at the beginning of October 1909, they sent a questionnaire to a number of journalists and well-known people in the artistic and literary world, asking for their opinion on the composer's true importance, his role, and his originality.[63] Only about thirty took up their pens, and even among that number, judging from the brevity of their responses, many backed out for different reasons (Maurice Barrès, Gaston Carraud, Camille Chevillard, Reynaldo Hahn, and Romain Rolland, among others). Their reactions were published in a small book, titled *Le cas Debussy*, and, as one might expect, they concentrated either solely on *Pelléas*, or less often on the *Prélude à l'après-midi d'un faune*, rarely on the *Nocturnes* and *La mer*, and almost never on the piano pieces or the songs.[64] While there are no surprises among the peremptory comments of the composer's ongoing opponents (such as Camille Bellaigue and Paul Flat), it is still interesting to read the ambivalent responses of Arthur Coquard (critic of *L'écho de Paris*), Jean d'Udine (who loved the *Nocturnes* and hated *La damoiselle élue*), and Camille Mauclair, the "literary chameleon"[65] who recalled that he had loved this music before the whole world did, but was now irritated by the Debussyists, and suddenly considered *Pelléas* to be "shifting sand."[66] Among those favorably disposed, the young Ernest Ansermet (who called himself the "correspondent of the Société internationale de musique") set the record straight most intelligently: "In my opinion, M. Debussy's work is the most important musical phenomenon since Wagner and the Russians. [. . .] Its influence is neither to be desired nor to be feared; it is unmistakable. [. . .] Already, M. Debussy's significant technical contribution has had ramifications for nearly all of today's composers."[67] Among the foreigners, we note only the reactions of three Germans: Siegmund von Hausegger, who agreed with Raphaël Cor that Debussy's music was weak in melody and rhythm, and that it lacked form; Felix Mottl, who deigned to enjoy the *Prélude à l'après-midi d'un faune* but admitted that *Pelléas* was quite far from his ideal; and Siegfried Wagner, who had heard only one act of *Pelléas*![68]

Was Debussy tempted to reply to this flood of second-rate literature? Perhaps he remembered the advice that Pierre Louÿs had given him long ago about Jean Lorrain's lampoon: "Don't argue with a journalist. No artist does that."[69]

Works for Piano

At the end of 1909, the year in which Nadar took an official photograph of Debussy and Henry de Groux painted his portrait, the composer finally completed some of his most important works. He sent one of the *Images* for orchestra, "Ibéria," to the engraver, and finished correcting the proofs for "Rondes de printemps" with Caplet. Since he had promised to write a piece for the clarinet *concours* at the Conservatoire, he began a *Rapsodie*, which he would finish within the required timeframe. The same month of December found him busily putting the final touches on the first book of *Préludes* for piano, nine of which he dated with surprising precision, from 7 December 1909 to 4 January 1910. He had sketched them over the previous few months, without giving the slightest hint to anyone that they were in progress. No longer was he using evocative titles such as *arabesques, estampes,* or *images*. This return to a classic genre-title for piano, without any dedications, resisted extramusical associations: the titles of the twelve preludes were indicated discreetly at the end of each piece, so as to minimize their impact on the performer—or even to allow him or her the freedom to imagine a different one. Having grown weary of hearing his music compared to visual images, Debussy nevertheless revealed in these titles a selection of his literary tastes (Baudelaire, "Les sons et les parfums tournent dans l'air du soir"; Leconte de Lisle, "La fille aux cheveux de lin"; Shakespeare, "La danse de Puck"), familiar tales and legends (Andersen, "Ce qu'a vu le vent d'ouest"; the Breton legend of Ys), imaginary scenes or landscapes ("La sérénade interrompue"; "Les collines d'Anacapri"), and images that he had picked up from reading or "snapshots" from daily life ("Des pas sur la neige"; "Voiles"; "Minstrels").

Debussy's works for piano—the great works of his maturity having begun with the *Images*—now formed a veritable repertoire. We have already observed that in his correspondence he appeared to be extremely discreet about this aspect of his compositions, as if they were only minor creations or of no great importance. When he received a copy of the *Hommage à Haydn*,[70] he commented to his publisher that "It will go up in smoke,"[71] and, when he announced the imminent release of the second book of *Préludes* to Robert Godet, he added: "Please think of this as a completely unpretentious calling card."[72] Even so, after finishing the first set of *Images*, he had written to Durand: "All modesty aside, I believe that these three pieces hold together well and that they will take their place in the piano literature... (as Chevillard would say) to the left of Schumann, or to the right of Chopin... as you like it."[73]

Debussy was very concerned with how performers understood his works. Since 1902, he had placed his confidence in Ricardo Viñes, who was something of an "official" pianist, but we must remember that the composer still insisted on hearing him before each performance. We lack expert assessments of his piano playing, but beyond the standard praise collected in the press, Jacques-Émile Blanche recalled the way in which Viñes interpreted Debussy's pieces, with "so much effort and diligence."[74] In any case, Debussy grew tired of him over the years; in a conversation with Segalen, he described Viñes's playing as "too dry,"[75] and he even uttered a more general complaint to Edgard Varèse: "One is often betrayed by so-called pianists! I can assure you of this, for you can't imagine how much my piano music has been distorted, to such an extent that I often have trouble recognizing it."[76] During the war, he would become even more vehement: "Pianists, for the most part, are bad musicians, and they chop the music into pieces—like a chicken."[77] Debussy's piano works had begun to make their mark in Japan during 1909: the American pianist Rudolph E. Reuter played the "Sarabande" in Tokyo on 24 November.[78]

It is surprising that Debussy's biographers have not been more interested in the pianos he owned. The testimonies, which were not always consistent, deserve to be discussed. According to Laloy, Debussy had a mahogany upright piano in his study on the avenue du Bois de Boulogne, which "the Pleyel company, always generous toward artists," had given him;[79] in 1907, Segalen heard Debussy perform the third *Chanson de Bilitis* "on an admirable Pleyel,"[80] and later George Copeland confirmed its presence.[81] In the composer's parlor, there was a black baby grand—a Blüthner "Aliquotflügel"—as we have already noted;[82] that piano, which Raoul Bardac inherited after Debussy's death, is preserved today at the Musée Labenche in Brive-la-Gaillarde. However, accounts do not agree on where this instrument was acquired. Maurice Dumesnil reported that the composer had bought it in Bournemouth;[83] yet there is no evidence that he ever went to this town on the English coast. Dolly de Tinan,[84] who would certainly have known best, recalled that it was acquired in Jersey in 1904.[85] More recently, however, Diane Enget Moore has made a compelling case for its purchase in Eastbourne.[86] A final question arises: did Debussy have a third piano—a Bechstein—in his study? In fact, three witnesses claimed to have seen it: a journalist (Gino G. Zuccala in 1910);[87] Alfredo Casella;[88] and Jacques Durand, who mentioned it when describing a letter that Debussy wrote to him on 29 May 1915 and which alluded to his "German piano."[89] Finally, Raoul Bardac, who made no mention of a Pleyel, was emphatic in citing a Blüthner and a Bechstein upright,[90] but we still do not know precisely when Debussy acquired these instruments.

Chapter Twenty-Three

Orchestral *Images* and Piano *Préludes*

1910

Premieres of "Ibéria" and "Rondes de printemps"

The important events in 1910 were the premieres (about ten days apart) of the second and third movements of the *Images* for orchestra, which had remained on Debussy's worktable for such a long time.[1] "Ibéria" was the first to be performed, at the Concerts Colonne on 20 February under the direction of Gabriel Pierné, triggering a few demonstrations "from the far left and the far right,"[2] and it was repeated the following Sunday. "Rondes de printemps" was conducted by the composer in the Salle Gaveau, at the Concerts Durand, on 2 March.[3]

Pierné had found "Ibéria" difficult to conduct at first, but Debussy felt, on 5 February, that he "already seemed to be getting a feel for its color."[4] However, at the performance, the composer deemed only the third part satisfactory: "the otherwise 'overtly Spanish' rhythm of the first part became 'rive gauche'[5] under the intelligent leadership of our young 'Kapellmeister,' and 'Les parfums de la nuit' came out tentatively, as if from under a cushion, no doubt so as not to upset anyone."[6] As the work was to be heard again on the following Sunday, Debussy requested another rehearsal, about which he would report to Caplet with atypical enthusiasm:

> Things are going better! The aforementioned young Kapellmeister and his orchestra have agreed to shed their feet for wings. . !
> You cannot imagine how naturally the "Parfums de la nuit" transitions to the "Matin d'un jour de fête." *It feels like it's been improvised...* And the entire buildup, the awakening of people and things... I see very clearly a watermelon merchant and some whistling kids... And yet,

look at how people can be mistaken, since some have viewed this as a "serenade."[7]

Upon hearing these two *Images*, the critics renewed their objections with, as was often the case, an absurd touch. Adolphe Jullien, the critic for *Les débats*, had misread the epigraph, drawn from Angelo Poliziano's *Canzoni a ballo*, at the head of "Rondes de printemps"; instead of "Vive le mai," he had read "Vive le mal," and in his article, he understandably questioned the work's joyful character.[8] Permit us, this once, to pass swiftly over the opinions of the anti-Debussyists, such as Jean Chantavoine, who reiterated that the composer was producing nothing more than "little trifles" or that he was now imitating his own imitators.[9] "There will come a day when these amusements cease to amuse," wrote Pierre Lalo, who detected in "Ibéria" only a "commonplace Spain."[10] Still, Debussy was indignant over a passage in Lalo's article that concerned his orchestration: "Oh, this abuse of the percussion and woodwinds—these oboes, these clarinets—and their endless nasal twang! Oh, these eternally stopped brass, these instruments, none of which is used in its true way and with its normal timbre, but which always seem to snigger with a puppet's voice! Oh, this music from a Tunisian café or from the rue du Caire!"[11] And the composer complained about it when writing to Caplet, who understood how innovative this subtle orchestration was. Debussy appreciated Charles Koechlin's article in the *Chronique des arts* and made sure to let him know that he had been particularly happy with his comments about the "Parfums de la nuit."[12] While Gaston Carraud[13] and Jean Marnold[14] identified a new style in the composer's work, Alfred Bruneau seemed won over this time and built up a string of adjectives, apparently for the sheer fun of it: for him, the work conveyed a "delicious poetry, an exquisite color, a captivating charm, a prestigious art," far from the "robust portrayals of Albéniz and Chabrier."[15] In his article, Laloy went even further than in his recent biography to establish the composer's position in history; he deemed the Symbolist and Impressionist phases "over" by 1904, making way for a new musical world whose equivalents were Paul Gauguin in painting and Paul Claudel in literature. To this end, he attempted to explain what was truly new in "Ibéria":

> Some melodies in this work are not only complete but also develop, generating other fertile tunes around them that interweave without concealing the main melody, which resembles the sturdy trunk of a leafy tree. And for this reason they are repeated, always in new ways. Two of these melodies, except for some secondary fragments, are enough to fill an entire section. Here, it is the opposite of what has just been described: throughout, the melody is predominant, intensified by the phrase and propelled by the rhythm. We can see how flexible this clarity is, however, in the central section, "[Les] parfums de la nuit," which is an exquisite contemplation where ideas emanate from

faraway places, draw near, take shape, fade, and return, transformed by an internal variation that changes all its details without losing its feeling.[16]

Laloy considered the "Rondes de printemps" to be "even more bold," developing "a single idea which passes through and runs among fresh melodic foliage, leading to a breathless dance, which spins for a moment, and then subsides and disperses into thin air. And the orchestra, having rejected the brightness of the brass, embodies, with the most luminous sounds, the diaphanous and yet precise elegance of a Corot landscape."[17]

Within this quite small band of music critics, a young writer named Jacques Rivière brought new clarity to the columns of the *Nouvelle revue française*. He tried to provide a literary analysis and translation of the impressions that Debussy's work awakened in him. In *Pelléas*, he had found "a marvelous world, a precious paradise,"[18] and in Debussy's "orchestral poems," starting with *La mer*, he detected a "guiding intelligence. [. . .] Only the most essential threads survive in the musical fabric; but they have been so aptly chosen that their simultaneous unfolding, and the unique ways in which the composer takes pains to connect them, replaces the voluptuous density of the earlier symphonies."[19]

When Gustav Mahler conducted the "Rondes de printemps" on 15 and 18 November in New York, the local critics expressed themselves much as did the Parisian press at the time of *La mer*—"disintegration of all form,"[20] "spasmodic" treatment,[21] "muddled sounds,"[22] "extravagant orchestral colors"[23]—although the audience seemed much more favorably disposed.[24]

Préludes, Book One, for Piano

For some months prior, a group of young composers had been feeling that the Société nationale de musique was becoming too conservative, and even too partisan. Many were Fauré's students: Charles Koechlin, Florent Schmitt, Jean Roger-Ducasse, André Caplet, Émile Vuillermoz, and especially Maurice Ravel. Despite the hostility of his friend Saint-Saëns regarding this group of composers, Fauré accepted the presidency of the new Société musicale indépendante (SMI).[25] The society's first concert (20 April) included dissonant pieces by Zoltan Kodály (which were booed) as well as a surprise: Maurice Ravel, whose relationship with Debussy had not yet improved, premiered the elder composer's *D'un cahier d'esquisses*, a piano piece that was by this time already six years old. The performance led Auguste Mangeot to surmise that this composition was "quite void of musical substance, [and that] the crafty M. Ravel, who interpreted it, had no difficulty in subsequently making it his own."[26]

As soon as he had access to letterhead stationery, Fauré wrote to Debussy, asking him to participate in another of the society's concerts. On 25 May, the composer played four of his own *Préludes*: "Danseuses de Delphes," "Voiles," "La cathédrale engloutie," and "La danse de Puck." A member of the audience, Paul Landormy, reported his impressions:

> He had an Érard piano brought in for the occasion; it was a rather old model, but one that was particularly suited to him—a slender baby grand, with a delicate sound and not much brilliance, but supremely 'distinguished.' One cannot imagine what he drew out of the relatively weak resources of this instrument. One cannot imagine the gentleness of his caressing strokes and the subtlety of his singing touch, which expressed so many things, while speaking so softly, nor can one imagine how his slightest intentions permeated, sometimes even incisively, the performance.[27]

Even those critics who had been rather hostile toward him made some surprising judgments about his pianistic talent. For example, Auguste Mangeot, who had found the four *Préludes* performed by Debussy on 25 May to be "remarkable," wrote: "Is there a pianist who has a sound more lovely than that of Debussy on the Érard? I don't think so. It would be a delight to hear him play Bach and Chopin."[28]

The first book of *Préludes* was not premiered in its entirety until Jane Mortier played it on 3 May 1911.[29] However, the composer had certainly not envisioned that these pieces would be performed as a set in a single concert.

Around this period of time, Debussy's works were beginning to be premiered outside of France. This was the case for "La fille aux cheveux de lin," performed by Franz Liebich in London (2 June 1910) and "Ce qu'a vu le vent d'ouest," played by Walter Rummel in Stockbridge, Massachusetts (26 July 1910).[30] The same would be true for the *Ballades de François Villon*, which Debussy had composed in May. Perhaps he had asked for Laloy's help, as he had for the *Chansons de Charles d'Orléans*,[31] in clarifying the meaning of certain words from the fifteenth century (for example, *musse, risse, greigneur*); in any case, he confided to a journalist from *Musica* that he had found it difficult "to attend to the [textual] rhythms and yet remain inspired."[32] He also implored his publisher to have the cover of the printed edition look more like parchment by making it more "yellowed" (*jaulni*),[33] wishing to stress the "aged" aspects of this trilogy.[34] It seems that these *Ballades* were premiered by Maggie Teyte at the Aeolian Hall in London on 18 November 1910.[35]

Fortified by his recent experience as an orchestral conductor, Debussy began, essentially for financial reasons, to aspire to some tours abroad. The first one would have taken him to America, but his meeting, in May 1910, with a M. Blumenberg about this subject came to naught.[36] On the other hand, thanks to the intervention of the Hungarian violinist Jenö Hubay and the pianist Theodor Szántó, a plan to travel to Austria-Hungary was seriously considered from the next month onward.

Foreign Composers in Paris

Debussy's renown throughout Europe increasingly led foreign composers to knock on his door when they found themselves in Paris. During the previous couple of years, he had thus met Manuel de Falla, who had become a friend of Ricardo Viñes. Debussy gave Falla advice on his *Trois mélodies* on poems by Théophile Gautier (which Durand had not wanted to publish) and especially on *La vida breve*, and recommended him to the publisher Lerolle. But Debussy declined a proposal that Falla conveyed to him on behalf of Isaac Albeniz's widow: to orchestrate a few pieces by the Spanish composer.[37]

In April, Gustav Mahler came to Paris to conduct his Second Symphony at the Trocadéro as part of the Société des grandes auditions, which was presided over by Countess Greffuhle. While rehearsals were underway, a reception was organized in Mahler's honor, to which the following were invited: Dukas, Fauré, Bruneau, Debussy, and the Clemenceaus, who were friends of the Austrian composer. In her memoirs, Alma Mahler gave a sensationalized account of this dinner, repeating the malicious gossip circulating in Paris about Debussy's private life and attributing the rumors to Lilly, who allegedly had received "poor treatment" from her husband and supposedly tried to poison herself.[38] However, Alma added one piece of information in particular that cannot possibly be true: during the concert on 17 April, she was said to have seen Debussy, Dukas, and Pierné "get up and leave in the middle of the second movement of Mahler's symphony."[39] It goes without saying that such behavior would have been entirely uncharacteristic of those three composers, who were not only too well mannered but also too well known to risk such a scene. Furthermore, no witnesses corroborated her story. In addition, Debussy must have known that Mahler had just conducted his three *Nocturnes* (February 1910) and the *Prélude à l'après-midi d'un faune* (10 March) in New York.[40] Finally, Alma added a comment that made her assertions only more improbable: "They didn't need to say anything, but they later explained that Mahler's work was too Schubertian for them, that even Schubert seemed too foreign, too Viennese, too Slavic, to them!"[41]

Meanwhile, a week of French music was being organized in Munich for the month of September. Two important honorary committees—one French, one German—included, among many other people, Romain Rolland and Laloy in the former, and Mahler and Strauss in the latter. The *S. I. M.* journal went out of its way to publish a special issue whose entire first part—comprising Charles Malherbe's comments on the concert programs—was written in German; the editorial staff paid tribute to the "very courteous gesture" of the Munich organizers who worked together for "the brotherhood of peoples."[42] In the programs (two of chamber music and two for orchestra), Saint-Saëns and Fauré took the lion's share, with six works each; for Debussy, there were two *Nocturnes*, but no songs or chamber music. These programs, which consisted of only "canonic works" that had already attained some degree of recognition, excited Debussy even less than did the conductor of his composition, Rhené-Baton, of whom he had a low opinion. He therefore decided not to go to Munich, giving his reasons to a journalist from *L'Ouest-artiste*,[43] to whom he revealed a certain xenophobia with respect not only to German music but also to "false-Italianism" and to the music of Scandinavia. "Like children, we [French people] clap our hands for a work that comes from afar," he said to the columnist; according to Debussy, the Munich concerts could only result in polite success and, moreover, "they come at a really bad time."[44] This short interview did not pass unnoticed and was reprinted in the 21 August issue of the *Paris-Journal* and in the 1 October issue of *Le courrier musical*.[45]

Toward the middle of the year, Debussy met an American violinist of Hungarian origin, Arthur Hartmann, who had been a child prodigy.[46] Hartmann presented him with a transcription of "La fille aux cheveux de lin" for violin and piano, and Debussy approved its publication by Durand.[47] He seems to have been impressed by Hartmann's instrumental talent, which he would soon compare to that of a Gypsy from Budapest,[48] and he attended a few of his concerts in Paris: "You are a rare man," Debussy wrote to him, "because you find ways to be a great virtuoso and, at the same time, a sensitive and consummate artist!"[49]

Leoni, the violinist who played in the bar at the Carlton Hotel, was a different kind of artist, although his style also resembled that of the Gypsies. For him, Debussy was said to have written *La plus que lente*, a waltz that he composed for piano but that Durand also published in a transcription for violin and piano. Leoni would never play this work.[50]

For a long time, Debussy had known the young English composer Cyril Scott—another unique figure, a musician who was drawn to Oriental philosophy and the occult. His first works—piano pieces and songs—had made something of a splash, and people readily described him as the "English Debussy."[51] Indeed, the French composer, to whom Scott had dedicated his Second Suite for piano, was "his master and his god," in the words of Mme de Saint-Marceaux.[52] When the German publisher Schott asked his opinion of Scott, Debussy wrote a surprisingly enthusiastic tribute on "his truly personal art, which deserves an enviable place in contemporary music," comparing the character of his music to "Javanese rhapsodies."[53]

The composer also continued to grant interviews to journalists, and it was not the French to whom he entrusted his true confessions. Thus, a rather long interview appeared in the 26 June issue of the *New York Times*, in which he replied to some very personal questions—not only on the way he composed, his career, and his ideas on art in general, but also on performers and the public.[54] The American journalist vividly portrayed Debussy's character and surroundings, describing the white walls, the antique vases and Oriental objects in his home, the meticulous order of his desk, and the uninterrupted succession of cigarettes smoked by his interviewee. Did he compose at the piano?

> No, I can't say I do. I don't know how to explain it exactly. [. . .] I don't think any composer knows how he does it. [. . .] There are days and weeks and often months that no ideas come to me.[55] [. . .] I never go to hear my work; I can't. It is too terrible for me. The interpretation is always so different from what I mean it to be. [. . .] Music is so much a part of myself that I do not recognize it when it is handled by others.[56] [. . .] A man portrays himself in his work, it is true, but only part of himself. In real life, I cannot live up to the ideals I have in music. I feel the difference there is in me between Debussy, the composer, and Debussy, the man.[57]

The isolation of his home near the Bois de Boulogne was thus no longer as intense as during the dark period of 1905, and Debussy remained very curious about new staged productions. He had already studied the score of *Salome* in Paris and in Brussels, and in May he declared to a journalist: "Richard Strauss was nothing but a frustrated Wagner, an artist doubling as a marvelous magician when conducting performances of his own works."[58] But Debussy was especially impressed by Igor Stravinsky's first ballet, *The Firebird*, a performance of which he attended with Paul-Jean Toulet on 2 July 1910.[59] He tempered his enthusiasm when writing to his publisher ("it's not perfect"), emphasizing its "extremely unusual rhythmic synchronization,"[60] but he insisted on meeting the young, twenty-eight-year-old Russian. Stravinsky described the evening of the premiere (25 June): "I was still on stage when the final curtain had come down, and I saw Diaghilev coming toward me, accompanied by a dark man with a sort of double forehead: it was Claude Debussy. The great composer congratulated me and invited me to dine with him."[61] A few months later, Stravinsky would begin to write *Petrushka*, with a photo set in front of him that Debussy had dedicated "To Igor Stravinsky, in complete artistic sympathy" (À Igor Stravinsky en toute sympathie artistique).[62]

Relationship with Emma in Crisis

Despite appearances, Claude's relationship with Emma went through a serious crisis during the first half of 1910. Rather mysterious references are found in the correspondence from this period, and authors have generally attempted to explain them away by minimizing their significance.[63] Quite naturally, Debussy confided in those with whom he was particularly close, including Caplet, Jacques Durand, and Laloy. Here are some excerpts, presented in chronological order to show how the events unfolded:

I am—as often happens with me—at a dangerous turning point in my life story, and we won't discuss it further.[64] (to Caplet, 23 March)

My life is always so sadly distressing. But I don't want to darken the sun that lights up your life at the moment.[65] (to Jacques Durand, 30 March)

I've continued this peculiar existence which is and will be my life from now on. People around me persist in failing to understand that I've never been able to live in the real world, which leads to that irresistible need to escape from myself into adventures; they may seem inexplicable because they reveal a man whom no one knows, and that man is perhaps the best part of me! Moreover, an artist is by definition a man who is used to dreaming and who lives among apparitions. . . How can one expect this same man to be able to conduct his daily life in strict observance of traditions, laws, and other barriers posed by the hypocritical and cowardly world?

All in all, I live with memory and regret—two sad companions! But they are faithful friends, more so than joy and happiness![66] (to Jacques Durand, 8 July)

I'm in an abominable mood, renouncing every form of happiness, unless it's what destroys me a little more every day.

That's why you haven't seen me, as I have no excuse to be unpleasant, mute, and without thoughts!

[. . .] It's not completely my fault, but I am rather miserable; it's even a bit like the Usher family, but this comparison simply doesn't hold up, because it's still the best I have of family![67] (to Laloy, 24 August)

I'm living in a time of anxiety, a bit like someone who might be awaiting a train in a dreary station! I want to get out, to go anywhere, but at the same time I'm afraid to leave! In short, I have to have a lot of patience to put up with myself![68] (to Jacques Durand, 25 September)

It is clear that family life was weighing on Claude. More than ever, Emma was high-strung and often ill; the responsibilities of the house, where her mother was also living, continually increased, as did the debts. Since 1909, Debussy had been resorting to the services of a financier by the name of Bertault, with whom he maintained a frequent correspondence that always focused on concerns relating to bills and due dates.[69] In this state of distress, did Claude go so far as to consider a separation? There is no mistaking this, given the following letter from Emma to a lawyer, postponing a meeting:

Sir,
    Please accept my most sincere apologies, but the terrible state in which I find myself, morally and physically, has completely prevented me from being at the meeting that you had so kindly arranged.

I'm still hesitating—I am waiting. . . It will cost me so much to separate from the person who makes me suffer so inexplicably—Alas, I will never lack for reasons.

Let me hope for your counsel when the time comes, and please accept, sir, my gratitude and my best wishes.

Emma Claude Debussy[70]

In reading the letters sent by Claude to Emma a few months later (from Budapest and Vienna), one finds only signs of great affection, without the slightest reference to recent storms. The crisis eased somewhat into a state of resignation. Claude was forty-eight years old and his health was failing. There was Chouchou and the fear of beginning a new life; in addition, he had seen friends distance themselves from him twice before, for similar reasons. So he stayed home, grumbling at times and retreating a bit into his solitude. Curiously enough, it was to a Roman journalist (four years later) that he would give his philosophy of life as an artist:

> It's no secret that family exerts an excessively powerful grip over me. And just in thinking about that extremely strong spiritual bond, more than once I've come to realize a very harsh truth: an artist should not get married. . .
>
> Yes, it's true! The immense adoration I devote to my wife and my little daughter means that I never regret for a single instant the step that I took; but I'm absolutely persuaded of this truth: an artist must aspire to be as free as possible in life. As for family, his father and mother are enough. A sister is already too much.[71]

A family event certainly contributed toward defusing the tension between husband and wife: after suffering for a long time, Claude's father died on 28 October. The composer was determined to inform his friends of the funeral service at Notre-Dame d'Auteuil.[72] This provided an opportunity to reestablish contact with Paul Dukas, and it was in a nostalgic tone that Debussy thanked him for his condolences, adding this characteristic remark: "I'd certainly ask you to come to see me, if I didn't fear that the atmosphere of my home would be less welcoming to you than in the past, or, in other words, that it would be less to your liking!"[73]

Maud Allan and *Khamma*

Was Debussy carried away by the success of the Ballets Russes season (*Scheherazade, The Firebird*) or had he harbored some regret for not having composed the music for *Masques et bergamasques*? In any case, on 30 September 1910 he signed a contract to write the music for a ballet, *Isis*, with a twenty-seven-year-old Canadian dancer, Maud Allan[74]—without any consultation with his exclusive publisher, Jacques Durand. Following musical studies with Ferruccio Busoni, Allan had performed after 1905 in the United States and in Vienna, Budapest, and London, where she was often compared to Isadora Duncan. Her greatest success had been *The Vision of Salomé*, a ballet with music by the Belgian composer Marcel Rémy.[75] We do not know the circumstances under which she approached Debussy, but one of the conditions of the contract was surely a determining factor in the composer's acceptance: upon signing, he was to receive a sum of 10,000 francs. In the month of December, the title of *Khamma* was substituted for that of *Isis*, as shown in Debussy's letter to Emma from Budapest, written on the 3rd of that month: "We must not forget Miss Maud Allan... *Khamma* (thoustra!)."[76]

Trip to Vienna and Budapest

Debussy's first foreign trip without Emma lasted about eight days and took him to Vienna and Budapest, "in order to play the orchestra in one and the piano in the other," he wrote to Caplet.[77] In fact, its primary purpose was to counteract "unabating 'poverty.'"[78] Edgard Varèse had tried to attract him to Prague as well, but to no avail.

The Vienna program was substantial: the *Petite suite*, the *Nocturnes*, *La mer*, "Ibéria," and the *Prélude à l'après-midi d'un faune*. Debussy was given only two rehearsals to prepare all these works for performance, and he even had to communicate to the orchestra through an interpreter, Dr. Angyan, a doctor of law. At times, he "wanted to say to them what Chouchou says to me [Debussy]: 'Look me in the eye.'"[79] Otherwise, he sang or made "Italian pantomime gestures."[80] The orchestra director, Ferdinand Löwe, who had conducted the *Prélude à l'après-midi d'un faune* in Vienna in July 1905, had assured Debussy that the musicians had already played *La mer* three times.[81] It was necessary to face the facts: "Chevillard was missed,"[82] and both *La mer* and the *Nocturnes* had to be removed from the program. However, Debussy succeeded in giving a performance of "Ibéria" on 2 December that even he considered "dazzling."[83] A few weeks later, speaking to a journalist from *Comœdia*, he opined that Austrian and German musicians were not necessarily superior to French musicians, but that they "worked more consistently and were more willing to give the necessary effort";[84] this did not prevent him from confiding to Emma that "the pretentiousness of the Viennese musicians seems to me to go beyond what's tolerable."[85] It was during a banquet given in Debussy's honor that the following famous exchange, reported by Rose Féart, took place: in a toast, an Austrian official congratulated him for having suppressed melody—which prompted an immediate reply on the composer's part: "On the contrary, sir, all my music strives to be nothing but melody!"[86] Another evening, he went to the Opéra to hear *Carmen*—oddly, a repetition of the production he had seen in the same place nearly thirty years earlier with Mme von Meck. "Yes," he wrote to Caplet, "*Carmen* is much better as 'action' (*mouvement*) than as 'color' (*accent*). In saying that, I'm not thinking of the unfortunate Micaëla, a period character who was probably imposed [on the librettists], but rather of Escamillo, whose grandiloquence is poor and without very distinct character, and also of certain patches of dialogue between José and Carmen."[87] At the Krantz hotel, where Debussy was staying, he remained very preoccupied with the harsh realities facing him in Paris, and gave his advice to Emma on a mysterious loan that she wanted to make to those he called the "vultures," and which would end up being a "bottomless pit."[88]

From 3 to 6 December 1910, he was in Budapest. There, in the huge, 1,500-seat Redoutensaal, he performed the *Estampes* and *Children's Corner* and accompanied Rose Féart in the *Proses lyriques*, while the Waldbauer Quartet played the String Quartet—extremely well, in his opinion.[89]

He reacted more positively to Budapest and the Hungarians than to the Viennese, although he noted with regret that the Danube was not blue.[90] Later he would tell Pierné that "their enthusiasm has something 'French' about it, which makes them more immediately likeable to us than our so-called Latin brothers."[91] His fondest memory was hearing the Gypsy violinist Radics in a "run-of-the-mill" café.[92] The intensity of Radics's art impressed him deeply, to the point that he was still speaking about it a long time afterward; he saw in it "the melancholy confession of a heart that suffers and smiles, almost at one and the same moment."[93] He also had contact with some young Hungarian composers, who were much less conservative than Viennese composers. His agent Gusztáv Bárczy arranged for him to meet Géza Vilmos Zágon, whose *Pierrot lunaire* would be heard in Paris.[94] Debussy was said to have attended a private performance in which the quartets of Béla Bartók and Zoltán Kodály were played.[95] What is certain is that Kodály had been familiar with Debussy's music ever since his visit to Paris in 1907, and that he had drawn Bartók's attention to it. That year Kodály even wrote a little piano piece—*Méditation sur un motif de Claude Debussy*—on a theme from the String Quartet, a tribute that was utterly unique at that time. At the end of 1909, Bartók was in Paris again and wanted to meet Debussy. The pianist Isidor Philipp was said to have advised him against it, assuring him that the composer hated everyone and that he would be rude to him![96]

When a Hungarian journalist came to interview him in Budapest, Debussy confessed that he was ashamed not to have paid more attention to Hungarian composers. Once back in Paris, however, the memory of Radics's performance inspired this fervent plea about what he had heard:

> In my opinion, this music should never be touched. Further, it should be protected, as much as possible, from the mishandling of "professionals." That

is why. . . [you should] have more respect for your Gypsies. They are not simply *entertainers*, whom one calls in to dress up a party, or to help one drink champagne! To tell the truth, their music is every bit as beautiful as your old embroidery, your lace. . . Why, then, don't you have the same respect for them? The same love?

Your young composers could profitably be inspired by them, not by copying them but by trying to adapt their freedom, their gift for evocation, for color, and for rhythm. Wagner's advice has been bad for much music and many countries. . . The folk music of one's country should be used only as inspiration, never as a compositional means. This is particularly true for your folk music. . . Love it as passionately as you please, but don't dress it in school clothes, don't put gold-rimmed eyeglasses on it![97]

Over a year later,[98] he reiterated the pleasure that the welcome in Budapest had given him, adding: "Nothing would make me happier, if life were not so fleeting, so harsh, than to return there—without music!"[99]

Proliferation of Concerts in Paris and Beyond

The musical scene in Paris of 1910 no longer resembled that of 1880 or 1900. It had developed a cosmopolitanism that proved to be open to quite varied European repertoires. Artistic life no longer revolved solely around the Pasdeloup or Colonne concerts. As for operatic productions, the public was less attracted to the Opéra and the Opéra-Comique than to Jacques Rouché's Théâtre des Arts and especially to the Grande saison of Astruc and Diaghilev. The growing number of concerts and recitals prompted the appearance of a *Guide du concert*, whose sole purpose was to list concerts by Touche, Sechiari, Monteux, Durand, Hasselmans, Domergue (Cercle musical), et al., compounding the stimulating competition between the Société nationale and the Société musicale indépendante.

Debussy would soon become troubled by such a proliferation: "When will they stop increasing the means of exposure, which are pointless and even dangerous!"[100] Nevertheless, during these years his works became established in solo and orchestral repertoires, albeit with somewhat predictable results. From a simple statistical point of view, the String Quartet was played the most (thanks especially to the Parent Quartet), followed more surprisingly by the *Danses sacrée et profane*, championed by performers on chromatic as well as traditional harps, and the *Prélude à l'après-midi d'un faune*, which the critics generally felt was interpreted best by the Colonne orchestra. In the realm of piano repertoire, "Jardins sous la pluie" was the most popular piece, followed by *L'isle joyeuse*. In 1910, a critic had reason to express amazement: "What a surprise! Debussy is becoming an object of study for students in the preparatory classes at the Conservatoire, at least in Mme Chéné's class."[101] As for the songs, they fell within the special purview of Jane Bathori and Émile Engel, and later that of Maggie Teyte. Those who were put off by the recent works continued to limit themselves to "Mandoline" or excerpts from *L'enfant prodigue*.

Only rarely did concerts in the provinces venture into the great symphonic works, apart from the *Prélude à l'après-midi d'un faune*. The *Nocturnes* were played more often (Pau and Vichy, 1903; Lyon, 1907; Nancy and Marseille, 1908; Toulouse, 1911), "Fêtes" and "Rondes de printemps" very seldom (Lyon, February and November 1911), and *La mer* apparently only once (Marseille, 1908).

Chapter Twenty-Four

Le martyre de saint Sébastien

1911

Debussy should have adamantly refused to consider any proposals for new works,[1] since he was determined to finish "Gigues" and to continue working on the Poe dramas and the *Préludes* for piano, in addition to having just agreed to a ballet commission. But then in Vienna he received an unexpected letter, written on beautiful paper in spectacular, large script and postmarked 25 November 1910 from Arcachon; in that letter, Gabriele D'Annunzio told him that he loved his music, discussed a "long-contemplated mystery play (*mystère*)," and asked him: "Do you like my poetry?"[2] Instead of waiting until he returned to Paris, Debussy responded from the Krantz hotel, where he was staying: "How could I possibly not love your poetry? The very thought of working with you already makes me feverish."[3] When he returned to Paris on 7 December, Debussy found that a sort of conspiracy had been organized to ensure his immediate acceptance. Accompanied by Gabriel Astruc, who played the role of impresario as director of the operatic season at the Châtelet, D'Annunzio had paid a visit to Emma and had no doubt used his most flowery rhetoric to win her over.[4] A few days later, Astruc wrote to her as follows: "Your gracious welcome and words of wisdom have given M. D'Annunzio and me confidence in the eventual success [of our project]."[5] In turning on the charm, D'Annunzio did not forget to include Chouchou.[6]

Origins of *Le martyre*

The matter was carried out so quickly that Debussy scarcely had time to think about it. On 9 December, he signed a contract to write the music for a *Saint Sébastien* (whose title did not yet include *Le martyre de*) that was to be a drama in four acts, comprising four symphonic preludes, three dances ("Charbons ardents," "Planètes," and "Passion de Notre Seigneur"—that is, Burning hot coals, Planets, and Passion of Our Lord), a "madrigal for 5 voices (optional)," and finally the "Lamentation des femmes veuves et Finale" (Lamentation of the widows and Finale). The deadlines were specified as follows: the piano score of the three dances created for Ida Rubinstein would be expected by the end of February 1911, with the orchestral score and parts "in time" for the rehearsals planned for late April. Debussy was to receive a sum of 20,000 francs—8,000 of which were granted right away—and a third of the box-office revenue, while retaining his rights to the score. Should the contract be broken, there would be no financial penalty.[7] In order to seal this slightly diabolical pact, Astruc organized a "very private little dinner" at the Café de Paris; in a letter to Emma on 9 December (the same day the contract was signed), he expressed his intention to introduce her and Claude to "the beautiful artist, Mme Ida Rubinstein," who would portray Saint Sebastien.[8]

The most surprising aspect of Debussy's decision was not only that it was made rapidly but that, for the first time in his life, he agreed to write music without having read one line of the accompanying text. What he also did not know was that this *Saint Sébastien* had already been offered to other composers before him.[9]

Since at least 1908, the Italian poet's imagination had been revolving around images of the saint tied to a tree and an archer who forges arrows, the sorts of *tableaux vivants* that push eroticism to nearly bizarre excess, as in: "He was lying down on the bed like the Syrian Adonis, and each wound was a mouth to be kissed by each woman [in the female chorus]."[10] These fantasies, linked to a fascination with the androgynous, would suddenly be distilled when D'Annunzio, "exiled" in Paris to escape his creditors, was taken by his chaperone Robert de Montesquiou to a performance of *Cléopâtre* at the Ballets Russes, starring the dancer Ida Rubinstein. At the end of the show, he rushed into her dressing room, clasped her beautiful bare legs, and kissed her feet;[11] he had found the "disturbing [androgynous] beauty" of his dreams.[12]

Even so, D'Annunzio, a former student at the University of Rome, took care to do his research. He knew the form of the dramatic Italian *laude* but wanted to investigate old French *mystères*. He sought out Gustave Cohen, the author of a work on stage direction in the religious theater of the Middle Ages, and asked him bluntly: "In *mystères*, were nude characters ever depicted, and did females ever play the role of males?"[13] The poet went to the Bibliothèque nationale, consulted the *Acta sanctorum*, and read especially a source from the thirteenth century—Jacobus da Voragine's *The Golden Legend*—from which he drew many images: the twin brothers Marcellien and Marc, the magic chamber, and the burning hot coals. He already knew that he would write in French and that his work would be complemented by music. First he contacted Roger-Ducasse, who withdrew, put off by the lack of time; then he approached Henry Février, who had just set a Maeterlinck drama to music. Ida Rubinstein supposedly suggested Florent Schmitt, the composer of the *Tragédie de Salomé*. Finally, D'Annunzio selected Debussy, who had been suggested by Robert de Montesquiou from the beginning.[14]

The story has been told and retold of how the meeting between these two men might have seemed almost miraculous, as their temperaments were polar opposites of each other, and their respective arts were so incompatible. However, it is not completely absurd to think that such a subject plunged the composer back into his old dreams of esotericism and awoke in him a degree of spirituality that had been latent in the original conception of the work. When interviewed by *Excelsior*, Debussy described D'Annunzio as "an artist with leadership in his blood. As soon as he appears, life enters with him, life vigorous and fertile."[15]

Concerts and Performers

While awaiting the text, which the poet was writing little by little at his retreat in Arcachon, Debussy had no lack of things to do. On 14 January, Viñes played three of the composer's *Préludes* at the Société nationale and accompanied Jane Bathori in the premiere of the *Promenoir des deux amants*. On the 16th, Prosper Mimart gave the first performance of Debussy's *Rapsodie pour clarinette* at the Société musicale indépendante, the same day that Marguerite Babaïan sang the *Trois ballades de François Villon* at the Salle des Agriculteurs. A few days later, a more personal event took place: on 25 January, Emma's daughter Dolly married a corporate administrator, Gaston Pochet Le Barbier de Tinan (a cousin of Jean!). It is to Debussy's credit that, within this same month, he took the time to welcome no fewer than three journalists and to give his opinion on a campaign led by a few French composers against the "invasion" of foreign music and the decentralization of musical life in France.[16] On 18 February, he experienced a painful revival of *Pelléas* at the Opéra-Comique, which included Marguerite Carré as Mélisande; Debussy felt obligated to congratulate her, since she was the wife of the director, but he would later say that she sang the role like some sort of "sad washerwoman!"[17] He had invited the Laloys and Gabriele D'Annunzio to his box, where he amused them "with his sarcastic remarks about the performers."[18]

In March, the succession of concerts was no less demanding. On the 5th, Debussy conducted the orchestral version of the *Trois ballades de François Villon* at the Sechiari concerts with a new singer, the American baritone Charles William Clark, who was replacing Jean Périer, as the latter was unavailable. Clark's interpretation was appalling, sung "with a dated French-American accent, and with a muffled voice that was equally American. Naturally, no one understood a word of this charming drollery, and... we'll have to try it again some other time! [. . .] We must not leave performances like these for posterity!" he wrote to Jean Périer, whom he asked to sing the Villon *Ballades* on the 25th at Charles Domergue's Cercle musicale.[19] On the same concert, he conducted Caplet's orchestration of *Children's Corner* as well as his own orchestration of Satie's *Gymnopédies* 1 and 3. Both of Satie's pieces were purportedly a success with the public and, according to their composer, their positive reception was said to have surprised Debussy. Satie would complain to his brother Conrad, "Why not leave me a small place in his shadow?"[20] At the end of the month, on the 25th, Debussy had to endure a lecture presented by Louis Schneider, who declared before the cosmopolitan audience at the Université des Annales that the composer's music was "of an amazing suppleness, almost imperceptible," and that "the same progressions that one hears in *Pelléas*" could be found in the trio of the Fates from Rameau's *Hippolyte et Aricie*.[21] No doubt Debussy was a little surprised to hear that, in his youth, his father's dream had been for him to "prepare for the navy school exams in order to become an ensign"![22] To ease Debussy's pain, Jean Périer sang the *Trois chansons de France*, Jane Bathori the *Chansons de Bilitis* and her students the *Chansons de Charles d'Orléans*, and Henri Etlin, a recent first-prize winner from the Conservatoire, played some of his *Préludes* for piano.[23]

The text for *Le martyre de saint Sébastien* had been arriving piecemeal at Debussy's home on the avenue du Bois de Boulogne since 11 January. Many changes were made to the original concept. The drama had become a "mystère" in five "mansions": Le cour des lys (The court of lilies), La chambre magique (The magic chamber), Le concile des faux dieux (The council of the false gods), Le laurier blessé (The wounded laurel), and Le paradis (Paradise). The third act—"the most significant, from a musical point of view"[24]—was the first to be finished by D'Annunzio.[25] The first mansion was completely done by the middle of February,[26] while the second was sent at the end of that month.[27] Debussy thus had only two months to compose his music! He wrote to D'Annunzio, "Now, any kind of music seems useless to me when placed alongside the ever-increasing splendor of your imagination. That is why it's not without a certain amount of terror that I see the moment approaching when I really must write something. . . Do I have it in me? Will I find what I want?"[28] A few weeks later, Debussy questioned the writer further: "Do you realize that [your text] is so lofty and goes so deep that it's daunting to find music for it?"[29] The composer had difficulty navigating his way through the profusion of stage directions. While writing the final choruses, he recalled the polyphonic composers whose works he had heard at the church of Saint-Gervais as a youth, and asked his publisher to send immediately a copy of Palestrina's *Missa Papae Marcelli*.[30] And to make clear that the haste required by this project had a detrimental effect on Debussy's desire for perfection in his compositional work, he explained to Caplet: "There's a type of coal that comes out of mines that is called 'all-purpose'. . . which describes my situation quite precisely."[31]

He was very fortunate to have Caplet at his side when the already-composed pages needed to be orchestrated. The (nearly complete) extant manuscript of the *Martyre* certainly shows the intervention of Caplet, as well as that of several copyists, but it would be wrong to assert, as has been frequently done, that Caplet took over for the composer in several parts of the work. In places, he developed the basic framework that had already been established according to Debussy's indications, relieving him from the heavy burden of notating the score by hand. But the treatment of the symphony orchestra (at times highlighting discrete instrumental groups), the extreme asceticism and transparency, and the musical language (restrained and yet expressive) clearly belong only to Debussy.

Rehearsals and the Premiere of *Le martyre*

Rehearsals began in April at the Théâtre du Châtelet, even before all the orchestral parts had been completed. A precise chronology is difficult to establish, since the letters exchanged by those principally involved generally lack dates. Émile Vuillermoz testifies that "most of the musicians considered this score as nothing more than a work for that particular occasion, a 'commission' dashed off by the composer at the last minute to satisfy the lavish whims of Mme Ida Rubinstein and Gabriel Astruc."[32] André Caplet conducted, Inghelbrecht prepared the chorus and the soloists (assisted by Chadeigne and Vuillermoz), Michel Fokine oversaw the choreography, and Léon Bakst designed the scenery and costumes. Gabriel Astruc went all out in marketing the work: a gigantic poster, four meters long, announced "150 artists, 350 performers, 500 costumes" and reproduced some of the costume designs. The price of the seats was also very high, from 20 to 150 francs. Ten gala performances were planned to be given from 20 May through 2 June. There was a very emotional moment "in the foyer of the theater, one morning in May, when a run-through had been organized with the orchestra, soloists, and choruses."[33] Vuillermoz reported that "until then, the orchestra had worked in the pit and the choruses [. . .] in the rehearsal room on the top floor.[34] [. . .] That day, the artists, generally blasé about rituals of this sort, were truly moved.[35] [. . .] It was an incomparable performance. Debussy himself, who rarely showed any emotion, could not maintain his usual demeanor of sarcastic benevolence, and wept quite openly."[36]

The staging, which was especially problematic, was carried out by Armand Bour and also to some extent by Bakst, who was so unconcerned with the sonorous outcome that he separated members of the chorus from one another in order to control his palette of colors more effectively. The fifth act, Paradise, was the most difficult to stage. In spite of the protestations of Debussy, who denounced "the poor relationship between the staging and the music" and suggested a "lunar" lighting, some torch bearers, and the return of seven seraphim positioned as angelic musicians at the moment of the resurrection of Sébastien's soul, the scene was weakened by a too-static solemnity.[37] In addition, the choruses, placed behind the scenery at the back of the enormous hall, could not hear the orchestra and thus did not have their intended impact.

External constraints also weighed on the production: on 16 May, the archbishop of Paris banned the work, stating that it distorted "in most improper terms the story of one of our most glorious martyrs,"[38] and on 22 May, the Catholic Church blacklisted all of D'Annunzio's works. To make matters worse, Berteaux, the minister of war, was killed in an airplane accident on the very morning of the dress rehearsal, and so the planned gala was replaced by a closed-door rehearsal for journalists only. The two artists penned a dignified response to the archbishop's condemnation: drafted by D'Annunzio and cosigned by Debussy, it claimed that the *Martyre* was a "profoundly religious work" and that it represented "the lyrical glorification not only of the admirable champion of Christ but of all Christian heroism."[39] Debussy expressed himself in a less bombastic style to journalists who came to interview him. To Henry Malherbe, he asserted, "I do not practice according to conventional rites. I worship the mysteries of nature."[40] And to René Bizet, he confessed, "I wrote my music as if it had been requested for a church. [. . .] I've put my theories into practice—if I may say so—in my music for the stage, which must be something other than the vague droning that generally accompanies verse or prose, and which should be united as one with the text."[41]

The gala of 21 May (converted at the last minute to a rehearsal for the press)[42] was slightly disrupted by the arrival of guests who had heard too late about the change of plans. On the premiere, which took place the following day, Mme de Saint-Marceaux commented in her journal as follows: "The plot is long and incomprehensible in certain parts, and the parallelism made in the second act between the Christian faith and pagan myths is very obscure for those who don't follow such things. Ida Rubinstein as mime is full of character. She speaks an incomprehensible language but [. . .] her face expresses what she doesn't know how to say."[43] Laloy, who deemed that D'Annunzio had no feel for the theater, was unable to hide his "eagerness to finally hear the music throughout those scenes where the conversation continued, despite one's sense that everything had been said, the words passing from one character to another like an inflated balloon. And when at last the orchestra and the choruses raised their harmonious voices, our enormous relief was marred by our fatigue; we were too worn out to match so much emotion."[44] Marcel Proust, seated next to Robert de Montesquiou, watched Ida Rubinstein's "sublime" legs in particular: "That was everything for me. But I found the piece very tedious, despite its moments, and the music pleasant but quite thin, very inadequate, truly crushed by the subject, the publicity, and the orchestra, which was just huge, considering that all it had to play were a few farts."[45]

The critics were somewhat confused when confronted with such a nontraditional production. Was it an oratorio, a mimed drama, or a ballet? In any case, there were fifty-five minutes of music, often laconic in nature, in a *mystère* that lasted more than four hours. "Strange work, in an unknown style, resisting categorization,"[46] noted Vuillermoz, who added that "the Debussyists were disconcerted and the Pelléastres divided," having confronted a score whose music was "so tangible and at the same time so ethereal."[47] One reviewer found that Debussy had "reinvented himself" (Louis Vuillemin)[48] and another that he had developed "a fullness of breath and a firmness of sound and inflection which, until then, we had not heard from him" (Gaston Carraud).[49] Two of them (Stœcklin and Carraud) made comparisons with *Parsifal*![50] Reynaldo Hahn pointed out that there was "a glaring disparity" between "the innate reserve" of the composer and the "flamboyant eloquence and luminous delirium of M. D'Annunzio."[51] Henri Ghéon, who had been one of the defenders of *Pelléas*, was spurred on by Gide to launch into a passionate criticism of D'Annunzio's work: "What a lot of ranting for two good screams! [. . .] A false work, flawed in its character and falsified in its essence. [. . .] The interior drama will perish under the weight of the picturesque scenery and the props."[52] He said next to nothing about the music, except that it showed a "remarkable expansion" of its composer's style.[53] Alfred Bruneau, whom Debussy insisted on thanking, appreciated the choral parts in particular, which, Bruneau wrote, reached "a new level of power," but he also praised "the preludes—hieratic and fanciful, religious and voluptuous—and the brilliant fanfares."[54] For Pierre Lalo, who conceded that the score had some fine qualities, it was "excellent music, but foreign to Debussy's true nature, incidental and parenthetical to his œuvre and to his art."[55] He declared himself surprised by the final chorus, "at times a huge Palestrina-like ensemble, at times interrupted by melodic and instrumental outbursts, more banal and more concerned with creating a big effect than one would expect in a work by M. Debussy."[56]

Neither Debussy nor anyone else would see this complete version of the *Martyre* again. The plan to give the work in Rome that same year, in celebration of the fortieth anniversary of Italian unity, failed, and instead became the subject of a two-year lawsuit.[57] Henry Russell, who had requested the right of first performance for the Boston Opera Company at the end of January, did not follow through. In fact, conscious of the *Martyre*'s hybrid tendencies and of his neglect in responding with musical passages to all the prompts in the text, Debussy soon began to think about revising it, which would have required him to add substantially more music. He even considered adapting it as a film, and corresponded with D'Annunzio about collaborating with a M. Péquin, a project that ultimately did not materialize.[58]

Trip to Turin

After the greuling undertaking of *Le martyre*, Debussy scarcely had time to return to his most treasured works, because he had promised to conduct one of a series of concerts in Turin that had been organized for an industrial exposition by a local lawyer, Giuseppe Depanis. D'Indy, Pierné, Edward Elgar, and Robert Kajanus (from Finland) had been invited as conductors for the other concerts. We do not always know the reasons—except when they were purely financial—that led Debussy to travel or not to foreign countries in order to conduct or oversee performances of his works. One such case involved *Pelléas*, which had been recently produced in Chicago (on 5 November 1910) and in Vienna (on 23 May 1911);[59] on the latter occasion, Hans Gregor conducted "an indiscreet, heavy, shrill orchestra," destroying "the intimate charm of this music."[60] "Ibéria" began to be performed more broadly as well: Gustav Mahler had conducted the American premiere in New York on 3 January 1911,[61] and Manuel de Falla and Franz Liebich had played the two-piano version in London on 24 May 1911.[62]

Debussy left for Turin with Emma and Chouchou on 19 June. Their week-long stay was recorded in some detail by Vittorio Gui.[63] The orchestra had been formed only recently and was by no means prepared. On the program were not only works by Debussy but also by other composers: the overture to *Gwendoline* by Chabrier; the symphonic poem *Sarabande* by Roger-Ducasse; and the prelude to the third act of Dukas's opera, *Ariane et Barbe-bleue*. The rehearsals began with the *Prélude à l'après-midi d'un faune*; Debussy, his eyes fixed on the score, exerted no leadership over the instrumentalists, who were unaccustomed to such repertoire. When they got to "Ibéria," things took a marked turn for the worse, so much so that it was decided by mutual agreement that the young Gui himself would see to the rehearsals—which he did, at times in the presence of the composer, to whom he gave the baton only on the day of the concert. But Debussy described a completely different picture of these sessions to Caplet and Durand:

> They've been working me hard! Six hours of rehearsal every day will surely make one sick of every kind of music, even one's own. And then, if you only knew how fundamentally indifferent they are to the music of Claude Debussy, and that at the first opportunity they'll return to their Puccini, Verdi, and all the others from the land where they speak the language of "si" (as our last national poet, G. d'Annunzio, wrote).[64]

A few months later, however, Debussy would have a chance to experience a deeper musical joy when Toscanini conducted *La mer* twice (28 and 29 September) in Turin, with "all his soul, all his intelligence, and all his *will*," as Leone Sinigaglia told him: "The audience, wary at the beginning (you can imagine! you know what I mean), was won over—in the end it was a great success."[65]

Stay in Houlgate

Upon his return to Paris, Debussy felt the impact of the pressure he had been enduring for many weeks; his doctor ordered him to rest for at least a month. "The *Martyre de Saint Sébastien* wiped me out more than I myself had realized, and the trip to Turin finished me off," he wrote to Durand on 13 July.[66] Considering a retreat to the seaside, he told Durand that he could not afford it, and that this was an additional subject of irritation and bickering with his wife. Within a few days, the publisher gave him the 3,000 francs that he needed as an advance for his orchestration of the *Rapsodie pour clarinette*, on which he planned to work during his summer vacation.

Debussy and his wife chose to spend a month by the beach at Houlgate, slightly west of Pourville. Nature and especially the sea were beautiful there, but the social atmosphere was almost unbearable. Photographs taken by Emma on the beach show Claude, dressed for the city, wearing a boater hat, and even seated on a kitchen chair. He confided to Caplet on 15 August that he was doing "nothing at all, not out of laziness but from a complete inability to think in that caravansary."[67] So he read 95-centime novels and discovered, of all things, the *Chroniques* by Jean de Joinville, the "delightful" biographer of Saint Louis.[68] From Durand, Debussy received the proofs of the orchestral score for the *Martyre*, which he and Caplet would correct.[69] The composer also declared to his publisher that he had "prepared almost completely" the orchestration of the *Rapsodie*.[70] But his soul was rarely at peace. In a letter sent to Durand, he let slip one of those comments that casts a very dark shadow on his relationship with his wife: "At the end of this holiday, we have to confess that we don't know why we came. Have we quite lost the ability to experience pleasure together?"[71] In the final days of their stay, however, the Debussys abandoned the crowded seaside and discovered the Norman countryside, "which is, quite simply, very beautiful, with meticulously maintained roads, homes with gardens going down to the sea, full of flowers and sizeable trees; no one around, no casino on the horizon."[72] They also visited Honfleur and Pont-l'Évêque.[73]

On their return to Paris, a new serious crisis caused friction between Claude and Emma. The English impresario Henry Russell wanted to present *Pelléas* (under Caplet's direction) at the Boston Opera Company, which he had founded. Russell had shown Debussy a scale model that gave an attractive preview of the scenery and the stage direction he had in mind. Dissatisfied with most of the productions he had attended, Debussy placed much hope in this performance and eagerly anticipated going to Boston with Caplet. Emma was firmly opposed, and he did not dare go against her will. He discussed the matter with Caplet, to whom he explained the agonizing atmosphere of these deliberations:

> We must give up all hope for the trip to Boston. . . There are obstacles whose form I sense perfectly but whose origin is unbeknownst to me. Perhaps you already know how much I loathe confrontations? It seems that everything is going against me, everything wounds me in this situation. And it seems only right that I should be helped, with the greatest possible affection! To tell you about my arguments and daily struggles has been so painful to me that I've put off writing to you as long as I could!
> The worst part is that I'm losing my sense of self in all this, and am forgetting that calm self-confidence which is an admirable strength, if one knows how to use it.[74]
> In short, I'm extremely demoralized.[75]

In this depressed state, Debussy attempted in vain to resume his composition on the Poe dramas. To Godet, he wrote on 18 December, "It feels like work, and the 'seams' are showing! The further I get into it, the more loathing I have for my *deliberate* mess, which is only a 'trompe-oreille';[76] the same goes for bizarre or amusing harmonies that are nothing more than parlor games."[77] And to Caplet, he wrote on 22 December: "It all seems deadly dull to me. For every measure that feels a bit free, there are twenty others that are stifled under the weight of a tone-deaf tradition,[78] from which, despite my efforts, I nevertheless acknowledge a hypocritical and cowardly influence."[79]

Satie, one of his most regular visitors, came to bring him the proofs of his *Morceaux en forme de poire*, which they corrected together.[80] In this Parisian life, which from then on offered Debussy more obligations than pleasures, he at least proved faithful to his friends. He went to see the exhibit of Henry de Groux, the Belgian painter who led such a bohemian life that he had been believed dead. Debussy offered an opinion of him that became well known only after his own death: "He teaches that one must disregard the unpleasant smoke of the censers and that, if necessary, it's useful to spit into them."[81] He also attended—out of friendship—the revival of a thirteenth-century drama, *Le chagrin dans le palais de Han* (Grief at the Han palace), adapted by Laloy with incidental music by Gabriel Grovlez, and on the same day, the premiere of the *Folies françaises ou les Dominos* (French follies or domino masks), a ballet, also by Laloy, on motifs by François Couperin and danced by Natalia Trouhanova.[82] While he was preparing to finally finish "Gigues," he went to hear *La mer* twice, first under the baton of Gabriel Pierné—"lamentable and embarrassing"—and then under that of Chevillard—"much better."[83] And, as the year drew to a close, he focused on the second book of *Préludes*, and sketched "Brouillards."

At the beginning of the catalog of his works that Durand published that year, we read the words of Charles Malherbe: "With a somewhat proud attitude and not without grace, he [Debussy] looks down from afar at the mediocrity passing by his feet, rushing toward success. He does not stoop to the crowd, whose coarseness disgusts him; he appeals to sensitive people and lures them to the heights, where he shows his free imagination."[84] Malherbe continues, "His art is subtle and complex; the deliberate vagueness of his lines, the flow of his harmonies, the iridescent reflections of his instrumentation, everything in it reveals a powerful appeal and charm that is irresistible: at first it astonishes, then it delights."[85]

But this did not prevent the usual negative comments from being repeated, such as those of Jean Poueigh in his overall opinion from the end of that year: for him, Debussy's work was not "the point of departure for new music. It was completely the opposite, a culmination rather than a beginning. An enchanting sunset but not a dazzling dawn. [. . .] It really seems that, since the *Prélude à l'après-midi d'un faune* [. . .] and *Pelléas* exhausted all the effects of a vocabulary and an artistic expression that were in themselves rather limited, these works will remain pinnacles that M. Debussy will not be able to attain or surpass again, unless he manages to revamp his style completely."[86]

Chapter Twenty-Five

The Year of the Ballets

1912

In 1912, the year during which he turned fifty, Debussy did not travel. It was also the year of the hundredth performance of *Pelléas*, which continued to make its way around the world: Nice (7 and 9 February),[1] Geneva (8, 12, 21, 26 March),[2] Boston (10, 13, 19, 22 January and 30 March),[3] and as far as Buenos Aires (12 August 1911).[4]

Debussy got back to work on *Khamma*, which, according to the terms of the initial contract, was about a year overdue, but which had been postponed by his work on the *Martyre*. The plot for this ballet-pantomime in three scenes had been conceived by the dancer, Maud Allan, and William Leonard Courtney, an English critic and academic. The action takes place in an ancient Egyptian temple dedicated to the sun god, Amun-Ra. The dancer Khamma sacrifices her life to persuade the great god to liberate the town, which has been besieged by invaders. She performs three dances before dropping dead and having her body blessed by the high priest. This subject hardly enthused Debussy, who had written to Godet that he "was hand-holding a child, without caring as much as he should have."[5] He repeated his opinion after having constructed the bulk of his score, writing to his publisher in January 1912: "Have you thought about the influence that a ballet libretto could have on the mind of a dancer? In looking at the libretto for *Khamma*—which I hope to play for you soon—a curious vegetation invades your brain and you [have to] forgive the dancers."[6] On 1 February, however, he appeared to be completely satisfied with his work: "When will you come to hear the new version of this curious ballet, with its trumpet calls, which signal a riot or a fire, and which send shivers down your spine?"[7] The piano score of *Khamma* would go to the engraver and the process of orchestration would begin.

More and more frequently during this period, Debussy met with performers, and his works were being played quite regularly. Ricardo Viñes described a dinner with the Laloys and Alexandre Charpentier's widow: "Of course, we didn't play any music and we hardly talked about it, as happens among true artists (which is to say that true artists speak the least about their own profession). Debussy and his wife chided me for not coming to see them more often; they like me very much. We spoke about the Chinese and their revolution."[8] On 26 February, Debussy agreed to a meeting with Alfredo Casella, a young Italian pianist and composer with rather cosmopolitan tastes who had studied with Fauré.[9] On 5 March 1912, at one of the Durand concerts,[10] Debussy accompanied Maggie Teyte in *Le promenoir des deux amants*;[11] in the same concert series (during March of the previous year), he had performed at the Salle Érard four of his *Préludes*: "Les sons et les parfums," "Le vent dans la plaine," "Des pas sur la neige," and "Minstrels" (which he had to repeat as an encore)—the last two for the first time. The performance of the *Préludes* sparked uneasy reactions among the most conservative individuals, people such as Luc Marvy, for whom "Le vent dans la plaine" gave the illusion of using "third- and quarter-tones."[12] On 12 March 1912, Viñes played the first set of *Images* and performed "La soirée dans Grenade" as an encore, confessing in his journal: "I was not very pleased with myself, especially because I knew that Debussy was in his box and that he never finds performances to his liking."[13] At that same concert, Debussy accompanied Maggie Teyte in the second series of *Fêtes galantes*.[14] On 19 March, Debussy received the pianist Édouard Risler, who was going to perform *Children's Corner* and *L'isle joyeuse* at the Durand concert of 26 March.[15] Finally, on 31 March, Henri Busser brought him the orchestration of *Printemps*, the symphonic suite that had constituted Debussy's second *envoi* from Rome but that he had modified from the version for piano, four hands.[16] Busser, who had taken about three years to complete this task,[17] claimed that during his visit, Debussy played some passages from *Le diable dans le beffroi* for him on the piano: "very picturesque, amusing, and completely different in feeling from his usual style."[18]

Another visit during the preceding weeks demonstrates that Debussy was as willing as ever to develop plans for operatic works. The visitor was Charles Morice, a writer who lived impecuniously as a journalist and lecturer but who had played an undeniable role at the beginning of the Symbolist movement and who had been the dedicatee of Verlaine's "Art poétique." Morice had brought to Debussy his recently published private edition of a "sung and danced poem, in the style of Verlaine";[19] the title, *Crimen amoris*,[20] was itself borrowed from Verlaine's long poem, which the latter had dedicated to Villiers de l'Isle-Adam and had included in his collection of poems titled *Jadis et naguère*. The script consisted of three parts: I. *Fête galante* ("Clair de lune,"[21] "Cortège," "Colloque sentimental," and "Un grand sommeil noir," drawn from *Sagesse*); II. *Crimen amoris*,[22] with the "Ballet of the Seven Deadly Sins,"[23] preceded by the text of "Vendanges" from *Jadis et naguère* and the "Sacrifice of Hell," during which the sins (Péchés) merge into the virtues (Vertus), and including passages from Verlaine's poem, "Crimen amoris," also from *Jadis et naguère*;[24] III. *Gaspard Hauser* (with several excerpts from *Sagesse*, alternating strophes from "Chevaux de bois" with those from "Gaspard Hauser").[25] In addition to gallant processions in brilliant moonlight, Morice envisioned a game between what was being heard backstage and what the audience saw onstage before having Lucifer collapse in the waves. Morice did not hesitate to stretch the imagination of the composer, who was required to write "epithelial rhythms"[26] or "a phrase in the orchestra expressing a desperate love, with brutal and sardonic dissonances, something like the caricature of true Love," or even to compel "the hymn of the orchestra to stop abruptly in raging discords that howl, hiss, roar, and growl."[27]

Debussy did not fail to suggest many changes to this script—especially in the third part—and, by 25 March, he had already spoken about it with Messager, who seemed impatient to get a copy of this work.[28] When the contract between Durand and the principal authors was signed on 21 May 1912, *Crimen amoris* had become an "operatic tale in three acts,"[29] and Morice was proceeding "on his own behalf and in the name of the beneficiaries of Paul Verlaine's estate,"[30] a detail that would turn out to be important. As before, it was announced that the work would appear on the Opéra's offerings for the 1912–13 season.[31]

Among the oddest premieres in Paris during March 1912 was Ernest Fanelli's work titled *Tableaux symphoniques*. The piece had been written nearly thirty years earlier by an obscure composer who was making a living as a copyist, and whom the press suddenly wanted to see as a forerunner of Impressionism because he had used the whole-tone scale as early as 1883! After this concert on 17 March, Maurice Ravel wrote with a touch of irony to set the record straight about this campaign, in which certain critics found a great opportunity to diminish the contribution of the purported leader of the Impressionists: "M. Debussy is customarily subjected to an attack of this kind every year. We already knew that the discovery of his harmonic system was due entirely to Erik Satie, that of his drama to Mussorgsky, and that of his orchestration to Rimsky-Korsakov. Now we know whence comes his Impressionism."[32]

L'après-midi d'un faune

Meanwhile, the Ballets Russes season was approaching. It would witness the premieres of *Le dieu bleu* (Reynaldo Hahn); *Thamar* (Balakirev), to which Debussy invited Toulet; Ravel's *Daphnis et Chloé*; but especially *L'après-midi d'un faune*, which marked Nijinsky's debut as a choreographer. Since 1910, the dancer had spent time at the Louvre, studying at length the Grecian urns (from the fifth and fourth centuries BCE) that depicted Dionysian processions of satyrs, their hands extended, and women being pursued, their arms raised.

This new language—this lateral concept of choreography, with its angular quality—was difficult to perfect, so much so that the production, at first planned for the 1911 season, had to be postponed until the following year. The rehearsals, which began in Monte Carlo in the spring, were long and painful; some claimed that there were sixty rehearsals, while others reported that there were one hundred twenty. In fact, the music of the *Prélude*, which had been chosen after some hesitation, did not completely suit Nijinsky; although he appreciated its color, he found it "too vague, too gentle for the movements he had conceived. It satisfied him in every way, except for its lack of angularity."[33] We would not know how Debussy learned about the preparation for the production had he not later confided the following remarks to an Italian journalist:

> I couldn't begin to imagine the style of choreography Nijinsky had devised for my work. I admittedly had a bad feeling about it, which is why, from time to time, I'd ask his permission to attend a stage rehearsal; but the distinguished dancer-choreographer always replied to me: it's too soon, wait until tomorrow. So, in order to get some accurate information, I spoke to my dear friend Igor Stravinsky.
>
> [. . .He] reassured me of the correlation between the music and the gestural expression, and I eventually calmed down. I cannot begin to describe to you my. . . terror when, at the dress rehearsal, I saw that the nymphs and fauns were moving on the stage like marionettes, or rather like cardboard cut-out figures, always facing sideways, with stiff and angular gestures, stylized in an archaic and grotesque manner! Can you imagine the disconnect between an undulating, lulling music, where curved lines abound, and a stage action where the people move like the figures on antique Greek or Etruscan vases, without grace or suppleness, as though their schematic gestures were governed by the laws of pure geometry?. . . An appalling "dissonance," with no possible resolution![34]

The performances were not a success at first. At the dress rehearsal on 28 May, the invited audience remained more or less unmoved. The premiere was marked by Rodin's enthusiasm but also by an uproar from music lovers who were deprived of the traditional ballet they expected. Success was assured by the well-known scandal that the faun's final gesture provoked. Debussy was wary of participating in that uproar, and—in spite of the financial benefits that future productions could bring him—he remained deeply critical of Nijinsky's choreography. He was not alone. Émile Vuillermoz focused in particular on denouncing the striking dissonance in the unnatural combination of the two arts:

> Debussy's music is not of the sort that knows how to obey; it constantly commands, and it disrupts the balance of the charming ballet [i.e., Debussy's music was not consonant with Nijinsky's choreography]. Debussy could not have endorsed this amusing linear stylization of the nymphs' postures.

There are no acute angles in the score. It is written in curves, in fluid turns, in arabesques of extraordinarily harmonious contours. And the music gets its revenge; it denounces the marionette gestures of the dancers with their wooden wrists, with scissor-like arms, which move, rolling along the sides of an invisible vase, shoulders facing forward and hips in profile! [. . .] The score mercilessly brings out all the defects of a production that has not considered its musical indications, one that would have been unobjectionable were the music more neutral.[35]

Igor Stravinsky

For Debussy, the most positive aspect of the Ballets Russes up to this time was the friendship he had established with Stravinsky over the previous months. On 16 June 1911, Stravinsky had dedicated a copy of his *Firebird* to Debussy: "For Monsieur Claude Debussy, from Igor Stravinsky, with admiration as always" (Pour Monsieur Claude Debussy, de la part de Igor Strawinsky qui l'admire comme tout).[36] In this same month of June, on the occasion of the performances of *Petrushka*, Debussy had invited the Russian composer and Satie to his home, where photos were taken of the three figures—two at a time—in front of the fireplace.[37] Reading the score piqued Debussy's interest once again in the music of this ballet, so much so that on 13 April 1912, he did not hold back his praise:

> Thanks to you, I've spent a lovely Easter holiday in the company of Petrushka, the terrible Moor, and the delightful ballerina. I imagine that you too must have spent some incomparable moments with these three dolls. . . and I don't know many things that are as good as what you call "le tour de passe-passe" [the magic trick][38]. . . In that passage there's a sort of sonorous magic, a mysterious transformation of mechanical spirits into human beings through a spell of which, thus far, you seem to be the sole inventor. Finally, there's a degree of orchestral *assuredness* that I have encountered only in *Parsifal*—I'm sure you'll understand what I'm trying to say! You will certainly go far beyond *Petrushka*, but you can already be proud of what this work represents.[39]

They exchanged letters even after Stravinsky returned to Russia. In a letter to Debussy on 4 November 1911, the Russian composer emphasized "the infinite admiration I have for you and for your creative genius."[40] About ten days after the premiere of the ballet version of *L'après-midi d'un faune*, Laloy invited the two composers to his Bellevue villa for a sight-reading session that might be called historic:

> As soon as he saw us, the Russian composer ran with outstretched arms to embrace the French master, who threw me a look over his shoulder that

showed how amused and yet moved he was. He [Stravinsky] had brought the reduction of his new work, *Le sacre du printemps*, for piano, four hands. Debussy agreed to play the lower part on the Pleyel piano that I still own. Stravinsky had asked permission to take off his collar. Gazing fixedly through glasses, diving into the piano, at times humming a passage instead of playing it, he led into a sonorous deluge the agile and soft hands of his partner, who followed without a hitch and seemed to make light of the difficulty. When they had finished, there was no more need for embraces or compliments. We were dumbfounded, knocked down as if struck by a hurricane that had come from the beginning of time to seize our life by its very roots.[41]

The "grande saison," as it was called, occupied Debussy more than he would have liked to admit. On 13 June, he went with Toulet to see Richard Strauss's *Salome* and, on the 20th, he heard *Tristan* at the Opéra; according to Busser's unnuanced account, Debussy argued about it with Dukas, who "completely admire[d]" the work, whereas Debussy claimed to find it "terribly boring."[42] Between these two dates, D.-E. Inghelbrecht conducted the concert version of *Le martyre de saint Sébastien* for the first time in France, under the auspices of the Société musicale indépendante; for the critics, this version seemed no more convincing than the earlier staged version of the work.[43] The world premiere of the concert version had been given in New York, on the previous 12 February, with the New Philharmonic Orchestra and the MacDowell Chorus under the direction of Kurt Schindler.[44] The full production of *Le martyre* that was conducted by Caplet at the Opera House in Boston on 30 March fell victim to unfortunate staging, made all the more incomprehensible because the program provided no explanation about the production; Mme Cevruti's mimes were deemed "grotesque" by the local *Sunday Herald*.[45]

The Origins of *Jeux*

During this period, the composer received a commission from Diaghilev for a ballet, which this time would be completed. Accounts concerning the birth of *Jeux* do not all agree, but it became a certainty by 18 June, when the contract for the work was signed by Diaghilev and Debussy.[46] The work's title was already established, the plot was purportedly by Nijinsky, and a sum of 10,000 francs was agreed upon for the composer, who promised to furnish the piano score by the end of August 1912 and the orchestral score by the end of March 1913. The initial idea for the story line may have originated during a stay in London, where, while having tea in Bedford Square at Lady Ottoline Morrell's home, Nijinsky and Bakst had purportedly been fascinated by some tennis matches, played by individuals dressed in white, standing out against the "dreaming garden trees."[47] Jacques-Émile Blanche, to whom Diaghilev had granted the title of "godfather" of his ballets, later claimed that he had played the role of "scribe" in drafting the scenario; but he gave several versions of it, showing his rather loose conception of the historical record.[48] As for Nijinsky, he connected this scenario with Diaghilev's sexual fantasies: "*Jeux* is the life of which Diaghilev dreamed. He wanted to have two boys as lovers. He often told me so, but I refused. Diaghilev wanted to make love to two boys at the same time. [. . .] In the ballet, the two girls represent the two boys, and the young man is Diaghilev. I changed the characters, as love between three men could not be represented on the stage."[49] The following is more or less the scenario for *Jeux* that Debussy probably received, sometime during July:

> In a park at twilight, a tennis ball is lost; a young man, then two young girls, hasten to look for it. The artificial luminescence of the tall electric street-lights, which casts a fantastical glow around them, gives them the idea of playing childish games: they seek each other, they hide from each other, they pursue each other, they quarrel with each other, and for no good reason they snub each other. The night is warm, the sky is bathed in a soft light; they embrace each other. But the spell is interrupted by a tennis ball thrown by some unknown mischievous hand. Surprised and frightened, the young man and the two young girls disappear into the nocturnal shadows of the park.[50]

Having interrupted the orchestration of "Gigues," Debussy must have composed the score for *Jeux* very quickly, since it was practically finished before the end of August. At the beginning of the month, Diaghilev and Nijinsky paid him a visit, but he did not want to play for them what he had already written, "unwilling to allow the Barbarians to stick their noses into my personal chemical experiments."[51]

During this time, what had become of the other ballet, *Khamma*? While the piano score was with the engraver and while Debussy told Durand that he was working on the orchestration, relations with Maud Allan had taken a sudden turn for the worse. The dancer opposed the publication of the music prior to the premiere of the ballet; in addition, she estimated that Debussy's score would not cover even half the time she had planned (40 minutes); finally, she asked that the work be dedicated not to Mme Jacques Durand, as the composer had suggested, but to her![52] Debussy rejected these demands, writing that he preferred to forgo any dedication whatsoever.[53] On 26 June, Maud Allan wrote a new letter, repeating the same points but adding that, while Debussy's music was "very beautiful," it did not fully fit with her scenario; she threatened to contact another composer if he persisted in refusing her requests.[54] On 16 July, Debussy drafted a short letter, haughtily reaffirming his refusal to accede to her demands concerning *Khamma*: "As I have written it, so will it remain!"[55] But it is unclear if he sought Durand's advice before sending the letter. The publisher had in fact taken over the negotiations in this controversy, which no one knew about at the time, and it was to him that Debussy expressed his deep disappointment in Maud Allan's behavior, on 12 September:

> Let me be frank about the rudeness of this young woman. It's unacceptable for her to express unfounded judgments and to convey them in language that would hardly be appropriate for addressing a bootmaker who might have misunderstood her order.
> I'm probably not philosophical enough, for I confess that I find this matter utterly revolting... Good grief! Here's someone who gives me such an insipid scenario that any half-wit could have come up with something better. Still, I'm finding a way, aided by God knows what, to write the music. And now this woman is giving me lessons in aesthetics, talking about her taste and that of the English—which really crosses the line.[56]

On 18 September, the piano "reduction" [*sic*][57] was registered at the legal deposit (for copyright purposes), but it was not sold commercially by Durand, who from this point forward was negotiating a compromise with the vindictive dancer.[58]

Summertime had passed once again without a restful stay at the seaside, and Chouchou complained to her father about it. Indeed, the year was terrible financially for Debussy. In spite of the substantial sums paid for the ballets, he seemed to be forced more than ever into seeking perilous loans. In order to fund them, he contacted a mutual insurance company which bore the paradoxical name of "The Future of the Proletariat" (L'avenir du prolétariat), but whose policies were by no means philanthropic, since they required him to transfer his royalties to the company. His debt to Durand, which in 1911 was 27,000 francs, would surpass 56,000 francs in 1914. On 30 October 1912, he nevertheless ventured to ask his publisher for a personal loan of 12,000 francs over four years, declaring himself sorry "to appear to be trading on our friendship."[59] Then, no longer knowing whom to approach, he tried to borrow from his professional contacts. He already owed 5,000 francs to Henry Russell, the man in Boston, who would never get his money back. He implored Laloy—probably in 1912—to find someone (Marnold was suggested) who would loan him 20,000 francs immediately.[60] "I don't know what else to do," he sighed.[61]

Critic for the *S. I. M.* Journal

It was at this juncture that Debussy decided to resume writing for the monthly *S. I. M.* journal, which had resulted from the merger of *Le mercure musical* and *La revue musicale*. The new editor, none other than Émile Vuillermoz, had had the idea to bring together Debussy and Vincent d'Indy, the former covering the Colonne concerts, the latter covering the Lamoureux concerts. The journal announced the news with a certain grandiloquence, expressing delight in seeing the composer "break, in our favor, his too-long silence that has saddened all those who know what penetrating, analytical perception and what luminous clairvoyance the creator of *Pelléas* brings to his assessments of the contemporary musical scene, within which he has known how to maintain such an absolute individualism."[62] One year later, André Gide would ask him in vain to take on the same role for the *Nouvelle revue française*. Debussy justified his decision to write for the *S. I. M.* to Godet, voicing his pessimism on the state of Parisian musical life: "One must faithfully try to put things back in their place [and] try to recover the values that arbitrary judgments and capricious interpretations have distorted. [. . .] We are becoming as foolishly fickle as some of the Viennese. . . And you can't imagine the standards of our so-called 'artistic productions'!"[63] Debussy's first article from November lacked a true prologue that presented the principles behind his criticism; nonetheless, in it he lamented the passivity of audiences as well as the "maniacal" ambition of artists, and he took up his old ideas again: "When will they stop increasing the means of exposure, which are pointless and even dangerous?"[64] His former readers could not have been surprised to reencounter his offhand manner and irony, whether concerning Beethoven's "Pastoral" Symphony, Berlioz's *Symphonie fantastique*, or Gustave Charpentier's *Impressions d'Italie*.[65] The following article, appearing in the December issue, was titled "Du respect dans l'art" (On respect in art) and began with some reflections on the hostile reception that part of the audience gave to a symphony by Théodore Dubois: "Must we all agree and accept that the official position of M. Théodore Dubois demands absolute respect? [. . .] In art, respect cannot be compulsory."[66] The venerable member of the Institut responded immediately to Debussy, criticizing the audience in the galleries who, during the performance, had demonstrated their displeasure "through jeers, cries, songs, and stupid and cruel sniggers"; Dubois concluded his letter with the following: "You are too great an artist, Sir, and you hold your art too sacred not to share" the opinion of the critics, who had denounced this public attitude.[67]

The turn of the new year would be marked by the commemoration of the hundredth performance of *Pelléas* at the Opéra-Comique, on 28 January 1913.[68] About a hundred guests—among them Dukas, Xavier Leroux, and Florent Schmitt[69]—were invited to this event. Albert Carré hosted a dinner at the Café Riche, during which he offered a toast, thanking M. Léon Bérard, the Under-secretary of State for the Fine Arts, for joining the admirers of Debussy's work.[70] Jacques Durand recalled that a government representative "celebrated the work and its composer," and "announced that the Minister had eclectic taste in art, having just awarded the Légion d'honneur rosette to d'Indy and Charles Lecocq. With this, he raised his glass and sat down. They had hoped for something more: Debussy had been made *chevalier* ten years before."[71]

The performance of *Pelléas*, meanwhile, had satisfied Debussy's taste less than ever; Marguerite Carré showed "staunch enthusiasm," Boulogne gave "a constant wobbling between two notes," and Jean Périer had nothing more "than the utmost goodwill."[72] That did not prevent Marcel Proust from listening to *Pelléas* "perpetually" on the théâtrophone:[73] "I can't make out a single word," he wrote to Reynaldo Hahn. "The passages I love the most are the ones without text. [. . .] When Pelléas emerges from the underground vaults with an 'Ah! I can finally breathe,' modeled on *Fidelio*, there are a few lines that are truly permeated by the freshness of the sea and the scent of the roses that the breeze wafts to him. Of course, there's nothing 'human' about it, but it's exquisitely poetic."[74]

Nearly a year earlier, *Pelléas* had been conducted (after many rehearsals) by André Caplet in Boston,[75] featuring Georgette Leblanc, who was called out for her "mannered acting" and tendency to hold "graphic pose[s]," as well as an excellent Golaud (Vanni Marcoux).[76] The staging, announced as having received "the warm approval of Debussy for the music and of Maeterlinck for the play,"[77] was described by Philip Hale as follows: "The various scenes did not occupy the whole of the stage as far as the eye of the spectator was concerned. He saw literally a stage picture, framed; or, rather, a series of dissolving pictures that came suddenly from the darkness and at the end of each scene gradually faded."[78] Amidst this contrasting landscape was an image that makes one smile: Chouchou had begun to take piano lessons with "a woman in black who," in the brutally frank words of her father, "looks like [a cross between] a drawing by Odilon Redon and a nihilist who sets off bombs."[79]

Chapter Twenty-Six:

Jeux; Travel to Russia

1913

> Why is there so much indifference for our great Rameau? And for Destouches, who is now practically unknown? And for Couperin, the most poetic of our harpsichordists, whose tender melancholy seems like a charming echo emanating from the mysterious background of landscapes where Watteau characters lament? This indifference becomes shameful, as it gives to other countries—so mindful of their glories—the impression that we scarcely value our own, given that not one of these illustrious Frenchmen appears on our concert programs, not even at this time of year when it is customary to move closer toward our forefathers.[1]

For his first column of 1913, Debussy thus resumed his panegyric, which he had not had occasion to lay out during the previous five years.[2] Moreover, a certain nostalgia emerged in his columns for the S. I. M.: nostalgia for *Parsifal* and Bayreuth;[3] for Ernest Chausson, whose "charming genius" was unable to be fulfilled;[4] for the Javanese and Vietnamese musics heard in 1889;[5] and for the "storytellers of ballads, fine-throated minstrels who innocently preserved the beauty of their legends."[6]

Debussy's interest in Asian musics was revitalized in May, when the pianist Walter Rummel proposed bringing some North Indian musicians—Sufis playing religious Islamic music—to the composer's home.[7] "I fear," Debussy replied, "that [we'd be] overtaxing your remarkable musician-philosopher by having him come with his group at what would be for them an abnormal hour. It would be simpler, I think, if he and his brother were to come here any day they want, around 5 p.m., which seems to be his usual time."[8] Debussy thus heard Inayat Khan, who at the time was touring in Europe with his two brothers and his cousin, and in turn played his own music for Khan. The younger brother, Musharaff Khan, was said to have shown Debussy how to play his instrument, the *vina*.[9] Gabriel D'Annunzio had published an enthusiastic account of the concert that Inayat Khan had given in Paris the previous winter, and it is likely that this experience led to the vague "Indian drama" project that D'Annunzio had contemplated undertaking with Debussy at one time[10]—in addition to the idea, also rather vague, of a "Persian ballet" that the composer had discussed with Toulet during the previous year.[11]

Indeed, Debussy's articles contained several allusions that showed an ever-attentive curiosity about contemporary signs of renewal. Reworking Francesco Pratella's manifesto,[12] Luigi Russolo had just brought out his *L'arte dei rumori: Manifesto futurista* (The Art of Noises: A Futurist Manifesto). "We are waiting with a straight face," Debussy commented in posing the question: "Will it ever achieve the already satisfying sonority of a steel mill operating at full steam?"[13] Nor did he ignore the early appearances of film music, and he mentioned the success at the Gaumont Palace of *L'agonie de Byzance* (The Agony of Byzantium), Louis Feuillade's spectacular grand drama recounting the capture of Constantinople. Henry Février and Léon Moreau had written a score for large orchestra, soloists, chorus, and organ for this silent film, prompting Debussy to write: "Let's apply the techniques of cinematography to pure music."[14]

Completion and Premiere of the *Images* for Orchestra

The completion of the score of "Gigues," dated 10 October 1912, was laborious, due to an "unfortunate accident" involving the manuscript, which Debussy mentioned to Durand on 23 July 1912,[15] and then subsequently due to the composition of other works, *Jeux* in particular. The proofs for "Gigues" were already extant at the beginning of 1913, although the work had still been announced by Durand as "Gigues tristes"; the score was not published, however, until December. Thanks to Caplet's attentive work, the reduction for piano, four hands, had appeared the previous year, and it has sometimes been suggested that the latter "collaborated" on the orchestration, which may or may not be the case.

We will recall that, in the initial plan (1903) for the orchestral *Images*, "Ibéria" came first in the triptych. Perhaps in order to provide a better balance to the set, Debussy ultimately chose to place the large Spanish section at the center of the structure, framed by "Gigues," whose slightly Scottish flavor was emphasized by the timbre of the oboe d'amore, and by "Rondes de printemps," whose character was more French.

The initial idea was for Caplet to conduct the premiere of these finally united *Images*, but he was in the United States. Then Chevillard came to mind, but the latter wanted to conduct only "Gigues," so Debussy agreed to approach Pierné, despite his reservations about that conductor's interpretation of "Ibéria"; he confessed to Durand that he had a soft spot for Pierné's

Colonne orchestra.[16] Ultimately, Debussy himself conducted the *Images* at the Concerts Colonne on 26 January 1913, in a manner "as exciting and vibrant as one could have wished," as he himself commented amusingly in the *S. I. M.*[17]

As usual, the critics were divided, some of them declaring their preference for "Gigues" (Carraud, Jemain),[18] while others thought that "Rondes de printemps" was the best (André Lamette).[19] Samazeuilh considered the use of folk themes to be incompatible with the subtlety of harmonic pursuits,[20] while Alfred Bruneau continued to be favorably disposed to "the refined, sensitive, and disturbing art of their composer."[21] By and large, the critics' reception was becoming considerably less negative than in the past. However, Maurice Ravel took up his pen to denounce strongly the trio of the old guard, always rather intractable, who merely skimmed the surface of Debussy's music:

> You have understood very well, you who superficially let yourselves succumb to the dazzling charm and exquisite freshness of the "Rondes de printemps"; you who feel moved to tears by that rustling "Ibéria," including its so deeply touching "Parfums de la nuit,"; by that harmonic splendor, so new and so refined; by all of that intense musicality; you are merely a writer or a painter. And you understand very well what contemptuous implications these terms have. [. . .] Only these [three critics] are "musicians" and "sensitive people": M. Gaston Carraud, to whom we owe three songs and a little symphonic poem; M. Camille Mauclair, who has clearly made himself known by literary and pictorial works; and M. Pierre Lalo, who has produced nothing at all.[22]

Debates continued to surface from time to time, with the aesthetics of the two camps in genuine opposition. In the November 1912 issue of the *S. I. M.*, d'Indy published an article—"Le bon sens" (Common sense)—in which he criticized the practices in vogue, summing up with this adage: "Aside from some arresting harmonies and some tantalizing orchestral timbres, there is nothing to recommend it"; according to him, Debussy and Ravel had been wrong in "allowing" these principles "to be established" by "their muftis and ulemas."[23] It was André Gedalge, Ravel's teacher, who replied to d'Indy by mocking that "mentality of another era, of a narrow, authoritative, and intolerant dogmatism."[24] At the end of the year, Alfredo Casella described "the Twilight of Franckism,"[25] triggered in his mind by the appearance of Debussy and the teaching of Fauré at the Conservatoire—comments that were strongly refuted by Auguste Mangeot.[26]

Shortly thereafter René Lenormand's *Étude sur l'harmonie moderne* (A Study of Modern Harmony) appeared. In that small technical work, Lenormand deemed that "by the boldness of his harmonies and also by their charm and musicality, Debussy could be considered as the leader of a new school."[27] After reading the manuscript of this study, which was packed with musical examples,

Debussy was nevertheless hardly enthusiastic about Lenormand's work; he was leery of how some might use "all those beautiful butterflies that are already a little crumpled by the [author's] analysis."[28]

Préludes, Book Two, and *La boîte à joujoux*

The composition of the second book of *Préludes* for piano was carried out in an even more discreet manner than that of the first book. On 7 January 1913, Debussy suddenly announced to Durand that he was working on the two pieces that were needed to complete the collection. But one of these, "Too-mai des éléphants," inspired by Rudyard Kipling, was proving to be, in his words, "impossible as a *Prélude*";[29] he therefore completed a replacement for it, perhaps "Les tièrces alternées."[30] This time, the composer did not wait for the publication of the second book to give its first performance, albeit a partial one. He played three *Préludes*—"Bruyères," "Feuilles mortes," and "La puerta del vino"—at the Salle Érard on 5 March, and, as acknowledged by Edmond Stoullig, received enthusiastic praise and even some flowers thrown by young girls, which the composer "picked up with the greatest pleasure."[31] On 5 April, he left it to Viñes to perform three other *Préludes* from Book Two at the Société nationale, after having the pianist play them first for him. By 19 April, the collection was commercially available; in addition to notational and typographical innovations (writing on three staves and using different sizes of notes), some allusions to Stravinsky's ballets can be discerned. This did not prevent an S. I. M. columnist from venturing to make bold comparisons: these pieces, he wrote, "link modern music to the tradition of our descriptive and picturesque French clavecinists."[32]

The titles of two of these *Préludes*—"Les fées sont d'esquises danseuses" (The fairies are exquisite dancers) and "Feuilles mortes" (Dead leaves)—had come to the composer's mind while he was paging through James Matthew Barrie's beautiful *Peter Pan* album, decorated with lovely illustrations by the English artist Arthur Rackham, a copy of which Godet had given as a gift to Chouchou. "Ondine" came from a work by Friedrich de la Motte Fouqué, illustrated again by Rackham. Other *Préludes* from this second collection alluded to an American clown who had just performed in Paris ("Général Lavine"); to Charles Dickens ("Hommage à S. Pickwick"); to a postcard received from either Manuel de Falla or Ricardo Viñes ("La puerta del vino"); and, more simply, to a small Egyptian funerary urn ("Canope") that Debussy kept on the mantel of his fireplace.

It was still with Chouchou in mind that Debussy accepted a proposal by André Hellé, an artist who worked for illustrated periodicals and the theater, to compose music for one of the first books written for children, *La boîte à joujoux* (The Toy Box).[33] This "ballet for children" was in reality a passionate drama transferred to a childlike universe, portraying puppets and soldiers, and ending with the happy marriage of a doll to a soldier. As soon as the contracts were drawn up, Debussy began working on it and remarked, on 25 July 1913, that he was wresting secrets from Chouchou's old dolls.[34] At about the same time, Satie dedicated to Chouchou the third of his *Croquis et agaceries d'un gros bonhomme en bois* (Sketches and provocations of a fat wooden mannequin). *La boîte à joujoux*, which recalls Mussorgsky's *Pictures at an Exhibition*, would be nearly finished by October in its version for piano, which apparently had no premiere in sight.

Premiere of *Jeux*

The "eighth" season of the Ballets Russes began at the brand-new Théâtre des Champs-Élysées on 15 May with the premiere of *Jeux*, a "danced poem"[35] that was presented alongside revivals of Stravinsky's *Firebird* and Rimsky-Korsakov's *Scheherazade*. Curiously, we know nothing about the relationship between Debussy and the conductor Pierre Monteux, who, while still a student, had played in the viola section at the premiere of *Pelléas*. This was not the first time that Debussy's music had been heard in this theater, hailed as "the temple of music,"[36] the construction of which was made possible by Gabriel Astruc's persistence. At the inaugural concert on 2 April 1913, Debussy had conducted the *Prélude à l'après-midi d'un faune*; the other composers who had been included on the very eclectic program likewise conducted their own works: Saint-Saëns (*Phaeton* and excerpts from *La lyre et la harpe*), d'Indy ("Le camp" from *Wallenstein*), Fauré (*La naissance de Vénus*), and Dukas (*L'apprenti sorcier*). On 5 May, also at this theater, Loïe Fuller had created, with her school of dance and the combined effects of colorful lights and veils, a choreographic adaptation of the *Nocturnes* (at least "Nuages" and "Sirènes," since "Fêtes" was played with the curtain closed). The scenery was by Fernand Ochsé, and the conductor was Inghelbrecht. Diaghilev had in fact considered choreographing "Fêtes" during the previous year.

The same day as the premiere of *Jeux*, Debussy published about forty lines in *Le matin*, where he seemed to embrace Nijinsky's scenario, which he described as being "made from that subtle 'triviality' on which I believe a balletic poem has to be based. [. . .] It has] everything necessary to give birth to rhythm in a musical atmosphere."[37] For once, he commended the Ballets Russes "for continually pushing the boundaries," for their performers—Karsavina and Schollar, as well as the "natural or acquired spontaneity" of Nijinsky—and finally even for Diaghilev, "that formidable and charming man who could make stones dance."[38]

The rehearsals, which suffered from being held so close to those for *Le sacre du printemps*, had been somewhat delayed and very tense, as Karsavina had trouble understanding Nijinsky's intentions, which were influenced by the pedagogical precepts of Émile Jaques-Dalcroze. Nijinsky's costume in particular (designed by Bakst, as was the scenery) became the subject of a quarrel with Diaghilev. In the atmosphere of these rehearsals, Debussy was seized by a feeling of disgust, just as he was whenever he was involved behind the scenes of the theater:

> I'd really have loved to get away from Paris, if only for a few days. There are too many Russians. . . the snobbery so mocked by artists has ultimately affected them, and they make use of it perhaps even more shamefully than do people in polite society, because for them, all it takes for something to be considered beautiful is that it hasn't been done before! This is the aesthetic for a novelty store! The saddest part in all of this is that ultimately the music suffers because of it.[39]

In Misia Sert's box, during the dress rehearsal, Gide, Cocteau, and Jacques-Émile Blanche could not hide their reservations from Diaghilev; Blanche considered the music to be "trivial"[40] or "innocuous."[41]

On 15 May, the audience was far from enthusiastic and rather ambivalent, offering only weak applause. As for the critical reception, it was true to form. *Le monde musical* described the score as a "pleasant-sounding little scherzo,"[42] but the reviews were unanimous in condemning Nijinsky's choreography. In the *S. I. M.*, Vuillermoz was the most scathing:

> Nijinsky has sinned against Debussy. His rendition of *Jeux* was a betrayal. Faced with the most delightfully quivering and capering score that has ever been offered to a choreographer, with the flight of the most supple and silky sonorous scarves that a composer has ever unfurled, and before an orchestra that one hears welling up from the dancer's feet with a fresh babbling of a spring, the director has not for a single moment lost his shameful theoretical composure. [. . .] Nijinsky has methodically applied his patented technique to this new score without deigning to listen to the desperate pleas of the music climbing from the depths where it is being held captive.[43]

Debussy's own words speak for themselves:

> Nijinsky's perverted genius indulges in a peculiar kind of mathematics. This fellow adds up thirty-second notes with his feet, demonstrates them with his arms, and then, as if suddenly paralyzed on one side, glares at the music as it passes by. It seems that this is called "stylized gesture". . . It's awful! It's even *Dalcrozian*; I consider Monsieur Dalcroze to be one of music's worst enemies! And can you imagine what havoc his method can wreak in the soul of a young savage like Nijinsky?[44]

It fell to a twenty-two-year-old critic, Roland-Manuel, to devote a commentary less influenced by choreographic events in one of his first reviews. It was published in a new periodical, *Montjoie!*, managed by Ricciotto Canudo, whose internationalist spirit had strongly displeased Debussy when Canudo visited him in 1910.[45] In his review, Roland-Manuel praised the work's ethereal orchestration, with "those delicious intertwinings of the winds and those silky slitherings of the strings. [. . .] Those sighs,] those delicate diversions, those whispered confidences, the composer of *Pelléas* possesses the secret for evoking them while maintaining an absolute simplicity."[46] Clearly, no score passed more unnoticed than that of *Jeux*. Well-nigh two generations elapsed before its subtle complexity was detected.[47] The individual who showed the most curiosity about it was Stravinsky, who, several months earlier, had read through the score of the work; he was the first to ask to see it, even before the orchestration was completed: "I'm waiting most eagerly," he wrote from Clarens on 13 December 1912, "for the proofs of your admirable *Jeux*."[48]

One of the most amazing confluences in the history of music thus took place in the month of May 1913 when, fourteen days after the premiere of *Jeux*, Monteux conducted the premiere of *Le sacre du printemps* in the same theater. It is important to recall Debussy's reactions to Stravinsky's work. After sight-reading it in Bellevue, an experience that haunted him "like a beautiful nightmare," he wrote in a letter to Stravinsky in November 1912 that he was awaiting the performance "like a greedy child who has been promised some sweets."[49] On 29 May 1913, the very day of the premiere, he warned Caplet: "*Le sacre du printemps* is an extraordinarily wild thing. . . It's savage music, so to speak, with every modern convenience!"[50] On 9 June, he received from Stravinsky the reduction of the work for piano, four hands, with the following dedication: "For my very dear friend Claude Debussy, in memory of the battle of 29 May 1913" (À mon très cher ami Claude Debussy en souvenir de la bataille du 29 mai 1913).[51] And on 23 June, he wrote to Caplet that he was saving for his next visit to Paris "a reading of the *Sacre du printemps*, which will not leave you indifferent."[52]

Georges Jean-Aubry later reported a comment that, he claimed, had come from the composer himself: "On the day after *Le sacre du printemps* (whose power he had experienced, about which he did not conceal his feelings, and which he admired), Debussy made this unforgettable comment to me: 'Still, French music would not be written like that!'"[53] Even later, in an interview with Robert Craft, Stravinsky wondered if Debussy was "not rather embarrassed by his inability to come to terms with the music of the *Sacre*."[54] At that time, Stravinsky had just completed a short and strange work for male chorus and large orchestra, *Le roi des étoiles*, based on a celestial text by Constantin Balmont. He dedicated the piece to Debussy, and had no doubt given him the manuscript.[55] When it appeared in 1913, Ravel planned to program it on a Société musicale indépendante concert, a performance that never took place, and it was surprisingly not until 1939 that the work was heard. Upon reading the score, Debussy could not hide his bewilderment:

> The music for *Le roi des étoiles* is nonetheless extraordinary... It's probably the "harmony of the eternal spheres" of which Plato speaks (don't ask me on what page!). And I see a possible performance of this cantata only in the "worlds" of Sirius and Aldebaran. As for our more modest planet, I daresay that it will remain as always, oblivious to this piece, even after the work is heard.[56]

We are inclined to believe that it was this work that led Debussy to feel that Stravinsky was leaning "dangerously toward Schoenberg."[57]

The "grande saison" ended with a "Debussy Gala," organized by Vuillermoz at the Comédie des Champs-Élysées on 19 June. Laloy noted "a room too narrow for the crowd that rushed in, and yet filled with a reverence appropriate to the most special intimacy."[58] After a "charming preamble" by Vuillermoz, read by the actor Signoret, Debussy and Viñes played Caplet's transcription of "Ibéria" for two pianos for the first time,[59] which also marked the last performance of a Debussy work entrusted to the Catalan pianist. In fact, the composer complained about it to Caplet in no uncertain terms: "Would that you were there, for you well know that I've continued to miss you, so much so that, with each sonority I so carefully crafted, we kept stumbling... And those tremolos that seemed to stir the silent pebbles."[60] Apart from three *Préludes*, also played by the composer, the program consisted of the following: three *Poèmes de Baudelaire*, sung by Gabriel Paulet;[61] the *Chansons de Charles d'Orléans*, performed under the direction of the composer by the Association Chorale de Paris (which had been founded by Inghelbrecht and Fernand Lamy); and the *Proses lyriques*, sung by Ninon Vallin. The soprano, who had been quite remarkable in the *Martyre*, also sang *Le promenoir des deux amants* in a way that enchanted Debussy: "There was reason to weep (Il y avait de quoi pleurer), similar to what your friend Pelléas says.[62] I don't know where she finds that captivating understanding of the curves that the music depicts through the words... but it's absolutely beautiful, and very simple."[63] Thanking Vuillermoz in his sardonic way for "the quite dizzying heights" to which his lecture had elevated Debussy, the composer informed him that after the gala, he had received a letter from an anonymous person who was asking to be reimbursed for the cost of his seat![64]

Financial Distress

After the whirlwind of the Ballets Russes season, the summer—another summer without a trip to the sea—brought its own litany of problems and troubles. Edgar and Lady Speyer had invited Debussy to London for a concert, with the added incentive of a large fee of 5,000 francs. The plan was to have Maggie Teyte sing the *Ballades de François Villon*. To his great regret, Debussy had to decline the invitation. This time Emma was seriously ill, suffering from "virtually no sleep and a bout of fever."[65] Dr. Crépel prescribed a cure at Vichy.[66] This news came at the worst possible time, especially since financial problems were more alarming than ever. To Henry Russell and a certain Crevel,[67] Debussy declared himself unable to manage the repayment of his debt, remarking that he had "absolutely no cash"[68] and was in "the most miserable financial difficulty."[69] On 12 July, he had to pay a large bill and asked Durand, as a matter of utmost urgency, for 6,000 francs.[70] On the same day, he wrote to Bertault, the financier, "I can't be in a greater bind, and really don't know what to do any more."[71] On 5 August, he wrote to Gabriel Astruc, to whom he had sent numerous pressing bills, that "tons of yapping dogs—politely called 'purveyors'—are after me."[72] And shortly thereafter, his seventy-six-year-old mother fell seriously ill, "from old age, from lack of care, and other miserable things"[73]—in fact, from arteriosclerosis. In these anxiety-filled days, the idea of suicide emerged for the first time: "I assure you that if I didn't have my little Chouchou, I'd blow my brains out, despite the cowardice or absurdity of such an act!"[74] In a letter to his publisher on 15 July, he pointed out the main cause of these difficulties—a cause that was much more constraining than the lack of money he had experienced with Gaby or Lilly:

> To struggle all alone is no big deal! But to struggle "with family" is horrible! Add to that the domestic requirements of a [life of] luxury that has been enjoyed for a long time, a life that one cannot understand has now become impossible to sustain.
>
> For me, I struggle only in the name of a certain point of honor that may be false but is explicable in the sense that I don't want one day to be reproached for having accepted the present situation only to capitalize on it for my own benefit (wonderful irony of things!).[75]
>
> It's perhaps my fault, because I only have energy for intellectual pursuits; in daily matters, I stumble over the slightest little stone, which anyone else would easily kick away! Anyway, I innately abhor all such discussions.[76]

What he did not dare discuss with Emma (accustomed to a lavish lifestyle as former wife of the banker Sigismond Bardac), he confided to Segalen, who had just returned from East Asia and who noted the composer's secret desire: "He dreams of moving to a suburb in order to have more peace and a less ridiculously expensive house."[77] Debussy had already complained about this insoluble problem to his publisher: "Ah! This avenue du Bois de Boulogne, which reeks of Brazilians and Americans, lacks a sense of the past. I also see my landlord, an alcoholic Englishman who would not fail to show me the door if ever he were to find an ostentatious parvenu with his millions!"[78]

It was in this ultra-gloomy context that the *Trois poèmes de Stéphane Mallarmé*—"Soupir," "Placet futile," and "Éventail"—were composed. Debussy had presented the manuscript of these songs to his publisher on 25 July, specifying "that those folks on the rue Saint-Jacques don't show this sort of item!"[79] A curious issue then suddenly arose that demonstrated how touchy he still was with respect to Ravel. Jacques Durand pointed out to Debussy that, in fact, it behooved him to request permission from Mallarmé's son-in-law, Dr. Edmond Bonniot, to set these poems to music. This was when Debussy realized that Ravel himself had, at the same time, composed songs on two of these poems: "Soupir" and "Placet futile." He exclaimed to Durand, "It's a phenomenon of extrasensory perception worthy of a call to the Academy of Medicine!"[80] More than likely, it was the reappearance of Mallarmé's *Poésies complètes* in the bookshops that had prompted this "return" to his work by each of the composers. Debussy wrote a fine letter to Bonniot, making a case for obtaining the rights to set these poems:

> I have devotedly maintained the most fervent admiration for the one [Mallarmé] who was "our master". . . He had, perhaps without knowing it, a considerable influence on the very quiet composer that I was at the time when he gave me the honor of welcoming me into his home. And [my] fervor increases with gratitude in remembering his benevolent reception of the music for *L'après-midi d'un faune*. I hope that these memories, among many others, will permit me to ask you—would you kindly facilitate the publication of these three songs?[81]

As for Ravel, he was able to announce to Roland-Manuel on 27 August: "We will soon attend a Debussy–Ravel competition. The other day, our publisher sent me a desperate letter, because Bonniot refused to accede the rights to the 'Soupir' and 'Placet futile' poems that Debussy has just set. I've settled everything."[82] Debussy's collection appeared on 18 October, and that of Ravel the following year.

Two older works received a new lease on life that year. *Printemps*, the symphonic suite from 1887, was conducted by Rhené-Bâton on 19 April at the Société nationale in a modified version. Henri Busser, having been charged with the orchestration, had entrusted to instruments the parts that originally would have been sung, and had given a rather extensive instrumental role to the piano. The *Marche écossaise*, also reorchestrated, was conducted by Inghelbrecht at the inaugural event (15 October, repeated on the 22nd) of the Nouveaux Concerts at the Théâtre des Champs-Élysées. On the opening concert, which attracted only a small audience, Debussy conducted "Ibéria" and Inghelbrecht conducted *La damoiselle élue* (Suzanne Vorska, soloist) in addition to works by Chabrier and Lalo. After only four months of existence, Gabriel Astruc's Théâtre des Champs-Élysées, which had forged ahead without the slightest subsidy, was already at an end. "I believe you're wrong to give up our theater," Debussy exhorted him. "People are certain to come down on you for this desertion.[83] In my humble opinion, it would be better to continue the struggle, and if you have to die, it's better to go out in style."[84]

Among the projects that thus came to naught was a revival of *Le martyre de saint Sébastien*, but Astruc's theater went out in style, just the same. The entire staff of the theater and the orchestra offered their director a performance in French of *Boris Godunov*, on which they had been working for a few weeks and which Debussy described in the *S. I. M.* as "admirable."[85] Vuillermoz was more pessimistic, burying Astruc's enterprise by declaring that the Parisian public was not ready to make a distinction between a meticulous performance—the result of many rehearsals—and a run-of-the-mill concert: "This miracle [*Boris Godunov*]," he concluded, "has interested no one."[86]

A much more unassuming event took place on 1 December in the Paris home of Louis Mors: the flutist Louis Fleury played Debussy's piece for solo flute in the background, at the beginning of the third act of *Psyché*, Gabriel Mourey's three-act play in verse. Of the incidental music that Mourey had been requesting since 1909, this piece was all that Debussy had written.[87] On 30 October, he had asked the writer to abandon "a few moans let out by the chorus" in the second act and to "keep to our first idea of 'La flûte de Pan'";[88] on 17 November, he had definitively given up on the idea of an accompaniment, and explained his thoughts about this to Mourey:

> Until today, I haven't yet figured out what's needed. . . for the reason that a flute singing on the horizon must immediately convey its emotion! What I mean is that we don't have the time to go back to it several times, and that all artifice becomes crude, and the design of the melodic line (not being able to count on any colorful interventions) can work to one's advantage. Would you please identify, very precisely, which poetic lines precede the entrance of the music?
> After numerous attempts, I believe that we have to stick with Pan's flute on its own, without any accompaniment. It's more difficult, but more natural.[89]

This work, which was not yet finished on 24 November and which would later be given the title of *Syrinx*, was to become one of the masterpieces of the flute repertoire.

Trip to Russia

Debussy was not able to attend Mourey's performance on 1 December because he was already on the train, embarking on the longest trip of his life. A tour of concerts in Russia had in fact been discussed for several months with Alexander I. Siloti, who occasionally gathered together an orchestra in Saint Petersburg, and then with Serge Koussevitsky, a double-bass player. The latter, thanks to his marriage to a wealthy woman, became a publisher and founded an orchestra that traveled on the Volga to give concerts in towns where no Western music had ever been heard. Debussy was especially struck by the fact that the audience did not applaud after hearing the works. His trip lasted for two weeks, between 1 and 16 December. It was the composer's longest absence ever from his home, which caused great dismay for Emma, as documented by the telegrams and letters sent during each stage of the tour.

The Russians were not as ignorant of contemporary French music as one might have thought. In 1910, Gabriel Fauré had been received there with much respect. The great symphonic institutions and contemporary music organizations of Saint Petersburg and Moscow had already programmed several Debussy works on their concerts, including the *Marche écossaise* and two of the *Nocturnes* in 1910.[90] The following year, Emil Cooper had conducted *La mer* with the Imperial Russian Musical Society.[91] Debussy himself knew, thanks to Durand, that his *Rapsodie pour clarinette* had been played there, and he was surprised at the "consternation" it had produced, "all the more since this work is certainly one of the most engaging pieces I've ever written!"[92] And Daniel Chennevière's little monograph, *Claude Debussy et son œuvre*, which was about to be released by Durand, was in the process of being translated into Russian.

Rimsky-Korsakov, who had considered the *Estampes* to be "poor and skimpy to the nth degree,"[93] was no longer alive to say that it would be better not to hear Debussy's music because one might get used to it and end up liking it. Among the younger generation, while Glazunov had appreciated the orchestration of the *Prélude à l'après-midi d'un faune* (which he found to be of a "spicy, artistically bizarre" character),[94] Nikolai Myaskovsky felt that Debussy was "an incomparable poet, perhaps the only important French composer—even, one might say, the only genius";[95] but he had tried in vain to persuade the young Sergei Prokofiev, who thought that Debussy's music was a meal that "strangely" lacked "fresh meat," to admire him.[96]

On 3 December, Debussy was welcomed at the train station in Moscow by a delegation of the town's Société musicale, a member of which gave a long speech. Then Koussevitsky whisked him away to his home far from the center of town, where he put him up in a "sumptuous" apartment.[97] The next day, Debussy had the orchestra work "with a lucid and exasperated fury. . . [. . .] the double basses are wonderful; I've never heard anything like them in any orchestra! [. . .] the 'Winds' are excellent musicians, but their sound is thick and brassy."[98] He communicated with the musicians through an interpreter named Zetlin, a "staunch Debussyist" whom he had met long ago at the home of the Princesse de Cystria, and through Mr. Forter, who was jealous of Zetlin.[99] Since *La mer* was "absolutely spot-on," Debussy decided not to perform

Printemps, which he felt would bring "an incompatible color" to the program; as for the *Nocturnes*, he had to work until two o'clock in the morning, correcting numerous errors in the orchestral parts.[100] On 6 December, Koussevitsky's orchestra was busy with a Busoni concerto "which lasts one hour and ten minutes... [...] Looking at the score, it's murky music in which the worst defects of Richard Strauss are exaggerated when used by someone who has none of his good qualities."[101] In the evening, Debussy attended with Diaghilev a performance of Mussorgsky's *The Fair at Sorochintsy* at the Moscow Art Theatre. This incomplete opera (based on a story by Gogol) had recently been heard for the first time, and in it Debussy noticed some "bits of music that were very well done!"[102] Was it at the end of this performance that Diaghilev took him to the Hermitage restaurant, where Gypsies sang their repertoire for them all night long?[103] He also had the opportunity to see his former piano student, Sonia von Meck (Nadezhda's daughter) again; she was now thirty years older and had become Princess Galitzine.

An anecdote concerning the composer's insomnia soon made the rounds in Moscow and was reported by Prokofiev.[104] Unable to sleep, Debussy went into a neighboring room, where there was a blackbird; to take his mind off things, he had some fun whistling one of his tunes to it, with such success that, upon leaving, the bird sang it "for anyone who wanted to hear it."[105] Sometime later, when informed of this little event, a high-ranking person from the conservatory in Saint Petersburg (who had also gone down to Koussevitsky's home) wanted to replicate the experience for himself; but the blackbird refused to learn his song, and the entire town knew it![106] Writing to Chouchou on 11 December, Debussy alluded only to "a bird who sings almost as well as Miss Teyte."[107]

Most of the details of his stay in Moscow, however, are given in the missives that Claude sent to Emma. In return, Emma sent despairing letters to him, which could only intensify his guilty conscience, and in his letter to her, he noted with bitterness certain painful passages that she had written:

> Your letter made me so sad that I've waited until now to reply to it...
>
> Such unfair and mean-spirited words... How can you think of such things? and are you suffering so much that you're forgetting that your poor Claude loves you? [...]
>
> Anyway, don't you know perfectly well why I'm making this trip..? [...]
>
> Surely you can feel how bitterly disillusioning it is to receive right in the heart these words that wound my best self, meaning, what I want to be for you..![108] (7 December)

> Do you realize that you wrote "I don't know how I can't bear a grudge against your music"... [?...] Between you and my music, if there's one that should be jealous, it's the music! And if I continue to make it and to love it, it's

surely because it—the same music that you treat so poorly—was responsible for my meeting you, loving you, and so on! You can be very sure that, were I no longer to write music, it would likely be you who'd stop loving me.[109] (8 December)

After spending two days determining the string bowings for the *Marche écossaise* and having his *Rapsodie* rehearsed by a clarinetist, who was "a very strong player but dumb as can be,"[110] Debussy traveled with Koussevitsky to St. Petersburg on 9 December. There he went to the Grand Hôtel d'Europe, directly across from the Noble Assembly Building, where the concert that he conducted before 2,500 people took place; it was, in his words, "a very beautiful performance."[111] Lazare Saminsky, who was present, remembered the composer's inexperience as a conductor: "A touching beauty emerged from that combination of an awkward technique with a convincing and personal interpretation of the highest order."[112] During the intermission, Debussy was so overwrought that he wept. Returning to Moscow on 12 December, he had to conduct the same program, which included two *Nocturnes, La mer*, and the *Prélude*; afterward, he thought that it had also "gone well."[113] A good twenty Russian musicians presented to the "illustrious master" a certificate, signed by each of them, in which they declared that their expectations of his visit had been fully met and that they had experienced days with him that they would "never forget," and some "insights that will forever enlighten our musical lives."[114] Incidentally, Alexander Scriabin happened to be in Moscow at the time; on that same 12 December, he gave a recital in which he premiered his opus 67 (*Two Preludes*) and opus 69 (*Two Poems*).[115]

Back in Paris, Debussy became aware of the aforementioned little book about his life and works by Daniel Chennevière, an eighteen-year-old student at the Conservatoire who had also studied philosophy at the Sorbonne.[116] That young author recognized in Debussy's work a Symbolist phase, followed by a period of "naturism";[117] he felt that, with his hero, "Classicism was dead forever."[118] Debussy had never read such extreme opinions of his work: "[The music of] Debussy," wrote Chennevière, "was the highest, indeed triumphal achievement of a musical upheaval that has undermined the most fundamental elements of Classicism, of European music.[119] [. . .] Thanks to Debussy, French music has reawakened from a century of sleep. [. . .] He has revitalized music. He has transformed its foundation (tonality), material, inspiration, and form. With a single stroke of his genius, he has carried out this unprecedented metamorphosis almost single-handedly.[120] [. . .] With Debussy, music is embarking on a new era. The future is linked with his name."[121]

In order to accurately perceive the breakthrough made by Debussy's compositions in Parisian musical life since 1902, one need only consult some statistical facts, based on nearly 7,000 works played in concerts in the French capital during the 1912–13 season. Of these, 204 works were by Debussy; that is to say, he ranked second among living composers, behind Saint-Saëns (279) and well ahead of Fauré (137), Massenet (98), d'Indy (49), Ravel (46), and Richard Strauss (32).[122]

Chapter Twenty-Seven

The Final Trips

1914

Under the malicious title of "Fécondité" (Prolificacy), *Le monde musical* had published the following few lines at the beginning of 1913:[1]

> Claude-Achille Debussy has promised to give us *Orphée* at the Astruc theater, *Crimen Amoris* at the Opéra, *Le Diable dans le Beffroi* and *La Chute de la Maison Usher* at the Opéra-Comique, not to mention *Tristan*, or the ballets, which for him are mere *Jeux*,[2] or the symphonic pieces, or the preludes.
> When will all of these lovely promises come to fruition?[3]

Beyond his intent to disparage, little did the journalist know that his list was quite out-of-date and incomplete.

From One Project to Another

While Segalen still believed in the *Orphée* project and revised it according to Debussy's indications, it was not a subject to which the composer could relate. Later, in the middle of the war, he warned the writer that "Orphée will not be singing."[4]

As for *Crimen amoris*, Debussy had grown weary of the pressure exerted on him by Charles Morice, and he contacted Laloy to come up with a more suitable libretto for this Verlaine-based project. On 27 January 1914, a new contract was signed between Durand and the three partners; the title of *Fête galante* replaced that of *Crimen amoris*, and Laloy's name would "potentially" be added to that of Morice as a collaborator on the libretto.[5] But the situation became more complicated very quickly: on 9 February, the Théâtre Idéaliste presented (in the Paris townhouse of Mme Oedenkoven) *Les Fêtes galantes, drame-ballet en deux actes. Vers d'Adrien Remacle adjoints au poème de Paul Verlaine. Musique de*

Adrien Remacle. This obscure composer claimed that Verlaine, while still alive, had endorsed his work and granted him "the exclusive right, identified in an official document, to write music for the *Fêtes galantes* poems."[6] On 23 March, the poet's son, Georges Verlaine, nevertheless confirmed to Morice "the right to a theatrical production with music by Monsieur Debussy on such Verlaine poems as you see fit to use."[7] Annoyed by the protracted legal wrangling, Debussy stashed the manuscript of this libretto in a drawer.[8]

Among the projects in progress that the journalist of the *Monde musical* article, cited at the beginning of this chapter, failed to mention was the ballet *Khamma*. Durand had found an amicable solution for delivering Debussy from his "Maud Allan nightmare":[9] Charles Koechlin was given the responsibility of completing the orchestration of the ballet, which he carried out during December 1912 and the first weeks of 1913, under the composer's supervision.[10] But, although this proposal was acceptable to the dancer, it did not help get the work performed on the stage.

Also pending were the plans, about which Debussy was not very enthusiastic, that Pierre-Barthélemey Gheusi, the new director of the Opéra-Comique, was considering for *La boîte à joujoux*. That theater or any other seemed to him poorly suited "for the angular gestures and burlesque appearance of the cardboard figures";[11] one would have to "present them in a slightly new way,"[12] with a stage director but not a ballet master[13]—in any case, not "to make a big deal out of nothing."[14] With D'Annunzio, Debussy pursued some similarly vague projects: not only the Indian drama to which we have alluded, but also a purely operatic version of *Le martyre de saint Sébastien*—in which the musical part would be expanded,[15] "and by a lot"[16]—as well as a film based on that work, about which we have only rather sketchy information.[17]

As if he did not already have enough projects on his worktable, Debussy signed a contract for a new ballet intended this time for an English stage. *Le palais du silence* was based on a libretto in one act by a Dutch Symbolist painter, Georges de Feure, with whom Debussy had associated more than twenty years earlier in the "Desboutin group."[18] The libretto dealt with a Chinese subject, portraying a mute prince, Hong-La, as the lover of a young captive princess, No-ja-li, whose name would ultimately be used as the title of the ballet. On 21 November 1913, Debussy set about to produce the piano score by 2 April 1914. Initially, he seemed to apply himself to the project, and, in a letter to his publisher on 6 January, he claimed that *Le palais du silence* was taking up all his time.[19]

On 5 February, Debussy participated in a very unusual concert with Arthur Hartmann at the Salle des Agriculteurs: he accompanied the violinist in transcriptions of "Il pleure dans mon cœur" (published in 1908) and two of the piano preludes, "La fille aux cheveux de lin" and "Minstrels." Even more curiously, the program included Grieg's Sonata for Violin and

Piano, op. 13. This choice suggests a tinge of remorse with respect to the Norwegian composer, whom Debussy had formerly treated cavalierly in *Gil Blas*,[20] and this at a time when certain members of the Schola Cantorum also poured their scorn on him (for example, Blanche Selva, in her book on *La sonate*).[21] In the *S. I. M.*, Debussy celebrated Grieg's "engaging melancholy[, . . .] the icy coolness of [Norway's] lakes, the urgent ardor of its hasty and sudden spring seasons."[22] Above all, he acknowledged that the friendship he had established with Hartmann was the impetus behind his participation in the concert. Together, they held on to the idea of a tour in the United States, in which the violinist would play a *Poème pour violon et orchestre* by Debussy, which had yet to be composed and which would never get beyond the early planning stage.[23]

Just when he was writing the 1 March article for the *S. I. M.*, which would be his last contribution to this journal, Debussy had on his desk the uncorrected proofs for *M. Croche antidilettante* that the publisher Dorbon had sent him. The idea of gathering his musical views into a single volume aligned with a plan that he himself had contemplated many years earlier. Pierre Louÿs had already encouraged him to undertake this project, and, running out of time, Debussy agreed to Laloy's idea of publishing a collection of his old articles. He had asked Laloy for his advice already at the end of 1906,[24] and on 11 February 1914, he asked for an hour with him in order to determine "how M. Croche was going to be put to rest."[25] At the end of May, Debussy again asked Dorbon to be patient, for he had not yet been able to carry out the "considerable revisions" he thought necessary to ensure that "this little book [. . .] would not be merely an assemblage of articles strung end to end."[26] The war would prevent the publication of the book, which was with the printers at Rassenfosse in Liège.[27]

Trip to Rome

Two new trips awaited Debussy, this time nearly back to back: the first was to Rome (18–24 February), the other to the Netherlands (26 February–2 March), both of which he would make with his typical lack of enthusiasm. It is true that, each time, he was momentarily escaping from a precarious financial situation. Monetary pressures were always rather acute, and during these months we find their traces yet again in the numerous despairing notes sent to "fat Bertault": "What will become of us among so many traps?" (26 December 1913);[28] "We have to get out of this situation" (6 January 1914);[29] "I don't know what to do or to whom I can turn anymore" (19 January);[30] "I see nothing but relentless work, with the terror of creditors ringing the doorbell" (20 January);[31] "At times I envy people who freeze to death" (24 January);[32] "Is there nothing more to hope for?" (13 February);[33] "I'm sinking more and more and have lost heart" (8 March);[34] and so on.

It was with this feeling of anxiety that he left for Rome, a city he had not seen for more than twenty-five years. Settled into his room in the "drearily cosmopolitan" Grand Hôtel de Russie, he felt "everything collapsing" around him.[35] For three days he received no news from Emma. He had to rehearse a program that included *La mer*, "Rondes de printemps," the *Prélude à l'après-midi d'un faune*, and the *Marche écossaise*. Two important figures from the Roman musical world tried to make his stay more pleasant: Count Enrico di San Martino, president of the Accademia Santa Cecilia, who had organized concerts of foreign music since 1911; and Bernardino Molinari,[36] artistic director of the Augusteo orchestra since 1912, who had been introducing the Roman public to the *Prélude à l'après-midi d'un faune* and "Ibéria" over the previous two years. Molinari, who was very open to the music of his time, kindly welcomed Debussy into his family and promised him that he would orchestrate *L'isle joyeuse*.

During a rehearsal, Debussy met with Alberto Gasco, a journalist from *La tribuna* and a composer originally from Naples, who considered the Augusteo concert to be a chance to make amends for the Roman fiasco of *Pelléas* in 1909.[37] Debussy confessed that he should not be regarded as a great orchestra conductor nor as a great pianist: "First of all, one must have certain specific qualities that I don't feel I possess," he told Gasco.[38] He was more forthcoming than he had been in previous interviews concerning the choreography for *L'après-midi d'un faune* or regarding *L'histoire de Tristan*: "The gossip surrounding my *Tristan* and the criticisms of this or that zealous friend have completely disgusted me, and I've decided not to deal with it any more. [. . .] What a beautiful subject, though!"[39] On the other hand, he expounded optimistically on the state of the Poe dramas: "Their composition is quite far along, except that in the two scores there are some [. . .] gaps—entire scenes without notes—that perhaps will be difficult to complete."[40]

The public reception of the Augusteo concert was rather mixed: favorable for *La mer*, with protests for "Rondes de printemps" and great success for the *Prélude à l'après-midi d'un faune*. Speaking to Gasco about his work, Debussy claimed to have been obsessed with "writing ever more musical music," concluding: "I say 'more music' much in the same way that Goethe referred to 'more light'!"[41]

Trip to the Netherlands

Back in Paris, Debussy barely had time to unpack his bags—only to find that he had forgotten his conducting batons in Rome—before resuming his demanding job as "positioner of sixteenth notes."[42] He had also promised to participate in the fourth *concert populaire* in Brussels, but had had to decline at the last minute—to the great displeasure of the "compositional youth" who were eager to celebrate him—leaving his works for Vincent d'Indy to conduct on his own.[43] On 26 February, Debussy arrived in Amsterdam, where he joined Gustave Doret—"more Swiss by the day, and arrogant as a prince consort"[44]—who had arranged for some concerts with the Concertgebouw and had prepared the orchestra. It was quickly decided to stick with the first two movements of the *Nocturnes*, since for "Sirènes" the only available singers were "some aging choristers who choose to sing out of tune."[45] The rest of the program included the *Prélude à l'après-midi d'un faune* and the *Marche écossaise*, to which Debussy had taken a real liking, plus three piano preludes, which he himself performed: "Danseuses de Delphes," "La fille aux cheveux de lin," and "La puerta del vino."[46]

We know about this Sunday-afternoon concert from a colorful description by Richard Van Rees, the president of the Concertgebouw:

> When he mounted the podium—led by the hand, so to speak, by his friend Doret, who accompanied him everywhere, served as his handler, and had to be seated at his side even when he conducted and when he played—the very large audience that filled the entire hall stood up spontaneously, as did the orchestra, and in this way gave an extraordinary and truly royal welcome to the great French master. To tell the truth, Debussy seemed awkward and unsure of himself on the podium, though not because of his external appearance, for his sturdy and handsome physique as well as his fine and noble facial features, with their hint of a Southern complexion, made a very congenial impression. But there was a faint cloud of weariness and boredom over his entire disposition, as with someone who suffers from homesickness, an affliction that never left him when he was far from home, so he said. [...]
>
> He was a poor conductor, but the very attentive orchestra intuitively followed his intentions, and the performance of his works was an enormous success. Debussy had the same success at the piano, even though some of the pieces were far from perfect, from a pianistic point of view. The concert ended with deafening applause, which seemed to exhaust the artist, who quickly left the podium, led by Doret.[47]

The same concert program had taken place at the Hague, in the presence of the Queen Mother; it had "gone well," except for a horn that had entered four measures too soon.[48] In Amsterdam, in the absence of Mengelberg (who was occupied with some concerts in Frankfurt), Richard Van Rees invited Debussy to dinner with a certain number of important people from the orchestra: "This man is nice," the composer wrote to Emma, "and he has splendid plans for *Pelléas*."[49] Having spotted a lovely little Empire clock while seated at the table, Debussy made a remark to his hostess that bordered on the impolite, which was unusual for him: "You will see me looking at it often, for each passing minute brings me closer to Paris!"[50] However, he relaxed after dinner, and Doret even had to insist that they leave around three o'clock in the morning, while smoking big Havana cigars.[51] The composer was especially happy to receive his fee of 1,500 francs, which would fill a hole in his nagging debts. But on the platform at the train station, as he was leaving, Gustave Doret was struck "by his forlorn air, by his indecision," and by his almost childlike anxiety.[52]

Debussy ended up missing, by three days, the premiere of the concert version of *Jeux*, performed in Paris under the direction of Pierné.[53] The latter had taken the opportunity to show the score to the administrators at the Académie des beaux-arts for the premiere, presenting it as a "symphonic work in a new form." The Colonne concerts gave a second performance of it during the following week,[54] which enabled Debussy to attend a rehearsal and to share his dissatisfaction with Pierné, albeit in a friendly way:

> I had the impression that the orchestra liked it much less than you did; was I perhaps mistaken? [...]
> It also seemed to me that the various episodes lacked continuity. The link between them may be subtle, but it exists nevertheless, doesn't it? Don't you know that as well as I do? And lastly, it's too loud in general.[55]

The press hardly recognized the novelty of Debussy's new work, in contrast with many critics who persisted in seeking a "second *Pelléas*."[56] One of the notable accolades came from Paul Le Flem, who, in one of his first reviews, showed enthusiasm for this "music of broken rhythms, conducive to an ever-changing choreography."[57]

Debussy the Pianist

On 21 March, the Société philharmonique devoted an entire concert to Debussy, who accompanied Ninon Vallin in the first performance of the *Trois poèmes de Mallarmé* and played a few of his pieces for piano. In addition to the String Quartet, performed by the Hayot Quartet, *Children's Corner* was also heard. One listener, the Japanese writer Shimazaki, paid particular attention to the latter work. In the little *Children's Corner* pieces, he saw the evocation of mysterious fairy tales, "of sounds resembling birds when they whistle and sing while calling to each other in the forest," when the pianist's fingers reached the high register of the keyboard; he found in that music "a new voice," quite different from the rest of the Western music he had heard in Paris up to that time.[58] Debussy as solo or collaborative pianist, whose performance Shimazaki curiously likened to "the aïnote"[59] in shamisen music, moreover found that he had new supporters among the French critics. The reviewer in *La critique musicale* wrote, "I admit that I prefer his playing to that of any other pianist. It is not about technical perfection as much as that his playing is simple and unassuming. The work is thus laid bare to the listener; it speaks for itself, it disappears."[60]

By a strange coincidence, this praise for Debussy's pianistic talent was mentioned at the very moment when the composer had just crushed the thumb of his left hand in the corridor door of the train going between Anvers and Brussels[61]—an accident that "nearly disabled him for two and a half months."[62] On 28 April, he made a short trip to Brussels, the only one he made solely as a pianist. Through Maurice Kufferath, he had been asked to participate in a private concert at the home of enthusiasts M. and Mme Frantz Wittouck. His String Quartet was performed there, as were the *Proses lyriques* and the *Chansons de Bilitis*, sung by Ninon Vallin, and the *Estampes*, two *Images*, and three *Préludes*, played by Debussy himself. *Le guide musical* praised his performance, "free from all mannerisms, it is even surprising in its simplicity. No emphasis on harmonic subtleties: the melodic lines are outlined in delicate strokes; no rhythmic distortion; no brilliance for its own sake. This great simplicity, which is initially disconcerting, quickly becomes captivating, and each page exudes a penetrating sense of clarity."[63]

About a month before the concert, Debussy contracted shingles, which caused him two weeks of suffering, to the point of having to ask his wife, at times, to write letters on his behalf.[64] There was still talk of producing *La boîte à joujoux* at the Opéra-Comique, but Loïe Fuller also wanted to be the first to perform it.[65] She had already danced with her veils in the *Nocturnes*, and thereafter staged excerpts from *Children's Corner*, first in Nice in March (with conductor Georges George)[66] and then at the Châtelet on 7 May (with Colonne's orchestra under the direction of Pierné).[67] As for *No-ja-li*, only a few sketches of it had been written,[68] and the director of the Alhambra in London, André Charlot, watched anxiously as the fateful day approached. Was it Durand who had the idea (as with *Khamma*) to ask Charles Koechlin to help Debussy? "Write it. I'll sign it," Debussy supposedly said to the young composer.[69] When this solution did not work out, Durand offered to Charlot the symphonic suite *Printemps*, as orchestrated by Busser. With only a few cuts, Debussy approved the score, and, once the delicate problems of rights were settled, his suite provided the musical basis for a ballet, *Spring*. This dance became part of the revue *Not Likely*, which was performed for the first time at the Alhambra on 4 May 1914, with costumes by Georges de Feure, designed in the style of the well-known couturier Paul Poiret![70] Thus, in a way, the types of productions that Pierre Louÿs had once envisioned for Debussy were coming to fruition.

An American Interview

Around this time, Debussy agreed to do an interview with Michel-Dimitri Calvocoressi (although he regarded him as Maurice Ravel's "personal lackey") for *The Etude*, a monthly magazine from Philadelphia. This would be the last interview the composer would grant, and it is particularly interesting because it concerns not the state of his projects nor *ad hoc* remarks but rather an "assessment of contemporary music" in Europe, including this comment in particular:

> I don't follow current events much. There comes a time in life when one wishes to concentrate, and now, I've made a rule for myself to hear as little music as possible.
> Take Arnold Schönberg, for instance. I've never heard any of his works. As my interest has been aroused by the things that are written about him, I decided to read through a quartet of his, but I haven't yet managed to do it.[71]

At least two of the composer's friends at this time—Godet and Varèse—might possibly have discussed Schönberg with him. Godet remembered having spoken with Debussy about the first two quartets (1905 and 1908), *Gurrelieder* (1911), and—if he was not mistaken—*Pierrot lunaire* (1912).[72] Varèse mentioned (from memory in 1962) the *Drei Klavierstücke*, op. 11 (1909), and the *Fünf Stücke* for orchestra, op. 16 (1909).[73] These two lists, which leave us in a state of some uncertainty, are not enough to explain any concrete basis of knowledge for Debussy's famous verdict: in a letter to Godet from 14 October 1915, he wrote that Stravinsky "is leaning dangerously toward Schönberg."[74]

The interview in *The Etude* was not limited to Schönberg and Germanic musics. Of the Hungarians, whom Debussy felt were "very close to us,"[75] he mentioned Bartók and Kodály, "young artists, extremely interesting, with many merits," who were "passionately finding their way."[76] He added that "a noteworthy feature of their music is the obvious affinity between its spirit and that of modern French music."[77] Regarding the Russians, Debussy described his encounters during his recent visit; he had not had the opportunity to hear their music, although he did know Stravinsky, who was "blessed with keen and fervent curiosity" and who "will calm down in due course."[78] As for the Italians, he mentioned none of the young members of the "generazione dell'Ottanta,"[79] whom he had no doubt heard in Paris, and was content to repeat his condemnation of opera composers who took pleasure in satisfying the public's "bad taste."[80] Finally, broaching the topic of Spain, Debussy had not one word for Manuel de Falla, although he knew his works very well, and cited only Albéniz, "the most typical. [. . .] The abundance of his imagination is positively stupendous, no less so than his ability to create atmosphere."[81]

Even if he was not up on current events, Debussy retained an appetite for the theater and stage productions. Did he not go to the Théâtre du Gymnase, at the beginning of January, to see *Samson*, the new play by Henri Bernstein?[82] When the German and Italian seasons opened at the Théâtre des Champs-Élysées in early May, he went with D'Annunzio to a performance of Verdi's *Otello*,[83] under the direction of Henry Russell and featuring Nelly Melba; we do not know his reaction to the late style of the Italian composer. He still yearned for one final bath of Wagnerism with *Die Meistersinger* and *Parsifal*, directed by Felix Weingartner (beginning of June), and with *Tristan*, under the baton of Albert Coates, after which he was said to have declared: "We're cleaning out our ears this evening!"[84] Meanwhile, he had braved a new revival of *Pelléas* at the Opéra-Comique,[85] the same evening as the premiere of *Parsifal* (3 June). Satisfied with Vanni Marcoux as Golaud,[86] he could not help but write to Alfred Maguenat, who had played Pelléas: "Sometimes your nerves get the better of you. But isn't that a sign of a sensitivity that does you honor?"[87] He continued to dream of another production of *Pelléas*, especially since he had met with Bernard Masselon, the director of the theater at Rouen, who was a little provincial but sensitive and generous. Debussy had approved Masselon's plans for the production, including the models for the scenery, which he found more suitable than those by Lucien Jusseaume and Eugène Ronsin (with which he had become disenchanted).[88] On 28 June (coincidentally, the day of the attack in Sarajevo that sparked World War I),[89] Debussy expressed his pleasure to Georges Rabani, a concert organizer, upon receiving the good news that the latter had just sent him about a planned tour in the United States.[90] But the composer was exhausted, and confessed to Durand: "Paris is becoming more and more odious to me. [. . .] Boredom has gnawed away at me too much in this house."[91]

The composer's last trip, a short one, was made while the onset of the war was accelerating in the Balkans. At the invitation of the Speyers, he went to London once again to conduct a concert at Queen's Hall, on 17 July, with a program that was no surprise: *Petite suite, Deux danses, Ariettes oubliées, Prélude à l'après-midi d'un faune,* and *Children's Corner.* Might he have had the curiosity to attend a performance of the revue *Not Likely* in order to find out what had become of his music (*Spring*) in that unusual venue?

Upon his return, he heard about the election of Charles Marie Widor as secretary in perpetuity of the Académie des beaux-arts (18 July) and congratulated him.[92] Widor then let it be known that he intended to support Debussy's candidacy as his successor in his previous position at the Institut de France, but at the meeting on 8 August, the Académie decided to defer the availability of this seat.[93]

These many months had hardly been favorable for composing. As Debussy wrote to Godet on 14 July, he had done nothing for four and a half months, adding this extremely pessimistic comment:

For a long time—I really must confess!—I've been losing myself, I feel dreadfully diminished! Ah! The "magician" that you [once] loved about me, where is he? He's no more than a sad conjuror, who soon will break his back in a final ungainly pirouette.[94]

However, in the final days of July, he completed the *Épigraphes antiques*, based on the incidental music originally written for the *Chansons de Bilitis* in 1901. Although he had dreamed of composing it as a suite for orchestra, he made a version for piano, four hands, which did not appear until February 1915.

Chapter Twenty-Eight

The War; Pourville

1914–15

On 1 August 1914, the same day of the military mobilization, Debussy wrote to some English men's clothiers in Paris (at the Carnaval de Venise shop) that, in light of the circumstances, he still could not pay a substantial bill of 1,963 francs and that he was appealing to their "kind generosity."[1] When war was declared by Germany, he wrote to Durand of his deep dismay: Raoul Bardac and Dolly's husband had been conscripted into military service, and he almost envied Satie, "who will have an important job defending Paris in his capacity as corporal."[2] Debussy described himself as no more "than a poor little atom hurled around by this terrible cataclysm."[3] And yet, when he contacted Inghelbrecht on 18 August, he momentarily regained his natural, rather sarcastic tone: "The war has cleansed Paris of all its foreigners, either by shooting them or by expelling them. It's instantly become a charming place.[4] For the time being, Raoul Bardac is in the motor service at Versailles, and Corporal Satie is defending Arcueil. Erlanger is at the disposal of the Minister of War, perhaps to clean the inkwells?"[5] Added to his note was this postscript: "In [18]70[6] they had Richard Wagner; in 1914 they have only Richard Strauss."![7]

Stay in Angers

On 31 August, the Germans were already at Compiègne, less than fifty miles north of Paris. Debussy asked Arthur Fontaine, an old friend who held an official position, for advice.[8] Emma was anxious and insisted that they leave Paris. As the government itself was retreating to Bordeaux on 3 September, Debussy decided the next day to ask for a safe-conduct pass to go to Angers "with 4 people."[9] During the trip, he covered the document issued by the railways with musical sketches for "Pour les notes répétées," one of his future *Études*.[10] After a "dreadful trip" and some "nightmarish sights," the Debussys first ended up at the

Hôtel des Trois Marchands—"a type of hostel for cattle dealers."[11] Fortunately, they encountered Charles Domergue, the founder of the Cercle musical, who had become a bicycle infantryman and who managed to find them a room at the Grand Hôtel. For almost a month, Debussy regretted having left Paris; he read the papers five times a day and played some piano (on a Bechstein), but suffered from what he called an "attack of enteritis" that confined him to bed for six days.[12] Writing to his pupil Nicolas Coronio, he expressed some anti-Germanic sentiments, which the circumstances would quickly exacerbate:

> I think we're going to pay dearly for the right to dislike the music of Richard Strauss and [Arnold] Schönberg. Concerning Beethoven, someone has just very fortunately discovered that he was Flemish! As for Wagner, people are bound to exaggerate! He will still be honored for having condensed centuries of music into a formula. That is really something, and only a German could attempt it. Our mistake was that we've tried to follow in his footsteps for too long.[13]

Back in Paris, he repeated himself in practically the same terms in another letter, with this variant: "As for Wagner, it's difficult to do away with him completely! I might add that he had enough genius that, little by little, one might forget his human weaknesses."[14]

Jacques Durand, who had spent the most dangerous weeks on the island of Noirmoutier with his associate and cousin, Gaston Choisnel, returned to Paris in October with the idea of undertaking a large-scale edition of classical compositions that would not be marred by editorial additions, as were numerous German editions (which, for that matter, were unattainable, due to the war). He secured the support of Saint-Saëns, Fauré, Dukas, and Debussy, while the publisher Maurice Senart independently enlisted Alfred Cortot, Guy Ropartz, and Blanche Selva for his own "Édition nationale," under the direction of Vincent d'Indy. A "united approach" did not work in the world of music publishing any more than it had succeeded in bringing together the Société nationale and the Société musicale indépendante. Debussy agreed to prepare a new edition of Chopin's works. Instead of composing a "Marche héroïque" or resuming work on the ballet *No-ja-li*, as André Charlot was requesting of him, he was happy to devote himself to this task—something that was a new experience for him and that brought him out of the stupor into which events had thrown him. He considered the Breitkopf edition of Chopin (Ignaz Friedmann) to be far superior to that of Peters (Hermann Scholtz), but he admitted his helplessness when confronted with three manuscripts, each giving a different version of the same work.[15] Furthermore, the publisher had done little to establish a critical apparatus for his collaborators.

Outside of this tedious editorial work, for which Debussy was not really equipped, the only creative activity that he continued during the last weeks of the year was a composition in homage to Albert I, the king of Belgium, and to his soldiers. Debussy wrote the short *Berceuse héroïque* for piano and orchestrated it almost immediately. "It was very tough," he confided to Godet, all the more so as the *Brabançonne*[16] instills no heroism in the hearts of those who haven't been "brought up with it."[17] Apart from that, he no longer knew music as it "was in the past"; even the "familiar sound" of the piano had become "unbearable."[18] On 9 January 1915, in a letter to Bernardino Molinari, he observed that "one concerns oneself with art only out of altruism. [. . .] One benefits from rekindling the slightly faded glories of old and from promoting to the rank of 'masters' some individuals [French composers] who certainly would not have expected any such thing to happen!"[19]

Amid the catastrophic effects of the war, Debussy soldiered on in his personal life. He went with Chouchou to the cinema on the Champs-Élysées to see *Le calvaire d'une reine*, and felt that Max Linder had "a lot more talent than Messieurs Chevillené and Piernard combined."[20] In fact, the Colonne and Lamoureux orchestras had merged in an attempt to maintain regular operations.[21] When not suffering from the flu,[22] Debussy saw Satie and Dukas, and he completed the revision of the Chopin *Études*, followed by those of the *Nocturnes* and the *Polonaises*. But he was "very sad" because his mother's condition was worse, as Dukas informed Robert Brussel on 12 March 1915.[23] On the 23rd of the same month, Debussy's mother passed away after a protracted illness, and he informed those who were still in Paris—Gabriel Fauré, Gabriel Pierné, Gabriel Astruc, Alfred Bruneau, Pierre-Barthélemy Gheusi, Désiré-Émile Inghelbrecht, Jean Périer, Jacques Rouché, Edgard Varèse, and of course Jacques Durand and Paul Dukas—and told many of them that the funeral would take place at Notre-Dame d'Auteuil.[24] Emma—whose mother also died, on 29 April, leaving her as the beneficiary of 5,000 francs from Osiris's estate—supported the work of Le vêtement du blessé (The Clothing of the Wounded).[25] A benefit concert for this group had been organized on 24 April, for which Debussy asked Ninon Vallin and Edmond Clément to sing a duet from *Carmen*.[26] In May, there was talk of a special performance of *Pelléas*—also to benefit the wounded—that was announced for 19 June "with any artists who still remain,"[27] along with Claire Croiza, who was asked to sing the role of Geneviève.[28] But the performance was postponed to the following season and was subsequently canceled.

The 11 March 1915 issue of *L'intransigeant* published an article under Debussy's name that was titled "Enfin seuls!. . ." (Alone at last!. . .) In part, it reflected ideas he had been expressing during the previous few months: "Since Rameau, we've no longer had a distinctly French tradition. [. . .] We have adopted compositional practices that are polar opposites to our spirit [. . .] and we were on the verge of condoning even more suspect naturalizations when the cannon interrupted, commanding our attention!"[29] But in many places the wording was not his, and it is almost certain that the initiative and the drafting of this article can be traced to Émile Vuillermoz, who had, incidentally, started one of his articles in the *S. I. M.* (15 June 1913) with the same words, "Alone at last!"[30]

An Unexpectedly Productive Summer

During the months that preceded his departure for the sea, Debussy's activities were rather sporadic but relatively varied: on 12 May, he went to the Société des auteurs (playwrights) in order to vote for Messager; a few days later, he attended a concert conducted by Alfredo Casella, in which the *Ballades de François Villon* were performed; and on 19 May, he, Emma, and Chouchou were granted a safe-conduct pass, no doubt to visit a house in Pourville that some friends were offering him for the summer. And then, something of a miracle unexpectedly happened: on 30 June, in response to Durand's proposal to work on an edition of some of J. S. Bach's compositions, Debussy announced that he had "a few ideas just now—we need not hasten to divulge them—I'd like to develop them into pieces for two pianos and *Fêtes galantes*. [. . .] I'd like to leave [Paris] as soon as possible. The house has been weighing heavily on my shoulders for some time now."[31] The pieces for two pianos were the *Caprices en blanc et noir*, which were sufficiently advanced by 7 July for him to propose that his publisher hear them.[32] But Fauré asked him to serve as a member of an *opéra-comique* jury at the Conservatoire, an invitation he declined (because Chouchou had the chicken pox),[33] although in June he had participated on the jury for operatic declamation (students in the classes of Pierre Léon Melchissédec, Jacques Isnardon, Luc Albert Saléza, and Eugène Gabriel Sizes).[34] As for Morice–Laloy's *Fête galante*, he gave it only very minimal attention, in light of the murky legal dispute surrounding Verlaine's estate and the fact that he had "other libretti to flog" (as Debussy would admit to Durand on 27 September)[35] and that Charles Morice seemed to him "a deceitful chap" and "the Jesuitical agent of this plot."[36]

Finally, on 12 July, the Debussys settled into the villa "Mon coin," in Pourville, which they knew well. It had a garden "with a relaxed naturalness" and from which the composer could catch sight of "a beautiful expanse of the sea, enough to imagine more of it beyond."[37] From the first days there, he felt renewed confidence, "changed the color" of the second *Caprice*,[38] and corrected the proofs for the Chopin edition. He had no access to a piano and did not miss it too much: "This absence [of an instrument] focuses the emotion by preventing it from digressing into improvisations."[39] On 22 July, he was happy to be able to send to Durand the second *Caprice*, in which Luther's hymn was castigated, in Debussy's words, "for brazenly straying into a French-style *Caprice*."[40] And he sent an amazing surprise: a "prospectus" that laid out a plan for "Six sonatas for various instruments, composed by Claude Debussy, French musician; the first being one for violoncello and piano."[41]

This return to chamber music in a traditional form—after more than twenty years—sparked various comments. The least credible was perhaps that of Jacques Durand, who claimed that it was the performance of Saint-Saëns's Septet for string quintet, trumpet, and piano at the Concerts Durand at the end of 1913 that supposedly triggered "a renewed sympathy for this form of musical expression"![42] It is obvious that the term "French musician" (*musicien français*), which Debussy had used already in November 1913 in a letter to Stravinsky,[43] puts us more certainly on the right path—that of the old-master tradition, of which he had only modest knowledge but which evoked in his mind "the form of the past, so supple (without the pomposity of modern sonatas)."[44] In any case, it was not a conversion to the principles of the Schola Cantorum; indeed, he would soon write that Vincent d'Indy was "the most Kraut-minded of all."[45] Around this time, he decided on the instrumentation for the six sonatas, including the last three that would never even be sketched: the fourth for oboe, horn, and harpsichord; the fifth for trumpet, clarinet, bassoon, and piano; and the sixth for "various instruments," including the double bass.

The speed with which the *Sonate pour violoncelle et piano* was conceived and developed is astonishing. Debussy announced to Durand on 5 August that he had sent it: "I like," he asserted, "its proportions and its form—almost classical, in the good sense of the word."[46] On the other hand, the composition of *En blanc et noir* underwent several modifications: a change of title,[47] passing from black to gray,[48] from Goya to Velázquez.[49] Then four measures of the second movement, crossed out at first, were restored[50] for "pressing reasons" of "proportions."[51] While correcting the proofs in November, the composer would express his regret that "the last page finishes abruptly."[52]

Debussy's letter of 5 August confirms that the *Études* were planned prior to *En blanc et noir*;[53] indeed, we saw some hints of them in his sketches from the trip to Angers. With the *Études*, Debussy suddenly took great care to note on a calendar their exact dates of composition—between 23 July and 29 September[54]— and he spoke a lot about this work with his publisher. For the dedication, he could not decide between Frédéric Chopin and François Couperin—he had so much "respectful gratitude" for each of them[55]—and he offered Emma on the occasion of his birthday, on 22 August, a sketch of "Pour les sixtes."[56] He was proud of "Pour les quartes," which contained "things never heard before,"[57] and of "Pour les dégres chromatiques," which gave new life to a "slightly worn-out procedure."[58] Several times, he expressed deep satisfaction—uncharacteristic for him—for what he had just produced: "I've put a lot of love and faith in the future of the *Études*";[59] "this music soars over the peaks of the performance";[60] "do not doubt its fierce rigor";[61] and "I confess that I'm pleased to have successfully completed a work that, in all modesty, will have a special place."[62]

No sooner had the *Études* been completed than he buckled down to work on the second *Sonate en trio*, about which he said, strangely enough, that it recalled "a very old Debussy, the composer of the *Nocturnes*."[63] He first sketched it for flute, oboe, and harp, but then he replaced the oboe with a viola.[64] Upon his return to Paris on 12 October, he brought the manuscript himself to his publisher,[65] after having worked "like a madman"[66] up to the last minute, like André Chénier "writing poetry before mounting the scaffold."[67]

Pourville, where his creative capacity had been reignited, was by no means in the middle of nowhere. There he had met Jane Bathori and Émile Engel, who gave a concert (that he did not attend), during which Engel sang "La Marseillaise."[68] It was also in Pourville that he visited Baron [Louis Bouchenez or Louis Bouchêne], the old actor whom he had no doubt formerly seen in Offenbach's *Les brigands* or *La Grande-Duchesse de Gérolstein*, and who was now tending to his flowers.[69]

To one and all, Debussy expressed his opinions on the war. Some of them were imbued with pervading patriotism, decrying "the atavism of barbarity" of the enemy,[70] who deliberately destroyed towns and cathedrals, and the "German taste, false and heavy, that seeps—God knows with what hidden hypocrisy—into our ways of thinking, listening, and even of feeling."[71] Other comments were even worse: "Will there never be a last German? I'm convinced that the soldiers reproduce among themselves!"[72] In addition, we hear his concerns for after the war: "The world will have to be cleansed of this bad seed."[73] Satie, who had apocalyptic views on the subject, concluded that Debussy "understands nothing about the war. For me," he explained to Paul Dukas, "this war is like an end of the world that is more asinine than the real one."[74]

Debussy implored Stravinsky on 24 October to be "a great Russian artist with all your might. It's a fine thing to belong to one's country, to be attached to its soil, just like the lowliest peasants."[75] That same day, the first performance of Debussy's *Berceuse héroïque* was given at a Colonne–Lamoureux concert conducted by Chevillard, whose lack of "expression" the composer once again deplored.[76] Unable to hear *Pelléas* in Paris, he received news of some mediocre performances of the work in Saint Petersburg, Russia, under the direction of the Polish conductor Grzegorz Fitelberg; just the same, he was flattered that the local critic Viacheslav Gavrilovich Karatygin had hailed the performance as "a milestone in the history of Russian musical culture."[77]

An Operation

Unfortunately, the respite granted by that miraculous summer would not continue. Debussy's illness became more critical and painful in November. Still, he participated in the entrance examinations for piano and harp at the Conservatoire. He even went to a rehearsal of the Colonne–Lamoureux orchestra that was to perform two *Nocturnes* on the 28th; at the beginning of "Sirènes," he pointed out that he did not hear the third horn and, if we are to believe Koechlin's account, declared: "I've had enough, I'm leaving!"[78] But on 26 November, Doctors Crépel and Desjardins, who had definitively diagnosed rectal cancer, decided to operate on him; he suffered "like a dog," as he wrote to Fauré.[79] On 2 December, he bravely went to Jacques Durand's new home to play *En blanc et noir* with Louis Aubert. The day before his operation, on 6 December, at 11:00 p.m., he left this moving note for Emma:

> As one never knows the outcome of even the simplest event, I must tell you one last time how much I love you and how sad I'd be if some ordinary accident were to prevent me from completing what I'd like to do to ensure your happiness, now as well as in the future.
> And you, my little darling who would be left, love me in the person of our little Chouchou. . . You are the two sole beings for whom I do not want to leave this life altogether.[80]

It was several weeks before he could get back to doing anything; the huskiness in his voice lasted even longer, and he continued to suffer, despite injections of morphine. The three doctors in his care assured him that he had been affected by a "rectitis" and that it would require a lot of patience, but he himself was aware that they were meting out "the truth in very small doses."[81]

The news of his illness got around Paris, even with former friends who no longer were in contact with him. Pierre Louÿs in particular learned about it, though we do not know how, and he overstated the grimness of the facts when informing his half-brother Georges on 28 December 1915: "The operation was performed six weeks ago.[82] His wife writes that he is lost, and that his suffering is terrible."[83]

Two short pieces had slightly preceded these events: an *Élégie* for piano, intended for a visitors' book dedicated to Queen Alexandra and published in facsimile by Mme Paul Alexandre Mellor in Paris; and the famous "Noël des enfants qui n'ont plus de maison" in its first version for voice and piano. Debussy would often be a little annoyed by the popular success of this Christmas song, and he was clearly aware of its slightly sensationalist character: "You can just picture it," he explained to Dukas: "The mother is dead, the father is at war; we have no more little clogs; we like bread more than toys; and to conclude: 'Victory to the children of France.' It doesn't get any more clever than that, does it? But it goes straight to the hearts of the townspeople."[84]

The end of that year saw the publication of the *Sonate pour violoncelle et piano* and *En blanc et noir*. There were no longer any critics around and scarcely any press coverage of cultural events to acknowledge the appearance of these works. Nevertheless, there was one composer—Saint-Saëns, no less—who penned his immediate reaction to the three pieces for two pianos, four hands: "It is *inconceivable*, and the door of the Institut must be barred at all costs to a man capable of such atrocities; it should be put next to the cubist paintings."[85]

Chapter Twenty-Nine

"The Factories of Nothingness"

1916–18

From this point forward, Debussy would stagnate in the "factories of nothingness"—a phrase borrowed from "our Jules" Laforgue[1]—and would lead an "existence that was circumscribed by a rubber ring."[2] Although he was given morphine over a period of four months, he noted that "the drugs have no lasting effect."[3] Since he was not able to leave the house, Emma told his most trusted friends about his condition and invited them to visit. Dukas came to see him on 12 January and tried to cheer him up; the next day, the Laloys came for lunch. And on the 14th, radium treatment began. Knowing that he would be incapacitated for a certain length of time, he chose some classic reading matter, asking his bookseller for Blaise Pascal's *Pensées* and his *Lettres provinciales*.[4] "He is better,"[5] Emma was able to report to Pasteur Vallery-Radot; but two weeks later the composer reported that he had been ill for seventy-three days![6] Even so, he met with Raphaël Martenot on 7 February to double-check the harp part in the *(Deuxième) Sonate en trio*.[7]

Debussy was probably not up-to-date on what was happening with his works outside of France. It seems that on 4 March, at the Aeolian Hall in London, his *Sonate pour violoncelle* was premiered by Mr. C. Warwick Evans, with Mrs. Alfred Hobday as accompanist;[8] a second performance, by Léonce Allard and Marie Panthès, followed on 9 March at the Saint-Pierre casino in Geneva.[9] England had clearly passed the torch to Switzerland, for in the same concert at the Saint-Pierre casino, Mme Rollan-Mauger sang the "Noël des enfants qui n'ont plus de maison" for the first time.[10]

Visits and an Invalid's Torments

Debussy was inundated more than ever with money problems, compounded by medicinal and pharmaceutical costs, as evidenced in some letters to Durand and to his regular "financiers." To one of them, Gaston Courty, he went so far as to claim that he had an engagement in 1917—in Buenos Aires, no less.[11] Segalen went to visit him on 3 May, and the next day he wrote to his wife, giving his personal medical opinion that the composer was "in remission from an extended and serious illness that, it must be understood, is incurable."[12] So Debussy went "back and forth between good and bad" days,[13] and at times found himself wishing that "we would move toward some hope for recovery."[14] But the evenings were "like a nightmare,"[15] and because of them he came to express the worst fear that might enter the thoughts of a creative person: that of no longer being able to satisfy "this desire always to go further, which took the place of bread and wine for me."[16]

He received the Inghelbrechts with Théophile Steinlen, who had made a lovely ink portrait of him two years earlier. He wrote some letters, one to honor the memory of Enrique Granados, who had died in a torpedo incident in the English Channel,[17] and another to Anton Zelling, who had devoted an article to Debussy, written in Dutch.[18] And Satie came to play backgammon with him in the afternoon. But his patience had limits: "One might wonder if this disease is not incurable?" he confessed to Durand. "It would be better to let me know about it right away, 'and then! oh! then!' (as poor Golaud says. . .) it wouldn't seem so long."[19]

On 3 July, he tried to fight back and made up his mind "to pay no heed, to work, and no longer to be at the beck and call of a slightly too authoritarian rectum!"[20] He even went to a recital by the pianist Francis Planté, who thanked him for having come and spoke to him "in a slightly disturbing way" about "Pagodes."[21] At the same time, the *Études* and the "reduction" of *Khamma* were being sold commercially. The tranquility of Debussy's remission was unfortunately short, for on 15 July, he received news that plunged him into a past that he had hoped was over: he was sentenced by a court order to remit a sum of 30,000 francs to his ex-wife Lilly, in order to guarantee alimony payments that the divorce decree had stipulated and with which he had been in arrears as far back as 1910. He begged his attorney for help:

> I'm so afraid of everything that has anything to do with business that I end up accepting every concession, but especially because I don't want to hear another word about Mme Texier; I'm not up to it, given that I've not yet recovered [from surgery] and that I still suffer a lot and experience hellish nights!
> Everyone seems to be against me in this venture. . . I'm well aware that an artist is far less interesting than a fashion model.

Just the same, I shouldn't be abandoned and left with only suicide as a way out.[22]

The past certainly continued to make demands on him. After some tours in New Zealand and Australia, Maud Allan resurfaced with the desire to dance *Khamma*! But Ernest Bloch, her orchestra conductor, wanted a version of it for a reduced orchestra of twenty musicians (instead of ninety, as originally planned). On 30 July, Debussy wrote to the dancer that it was impossible for him to undertake such a task: "What would you do," he replied to her, "if you were asked to dance with just one arm and one leg?"[23] He had written to Bloch on 28 July, giving him complete freedom and offering a suggestion: "There's a piano in my score, and perhaps you will find your salvation in it. . . !"[24] In the end, Maud Allan never did dance *Khamma*.

While some "student buglers" were blaring away under the windows of Debussy's house,[25] he turned back to *La chute de la maison Usher* and proposed the "definitive" version of the libretto to his publisher, no doubt hoping to justify some advances. Indeed, he found, more than ever, "curious similarities" between his dwelling and the house of Usher: "Apart from the fact that I do not have Roderick Usher's mental instability, nor his passion for Carl Maria von Weber's *La dernière pensée*, we do share a certain hyper-sensitivity. . . on that subject, I could give you details that would make your beard fall out."[26] In fact, this pursuit of a musical embodiment of anguish, which had haunted him for so many years, was clearly an impossible dream. He hung on to it just as he was clinging on to life, but he felt this failure as the worst possible humiliation. When Paul Dukas visited Debussy, he was struck by the tragic impression of this lost creativity when the composer described the current state of the libretto to him. In two letters to Paul Poujaud, Dukas wrote that, all things considered, he shared the attitude of the musical world toward the evolution of Debussy's work in recent years:

> Poor Claude! He upsets me to the very core of my being. I find this "penance" exaggerated and pathetic.[27] (31 July 1916)

> His dramatic idea is absolutely fine, and especially so if the music turns out as he wishes, but I believe that it's the music in particular that is unsatisfactory to him, although he's written a lot of it. I have the impression that his editorial work has tarnished the fine musical intuition which guided him in the past, and that he no longer has that self-confidence which brought us the *Faune* and *Pelléas*. It's obvious that he wants to get back into the swing of things. . . to see people again, to chat a bit. I did my best to cheer him up, but the atmosphere is hardly *uplifting*.[28] (11 March 1915)

"To see people again, to chat a bit." The circumstances were challenging: Emma and Chouchou came down with whooping cough and the doctors advised a change of scene, while Debussy himself "watched the days go by, minute by minute, like cows watching the passing trains."[29] Or else he was reduced to exercising "patience" or trying to play the *Études*: "I was more successful with the first half than with the second half," he confessed to Walter Rummel.[30]

Stay in Le Moulleau

On 11 September, the Debussys left for Le Moulleau (near Arcachon) to stay at the Grand Hôtel, where there was "neither gas nor electricity,"[31] but which was "an incomparable place as far as the scenery and natural light were concerned."[32] At the hotel, an Érard piano was soon made available to the composer; but unfortunately, there were several pianos on each floor, and he had never "heard so much bad music at once,"[33] as he wrote to Paul Dukas, including "some Franck and some Duparc,"[34] as he wrote to Walter Rummel. He even began to miss the buglers from the Bois de Boulogne! To Durand, he spoke of a pianist who had "attempted the 'Danseuses de Delphes' that morning—to make amends, the pianist immediately continued with a performance of Tchaikovsky's *Romance*, this latter rendering being superior."[35] And to Godet, the composer wrote about a "young girl whom I don't know and to whom I swear to you I've never done the least harm, who plays Franck for a good part of the afternoon... Good lord! When there is the sea, and sunsets to weep for! If I were the sun, I'd sleep elsewhere!"[36] Whenever he needed a break, he would go for a walk with Chouchou in the pine forest nearby, where Emma took photographs of them.

One visit in particular disturbed him: that of Louis Rosoor, a cellist and professor at the Conservatoire in Lille. Seeing the evocation of the Italian commedia dell'arte characters in Debussy's *Sonate pour violoncelle et piano*, Rosoor did not hesitate to give it a title: "Pierrot fâché avec la lune" (Pierrot angry with the moon).[37] Faced with such a characterization, Debussy was seized with true indignation; he wrote to Durand, "For a moment, he made me regret having written a sonata and made me question the validity of my writing! [. . .] This episode has deeply disturbed me; it's full of implications and I'm no longer surprised that my poor music is so often misunderstood."[38]

A final modest breakthrough occurred just before their departure, which Debussy shared with Durand on 17 October: "Recently, while on a walk at Cap Ferret, I found the 'cellular' motivic idea for the finale of the Sonata for violin and piano."[39] But this finale would continue to give him trouble for several months.

On 28 October, he let Henri Busser know that he had "returned from Arcachon in better shape" and that he was troubled[40] by Busser's proposal to orchestrate the "Noël des enfants," even though he himself had begun to sketch one possibility.[41] Debussy added, "In its place, I've dreamed of children's voices—women's voices immediately become falsely dramatic, or else something worse: they imitate little girls."[42]

The end of 1916 was marked by three concerts of his works. The first, at Durand's, occasioned the premiere of the *Sonate pour flûte, alto et harpe*, performed by Albert Manouvrier, Darius Milhaud,[43] and Jeanne Dalliès; Debussy took it as an opportunity to convey to his publisher his dissatisfaction with the chromatic harp, "which does not have the sonorous weight of the pedal harp."[44] The second concert was devoted to four of his *Études*, played for the first time by Walter Rummel at the home of Countess Orlowska to benefit the Aide affectueuse aux musiciens (Friendly assistance to musicians) fund.[45] Finally, the third concert, on 21 December at the home of Mme Georges Guiard, was organized for the Vêtement du prisonnier de guerre (Clothing of the prisoners of war) fund. There, Debussy and Roger-Ducasse played *En blanc et noir*; this was not a premiere, however, because that work had first been performed by Walter Rummel and his wife Thérèse Chaigneau, at the home of the Princesse de Polignac on the previous 22 January.[46]

In this context, Debussy showed only a passing interest in Gabriel Fauré's attempts to unite the two rival music societies, the Société nationale de musique and the Société musicale indépendante. To the elder composer, Debussy responded skeptically on 9 February 1917: "For the Société nationale... it's a very delicate situation! [...] Mustn't you in fact admit that musicians are really particularly oblivious? In order to fight [for a common cause], they must be united! Have they ever been of one accord?"[47] However, on 15 March 1917, when Fauré issued his "Appel aux musiciens français" (Appeal to French musicians) in *Le courrier musical*,[48] Debussy agreed to add his signature.

Always curious about the works of Stravinsky (who was living in Morges, Switzerland, at that time), Debussy went on 10 January 1917 to the Opéra, where a "ballet blanc"[49] of the Russian composer's *Les abeilles* was on the program. In fact, this was the *Scherzo fantastique* (1907–8), a work from Stravinsky's youth for which a scenario, based on Maeterlinck's *La vie des abeilles*, had been conceived. When some people caught sight of Debussy on the set, they nonchalantly asked him if all was well now (as if they were unaware of the severity of his illness).[50]

He continued to participate in a few juries (the Lasserre prize), to receive composers (Lili Boulanger)[51] and some performers (Claire Croiza),[52] and to contemplate a concert tour of England and Scotland.[53] He even agreed to go to Madrid to conduct a concert of his works, at the invitation of the recently formed Sociedad nacional de música, an organization that had programmed (on one of its concerts in 1915) his quartet, of which Adolfo Salazar had made a detailed analysis. In Madrid, Manuel de Falla had paved the way for Debussy, having published in 1916 an impassioned article extolling the significance of his Parisian friend; Debussy's role, he asserted, was not so much to restore the musical tradition of his country as it was to achieve "one of the most outstanding feats in the history of contemporary music."[54] But what doctor would have allowed such a trip for Debussy?

On 9 March, his *Sonate en trio* was publicly performed in a benefit concert at the Salle Laurent,[55] and in the middle of the same month, Gaston Poulet and his colleagues came to his home to rehearse his quartet.[56] On the 17th, Claire Croiza participated in a concert that Debussy organized once again for the Aide affectueuse aux musiciens fund.[57] Finally, on 24 March, Claire Croiza and Walter Rummel gave an afternoon concert for the Vêtement du blessé (Clothing of the Wounded) fund.[58] Around the same time, the idea of performing *Jeux* at the Trocadéro suddenly materialized, on the initiative of the Beaux-Arts under-secretary of state, but the project got bogged down with problems of royalties; besides, Debussy felt that the Trocadéro was "a hundred times too large," declaring his preference for the Palais Garnier.[59] On 15 April, he was able to inform Durand that he had finished the edition of J. S. Bach's sonatas for violin and piano—work that was disillusioning, he confessed, faced with "several hundreds of pages where one must trudge through a thicket of joyless measures which unfold mercilessly, each with its own little rascally 'subject' and 'counter-subject.'"[60]

Debussy was surprised to note certain belated converts to his music. Jean d'Udine, who had criticized the rhythmic poverty of *La mer*[61] and had judged "Ibéria" as "petty, thin, skimpy, small,"[62] wrote to the composer on 27 April that he had been seized by a "lively passion" for his *Deux danses* and was still hoping to convert him to the "rhythmic exercises" of Dalcroze, while assuring him of his "slight remorse" and "very complex feelings."[63]

Satie: *Parade*

Among the group of Debussy's oldest friends who came to support him in his distress was Satie, whose relationship with him was in the process of changing. In spite of the circumstances, Satie came out of the shadows, as it were. Some concerts bringing together music and exhibits of paintings took place at the home of Mme Bongard and especially in the studio of the Swiss painter Émile Lejeune, founder of the Lyre et palette society; these included programs of Satie and Ravel (under the auspices of the Lyre et palette society on 18 April 1916), and Satie and Granados (at the home of Mme Bongard on 30 May), with Jane Bathori and Ricardo Viñes performing. Artists such as Matisse and Picasso illustrated the programs, and Jean Cocteau wrote an "Hommage à Satie."[64] In particular, Satie had been composing for Diaghilev (since May 1916) the ballet *Parade*, based on an idea from Cocteau, and the Princesse de Polignac had just commissioned him for *Socrate* (January 1917). Did Satie show Debussy what he was writing at the time? One can imagine the extreme misgivings the latter might have felt regarding the aesthetic of *Parade*, a work that would suddenly propel his friend to center stage. As we have already noticed, Debussy's illness had not destroyed all traces of his natural irony; it certainly had an effect on the new Satie. In any case, the famous quarrel between the two men must date from the time before the rehearsals for *Parade*, as is evidenced by this letter of 8 March 1917, from Satie to Emma:

> Really, it would be better that the "Precursor"* remain at home from now on—in the distance.
> Best wishes—
>
> ES
>
> P.S. What snow! I hope that you all are well. I will write often. I love you all— very much.
> *Tiresome teasing, and repeated over and over. Really!
> Quite unbearable, in any case.[65]

It is likely that Debussy did not attend the eventful premiere of *Parade* on 18 May 1917. However, a letter to Arthur Dandelot seems to imply that he had been at the Théâtre du Châtelet two days before, and that he had tried in vain to thank Diaghilev for a production that had included *The Firebird* (Stravinsky), *The Good-Humored Ladies* (Domenico Scarlatti, arranged Vincenzo Tommasini), *Les contes russes* (Anatoly Liadov), and the *Prince Igor* (Alexander Borodin) dances.[66] On 25 May, he returned to the theater, where *Petrushka*, *The Good-Humored Ladies*, *Las meninas*, and, astonishingly enough, *Parade* were on the program. In his congratulatory letter to Diaghilev, he mentioned only *Las meninas*, which he called an "amazing feat" for having reclad the distinctly French charm of Fauré's *Pavane* in "Spanish seriousness," and *Petrushka*, which he deemed "a true masterpiece."[67] Debussy wrote not one word on *Parade*— neither in this letter nor to any of his later correspondents.

In the previous months, the composer had completed his third sonata, the *Sonate pour violon et piano*, whose "cellular idea" was born at Arcachon (as we have seen), but only after much turmoil and regret. At the beginning of April, he wrote again to Dukas: "I'm between a thousand worries and a dozen ways to finish a sonata for violin and piano."[68] However, the work was given its premiere a month later, on 5 May, at a benefit concert for blind soldiers. A young composer who attended it, Francis Poulenc, described the scene "in the half-filled Salle Gaveau. At [Debussy's] entrance on stage, he was given an ovation, but at the conclusion [of the performance], he was met with only polite applause."[69]

Even though Debussy found it difficult to get to the Conservatoire by 9:00 a.m. for the examinations, as he explained to Fauré,[70] he still tried to make plans, meeting with Firmin Gémier before a performance of *Shylock* and telling him about his long-held desire to compose incidental music for *As You Like It*, as adapted by Paul-Jean Toulet.[71] This was an opportunity to renew his correspondence with Toulet,[72] who was now retired in Guéthary but who remained his only "fun-loving" friend: "The vocal component can play a big role in *As You Like It*. . . I plan to include all of the 'songs' that decorate the text,"[73] Debussy told him, thus confirming his desire to "work on subjects that *Pelléas* had previously precluded for him."[74] He led Toulet to believe that they would be able to discuss the matter together, since he soon would be going to the Basque country, not far from where the writer was living.

Before leaving Paris, Debussy had time to attend a recital of J. S. Bach, Chopin, and Mussorgsky, along with his own works, performed by Walter Rummel. However, he declined the Marquise de Clermont-Tonnerre's invitation to the opening of her pavilion in Passy, during which she had the *Sonate pour flûte, alto et harpe* performed "under the terrace's supporting walls, which amplify the sound."[75] But at the end of June, a special pleasure was awaiting him. Bernardino Molinari came to Paris to conduct three French-Italian concerts with the Conservatoire orchestra; the audience was sparse, but the interpretation of *La mer* brought Debussy great satisfaction, thanks to the conductor, who was "something of a sorcerer who shook off the apathy of the orchestra."[76] And, in addition to Saint-Saëns's "Organ Symphony" (no. 3 in C Minor, op. 78), the concerts included some works—by Giuseppe Martucci and Edward Elgar, as well as Ottorino Respighi's cantata *Aretusa*—that were far from his own musical horizon (though whether he sat through them is not known).[77]

The Chalet Habas

On 3 July, the family arrived in Saint-Jean-de-Luz and settled into the "Chalet Habas," rented from an English colonel (Nicoll) who left some war souvenirs there. Although the chalet did not afford a view of the sea, which was fifteen minutes away by foot, one could catch sight of the foothills of the Pyrenees in the distance and there enjoy a "Biblical calm, an extraordinary silence (in the words of Maeterlinck)."[78] Debussy soon became aware of the presence of "illustrious pianists" in the region, including Ricardo Viñes, Joaquin Nin, and Marguerite Long;[79] "however," he added, "I have the advantage of staying in a place far enough removed that I don't hear them."[80] On the other hand, he was approached by Mme Carlos Petit-Ducourau to participate in the activities of a "group à la Schola," but which was a rival of that institution: "There's a little region, where the air is sweet and gentle, that is divided by different ways of performing Gregorian and Palestrinian chant, under the permanently closed eye of the late Charles Bordes! [. . .] Breaking news: I've been told that Mme Blanche Selva has arrived. . . God moves in mysterious ways. In a word: It's a big Ocean out there!"[81]

In order to demonstrate his independence from all organized musical establishments, Debussy agreed to accompany Gaston Poulet, performing his last Sonata both in Saint-Jean-de-Luz and Biarritz—the final public concerts in which he would participate: "They wanted us to play the 'Intermezzo' again as an encore, which I categorically refused to do, first and foremost out of respect for compositional unity; in that case, we would have had to repeat the entire sonata."[82] On 25 and 27 September, Francis Planté, another pianist who was in the region, gave two recitals under the auspices of the Charles Bordes Society. Debussy commented on them to Durand, while slipping in a cutting remark about Ravel:

> That man [Planté] is prodigious—he's even a little terrifying: at the first concert, he broke a hammer; at his age (78 years), it was remarkable! He played—very well—the "Toccata" (from *Pour le piano* by Claude Debussy), and performed—also marvelously well—Liszt's *Feux follets*. Much less successful was Ravel's *Jeux d'eau*. This piece, with its butterfly wings, can't withstand the weight (or the feet, if you prefer) of the virtuoso.[83] He's going to play "Reflets dans l'eau" and "Mouvement" in the second concert, and has asked me for advice. Doesn't this humility tell me something worthwhile?[84]

One cannot help but compare this unproductive three-month stay with the one in 1915 that went so far beyond Debussy's expectations: "I had planned to write, along the lines of the set of sonatas, a set of little 'concerti' for piano, employing certain orchestral groupings. It's moving along, but not well,"[85] he wrote. For some time now, he had no longer even considered commenting on the events of the war. After the abdication of Tsar Nicolas II and a little before the armistice of Brest-Litovsk, he confessed that he understood nothing of what was happening in "mysterious Russia"![86] And the family's return to Paris took place under the worst conditions: "international hassles" at Saint-Jean-de-Luz, and an interminable wait at the drafty train station in Bordeaux, in pouring rain.[87]

The Last Months

At the end of October, having returned home (he wrote that his garden, "lost under the dead leaves, seemed abandoned"),[88] Debussy was still able to be somewhat active. He asked Gaston Poulet to come over to play his last sonata for Caplet, who was on leave from the warfront.[89] But he was not able to attend the performance of his *Prélude à l'après-midi d'un faune*—that "old war horse, now promoted to a more calm fate"—and apologized to the conductor, his friend Alfred Bruneau.[90] As Chouchou was no longer making "noticeable progress" at the piano, he dismissed her teacher, thanking her in terms that were a model of diplomacy.[91] And to the long missives that Godet sent him, he replied: "Music has completely abandoned me."[92] However, he still displayed some final, critical acumen when commenting on Walter Rummel's candidacy for a position at the Conservatoire in Geneva:

> Isn't he a bit too young? And will the young pianists of Geneva take him seriously? (Couldn't he at least wear glasses?) Still, in all sincerity, I wish him success. Here, in Paris, I'm afraid he might not be able to do much more! You know how people stick to their opinions! They will never admit that, having been born in Berlin, he might not remain German through and through. Note that, if he doesn't watch out, "Kultur" will overcome him, as will his taste for deep discussions—as deep as 40 degrees below sea level.[93]

On 1 November, Debussy wrote his last letter to his publisher in which he claimed that he was working on the operatic version of *Le martyre* with Laloy: "Isn't it strange that in those 3,995 and some-odd lines, there's so little substance? Just words, words. . ."[94] The previous year, Laloy had handed him the text of an *Ode à la France*, which was written in the same vein as the *Berceuse héroïque* and the "Noël." Debussy sketched about fifteen pages of a short score, notated on four staves, but no other individuals were privy to this source, and thus able to attest to the reliability of the completion that was made after his death.[95]

From then on, he was confined to bed by his illness. On 23 January 1918, Godet wrote to Debussy, mentioning that he heard from Walter Rummel that the composer had been bedridden "for several weeks."[96] In that very long letter, Godet spoke of literature he had been reading, of the poor quality of the concerts of French music that Pierre Sechiari had just given in Switzerland, of a short essay comparing Chopin and Debussy that he was in the process of completing, and especially of many questions concerning the corrected score of the *Nocturnes*, which Ernest Ansermet was preparing to conduct in Geneva.[97] Was Debussy himself able to read this letter from beginning to end? It was difficult for Emma to reply to these sorts of questions on his behalf. However, she gave some news to Toulet's wife, Marie, in mid-winter:

> Claude is feeling much better and is getting up a bit—very briefly—each morning.
> Nights are better with morphine. He looks rather well and his appetite is fairly good—though it will take a long time for his energy to return. [. . .]
> Here, often without coal, the house is unbearable, except for Claude's room.
> Chouchou is well and sleeps peacefully. She is rather poorly brought up, but where would I find the time to try to curb her bad manners?[98]

On 8 February 1918, Pasteur Vallery-Radot wrote to Toulet that the news about Debussy's cancer had spread throughout Paris and that Emma knew the truth, even if she still wanted "to feign ignorance."[99] He had seen the invalid in his bed, "much thinner, but not too depressed."[100] When did Debussy write his last, incomplete note to Emma, in pencil with an unsteady hand? Probably on 1 January: "My little darling, the years pass by, and look alike—that's nothing new, even in these times of constraint. . ."[101]

On 21 March, Jacques Rouché challenged the conditions of the war by mounting a sumptuous production of Rameau's *Castor et Pollux*—amid the German offensive and the bombardment of Paris[102]—which brought back Debussy's enthusiasm for the Schola's performance of this work in 1903.[103] On the 17th, when Pierné conducted "Ibéria," did he know that he was saying a final farewell to his classmate from Rome?

Two eyewitness accounts of the composer's last days are extant: that of Jacques Durand, who went to the Bois de Boulogne on 23 March; and that of Chouchou in a letter to Raoul Bardac—astonishing in its expression, heart-rending in its tragic spontaneity. Durand recorded his memories as follows:

> I knew that his days were numbered: the ravages of his suffering were visible on his face, so expressive. Catching sight of me, Debussy conveyed his happiness; he wanted to speak with me in private. First, he told me of the horror of the previous night, when, seeing the danger of the bombing, he didn't have the strength to get up to take shelter in the cellar with his family, and they didn't want to leave him. [. . .] I tried to cheer him up, to get him to foresee some future improvement in his condition. He thanked me and then, watching me fixedly with his deep eyes, which were already looking to the great beyond, he told me that it was all over, that he knew it, that it was a question of hours, very short now. [. . .] Faced with my denial, he gave me a sign that he wanted to embrace me; then he asked me to give him a cigarette, his final consolation.[104]

Debussy passed away on 25 March.[105] Fourteen days later, Chouchou, twelve and a half years old at the time, wrote to her brother:

> My dear Raoul,
> Did you receive the last telegram? Yes, you must have. It was I who thought to send you the first one. I wrote it and then, thinking that one would have to show several identity papers at the post office and that I don't have them because I'm a little girl, I asked Dolly to send it. She came here because I asked her, seeing the utterly distraught face of my poor Mama! As soon as she left, Mama was called to Papa's side because the nurse thought his condition was "very bad"!—We quickly sent for two doctors, both of whom said to give him an injection so he wouldn't suffer. You know that I understood—Roger-Ducasse, who was there, said to me: "Come, Chouchou, kiss your father."

Then all of a sudden I knew it was over. When I returned to his bedroom, Papa was sleeping and breathing regularly but very shallowly. He continued to sleep in that way until 10:15 in the evening and at that hour, gently, angelically, he went to sleep forever. I can't tell you what happened after that. A flood of tears welled up in my eyes, but I immediately fought them back on account of Mama. All night long, alone in Mama's big bed, I couldn't sleep for a single minute. I had a fever and my dry eyes searched the walls, and I could not bring myself to believe that it was true!!!

The next day, far too many people came to see Mama who, by the end of the day, could no longer hold it together—it was a release for her and for me. Thursday arrived, the Thursday when he was to be taken away from us forever! I saw him one last time in that horrible box—on the ground. He seemed happy, oh so happy, and this time I didn't have the strength to hold back my tears and, nearly collapsing, I could not embrace him. At the cemetery, Mama naturally could not have handled herself better and, as for me, all I could think of was: "I mustn't cry because of Mama." I mustered all my courage. From where did it come? I don't know. I didn't shed a single tear; tears stifled are worth as much as tears shed, and now, it is night forever. Papa is dead! Those three words, I don't understand them, or rather I understand them all too well. And to be completely alone here, to struggle with Mama's indescribable grief, is truly terrible—it has made me forget my own sorrow for a few days, but now I sense it even more poignantly—oh you who are so far away, think a bit about your poor little sister who would like to embrace you so much and to tell you how much she loves you. Do you understand everything that I'm feeling but can't put into words?

A thousand tender kisses and all the affection of your little sister,

Chouchou[106]

"On Friday, the 29th," wrote Laloy, "he was carried to a temporary vault in Père-Lachaise, through gray and cold weather. About fifty people had gathered in the garden outside of his house, but most of them slipped away en route, and we were barely twenty by the time we arrived at the cemetery."[107] As Debussy had been neither a functionary nor a member of the Institut, there was, fortunately, no official speech.

Postlude

Debussy's death led to no "holy alliance" with the critics,[108] who devoted a few truncated articles to him in the papers, which provided only a little space for nonmilitary news. Camille Bellaigue, his former friend from the Conservatoire, renounced none of his core criticisms of Debussy's music—the absence of melody, rhythm, and form: "More than any other composer of his time, [Debussy] drank from his cup, which, once again, was not large but of a fine crystal, where vague and changing colors played out in iridescent reflections."[109] Although Henri Quittard proved to be more objective, he emphasized that "as exquisite as were his [Debussy's] works, perhaps they were not the kind of compositions from which a lasting tradition can develop."[110] In *Le temps*, Pierre Lalo further developed his comments, while reserving his praise strictly for the works whose merits he himself had extolled, which is to say, those up to and including *Pelléas*. He took care not to mention any works by Debussy that had been composed after 1902, if only not to judge them as a whole, while asserting that they did not have the same qualities and that their musical language became fossilized "in formulae, at times."[111] Finally, he wrote that "while not all of the qualities of French genius are included in his music, all the qualities of his music are of the purest essence of French genius."[112] Just the same, there was a more eloquent advocate in Gaston Carraud: in spite of his reservations about the "rarefied" nature of Debussy's work and the idea that it suited only a limited public,[113] Carraud recognized its quintessential element, knowing that Debussy had "reversed the very notion of musical art, turned its path on its head, opened a horizon of potentially limitless innovations, and, in the process, created utterly new means of musical expression."[114]

Notes

Preface to the Translation and Revised Edition

1. "Petite mienne" was Debussy's term of endearment for his wife Emma Bardac. The poem was a tongue-in-cheek message from "C. D." designed to bolster my courage, assuring me that I "corrected his work so well."

Introduction

1. MR: See Debussy's letter to André Caplet, written on 17 November 1911, in *C*, 1463.
2. MR: See Debussy's letter of 11 December 1911 to Caplet in *C*, 1473.
3. MR: See Debussy's letter of 15 June 1916 to Robert Godet in *C*, 2002.
4. MR: The present edition retains citations from Claude Debussy, *Monsieur Croche et autres écrits*, rev. ed. François Lesure (Paris: Gallimard, 1987). However, rather than citing the letters published in numerous disparate sources that were available at the time when Lesure's biography appeared, the present edition references the letters as published in Claude Debussy, *Correspondance, 1872–1918*, ed. François Lesure and Denis Herlin (Paris: Gallimard, 2005), which appeared after Lesure's death.
5. MR: Debussy had planned to collaborate with René Peter and Régine Dansaert (the sister of Alice Peter, who was the wife of René's brother Michel), on this play, but ended up writing it himself. It centers on the artistic rivalry that results when an esoteric society, the *Frères en art*, is formed to prevent the commercial exploitation of their work. See pp. 152–53 for further details.

1. An Unsettled Childhood: 1962–72

1. Henri-D. Reynaud, "Hommage de la Bourgogne à Claude Debussy," *Beaux-Arts* (6 August 1948): 7. [The original article may be accessed in the Fonds François Lesure (Claude Debussy archives), département de la Musique, Bibliothèque nationale de France, uncatalogued documents, carton I/6(17); hereafter, this source will be abbreviated as Fonds FL, BnF.] Most of the official civil documents write "de Bussy" in two words.
2. MR: Reynaud, "Hommage," 7.

3. Marcel Dietschy, *La passion de Claude Debussy* (Neuchâtel: Éditions de la Baconnière, 1962), expanded upon Léon Vallas's research regarding the origins of Debussy's family. Unless otherwise indicated, the information given in this chapter is borrowed from Dietschy, as is the family tree provided here. MR: See the Dietschy material in DOSS-05.03 and DOSS-05.15 in the Centre de documentation Claude Debussy (hereafter abbreviated as CDCD) for further details on Debussy's ancestors.

4. The father of Victorine (Manuel-Achille's wife and Achille-Claude's mother) died in 1859 at the nursing home in Clermont (Oise), perhaps suffering from paretic neurosyphilis. His mother was from Tonnerre. MR: The references to Manuel-Achille's fondness for *Le pré aux clercs* and *La fille du régiment* are based on René Peter, *Claude Debussy*, rev. ed. (Paris: Gallimard, 1944), 99.

5. MR: A copy of the marriage certificate of 30 November 1861 is among the Dietschy material at the CDCD in DOSS-05.15.

6. For the baptism of Adèle (Achille-Claude's sister), the witnesses were, on 24 July 1863, the same umbrella merchant Fabre and the hairdresser Girard, rue au Pain. MR: A copy of Achille-Claude's birth certificate may be found in Fonds FL, BnF, carton I/6(17).

7. MR: See Fonds FL, BnF, carton I/6(17).

8. The alleged confessions that Debussy was said to have made to Henry Malherbe at the time of *Le martyre de saint Sébastien* [see the interview, from the 11 February 1911 issue of *Excelsior*, in Claude Debussy, *Monsieur Croche et autres écrits*, rev. ed. (Paris: Gallimard, 1987), 323–25] are complete rubbish: "At the age of ten, he was too absorbed in his preparation for his entrance examination into the Conservatoire to pursue diligently his catechism lessons. A debate on this subject erupted between Claude Debussy's mother and the parish priest at St.-Germain. The child had to give up his first communion"; see Henry Malherbe, "Le 'Martyre de Saint Sébastien' est-il toujours à l'index?" *Les lettres françaises* 8, no. 221 (19 August 1948): 6.

9. The factors in this controversy may be found in Henry Prunières, "Autour de Debussy," *La revue musicale* 15, no. 146 (May 1934): 349–58; continuing in *La revue musicale* 15, no. 147 (June 1934): 21–36; and in *La revue musicale* 15, no. 149 (September–October 1934): 189–94.

10. Dietschy, *Passion de Claude Debussy*, 10. MR: William Ashbrook and Margaret G. Cobb, in their English translation of Marcel Dietschy, *A Portrait of Claude Debussy* (Oxford: Oxford University Press, 1990), 9, translate *l'arsouille* as "the blackguard."

11. Emmanuel was said to have left his parents early on, leading a wandering life and ending up as a farmhand.

12. Jean-Yves Mollier, *L'argent et les lettres: Histoire du capitalisme d'édition, 1880–1920* (Paris: Fayard, 1988). MR: See pp. 121–49, in particular.

13. MR: The battle of Sedan, in the Ardennes, took place on 2 September 1870.

14. Dietschy, *Passion de Claude Debussy*, 12, and Dietschy, *Portrait of Claude Debussy*, 12. MR: Dietschy points out that Achille's younger sister had signed Alfred's baptismal certificate, remarking that it is likely that the firstborn, had he been present, would have signed it as well.

15. Our emphasis. The letter from 20 April 1909 [*C*, 1172; misdated in FL 2003 as 1905] was written for a local journal (published in Nice), the *La revue des lettres et des arts*, in reply to an inquiry: "When you go to the Riviera, can you work there?" MR: Debussy wrote to Jean Veillon, the chief editor of the journal, and his letter was published in "Réponses à l'enquête," *La revue des lettres et des arts* 2, no. 5 (1 May 1909): 297.

16. Letter of 24 March 1908 [in *C*, 1076].

17. How credible is an opinion shared by Adèle Debussy, when she was seventy-four years old, with a journalist from *L'intransigeant*: "My aunt, who lived in Cannes, was a very good musician"? MR: See especially p. 3 in Pierre Bret, "Il y a vingt ans, Debussy mourait," *L'intransigeant* (4 March 1938): 1 and 3.

18. MR: See Louis Laloy, *Claude Debussy* (Paris: Les bibliophiles fantaisistes, 1909), 11.

19. MR: Dietschy, *Passion de Claude Debussy*, 12, and Dietschy, *Portrait of Claude Debussy*, 12.

20. MR: Laloy, *Claude Debussy*, 11.

21. Adèle's memories are also entirely untrustworthy concerning this matter: "His first teacher at Cannes was an Italian who said to his mother, after several lessons: 'He will go far, your child.'" MR: See Bret, "Il y a vingt ans, Debussy mourait," 3.

22. In a conversation with Victor Segalen on 8 October 1907, Debussy was more precise, yet at the same time more evasive: "It could have gone either way. My father determined that I should go to the Borda. ["Going to the Borda" meant going to the Naval Academy in Brest. The origin of this generic term is discussed in *Histoire de l'école navale* (Paris: Maison Quantin, 1889), 196. Borda was also the name given to French ships, typically used as school ships by the École Navale once they were decommissioned; see *Jean-Michel Roche, Dictionnaire des bâtiments de la flotte de guerre française de Colbert à nos jours. Tome 1: 1671–1870* (France: Group Retozel-Maury Millau, 2005), 79. An illustration of one of these ships may be found in *Histoire de l'école navale*, 256.] Then he met someone. . . I don't know how it happened. 'Ah! He plays that? Perfectly —But you have to make him study music. . .' etc. . . Then my father was determined that I was meant to be a musician exclusively, like someone who knows nothing about it." See Annie Joly-Segalen and André Schaeffner, eds., *Segalen et Debussy* (Monaco: Éditions du Rocher, 1961), 70–71 [reprinted in Annexe 1 of *C*, 2199].

23. Madame Gerard de Romilly, "Debussy professeur, par une de ses élèves (1898–1908)," *Cahiers Debussy*, nouv. sér. 2 (1978): 5. "At times when he felt like speaking," wrote Jean Lépine, "he claimed that he would have loved to have become a painter. And he had bought a square palette 'to be unlike everyone else'"; see Jean Lépine, *La vie de Claude Debussy* (Paris: Albin Michel, 1930), 84.

24. David Grayson, "Claude Debussy Addresses the English-speaking World: Two Interviews, an Article, and The Blessed Damozel," *Cahiers Debussy*, nouv. sér. 16 (1992): 27.

25. MR: Louis-Adolphe Thiers served as Head of State, then provisional President of France, from 1871 to 1873.

26. MR: Patrice de MacMahon, Duke of Magenta and Marshal of France, led the Versailles troops in the suppression of the Paris Commune. He would go on to

serve as Chief of State from 1873 to 1875 and as President of the Third Republic from 1875 to 1879.

27. MR: The sentence in parentheses, mentioned in FL 2003 in the first paragraph under "The Commune" section but not within the citation of Mme Debussy's letter, is taken from Edward Lockspeiser (*Debussy: His Life and Mind* [Cambridge: Cambridge University Press, 1978], 1:18n1), who consulted the dossier of Captain de Bussy at the *Bureau historique de l'armée*. In the sentence immediately preceding the one in parentheses, the dates of Manuel's employment—from 15 December to 15 March (not 15 February, as in FL 2003)—are also corrected by Lockspeiser.

28. MR: The text of this letter is faithfully transcribed by Lockspeiser in *Debussy: His Life and Mind*, 1:18n1, and by Dietschy in DOSS-05.15 in the CDCD.

29. These facts have been established by Marcel Dietschy, "The Family and Childhood of Debussy," *The Musical Quarterly* 46, no. 3 (July 1960): 301–14.

30. In March 1870, Sivry was at the Monnaie in Brussels—along with Villiers de l'Isle Adam, Catulle Mendès, and Judith Gautier—to attend a performance of *Lohengrin* (Alan William Raitt, *Villiers de l'Isle Adam et le mouvement symboliste* [Paris: Librairie José Corti, 1965], 305). At the time of his arrest, on 5 July 1871, he was the orchestra conductor at Néris, a spa near Montluçon.

31. MR: The child bride of Paul Verlaine, Mathilde's memoirs were first published in Mathilde Mauté and François Porché, *Mémoires de ma vie* (Paris: Flammarion, 1935).

32. There is no mention of Debussy as a student of her mother in the manuscript of Mathilde's memoirs, except on a small piece of paper in another hand (probably written subsequently), inserted between two pages. MR: The manuscript of her memoirs, to which Lesure refers, has not been found among the materials in the Fonds FL, BnF; rather, in carton I/6(17) there is a photocopy of pp. 56–61, a passage on Mathilde's parents, of the published memoirs. On pp. 176–77 of *Mémoires de ma vie*, Mathilde recounts that her brother Charles met Debussy's father and that he and her mother "were the first to discover the astonishing musical disposition of the child and to urge his family to nurture him along this path."

33. [See Debussy's letters to Jacques Durand from 27 January 1915 and 1 September 1915 in *C*, 1871 and 1927, respectively.] Jean-Jacques Eigeldinger, *Chopin vu par ses élèves*, 3rd ed. (Neuchâtel: Éditions de la Baconnière, 1988), 191n121, could not find any further information confirming the fact that Madame Mauté had been Chopin's pupil. Debussy himself wrote in the preface of his revision of Chopin's Works that the latter "had many pupils [. . .] more than have been attributed to him, no doubt." MR: See Debussy's "Préface" to Frédéric Chopin, *Œuvres complètes pour piano: Valses* (Paris: A. Durand & fils), 1915.

34. MR: See Paul Verlaine, *Confessions*, in *Œuvres poétiques complètes* (Paris: Gallimard, 1962), 1350; see also his eulogistic poem, "A Madame Marie M. . . ," on p. 1020.

35. MR: Victor Henri de Rochefort-Luçay, known as Henri Rochefort, was a writer with radical political views who favored the Commune and who was imprisoned off and on for his extremist activity. He founded and wrote for *La lanterne*, *La Marseillaise*, and *L'intransigeant*, and as a Boulangist, followed General Boulanger into exile in 1889. In 1895, he returned to Paris and became involved

as an anti-Dreyfusard. For further details on his radical publication activities, see Henri Avenel, *Histoire de la presse française depuis 1789 jusqu'à nos jours* (Paris: Ernest Flammarion, 1900), 564–66, 576–78, 720–22, and 758–61.

36. MR: *Le rappel*, founded in 1869 by Victor Hugo and Henri Rochefort, among others, was a mouthpiece for radical Republican views; see Avenel, *Histoire de la presse française*, 573–76.

37. MR: The original report, signed by "P." and addressed to "M. le Général, préfet de Police," may be found in the Archives of the Préfecture de Police de Paris, Dossier B a 1271. A copy of this report is available among the Dietschy material in the CDCD, DOSS-03.20.

38. MR: The Mettray Penal Colony, in Indre-et-Loire, near Tours, was a private reformatory, established for the rehabilitation of young male delinquents. It is described by Matthew Davenport Hill in *Mettray, A Letter from the Recorder of Birmingham to Charles Bowyer Adderley, Esq., M.P.* (London: A. and G. A. Spottiswoode, 1855).

39. MR: This is likely a reference to Auguste Jean Marie Vermorel, a radical and socialist journalist who worked for *La presse*, *La liberté*, *Le courrier français*, and the *Réforme*, and who was imprisoned for his anti-government stance; see Bernard Noël, *Dictionnaire de la Commune* (Paris: Flammarion, 1978), 278–79.

40. MR: The Association internationale des travailleurs was a Socialist labor movement whose ideas were influenced by the theories of Karl Marx, among others. For further details, see Augustin Souchy, *L'encyclopédie anarchiste* (Paris: La librairie internationale), s.v. "Association internationale des travailleurs," 1:154–60. Various addresses made by Marx may be accessed at the French language portal of the Marxists Internet Archive, https://www.marxists.org/francais/ait/index.htm, or on the general archive website, https://www.marxists.org, both accessed 16 January 2019.

41. MR: This reference is likely to the radical Comité de vigilance de Montmartre, also known as the Comité de vigilance des citoyennes du XVIIIe arrondissement; for details, especially on the women involved in this movement, see Martin Phillip Johnson, *The Paradise of Association* (Ann Arbor: University of Michigan Press, 1999), 241–43.

42. MR: This reference is to Nina de Callias, or Nina de Villard, who was an amateur pianist and poet, the lover of Charles Cros, and the subject of Édouard Manet's oil painting, *La dame aux éventails*, in 1873. Parnassian poets and Republicans who would become involved with the Commune frequented her salon on the rue Chaptal, but with the onset of the political crisis in Paris in 1870, she and her mother fled to Geneva, where they would spend three years. It was at her home that Mathilde Mauté would meet Verlaine; see Mauté, *Mémoires de ma vie*, 39–43. From her memoirs, it is clear that Mathilde's relationship with Verlaine was encouraged by her brother Charles de Sivry, who was a friend and admirer of the poet. For further details on the life of Nina de Callias, see "*The Lady with the Fans*: Nina de Callias, Manet's Model," Musée d'Orsay, https://www.musee-orsay.fr/en/events/exhibitions/archives/exhibitions-archives/article/span-classitaliquenoirla-dame-aux-eventails-span-nina-de-callias-modele-de-manet-4004.html, accessed 16 January 2019.

43. Archives Préfecture de police de Paris, B a. 1271 (Dossier Sivry). MR: A copy of this report is available in the Dietschy material at the CDCD, DOSS-03.20.

44. MR: See Laloy, *Claude Debussy*, 11–12.

45. Joly-Segalen and Schaeffner, *Segalen et Debussy*, 107.

46. See especially [pp. 104–5 and 145 in] André Vial, *Verlaine et les siens: Heures retrouvées; Poèmes et documents inédits* (Paris: A. G. Nizet, 1975), and [pp. 56–61, 69–79] in Pierre Petitfils, *Album Verlaine* (Paris: Gallimard, 1981). MR: The relationship between Charles de Sivry, Nina de Callias, and Paul Verlaine is elucidated on pp. 56–61; see n42.

47. MR: Rimbaud's stormy homosexual relationship with Verlaine is well documented.

48. It is difficult to go along with Léon Vallas, *Claude Debussy et son temps* (Paris: Éditions Albin Michel, 1958), 103, when he claims that Debussy met Verlaine at Mallarmé's home.

49. MR: See Debussy's letter to Paterne Berrichon from 10 March 1901 in *C*, 588.

50. MR: Paul Vidal, in his "Souvenirs d'Achille Debussy," *La revue musicale* (1 May 1926): 13 (109), described her as "passionately devoted to her son, and very fanatical about him."

51. Archives nationales, AJ/37/322. MR: Upon the death of Berlioz in 1869, David took over his position at the Institut, serving as librarian at the Conservatoire.

2. Failure of a Pianist: 1872–79

1. MR: See Debussy's letter of 25 November 1909 in *C*, 1224.

2. MR: In 1801, the first stone of the Conservatoire library was laid, under the leadership of the director at the time, Bernard Sarrette. See Constant Pierre, *Le Conservatoire national de musique et de déclamation* (Paris: Imprimerie nationale, 1900), 141.

3. MR: See the official document, from 14 November 1881, that outlines the plan to build a new theater, library, and museum, and to enlarge the facilities on the site of the rue du Faubourg-Poissonnière, in Pierre, *Conservatoire national*, 326–27.

4. MR: In 1911, under the directorship of Gabriel Fauré, the Conservatoire moved to 14 rue de Madrid.

5. MR: See the letter from Ambroise Thomas, written on 26 August 1871, and the subsequent official action taken on 14 September 1871, in Pierre, *Conservatoire national*, 302–4.

6. MR: See Ambroise Thomas's notice of 31 August 1871 in Pierre, *Conservatoire national*, 310.

7. MR: See Ambroise Thomas's request of 30 September 1873, followed by the official notice on 13 October 1873, in Pierre, *Conservatoire national*, 310–11. On 26 November, Thomas issued the decree that orchestra rehearsals were to begin on 1 December, and that they would be held on Mondays at 10:00 a.m.

8. MR: See Pierre, *Conservatoire national*, 397–98.

9. Julian Tiersot, "Souvenirs," *Le ménestrel* 78, no. 45 (9 November 1912): [353].

10. Camille Bellaigue, *Souvenirs de musique et de musiciens* (Paris: Nouvelle librairie nationale, 1921), 35.

11. It is very difficult to trust his sister Adèle's later statement: "My father also played the piano, even fairly well for an amateur." MR: See especially p. 3 in Pierre Bret, "Il y a vingt ans, Debussy mourait," *L'intransigeant* (4 March 1938): 1 and 3.

12. MR: FL 2003 ascribes this description to Robert de Montesquiou. However, its attribution to Régnier is clearly established by Denis Herlin on p. 200 in "Le 'pâtre calabrais' et le poète ou la rencontre de Debussy et de Henri de Régnier," in *Henri de Régnier, tel qu'en lui-même enfin?* ed. Bertrand Vibert (Paris: Classiques Garnier, 2014), 199–214.

13. Jean Lépine [describes Debussy's character and physical traits in] *La vie de Claude Debussy* (Paris: Albin Michel, 1930), [see especially pp. 19 and 40]. The memories of Raymond Bonheur, Gabriel Pierné, and Paul Vidal may be found in *La revue musicale* (1 May 1926): 3–16 (99–112). MR: See also Bellaigue, *Souvenirs de musique*, 35; Julien Tiersot, "Adieux au vieux Conservatoire," *Le ménestrel* 78, no. 43 (9 November 1912): 353; and Léon Daudet, *Salons et journaux: Souvenirs des milieux littéraires, politiques, artistiques et médicaux de 1880 à 1908*, 4ème sér. (Paris: Nouvelle librairie nationale, 1917), 307–8.

14. Archives nationales, AJ/7/238/1. MR: John Clevenger, in his dissertation, "The Origins of Debussy's Style" (PhD diss., University of Rochester, 2002), provides a useful summary of all of Debussy's professors' reports. For Duvernoy's assessments of 29 January and 11 June 1873, see Clevenger, "Origins of Debussy's Style," 178.

15. Léon Vallas, "Achille Debussy jugé par ses professeurs," *Revue de musicologie* 34, nos. 101–102 (July 1952): 47, offered an incomplete account, neglecting the opinions of the jury members who were not his professors. MR: See also Clevenger, "Origins of Debussy's Style," 178.

16. MR: Bellaigue's comment is recorded in his *Souvenirs de musique*, 35.

17. MR: The information on Marmontel as a teacher comes from Bellaigue, *Souvenirs de musique*, 34.

18. MR: For Marmontel's report on Debussy's solfège exam from 17 January 1873, see Clevenger, "Origins of Debussy's Style," 181.

19. MR: Reported in Vallas, "Achille Debussy jugé par ses professeurs," 46, and in Clevenger, "Origins of Debussy's Style," 181.

20. Archives nationales, AJ/37/239/3. MR: See Marmontel's report on Debussy's solfège exam from 11 June 1874 in Clevenger, "Origins of Debussy's Style," 182.

21. MR: See Vallas, "Achille Debussy jugé par ses professeurs," 46, and Clevenger, "Origins of Debussy's Style," 182.

22. MR: See Vallas, "Achille Debussy jugé par ses professeurs," 47 (where the date, which is repeated in FL 2003, is given as 28 June and the word "musical" is omitted), and Clevenger, "Origins of Debussy's Style," 178.

23. MR: See Weber, "Critique musicale: Les concours publics du Conservatoire," *Le temps* (25 August 1874): [2]. Debussy was not mentioned by name in this report; rather, Weber wrote that "the youngest pupil is not yet twelve years old; he was given a second honorable mention, because one must be much more lenient with the young." Debussy had been mentioned by name, however, in a previous report cited in "Faits divers," *Le temps* (27 July 1874): [2].

24. MR: Henry Cohen, "Distribution des prix au Conservatoire," *L'art musical* 14, no. 32 (12 August 1875): 251.

25. Gaston Escudier, "Discours de M. de Cumont," *L'art musical* 13, no. 33 (13 August 1874): 264. [Also quoted in *Le ménestrel* 40, no. 36 (9 August 1874): 284, and in the *Revue et gazette musicale* 41, no. 32 (9 August 1874): 250.]

26. MR: See Clevenger, "Origins of Debussy's Style," 182.

27. Léon Vallas, "Achille Debussy jugé par ses professeurs," 47, erroneously switched the two opinions of 15 January and 9 June. [See also Clevenger, "Origins of Debussy's Style," 182.] César Destefani, whose studies at the Conservatoire were limited to solfège, would become a violinist at the Théâtre-Italien.

28. MR: Marmontel's assessments of 22 January and 22 June 1875 may be found in Vallas, "Achille Debussy jugé par ses professeurs," 47, and in Clevenger, "Origins of Debussy's Style," 179. For the June exam, the students performed Chopin's Rondo in E-flat Major, op. 16.

29. MR: The two second prizes were awarded to Victor-Auguste Dolmetsch and Charles-Henri-Jacques Dusautoy; see Pierre, *Conservatoire national*, 587, 742, and 748.

30. MR: Pierre, *Conservatoire national*, 795 lists Léon-Lucien-Henri Lemoine as the grandson and successor of the publisher Jean-Henri Lemoine; FL 2003 reports in error that "L. Lemoine," the "son" of the publisher, received one of the first honorable mentions.

31. [The results of the *concours* were reported in *L'art musical* 14, no. 30 (29 July 1875): 235, and in *Le ménestrel* 41, no. 36 (8 August 1875): 284.] Much later, Satie deemed that no one played Chopin better than Debussy (Erik Satie, *Ecrits*, ed. Ornella Volta [Paris: Éditions Champ libre, 1977], 68). It was Chopin's first Ballade that he played in 1875 [confirmed by Clevenger; see "Origins of Debussy's Style," 197], and not the second, as reported by most of his biographers.

32. MR: See Gabriel Pierné, "Souvenirs d'Achille Debussy," *La revue musicale* (1 May 1926): 11 (107).

33. MR: See Raymond Bonheur, "Souvenirs et impressions d'un compagnon de jeunesse," *La revue musicale* (1 May 1926): 5 (101).

34. MR: Prévost and Bourbonneux both offered afternoon tea.

35. MR: See Pierné, "Souvenirs d'Achille Debussy," 11 (107).

36. MR: Pierné, "Souvenirs d'Achille Debussy," 11 (107). Jean-Louis-Ernest Meissonier (1815–91) was a classicist painter who excelled initially in miniature portraits and later in military themes. On 24 May 1884, an exhibition of his collected works, including 146 items (paintings, sculpture, and engravings), had been shown at the Petit Gallery in Paris; see further details from the Rehs gallery at Janet Whitmore, "Biography – Jean Louis Ernest Meissonier (1815–1891)," Rehs Galleries, Inc., http://www.rehs.com/Jean_Louis_Ernest_Meissonier_Bio.html, accessed 16 January 2019.

37. MR: Bellaigue, *Souvenirs de musique*, 37.

38. Léontine Mendès was not really a classmate; she would go on to perform her debut at the Opéra-Comique the following year. She was further along in her studies at the Conservatoire, given that she won a second prize several months after the concert at Chauny and a first prize in *opéra-comique* in 1877.

39. MR: Henry Cohen, "Concours du Conservatoire," *L'art musical* 16, no. 30 (26 July 1877): 235.

40. MR: See pp. 35–37 and 39–41 for more information on Achille's first serious muse, the high soprano Mme Marie Vasnier.

41. MR: Copies of the program may be found in Fonds FL, BnF, cartons I/6(1) and I/6(3).

42. MR: The fantasy on Meyerbeer's *L'Africaine* was arranged by L. Girard and performed by the Fanfare des Manufactures. The "grande fantaisie" on Meyerbeer's *Robert le diable* was composed by Allard for violin and performed by M. Mansart (conductor of the brass band). And the fantasy from Verdi's *La traviata* for "piston" was arranged by Jean-Baptiste Arban and performed by M. Quinard.

43. Called a "well-known cellist/composer" by *Le ménestrel* in 1884, Samary offered to Carvalho, without success, his comic opera in one act, *Le chien de garde*. He excelled "in organizing musical and dramatic evenings," and was said to have had "numerous artistic connections" (according to *Le ménestrel* 43, no. 4 [24 December 1876]: 31).

44. MR: This piece, sung by M. Fleury, might be translated as "Where's my velocipede?" referring to an old-fashioned style of bicycle. In addition to the works mentioned, the second half of the concert opened with a fantasy by Tilliard on Vincenzo Bellini's *Norma*, performed by the brass band, and included another fantasy for piano, arranged by René Favarger from Carl Maria von Weber's *Oberon* and performed by M. A. Geffrin (the conductor of the Chauny choral union). As well, Mlle Mendès sang a *Sérénade* by Gaetano Braga, accompanied by cellist M. Samary. Finally, the Chauny choral union performed Lindpaintner's *Le drapeau de la France* on the first half of the concert, and Laurent de Rillé's *Chœur de buveurs* on the second half.

45. MR: This review, authored by "A.-R.," is cited in Henri Borgeaud, "Deux concerts à Chauny (Aisne) en 1876 avec M. de Bussy," *Revue de musicologie* 48, no. 125 (July–December 1962): 97.

46. MR: This review, authored by "E. L." in the 19 January 1876 issue of *La defense nationale*, is also cited in Borgeaud, "Deux concerts à Chauny," 97.

47. Borgeaud, "Deux concerts à Chauny," 98 [the critic this time was "J. B." and the review appeared in the 22 March 1876 issue of *La défense nationale*]. Vallas (*Claude Debussy et son temps* [Paris: Éditions Albin Michel, 1958], 18) claimed that these press clippings were preserved in the Bibliothèque de l'Opéra, but they have not been found there.

48. MR: See Vallas, "Achille Debussy jugé par ses professeurs," 47, and Clevenger, "Origins of Debussy's Style," 182. FL 2003 reported the date of Lavignac's assessment as three days before, rather than after, the Chauny concert.

49. MR: See Vallas, "Achille Debussy jugé par ses professeurs," 47–48, and Clevenger, "Origins of Debussy's Style," 179.

50. Maurice Emmanuel, Pelléas et Mélisande *de Claude Debussy: Étude historique et critique, analyse musicale* (Paris: Paul Mellottée, Éditeur, [1926]); repr. as Pelléas et Mélisande *de Claude Debussy: Étude et analyse* (Paris: Éditions Mellottée, 1950), 12. Alfred Bruneau sketched a fierce portrait of this guard in his "Souvenirs inédits," *Revue internationale de musique française* 7 (1982): 27 and 29.

51. MR: See Vallas, "Achille Debussy jugé par ses professeurs," 47, and Clevenger, "Origins of Debussy's Style," 183.

52. MR: See Vallas, "Achille Debussy jugé par ses professeurs," 48, and Clevenger, "Origins of Debussy's Style," 179. FL 2003 reported the date of 22, rather than 20, June.

53. MR: Pierre, *Conservatoire national*, 554, lists two additional first-prize winners: Jean-Rodolphe Gésus and Amédée-Gustave Sujol. Thus, a total of five candidates earned a first-prize medal in solfège in 1876.

54. Henry Cohen, "Distribution des prix au Conservatoire," *L'art musical* 15, no. 32 (10 August 1876): 249.

55. Bellaigue, *Souvenirs de musique*, 41.

56. Octave Fouque, "Concours publics du Conservatoire," *Revue et gazette musicale* 45, no. 51 (30 July 1876): 242.

57. Louis Laloy, *La musique retrouvée, 1902–1927* (Paris: Librairie Plon, 1928), 122.

58. MR: The one work he is known to have performed for the instrumental-ensemble class, in June 1875, was the third movement of Beethoven's Trio in B-flat Major, op. 11; see Clevenger, "Origins of Debussy's Style," 254. On pp. 267–68, Clevenger describes the typical repertoire expected of the students in this class, as well as Debussy's spotty attendance in it; Baillot's reports, cited in Clevenger, "Origins of Debussy's Style," 183, show that Debussy attended class in 1874–75 and in fall 1875, but that he dropped out for the last two months, and then attended on and off again during the spring of 1879. At the very least, the instrumental-ensemble class afforded the young pianist a foundation in playing chamber music, an experience that would have served him well for his first concerts in Chauny as well as in his future summer employment, performing in resident trios for Mme Wilson Pelouze at Chenonceaux and for Mme von Meck in Russia.

59. MR: Pierre Baillot (1771–1842) was an esteemed violinist who taught at the Conservatoire for many years and whose *L'art du violon* (1834) had a profound influence on violin instruction, both with respect to technique and performance practice, at the time. His son, René-Paul, was born in 1813 and thus would not yet have been a seventy-year-old in 1876–77, as claimed in FL 2003.

60. MR: See Pierné, "Souvenirs d'Achille Debussy," 10 (106).

61. MR: See Bellaigue, *Souvenirs de musique*, 35.

62. Archives nationales, AJ/37/238/1 [notebook of Henry Duvernoy]. MR: See also Duvernoy's and Fissot's reports in Clevenger, "Origins of Debussy's Style," 178–80. FL 2003 states that Duvernoy commented twice on Debussy's intelligence over the years, but three reports are cited in Clevenger.

63. MR: See Vidal, "Souvenirs d'Achille Debussy," 12 (108).

64. [See Pierné, "Souvenirs d'Achille Debussy," 10 (106).] A little later, Marguerite Vasnier ("Debussy à dix-huit ans," *La revue musicale* [1 May 1926]: 17 [113]) noted his manner of playing "as pounding and at times also very sweet and very singing."

65. MR: For Marmontel's assessments of 31 January and 21 June 1877, see Vallas, "Achille Debussy jugé par ses professeurs," 48, and Clevenger, "Origins of Debussy's Style," 179–80.

66. Charles Bannelier, "Concours du Conservatoire," *Revue et gazette musicale* 44, no. 30 (29 July 1877): 236. Georges Mathias had served as a professor at the Conservatoire since 1862. He had been a student of Kalkbrenner and, for several years, of Chopin. Those two schools of piano pedagogy would be at odds with each other for some time. Among the most notable of Mathias's students were Raoul Pugno and Isidore Philipp; among the most atypical, Erik Satie.

67. MR: Bannelier, "Concours du Conservatoire," 237.

68. MR: Just after leaving the Conservatoire, Guitry would appear in Alexander Dumas *fils*'s *La dame aux camélias* (which became known as *Camille* in English). After 1918, he frequently acted in plays written by his son, Sacha Guitry, who was not only a playwright but also an actor in film and on the stage, as well as a director and screenwriter.

69. MR: See Henri Moreno, "Conservatoire national de musique et de déclamation: Distribution des prix, année scolaire 1876–1877," *Le ménestrel* 43, no. 36 (5 August 1877): 281–84. The date of the ceremony is given as 6 (rather than 4) August in FL 2003.

70. Yves Lado-Bordowsky, "Une signature de Debussy en 1877," *Cahiers Debussy*, nouv. sér. 15 (1991): 51–53.

71. MR: Vallas, "Achille Debussy jugé par ses professeurs," 48, although FL 2003 reports the date as 27 November 1877. However, Clevenger, "Origins of Debussy's Style," 135–36, points out that Durand's course in 1877–78 was actually a class in harmony and accompaniment (it was not until director Thomas's curricular changes in fall 1878 that the course focused solely on harmony instruction), and that Achille had already audited this class in 1876–77. He thus studied harmony for a total of four years under Durand.

72. MR: Clevenger, "Origins of Debussy's Style," 158, provides further details. Apparently, Durand had been injured in a street altercation with "a certain Davison," and even though he "won the ensuing court case, which stipulated a fine and two months of prison time for the assailant, the incident resulted in embarrassing press coverage" and led to his resignation.

73. MR: See Vallas, "Achille Debussy jugé par ses professeurs," 48, and Clevenger, "Origins of Debussy's Style," 184.

74. Claude Debussy, *Monsieur Croche et autres écrits*, rev. ed. (Paris: Éditions Gallimard, 1987), 288 and 65 [See also Claude Debussy, *Debussy on Music*, trans. Richard Langham Smith (New York: Alfred A. Knopf, 1977), 237 and 84]. On a little piece of paper that I [Lesure] own, Debussy noted, no doubt at the time when he was appointed to the Conseil supérieur of the Conservatoire: "reduce harmony studies to one year."

75. MR: For Durand's comments from 19 June 1878, see Vallas, "Achille Debussy jugé par ses professeurs," 47, and Clevenger, "The Origins of Debussy's Style," 184.

76. MR: Antoine Banès, "Les concerts," *Le Figaro* (19 April 1920): 3.

77. MR: Banès, "Les concerts," 3.

78. MR: See Vallas, "Achille Debussy jugé par ses professeurs," 48, and Clevenger, "Origins of Debussy's Style," 184.

79. MR: See Vallas, "Achille Debussy jugé par ses professeurs," 48, and Clevenger, "Origins of Debussy's Style," 180. While FL 2003 follows Vallas in ascribing the date of this assessment to 20 January (possibly mistakenly taking the number 20 from the date of the June exam that year), Clevenger cites it as 25 January.

80. MR: For Marmontel's opinion of 20 June 1879, see Vallas, "Achille Debussy jugé par ses professeurs," 48, and Clevenger, "Origins of Debussy's Style," 180.

81. MR: Pierre, *Conservatoire national*, 588, lists two first-prize winners: Bellaigue and Paul-Auguste-Désiré Fournier, for 1878, although only Bellaigue is mentioned in Clevenger, "Origins of Debussy's Style," 140.

82. MR: See A. Landély Hettich, "Concours publics du Conservatoire," *L'art musical* 17, no. 31 (1 August 1878): 245.

83. MR: Pierre, *Conservatoire national*, 588, lists O'Kelly in addition to Pierné for the second-place medal in 1878, although only Pierné is mentioned in Clevenger, "Origins of Debussy's Style," 140.

84. MR: See Landély Hettich, "Concours publics du Conservatoire," 245.

85. Archives nationales, AJ/37/238/2. MR: See Clevenger, "Origins of Debussy's Style," 180.

86. MR: See Vidal, "Souvenirs d'Achille Debussy," 12 (108). Lesure points out that Vidal hailed from the friendly city of Toulouse.

87. MR: Vidal, "Souvenirs d'Achille Debussy," 12 (108).

88. AJ/37/102–4, 158–60. See François Lesure, "Raymond Bonheur: Un ermite, ami de Debussy (1861–1939)," *Cahiers Debussy* 17–18 (1993–94): 65–66.

89. MR: See Bonheur, "Souvenirs et impressions," 3–4 (99–100).

90. François Lesure, "Quatre lettres de René Chansarel à Debussy (1889)," *Cahiers Debussy*, nouv. sér. 4–5 (1980–81): 51–56. Chansarel would go on to obtain a first prize in piano in 1883. MR: See Pierre, *Conservatoire national*, 588.

91. MR: This assessment was rendered on 4 February 1879; see Vallas, "Achille Debussy jugé par ses professeurs," 48, and Clevenger, "Origins of Debussy's Style," 180.

92. MR: See Vallas, "Achille Debussy jugé par ses professeurs," 48, and Clevenger, "Origins of Debussy's Style," 184.

93. MR: See Vidal, "Souvenirs d'Achille Debussy," 12 (108).

94. MR: See Bonheur, "Souvenirs et impressions," 3 (99).

95. MR: See Charles Bannelier, "Conservatoire national de musique et de déclamation: Concours publics," *Revue et gazette musicale* 46, no. 30 (27 July 1879): 244.

96. MR: See Léonce Dupont, *Tours et Bordeaux: Souvenirs de la République à outrance* (Paris: E. Dentu, 1877), 60. Marcel Dietschy, *La passion de Claude Debussy* (Neuchâtel: Éditions de la Baconnière, 1962), 33n14 (and Marcel Dietschy, *A Portrait of Claude Debussy*, trans. William Ashbrook and Margaret G. Cobb [Oxford: Oxford University Press, 1990], 26n14), cites a source for this description of Mme Pelouze, from the December 1887 issue of a journal titled *Le curieux*. In fact, there is a brief notice on "M. Wilson," *Le curieux* 2, no. 45 (December 1887): 336, that mentions Wilson's sister as the wife of the deceased Eugène Pelouze and the mistress of M. Grévy; it also notes that she lives in the Chenonceaux château, but includes no physical description of her.

97. MR: Edward Lockspeiser, *Debussy: His Life and Mind* (Cambridge: Cambridge University Press, 1978), 1:36, cites this description of Mme Pelouze, adding that she was "wearing a diamond tiara." Lockspeiser based his information on Robert de Bonnières, *Mémoires d'aujourd'hui* (Paris: Paul Ollendorff, 1883), 91, in which there is a reference to "la belle Américaine" who "wore a crescent of diamonds on her forehead" and was described as being "fragrant as a heady magnolia flower." It should be noted that Mme Pelouze was never mentioned by name in Bonnières's memoir; in fact, he stated explicitly that he did not know her actual name and nationality, but only that she stood out among several women with amorous connections to Jules Grévy.

98. Émile Maillard, *L'art à Nantes au XXe siècle* (Paris: Librairie des Imprimeries réunies, [1888]), 135–36.

99. MR: Charles Auguste Émile Durand adopted the name of Carolus-Duran when he began to exhibit at the Salon. Well known for his portraits of high-society individuals, he also taught, among others, John Singer Sargent and James Carroll Beckwith; see further information on Carolus-Duran, as well as his portrait by Sargent, at the Clark Museum website, http://www.clarkart.edu/Art-Pieces/6161.aspx, accessed 16 January 2019.

100. Mme Pelouze took Nicasio Jimenez with her to Bayreuth in 1883.

101. Charles Richard, *Chenonceaux et G. Flaubert* (Tours: Deslis Frères, 1887); René Martineau, *Promenades biographiques* (Paris: Librairie de France, 1920), [especially pp. 7–16].

102. MR: See Laloy, *La musique retrouvée*, 125–26.

103. The lists of French pilgrims to Bayreuth drawn up by Albert Lavignac (*Le voyage artistique à Bayreuth* [Paris: Librairie Delagrave, 1937], 549–57) should be verified against other sources, as recorded, for example, in Léon Vallas, *Vincent d'Indy* (Paris: A. Michel, [1946]), 1:220 [or in Myriam Chimènes, *Mécènes et musiciens: Du salon au concert à Paris sous la IIIe République* (Paris: Librairie Arthème Fayard, 2004), 462]. Toché was also a fervent Wagnerian and collaborated, with Henri Fantin-Latour, in the *Bayreuther Festspiel Blätter* (1884).

104. MR: See Vidal, "Souvenirs d'Achille Debussy," 13 (109). Note that Vidal made this statement with respect to Achille's experience in summer 1879, but that he erroneously referenced Mme von Meck instead of Mme Pelouze. Achille would begin to work for Mme von Meck in the following summer of 1880.

105. Paul Poujaud confided to Vallas that around 1877 he had met in the Conservatoire library a young student whose physical appearance—shape of the head, black hair, sharp eyes—as well as his "little bohemian" style, had struck him (Vallas, *Achille-Claude Debussy* [Paris: Presses Universitaires de France, 1944, repr. 1949], 4).

3. Birth of a Composer: 1880–82

1. MR: While Georges Jean-Aubry began a catalog of Debussy's works in 1907, he first published one (with Debussy's consent) in the concert program of the Cercle de l'art moderne at Le Havre on 22 April 1908. In January of that year,

Debussy had reviewed Jean-Aubry's catalog but confessed that he could not remember the precise dates of his works (see letter of 3 January 1908 in *C*, 1048–49). Louis Laloy made several emendations to this list in 1909, publishing his own catalog in *Claude Debussy* (Paris: Les bibliophiles fantaisistes, 1909), 101–5. Upon the composer's death in 1918, Jean-Aubry completed the catalog and published it in pp. 206–9 of Georges Jean-Aubry, "Some Recollections of Debussy," *The Musical Times* (1 May 1918): 203–9. It was subsequently finalized and printed in his *La musique et les nations* (Paris: Les Éditions de la Sirène, 1922), 247–55.

2. MR: While this point is true in a general sense, especially for some of the earlier works, Debussy painstakingly recorded the completion, including even the hour of the day, of some of his later manuscripts. Examples include the short score for *La mer*, which is dated "Dimanche 5 mars à 6 h. du soir," and the orchestral preparation for *Jeux*, which is dated at the end "28.3.13 midi" and "24.4.13 6 h."

3. MR: Paul Vidal, "Souvenirs d'Achille Debussy," *La revue musicale* (1 May 1926): 12–13 (108–9).

4. The manuscript of "Madrid" (lacking the text) curiously bears a joint dedication to Paul Vidal and François-Henri-Alexandre Passérieu (a student from Marseilles who studied voice at the Conservatoire). MR: This manuscript is currently housed in the Frederick R. Koch Collection at the Beinecke Rare Book & Manuscript Library at Yale University.

5. MR: Vidal, "Souvenirs d'Achille Debussy," 12 (108).

6. MR: Vidal recounted the entire story in "Souvenirs d'Achille Debussy," 13 (109).

7. MR: See Laloy, *Claude Debussy*, 13.

8. MR: See Maurice Emmanuel, *Pelléas et Mélisande de Claude Debussy: Étude historique et critique, analyse musicale* (Paris: Paul Mellottée, Éditeur, [1926]); repr. as *Pelléas et Mélisande de Claude Debussy: Étude et analyse* (Paris: Éditions Mellottée, 1950), 19.

9. Emmanuel was registered in the class of Théodore Dubois on 6 December 1881 (Archives nationales, AJ/37/105). There could be several reasons for questioning the accuracy of Maurice Emmanuel's memory. The news that he reported was not always firsthand. It was at Marmontel's home on the rue Blanche (where he was readily welcomed) that he noted "these new harmonies" by Achille, which the master of the house offered to guests such as Ernest Reyer, Ernest Guiraud, and Émile Réty. Emmanuel adds that "this took place in the years following 1880." What was firsthand, however, were the harmonic fantasias played by Achille in Léo Delibes's class—with freedoms that seemed to enchant the future musicologist [Emmanuel] and that he hastened to share at Marmontel's gatherings.

10. MR: See Emmanuel, *Pelléas et Mélisande de Claude Debussy*, 19–20.

11. MR: See Léon Vallas, "Achille Debussy jugé par ses professeurs," *Revue de musicologie* 34, nos. 101–102 (July 1952): 49; and John Clevenger, "The Origins of Debussy's Style" (PhD diss., University of Rochester, 2002), 185.

12. Kaiser hailed from the Lorraine region and went on to coach solfège at the Conservatoire.

13. MR: The annual *concours*, or examination periods, occur near the end of the academic year.

14. Rather than the romanticized work of Catherine Drinker Bowen and Barbara von Meck (*Beloved Friend: The Story of Tchaikowsky and Nadejda von Meck* [New York: Random House, Inc., 1937; French trans., Paris, 1940]), one might consult the correspondence between Tchaikovsky and Nadezhda von Meck, published by Vladimir A. Zhdanov and Nikolai T. Zhegin in three volumes (Moscow: Academia, 1934–36). Edward Lockspeiser published excerpts from the correspondence concerning Debussy (in French) for the first time in "Debussy, Tchaïkovsky et Mme von Meck," *La revue musicale* 16, no. 160 (November 1935): 245–52, and 18, no. 177 (October 1937): 217–21. (Lockspeiser did not convert the dates to the Gregorian calendar [nor did Zhdanov and Zhegin; rather, they reported the date according to the Julian calendar, also known as the "Old Style," used in Russia at the time].) MR: All of the dates in this chapter have been converted to the Gregorian calendar. Because the Tchaikovsky–von Meck correspondence is published in Russian and thus less accessible to English readers, whenever possible we cite both the original Russian source as well as Lockspeiser's articles, which were published immediately after the appearance of the respective volumes—vol. 1: 1876–78 (published in 1934); vol. 2: 1879–81 (published in 1935); and vol. 3: 1882–92 (published in 1936)—of *P. I. Chaikovskii: Perepiska s N. F. von-Mekk*. In addition, whenever possible, we have translated the text from the original Russian directly into English, rather than via a French translation; I am grateful to Olga Shupyatskaya for her invaluable assistance with the Russian–English translations.

15. MR: See Mme von Meck's letter of 16 November 1878 in Zhdanov and Zhegin, *P. I. Chaikovskii*, 1:472.

16. MR: The date of Mme von Meck's letter is 22 July 1880, one month before Achille's eighteenth birthday. See Zhdanov and Zhegin, *P. I. Chaikovskii*, 2:374, and Lockspeiser, "Debussy, Tchaïkovsky et Mme von Meck," *La revue musicale* (November 1935): 246.

17. MR: In a letter dated 19 August 1880, Mme von Meck noted that Achille was Massenet's pupil and that he "has already finished the Conservatoire with a first prize" (see Zhdanov and Zhegin, *P. I. Chaikovskii*, 2:394, and Edward Lockspeiser, "Debussy, Tchaïkovsky et Mme von Meck," *La revue musicale* [November 1935]: 247). On 20 September, she wrote from the Villa Oppenheim that Achille's recent compositions were "echoes of his professor, Massenet" and that his recent trio "is very nice but it is again reminiscent of Massenet" (see Zhdanov and Zhegin, *P. I. Chaikovski*, 2:408, and Edward Lockspeiser, "Debussy, Tchaïkovsky et Mme von Meck," *La revue musicale* [November 1935]: 248).

18. MR: See Debussy's letter to Chausson, who himself was traveling to Arcachon, from 23 October 1893 in *C*, 168. And in fall 1916, near the end of life, Debussy returned to Le Moulleau in Arcachon, mentioning the pine trees in letters to Jacques Durand on 14 September (*C*, 2026) and to Roger-Ducasse on 23 September (*C*, 2029).

19. Mme von Meck's letter dates from 10 August. MR: See Zhdanov and Zhegin, *P. I. Chaikovskii*, 2:389.

20. MR: See Mme von Meck's letter of 19 August 1880 in Zhdanov and Zhegin, *P. I. Chaikovskii*, 2:394, and in Lockspeiser, "Debussy, Tchaïkovsky et Mme von Meck," *La revue musicale* (November 1935): 247.

21. For all the possibilities, see André Schaeffner, "Debussy et ses rapports avec la musique russe" in *Essais de musicologie et autres fantaisies* (Paris: Le Sycomore, 1980), republished in *Variations sur la musique* (Paris: Librairie Arthème Fayard, 1998).

22. Perhaps the arrangement for piano, four hands, of the *Suite pour piano*, op. 43.

23. MR: FL 2003 ascribed the date of 18 August to Mme von Meck's letter, which was in fact completed on 19 August 1880. See Zhdanov and Zhegin, *P. I. Chaikovskii*, 2:394, and Lockspeiser, "Debussy, Tchaïkovsky et Mme von Meck," *La revue musicale* (November 1935): 247.

24. MR: See Mme von Meck's letter of 11 October 1880 in Zhdanov and Zhegin, *P. I. Chaikovskii*, 2:421, and in Lockspeiser, "Debussy, Tchaïkovsky et Mme von Meck," *La revue musicale* (November 1935): 251.

25. MR: See Tchaikovsky's letter of 22 October 1880 in Zhdanov and Zhegin, *P. I. Chaikovskii* 2:429, and in Lockspeiser, "Debussy, Tchaïkovsky et Mme von Meck," *La revue musicale* (November 1935): 248, although Lockspeiser gives the date as 20 October.

26. MR: This photograph is reproduced in François Lesure, *Debussy: Iconographie musicale* (Geneva: Minkoff & Lattès, 1980), 34.

27. MR: See Tchaikovsky's letter of 26 October 1880 in Zhdanov and Zhegin, *P. I. Chaikovskii* 2:431, and in Lockspeiser, "Debussy, Tchaïkovsky et Mme von Meck," *La revue musicale* (November 1935): 249n1.

28. MR: This letter dates from 12 November 1880. See Zhdanov and Zhegin, *P. I. Chaikovskii*, 2:441, and Lockspeiser, "Debussy, Tchaïkovsky et Mme von Meck," *La revue musicale* (November 1935): 249.

29. Letter of 25 October 1880 [see Zhdanov and Zhegin, *P. I. Chaikovskii*, 2:430, and Lockspeiser, "Debussy, Tchaïkovsky et Mme von Meck," *La revue musicale* (November 1935): 249–50].

30. MR: See Madame von Meck's letter of 15 November 1880 in Zhdanov and Zhegin, *P. I. Chaikovskii*, 2:445.

31. MR: See Madame von Meck's letter of 26 October 1880 in Zhdanov and Zhegin, *P. I. Chaikovskii*, 2:431.

32. MR: See Mme von Meck's letter of 5 November 1880 in Zhdanov and Zhegin, *P. I. Chaikovskii*, 2:437, and in Lockspeiser, "Debussy, Tchaïkovsky et Mme von Meck," *La revue musicale* (November 1935): 248.

33. See Mme von Meck's letter of 12 November 1880 [in Zhdanov and Zhegin, *P. I. Chaikovskii*, 2:441, and in Lockspeiser, "Debussy, Tchaïkovsky et Mme von Meck," *La revue musicale* (November 1935): 250].

34. A letter from Gustave Charpentier (June 1882) tells rather bluntly how Massenet, a member of the jury, "recruited" certain students at the time of their examinations in harmony: "Come to my class next fall; I'm counting on it, all right?" (Gustave Charpentier, *Lettres inédites à ses parents: La vie quotidienne d'un élève du Conservatoire, 1879–1887*, ed. Françoise Andrieux [Paris: Presses Universitaires de France, 1984], 81).

35. Archives nationales, AJ/37/159/5 (year 1880–81). When in 1894 Debussy went to Brussels to give a concert, certain critics introduced him as a student of

Franck, and one of them even specified that he "had been the disciple of the composer of the *Béatitudes* for scarcely six months"; see "À la Libre Esthétique: Œuvres musicales de M. Claude-A. Debussy," *L'art moderne* 14, no. 9 (4 March 1894): 66–67.

36. MR: See Vidal, "Souvenirs d'Achille Debussy," 14 (110).

37. MR: Vidal, "Souvenirs d'Achille Debussy," 14 (110).

38. MR: This remark may be found already by 13 April 1903 in *Gil Blas* (see Claude Debussy, *Monsieur Croche et autres écrits*, rev. ed. [Paris: Gallimard, 1987], 149; and Claude Debussy, *Debussy on Music*, trans. Richard Langham Smith [New York: Alfred A. Knopf, 1977], 173). It is also found in Claude Debussy, "Les 'Béatitudes' jugées par Debussy," *Revue musicale de Lyon* 5, no. 26 (12 April 1908): 754–55.

39. MR: Debussy, *Monsieur Croche*, rev. ed., 149, and Debussy, *Debussy on Music*, 173.

40. Emmanuel, in Pelléas et Mélisande *de Claude Debussy*, 33n, categorically asserts that Debussy attended not a single one of these lessons.

41. [In other words, Cuignache took three years in all, as reported in FL 2003, to earn a first medal in solfège.] After twelve years of study, Cuignache became a professor of solfège at the Conservatoire in 1896 [see Constant Pierre, *Le Conservatoire national de musique et de déclamation* (Paris: Imprimerie nationale, 1900), 441] and a rehearsal coach at the Opéra-Comique [in 1898; see the entry for 15 January 1898 in Jean Raphanel, *Histoire au jour le jour de l'Opéra-Comique*, 1re sér.: 1 January–30 June 1898 (Paris: Bibliothèque de "la vie théâtrale," 1898), 11]. In 1923, Cuignache conducted the *Prélude à l'après-midi d'un faune* as director of the Concerts classiques in Biarritz.

42. MR: The notice for the classes, to begin on 16 November at the Flaxland salons at 40 rue Neuve-des-Mathurins, appeared in *Le ménestrel* 47, no. 48 (30 October 1881): 383. Gustave-Alexandre Flaxland founded a publishing house in 1847, but in December 1869, he sold his entire catalog to Durand, Schoenewerk et Cie. and turned his full attention to the manufacturing of pianos.

43. *Revue et gazette musicale* 46, no. 1 (5 January 1879): 8; *Le monde artiste* 21, no. 44 (5 November 1881): 8; *Le ménestrel* 48, no. 16 (19 March 1882): 127; 50, no. 10 (10 February 1884): 88 [this review specifically mentions Mme Vasnier and M. Debussy]; 51, no. 17 (29 March 1885): 135; and 51, no. 28 (14 June 1885): 223. In addition, we find a note on Mme Moreau-Sainti in the Album Mariani [a publication sponsored by the inventor of Mariani wines; in vol. 1 of Angelo Mariani, *Figures contemporaines tirées de l'Album Mariani* (Paris: Flammarion, 1894), Mme Moreau-Sainti endorses Mariani wine, writing: "A singer without Mariani coca is a violinist without rosin."] She was still giving evening performances in 1893 (*Le ménestrel* 59, no. 11 [12 March 1893]: 88). MR: A notice for her voice classes, held at that time on Fridays from 3:00 to 6:00 p.m. at 11 rue Gounod, appeared in *Le ménestrel* 60, no. 2 (14 January 1894): 16. An additional notice about Gaston Bérardi's *Légende tsigane*, performed in chorus by Moreau-Sainti's pupils, appeared in *Le ménestrel* 54, no. 18 (29 April 1888): 144.

44. Legally, her full first name was Marie Blanche [and her maiden name appears as Marie Blanche Adélaïde Frey on the birth certificates of her children, Marguerite Félice Louise and Maurice Henri Félix; see the Dietschy material in DOSS-04.78 at the CDCD].

45. [Most biographers call him Eugène-Henri. He is listed as Henri Eugène Alfred Vasnier on the birth certificates of his children; see the Dietschy material in DOSS-04.78 at the CDCD.] Curiously, Victor I. Seroff [in his *Claude Debussy; Debussy, Musician of France*, translated from English by Roger Giroux (Paris: Éditions Buchet/Chastel, Corrêa, 1957), 57,] uses the first name of Pierre for him, while Dietschy calls him Eugène. His death certificate, as well as his publications, proves that his customary first name was Henri.

46. MR: He authored, for example, an extract as "Henri-A. Vasnier" in the *Mémoires de la société nationale des antiquaries de France* 65 (1906) titled "Observations sur la reconstitution des frises rapportées de la Susiane par la mission Dieulafoy," and his name appeared as "H.-A. Vasnier" in another publication, "Conservation et commerce des œuvres d'art," in *L'hellénisme* 7 (July 1909): 15–23.

47. MR: His "blazing eyes" were noted by Paul Vidal in "Souvenirs d'Achille Debussy," 12 (108).

48. Yves Lado-Bordowsky, "La chronologie des œuvres de jeunesse de Claude Debussy (1879–1884)," *Cahiers Debussy*, nouv. sér. 14 (1990): 3–22.

49. MR: See André Suarès, *Debussy* (Paris: Émile-Paul frères, 1922), 133.

50. MR: For Guiraud's comments from 31 January and 26 June 1881, see Vallas, "Achille Debussy jugé par ses professeurs," 49, and Clevenger, "Origins of Debussy's Style," 186.

51. MR: See letter of 24 May 1881 in Zhdanov and Zhegin, *P. I. Chaikovskii*, 2:510, and in Lockspeiser, "Debussy, Tchaïkovsky et Mme von Meck," *La revue musicale* (November 1935): 250.

52. MR: FL 2003 faithfully renders Mme von Meck's return address, giving the Julian calendar date (also known as the "Old Style") of 8 February as well as its Gregorian equivalent (or "New Style," used by European countries at the time and adopted in Russia after 1918) of 20 February.

53. The manuscript, preserved today at the Glinka Museum in Moscow, comprises only the third movement of this Symphony, an Allegro. MR: The score—for piano, four hands—is dated December 1880–January 1881.

54. The daughters were Julia, the oldest; Sonia, whom, according to a persistent legend, Achille had courted (see François Lesure, *Claude Debussy: Biographie critique* [Paris: Fayard, 2003], 457); and Ludmilla, the youngest, born in 1872. MR: Mme von Meck's letter is reprinted in *C*, 11–12.

55. MR: FL 2003 mistakenly attributes Dubois's remarks from the exams for the composition class to those of the first round of the *concours* in June 1881.

56. Archives nationales AJ/37/237/1 (notebook of Dubois). MR: See Clevenger, "Origins of Debussy's Style," 186.

57. MR: See Vidal, "Souvenirs d'Achille Debussy," 13 (109).

58. The sole opinion on Tchaikovsky's music later conveyed by Debussy was on the occasion of a Concert Colonne on 15 March 1903, in which Leopold Auer played the *Sérénade mélancolique* for violin; Debussy called it, as he did a Brahms concerto, "boring rubble." MR: See Debussy's review, "Au concert Colonne," from *Gil Blas* (16 March 1903), in Debussy, *Monsieur Croche*, rev. ed., 126, and in English translation in Debussy, *Debussy on Music*, 146.

59. MR: FL 2003 mistakenly cites this obituary as having appeared in *La revue blanche*. In fact, it comes from "À la Schola Cantorum," *Gil Blas* (2 February 1903); see Debussy, *Monsieur Croche*, rev. ed., 94, and in English translation in Debussy, *Debussy on Music*, 114.

60. MR: *Les cloches de Corneville* is an opéra comique by Robert Planquette that was premiered on 19 April 1877 at the Théâtre des Folies-Dramatiques.

61. MR: FL 2003 erroneously states that "Triolet à Philis" and "Souhait" were drawn from Banville's collection of *Les Stalactites* rather than from his *Les Cariatides*. The text for "Nuit d'étoiles" (1880), Debussy's first published song, was drawn from Banville's *Stalactites*.

62. Nicolas von Meck's memoirs were published by Lockspeiser in his first *Debussy* (London: J. M. Dent & Sons, 1936), 279–81. MR: It is perhaps worth noting that Lockspeiser translated Debussy's *air songeur* as a "longing" look rather than a "pensive" one, as I have translated it.

63. MR: See Vidal's letter of 12 July 1884 to Mme Henriette Fuchs in François Lesure, "Debussy de 1883 à 1885 d'après la correspondance de Paul Vidal à Henriette Fuchs," *Revue de musicologie* 48, no. 125 (July–December 1962): 100.

64. MR: "Ici-bas" was composed by Lucien Hillemacher (1860–1909) and Paul Hillemacher (1852–1933) and published by Alphonse Leduc (plate number A.L. 6585). In 1932, Max Eschig published it under Debussy's name, in a collection of *Quatre mélodies* that included (in order) "Rondeau," "Chanson d'un fou" (actually by Émile Pessard), "Ici-bas," and "Zéphyr" (Banville's "Triolet à Philis").

65. MR: See Louis Laloy, *Debussy* (Paris: Aux Armes de France, 1944), 6 [reprint of Laloy's *Claude Debussy*, Paris: Les bibliophiles fantaisistes, 1909].

66. See Debussy's letter of 21 November 1910 to André Caplet [in *C*, 1331–32].

67. MR: Cited in Vallas, "Achille Debussy jugé par ses professeurs," 49, and in Clevenger, "Origins of Debussy's Style," 186.

68. MR: Mélanie Hélène Bonis was known professionally as Mel Bonis; FL 2003 here (following Vallas in his "Achille Debussy jugé par ses professeurs," 49) cites both her given name and the full name by which she was commonly known. See Pierre, *Conservatoire national*, 703.

69. MR: See Vallas, "Achille Debussy jugé par ses professeurs," 49, and Clevenger, "Origins of Debussy's Style," 186.

70. Raymond Bonheur, "Souvenirs et impressions d'un compagnon de jeunesse," *La revue musicale* (1 May 1926): 5n3 (101n3).

71. MR: The complete score of "Les elfes" was brought to light by Denis Herlin, ed., in *Quatre nouvelles mélodies* (Paris: Durand, 2012), 11–22.

72. MR: The phrase "Avec le gracieux concours de Mme Vasnier et de Mr Achille de Bussy" was printed on the program; see n73.

73. The program was reproduced in *La revue musicale* (1 May 1926): 18 (114); and in Margaret G. Cobb, *The Poetic Debussy*, 2nd ed. (Rochester, NY: University of Rochester Press, 1994), illustration no. 3, inserted after p. [194]. MR: As the manuscript of the *Nocturne et Scherzo*, which is for violoncello and piano, postdates this performance, it is likely that the work was originally composed for violin and piano, and that the extant manuscript is actually a transcription of what Thieberg and Debussy played in May 1882; see Lesure, *Claude Debussy: Biographie critique*, 486.

74. MR: Marius Dillard's "Rondel chinois" was published in the 5 May 1878 edition of the *Union littéraire des poètes et prosateurs* as the result of his winning a poetry competition. The eighteen-year-old poet would subsequently make his living in Rouen as a journalist. See Denis Herlin, "Les mélodies de Debussy," 24 and 176, in *Claude Debussy: Intégrale des mélodies*, Ligia LIDI 0201285–14, 4 CDs.

75. MR: The original dedication of the "Rondel chinois" is a clever pun on the word "chinois": "À Mme Vanier [sic], la seule qui peut chanter et faire oublier tout ce que cette musique a d'inchantable et de chinois." In French, the phrase "pour moi, c'est du chinois" is the equivalent of "It's Greek to me" in English.

76. This receipt is reproduced in facsimile by Maurice Boucher in *Claude Debussy* (Paris: Éditions Rieder, 1930), plate 5. Bulla himself made arrangements (notably of Mendelssohn).

4. The Path to the Prix de Rome: 1882–84

1. On 12 April 1882, he had composed for his beloved a song on a text by Banville, "Le lilas," commemorating the springtime blooming of the lilacs.

2. In addition to the score for voices and orchestra, Debussy made a reduction of the work for chorus and two pianos. Pierné handled the same text, but without accompaniment. MR: For a discussion of the sources as well as an analysis of "Salut printemps," see Marie Rolf, "Debussy's Rites of Spring," in *Rethinking Debussy*, ed. Elliott Antokoletz and Marianne Wheeldon (Oxford: Oxford University Press, 2011), 3–10.

3. Archives nationales, AJ 37/237/1. MR: See Dubois's report from 26 June 1882 in John Clevenger, "The Origins of Debussy's Style" (PhD diss., University of Rochester, 2002), 186.

4. MR: See Clevenger, "Origins of Debussy's Style," 186, and facsimile 243 in Fonds FL, BnF, carton I/6(1).

5. MR: This poem came from Armand Renaud's collection, *Les nuits persanes*—hence Debussy's subtitle. In 1872, Camille Saint-Saëns had published six *Mélodies persanes*, op. 26 (Paris: G. Hartmann), drawn from the same collection of poetry.

6. MR: "Le triomphe de Bacchus à son retour des Indes" is one of the later poems in Banville's *Les Stalactites*.

7. MR: See Constant Pierre, *Le Conservatoire national de musique et de déclamation* (Paris: Imprimerie nationale, 1900), 806.

8. MR: The second honorable mention shared by Missa and Debussy was for the *concours* in counterpoint and fugue; see Pierre, *Conservatoire national*, 536.

9. This is the only award that Missa (1861–1910) would receive at the Conservatoire—which did not prevent him from performing *comique* or *bouffe* operas nearly every year after 1886. He was the organist at Saint-Thomas d'Aquin. MR: See Debussy's review, "À propos de 'Muguette,'" *Gil Blas* (23 March 1903) in Claude Debussy, *Monsieur Croche et autres écrits*, rev. ed. (Paris: Gallimard, 1987): 131–32; and in Claude Debussy, *Debussy on Music*, trans. Richard Langham Smith (New York: Alfred A. Knopf, 1977), 153–54.

10. MR: See Marguerite Vasnier, "Debussy à dix-huit ans," *La revue musicale* (1 May 1926): 19 (115).

11. MR: See Madame von Meck's letter to Tchaikovsky from 9 September 1882 in Vladimir A. Zhdanov and Nikolai T. Zhegin, eds., *P. I. Chaikovskii: Perepiska s N. F. von-Mekk*, 3 vols. (Moscow: Academia, 1934–36), 3:94.

12. MR: See Madame von Meck's letter to Tchaikovsky from 2 September 1881 in Zhdanov and Zhegin, *P. I. Chaikovskii*, 2:544.

13. Paul Vidal's memories, published in "Souvenirs d'Achille Debussy," *La revue musicale* (1 May 1926): 13 (109), are inaccurate on this point. *Tristan* was not given in Vienna that year, but rather on 4 October 1883.

14. The date on the manuscript of "Mandoline" is 25 November; that of "En sourdine" is "Vienne = 16. Sep. 82." The latter date was probably recopied by Achille from an earlier manuscript, since he did not leave for Vienna until October.

15. MR: See Madame von Meck's letter to Tchaikovsky from 17 July 1884 in Zhdanov and Zhegin, *P. I. Chaikovskii*, 3:287.

16. Reproduced in an article by Arnold Schœnberg, "Conviction ou connaissance," *Musique* 1, no. 4 (15 January 1928): 157. MR: The original dedication reads as follows: "Je vous la souhaite bonne et heureuse," and "Parmi les souhaits qui montent vers vous, permettez moi [sic] de former celui-ci: que vous soyez toujours celle qui a donné la forme revèe [sic] par les musiciens en delire [sic] a [sic] la pauvre musique de celui qui sera toujours votre ami et compositeur dévoue [sic]."

17. MR: Georges Favre, *Compositeurs français méconnus: Ernest Guiraud et ses amis Émile Paladilhe et Théodore Dubois* (Paris: La Pensée universelle, 1983), 36–37.

18. Favre, *Compositeurs français méconnus*, 37.

19. MR: See Clevenger, "Origins of Debussy's Style," 187, and facsimile 413 in Fonds FL, BnF, carton I/6(1).

20. MR: This collection, known as the Recueil Vasnier, is among the holdings of the Bibliothèque nationale de France, département de la Musique (Ms Gr-Res 17716 [1–9]). Formerly owned by Henry Prunières, the Recueil Vasnier was published in facsimile by the Centre de documentation Claude Debussy in 2011. A critical edition of the thirteen songs in the collection is available in the *Œuvres complètes de Claude Debussy*, sér. II, vol. 2, ed. Marie Rolf (Paris: Durand, 2016).

21. MR: FL 2003 states that "Séguidille" was given to Marie "a few months earlier," but the precise date of this song is difficult to determine, since the sole complete manuscript of the composition bears no date. That said, it was initially intended to be a part of the Recueil Vasnier, and in fact one folio, containing a draft of the song, was excised from the volume. This folio followed the only other song in the collection that was also based on a poem by Théophile Gautier: "Coquetterie posthume." The latter bears the date of "31. Mars. 83." and so it is reasonable to conclude that "Séguidille" was composed between the first half of 1883 and the first half of 1884, during which time the Recueil Vasnier was completed. "Séguidille" was not published until 2014, in an edition by Marie Rolf (Paris: Durand); it is also included in Rolf, *Œuvres complètes de Claude Debussy*, sér. II, vol. 2, 66–75.

22. MR: See the report in "Paris et départements," *Le ménestrel* 49, no. 29 (17 June 1883): 231.

23. MR: See Vasnier, "Debussy à dix-huit ans," 21 (117).

24. MR: Cited in Marcel Dietschy, *La passion de Claude Debussy* (Neuchâtel: Éditions de la Baconnière, 1962), 42–43. See also the English translation by William Ashbrook and Margaret G. Cobb, *A Portrait of Claude Debussy* (Oxford: Oxford University Press, 1990), 35.

25. Ernest Reyer, "Revue musicale: Académie des Beaux-Arts," *Journal des débats politiques et littéraires* (28 October 1883): (2).

26. B. W., "Concours de l'Institut," *L'art musical* 22, no. 26 (28 June 1883): 201.

27. MR: See Édouard Noël and Edmond Stoullig, *Les annales du théâtre et de la musique* (Paris: G. Charpentier et Cie, 1884), 318.

28. Vidal, "Souvenirs d'Achille Debussy," 15 (111).

29. MR: Bourget married Minnie David in 1890.

30. A remark reported without reference by Edward Lockspeiser, *Debussy: His Life and Mind* (Cambridge: Cambridge University Press, 1978), 1:67. [The citation originally appeared in Henry Prunières, "À la Villa Médicis," *La revue musicale* (1 May 1926): 25n2 (121n2).] Bourget would grant the right to set these two poems to music only on 29 October 1892, for 50 francs (Léon Vallas, *Claude Debussy et son temps*, [Paris: Éditions Albin Michel, 1958], 41n1).

31. MR: Baudelaire is often credited with coining the term "modernity" to suggest the ephemeral and fleeting experiences of life, especially during a given period of time, and art's ability not only to reflect this experience but also to distill its eternal and immutable qualities. His essay "Le peintre de la vie moderne" was published in three consecutive issues of the *Figaro*, on 26 and 29 November and 3 December 1863. See especially the section on "La modernité" in *Le Figaro* (26 November 1863): 4–5; and in English translation in Charles Baudelaire, *The Painter of Modern Life and Other Essays by Charles Baudelaire*, trans. and ed. Jonathan Mayne (London: Phaidon, 1964), 12–15.

32. MR: See Vasnier, "Debussy à dix-huit ans," 20 (116).

33. See p. 98 of François Lesure, "Debussy de 1883 à 1885 d'après la correspondence de Paul Vidal à Henriette Fuchs," *Revue de musicologie* 48, no. 125 (July–December 1962): 98–101.

34. MR: To the present day, the École des mines remains one of the top engineering schools in France.

35. MR: See François Lesure, "Debussy et la Concordia (1883–1885)," *Cahiers Debussy* 3 (1976): 3. An extract of the statues of the Concordia, reprinted in a program booklet of a performance of J. S. Bach's *Matthäus-Passion* on 16 May 1888 (see "Programmes—Association Concordia" at the BnF, département de la Musique), reiterates this citation but specifies that the Concordia's purpose was to study both "old and new" choral masterpieces.

36. Vallas, *Claude Debussy et son temps*, 55, asserts that every week, Achille had "a meeting followed by long conversations" with Gounod at the Concordia.

37. MR: This information is taken again from an extract of the statues of the Concordia, reprinted in a program booklet of a performance of J. S. Bach's *Matthäus-Passion* on 16 May 1888; see "Programmes—Association Concordia," BnF, département de la Musique.

38. MR: The Mendelssohn performance of 21 December 1882 had been reported by Gaston Dubreuilh in *Le ménestrel* 49, no. 5 (31 December 1882): 39,

while that of Gounod's *Rédemption* was mentioned in *Le ménestrel* 49, no. 28 (10 June 1883): 223, and in a notice by Edmond de Pressensé in "Revue du mois," *Revue chrétienne* 30 (April 1883): 253–54. On 16 May 1883, the Concordia had performed the *Chœurs d'Ulysse*, composed in 1852 by Gounod on texts by François Ponsard; see L. A. Bourgault-Ducoudray, "Concerts et soirées," *Le ménestrel* 49, no. 26 (27 May 1883): 207. We might add that *Athalie* and Robert Schumann's *Paradis et la Péri*, as well as Charles-Ferdinand Lenepveu's *Laudate*, were performed in early February 1885, shortly after Debussy left for Rome, as per a notice in *Le ménestrel* 51, no. 10 (8 February 1885): 80. Two months later, the Concordia celebrated the 200th anniversary of J. S. Bach's birth with a concert that included a cantata as well as his *Magnificat*, in which Mme Fuchs sang as a soloist; see the notice in *Le ménestrel* 51, no. 21 (26 April 1885): 167.

39. MR: See Henriette Fuchs, "Le bi-centenaire de Bach," *Revue chrétienne* 32 (1885): 846.

40. [*C*, 14].

41. MR: *C*, 14. According to Lesure and Herlin, this telegram may have been written in December 1883.

42. MR: *C*, 15. Lesure and Herlin ascribe a date of the end of December 1883 for this note.

43. A partial citation of Vidal's letter may be found in Lesure, "Debussy et la Concordia," 5. MR: A full citation is given in Lesure, "Debussy de 1883 à 1885," 98–99.

44. MR: This concert, which took place in the Salle Érard, was reported in "Nouvelles diverses: Concerts et soirées," *Le ménestrel* 50, no. 7 (13 January 1884): 55. Other works performed included compositions by Schumann, Saint-Saëns, Ritter, and George Frideric Handel. "M. Ch.-M. Widor" conducted the chorus and orchestra, and "M. de Bussy" was listed as the accompanist. The original program may be seen in "Programmes—Association Concordia," BnF, département de la Musique, and a photocopy of the program, along with a review by Henry Fouquier in *Le clarion* (4 February 1884), may be found within the Dietschy material, in DOSS-2.32 of the CDCD.

45. MR: A photocopy of the actual concert program is preserved in Fonds FL, BnF, carton I/6(11) and also among the Dietschy material in DOSS-2.32 of the CDCD. The choruses were conducted by Charles-Marie Widor, and the "Accompagnateur" was listed as "M. De Bussy." The event was favorably reviewed in "Nouvelles diverses: Concerts et soirées," *Le ménestrel* 50, no. 15 (9 March 1884): 119.

46. MR: This concert was reviewed in "Nouvelles diverses: Concerts et soirées," *Le ménestrel* 50, no. 20 (13 April 1884): 159.

47. MR: This concert, given in the Salle Érard, also included excerpts from Lenepveu's *Velléda*. It was a benefit concert for the Miséricorde, chaired by Mme la maréchale de MacMahon (the widow of Patrice MacMahon, who had served as President of the Third Republic from 1875 until his death in 1879), and was reviewed in "Nouvelles diverses: Paris et départements," *Le ménestrel* 50, no. 26 (25 May 1884): 206.

48. MR: *C*, 15–16; according to Lesure and Herlin, this letter was written after 14 January 1884.

49. "Nouvelles diverses: Concerts et soirées," *Le ménestrel* 50, no. 11 (10 February 1884): 88.

50. MR: See Vidal's letter of 12 July 1884 to Henriette Fuchs in Lesure, "Debussy de 1883 à 1885," 99.

51. Jacques Durand, *Quelques souvenirs d'un éditeur de musique* (Paris: A. Durand & fils, 1924), 1:28.

52. MR: This quote is from p. 224 of Maurice Emmanuel, "Debussy inconnu," *Revue Pleyel* 43 (April 1927): 223–25.

53. MR: The *plein jeu* is a mixture stop, with pipes sounding in octaves and fifths at least two octaves above the key that is depressed, and the *cornet, nazard,* and *tierce* engage the higher harmonics (octaves, third, and fifths) above the depressed key.

54. Emmanuel, "Debussy inconnu," *Revue Pleyel* 43 (April 1927), 224.

55. MR: This quote is taken from Léo Dilé's French translation of Lockspeiser: *Debussy: Sa vie et sa pensée* (Paris: Fayard, 1980), 84. However, it appears to be a mélange that has been extracted from several Emmanuel sources; see details in the following notes.

56. MR: Emmanuel alludes to the buses along the faubourg Poissonière in Pelléas et Mélisande *de Claude Debussy: Étude historique et critique, analyse musicale* (Paris: Paul Mellottée, Éditeur, [1926]), repr. as Pelléas et Mélisande *de Claude Debussy: Étude et analyse* (Paris: Éditions Mellottée, 1950), 39; and in "Debussy inconnu," *Revue Pleyel* 41 (February 1927): 156.

57. MR: This passage comes from Emmanuel's Pelléas et Mélisande *de Claude Debussy,* 103.

58. This passage is paraphrased from p. 45 of Maurice Emmanuel, "Les ambitions de Claude-Achille," *La revue musicale* (1 May 1926): 43–50 (139–46); see also p. 36 in the reprint, *La revue musicale* 258 (April 1964): 33–40.

59. David Grayson, "Claude Debussy Addresses the English-speaking World: Two Interviews, an Article, and *The Blessed Damozel,*" *Cahiers Debussy,* nouv. sér. 16 (1992): 27.

60. Vallas, *Claude Debussy et son temps,* 55–56.

61. MR: See Vidal's letter to Henriette Fuchs, from 30 May 1884, in Lesure, "Debussy de 1883 à 1885," 99.

62. MR: See Pierre, *Conservatoire national,* 539, as well as Durand, *Quelques souvenirs,* 1:29–30.

63. MR: See Durand, *Quelques souvenirs,* 1:30.

64. MR: See Rés. Vmc. Ms. 140 (listed in FL 2003 as "recently rediscovered," and apparently acquired by the département de la Musique of the BnF in 1998).

65. MR: Emmanuel, Pelléas et Mélisande *de Claude Debussy,* 16.

66. MR: Cited in Dietschy, *Passion de Claude Debussy,* 45, and in Dietschy, *Portrait of Claude Debussy,* 37.

67. MR: See Arthur Pougin, "Nouvelles diverses: Paris et départements," *Le ménestrel* 50, no. 31 (29 June 1884): 247; and Arthur Pougin, "Étranger: France (Correspondance particulière)," *Le guide musical* 30, nos. 28 and 29 (10 and 17 July 1884): 202–3.

68. MR: A. Héler and Landely were both pseudonyms for Amédée Louis Hettich (1856–1937), a music journalist, publisher, and voice teacher who was

known for his collection of 140 *Vocalises-Études* by many different composers, published in fourteen volumes in 1905. See Pierre, *Conservatoire national*, 775.

69. MR: A. Héler, "Concours de l'Institut," *L'art musical* 23, no. 10 (15 July 1884): 73–74.

70. MR: Charles Darcours, "Notes de musique: Le Prix de Rome," *Le Figaro* (2 July 1884): 6.

71. See André Suarès and Romain Rolland, "Cette âme ardente. . . Choix de letters de André Suarès à Romain Rolland," *Cahiers Romain Rolland* 5 (1954): 206. Debussy himself, at the idea of revisiting this score in 1907, wrote to Durand: "It must nevertheless be corrected, as I'm fairly sure that the 'original' orchestration reeks of 'the competition,' 'the Conservatoire,' and the boredom. . ." [See his letter of 17 July 1907 in *C*, 1015.]

72. MR: See Jean Ritz, "Nouvelles diverses: Paris—Une épave," *Le progrès artistique* 7, no. 323 (11 July 1884): 2.

73. MR: See Claude Debussy, "Les impressions d'un Prix de Rome," *Gil Blas* (10 June 1903): [1]. Reprinted in Debussy, *Monsieur Croche*, rev. ed., 189, and in English translation in *Debussy on Music*, 211–12.

74. Before 1863, the duration of the residents' stay would have been as long as five years. MR: The Prix de Rome winners were expected to spend usually three years, with at least two of them in residence, at the Villa Medici. Concomitantly, they received four years of financial support, with the expectation that they would send an annual composition to the Institut; see Clevenger, "Origins of Debussy's Style," 131. The rules, procedures, and many details of the Prix de Rome were discussed at length by Henri Rabaud, a former Prix de Rome winner in composition and director of the Conservatoire from 1922 to 1941; see "La défense du prix de Rome par un ancien pensionnaire," *La revue de Paris* 12, no. 2 (15 March 1905): 373–418, an article that was reprinted in *Le concours du prix de Rome de musique* (1803–1968), ed. Julia Lu and Alexandre Dratwicki (Paris: Symétrie, 2011), 803–30.

75. Maurice Dangremont was a Brazilian violinist who was performing by the age of nine (1877).

76. MR: This letter—excerpted in Autographs et Documents divers, Hôtel Drouot, 18 December 1969, a copy of which is in the Fonds FL, BnF, carton I/6(1)—is reproduced in Lesure, "Debussy de 1883 à 1885," 99–100.

77. This increase plus an allowance of 75 francs for the composers was announced in *Le ménestrel* 50, no. 18 (30 March 1884): 142. Marcel Dietschy gives different amounts prior to that decision; see his *Passion de Claude Debussy*, 56n5 [and *Portrait of Claude Debussy*, 40n6].

78. Vincent d'Indy won the first prize, out of seventeen applicants, with *Le chant de la cloche*.

79. MR: In their communications with each other, Gounod was now addressing Debussy as "tu" rather than the more formal "vous."

80. A fragment of this letter is reproduced in facsimile by Maurice Boucher in *Claude Debussy* (Paris: Éditions Rieder, 1930), plate 11.

81. MR: A report on Saint-Saëns's very academic and boring speech was given by A. Héler in "À l'Académie," *L'art musical* 23, no. 17 (31 October 1884): 129–30.

82. Cited on pp. 38–39 of Alfred Bruneau, "Souvenirs inédits," *Revue internationale de musique française* 7 (February 1982): 9–82.

83. MR: His mother Charlotte was the daughter of Charles Lucien Bonaparte and Zénaïde Bonaparte. His father was Pietro Primoli, Count of Foglia. Giuseppe collected art and items connected to the Bonaparte side of his family, and eventually donated them to the city of Rome; today, these treasures are housed in the Museo Napoleonico.

84. About Primoli, see Marcello Spaziani's edition of Primoli, *Pages inédites* (Rome: Edizioni di storia e letteratura, 1959), and Marcello Spaziani, *Con Gégé Primoli nella Roma bizantina* (Roma: Edizioni di storia e letteratura, 1962). Princess Mathilde was said to be the Princess of Parma in *The Remembrance of Things Past*. MR: See George D. Painter, *Marcel Proust: A Biography* (New York: Random House, 1989), 1:97.

85. MR: Lesure and Herlin posit a date of November 1884 for this letter; see *C*, 19.

86. [*C*, 20.]

87. MR: See Debussy's letter from 15 January 1885 to Henriette Fuchs in *C*, 21.

88. MR: See Lesure, "Debussy et la Concordia," 5.

89. MR: Debussy referred to Claudius Popelin's advice in a letter to him from 24 June 1885; see *C*, 31.

5. The Villa Medici: 1885–87

1. The dates of Debussy's letters to Vasnier, as Henry Prunières published them in "À la Villa Médicis," *La revue musicale* (1 May 1926): 23–42 (119–38), are often incorrect, with frequent confusion between 1885 and 1886. MR: These errors have been corrected in *C*.

2. MR: See Claude Debussy, "Les impressions d'un Prix de Rome," *Gil Blas* (10 June 1903): [1]. Reprinted in Claude Debussy, *Monsieur Croche et autres écrits*, rev. ed. (Paris: Gallimard, 1987), 189; and in Claude Debussy, *Debussy on Music*, trans. Richard Langham Smith (New York: Alfred A. Knopf, 1977), 212.

3. René Patris d'Uckermann, *Ernest Hébert, 1817–1908* (Paris: Éditions de la Réunion des musées nationaux, 1982), 176.

4. MR: See Achille's letter to Henri Vasnier from the beginning of February 1885 in *C*, 22–23.

5. MR: Mentioned in Vidal's letter to Henriette Fuchs from 15 April 1884; see François Lesure, "Debussy de 1883 à 1885 d'après la correspondence de Paul Vidal à Henriette Fuchs," *Revue de musicologie* 48 (July–December 1962): 99.

6. MR: See Vidal's memoirs in Henri Rebois, *Les grands Prix de Rome de musique à l'Académie de France* (Paris: Firmin-Didot et Cie, 1932), 78.

7. MR: See Vidal's letter to Henriette Fuchs from 16 February 1885 in Lesure, "Debussy de 1883 à 1885," 100.

8. MR: Lesure, "Debussy de 1883 à 1885," 100–101.

9. Reproduced in François Lesure, *Claude Debussy: Iconographie musicale* (Geneva: Minkoff & Lattès, 1980), 36. MR: Given the title of his winning

composition for the Prix de Rome (*L'enfant prodigue*), Debussy's description of himself as "l'enfant prodigue" is an obvious *double entendre*.

10. MR: The photo is inserted between pp. 48 and 49 of Léon Vallas, *Claude Debussy et son temps* (Paris: Librairie Félix Alcan, 1932).

11. MR: Henry Prunières, in "À la Villa Médicis," *La revue musicale* (1 May 1926): 23 (119), pointed out that many painters, sculptors, and architects favored Debussy's cantata, while most of the composers were less enthusiastic.

12. Gabriel Pierné, "Souvenirs d'Achille Debussy," *La revue musicale* (1 May 1926): 11 (107).

13. Paul Vidal, "Souvenirs d'Achille Debussy," *La revue musicale* (1 May 1926): 15 (111).

14. MR: See Vidal's remembrance of this event in Rebois, *Les grands Prix de Rome de musique*, 61.

15. Vidal clearly asserted this in his second set of memoirs, published in Rebois, *Les grands Prix de Rome de musique*, 61, though he had not included this information in the recollections he had entrusted to the *Revue musicale*. The members of the Institut were not completely blind to the artistic benefits that the young musicians could look forward to while in Rome. A few weeks before Achille's departure, Saint-Saëns noted in front of his colleagues at the Académie that if the residents did not draw much benefit from these years, it was partly due to the fact that they had little occasion to hear music in Rome (Archives Académie des beaux-arts, 2 E-17, meeting of 27 September 1884 [see Lesure's notes in Fonds Lesure, BnF, carton I/6(11)]). If one looks at the programs from the Apollo, Argentina, and Costanzi theaters for the year 1886, one finds *Les Huguenots*, *Faust*, *Rigoletto*, *Don Giovanni*, *Otello*, and *Les pêcheurs des perles*. It seems that, in addition to hearing *Lohengrin* and *Aida*, Achille attended a performance of Donizetti's *La favorite* at the Argentina in April 1886.

16. MR: Achille expressed his despondency in these exact terms in his letter to Henri Vasnier from 23 April 1885; see *C*, 26.

17. [*C*, 23.]

18. MR: FL 2003 gives the date of the letter as 5 May 1885; however, Debussy also writes "Wednesday" along with the date. As explained by Lesure and Herlin in *C*, 27n2, 5 May was a Tuesday. Furthermore, as Debussy alludes to the first fifteen days of the month at the beginning of the letter, Lesure and Herlin logically ascribe a date of 20 May to it; see *C*, 27.

19. Marcel Dietschy, *La passion de Claude Debussy* (Neuchâtel: Éditions de la Baconnière, 1962), 56–57n9. MR: See also the English translation by William Ashbrook and Margaret G. Cobb, *A Portrait of Claude Debussy* (Oxford: Oxford University Press, 1990), 43n9.

20. Her journal is preserved in the Musée Hébert in Paris. MR: Because the museum (in the Hôtel de Montmorency at 85 rue du Cherche-midi) has been closed, all of the entries in Gabrielle Hébert's journal have been corroborated against notes carefully taken by Denis Herlin. I am grateful to him for sharing them with me. All subsequent references to Mme Hébert's journal have been confirmed by Herlin's notes but are not footnoted individually, to avoid encumbering the text.

21. [From Debussy's "Les impressions d'un Prix de Rome," *Gil Blas* (10 June 1903); reprinted in] Debussy, *Monsieur Croche*, rev. ed., 189, [and in English translation in *Debussy on Music*, 212].

22. MR: D'Uckermann, *Ernest Hébert*, 177.

23. D'Uckermann, *Ernest Hébert*, 178.

24. MR: See Debussy, *Monsieur Croche*, rev. ed., 176, and Debussy, *Debussy on Music*, 199.

25. This is how the German woman referred to her husband—as "Alles" [Everything] or even "Mon Alles" [My All].

26. MR: The Acqua acetosa is a mineral spring in Rome, located at a beautiful site near a beach on the Tiber River, where picnickers would often come to drink the water.

27. MR: D'Uckermann, *Ernest Hébert*, 178, notes that Princess Scilla was an old friend of the Héberts.

28. [According to Annie et Gabriel Verger, *Dictionnaire biographique des pensionnaires de l'Académie de France à Rome* (Dijon: Échelle de Jacob, 2011): 2:875 and 3:1138, Jules-Jacques] Jean Labatut was a sculptor and Henri Naudé an engraver.

29. Henri Deglane was an architect and William Barbotin an engraver. MR: Mme Castellani may have been a member of the famous jewelry family.

30. [*C*, 33.] In his *Souvenirs de jeunesse (1866–1900): Pages choisies* (Lausanne: La guilde du livre, 1947), 78–81, Romain Rolland, who was a boarder at the Farnese palace between 1889 and 1891, drew a rather warm portrait of Ernest, whom he also accompanied at the piano, but a less flattering one of Gabrielle, "his lovely Rubenesque wife, blond, pink, large and fat, who did not even try to conceal her arrogant disdain for the French; she treated the young artists a little less well than she did her little curs who, at her soirees, blocked the seats of the parlors, pissing on the precious Gobelin tapestries and nipping at the calves of the arriving guests." On 5 June 1905, the report in Mme de Saint-Marceaux's journal would be even less flattering: "This Hébert woman is an odious creature, a jealous and vulgar German, the illegitimate daughter of a German prince, they say, who has slept with the boarders at the Villa Medici; she is bitter and mean." MR: See Marguerite de Saint-Marceaux, *Journal, 1894–1927*, ed. Myriam Chimènes et al. (Paris: Librairie Arthème Fayard, 2007), 396.

31. MR: See Louis Laloy, *Claude Debussy* (Paris: Les bibliophiles fantaisistes, 1909), 17.

32. The count typically had his guests sign their names on these Japanese scrolls. An exhibit in Rome was devoted to them. See Maria Elisa Tittoni Monti et al., *Frammenti di un salotto: Giuseppe Primoli, i suoi kakemono e altro* (Rome: Marsilio Editori, 1983), 77.

33. Remember that in her memoirs ("Debussy à dix-huit ans," *La revue musicale* [1 May 1926]: 17 [113]), Marguerite Vasnier described the long strolls and the croquet parties in the park at Saint-Cloud, during the period when Debussy was going to the Vasniers' home at the Ville-d'Avray, just a short distance south of Saint-Cloud, in the summertime. MR: Debussy's tempo marking, alluding to the fair at Saint-Cloud, is likely intended to conjure up the continuous, circular rhythm of a carousel with its wooden horses.

34. The Vasniers spent their vacation in Dieppe, as they would in 1887, in the villa of the painter Armand Constant Mélicourt. Edgar Degas and Jacques-Émile Blanche also happened to be there.

35. MR: FL 2003 gives the time as 6:00 in error.

36. MR: For Debussy's letter of 24 June 1885, see *C*, 31.

37. MR: See Achille's letter to Claudius Popelin from August 1885 in *C*, 35.

38. MR: See Achille's letter to Henri Vasnier from the beginning of September 1885 in *C*, 37.

39. MR: See Achille's letter to Gustave Popelin from the beginning of July 1885 in *C*, 34.

40. This portrait was reproduced [and inserted between pp. 24 and 25] in the *Revue musicale* (1 May 1926). The Netherlands Institute in Paris houses Henri Vasnier's letter (23 November 1885) asking Paul Baudry to make the portrait of his wife. MR: According to Charles Ephrussi, *Paul Baudry, sa vie et son œuvre* (Paris: Ludovic Baschet, 1887), 274, Baudry's painting of Mme Vasnier was his last portrait, and an incomplete one at that, before his death in 1886. His reputation had been established since the period during which he had painted the elaborate foyer within the Opéra Garnier, which had opened in 1875. Hébert and Baudry had known each other for a long time; they each had won a Prix de Rome and thus lived at the Villa Medici, beginning in 1840 for Hébert and in 1850 for Baudry. It would have been quite natural for these old friends to be dining together in Paris and gossiping about mutual acquaintances.

41. MR: In his private notes, Marcel Dietschy described M. Vasnier as a "very closed, cold" individual who "knew about the liaison between Debussy and [his] wife and was closing his eyes"; see DOSS-04.78 in the Dietschy material at the CDCD. In *Passion de Claude Debussy*, 38, Dietschy softened his language somewhat, describing M. Vasnier as "un homme froid, secret" and his wife as the opposite: "une de ces femmes de tempérament, dont le mari finit par prendre son parti de n'être qu'un mari." Ashbrook and Cobb, in *Portrait of Claude Debussy*, 31, translate this passage as follows: "M. Vasnier was a cold man, secret" and "Mme Vasnier was the exact opposite of her husband. She was one of those women of character whose husbands end up being only husbands."

42. MR: While FL 2003 suggested a date from the end of 1886 for this letter, Lesure and Herlin ascribe the date of December 1885, based on Debussy's handwriting; see *C*, 47–48. FL 2003 also states that M. Vasnier's letters to Debussy stopped by the end of the summer of 1886; however, they appear to have tapered off already by the beginning of that year, following the Hébert's lunch with Baudry in Paris in December 1885.

43. MR: The Académie responded to the first part of his work on *Zuleima*: "We note with regret that this boarder today seems to be preoccupied solely with creating the strange, the bizarre, the unintelligible, the unplayable. In spite of several passages that do not lack a certain character, the work's vocal part offers no interest, in terms of either the melody or the declamation." See the transcript of the report in François Lesure, *Claude Debussy: Biographie critique* (Paris: Fayard, 2003), 572; the contents of this report have been confirmed by Denis Herlin.

44. *L'art en Italie*, reprinted in *Le ménestrel* 52, no. 21 (25 April 1886): 169, announced *Diane au bois* as the *envoi* on which Debussy was working.

45. MR: Lesure is likely referring to the composition of either Bourget's "Romance (L'âme évaporée et souffrante)" or his "Les cloches," neither of which was published until 1891 by Durand–Schoenewerk.

46. Letter of 7 October from Vidal to Henriette Fuchs. [This letter is not reproduced in Lesure, "Debussy de 1883 à 1885."] Certain Villa Medici boarders knew better than Debussy how to profit from their connections in order to gain admittance into Roman salons. Pierné would often go to Mme Hegermann-Lindencronne, the wife of a Danish minister; there he met Edvard Grieg and performed two-piano improvisations with Franz Liszt. Paul Vidal attended Mme Egerton Castle's salon, a decidedly Wagnerian circle, where he got to know Joseph Rubinstein, Countess Doenhoff, and a pianist friend of Wagner, Malwida von Meysenbug. And for two years he audited the piano class that Liszt still gave—which Achille could have done just as well, if he had not decided that Roman society was "closed and unwelcoming to the young residents whose youthful and very French independence mixed badly with the coolness of the Romans." See Debussy, "Les impressions d'un Prix de Rome," *Gil Blas* (10 June 1903); reprinted in Debussy, *Monsieur Croche*, rev. ed., 190, [and in Debussy, *Debussy on Music*, 213].

47. MR: This is likely a pun on an *étouffe chrétien*, a heavy dish that is very rich and hard to digest. A traditional *galette des rois* for Twelfth Night could easily qualify, for it is often made with frangipane, a mixture of butter, sugar, eggs, and almond paste. The cake comes with a crown on top, which is awarded to the person who finds the *fève*, or charm, within the piece given him or her. Debussy's reference to an *étouffe coquin* implies that the Twelfth Night cake will "stuff the rascals."

48. MR: Princess Wittgenstein's forty-year relationship with Franz Liszt is well known.

49. MR: See Rebois, *Les grands Prix de Rome de musique*, 60.

50. On 1 September 1915, Debussy still remembered "that art of making a sort of *breathing* with the pedal that I had observed in Liszt's playing, when I was able to hear him, while in Rome." MR: See his letter to Jacques Durand in *C*, 1927.

51. MR: D'Uckermann, *Ernest Hébert*, 181.

52. Needless to say, Victor I. Seroff (*Claude Debussy* [Paris: Éditions Buchet/Chastel, 1957], 68) and Dietschy (*Passion de Claude Debussy*, 52, and *Portrait of Claude Debussy*, 42) did not furnish their source in reporting the episode of Loulou's nightly visits to Debussy in his room. René Peter (*Claude Debussy*, rev. ed. [Paris: Gallimard, 1944], 21) was the first to tell the story, without revealing the name of Debussy's seductress. One can scarcely believe George Painter, the Marcel Proust historian, when he suggests that Mme Hochon was one of the models for Mme Verdurin in *À la recherche du temps perdu*; see George D. Painter, *Marcel Proust: A Biography* (New York: Random House, 1989), 1:195. MR: Hébert, who apparently studied with Jean-Auguste-Dominique Ingres, painted a portrait of Louise Lefuel Hochon; housed at the Musée Hébert (closed at present), one can view it on various websites, including Wikimedia Commons, https://commons.wikimedia.org/wiki/Category:Ernest_Hébert, accessed 16 January 2019.

53. MR: See *C*, 49–50. This is the last known letter from Achille to Henri Vasnier.

54. MR: See Rebois, *Les grands Prix de Rome de musique*, 60.

55. Adoré Floupette was the collective pseudonym adopted by Henri Beauclair and Gabriel Vicaire for this charming, decadent hoax in verse, including lines such as "L'alme fragilité des nonchaloirs impies / A reflété les souvenirs glauques d'Éros." MR: From the poem titled "Andante" (which is part of a set of poems collectively titled *Symphony in Green Minor*), these lines are translated as "The august reprobates of listless accidie / Reflect pale souvenirs of Eros, glaucous-glazed." See Adoré Floupette, *The Deliquescences*, trans. Stanley Chapman (London: Atlas Press, 2007), 53. The Vidal quote is from Rebois, *Les grands Prix de Rome de musique*, 60.

56. MR: See Paul Vidal, "Souvenirs d'Achille Debussy," *La revue musicale* (1 May 1926): 11 (107).

57. MR: A detailed account of the entire episode is given in René Peter, *Claude Debussy*, rev. ed. (Paris: Librairie Gallimard, 1944), 109–13.

58. MR: Tiberius Claudius Caesar Britannicus, the son of the Roman emperor Claudius, was the heir apparent to the throne of the Roman empire. However, when his father remarried, his older stepbrother Nero came into power, and Britannicus was apparently murdered just before turning fourteen. He is often depicted in sculpture with curly bangs combed over his forehead.

59. A. Montaux, "Journal d'un musicien," *Le ménestrel* 62, no. 33 (16 August 1896): 262.

60. MR: FL 2003 dates this letter at the end of 1885. However, based on Debussy's handwriting and also the fact that he changed the date of "1886" to "1887" in this passage, a date of 1 January 1887 has been established by Lesure and Herlin; see *C*, 57.

61. MR: See Debussy's letter to Émile Baron, sent from the Villa Medici possibly in 1886, in *C*, 56.

62. MR: See his letters to Baron from September 1886, 23 December 1886, and 9 February 1887 in *C*, 51–52, 55, and 59–60, respectively.

63. MR: The date of September 1886 is suggested in *C*, 50–51; however, in a personal letter to MR, Denis Herlin posits that, taking the style of Debussy's handwriting into account, the letter could have been written as late as the end of November.

64. [Debussy's letter to Baron, from perhaps September 1886, is in *C*, 51.] Achille would leave Rome at least twice during his stay, to go to Orvieto and to Naples. In his conversations with Guiraud a few years later [see "Transcription littérale des notes au crayon du carnet de Maurice Emmanuel (1889–1890)," in *Inédits sur Claude Debussy*, Collections Comœdia-Charpentier (Paris: Les Publications Techniques, 1942), 32], he pointed out what he had liked the most in Italy: in Orvieto, Luca Signorelli's *La resurrezione dei morti* ("not because of the trumpets"); in Rome, Raphaël's *Loggie* ("not the *Stanze*"); and in Santa Sabina, Giovanni Battista Salvi da Sassoferrato's *La Madonna del Rosario*. In "Les impressions d'un Prix de Rome," *Gil Blas* (10 June 1903), Debussy complained, with respect to these travels in Italy, of the "lack of contacts [with people] in the cities where one is treated too

much like a foreigner," except by the "smiling young girls" who sell postcards [see Debussy, *Monsieur Croche*, rev. ed., 190, and Debussy, *Debussy on Music*, 213].

65. MR: Désiré-Maurice Ferrary won a Prix de Rome in sculpture in 1882, and Alexis Axilette won his Prix de Rome in painting in 1885.

66. MR: All three of these men were Prix de Rome winners from 1883: Gaston Redon in architecture, Marcel Baschet in painting, and Henri-Édouard Lombard in sculpture.

67. MR: Various people typically attended these dinners; many of their names have been omitted in order to focus on Debussy's frequent presence and to avoid encumbering the text.

68. MR: Henri Pinta won a Prix de Rome in painting in 1884.

69. The Countess Mélanie de Pourtalès, whose portrait Hébert would later make.

70. MR: Joseph-Antoine Gardet and Hector d'Espouy were Prix de Rome winners in 1885 for sculpture and in 1884 for architecture, respectively.

71. Augustin Savard had recently arrived at the Villa and was himself a staunch Wagnerian. He remembered having heard Debussy play *Tristan* at the piano in his room, and he played Achille's second *envoi* from Rome, *Printemps*, with him at the Héberts. See Rebois, *Les grands Prix de Rome de musique*, 63–64.

72. MR: This information is gleaned from the report of the Académie des beaux-arts, cited at length in Vallas, *Claude Debussy et son temps* (Alcan, 1932), 62, as well as in the later edition of this biography (Éditions Albin Michel, 1958), 80. The report is also given in full in Lesure, *Claude Debussy: Biographie critique*, 573, and has been confirmed by Denis Herlin. A short score of an orchestral work condenses the primary musical material on only three or four staves.

73. This was a photographic reproduction of his *Vierge à l'enfant* with the following dedication: "To our very dear and much missed composer Debussy, his friend H. . . , Rome, 2 March 1887." It was shown in the exhibition at the Bibliothèque nationale in 1962 [see item 41 in *Claude Debussy* (Paris: Les presses artistiques, 1962), 26].

74. Pierné's career started with a bang: Pasdeloup and Colonne played his works, and the publisher Leduc announced that he had obtained exclusive rights to publish them.

75. The performers in this concert on 13 March were Mesdames Leroux and Boidin-Puisais, and Messieurs Van Dyck, Blauwaert, and Mauguière.

76. For a long time, Mounet-Sully wanted to revive *Hamlet*. Mounted as a lavish production, this adaptation included some cuts and appreciably altered the denouement of Shakespeare's work.

77. [*C*, 61–62.]

6. Beginning of the Bohemian Period: 1887–89

1. MR: See Debussy's letter of 17 March 1887 to Ernest Hébert in *C*, 61.

2. MR: See Marguerite Vasnier, "Debussy à dix-huit ans," *La revue musicale* (1 May 1926): 21 (117).

3. MR: Le Bas-Fort-Blanc is a section on the western side of Dieppe, nestled under the cliffs along the water; see Wendy Baron, *Sickert: Paintings and Drawings* (New Haven, CT: Yale University Press, 2006), 462.

4. Jacques-Émile Blanche, *La pêche aux souvenirs* (Paris: Flammarion, 1949), 224. MR: The portrait of Marie Vasnier that is perhaps best known is the one by Jacques-Émile Blanche; see François Lesure, *Debussy; Iconographie musicale* (Geneva: Minkoff & Lattès, 1980), 35. It depicts a more commanding presence, with her head tilted back and her right hand on her hip, compared to Paul Baudry's earlier portrayal of her as softer and more approachable, with hands gently folded in front of her; see André Gauthier, *Debussy: Documents iconographiques* (Geneva: Pierre Cailler, 1952), plate 8.

5. According to Dietschy's manuscript notes on Popelin [see DOSS-03.78 at the CDCD].

6. MR: David Grayson provides a great deal of information about Jeanne Andrée in "'Paysage sentimental': 'Si doux, si triste, si dormant . . . ,'" in *Debussy's Resonance*, ed. François de Médicis and Steven Huebner (Rochester, NY: University of Rochester Press, 2018), 111–12.

7. MR: See Debussy's letter of 24 June 1885 to Claudius Popelin in *C*, 32.

8. Apparently the two were very close. Achille had sent his photo from the Villa Medici to Alfred in 1886: "To Frèdo his Chilo" (reproduced on the cover of François Lesure, *Claude Debussy avant* Pelléas *ou les années symbolistes* [Paris: Klincksieck, 1992]).

9. Margaret G. Cobb, "Au temps de *La damoiselle élue*," *Cahiers Debussy* 12–13 (1988–89): 48–53. During the war, Alfred's knowledge of the language would be used on the English front.

10. MR: *La damoiselle élue* was completed in Paris in 1888, well over a year after Achille's return from Rome.

11. MR: FL 2003 erroneously lists a single performance of *Lohengrin* at the Éden in Paris on 3 May 1887. Charles Lamoureux conducted the premiere in April, and Ernest Van Dyck sang the role of Lohengrin, as he did when it was finally produced at the Palais Garnier on 16 September 1891. The role of Elsa in the latter production was sung by **Rose Caron**. The performance thus featured two singers who earlier had sung in Debussy's *L'enfant prodigue*.

12. MR: See Alfred Ernst, "Le wagnérisme en 1888," *Revue wagnérienne* (15 July 1888): 294.

13. MR: See Jean Moréas, "Le symbolisme," *Le Figaro*, supplément littéraire (18 September 1886): 1–2.

14. MR: See Robert Brussel, "Claude Debussy et Paul Dukas," *La revue musicale* (1 May 1926): 94 (190).

15. MR: Brussel, "Claude Debussy et Paul Dukas," 94 (190).

16. MR: The original French is "Toute la lyre," a phrase that may have entered common parlance. Debussy used it two months earlier in a letter to Hébert from March 1887 (see *C*, 61–62); see also Albert Samain's use of it in 1894 on p. 376n42. "Toute la lyre" is the title of a posthumous collection of poetry by Victor Hugo that is organized into seven sections, each representing a "string" of the lyre. (I am grateful to Helen Abbott for pointing out this source.) Although these poems

were published (in two volumes) in 1888 and 1893, their collective title had been announced by Hugo himself already in the 1870s. It is thus conceivable that Debussy would have known and deliberately echoed Hugo's distinctive turn of phrase.

17. [This quotation, as well as much of the information in this paragraph, comes from a] letter from Dukas to Léon Vallas of 15 March 1929. MR: A copy of this letter is in the Fonds Lesure, BnF, carton I/4(5).

18. MR: See René Peter, *Claude Debussy*, rev. ed. (Paris: Gallimard, 1944), 27–28.

19. Dukas remarked that Achille had a private entrance there and that "some birds, outside of their abandoned cages, would flutter through the rooms" (Brussel, "Claude Debussy et Paul Dukas," 96 [192]).

20. [See *C*, 66.] Before leaving for Rome, Debussy asserted that he had tried in vain to sell some music (letter to Primoli, likely from November 1884 [*C*, 19]). In 1888, Veuve Girod copublished with the *Revue indépendante* the six *Litanies* by Édouard Dujardin (words and music).

21. Vallas and others wrongly give the date of 1889 for this inscription.

22. In his note to d'Indy, Fauré wrote that he had taken great pleasure in chatting with "Bréville, Husson, and Bagès." It is hard to believe that he could have written to composer Léon Husson for Debussy. As for Bréville, he commented on Debussy's commitment: "This is the best part of our letter." See the facsimile in *S. I. M.* 9, no. 5 (15 May 1913), [inserted after p. 44, "Une lettre française de Bayreuth"].

23. MR: La Coupole here refers to the Académie française, which is located in the Palais de l'Institut de France, a landmark building in Paris that is topped by a beautiful dome.

24. MR: The quotes from the Académie des beaux-arts are cited in Léon Vallas, *Claude Debussy et son temps* (Paris: Éditions Albin Michel, 1958), 80. A full transcript of the report is given in François Lesure, *Claude Debussy: Biographie critique* (Paris: Fayard, 2003), 573.

25. MR: From Louÿs's notes, given by Georges Serrières to be sold at Coulet et Faure, auction catalog 58 (Paris, October 1959); see DOSS-03.02 ("Notes de la main d'un inconnu, rapportant des souvenirs de Pierre Louÿs sur Debussy"), 2, among the Dietschy materials in the CDCD. See also Marcel Dietschy, *La passion de Claude Debussy* (Neuchâtel: Éditions de la Baconnière, 1962), 65 (and William Ashbrook and Margaret G. Cobb's English translation of Dietschy, *A Portrait of Claude Debussy* [Oxford: Oxford University Press, 1990], 53), as well as Lesure, *Claude Debussy avant Pelléas*, 215.

26. MR: Citation from the archives of the Académie de France in Rome, and confirmed by Denis Herlin. A more developed, internal report that preceded the public version reads as follows: "The text chosen by M. Debussy is in prose and rather obscure; but his musical setting of it lacks neither poetry nor charm, although it still manifests those consistent tendencies toward vagueness in its expression and forms, for which the Académie has already had occasion to reproach the composer. Here, however, his inclinations and these procedures are markedly more restrained and seem, up to a point, justified by the very nature and indeterminate character of the subject." This assessment is cited in Vallas, *Claude*

Debussy et son temps, 81, and paraphrased in Lesure, *Claude Debussy: Biographie critique*, 573.

27. His letter from 30 April 1887 is reproduced in Albert Samain, "Lettres à Raymond Bonheur," in *Revue de l'histoire de Versailles* (1959–60): 6; [see also Albert Samain, *Des lettres, 1887–1900* (Paris: Mercure de France, 1933), 3]. David Grayson has studied the problems connected to the translations of *La damoiselle élue*, as well as the changes brought to the successive editions of the score, in "Claude Debussy Addresses the English-speaking World: Two Interviews, An Article, and *The Blessed Damozel*," *Cahiers Debussy* 16 (1992): 35–44.

28. Archives of the Académie des beaux-arts, 2 E. 17, minutes of 29 September 1888 [see Fonds FL, BnF, carton I/6(11)]. The following year, when Savard was late for the same obligation, the minutes of the Académie reported: "It will remain to be decided if M. Debussy should be released from this obligation which he shirked last year" (29 June 1889). Even so, Debussy intimated to Godet on Christmas Day in 1889 that he was planning a "Festival Debussy" there for the following year [see *C*, 81].

29. [See copy of the Archives of the Académie des beaux-arts, 2 E. 17, minutes of 6 October 1888 in Fonds FL, BnF, carton I/6(11).] Marty's *Ouverture de Balthazar* was performed at the public concert on 20 October, before Camille Erlanger's cantata [presumably referring to his *Velléda*].

30. MR: Autograph letter from Delibes to Erlanger, dated 7 December 1890, in the Beinecke Rare Book & Manuscript Library, Yale University. Interestingly, Delibes refers to Debussy's work as "*La Demoiselle au ciel*." I am grateful to Pauline Girard for providing information on the source of this letter.

31. Emmanuel Chabrier, *Correspondance*, ed. Roger Delage, Frans Durif, and Thierry Bodin (Paris: Klincksieck, 1994), 591.

32. For an analysis of this novel, see Edward Lockspeiser, *Debussy: His Life and Mind* (London: Cassel, 1962–65), 1:104–7.

33. Paul Vidal wrote in 1884, concerning the boarders at the Villa Medici: "We are just about managing to get along, and our strongest connecting link is perhaps the friendship and the admiration that we have for Bouchor" (François Lesure, "Debussy de 1883 à 1885 d'après la correspondence de Paul Vidal à Henriette Fuchs," *Revue de musicologie* 48 [July–December 1962]: 99).

34. MR: See Debussy's letter to Godet from 27 October 1893 in *C*, 172, and especially Lesure and Herlin's remarks in *C*, 172n1.

35. The details in this paragraph and many others that follow are taken from Robert Godet's introduction in Claude Debussy, *Lettres à deux amis*, ed. Robert Godet and Georges Jean-Aubry (Paris: J. Corti, 1942). Camille Benoit appears beside Chabrier and d'Indy in the famous group portrait painted by Fantin-Latour in 1885, *Autour du piano* (in the salon of the judge Antoine Lascoux). MR: Further information, including the identity of the other individuals portrayed in the picture, is given by the Musée d'Orsay: http://www.musee-orsay.fr/de/kollektionen/werkkatalog/notice.html?no_cache=1&nnumid=000214&cHash=34e19f6012, accessed 16 January 2019.

36. MR: Lockspeiser, in *Debussy: His Life and Mind*, 1:140, describes the Taverne Pousset as "a small mock-medieval restaurant with somber furnishings

and stained-glass windows," where a "celebrated Munich beer" was served. In 1897–98, Édouard Niermans, the Dutch-born Parisian architect who had constructed the Dutch pavilions (including a "Taverne Hollandaise") at the 1889 World's Fair, built a second Taverne Pousset, at 14 boulevard des Italiens, in art-nouveau style (hence the differentiation between "le petit Pousset"—a homonym for "Tom Thumb," the "petit poucet" in one of Charles Perrault's fairy tales—and "le grand Pousset"). For beautiful illustrations of the latter site, see Jean-François Pinchon, *Édouard Niermans: Architecte de la Café-Society* (Liège: Mardage, 1991), 41 and 120–27. The highly decorated menu for the Taverne Hollandaise at the 1889 World's Fair is reproduced on p. 31 of this source.

37. See the entry for 3 July 1894 [in Edmond and Jules de Goncourt, *Journal: Mémoires de la vie littéraire, 1894–95*, ed. Robert Ricatte (Monaco: Les Éditions de l'Imprimerie nationale de Monaco, 1956–58), 20:93].

38. The music [by Sivry appeared in the 3 April 1898 issue of *Les quat'z'arts* and] is reproduced by Eric Frederick Jensen in "Adventures of a French Wagnerian: The Work of Villiers de l'Isle-Adam," *Music Review* (1990): 196–97. MR: On p. 195, Jensen gives a similar version, albeit unaccompanied, of Villiers's "La mort des amants" made by Judith Gautier, which was published in Fernand Clerget, *Villiers de l'Isle-Adam* (Paris: Société des Éditions Louis-Michaud, [1913]), 71. Other versions are identified and discussed by Helen Abbott in *Parisian Intersections: Baudelaire's Legacy to Composers* (Bern: Peter Lang, 2012); see especially pp. 71, 83–102, and 175–86.

39. MR: Villiers described himself as an "apprenti-musicien" on the flyleaf of a presentation copy of his *Contes cruels* for Chabrier; see Jensen, "Adventures of a French Wagnerian," 188.

40. MR: Villiers died of stomach cancer on 19 August (not 18 August, as reported in FL 2003) 1889.

41. Vallas, *Claude Debussy et son temps*, 140, writes enigmatically: "This document, certainly of great interest, lies unknown in a private collection." On the Symbolist conception of *Axël*, see Alan William Raitt, *Villiers de l'Isle-Adam et le mouvement symboliste* (Paris: Librairie José Corti, 1965), 131–41.

42. [See Samain's letter to Bonheur from 3 March 1894 in] Samain, "Lettres à Raymond Bonheur," 29.

43. MR: See the entry for Pousset in the index to Goncourt, *Journal, 1896*, ed. Ricatte, 22:246.

44. MR: See the entry for 10 April 1892 in Goncourt, *Journal, 1891–1892*, ed. Ricatte, 18:164.

45. Bernard Lazare, [*Figures contemporaines* (Paris: Perrin et Cie, 1895), 31.]

46. See entry for 3 January 1889 [in Goncourt, *Journal, 1887–1889*, ed. Ricatte, 15:223].

47. [See entry for 18 October 1891 in] Jules Renard, *Journal* (Paris: Gallimard, 1935), 72.

48. See the text in François Lesure, "Le 'jeune Prix de Rome' de Mendès," *Cahiers Debussy* 6 (1982): 36–40. MR: In August 1876, the month in which this article first appeared in *Le gaulois*, Achille would have just turned fourteen; at this

time, he was studying at the Conservatoire but certainly not yet strongly affected by Wagner's music.

49. Alfred Cortot, "Un drame lyrique de Claude Debussy," in *Inédits sur Claude Debussy,* Collections Comœdia-Charpentier (Paris: Les Publications Techniques, 1942), 12–16.

50. MR: Raymond Bonheur, "Souvenirs et impressions," *La revue musicale* (1 May 1926): 4 (100).

51. MR: Godet describes "le père Thommen" and his bistro in his introduction to Debussy, *Lettres à deux amis,* 46–49.

52. In the *Frères en art,* a theatrical play written by Debussy around 1900, one notices this dialogue between two characters, Ralan (a sculptor) and Maltravers (a painter): "What a musician this Rollinat is! —No! What a poet! —Ah!. . ." (see Lesure, *Claude Debussy avant* Pelléas, 241).

53. Henri Willette, *Georges Lorin et Rollinat: Conversation avec Lorin* (Paris: Sansot, [1928]); and Régis Miannay, *Maurice Rollinat: Poète et musicien du fantastique* (Châteauroux: Éditions Minard, 1981), 229, 282–83, 296–97, 430, 501, and 504–505. MR: The Goncourt journal is sprinkled with references to Rollinat from 1883 to 1894; while the Goncourts viewed him as odd and macabre and looked askance at his relationship to the Callias circle, they also pointed out the success of his populist music and his relationships with singers such as Reynaldo Hahn, Yvette Guilbert, and Émile Engel. See also Godet's introduction to Debussy, *Lettres à deux amis,* 50–52, as well as pp. 13–15 in Harold B. Segel, *Turn-of-the-century Cabaret: Paris, Barcelona, Berlin, Munich, Vienna, Cracow, Moscow, St. Petersburg, Zurich* (New York: Columbia University Press, 1987); the entire first chapter (pp. 1–83) of Segel's book is devoted to Parisian cabarets such as the Chat Noir.

54. MR: A brief synopsis of this work, titled *Blanc et noir,* is given in Paul Hugounet, *Mimes et Pierrots: Notes et documents inédits pour server à l'histoire de la pantomime* (Paris: Librairie Fischbacher, 1889), 243–44. The last chapter of this book, covering pp. 237–51, is devoted to a discussion of the Cercle funambulesque, whose primary purpose was to present classical pantomime that featured *commedia dell'arte* characters and music by young composers.

55. Yves A. Lado-Bordowski, "*L'archet.* Un 'croquis musical' de Debussy [1881]," *Cahiers Debussy* 16 (1992): 3–21. MR: It was not until 2012 that "L'archet" was published, in an edition by Denis Herlin (Paris: Durand).

56. MR: Godet, introduction to Debussy, *Lettres à deux amis,* 71.

57. MR: Godet, introduction to Debussy, *Lettres à deux amis,* 76.

58. Robert Godet, "En marge de la marge," *La revue musicale* (1 May 1926): 63–64 (159–60).

59. MR: See "Echos," *La presse* (2 June 1894): [2]. Proust's remark, noted also in his letter to Robert de Montesquiou, was made upon hearing Bagès sing at the home of the latter; see Marcel Proust, *Correspondance,* tome 1: 1880–95, ed. Philip Kolb (Paris: Librairie Plon, 1970), 1:301n3.

60. MR: It should be noted that Mme de Saint-Marceaux's comment on Bagès's singing was not contemporaneous with that of Proust. Rather, she wrote it in her diary a decade later; see the entry for 23 February 1904 in Marguerite de

Saint-Marceaux, *Journal, 1894–1927*, ed. Myriam Chimènes et al. (Paris: Librairie Arthème Fayard, 2007), 335.

61. MR: See Camille Bellaigue, "Revue musicale," *Revue des deux mondes* 92 (1 March 1888): 458.

62. [See Pierre de Bréville, "Les fioretti du père Franck," *Mercure de France* 68, no. 242 (15 July 1907): 304–5. Franck was most likely alluding to his perception of Debussy's music as incapable of being grasped easily or even perhaps as ultra-refined. Lockspeiser, in *Debussy: His Life and Mind*, 1:126, translates this quote as "the split hairs of music" or "the nerves of music" and adds that, although this description "meant to convey his (Franck's) irritated censure of Debussy's style," it "defines precisely its compelling, nervous appeal."] According to a disclosure from d'Indy to Guillaume Lekeu, César Franck used the word *Raca* [i.e., "worthless"; see Matthew 5:22] in mentioning Debussy (Brussel, "Claude Debussy et Paul Dukas," 96 [192]).

63. MR: See Julien Tiersot, "Les nouvelles: Concerts et soirées," *Le ménestrel* 55, no. 6 (10 February 1888): 47.

64. Balthazar Claes, "Chronique de la semaine: Paris—Théâtres et concerts," *Le guide musical* 35, no. 6 (7 February 1889): 45.

65. MR: Jacques Durand's memories of this event may be found in Jacques Durand, *Quelques souvenirs d'un éditeur de musique* (Paris: A. Durand & fils, 1924), 1:59.

66. Henri Busser, *De* Pelléas *aux* Indes galantes (Paris: Librairie Arthème Fayard, 1955), 47. MR: Busser would later conduct *Pelléas et Mélisande*, and orchestrate Debussy's *Petite suite* as well as his *Printemps*.

67. [*C*, 70.]

68. Fabrice Touttavoult, *Confessions: Marx, Engels, Proust, Mallarmé, Cézanne* (Paris: Éditions Belin, 1988), 127–29. MR: Debussy's turn of phrase, "n'importe où hors du monde," comes from the title of one of Baudelaire's prose poems in *Le spleen de Paris*, published posthumously in 1869. (My thanks to Helen Abbott for pointing out this connection.) The title of Baudelaire's poem was in English, followed by the French phrase (in smaller letters), which itself was derived from an 1844 poem by Thomas Hood titled "Bridge of Sighs." Hood's poem was quoted in its entirety by Edgar Allan Poe in his essay "The Poetic Principle," which Debussy possibly knew.

69. Dietschy, *Passion de Claude Debussy*, 80n22, and Dietschy, *Portrait of Claude Debussy*, 56.

70. MR: See Chansarel's letter to Debussy from 24 April 1889 in *C*, 73. In *C*, 73n2, Lesure and Herlin point out that Verlaine used the word for "lowlife"—*pouacre*—as the title of one of his poems; dedicated to Jean Moréas, it was first published in *Le chat noir* 2, no. 84 (18 August 1883): 126, and reprinted the next year in *Jadis et naguère* (Paris: Léon Vanier, 1884).

71. MR: See Chansarel's letter to Debussy from 16 May 1889 in *C*, 75.

72. MR: See Peter, *Claude Debussy*, 122–25.

73. MR: This is how René Chansarel referred to his own pianism in a letter to Debussy from 24 April 1889; see *C*, 73.

74. MR: See Annegret Fauser, *Musical Encounters at the 1889 Paris World's Fair* (Rochester, NY: University of Rochester Press, 2005).

75. MR: This song was originally composed by Louis-Victor Simon, on a text written in 1780 by Fabre d'Églantine, for a one-act opéra comique titled *Laure et Pétrarque*.

76. MR: These words were used by Georges Jean-Aubry in his long interview with Robert Godet; see Godet's introduction to Debussy, *Lettres à deux amis*, 80.

77. MR: The Vietnamese title of this drama was Ly-Tieng-Vuong, as cited by Fauser, *Musical Encounters*, 186, from Hippolyte Lemaire, "Théâtres," *Le monde illustré* 33, no. 1681 (15 June 1889): 399.

78. MR: This group of performers is discussed and illustrated in Fauser, *Musical Encounters*, 191–92.

79. Reproduced in Lesure, *Claude Debussy: Iconographie*, 40 [as well as in Fauser, *Musical Encounters*, 192]. MR: Debussy's quote comes from his article "Du gout," *S. I. M.* (15 February 1913), which is reprinted in Claude Debussy, *Monsieur Croche et autres écrits*, rev. ed. (Paris: Gallimard, 1987), 229; and in Claude Debussy, *Debussy on Music*, trans. Richard Langham Smith (New York: Alfred A. Knopf, 1977), 278.

80. Anik Devriès, "Les musiques d'Extrême-Orient à l'Exposition universelle de 1889," *Cahiers Debussy*, nouv. sér. 1 (1977): 24–37. A program from the Annamite theater is preserved at the Bibliothèque historique de la Ville de Paris.

81. MR: See Camille Saint-Saëns, "Le 'Rappel' à l'Exposition: Les instruments de musique," *Le rappel* (10 October 1889): [2].

82. MR: Robert Godet, "En marge de la marge," 55 (151).

83. MR: Fauser, *Musical Encounters*, 166, spells the dancers' names as Wakiem, Seriem, Taminah, and Soekia.

84. Goncourt disagreed with the rest of Paris: "That dance is in no way gracious, voluptuous, or sensuous; it consists completely of gesticulations of the wrists, and it is executed by women whose skin looks like flannel and who are oily as if from the nasty grease of rats that have fed on sewage eels" (see entry of 24 May 1889 [in Goncourt, *Journal, 1889–1890*, ed. Ricatte, 16:79]). As for Joris-Karl Huysmans, he noticed especially their dirty feet.

85. Debussy, *Lettres à deux amis*, 81.

86. MR: In a letter to the publisher Schott, Debussy compared the compositional unfolding of Cyril Scott's works to Javanese rhapsodies, which develop not in a traditional form but rather according to a fantasy of "innumerable arabesques"; see *C*, 1315–16n4. Similarly, Debussy referenced the arabesque several times with respect to the music of Bach. See, for example, his use of the term "the capricious arabesque" in his article, "Du gout," *S. I. M.* (15 February 1913), which is reprinted in Debussy, *Monsieur Croche*, rev. ed., 229, and in Debussy, *Debussy on Music*, 278. See also his mention of "the adorable arabesque" in his letter from October 1902 to the journal *Musica* in *C*, 690, and in the survey titled "L'orientation musicale" by Charles Joly that was published that same month in *Musica*, reprinted in Debussy, *Monsieur Croche*, rev. ed., 65, and in Debussy, *Debussy on Music*, 84.

87. MR: The contents of these programs are reproduced in Fauser, *Musical Encounters*, 321–22.

88. Note Pierre Louÿs's manuscript on "Debussy sur Wagner" (reproduced by Paul-Ursin Dumont, *Pierre Louÿs: L'ermite du hameau*, [Vendôme: Libraidisque, 1985], 105).

89. Étienne Destranges, *Dix jours à Bayreuth (fêtes de 1889)* (Paris: Tresse et Stock, 1889), 39–40.

90. Dukas's presence was not pointed out by Lavignac, but the composer had kept his tickets for the performances of 11 August (*Parsifal*) and 12 August (*Tristan*). See item 11 in *Paul Dukas*, 1963 exhibition catalog, ed. François Lesure (Paris: Bibliothèque nationale, département de la Musique, 1965), 5.

91. See Arthur Hoérée, "Entretiens inédits d'Ernest Guiraud et de Claude Debussy," in *Inédits sur Debussy*, Collections Comœdia-Charpentier (Paris: Les Publications Techniques, 1942), 33, where a short excerpt of a letter, otherwise unknown and dated erroneously as September 1890, was published. MR: See his letter from the beginning of August 1889 in *C*, 78; Lesure and Herlin saw only a copy of this letter from Maurice Emmanuel.

92. The text of these notebooks had first been published in excerpts by Maurice Emmanuel in his Pelléas et Mélisande *de Claude Debussy: Étude historique et critique, analyse musicale* (Paris: Paul Mellottée, Éditeur, [1926]), repr. as Pelléas et Mélisande *de Claude Debussy: Étude et analyse* (Paris: Éditions Mellottée, 1950); and in "literal transcription" by Arthur Hoérée in "Entretiens inédits d'Ernest Guiraud et de Claude Debussy," 27–33. In 1889, Emmanuel was a private pupil of Guiraud. We find a more precise account of the circumstances of these conversations in Maurice Emmanuel, "Mes avatars," *Zodiaque* 139 (January 1984): 15–38. [According to Emmanuel, "Mes avatars," 17–18, Réty advised him to leave Delibes's class and to study secretly with Guiraud. For two years, Emmanuel would go to Guiraud's house at 11:00 a.m. The teacher would wake up at noon and take his pupil to lunch at a nearby bistro; by 2:00 p.m., they would return to Guiraud's home, where he would correct Emmanuel's fugues and choruses, and give him lessons in orchestration. On p. 18, Emmanuel reminisced:] "In 1889 I had the opportunity to have lunch with Debussy more than ten times after his return from Rome, when Guiraud took him along with me to a restaurant. At first, I was rather embarrassed. How should I explain my presence with the master when I was not his student? I was reduced to silence, and must have looked like a fool to Debussy. But I was not deaf, and the conversations between the Prix de Rome winner and his composition teacher seemed to me so lively and of such significance that I took note of them, as accurately as possible."

93. MR: See Emmanuel, Pelléas et Mélisande *de Claude Debussy*, 35.

94. MR: Emmanuel, Pelléas et Mélisande *de Claude Debussy*, 36.

95. MR: Emmanuel, Pelléas et Mélisande *de Claude Debussy*, 35.

96. MR: Emmanuel, Pelléas et Mélisande *de Claude Debussy*, 35–36.

97. MR: See Debussy's letter to Henri Vasnier from 4 June 1885 in *C*, 29.

98. MR: Debussy's letter to Henri Vasnier from 4 June 1885 in *C*, 29.

99. MR: See Debussy's letter to Henri Vasnier from 19 October 1885 in *C*, 42–43.

100. Letter from Adrien Dukas to Paul Dukas, 6 December 1889, BnF, W-49(50).

101. [*C*, 82.]

102. MR: See Debussy's letter to Robert Godet from 14 October 1889 in *C*, 79.

7. From Baudelaire to Mallarmé: 1890–91

1. Georges Servières, "Lieder français, III: Cl.-Ach. Debussy," *Le guide musical* 41, nos. 37 and 38 (15 and 22 September 1895): 682–83.

2. MR: Victor Debay sang some of the *Cinq poèmes* in Lyon on 20 February 1903, and Camille Fourrier sang "Le jet d'eau" at a Mathurins concert on 15 May 1905. Finally, Jeanne Raunay sang "Le jet d'eau" and "Recueillement" in Paris on 7 December 1905.

3. MR: See André-Ferdinand Herold, "Quelques mots sur Stéphane Mallarmé," *L'ère nouvelle: Organe de l'entente des gauches* (21 December 1925), [3], in which Herold recalled that "one day I invited him [Mallarmé], along with several friends, to come hear the *Cinq poèmes de Baudelaire* that Debussy had just finished and that had not yet been published."

4. MR: According to Lesure, this event occurred in February 1890, though the date for Chausson's soiree has not been corroborated by any source.

5. Paul Vidal, "Souvenirs d'Achille Debussy," *La revue musicale* (1 May 1926): 16 (112). According to Godet (notes about Vallas's book), Chausson said of "La mort des amants": "Isn't it terribly melodic?" MR: Reported also by Henry Prunières in "Autour de Debussy," *La revue musicale* 15, no. 147 (June 1934): 22.

6. MR: *Méphistophéla* was published in 1890 by E. Dentu in Paris.

7. MR: See the 9 March 1890 entry (not 8 March, as reported in FL 2003) in Willy, *Lettres de l'ouvreuse: Voyage autour de la musique* (Paris: Léon Vanier, 1890), 174. Henry Gauthier-Villars adopted several different pseudonyms, among them "Willy" and "l'ouvreuse." This volume was a collection of many of the reviews he wrote in the guise of "l'ouvreuse" (the usherette). He also worked with several different ghostwriters, among them Jean de Tinan, Curnonsky, Émile Vullermoz, Paul-Jean Toulet, Lugné-Poe, and Colette, his wife.

8. The printed program included two tempo markings that were different from the final version: I. Allegro moderato. II. Andante et final. MR: In fact, the *Fantaisie pour piano et orchestre* was never performed during Debussy's lifetime, and the composer revised it over a long period of time. For details, see the avant-propos/foreword in Claude Debussy, *Fantaisie pour piano et orchestre (2e version), Œuvres complètes de Claude Debussy*, sér. V, vol. 2 bis, ed. Jean-Pierre Marty with the collaboration of Denis Herlin and Edmond Lemaître (Paris: Durand, 2007), xi–xii and xv–xvii.

9. MR: See Debussy's letter to Vincent d'Indy from 20 April 1890 in *C*, 87.

10. MR: The text of the contract is given in *C*, 87–88.

11. [For the information and quotations in this paragraph, see] Robert Godet, "En marge de la marge," *La revue musicale* (1 May 1926): 68–69 (164–65).

12. MR: The manuscript of *Rodrigue et Chimène*, formerly in the collection of Alfred Cortot, now is part of the Robert Owen Lehman collection, on deposit at The Morgan Library & Museum, New York.

13. MR: Pierre Corneille (1606–84), known as the father of classical drama in France, wrote *Le Cid*, based on a play by Guilhen de Castro and on which Mendès's *Rodrigue et Chimène* was in turn based.

14. [As announced in "Nouvelles de partout,"] *Journal de musique* 3, no. 134 (21 December 1878): 3–4.

15. MR: See n13.

16. MR: "Nouvelles de partout," *Journal de musique* (21 December 1878), 4.

17. MR: See "Nouvelles diverses," *L'art musical* 18, no. 26 (26 June 1879): 206–7. As a composer, Gevaert won the Belgian Prix de Rome. However, he is perhaps best known today as a teacher and author of a treatise on instrumentation and a book on harmony. He also served as director of the Conservatoire royal de Bruxelles from 1871 to 1908.

18. [The name of Émile Pessard was mentioned in] "Nouvelles de partout," *Journal de musique* 3, no. 135 (28 December 1878): 4. In the "Nouvelles de partout" section of successive issues of the *Journal de musique*, 3, nos. 136–38 (4 January 1879, p. 4; 11 January 1879, p. 3; and 18 January 1879, p. 4), [the names of Massé, Bizet, and Maillard appeared. The notice in the 4 January issue reiterated what was published in] *L'art musical* 18, no. 1 (2 January 1879): 6, [where Louis Gallet claimed to have co-written a libretto on *Le Cid* with Édouard Blau, mentioning that since 1873 the Opéra had been planning to produce it, with music by Massenet]. Finally, in *L'art musical* 18, no. 2 (9 January 1879): 15, [Aimé Maillard was cited as the fifth composer known to be working on *Le Cid*]; see also "Nouvelles diverses: Paris et départements," *Le ménestrel* 45, no. 6 (5 January 1879): 46.

19. MR: See Chabrier's letter to Ernest Van Dyck, from 7 April 1888, in Emmanuel Chabrier, *Correspondance*, ed. Roger Delage, Frans Durif, and Thierry Bodin (Paris: Klincksieck, 1994), 483.

20. MR: See Chabrier's letter to Wilhelm Enoch, from possibly 25 July 1886, in Chabrier, *Correspondance*, 371.

21. MR: It should be noted that Chabrier did not complete his lyric drama, *Briséïs*, based on a libretto by Mendès and Ephraïm Mikaël.

22. MR: These oft-cited remarks from Debussy to his teacher Guiraud were reported by Maurice Emmanuel. See Maurice Emmanuel, Pelléas et Mélisande *de Claude Debussy: Étude historique et critique, analyse musicale* (Paris: Paul Mellottée, Éditeur [1926]); repr. as Pelléas et Mélisande *de Claude Debussy: Étude et analyse* (Paris: Éditions Mellottée, 1950), 35.

23. MR: Emmanuel, Pelléas et Mélisande *de Claude Debussy*, 35.

24. Information provided by Mme and M. Sylvie and Pierre Hottinguer, as well as by Mme Jean de Crevecœur.

25. MR: Rose Depecker had studied piano with Félix Le Couppey, who died in 1887. She also won a first prize in harmony in 1887 and a first prize in counterpoint and fugue in 1892; see Constant Pierre, *Le Conservatoire national de musique et de déclamation* (Paris: Imprimerie nationale, 1900), 738.

26. MR: See the "Chronique de la semaine," *Le monde artiste* 30, no. 10 (9 March 1890): 158. FL 2003 reports that the event took place on 9 March, but that was the date of the review which came out on Sunday, the day after the recital that took place on Saturday at the Salle Érard.

27. *Le ménestrel* 56, no. 18 (4 May 1890): 144. In 1895, she published a few songs and, three years later, she married the explorer Émile Gentil.

28. MR: The description of Gaby in this paragraph is taken from Henri Pellerin, "Claude Debussy et le Pays d'Auge," *Le Pays d'Auge* 7, no. 5 (May 1957): 8.

29. Pellerin, "Claude Debussy et le Pays d'Auge," 8. MR: Pellerin's full article is informative; it begins in *Le Pays d'Auge* (May 1957): 1–16, and continues in *Le Pays d'Auge* (June 1957): [1–11].

30. MR: For further information on Mercier, see Debussy's letter to Robert Godet from 25 December 1899 in *C*, 80–83, and especially *C*, 82n2.

31. MR: René Peter was a young student of Alfred Stevens, who had painted his portrait in 1880; *René Peter, enfant* may now be viewed at the Musée d'Orsay in Paris. See http://www.musee-orsay.fr/fr/collections/catalogue-des-oeuvres/notice.html?nnumid=21051, accessed 16 January 2019. See also letters from Alfred Stevens and Puvis de Chavannes concerning René's paintings, in *Les Autographes: Autographes, lettres et manuscrits, documents et souvenirs* 141 (Paris, Noël 2015), item 276.

32. MR: See Robert de Montesquiou, *Diptyque de Flandre, triptyque de France* (Paris: Éditions E. Sansot, 1921), 9; the first section of this book is devoted to Alfred Stevens, identifying him as "le peintre aux billets." A few examples may be seen in plates 17 ("La lettre de faire-part"), 23 ("Le billet"), and 45 ("Souvenirs et regrets") in François Boucher, *Alfred Stevens* (Paris: Éditions Rieder, 1930).

33. MR: See the entry for 11 August 1892 in Edmond et Jules de Goncourt, *Journal: Mémoires de la vie littéraire, 1891–1892*, ed. Robert Ricatte (Monaco: Les Éditions de l'Imprimerie nationale de Monaco, 1956–58), 18:229.

34. MR: See Boucher, *Alfred Stevens*, 29–31 and 35.

35. Boucher, *Alfred Stevens*, 30; Camille Lemonnier, *Alfred Stevens et son œuvre, suivi des impressions sur la peinture* (Brussels: Librairie nationale d'art et d'histoire G. van Oest et Cie, 1906), 23.

36. MR: See the entry of 11 August 1892 in Goncourt, *Journal, 1891–1892*, ed. Ricatte, 18:229.

37. MR: See Boucher, *Alfred Stevens*, 30, and Lemonnier, *Alfred Stevens et son œuvre*, 29.

38. MR: See the entry of 1 August 1892 in Goncourt, *Journal, 1891–1892*, ed. Ricatte, 18:228.

39. See the 6 March 1895 entry in Goncourt, *Journal, 1895–1896*, ed. Ricatte, 21:21.

40. MR: Cited in *C*, 2227.

41. The break with his parents did not last long. In July 1895, Claude postponed an appointment with Pierre Louÿs in order to be present for his mother's birthday party. On 11 September 1897, he wrote to Hartmann that his father was "not at all well" and that his mother was "calling him back to be close to his father" [*C*, 363]. After *Pelléas*, he painted this picture of his family for his wife, Lilly: "Welcomed, yesterday evening, at the home of the old Debussys. Mother had that stiff cordiality which is one of the hallmarks of her nature. . . 'La Trouille' [the nickname for his portly sister, Adèle] has grown considerably, no longer a little 'marmite' [cooking pot] but quite a large-sized 'pot-au-feu' [stockpot]. And Alfred continues to twirl his moustache in the grim manner of a bored noncommissioned officer who is waiting for the directory to come out!" See his letter from 1 June 1903 [in *C*, 737].

42. [*C*, 93.]

43. MR: FL 2003 gives his last name as "Limé," but Denis Herlin, in his article titled "À la Librairie de l'Art indépendant: Musique, poésie, art et ésoterisme," in *Histoires littéraires* 17, no. 68 (October–December 2016), 9n3, establishes the spelling of his last name as Limet.

44. MR: The "Bloody Week" at the end of the Commune culminated in a massacre at the Père-Lachaise Cemetery, where many Communards were slaughtered on 28 May 1871.

45. MR: According to FL notes taken from AJ/37/102 [in Fonds FL, BnF, carton I/6(4)], Bailly enrolled at the Conservatoire on 25 November 1877. Herlin, "À la Librairie de l'Art indépendant," 9n4, mentions a calling card in which Bailly described himself as a "music teacher" and a "former student at the Paris Conservatoire"; see BnF, département de la Musique, Ms. 11173. His name does not appear in Pierre, *Conservatoire national,* implying that he won no prizes while a student there.

46. MR: The logistics in which Bailly had essentially two addresses and two entrances for what was the same location are discussed by Jacques Brieu in his "Edmond Bailly," *Mercure de France* 120, no. 451 (1 April 1917): 554.

47. MR: Herlin, "À la Librairie de l'Art indépendant," 10–11, explains how Bailly thus sold prints, books, and music while also publishing new books, poetry, and music from the Librairie de l'art indépendant. In an appendix to his article, on pp. 40–55, Herlin gives a full catalog of the literary publications of the Librairie de l'art indépendant.

48. MR: Joscelyn Godwin mentions two additional works composed by Bailly for voice and piano: "La tristesse d'Ulad" (1898) and "Larmes" (1901); see Godwin, *Music and the Occult: French Musical Philosophies, 1750–1950* (Rochester, NY: University of Rochester Press, 1995), 153. Note that Debussy set Mallarmé's "Apparition" ten years before Bailly's version appeared, and that he, too, was captivated by the poetry of Charles d'Orléans, composing choral works in 1898 and 1908, significantly later than the d'Orléans settings of Bailly. Herlin, in "À la Librairie de l'Art indépendant," 32–33, makes the important observation that Debussy even worked with the same edition of d'Orléans's texts (by Champollion-Figeac) that was used by Bailly.

49. Henri de Régnier, *Vues* (Paris: Le Divan, 1926), 83–87; *Les nouvelles littéraires* (8 May 1926), [1]; and "Souvenirs sur Debussy," *La revue musicale* (1 May 1926): 89–91 (185–97).

50. MR: See Debussy's letter to Chausson from August 1893 in *C,* 147–48.

51. An extensive article by Edmond Bailly, "Le monde sonore. Le son. Harmonie des sphères. Voix de la nature," appeared in *Le guide musical* 37, no. 8 (22 February 1891): 57–59, and was continued in *Le guide musical* 37, no. 9 (1 March 1891): 65–67, in *Le guide musical* 37, no. 10 (8 March 1891): 73–75, and in *Le guide musical* 37, no. 11 (15 March 1891): 81–82.

52. MR: The cover of this journal, published by the Librairie de l'art indépendant, described it as a "revue documentaire de la tradition ésotérique et du symbolisme religieux."

53. MR: See Debussy's letter to Baron from September 1886 in *C,* 52.

54. MR: Gabriel Vicaire and Henry Beauclair [Adoré Floupette], *Les déliquescences d'Adoré Floupette* (Paris: Léon Vanier, 1885). For further details on this collection of decadent poetry, see p. 371n55.

55. MR: See Debussy's letter to André Poniatowski from February 1893 in *C*, 117.

56. MR: The original French here is "5 h à 7 h," translated literally as "5 o'clock to 7 o'clock"—in other words, the cocktail hour. Debussy's dedication of *La damoiselle élue*, from May 1893, reads: "This manuscript is offered to Bailly in memory of many times between 5 and 7 o'clock that were for me and will always be for me a precious aesthetic, and also for my sincere friendship" (Ce manuscrit est offert a [*sic*] Bailly en souvenir de beaucoup de 5h a [*sic*] 7h qui me furent et me seront toujours de précieuse esthétique, et aussi pour ma sincere [*sic*] amitié).

57. Victor-Émile Michelet, *Les compagnons de la hiérophanie* (Paris: Dorbon-Aîné, 1937), 73. Raymond Bonheur claimed that Debussy's acquaintance with the Librairie came about as a result of "a fortuitous combination of circumstances," which remains mysterious [see Raymond Bonheur, "Souvenirs et impressions d'un compagnon de jeunesse," *La revue musicale* (1 May 1926): 8 (104)].

58. Marius Richard, "Debussy inédit," *La liberté* (12 [*recte* 11] and 13 December 1931). MR: See especially p. 2 of the 13 December 1931 issue, titled "Souvenir sur Debussy: Une controverse musicale."

59. Marc Bredel, *Erik Satie* (Paris: Éditions Mazarine, 1982), 84 and 90.

60. Erik Satie, *Écrits*, rev. ed. Ornella Volta (Paris: Éditions Champ Libre, 1981), 68.

61. One cannot trust Lockspeiser, who, relying on Edmond Haraucourt's vague mixture of peoples' remarks, contended that Claude-Achille frequented the Chat Noir a little after 1881 and that he showed off at the piano in the company of Maurice Rollinat, Georges Fragerolle, Paul Delmet, and Marie Krysinska; [see Edward Lockspeiser, *Debussy: His Life and Mind* (London: Cassel, 1962–65), 1:144]. The same imagined events reappear in Stefan Jarocinski, *Debussy, impressionisme et symbolisme*, trans. Thérèse Douchy (Paris: Éditions du Seuil, 1970), 96–97.

62. MR: See Maurice Donnay, *Autour du Chat Noir* (Paris: Bernard Grasset, 1926), 28.

63. MR: The script of *Ailleurs*, premiered at the Chat Noir on 11 November 1891, with scenery by Henri Rivière, is reproduced in Donnay, *Autour du Chat Noir*, 135–92.

64. MR: Maurice Mac-Nab, one of the regulars at the Chat Noir, went so far as to publish a very limited edition of amusing *Poèmes mobiles* together with his *Monologues*, with many illustrations by the author (Paris: Léon Vanier, 1886). I am grateful to Peter Bloom, who suggested the connection between the "mobile poems" and the "incongruous poems" of Mac-Nab.

65. Robert Godet, in Claude Debussy, *Lettres à deux amis*, ed. Godet and Georges Jean-Aubry (Paris: Librairie José Corti 1942), 50, was the first to correct this myth.

66. See the entry of 21 November 1891 in Goncourt, *Journal, 1891–1892*, ed. Ricatte, 18:96.

67. Autograph letter from Camille Benoit to Paul Dukas, BnF, département de la Musique, W-48 (74).

68. MR: See Donnay, *Autour du Chat Noir*, 31–32. The text of the song's refrain was as follows: "Café, liqueur universelle / Nectar aimé des dieux / Ton suave

arome recèle / Un pouvoir mystérieux." (Coffee, universal liquor / Beloved nectar of the gods / Your mellow aroma holds / A mysterious power.) FL 2003 states that the chorus was an improvised fugue on this song; however, there is no mention of a fugue in Donnay's account.

69. MR: The quotation in FL 2003 is "pour soi tout seul." This citation was most likely taken from a letter that Pierre Louÿs had written to his half-brother Georges Louis on 16 April 1890. In it he referenced the notion of writing for the public, but believed that his works should be kept "pour soi seul"; see Pierre Louÿs and Georges Louis, *Correspondance croisée, 1890–1917* (Paris: Honoré Champion, 2015), 1:20. Georges Jean-Aubry, in his Introduction to Claude Debussy and Pierre Louÿs, *Correspondance de Claude Debussy et Pierre Louÿs* (1893–1904), ed. Henri Borgeaud (Paris: Librairie José Corti, 1945), 7, posits that the friendship between Debussy and Louÿs did not blossom until 1893, three years after the publication of the *Cinq poèmes*. Thus, given that FL 2003 purports that this remark was made by Louÿs in 1890–91, it could hardly have been addressed to Debussy. That said, Louÿs wrote to Debussy on 24 July 1896 in similar terms: "One must write: 1° For oneself." See *C*, 320.

70. Richard, "Souvenir sur Debussy: Une controverse musicale," cited on p. 385n58. Eighteen years later, the tailor nevertheless demanded his due; see Debussy's letter to Durand, possibly from 1908, [in *C*, 1141–42].

71. MR: See Herold, "Quelques mots sur Stéphane Mallarmé," [3]. As Denis Herlin points out in his facsimile edition of Debussy's *Prélude à l'après-midi d'un faune* (Paris: Bibliothèque nationale de France, Brepols Publishers, 2013), 8n20, Herold was well aware of Mallarmé's taste in music and invited him to musical gatherings at his home (see p. 381n3). Mallarmé's letter to Herold from 28 February 1890 references this exchange; see Stéphane Mallarmé, *Correspondance*, ed. Henri Mondor and Lloyd James Austin (Paris: Gallimard, 1959–85), vol. 11 (supplément): 53. According to Jacques Robichez, *Le symbolisme au théâtre* (Paris: L'Arche, 1957), 89–91, the Théâtre d'Art came into its own by November 1890, following the short-lived previous merger of Fort's Théâtre Mixte with Louis Germain's Théâtre Idéaliste. Readers interested in the formation and early productions of the Théâtre d'Art will want to consult Robichez, *Le symbolisme au théâtre*, 86–92 and 110–41. For details on Lugné-Poe's involvement as an actor at Fort's Théâtre d'Art, the beginnings of his own Théâtre de l'Œuvre, and the premiere of Maurice Maeterlinck's play, *Pelléas et Mélisande*, see Robichez, *Le symbolisme au théâtre*, 158–75 and 188–96.

72. MR: See Jean-Michel Nectoux, "Debussy et Mallarmé," *Cahiers Debussy* 12–13 (1988–89): 54.

73. Louÿs felt that he went there not "to listen but rather to write. The sound of the orchestra excited his imagination, but without his being concerned about knowing if they were playing [Jean-Philippe] Rameau's 'Tambourin' or [Richard Wagner's] *Siegfried's Idyll*." (Jean-Paul Goujon, "Pierre Louÿs et Wagner," in *Littératures* [Toulouse: 1988], 152.)

74. MR: See Mallarmé's letter of 29 November 1890 to Edmond Deman in Mallarmé, *Correspondance*, 4:165.

75. MR: Herold, "Quelques mots sur Stéphane Mallarmé," [3].

76. MR: See Stéphane Mallarmé, *Œuvres complètes: Poésies*, ed. Carl Paul Barbier and Charles Gordon Millan (Paris: Flammarion, 1983), 269.

77. Nectoux, "Debussy et Mallarmé," *Cahiers Debussy* (1988–89), 58 and 65n21.

78. MR: Debussy's letter to Godet from 12 February (not 13 February, as reported in FL 2003) is in *C*, 95–96.

79. As reported by Prince Poniatowski [in *D'un siècle à l'autre* ([Paris]: Presses de la cité, 1948), 242.]

80. Louis Laloy, *La musique retrouvée* (Paris: Librairie Plon, 1928), 121. MR: The phrase "bien tassée" refers to the way a drink of absinthe is prepared. Concentrated absinthe is poured into a glass, on top of which rests a slotted spoon that holds a lump of sugar. Water is gradually poured over the sugar, thus diluting the absinthe, to the drinker's taste. Absinthe that is "bien tassée" is quite potent, as it involves very little water in its preparation.

81. Letter from Camille Mauclair to Gabriel Astruc (BnF, département de la Musique, Lettre de Camille Mauclair à Gabriel Astruc, Paris, [1932], 2). On p. 66 of "Le souvenir de Claude Debussy," *Terres latines* 4, no. 3 (March 1936), 66–67, Mauclair states that he had known the composer at Mallarmé's [salon, but in his letter to Astruc, he claims that he met Debussy through their mutual friend, Pierre Louÿs].

82. [See in particular p. 133 of] Julien Tiersot, "La semaine sainte à l'église Saint-Gervais," *Le ménestrel* 58, no. 17 (26 April 1892): 132–33, where the author noted the presence of Mallarmé, Gounod, and even Péladan for the concerts during Holy Week.

83. MR: Debussy's letter to Marie Mallarmé was dated on 12 September 1898, which was three days after Mallarmé's death (not one day later, as reported in FL 2003); see *C*, 418.

84. MR: The contract is reprinted in *C*, 94.

85. MR: The contract is reprinted in *C*, 97–98.

86. MR: This contract is reprinted in *C*, 99–100.

87. MR: The less formal contract with Hamelle is reprinted in *C*, 101–2.

88. MR: Read sent a letter, written in French, to Debussy on 24 January 1891, in which he gave his permission for publication of the *Marche des anciens comtes de Ross* and also attached a note that explained the origin of the march, information that appeared on the title page of the composition. See Marie Rolf, "General Meredith Read and Claude Debussy's *Marche écossaise*," *The Musical Quarterly* 95, nos. 2–3 (Summer–Fall 2012): 271.

89. MR: FL 2003 repeats the story about Alphonse Allais and misidentifies Read as a "Scottish general." For a detailed explanation of the origins of the *Marche écossaise*, see Rolf, "General Meredith Read and Claude Debussy's *Marche écossaise*," 252–98.

90. MR: See Godet's introduction in Debussy, *Lettres à deux amis*, 40–45.

91. See in particular Victor Seroff, *Claude Debussy* (Paris: Éditions Buchet/Chastel, Corréa, 1957), 150; Anne Rivière, *L'Interdite: Camille Claudel, 1864–1943* (Paris: Éditions Tierce, 1983), 20–21, fictionalized; Reine-Marie Paris [identified as Reine-Marie Nouel in FL 2003], *Camille Claudel, 1864–1943*, ed. Jean Pavlevski (Paris: Economica, 2012), a corrected version of the 1984 edition published by Gallimard [see as well the English translation: Reine-Marie Paris, *Camille: The Life of Camille Claudel, Rodin's Muse and Mistress*, trans. Liliane Emery Turk (New York:

Henry Holt and Company, 1988)]; *"L'âge mur" de Camille Claudel* (Paris: Éditions de la Réunion des musées nationaux, 1988), 19–26 and 60, from the Dossiers of the Musée d'Orsay. MR: In the latter source, André Tissier claims that Claudel met Debussy for the first time at Mallarmé's salon (p. 19) and that she took Debussy to the Exposition universelle, where they both discovered Hokusai's *Wave off Kanagawa* (p. 21). In the 1897 Salon, Claudel would appropriate Hokusai's idea in her sculpture titled *La vague*, and in 1905, Debussy would request that a variant of Hokusai's wave be reproduced on the cover of the first edition of *La mer*.

92. See the entry of 8 March 1894 in Goncourt, *Journal, 1894–1895*, ed. Ricatte, 20:19.

93. Jules Renard, *Le journal de Jules Renard* (Paris: François Bernouard, 1927), 1:261, describes a dinner on 19 March 1895 at Paul Claudel's home: "She [Camille] hates music, saying out loud what she thinks, and her brother rages, staring at his plate, and one senses his fists clenching in anger."

94. MR: See Godet's introduction in Debussy, *Lettres à deux amis*, 41.

95. MR: See Godet, "En marge de la marge," 72 (168).

96. MR: See Godet's introduction in Debussy, *Lettres à deux amis*, 44.

97. MR: See Godet's introduction in Debussy, *Lettres à deux amis*, 44.

98. See pp. 199–200.

99. MR: See pp. 736n1 and 746n1 in Mathias Morhardt, "Mlle Camille Claudel," *Mercure de France* 25, no. 99 (March 1898): 709–55.

100. [See Suarès's letter from 14 January 1890 in André Suarès and Romain Rolland,] "Cette âme ardente. . . Choix de lettres de André Suarès à Romain Rolland (1887–1891)," *Cahiers Romain Rolland* 5 (1954): 206.

101. MR: Suarès, "Cette âme ardente. . . ," 206.

102. MR: The questionnaire, from 16 February 1889, is reproduced in *C*, 67–68.

103. MR: See Godet, "En marge de la marge," 76 (172). Debussy's advocate and colleague at the Société nationale de musique, Ernest Chausson, would set five of Maeterlinck's *Serres chaudes* in 1893–96.

104. Octave Mirbeau, "Maurice Maeterlinck," *Le Figaro* (24 August 1890): [1].

105. MR: Denis Herlin traces Huret's involvement in this exchange in greater detail; see his *"Pelléas et Mélisande* aux Bouffes-Parisiens," in Pelléas et Mélisande *cent ans après: Études et documents*, ed. Jean-Christophe Branger, Sylvie Douche, and Denis Herlin (Paris: Symétrie, 2012), 45–46.

106. MR: Herlin, *"Pelléas et Mélisande* aux Bouffes-Parisiens," 45n23, speculates that this mutual friend must have been Octave Maus, who was a passionate supporter of d'Indy's work.

107. Published by Léon Vallas in [a letter appearing under] "Correspondance," *Le temps* (28 September 1942): 2, and excerpted in his *Achille Claude Debussy* (Paris: Presses Universitaires de France, 1944), 213–14.

108. Gabriel Mourey, "Souvenirs sur Debussy," *Cahiers Debussy* 15 (1991): 56–57.

109. [Paul Adam's 1892 letter to Gabriel Mourey is excerpted in] a Drouot auction catalog (Paris, 16 October 1991), item 118.

110. MR: This is a veiled reference to the journal *Le centaure*, which published only two issues in 1896. Many of Debussy's friends—writers such as Herold, Régnier,

Louÿs, Paul Valéry, André Lebey, Jean de Tinan, and André Gide—were involved with this publication.

111. MR: See Louÿs's letter to George Louis from 17 September 1891 in Louÿs and Louis, *Correspondance croisée, 1890–1917*, 1:108.

112. MR: Willy, *Bains de sons, par l'ouvreuse du cirque d'été* (Paris: H. Simonis Empis, 1893), 150. Willy's invented adjective plays on Baudelaire's well-known collection of poems from which Debussy drew for his *Cinq poèmes de Baudelaire*.

113. MR: This reference is to the *Trois mélodies de Verlaine*, which include "La mer est plus belle," "Le son du cor s'afflige," and "L'échelonnement des haïes."

114. MR: This reference is to the *Fêtes galantes*, series I, published in 1903 by Fromont.

8. Esotericism and Symbolism: 1892

1. MR: Constant Pierre, *Le Conservatoire national de musique et de déclamation* (Paris: Imprimerie nationale, 1900), 450, specifies that Marty was a professor of vocal ensembles.

2. MR: See Raymond Bonheur, "Souvenirs et impressions d'un compagnon de jeunesse," *La revue musicale* (1 May 1926): 5 (101).

3. MR: In addition, two sessions each were devoted to Cécile Chaminade (introduced by Roger Milès), Georges Hüe (introduced by Léonce Détroyat), and Vincent d'Indy (introduced by Henry Bauër). The concerts, collectively titled "One Hour of New Music," were held at the Théâtre d'Application. See "Nouvelles diverses: France," *L'art musical* 31, no. 1 (15 January 1892): 6.

4. MR: See Debussy's letter from February 1893 to André Poniatowski in *C*, 115.

5. Henri Moreno (that is to say, Heugel), "Semaine théâtrale," *Le ménestrel* 58, no. 25 (19 June 1892): 196. Chabrier seems to have been similarly inclined; he made mention of "sick" music to his publisher, Enoch.

6. [*C*, 103.]

7. MR: This exchange was reported by Robert Godet in "En marge de la marge," *La revue musicale* (1 May 1926): 70 (166).

8. Amédée Gastoué, *L'église et la musique* (Paris: B. Grasset, 1936), 60. The trip that Debussy is said to have made to the Abbey of Solesmes in 1893 may be regarded as legend; see François Lesure, *Claude Debussy: Biographie critique* (Paris: Fayard, 2003), 459.

9. MR: See the notice in "Courrier des théâtres," *Le Figaro* (2 March 1892): 6.

10. Later, in a letter to Félix Fenéon from April 1907, Jules Bois himself seemed to repudiate somewhat his youthful behavior: "I've never been an occultist in the activist and somewhat mystical sense of the word." See Charavay catalog, unidentified number; confirmed by FL notes in BnF, Fonds Lesure, carton I/6(15).

11. MR: See Debussy's letter to Bois from the middle of March 1892 in *C*, 105. In *C*, 105n4, Lesure and Herlin point out Debussy's allusion to Camille de

Sainte-Croix's novel-like story, *La mauvaise aventure*, in 1885. Henri Quittard ultimately composed the music for Bois's *Les noces de Sathan*; at its performances on 28 and 30 March 1892, Lugné-Poe played the role of Satan.

12. Christophe Beaufils, *Le Sâr Péladan, 1858–1918: Biographie critique* (Paris: Aux amateurs de livres, 1986), 89–92; Robert Orledge, *Satie the Composer* (Cambridge: Cambridge University Press, 1990), especially 106–8. MR: Orledge, *Satie the Composer*, 46, explains that "the subtitle 'Wagnérie Kaldéenne' for *Le fils des étoiles* was a misleading afterthought that appears in neither Satie's manuscript nor Péladan's autograph scenario," both of which are instead titled "Pastorale Kaldéenne." One might add that Satie composed the music for Jules Bois's second esoteric drama, *La porte héroïque du ciel*, and that this work was performed at Lugné-Poe's Théâtre de l'Œuvre in 1894.

13. P. Contamine de Latour, "Erik Satie intime: Souvenirs de jeunesse," *Comœdia* (6 August 1925): 2.

14. MR: See *C*, 2226.

15. MR: Satie's dedicated score may be viewed online at the website of the BnF, IFN-52000613.

16. MR: In 1888, Joséphin Péladan, Stanislaus de Guaita, and Gérard Encausse (whose pseudonym was Papus) founded the Ordre de la Rose+Croix Kabbalistique in Paris. Péladan subsequently broke from this group for theological reasons, founding his own order, the Rose+Croix Catholique, and Papus Martinist founded a Martinist order. See John Michael Greer, *The New Encyclopedia of the Occult* (St. Paul, MN: Llewellyn Publications, 2004), 211–12, 360–61, and 365.

17. MR: See p. 227 of Laurent Tailhade, "*Quand les violons sont partis* par Édouard Dubus," *L'initiation* 5, no. 15 (June 1892): 227–30.

18. MR: Debussy's original words were "le plus humble des groins." As pointed out by Lesure and Herlin in *C*, 106n2, Tailhade would go on to publish a work in 1899, titled *À travers les groins*, that created a stir.

19. MR: See Debussy's letter of 19 June 1892 in *C*, 106.

20. MR: Errors in both the spelling of Tailhade's name (as Taillhade) and Debussy's signature (as L. Debussy) were printed in "Correspondance," *L'initiation* 5, no. 16 (July 1892): 95–96.

21. Letter of 18 December 1911 [in *C*, 1470]. The two men did not meet in person until the time of *Pelléas*.

22. See Léon R. Schidlof, *Dossiers secrets d'Henri Lobineau* (Paris: Philippe Toscan du Plantier, 1967 [mimeographed]), [12]; see also Gérard de Sède, *Signé Rose+Croix: L'énigme de Rennes-le-Château* (Paris: Librairie Plon, 1977, [28]), which considers the relationship between Debussy and the singer Emma Calvé. MR: Calvé was an occultist who had several amorous liaisons with other occult figures, among them Jules Bois. Schidlof was a genealogist whose pseudonym was Henri Lobineau.

23. Robert Orledge, *Debussy and the Theatre* (Cambridge: Cambridge University Press, 1982), 46–47; Roy Howat, *Debussy in Proportion: A Musical Analysis* (Cambridge: Cambridge University Press, 1983), 170; and Orledge, *Satie the Composer*, 41.

24. These individuals all circulated within what FL 2003 calls the "Desboutin group," referring to the painter, Marcellin Desboutin.

25. MR: De Feure, whose birth name was Georges Joseph Van Sluijters, was born in Paris; his Dutch father, Jan Hendrik, was an architect who worked for aristocratic families in the area of Paris between the Parc Monceau and the Arc de Triomphe. Georges de Feure wrote the scenario for a ballet to be composed by Debussy, *Le palais du silence*, or *No-Ja-Li*; see p. 310. Further information on de Feure's Symbolist leanings may be found in Ian Millman, "Georges de Feure: The Forgotten Dutch Master of Symbolism and Art Nouveau," *Tableau Fine Arts Magazine* 6, no. 1 (September–October 1983): 41–47; a photocopy of this article is located at the BnF, Fonds Lesure, carton I/6(15). See also Ian Millman, *Georges de Feure, maître du symbolisme et de l'art nouveau* (Paris: ACR Édition, 1992), which is replete with beautiful reproductions of de Feure's art.

26. FL 2003 cites the unpublished souvenirs of Georges de Feure, communicated by his widow to Henri Borgeaud. Dépaquit, who would become the first mayor of the free Commune of Montmartre (founded on 11 April 1870), was an illustrator who wrote the script of a pantomime-ballet, *Jack-in-the-box*, for Satie. MR: The composer referred to the project as "more of a 'clownerie' than a pantomime," and he called his score a "suite anglaise"; see Orledge, *Satie the Composer*, 282.

27. MR: This quote comes from Debussy's dedication to Denis of a copy of the newly published score, in July 1893; see *C*, 2220. As for the composer's letter to Denis, Lesure and Herlin ascribe to it the date of 10 June (although FL 2003 gives the month as July) 1893; in his thank-you note, Debussy referred to a proof of Denis's cover illustration, calling it "a beautiful thing"; see *C*, 139.

28. MR: Debussy's contract with Paul Dupont, dated 27 July 1892, is reproduced in *C*, 107. Note that in Dupont's publication, "*(Interlude)*" appeared as a subtitle to the *Nocturne*.

29. MR: Announcements appeared, under the title of "Le Figaro musical," on the front pages of *Le Figaro* (20 August 1892) and *Le Figaro* (24 August 1892), and a brief review by Charles Darcours was published in "Le Figaro musical," *Le Figaro* (22 August 1892): 2.

30. MR: These two poems were not titled individually; rather, they appeared under the collective title of *Proses lyriques*, by "C. A. Debussy," in *Entretiens politiques et littéraires* 5, no. 33 (December 1892): 269–71.

31. Bonheur, "Souvenirs et impressions," 6 (102).

32. MR: This reference, made in 1910, is presumably to Marie François Sadi Carnot, who was the President of France from 1887 until his assassination in 1894.

33. It has generally been assumed that Debussy made a mistake in situating that visit at the rue de Londres, and that it had taken place at the rue Gustave Doré. The details given on the furnished apartment, added to what we now know of the relationship between the two men from 1890, lead us to believe that his memory was perfectly reliable.

34. Letter of 25 March 1910 to Georges Jean-Aubry [in *C*, 1261].

35. MR: Two authors who have presented analyses that correlate Debussy's music closely with Mallarmé's text include Arthur B. Wenk, *Claude Debussy and the Poets* (Berkeley: University of California Press, 1976), 148–70; and David J. Code,

"Hearing Debussy Reading Mallarmé: Music *après Wagner* in the *Prélude à l'après-midi d'un faune*," *Journal of the American Musicological Society* 54, no. 3 (Fall 2001): 493–554.

36. MR: See Debussy's letter to Poniatowski from 9 September 1892 in *C*, 110.

37. [*C*, 109.] This is the earliest known letter in which Achille abandoned his first name in his signature.

38. MR: See Debussy's letter to Poniatowski from 9 September 1892 in *C*, 110.

39. MR: See Debussy's letter to Poniatowski from 5 October 1892 in *C*, 111–12.

9. The Chausson Year: 1893

1. MR: See Debussy's February 1893 letter to André Poniatowski in *C*, 115.

2. MR: These were Debussy's own words; see his February 1893 letter to André Poniatowski in *C*, 117.

3. MR: See André Poniatowski, *D'un siècle à l'autre* (Paris: Presses de la Cité, 1948; repr. 1984), 310.

4. MR: Poniatowski, *D'un siècle à l'autre*, 310.

5. Poniatowski, *D'un siècle à l'autre*, 307–10. Again, the letter from Debussy that (discreetly) mentions this support is dated February 1893 [*C*, 113–17].

6. MR: Poniatowski, *D'un siècle à l'autre*, 113–14.

7. Julien Tiersot, "Revue des grands concerts," *Le ménestrel* 59, no. 16 (16 April 1893): 125.

8. See the review in "Concerts: Société nationale," *Le progrès artistique* 16, no. 778 (23 April 1893): 3.

9. MR: Charles Darcours, "Notes de musique," *Le Figaro* (12 April 1893): 5.

10. MR: Darcours, "Notes de musique," 5.

11. MR: Willy, "Lettre de l'ouvreuse," *L'écho de Paris* (11 April 1893): 3.

12. Léon Vallas gives longer excerpts from some of these articles in *Claude Debussy et son temps* (Paris: Éditions Albin Michel, 1958), 150–52 [and 133].

13. BnF, département de la Musique, Rés. F. 994 E, 2.

14. *Archives d'Eugène Bertrand*, auction catalog, Thierry Bodin, expert (La Varenne-Saint-Hilaire, 18 March 1990), item 34. MR: The text of the letter is not in the catalog itself, but FL wrote it by hand into his copy of the catalog, now in the Fonds Lesure, BnF, carton I/5(15).

15. Michel Stockhem, "Lettres d'Ernest Chausson à Eugène Ysaÿe," *Revue belge de musicologie* 42 (1988): 249.

16. MR: H. Moreno was the pseudonym for Henri Heugel, the publisher of music as well as, for many years, *Le ménestrel*.

17. MR: H. Moreno, "*La Walkyrie* de Richard Wagner, première représentation à l'Opéra," *Le ménestrel* 59, no. 20 (14 May 1893): 153.

18. Henri de Régnier, [Œuvres diverses,] BnF, Mss. 14976, fol. 111. MR: See the journal entry for 11 May in Henri de Régnier, *Les cahiers inédits, 1887–1936*, ed. David J. Niederauer and François Broche (Paris: Éditions Pygmalion/Gérard Watelet, 2002), 336.

19. MR: See Debussy's letter of 7 May 1893 to Chausson in *C*, 126–27.

20. [*C*, 126.]

21. [*C*, 130.]
22. [*C*, 132.]
23. [*C*, 136.]
24. [*C*, 140.]
25. [*C*, 144.]
26. [*C*, 145.]

27. MR: Chausson asked Bonheur, in a letter from 8 June 1893, to bring the orchestral score of Rimsky-Korsakov's *Antar*; see Ernest Chausson, *Écrits inédits: Journaux intimes, roman de jeunesse, correspondance*, ed. Jean Gallois and Isabelle Bretaudeau (Monaco: Éditions du Rocher, 1999), 345.

28. MR: See Chausson's letter of 10 May 1893 to Ysaÿe in Stockhem, "Lettres d'Ernest Chausson à Eugène Ysaÿe," 249.

29. [See Chausson's letters from 9 June and 28 June 1893 in] Stockhem, "Lettres d'Ernest Chausson à Eugène Ysaÿe," 252–53. The work was not programmed in Brussels after all.

30. Letter from Satie to his brother Conrad, 28 June 1893 (Robert Orledge, *Satie the Composer* [Cambridge: Cambridge University Press, 1990], 49).

31. See Chausson's letter of 12 October 1893 [and sent from Royan, two hours north of Arcachon, in *C*, 164.] MR: As Lesure and Herlin point out in *C*, 163n2, this letter was dated as 19 October in Ernest Chausson, "Dix lettres d'Ernest Chausson à Claude Debussy (1893–1894)," *Revue de musicologie* 48, no. 125 (July–December 1962): 49–60. However, we know that Chausson had already gone farther south to Arcachon by 17 October, from a letter that he had written to Lerolle on that date; thus, since Chausson had written the letter in question on a Thursday, and since in it he stated that he was leaving for Arcachon the next day, Lesure and Herlin surmise that the correct date must be 12 October, from the previous week.

32. MR: See Chausson's letter of 19 July 1893 in *C*, 145.

33. MR: See Debussy's letter to Chausson from 4 June 1893 in *C*, 132.

34. See Chausson's letter of 18 December [in *C*, 181].

35. MR: See Chausson's letter of 19 July 1893 in *C*, 144–45.

36. MR: See Debussy's letter of 9 July 1893 in *C*, 143–44.

37. MR: This passage is quoted in part in Jean Gallois, *Ernest Chausson* (Paris: Librairie Arthème Fayard, 1994), 347.

38. Marcel Dietschy and André Schaeffner disagreed on this issue in particular; see André Schaeffner, "Debussy et la musique russe," *Musique russe I* (1953, republished with several modifications in *Essais de musicologie et autres fantaisies* [1980], 157–206; reprinted in *Variations sur la musique* [Paris: Librairie Arthème Fayard, 1998], 255–303). Laloy stated that Brayer had played *Boris* to Debussy before his second sojourn to Bayreuth. MR: Marcel Dietschy, in *La passion de Claude Debussy* (Neuchâtel: Éditions de la Baconnière, 1962), 72–76 (and in William Ashbrook and Margaret G. Cobb's English translation of Dietschy, *A Portrait of Claude Debussy* [Oxford: Oxford University Press, 1990], 60–64), lays out the arguments made by various authors concerning the origins of Mussorgsky's influence on Debussy. He makes the point that Debussy's exposure to Mussorgsky helped mollify his obsession with Wagner. The passages cited in FL 2003 come from Raymond Bonheur,

"Souvenirs et impressions d'un compagnon de jeunesse," *La revue musicale* (1 May 1926): 7n2 (103n2)–8 (104).

39. MR: Lugné-Poe [Aurélian-Marie Lugné] recorded his memories of the premiere in *La parade. I. Le sot du tremplin: Souvenirs et impressions de théâtre* (Paris: Librairie Gallimard, 1930); see especially pp. 244–30.

40. Claude Debussy, "Pourquoi j'ai écrit 'Pelléas,'" in *Monsieur Croche et autres écrits*, rev. ed. (Paris: Éditions Gallimard, 1987), 62; and in English in Claude Debussy, *Debussy on Music*, trans. Richard Langham Smith (New York: Alfred A. Knopf, 1977), 74–75. See also Louis Laloy, *Claude Debussy* (Paris: Les bibliophiles fantaisistes, 1909), 28.

41. Jacques Robichez, *Le symbolisme au théâtre: Lugné-Poe et les débuts de l'Œuvre* (Paris: L'Arche, 1957), 171n65. MR: FL 2003 cites p. 158 in error.

42. MR: Robichez lists many more figures that were well known in Parisian society in his *Le symbolisme au théâtre*, 170n58.

43. Letter of 21 May 1893, cited on p. 340 of François Lesure, "Claude Debussy, Ernest Chausson et Henri Lerolle," in *Humanisme actif* (Paris: Hermann, 1968), 1:337–44. Tola Dorian had insisted that the program mention that she had made use of Paul Vogler's sets.

44. MR: See Stéphane Mallarmé, *Divagations* (Paris: Bibliothèque-Charpentier, Eugène Fasquelle, éditeur, 1897), 221.

45. MR: A facsimile of this letter is given in Denis Herlin, "*Pelléas et Mélisande* aux Bouffes-Parisiens," in Pelléas et Mélisande *cent ans après: Études et documents*, ed. Jean-Christophe Branger, Sylvie Douche, and Denis Herlin (Paris: Symétrie, 2012), 54.

46. MR: Gustave Charpentier, in "Hommage à Claude Debussy: Sa jeunesse et sa mort," *Chantecler* 3, no. 100 (24 March 1928): 1, claimed that Debussy told him that the work was "so antithetical to what I wanted to express. The traditional aspect of the subject calls for music that does not belong to me."

47. [Letter from Paul Dukas to Vincent d'Indy, dated 1 October 1893; see Georges Favre, "Une lettre de Paul Dukas à Vincent d'Indy,"] *La revue musicale* 25, no. 209 (March 1949): 7.

48. MR: Teresa Davidian, in "Debussy's *Fantaisie*: Issues, Proofs, and Revisions," *Cahiers Debussy* 17–18 (1993–94): 15–33, argues that the primary reason for the composer's decision to shelve this work was his dissatisfaction with its orchestration.

49. *L'idée libre*, a periodical in which Régnier and Bailly notably collaborated, announced this article in its issue of 10 September 1893, and then in the five following issues, up to February 1894. Commenting on this title, Pierre Louÿs wrote that it "is more than an homage. It is an obsession; it's haunting." MR: See a facsimile of Louÿs's manuscript in Paul-Ursin Dumont, *Pierre Louÿs, l'hermite du hameau* (Vendôme: Libraidisque, 1985), 105.

50. [*C*, 152.]

51. MR: See Debussy's letter to Chausson from 3 September 1893 in *C*, 156.

52. MR: See Debussy's letter to Chausson from 2 October 1893 in *C*, 160.

53. MR: See Debussy's letter to Chausson from 2 October 1893 in *C*, 160–61.

54. MR: Chausson, in a letter to Debussy from 12 October 1893, mentioned that "Bonheur is absolutely in love with your scene from *Pelléas et Mélisandre* [*sic*]";

see *C*, 165. And Debussy mentioned Lerolle's comments on "some extraordinary things in *Pélléas* [*sic*]" in a letter to Chausson from 23 October 1893; see *C*, 169.

55. Georges Jean-Aubry placed their meeting at the Auberge du Clou in 1893 (see his introduction in Claude Debussy and Pierre Louÿs, *Correspondance de Claude Debussy et Pierre Louÿs (1893–1904)*, ed. Henri Borgeaud [Paris: Librairie José Corti, 1945], 9). But a manuscript by Louÿs unambiguously specifies that "he got to know me at Mallarmé's" (reproduced by Dumont, *Pierre Louÿs, l'hermite du hameau*, 105), and a dedication of *Aphrodite* to the composer clearly confirms the following: "[. . .] so that the dates of this book will remind him of the first four years of our friendship, 1892–1895" (pour que les dates de ce livre lui rappellent les quatres premières années de notre amitié, 1892–1895). A facsimile of Louÿs's dedication appears in *Livres anciens et modernes, comprenant la bibliothèque du Comte et de la Comtesse Guy du Boisrouvray*, auction catalog (Monte-Carlo, Sotheby's, 16 October 1989), item 58. MR: This copy was subsequently sold in June 1992; see the auction catalog of the Librairie Lardanchet, item 203, mentioned in *C*, 310n1.

56. See Debussy's letter to Chausson [from 16 November 1893] in *C*, 176. The version reported much later by Louÿs stressed Debussy's shyness on that occasion. [See the letter from Louÿs to his half-brother Georges Louis, written on 19 April 1914, in Pierre Louÿs and Georges Louis, *Correspondance croisée, 1890–1917* (Paris: Honoré Champion, 2015), 4:1997–98, and cited in *C*, 176n1.] Camille Mauclair ("Claude Debussy et les poètes" in the program of the Festival Claude Debussy, 17 June 1932) claimed a personal role in obtaining that authorization, but his version is not credible, given the chronology of events.

57. Régnier's journal may be found at the BnF, Mss., nouv. acq. fr. 14976, fol. 137v. MR: See also his entry from August 1893 in Régnier, *Les cahiers inédits, 1887–1936*, 349.

58. Letter of 15 August 1893 [from Debussy to Chausson in *C*, 149].

59. MR: The contract for the String Quartet is reprinted in *C*, 165–66.

60. MR: See Debussy's letter to Chausson from 23 October 1893 in *C*, 168. Durand's publication office was located at the place de la Madeleine.

61. MR: See Chausson's letter to Lerolle from 28 November 1893 in Lesure, "Claude Debussy, Ernest Chausson et Henri Lerolle," 340 [as well as in Chausson, *Écrits inédits*, 365].

62. MR: See Debussy's letter to Dukas from 11 January 1894 in *C*, 186.

63. MR: For further details and illustrations, see Louis Laloy, *La musique retrouvée* (Paris: Librairie Plon, 1928), 68, and "Saint Gervais," *Autour de Charles Bordes*, 3 April 2013, http://charles-bordes.over-blog.com/article-saint-gervais-116768870.html.

64. MR: Yvonne, the older of the two sisters, was said to embody in a way Debussy's "damoiselle élue"; see Jean-Michel Nectoux, *Harmonie en bleu et or: Debussy, la musique et les arts* (Paris: Librairie Arthème Fayard, 2003), 76, for a discussion of her interaction with and influence on the composer, who would dedicate in 1894 the manuscript of his *Images oubliées* for piano to her. A reproduction of the Renoir portrait of the sisters (1897) that is housed at the Musée de l'Orangerie in Paris appears on p. 76, and a reproduction of Denis's portrait of Yvonne (also from 1897) appears on p. 83.

65. MR: Debussy's dedication on the fan reads: "To Miss Yvonne Lerolle, in remembrance of her little sister Mélisande" (À Mademoiselle Yvonne Lerolle en souvenir de sa petite sœur Mélisande). In other words, Yvonne reminded Debussy of Mélisande. See Nectoux, *Harmonie en bleu et or*, 77.

66. The fan is reproduced on the cover of Claude Debussy, *Correspondance, 1894–1918* (Paris: Hermann, 1993) [as well as in Jean-Michel Nectoux, *Debussy, la musique et les arts*, exhibition catalog (Paris: Musée d'Orsay, 2012), 45].

67. MR: See J. G. R., "Les concerts à Paris," *Le guide musical* 40, no. 2 (7 January 1894): 35.

68. MR: L'ouvreuse du cirque d'été, "Lettre de l'ouvreuse," *L'écho de Paris* (2 January 1894): 3.

69. MR: See "Le quatuor Ysaÿe à Paris," *L'art moderne* 14, no. 1 (7 January 1894): 5.

70. MR: See Paul Dukas, *Les écrits de Paul Dukas sur la musique* (Paris: Société d'éditions françaises et internationales, 1948), 176.

71. MR: See Debussy's letter to Chausson from 5 February 1894 in *C*, 192.

72. See letter of 16 March 1902 in Albéric Magnard, *Correspondance (1888–1914)*, ed. Claire Vlach (Paris: Société française de musicologie, 1997), 185.

10. A "Fairy Tale" Gone Awry: 1894

1. A written invitation to these performances is preserved in the Bibliothèque Jacques Doucet. According to Ernest Chausson, *Écrits inédits: Journaux intimes, roman de jeunesse, correspondance*, ed. Jean Gallois and Isabelle Bretaudeau (Monaco: Éditions du Rocher, 1999), 376, and Léon Vallas, *Achille-Claude Debussy* (Paris: Presses Universitaires de France, 1949), 94 [*recte* 34], Debussy received the sum of 1,000 francs for the first act of *Parsifal* alone. MR: It was likely for a performance at Mme Escudier's home that Debussy annotated a French translation in Chausson's personal first-edition score of *Parsifal*, often changing the rhythm of the vocal line to accommodate the French text; this score was sold by Sotheby's in 2014 (see *Music, Continental and Russian Books and Manuscripts* [London, Sotheby's, 20 May 2014], item 226) and has subsequently been advertised by Michel Scognamillo, *Livres précieux ou curieux, autographes, musique & photographies* (Paris, Librairie Métamorphoses), item 21. Lerolle's fascinating description of the session chez Mme Escudier in which Debussy performed the first act of *Parsifal* is given in Chausson, *Écrits*, 376, and reproduced in *C*, 192.

2. MR: See Marguerite de Saint-Marceaux, *Journal, 1894–1927*, ed. Myriam Chimènes *et al.* (Paris: Librairie Arthème Fayard, 2007), 77.

3. Saint-Marceaux, *Journal*, 77. The atmosphere of this salon was notably described by Miguel Zamacoïs, *Pinceaux et stylos* (Paris: Librairie Arthème Fayard, 1948), 201–7, and by Jean-Michel Nectoux et al., *Une famille d'artistes en 1900: Les Saint-Marceaux*, Les Dossiers du Musée d'Orsay (Paris: Réunion des musées nationaux, 1992), 87–88.

4. MR: The opening chorus of Charles Gounod's *Mireille* (1864) begins with the words, "Chantez, chantez, Magnanarelles."

5. MR: See Debussy's letter to Chausson from 5 February 1894 in *C*, 191.
6. She had sung the role of Saint Cécile in Chausson's *La légende de sainte Cécile* at the Société nationale on 4 March 1893.
7. MR: J. G. R., "Chronique de la semaine," *Le guide musical* 40, no. 9 (25 February 1894): 199.
8. MR: See F. M., "Les grands concerts, *Le progrès artistique* 17, no. 816 (22 February 1894): 5.
9. MR: See "Bruits qui courent," *L'art musical* 33, no. 8 (22 February 1894): 63.
10. According to Willy. MR: See the entry of 16 February 1890 in his *Lettres de l'ouvreuse: Voyage autour de la musique* (Paris: Léon Vanier, 1890), 133.
11. Georges Servières, "Lieder français. III: Cl.-Ach. Debussy," *Le guide musical* 41, nos. 37 and 38 (15 and 22 September 1895): 683. In "De fleurs," Servières wrongly juxtaposed the "greenhouse of sorrow" with "redeeming hands."
12. Étienne Destranges, *Consonnances et dissonances* (Paris: Fischbacher, 1906), 164.
13. MR: Debussy himself served as her accompanist; see Albert Van der Linden, "Le premier concert Debussy en Belgique (1894)," *Miscellanea musicologica Floris Van der Mueren* (Ghent: Louis van Melle, 1950): 194.
14. [The information in this paragraph comes from a circular that was dated 1 February 1894; see] "La damoiselle élue" auction catalog (Brussels, Pascal de Sadeleer, 20 November 1993), item 144. MR: See also Van der Linden, "Le premier concert Debussy en Belgique (1894)," 193. This source chronicles many of the reviews following the 17 February concert.
15. Letter of 8 March 1894 to Chausson [in *C*, 200].
16. MR: See "La damoiselle élue" auction catalog, item 144.
17. MR: Gevaert was said to have made this remark to Ysaÿe, cited in Van der Linden, "Le premier concert Debussy en Belgique (1894)," 198.
18. MR: Solvay's original review in the 3 March 1894 issue of *Le soir* was reprinted in "Nouvelles diverses: Étranger," *Le ménestrel* 60, no. 9 (4 March 1894): 69.
19. MR: This critic, presumably reporting in the 5 March 1894 issue of *Le patriote*, is cited in Van der Linden, "Le premier concert Debussy en Belgique (1894)," 199.
20. MR: Maurice Kufferath, "Chronique de la semaine: Bruxelles," *Le guide musical* 40, no. 10 (4 March 1894): 227–28. A reduced version of Kufferath's review appeared in the 10 March 1894 issue of *L'indépendance belge*.
21. Kufferath, "Chronique de la semaine: Bruxelles," 227.
22. ["À la Libre Esthétique: Œuvres musicales de M. Claude-A. Debussy," *L'art moderne* 14, no. 9 (4 March 1894): 67.] See also Van der Linden, "Le premier concert Debussy en Belgique (1894)," 196.
23. MR: See his letter from around 24 February 1894 in *C*, 198.
24. Letter of 3 July 1922 from Lucien Daudet to Marcel Proust. See *Bibliothèque G. T. Livres et autographes*, auction catalog (Paris, Drouot, 24 November 1986), last part of item 172.
25. MR: See Chausson's letter to Lerolle from 28 February 1894 in François Lesure, "Claude Debussy, Ernest Chausson et Henri Lerolle," in *Humanisme actif* (Paris: Hermann, 1968), 1:341, and in *C*, 197n2.

26. Letter of 25 February 1894 from Lerolle to Chausson, in Lesure, "Claude Debussy, Ernest Chausson et Henri Lerolle," 341, [and in *C*, 197n2].

27. The original manuscript of this letter seems to have been destroyed. I [Lesure] found a copy of it among the papers of Georges Jean-Aubry. [See *C*, 199–200.]

28. MR: See Debussy's letter to Lerolle, from around 24 February 1894 in *C*, 196–97.

29. MR: This passage comes from Debussy's letter of 16 March 1894; see *C*, 202.

30. MR: Saint-Marceaux mentions a "haute casquette," which presumably refers to the hats worn by butchers' assistants, according to Lucien Maillard, "Debussy par lui-même ou les chemins du désir," *Traversières Magazine* 120 (2017): 10.

31. MR: Saint-Marceaux, *Journal*, 79–80.

32. MR: See Chausson's letter to Lerolle in Lesure, "Claude Debussy, Ernest Chausson et Henri Lerolle," 342.

33. These performances were later resumed at the home of Mme Godard-Decrais. See p. 141.

34. MR: Saint-Marceaux, *Journal*, 80.

35. MR: See Pasteur Vallery-Radot, *Tel était Claude Debussy* (Paris: René Julliard, 1958), 41–43. Also cited in full in *C*, 203–4n4.

36. Paris, private collection. MR: Chausson's reaction is also transcribed in Lesure, "Claude Debussy, Ernest Chausson et Henri Lerolle," 342–43, where the letter is dated 6 April 1894; and in *C*, 202n2, where the letter is dated 5 April 1894.

37. [This quote is from a letter to Jean Stevens, in a private collection; see *C*, 203–4n4.] Louÿs would soon find himself juggling even more acrobatic delicate situations, between his mistress Marie [de Régnier, daughter of José-Maria de Heredia and wife of Henri de Régnier], his wife Louise de Heredia [sister of Marie de Régnier], and his Moorish mistress Zohra.

38. MR: See Lerolle's letter to Chausson from 13 March 1894 in Lesure, "Claude Debussy, Ernest Chausson et Henri Lerolle," 342. FL 2003 dates Lerolle's comment erroneously to "two days" after 11 May, probably confusing 13 May and 13 March.

39. In an undated letter to Pierre Louÿs, Debussy declined an invitation because "Gaby had several hats to finish and she needed my opinion on their arrangement." [See *C*, 232.]

40. MR: See Debussy's letter to Lerolle from 28 August 1894 in *C*, 219.

41. Letter of 10 December 1894 [in *C*, 227].

42. Jacques Durand, *Quelques souvenirs d'un éditeur de musique* (Paris: A. Durand & fils, 1924), 1:74.

43. Jean-Paul Goujon, *Jean de Tinan* (Paris: Plon, 1991), 97.

44. MR: As reported by Curnonsky; see Claude Debussy and Pierre Louÿs, *Correspondance de Claude Debussy et Pierre Louÿs (1893–1904)*, ed. Henri Borgeaud (Paris: Librairie José Corti, 1945), 38n2. Louÿs mentioned the Natansons and Robert in his letter to Debussy on 31 May 1894; see *C*, 208. And he referred to Robert's weakness for absinthe in a letter to Debussy from 29 July 1894; see *C*, 218.

45. MR: This lunch took place on 24 July 1894; see Valéry's letter to Gide from 27 July 1894 in André Gide and Paul Valéry, *Correspondance, 1890–1942*, ed. Peter Fawcett (Paris: Éditions Gallimard, 2009), 715–16. See also Debussy's letter to Lerolle from 28 August 1894 in *C*, 220.

46. This first version for orchestra has unfortunately not been found. Guy Ropartz performed it in Nancy in January 1910 [see F. L., "Correspondances: Nancy," *Le guide musical* 56, no. 6 (16 January 1910): 115]. See Michel Stockhem, "Lettres d'Ernest Chausson à Eugène Ysaÿe," R*evue belge de musicologie* (1988), 249n17.

47. MR: See Debussy's letter of 20 August 1894 to Pierre Louÿs in *C*, 218–19.

48. MR: See Debussy's letter from 28 August 1894 in *C*, 220. The boy Yniold cries out to his father, "petit père," numerous times in the course of this act.

49. MR: See Debussy's letter to Lerolle from 28 August 1894 in *C*, 220.

50. MR: See Debussy's letter of 22 September 1894 in *C*, 222.

51. MR: See Debussy's letter of 22 September 1894 to Ysaÿe in *C*, 222.

52. Alfred Bruneau, *Massenet* (Paris: Librairie Delagrave, 1935), 21.

53. Anik Devriès and François Lesure, *Dictionnaire des éditeurs de musique français* (Genève: Éditions Minkoff, 1988), 2:212.

54. MR: See *C*, 224 for the text of the contract between Debussy and Hartmann.

55. Lesure, "Claude Debussy, Ernest Chausson et Henri Lerolle," 344.

56. MR: See François Lesure's transcription of Koechlin's memories in Charles Koechlin, "Souvenirs sur Debussy," *Cahiers Debussy*, nouv. sér. 7 (1983): 4.

57. Charles Koechlin, "*Pelléas et Mélisande*," [ed. Aude Caillet, *Cahiers Debussy* 27–28 (2003–4), 31–123; see in particular p. 34]. We know this information from two of Debussy's letters to Le Grand. MR: See these letters to Le Grand—one that Lesure and Herlin believe is from 17 June 1894 and the other that they posit is from 7 July 1894—in *C*, 209 and 211, respectively.

58. MR: See Koechlin, "Souvenirs sur Debussy," *Cahiers Debussy* (1983), 5.

59. See Koechlin, "Souvenirs sur Debussy," *Cahiers Debussy* (1983), 5.

60. Charles Koechlin, *Debussy* (Paris: Henri Laurens, 1941), 101.

61. Gustave Doret, *Temps et contretemps* (Fribourg, Éditions de la Librairie de l'Université Fribourg, 1942), 94–96.

62. MR: See Debussy's note to Mallarmé from 20 December 1894 in *C*, 228.

63. MR: Gustave Robert, "Musique," *Revue illustrée* 19, no. 218 (1 January 1895): [2]. This early review is not cited in FL 2003, but it appeared immediately after the premiere.

64. MR: Gustave Robert, "Musique," *Revue illustrée* 20, no. 239 (15 November 1895): [1–2]. This citation is noted in FL 2003.

65. MR: Charles Darcours, "Notes de musique," *Le Figaro* (26 December 1894): 7.

66. MR: Auguste Goullet, "La musique à Paris," *Le soleil* (24 December 1894): [3]. Léon Vallas discusses many other reviews of the initial performances of the work during 1894–95 in *Claude Debussy et son temps* (Paris: Éditions Albin Michel, 1958), 184–88.

67. [See his letter to Debussy from 22/23 December 1894 in *C*, 229.] Charles Koechlin likewise revealed that "the performance left much to be desired, aggravated by the raw acoustics of the Salle d'Harcourt"; see Koechlin, *Debussy*, 13.

68. MR: See Debussy's letter to Henri Gauthier-Villars from 10 October 1895 in *C*, 278. FL 2003 cites Mallarmé's last line as "Couple, adieu, je vais voir ce que tu devins."

69. MR: See Mallarmé's letter to Debussy from 23 December 1894 in *C*, 230.

11. Pierre Louÿs; The Lean Years: 1895–96

1. MR: The colonnes Morris are the kiosks in Paris on which posters advertising cultural events are displayed.

2. MR: The French is "avec toute ma sympathie pour Pierre Louÿs"; see Claude Debussy and Pierre Louÿs, *Correspondance de Claude Debussy et Pierre Louÿs (1893–1904)*, ed. Henri Borgeaud (Paris: Librairie José Corti, 1945), 27.

3. MR: Biskra was a common vacation spot in Algeria, especially in winter. In summer 1894, Louÿs met his friend André Gide instead of Debussy in Biskra; there he worked on his *Chansons de Bilitis*, which he dedicated to Gide "with a special reference to 'M.b.A,' that is to say, to Meriem ben Atala." See Herbert Peter Clive, *Pierre Louÿs (1870–1925): A Biography* (Oxford: Clarendon Press, 1978), 106. Louÿs also spent time in Algeria during July and August 1894 with André-Ferdinand Herold, and their experiences were memorialized in A.-F. Herold and Pierre Louÿs, *Journal de Meryem, 1894*, ed. Jean-Paul Goujon (Paris: Éditions du Limon, 1996).

4. In addition to the biographies of Pierre Louÿs by Robert Fleury (*Pierre Louÿs et Gilbert Voisin: Une curieuse amitié* [Paris: Éditions Tête de Feuilles, 1973]), Giorgio Mirandola (*Pierre Louÿs* [Milano: Mursia, 1974]), Clive (*Pierre Louÿs*), and Paul-Ursin Dumont (*Pierre Louÿs, l'ermite du hameau* [Vendôme: Libraidisque, 1985]), we might draw attention especially to that of Jean-Paul Goujon (*Pierre Louÿs: Une vie secrète (1870–1925)* [Paris: Fayard, 2002]).

5. [Cited on p. 154 in] Jean-Paul Goujon, "Pierre Louÿs et Wagner (avec 6 lettres inédites)," *Littératures* 18 (University of Toulouse Press, 1988), 151–70.

6. MR: See his letter from Algeria, 20 March 1897, in Pierre Louÿs, *La femme et le pantin* (Brussels: Éditions du Nord, 1936), xviii. In this same letter, Louÿs listed Mallarmé, Swinburne, Leo Tolstoy, José-Maria de Heredia, Pierre Loti, and Gabriele D'Annunzio as the contemporary writers he admired the most.

7. MR: See the photo of Louÿs at his harmonium in François Lesure, *Debussy: Iconographie musicale* (Geneva: Minkoff & Lattès, 1980), 67.

8. MR: The Parisiana was a café-concert located in the second arrondissement of Paris.

9. Jean-Paul Goujon, *Jean de Tinan* (Paris: Plon, 1991), 135–36 and 243.

10. Letter from Fargue to Auguste Martin in a catalog of an exhibition at the Opéra-Comique titled *Claude Debussy, chronologie de sa vie et de ses œuvres* (Paris: May 1942), ix; republished in Léon-Paul Fargue, "Un portrait de Debussy," *Cahiers Debussy* 15 (1991): 60–61.

11. Goujon, *Jean de Tinan*, 188 and 190.

12. MR: See, for example, Debussy's letters to Louÿs from 9 and 31 March 1897 in *C*, 348.

13. MR: See Gaby's letter of 23 January 1897 in *C*, 338–39.

14. MR: See *C*, 300 for an undated letter from Debussy to Louÿs in which he reports being "up to his neck" in "a black, green, and multi-colored mess," and in which he asks his friend to grant him "the favor of one LOUIS!!!" In his plea, Debussy of course was punning on Louis/Louÿs.

15. Anik Devriès and François Lesure, *Dictionnaire des éditeurs de musique français* (Genève: Éditions Minkoff, 1988), 2:212.

16. MR: See Debussy's letter to Louÿs from 11 October 1900 in *C*, 570.

17. MR: Louÿs biographers such as Clive appear to have followed Robert Cardinne-Petit's claim; see his *Pierre Louÿs inconnu* (Paris: Éditions de l'Élan, 1948), 176.

18. MR: In his letter of 12 October 1895, Debussy informed Louÿs that Gaby would be waiting for him with the ticket; see *C*, 280.

19. MR: Here Louÿs was referring to Alfred Vallette, a publisher who in 1890 revived the *Mercure de France*, a Symbolist mouthpiece. Louÿs's *Aphrodite* would be published by the *Mercure de France* (as a serial titled *L'esclavage*) in 1896, and Vallette would go on to publish works by Mallarmé, Proust, Gide, and Jarry. Incidentally, Vallette married the novelist Rachilde [Marguerite Vallette-Eymery].

20. MR: See Louÿs's letter to Debussy from 13 October 1895 in *C*, 281.

21. MR: See Debussy's letter to Louÿs from 17 October 1895 in *C*, 283.

22. L'ouvreuse du Cirque d'été, "Lettre de l'ouvreuse," *Écho de Paris* (13 [*recte* 15], October 1895): 3.

23. MR: Victorin Joncières, "Revue musicale," *La liberté* (20 October 1895): [1].

24. Joncières, "Revue musicale," [1], cited in n23.

25. MR: Alfred Bruneau "Les concerts: Concerts Colonne," *Le Figaro* (14 October 1895): 3.

26. MR: Amédée Boutarel "Paris et départements: Concerts du Châtelet," *Le ménestrel* 61, no. 42 (20 October 1895): 336.

27. MR: Isidor Philipp, "Revue des grands concerts: Concerts Colonne," *Le ménestrel* 61, no. 43 (27 October 1895): 340.

28. MR: Hugues Imbert, "Chronique de la semaine: Paris—Réouverture des Concerts-Colonne," *Le guide musical* 41, no. 42 (20 October 1895): 782.

29. MR: Hugues Imbert, "Chronique de la semaine: Paris—Deuxième Concert-Colonne," *Le guide musical* 41, no. 43 (27 October 1895): 803.

30. Henry Eymieu, "La musique moderne dans les grands concerts: Concerts Colonne," *Le monde artiste* 38, no. 27 (3 July 1898): [419].

31. MR: Alfred Ernst, "La vie musicale," *Revue encyclopédique* 121 (15 December 1895): 466.

32. MR: Hirsch's article appeared in "Musique," *Mercure de France* 16, no. 71 (November 1895): 255.

33. MR: See Debussy's letter to Charles-Henry Hirsch in *C*, 286.

34. *Lettres autographes et documents: Archives de la famille Hérold*, auction catalog (Paris, Hôtel Drouot, 12 June 1991), item 178. MR: Lesure must have seen the original letter, as this quotation did not appear in the catalog. See also p. 402n44.

35. [The plot was outlined on 19 April 1895 in a letter from Louÿs to Debussy; see *C*, 252–54.] A letter from 12 April already indicated the form of the first act [see *C*, 250–51].

36. [A summary of the plot is given in] Debussy and Louÿs, *Correspondance de Claude Debussy et Pierre Louÿs*, 185–89. MR: The "Dame verte" is a sylph or peri, something like a goddess of the woodland fairies. In the story, her attraction, signifying the allure of Nature, is set up as a foil to the strict mores of the Church. While Cendrelune, with the help of the saints, initially resists the temptations of Nature, when she ultimately realizes that Nature is represented by her own mother, she capitulates, and everyone lives happily ever after.

37. MR: See Louÿs's letter to Debussy from 12 May 1895 in *C*, 257.

38. MR: See Louÿs's letter to Debussy from 21 May 1898 in *C*, 404.

39. MR: See Louÿs's letter to Debussy from 14 January 1896 in *C*, 303.

40. MR: See Debussy's letter to Louÿs in *C*, 313.

41. MR: See Debussy's letter to Louÿs from 27 December 1897 in *C*, 378. More than a decade later, Ravel would compose music for the ballet of *Daphnis et Chloé*, commissioned by Diaghilev for the Ballets Russes, who premiered the work on 8 June 1912 at the Théâtre du Châtelet.

42. MR: See François Coppée, "Pierre Louÿs," *Le journal* (16 April 1896): [1].

43. Letter of 10 April 1896 [from Debussy to Louÿs in *C*, 310].

44. *Lettres autographes et documents: Archives de la famille Hérold*, item 178. MR: Lesure must have seen the original letter, as details of its contents did not appear in the catalog. See also p. 401n34. The story of Yvette Guilbert's proposal to Louÿs concerning the role of Chrysis may be found in Dumont, *Pierre Louÿs, l'ermite du hameau*, 194–95.

45. MR: See Louÿs's letter to Debussy from 4 November 1897 (date deduced by Lesure and Herlin) in *C*, 372.

46. Louÿs's response to the question posed in the article's title, "What should one put under the music: beautiful lines, bad ones, free verse, prose?" was published in the periodical *Musica* (March 1911). Both Louÿs's and Debussy's responses are reproduced in Debussy and Louÿs, *Correspondance de Claude Debussy et Pierre Louÿs*, 197–200.

47. Louÿs's translation had been published in *L'esprit français* 3, nouv. sér. no. 63 (10 September 1931): 238–39, and was reprinted in Debussy and Louÿs, *Correspondance de Claude Debussy et Pierre Louÿs*, 190–91; [Pierre Louÿs, *Les poëmes, 1887–1924*, ed. Yves-Gérard Le Dantec (Paris: Éditions Albin Michel, 1945), 206–7; and on pp. 14–15 of Denis Herlin, "Une œuvre inachevée: *La saulaie*," *Cahiers Debussy* 20 (1996): 3–23]. We also have the three-page manuscript, in Debussy's hand, of Louÿs's translation in French; see BnF, département de la Musique, Rés. Vmb. Ms. 19. MR: FL 2003, 167n17, identifies the sonnets as numbers 24, 25, and 27 of the poem, while Herlin correctly identifies them as numbers 49, 50, and 52.

48. Three pages, at the conservatoire in Saint-Germain-en-Laye and at Stanford University[, as well as one that was sold at Sotheby's in 1988, identified erroneously as an extract from the *Nocturnes*; see Sotheby's, "Fine Books, Manuscripts, and Original Drawings" (New York: 14 December 1988), lot 205. These sources are discussed at length in Herlin, "Une œuvre inachevée: *La saulaie*," 8. Herlin, 16–23, also includes facsimiles and a transcription of the three pages. A facsimile of the Stanford source was also reproduced at the end of the book by Edward Lockspeiser, *Debussy et Edgar Poe: Manuscrits et documents inédits* (Monaco: Éditions du Rocher,

1962), [102–3]. In 2006, composer Robert Orledge reconstructed and completed the work].

49. [*C*, 326.]

50. MR: See Debussy's letter to Ysaÿe from 13 October 1896 in *C*, 326. As Lesure and Herlin point out in *C*, 326n4, Debussy often described his compositional work in these terms.

51. [*C*, 524.]

52. [*C*, 531.]

53. Clive, *Pierre Louÿs*, 10–11.

54. MR: While FL 2003 claims that Debussy "did not share Louÿs's enthusiasm" for Bizet's opera, the composer, in his maturity, acknowledged its validity as "action" (between the characters) more than as reflecting the "color" (of Spain); see his comments to André Caplet in a letter from 14 February 1911 in *C*, 1391. However, *Carmen* clearly made an indelible impression on him as a youth when he saw and heard it with Mme von Meck in 1882. Readers will recall that it was Debussy's own teacher, Ernest Guiraud, who composed the recitatives for *Carmen* and who compiled twelve numbers from it into two orchestral suites, in 1882 (two years after Debussy had begun to study with him) and in 1887. See the avant-propos/foreword in Claude Debussy, "Séguidille," ed. Marie Rolf (Paris: Durand, 2014), i–iii (in French) and iv–vi (in English).

55. [*C*, 330–31.]

56. Letters of 23 December 1894 and 29 October 1896 [in *C*, 229 and 330, respectively.]

57. [See Louÿs's letter to Debussy from 29 October 1896 in *C*, 331.]

58. MR: Feuillet's work could be categorized as somewhere between Romanticism and Realism. A popular novelist and dramatist during the Second Empire, he was best known for his "distinguished and lucid portraiture of life," sensitive depictions of female characters, analyses of characters' psychologies and feelings, and his excellent, reserved but witty prose style. See *1911 Encyclopedia Britannica*, vol. 10, s.v. "Octave Feuillet," by E. G., available via Wikisource, https://en.wikisource.org/wiki/1911_Encyclop%C3%A6dia_Britannica/Feuillet,_Octave, accessed 16 January 2019.

59. Letter of 24 July [1896 in *C*, 319–20].

60. Letter of 28 July [1896 in *C*, 320]. MR: Debussy's retort calls attention to the fact that Louÿs's comments did not square with his usual rhetoric, as exemplified by Louÿs's diary entry from 15 April 1890: "I want to be celebrated amidst a small group of friends, I want to be loved by twenty people and even that is a lot." See Pierre Louÿs, *Œuvres complètes* (Paris: Éditions Montaigne, 1929–31), 9:278.

61. Henri Rambaud, "Un musicien et un poète: Debussy et Pierre Louÿs," *Contrepoints* 4 (May–June 1946): 18.

12. *Pelléas*—The Long Wait: 1895–98

1. Francis Jammes and Arthur Fontaine, *Correspondance, 1898–1930*, intro. and notes by Jean Labbé (Paris: Gallimard, 1959), [9].

2. MR: See Debussy's letter of 28 August 1894 to Henry Lerolle in *C*, 221.

3. MR: See Debussy's letter of 23 September 1895 to Henry Lerolle in C, 272.

4. MR: Madame Gérard de Romilly, "Debussy professeur, par une de ses élèves (1898–1908)," *Cahiers Debussy*, nouv. sér. 2 (1978): 3.

5. MR: Romilly, "Debussy professeur," 4.

6. MR: Romilly, "Debussy professeur," 4.

7. MR: Romilly, "Debussy professeur," 5–6.

8. Romilly, "Debussy professeur," 4. Raoul Bardac commented on Debussy's teaching: "I worked with Claude. It wasn't a lesson from professor to student, but rather a relationship between master and disciple. The sessions were spent in conversations or performances of old or contemporary pieces, and in examining some general problems that the knowledge of music poses." ("Souvenirs de Raoul Bardac sur Claude Debussy, lus à la radio pour le 30ème anniversaire de sa mort en 1948.") MR: A typescript of this talk, dated 18 March 1948, is located in BnF, Fonds Lesure, carton II/1(3).

9. MR: Romilly, "Debussy professeur," 8.

10. MR: Gustave Samazeuilh, "Le quarantenaire de *Pelléas*," *L'information musicale* 2, no. 70 (15 May 1942): 937. An original copy of this issue is available in BnF, Fonds Lesure, carton I/6(12). Samazeuilh adds that he first met Debussy in 1896 at Chausson's home on the boulevard de Courcelles.

11. Samazeuilh, "Le quarantenaire de *Pelléas*," 937. MR: The excerpts from *Pelléas* heard by Samazeuilh on that occasion included the first versions of the tower scene, the duet, and the death of Mélisande.

12. MR: The slapstick antics of Foottit and Chocolat were often featured at the Nouveau Cirque and memorialized by artists such as Toulouse-Lautrec and writers such as Colette; see Barry Anthony, "George Footit and Raphaël 'Chocolat' Padilla," *Who's Who of Victorian Cinema*, revised by Stephen Herbert December 2012, http://victorian-cinema.net/footit. Historic clips of their work may be viewed on YouTube.

13. André Lebey, *Jean de Tinan: Souvenirs et correspondence* (Paris: Henri Floury, 1922), 75.

14. [See an undated letter from Debussy to Léon Daudet in] Charavay catalog 753 (Paris, October 1974), item 36158.

15. MR: Réné Peter, *Claude Debussy*, rev. ed. (Paris: Gallimard, 1944), 93.

16. Henri Pellerin, "Claude Debussy et le Pays d'Auge," in *Le Pays d'Auge* 7, no. 5 (May 1957): 1–16 and *Le Pays d'Auge* 7, no. 6 (June 1957): 1–11. Pellerin questioned Gaby during the last years of her life about her relationship with Debussy, but unfortunately mixed up these confidences with the fictionalized comments from Seroff's book [Victor Seroff, *Debussy, Musician of France* (New York: Putnam, 1956); Victor I. Seroff, *Claude Debussy*, trans. from English by Roger Giroux (Paris: Éditions Buchet/Chastel, 1957)].

17. Catherine Stevens's "Notes" on Debussy were written up, at René Peter's request, and may be accessed among the Dietschy materials in DOSS-04.49 and in DOSS-03.02 at the CDCD. MR: In addition to the circumstances surrounding the aforementioned marriage proposal, Catherine recalled that Debussy would visit her family two to three times a week around the end of 1895 and the beginning of 1896, but that after her polite refusal, the frequency of his visits declined. She

remembered that he played various drafts of *Pelléas* for the family and that she shared with the composer a love of both Javanese and Russian music. Finally, she remarked on his cheerful disposition, despite his own difficult financial state.

18. MR: See Debussy's letter of 9 August 1896 (not 19 August, as reported in FL 2003) to Louÿs in *C*, 322, and Gaby's letter of 23 January 1897 to Louÿs in *C*, 338.

19. Letter to Pierre Louÿs, 9 February 1897 [in *C*, 342]. Marcel Dietschy searched the daily newspapers in vain for various facts alluding to this suicide attempt. MR: This search was repeated by Lesure and Herlin, who confirm that no notice of Gaby's suicide attempt appears in the issues of *Le petit journal* between January and March 1897; see *C*, 342n2.

20. Dietschy, who more or less follows Seroff here, asserts that this event caused the parting of ways with Chausson, Lerolle, and Ysaÿe. In fact, Debussy had been cool toward Chausson for a long time, for reasons that are known, and had kept Ysaÿe at arm's length. As for Lerolle, several letters show that they remained very close and that Lerolle even gave him financial help in the following months.

21. MR: *C*, 348. See also p. 132 in the present volume.

22. MR: See Debussy's letter from 9 February 1897 to Louÿs in *C*, 342.

23. Henri Pellerin, "Claude Debussy et le Pays d'Auge," *Le Pays d'Auge* 7, no. 6 (June 1957): 5.

24. MR: See Debussy's letter of 27 March 1898 to Louÿs in *C*, 394–95.

25. Letter of 20 April 1898 [in *C*, 396].

26. MR: See Debussy's letter of 21 April 1898 in *C*, 398. FL 2003 states that this letter was received "several days later" when, in fact, it was written the next day (see n25).

27. MR: See Louÿs's letter of 5 May 1898 to Debussy in *C*, 400.

28. MR: See p. 4 in René Peter, "Debussy et l'amour," *Comœdia* 2, no. 54 (4 July 1942): 1 and 4.

29. MR: Peter, "Debussy et l'amour," 4. Note that Peter wrote about Alice's sense of "poetic" life, not "practical" life, as cited in FL 2003.

30. MR: Denis Herlin, "Un cercle amical franco-belge de Debussy: les Dansaert, les Loewenstein et les Peter," in *Bruxelles ou la convergence des arts*, ed. Malou Haine and Denis Laoureux (Paris: Vrin, 2013), 198–213. FL 2003, in contrast, suggests that the letters sent by Debussy to Alice Peter from 1897 to 1899 lack any emotional warmth, to the point that one can be certain that the "romantic complications" about which he spoke with Hartmann on 14 July 1898 concerned someone else.

31. MR: See Debussy's letter to d'Indy from February 1895 in *C*, 244.

32. MR: See Debussy's letter to Henry Lerolle from 23 September 1895 in *C*, 272.

33. See Debussy's letter to Henry Lerolle from 23 September 1895 [in *C*, 272]. MR: Balzac's story concerns a married woman's lover, who dies while hiding in a closet that has been bricked up by the woman's husband, in a fit of pique.

34. MR: This theme resembles that of Madeline's entombment within the family house in Edgar Allan Poe's *The Fall of the House of Usher*, a work that Debussy would contemplate setting already in the 1890s and on which he continued to work from 1908 to 1917. In recent times, a number of musicians have made completions

of this work, among them Carolyn Abbate (1977), Juan Allende-Blin (1977), and Robert Orledge (2004).

35. MR: See Debussy's letter to Pierre Louÿs, dated April 1895 (according to Lesure and Herlin), in *C*, 254.

36. MR: See Debussy's letter to Bonheur from 9 August 1895 in *C*, 267. Debussy's original French is a play on words: his phrase, *jeu d'enfer* (game from hell), is a twisted variant of *jeu d'enfant* (child's play).

37. [*C*, 267–68.]

38. Letter to Lerolle of 17 August 1895 [see *C*, 268].

39. Letter from Samain to Raymond Bonheur of 27 April 1894 (Albert Samain, "Lettres à Raymond Bonheur," *Revue de l'histoire de Versailles et de Seine-et-Oise* [1959–60]: 33).

40. See the notice under "Gazette théâtrale," *Écho de Paris* (12 October 1895): 3.

41. See Debussy's letter to Julia Robert from late November–early December 1895 in *C*, 291.

42. Letter to Hartmann [from Debussy, sent sometime around September to the beginning of October 1895; see *C*, 273].

43. MR: FL 2003 cites the date of 19 October 1895 for this letter; however, Lesure and Herlin give the date as 17 October in *C*, 284–85.

44. MR: This undated letter was in the Honegger collection, and I am grateful to Denis Herlin for sharing a copy of it with me.

45. MR: See Debussy's letter from 26 November 1895 in *C*, 288–89. Jehin was born in Belgium and studied at the Brussels Conservatory. He spent most of his career conducting opera with the Casino Orchestras in Monte Carlo and at Aix-les-Bains, and was married to mezzo-soprano Blanche Deschamps-Jehin.

46. The date of the plan to perform *Pelléas* at Robert de Montesquiou's Pavillon des Muses, in Neuilly, remains uncertain, but it was probably in 1895 or 1896. The Pavillon was decorated with canvases by Whistler, Stevens (*L'intérieur d'atélier*), and Besnard, as well as with Japanese scroll paintings. Among the socialites who flocked to the place was Louise Hochon (the guest at the Villa Médici who had initiated a brief amorous liaison with Achille).

47. See Debussy's letter to Eugène Ysaÿe from 13 October 1896 [in *C*, 325–26].

48. MR: Ysaÿe's letter to Debussy, from 17 October 1896, is in *C*, 327–29.

49. MR: Debussy's response to Ysaÿe, written on 17 November 1896, may be found in *C*, 333.

50. [Debussy's letter to Hartmann is in *C*, 414–15.]

51. [*C*, 414–15.] According to Koechlin, Debussy would subsequently describe Fauré's score as a "fileuse [spinning song] for seaside resort casinos." MR: See Koechlin's letter to Gabriel Astruc, 6 July 1931, BnF, département de la Musique, Bob-20828. It is important to understand that in act 3, scene 1 (a scene that Debussy cut), Mélisande is working at her spinning wheel while she is talking with Pelléas and Yniold. Fauré thus fashioned a spinning song for his incidental music to Maeterlinck's play. Koechlin had a deep knowledge of Fauré's score, as the latter had asked him to help with the orchestration of the work. For further context and analysis of the *Pelléas* connections between Fauré, Koechlin, and Debussy, see Jean-Michel Nectoux, *Gabriel Fauré: A Musical Life*, trans. Roger Nichols (Cambridge: Cambridge University Press, 1991), 149–62.

13. From Bachelorhood to Marriage: 1897–99

1. BnF, département de la Musique, Rés. F. 994.B (3.13) [contains copies of the programs for the Société nationale concerts on 1 February 1896 at the Salle Pleyel and on 23 January 1897 at the Salle Érard], on which Debussy had played the piano part in Guillaume Lekeu's Piano Quartet in B Minor; [the performance on 1 February 1896 was listed as a premiere. See also the entries for 1 and 2 February 1896 and 23 January 1897 in Michel Duchesneau, *L'avant-garde musicale et ses sociétés à Paris de 1871 à 1939* (Liège: Mardaga, 1997), 256 and 257.] Between 1900 and 1902 Debussy was still part of the committee of the Société; [the list of members is also documented in BnF, département de la Musique, Rés. F. 994.B (3.13)].

2. MR: See Debussy's letter to Georges Hartmann from 31 December 1897 in *C*, 381.

3. MR: Paul Verlaine died on 8 January 1896.

4. MR: Presumably because the *Divagations* mixed prose poems, criticism, and "rambling" qualities in a quintessentially Symbolist manner.

5. MR: See *C*, 418. Pierre Louÿs described Mallarmé's passing in vivid detail, in a letter to his half-brother Georges Louis, written on 13 September 1898: "Mallarmé died suddenly, while strolling in his garden with his doctor. He was complaining of swollen tonsils, and wanted to explain that this condition hampered his breathing: to show this, he took in a deep breath, his uvula got caught between his tonsils, and he suffocated to death. What an odd way to die!" See Pierre Louÿs and George Louis, *Correspondance croisée, 1890–1917*, ed. Gordon Millan (Paris: Honoré Champion, 2015), 1:564.

6. MR: See Debussy's letter of 9 February 1897 in *C*, 343.

7. MR: See his letter to Georges Hartmann from 14 September 1897 in *C*, 363.

8. MR: See his letter from 9 May 1897 in *C*, 352.

9. MR: See Louÿs's letter to Debussy from the end of May 1897 in *C*, 353–54.

10. MR: This is how René Peter referred to himself in his *Claude Debussy*, rev. ed. (Paris: Gallimard, 1944): 13.

11. MR: The manuscript of Debussy's "Berceuse" is housed in the Library of Congress in Washington, DC. This unaccompanied song has been recorded by François Le Roux in Claude Debussy, *Intégrale des mélodies*, Ligia, LIDI 0201285-14.

12. MR: See René Peter, *La tragédie de la mort*, preface by Pierre Louÿs, 2nd ed. (Paris: Édition du Mercure de France, 1899). The work was dedicated "to Claude Debussy / Versailles. —August 1896."

13. MR: For further information, see Robert Orledge, *Debussy and the Theatre* (Cambridge: Cambridge University Press, 1982), 241 and 244–45.

14. MR: Debussy's original manuscript of this play is housed in the BnF, département de la Musique; see n17.

15. MR: FL 2003 identifies the recipient of this letter as Alice Peter; however, this error is corrected in *C*, 405, which establishes the recipient as Alice's sister, Régine Dansaert, who worked with René Peter on various theatrical projects.

16. While Debussy could have begun to write the play in 1898, the latest date after which he could no longer have been interested in such attempts is clearly 1901—when the fate of *Pelléas* was decided.

17. In the 43-page manuscript, Rés. Vma. Ms. 1062 (also available online), after the second scene (on p. 5), the handwriting is different (apparently penned later). The incomplete state of the play is confirmed by the fact that Ancelac, who is listed in the general cast, does not appear in the text that has been preserved and published in full by François Lesure, *Debussy avant* Pelléas *ou les années symbolistes* (Paris: Klincksieck, 1992), 229–52.

18. Edward Lockspeiser, "*Frères en art*, pièce de théâtre inédite de Debussy," *Revue de musicologie* 56, no. 2 (1970): 165–76. Jean Barraqué, in his *Debussy* (Paris: Éditions du Seuil, 1962), 104, sees the play, indefensibly, as "a charge against the Société nationale and its leaders."

19. MR: See scene 6 in the first tableau of *F. E. A.*, where Redburne cites Mallarmé as a fan of Maltravers, in Lesure, *Claude Debussy avant* Pelléas, 238.

20. MR: See scene 6 in the first tableau of *F. E. A.* in Lesure, *Claude Debussy avant* Pelléas, 239.

21. MR: See the third tableau of *F. E. A.* in Lesure, *Claude Debussy avant* Pelléas, 249.

22. MR: See scene 6 in the first tableau of *F. E. A.* in Lesure, *Claude Debussy avant* Pelléas, 238.

23. MR: In a *pièce à clefs*, the characters are real, although their names are fictitious.

24. Léon Vallas published a few excerpts from the poems of these *Nuits blanches*, based on [Debussy's notes on eight pages of] a little notebook that Lilly had kept (see "Debussy, poëte," *Les nouvelles littéraires* 12, no. 548 [15 April 1933]: 10). Lockspeiser (following Vallas) joined the texts of two of these *Nuits* in his *Debussy: His Life and Mind* (Cambridge: Cambridge University Press, 1978), 1:131.

25. These two *Nuits blanches* were played on the radio for the first time on 18 October 1991; broadcast by France-Musique, they were sung by François Le Roux and accompanied by Noël Lee.

26. Camille Bellaigue, "Revue musicale: Quelques chansons," *Revue des deux mondes* 67, no. 143 (15 October 1897): 933.

27. MR: See Debussy's letter to Pierre de Bréville from 24 March 1898 in *C*, 394.

28. In his concerts at the Conservatoire in Nancy, Ropartz would program the *Prélude à l'après-midi d'un faune* for the first time on 7 November 1897.

29. [*C*, 578.]

30. MR: Debussy wrote first on 12 April 1901 to Pierre de Bréville (see *C*, 592), and then on the next day to the soloist Blanche Marot (see *C*, 593) to cancel the performance of the *Proses lyriques*.

31. MR: See *C*, 446. In *C*, 446n3, Lesure and Herlin point out that Debussy's final sentence is a riff on Molière, from act 3, scene 3 of *Tartuffe*.

32. MR: See Louÿs's letter to Debussy from 29 January 1899 in *C*, 455, and the entry for 30 November 1901 in Ricardo Viñes's journal (this unpublished source was kindly provided to me by Denis Herlin). Siegfried Bing's famous gallery, La Maison de l'Art Nouveau, opened in Paris in 1895 and featured entire rooms designed in Art Nouveau style. He sold decorative arts from East Asia in addition to glassware by Louis Comfort Tiffany and fabrics by William Morris.

33. Henri Pellerin, "Claude Debussy et le Pays d'Auge," *Le Pays d'Auge* 7, no. 6 (June 1957): 6.

34. MR: This passage rhymes in the original French: "ainsi le chèvre<u>pied</u> arrache à la <u>haie</u> sa ronce préf<u>érée</u>."

35. Colette, Gabrielle Sidonie, *Mes apprentissages* (Paris: J. Ferenczi et Fils, 1936), 206. [At the end of this passage, Colette was implying that she felt Debussy's acknowledgement and acceptance of her in his simple quip, "Bonne mémoire!"] In a letter, the autograph of which I [Lesure] own, she gives a slightly different version of the scene: "Upon returning to Louis de Serre's home, Debussy was ecstatic. He sang bits and pieces of this new music, with glissandos on the piano, and imitated the drums on a window and the glockenspiel on a crystal vase. He buzzed like a swarm, his amazing face laughing from ear to ear, and we found him handsome."

36. MR: See his letter to Chausson from 5 May 1899 in *C*, 475.

37. MR: See Louÿs's letter to Debussy from 12 June 1899 in C, 495. Louÿs was planning to place a wreath on Chausson's grave, and was offering to include Debussy's card along with his own. FL 2003 writes that Chausson died "three months" after his invitation to Debussy on 5 May, but the time period was actually under six weeks.

38. [*C*, 465.]

39. MR: Debussy used this affectionate name for her when he dedicated the short score of his *Nocturnes* "à ma petite Lilly-Lilo" (to my little Lilly-Lilo).

40. MR: See René Peter, "Debussy et l'amour," *Comœdia* 2, no. 54 (4 July 1942): 1 and 4.

41. MR: Peter, *Claude Debussy*, rev. ed., 41.

42. Until July, Lilly's residence was at 12 rue de Berne. The correspondence between Claude and Lilly, later owned by Émile Vuillermoz, is now on deposit [at the Beinecke Rare Books & Manuscript Library, Yale University, as part of the Frederick R. Koch Collection, box 19, folder 298–303.]

43. [*C*, 468.]

44. [*C*, 468–69.]

45. MR: See Debussy's letter to Lilly from 27 May 1899 in *C*, 485.

46. MR: Lesure's description of Lilly's voice as "une petite voix blanche" comes from p. 3 of a letter by Lucien Monod to Dietschy, dated 2 May 195; see Fonds Lesure, BnF, carton I/6(9). Incidentally, Lucien made three portraits of Lilly, and she served as godmother to Jacques, one of his sons.

47. MR: "C'est un oiseau qui vient de France" was a popular tune well known in France during the period between the wars of 1870 and 1914. Composed by Frédéric Boissière on a text by Camille Soubise, the song contains a refrain whose last line is the same as the title, "This is a bird who comes from France."

48. Letter of 2 June 1903 [in *C*, 738. Mélisande's hair song opens act 3, scene 1 of *Pelléas et Mélisande*.]

49. MR: See his letter to Lilly from 19 July 1904 in *C*, 854.

50. "My temperament often collides with yours," Debussy wrote to her on 24 July 1904 [*C*, 854], and here we can reconstruct the sequence of events from a few lines sketched in pencil, four years later, in a small notebook and perhaps intended for his lawyer with a view to his divorce from Lilly: "Constant concealment [. . .]

only seeking a slightly better *situation*—is moreover mistaken and avenges herself by exerting a daily tyranny on my thoughts and my relationships—concrete proof in my output of these last four years." MR: See BnF, département de la Musique, Rés. Vmf. Ms. 53, 4r-v.

51. A certain friendship had developed between the two young women. During the month in which he married Lilly, Debussy offered Gaby, as a farewell gift, a manuscript of the *Prélude à l'après-midi d'un faune*: "To my dear and good little Gaby / the sure affection of / her devoted / Claude Debussy / October 1899" (à ma chère et tres [*sic*] bonne petite Gaby / la sûre affection de / son dévoué / Claude Debussy / Octobre 1899). MR: This manuscript now resides in the Robert Owen Lehman collection, on deposit at The Morgan Library & Museum in New York.

52. MR: According to Denis Herlin, "Un cercle amical franco-belge de Debussy: les Dansaert, les Loewenstein et les Peter," in *Bruxelles ou la convergence des arts*, ed. Malou Haine and Denis Laoureux (Paris: Vrin, 2013), 198–213. Lilly recalled finding a letter from Alice Peter in June 1899 that showed that Debussy had not yet completely broken off their relationship.

53. See his letter to Lilly from 1 May 1899 [in *C*, 472].

54. See his letter of 5 May 1899 to Lilly [in *C*, 474].

55. See his letter from 8 May [in *C*, 476]. MR: In this letter, Debussy concluded that Lilly was "afraid" of him, hence her smiles mixed with tears.

56. MR: See Debussy's letter to Lilly from 19 May 1899 in *C*, 480, in which he objected to the phrases that Lilly apparently used in her previous letter to him, claiming that he would have set her straight immediately if she had only expressed her reservations when they were together in person.

57. See Louÿs's letter to Debussy from 15 May 1899 [in *C*, 478–79].

58. MR: See Debussy's letter of 16 May to Louÿs in *C*, 479.

59. MR: His first letter is dated 22 May 1899; see *C*, 481. In his letter from 26 May, he remarks that Lilly has been gone for five days; see *C*, 484.

60. MR: See his letter of 24 May in *C*, 483.

61. MR: Her words are referenced in a letter from Debussy to Lilly, dated 27 May; see *C*, 485.

62. MR: See his letter to Lilly from 2 June 1899 in *C*, 491.

63. MR: See his letter of 29 May 1899 in *C*, 488. Debussy wrote to Lilly, "Il me semble qu'il y a cent ans que je ne t'ai plus vue," echoing the words that Pelléas sings to Mélisande in act 4, scene 4: "On dirait par moments qu'il y a cent ans que je ne l'ai plus vue."

64. MR: See Debussy's letters to Eugène Fromont and to Georges Hartmann from 2 June 1899 in *C*, 491 and 492, respectively.

65. MR: See his letter from 2 June 1899 in *C*, 491.

66. MR: See his letter from 11 June 1899 in *C*, 494. The opening lines of Verlaine's "Green," though worded more formally (using the "vous" instead of "tu" form of address), are: "Voici des fruits, des fleurs, des feuilles, et des branches / Et puis voici mon cœur qui ne bat que pour vous." (Here are fruits, flowers, leaves, and branches / And here is my heart that beats only for you.)

67. MR: See the first of the two letters that Debussy sent to Louÿs on 17 June 1899 in *C*, 502.

68. MR: See his letter to Lilly from 17 June 1899 in *C*, 500–501.

69. MR: Debussy used these words in his letter to Lilly from 21 June 1899; see *C*, 505.

70. MR: Debussy's letter is undated, but Lesure and Herlin surmise that it must be from July–August 1899, based on the color of Debussy's stationery; see *C*, 514.

71. MR: See the second of two letters that Debussy sent to Louÿs on 17 June 1899 in *C*, 502.

72. MR: In a letter to Debussy from 12 June 1899, Louÿs wrote that he believed Bourdeau to be a bassoon professor at the Conservatoire! Indeed, Eugène Bourdeau was appointed professor of bassoon in October 1891, and since 1867 he had been playing in the orchestra at the Opéra-Comique. As a student at the Conservatoire, he had earned first prize in the *concours* in 1868. See Constant Pierre, *Le Conservatoire nationale de musique et de déclamation* (Paris: Imprimerie nationale, 1900), 439 and 706.

73. Besides the march, the musical program desired by Louÿs had consisted chiefly of works by J. S. Bach. The columnist for the *Figaro* mixed up different parts of the program, writing: "During the mass, M. Noté sang the *Marche nuptiale* by C. Debussy." MR: It is quite possible that Debussy ended up composing a song rather than an organ piece for Louÿs's wedding. See "Le monde et la ville: Mariages," *Le Figaro* (25 June 1899): 2. This notice listed numerous members from high society who attended the wedding. Among the witnesses were François Coppée and Henri de Régnier.

74. MR: See Debussy's letter to Louÿs from 13 June 1899 in *C*, 497.

75. MR: The original text is "j'aime de tout mon siècle" and not the more idiomatic "j'aime de tout mon cœur," as cited in FL 2003; see Debussy's letter to Hartmann from 3 July 1899 in *C*, 510.

76. MR: Here, FL 2003 prints another more idiomatic phrase—that Lilly has "les plus beaux cheveux du monde qui rendent possibles les comparaisons les plus excessives"—rather than the more complete phrase that mentions Lilly's eyes in addition to her hair: "les plus beaux cheveux du monde et des yeux qui rendent poussives les comparaisons les plus excessives," which is clearly in *C*, 510; the latter has been independently verified by Denis Herlin, who carefully examined the original letter.

77. MR: See Debussy's letter to Desjardins from 4 September 1899 in *C*, 516.

78. MR: Madame Gérard de Romilly, "Debussy professeur, par une de ses élèves (1898–1908)," *Cahiers Debussy*, nouv. sér. 2 (1978): 8.

79. MR: An "omnibus" in Paris during this time would have been a carriage drawn by horses.

80. Romilly, "Debussy professeur," 9. Note that, at the premiere of *Pelléas*, Debussy's parents were seated in the box of Mme and Mlle de Romilly; the latter became the wife of Lieutenant Gérard on 9 July 1901.

81. [The letter from Fontaine to Jammes dates from October 1899; see] Francis Jammes and Arthur Fontaine, *Correspondance, 1898–1930* (Paris: Gallimard, 1959), 33.

82. See Debussy's letter to Hartmann from 18 December 1899 [in *C*, 524].

83. Letter of 28 April 1903 [in *C*, 727]. MR: As noted by Lesure and Herlin in *C*, 727n1, the phrase "le petit être mystérieux" comes from one of Arkel's lines

in act 5 of *Pelléas*. FL 2003 states that this letter from London was penned "a few months" after the wedding, but it was actually written well over two years later.

84. MR: See Debussy's letter of 25 June 1898 in *C*, 408.

85. MR: See Debussy's letter to Godet from 5 January 1900 in *C*, 531.

86. MR: The full dedication of the manuscript, now housed at the Library of Congress in Washington, DC, reads: "Ce manuscrit appartient a [sic] ma petite Lilly-Lilo / tous droits réservés, il marque aussi la joie / profonde et passionnèe [sic] que j'ai d'etre [sic] / son mari / Claude Debussy / petit janvier de 1901."

14. *Nocturnes*: 1900–1901

1. MR: See pp. 103 and 105 in the present volume.

2. MR: See *C*, 220. Paul Landormy's program notes, written for a performance of the *Nocturnes* at the Concerts Colonne on 14 December 1913, are rather unique in their emphasis on different orchestral groupings within each movement; see the Programmes Colonne: 1913 dossier at the BnF, département de la Musique.

3. MR: See Théodore Duret, *Histoire de J. Mc. N. Whistler et de son œuvre* (Paris: H. Floury, 1904), 176–77. Duret writes, "Whistler's nocturnes leave the subject in an indeterminate state, under a general guise of atmosphere or shadow, which is worthy in itself and which becomes the core of the painting, and in Debussy's nocturnes, the melody or musical motif also remains enveloped in an indefinite and continuous harmony, which forms the very framework of the composition."

4. MR: Camille Mauclair was one of these individuals; see Claude Debussy, *Nocturnes*, in *Œuvres complètes de Claude Debussy*, sér. V, vol. 3, edited Denis Herlin (Paris: Durand, 1999), xiii and xxi.

5. Michel Stockhem, "Lettres d'Ernest Chausson," *Revue belge de musicologie* 42 (1988): 257.

6. MR: See Debussy's letter to Lerolle from 23 September 1895 in *C*, 272.

7. [*C*, 408.]

8. [*C*, 419.]

9. MR: See his letter to Hartmann from 16 November 1898, referencing the run-through that he had given his publisher during the previous week, in *C*, 428.

10. [*C*, 448 and 465, respectively.]

11. MR: See Debussy's letters to Hartmann from around 13 June 1899 and from 24 September 1899 in *C*, 496 and 518, respectively.

12. MR: Debussy's letter to Hartmann dates from the beginning of December 1899; see *C*, 523.

13. MR: For discussions on the changes made in the *Nocturnes*, see the avant-propos/foreword in Debussy, *Nocturnes*, ed. Herlin, xi–xvii and xix–xxv, as well as two articles in particular by Denis Herlin: "Le dédale des corrections dans 'Sirènes,'" *Cahiers Debussy* 12–13 (1988–89): 82–99; and "Sirens in the Labyrinth: Amendments in Debussy's *Nocturnes*," in *Debussy Studies*, ed. Richard Langham Smith (Cambridge: Cambridge University Press, 1997), 51–77.

14. MR: Maurice Emmanuel, *Pelléas et Mélisande de Claude Debussy: Étude historique et critique, analyse musicale* (Paris: Paul Mellottée, Éditeur, [1926]), repr. as *Pelléas et Mélisande de Claude Debussy: Étude et analyse* (Paris: Éditions Mellottée, 1950), 44.

15. MR: Carré would have gone to Debussy's apartment on the rue Cardinet, where he was living at the time.

16. Albert Carré, *Souvenirs de théâtre* (Paris: Librairie Plon, 1950), 275.

17. The stir surrounding *Pelléas* in professional circles was so emphatic that Constant Pierre, in his summary of the Conservatoire that appeared in 1900, mentioned it already among Debussy's works, next to *Chimène*. MR: In addition, a notice in *Le guide musical* 46, nos. 33–34 (9 and 16 August 1900): 597, listed "*Péléas* [*sic*] *et Mélisande*, six tableaux de M. Debussy" among the unpublished works received by the Opéra-Comique and planned to be produced during the following season.

18. MR: Hartmann's letter to Debussy, in which he encouraged the composer to get back to work on the piano reduction and the orchestral score of *Pelléas*, is dated on 4 January 1990; see *C*, 530.

19. MR: See Debussy's letter to Hartmann in *C*, 538.

20. MR: The French phrase is "terrible homme," a twist on the commonly used phrase, "enfant terrible." Hartmann used this phrase to describe Debussy in his letter to the composer from sometime between 20 and 23 September 1899; see *C*, 517.

21. MR: Hartmann's letter reads "dernier carat" (at the latest) in *C*, 548, although FL 2003 quotes this phrase as "dernier avril" (end of April).

22. MR: FL 2003 erroneously cites "et la grâce que je *vous* souhaite" rather than "et la grâce que je *nous* souhaite"; see *C*, 548.

23. Hartmann's letter from 28 March 1900 [is given in *C*, 548].

24. MR: See the letter from Debussy to Hartmann of 4 February 1900 in *C*, 539. Debussy's letter to Louÿs, from 6 February 1900, similarly alludes to performing *Pelléas* in Japan, far away from the Parisians who were enjoying Charpentier's work; see *C*, 540.

25. MR: See the entry for 4 March 1900 in Ricardo Viñes, "Le journal inédit de Ricardo Viñes," trans. and ed. Nina Gubisch, *Revue internationale de musique française* 1, no. 2 (June 1980): 222.

26. MR: See his letter of 10 April 1900 in *C*, 554.

27. MR: Hugues Imbert, "Chronique de la semaine: Paris—Concerts Lamoureux," *Le guide musical* 46, no. 12 (25 March 1900): 271. Louÿs had claimed that his *Chansons de Bilitis* were translated from ancient Greek poems, a hoax that fooled even many scholars for several years.

28. MR: See Debussy's letter of 25 April 1900 in *C*, 557.

29. MR: See Debussy's letter to Lilly from 25 April 1900 in *C*, 556.

30. In July, did the Debussys make a three-week sojourn to Bichain, as Marcel Dietschy claims? There is no evidence to confirm this assertion.

31. MR: Presumably following a miscarriage or an abortion.

32. MR: See Debussy's letter to Louÿs from 25 August 1900 in *C*, 566.

33. Arthur Dandelot, "Exposition de 1900: Deuxième séance officielle de musique de chambre," *Le monde musical* 12, no. 11 (10 [*recte* 30] June 1900): 195.

34. MR: See the penultimate verse of Rossetti's poem, originally published in *The Germ*, a source that is available in facsimile: *The Germ: The Literary Magazine of the Pre-Raphaelites* (Oxford: Ashmolean Museum, 1992): 80–83.

35. MR: See his letter of 24 August 1900 in *C*, 565.

36. Adolphe Jullien, "Revue musicale," *Journal des débats* (2 September 1900): [1].

37. MR: Alfred Bruneau, "La musique à l'Exposition," *Le Figaro* (24 August 1900): 5.

38. MR: Bruneau, "La musique à l'Exposition," 5.

39. MR: Arthur Dandelot, "Exposition de 1900: 7e grand concert officiel," *Le monde musical* 12, no. 16 (30 August 1900): 259.

40. L. P., "Chronique de la semaine: Paris—Septième Grand Concert officiel au Trocadéro," *Le guide musical* 46, no. 35 (21 August 1900): 616.

41. MR: Incidentally, Pierre Lalo would marry Noémi Fuchs, the daughter of Henriette and Edmond Fuchs, from the Concordia choral society.

42. MR: Pierre Lalo, "La musique," *Le temps* (28 August 1900): [3].

43. MR: See Debussy's letter of 27 August 1900 to Pierre Lalo in *C*, 567. As Lesure and Herlin point out in *C*, 567n1, *Le temps* came out in the evening, so the date of 28 August for Lalo's article actually was seen by Debussy on 27 August; clearly, his letter to Lalo was a spontaneous response.

44. MR: See Debussy's letter to Louÿs from sometime before 9 December 1900 in *C*, 575.

45. MR: See the entry for 9 December 1900 in Viñes, "Le journal inédit," 222.

46. MR: See the entry for 9 December 1900 in Marguerite de Saint-Marceaux, *Journal, 1894–1927*, ed. Myriam Chimènes et al. (Paris: Librairie Arthème Fayard, 2007), 230.

47. MR: See his letter from 16 December 1900 in *C*, 576.

48. Pierre de Bréville, "Revue du mois: Musique," *Mercure de France* 37, no. 133 (January 1901): 215.

49. Jean D'Udine, "Les grands concerts," *Le courrier musical* 3, no. 17 (15 December 1900): 8.

50. Alfred Bruneau, "Les concerts," *Le Figaro* (10 December 1900): 4.

51. Gaston Carraud, "Les concerts," *La liberté* (11 December 1900): 2.

52. "Choses et autres: Concerts," *La vie parisienne* 38, no. 50 (15 December 1900): 705.

53. MR: Paul Dukas, "Chronique musicale: Concerts Lamoureux," *La revue hebdomadaire* 10, no. 3 (2 February 1901): 277. The contents of this review are cited in full in Paul Dukas, *Les écrits de Paul Dukas sur la musique* (Paris: Société d'éditions françaises et internationales, 1948), 529–33 (see in particular pp. 532–33), and excerpted in *C*, 585n2.

54. MR: See Debussy's letter of 11 February 1901 in *C*, 585.

55. MR: Debussy was suggesting that he was thinking in terms of pure expression rather than about musical technique.

56. MR: See Debussy's letter of 11 February 1901 to Dukas in *C*, 586.

57. MR: See his letter of 5 May in *C*, 596.

58. MR: Possibly a reference to Risler's premiere of Dukas's sonata, which took place at the Salle Pleyel on 10 May 1901. Recall that Debussy mentioned

this concert briefly in his column of 1 June 1901 in *La revue blanche* (see Claude Debussy, *Monsieur Croche et autres écrits*, rev. ed. [Paris: Gallimard, 1987], 47; and Claude Debussy, *Debussy on Music*, trans. Richard Langham Smith [New York: Alfred A. Knopf, 1977], 41–42).

59. François Caradec, *Feu Willy: Avec et sans Colette* (Paris: Carrère-Lafon, 1984), 100.

60. MR: See Maeterlinck's note to Debussy from 30 May 1901 in *C*, 599.

61. Madame Gérard de Romilly, "Debussy professeur, par une de ses élèves (1898–1908)," *Cahiers Debussy*, nouv. sér. 2 (1978): 7.

62. [See Leblanc's letter to Debussy from the end of 1901 in *C*, 633.] Auguste Martin, *Claude Debussy: Chronologie de sa vie et de ses œuvres*. Catalog of the Exposition Debussy (Paris, Opéra-Comique, 17 May 1942), 56, item 248. In her *Souvenirs: 1895–1918* (Paris: Bernard Grasset, 1931), in which many details are not very credible, Georgette Leblanc relates the scene of the reading of *Pelléas* at Maeterlinck's home, "at the end of 1901" [p. 166; see the entire passage on pp. 165–175. On pp. 169–70 of this source, as well as on p. 83 of] Georgette Leblanc, "Debussy souvenirs (1895–1918)," *Silences* 4 (Paris: Éditions de la Différence, 1987): 81–85, the author claims that afterward there were "two or three rehearsals at my home and two in the evenings at his place, on the sixth floor of the rue Cardinet," that Debussy was "delighted" with her interpretation, and that they "understood" each other perfectly. She had been taken aback by his "way of behaving" when she knew that Mary Garden had been chosen. MR: See also Janet Flanner's English trans. of Leblanc's *Souvenirs* (New York: E. P. Dutton, 1932), 167–78.

63. MR: Both Toulet and Curnonsky served as ghostwriters for Willy.

64. André Schaeffner reviewed the recent publications of books on Debussy by Yvonne Tienot and Oswald d'Estrade-Guerra, Lockspeiser (*Debussy et Edgar Poe*), Annie Joly-Segalen and André Schaeffner, Marcel Dietschy, and the 1962 Debussy exposition at the Bibliothèque nationale in *Revue de musicologie* 48, no. 125 (July–December 1962): 174–75. [Here Schaeffner was citing Marcel Dietschy, *La passion de Claude Debussy* (Neuchâtel: Editions de la Baconnière, 1962), 155 (see also *A Portrait of Claude Debussy*, trans. Willliam Ashbrook and Margaret G. Cobb [Oxford: Oxford University Press, 1990], 123). FL 2003 also references] Curnonsky [Maurice-Ed. Sailland], *Souvenirs littéraires et gastronomiques* (Paris: Éditions Albin Michel, 1958), 108 [various anecdotes on Debussy appear on pp. 107–12].

65. MR: See his letter from 31 August 1901 in *C*, 616.

66. MR: *C*, 616. This could be an allusion to Jean-François Millet's *The Gleaners*.

67. MR: See Debussy, *Monsieur Croche*, rev. ed., 54, and Debussy, *Debussy on Music*, 51.

68. MR: See Debussy's letter to Maurice Curnonsky, written from Bichain and dated by Lesure and Herlin to around 8 September 1901 in *C*, 619. In this letter, Debussy reiterated the turn of phrase about the Angelus that had so captivated him (see n66 and n67), this time using an adjective to describe the country's "<u>good</u> men."

69. MR: This couplet is extracted from Louÿs's much longer letter in verse; see *C*, 563.

70. MR: Herlin and Lesure posit a date of 7 November 1901 for this letter; see *C*, 624.

71. MR: See Jacques d'Offoël, "Chronique de la semaine: Paris—Concerts Lamoureux," *Le guide musical* 47, no. 44 (3 November 1901): 794. The outcry of the audience was mentioned in Olivier Berggruen, "Revue des grands concerts: Concerts Lamoureux," *Le ménestrel* 67, no. 44 (3 November 1901): 349. Arthur Dandelot, in "Concerts Lamoureux," *Le monde musical* 13, no. 20 (31 October 1901): 316, reported that Debussy's music "can't please everyone." Finally, in an article published in *La revue blanche* on 15 November 1901, Debussy referred to the Lamoureux performance and to writing music that ran the risk of displeasing some listeners; see Debussy, *Monsieur Croche*, rev. ed., 56, and Debussy, *Debussy on Music*, 53.

72. MR: Louis Laloy, *La musique retrouvée, 1902–1927* (Paris: Librairie Plon, 1928), 93.

73. Laloy, *La musique retrouvée*, 94. [The entire episode appears on] pp. 93–95.

74. MR: See his review of 15 November 1901 in Debussy, *Monsieur Croche*, rev. ed., 56, and Debussy, *Debussy on Music*, 53.

75. MR: Charles Joly, "Les Concerts," *Le Figaro* (28 October 1901): 4.

76. MR: Dandelot, *Le monde musical* review cited in n71.

77. MR: D'Offoël, *Le guide musical* review cited in n71.

78. MR: Jean Marnold, "Les 'Nocturnes' de Claude Debussy," *Le courrier musical* 5, no. 5 (1 March 1902): 68. Marnold's extensive analysis of the *Nocturnes* was published in the following issues of *Le courrier musical*: 5, no. 5 (1 March 1902): 68–71; 5, no. 6 (15 March 1902): 81–84; 5, no. 9 (1 May 1902): 129–33; 5, no. 21 (15 December 1902): 293–95; 6, no. 2 (15 January 1903): 18–19; and 6, no. 4 (15 February 1903): 49–52.

79. MR: Pierre Lalo, "La musique," *Le temps* (7 November 1901): [3].

80. MR: See Debussy's letter to Pierre Lalo from around 10 November 1901 in *C*, 625–26.

15. The Composer as Critic: 1901–3

1. MR: See his letter to Georges Louis from 23 January 1901 in Pierre Louÿs and Georges Louis, *Correspondance croisée, 1890–1917* (Paris: Honoré Champion, 2015), 2:828.

2. MR: See Debussy's letter to Louÿs from around 19 January 1901 in *C*, 582.

3. MR: Ed. L., "Les Chansons de Bilitis *au Journal*," *Le journal* (8 February 1901): 2.

4. In the publication of that work, the two first movements were dedicated to Mlle Worms de Romilly and to Mme Eugène Rouart (Yvonne Lerolle). Only the third movement was dedicated to Coronio.

5. Letter from Martin du Gard to Pasteur Vallery-Radot of 18 March 1958. MR: See *Lettres et manuscrits autographes, documents historiques à Piasa*, auction catalog (Paris, 6 March 2007), lot 231.

6. Maurice Ravel, *Maurice Ravel: Lettres, écrits, entretiens*, ed. Arbie Orenstein (Paris: Harmoniques/Flammarion, 1989), 64. In 1900, Ravel had sent his *Épigrammes de Clément Marot* to Debussy with his "warm regards and admiration."

7. MR: Debussy would also dedicate to Garban, "en réelle sympathie" (in true friendship), a score of the *Prélude à l'après-midi d'un faune*; see *C*, 2221.

8. [*C*, 613.]

9. On the political leanings of *La revue blanche*, see Claude Debussy, *Debussy on Music*, ed. Richard Langham Smith (New York: Alfred A. Knopf, 1977), 3–12; and [especially pp. 262 and 292–96 of] Arthur Basil Jackson, *La revue blanche (1893–1903): Origine, influence, bibliographie* (Paris: M. J. Minard, 1960).

10. MR: See p. 114 in the present volume.

11. MR: This letter is cited in Paul Dukas, *Correspondance de Paul Dukas*, ed. Georges Favre (Paris: Éditions Durand, 1971), 20–21.

12. MR: See his review from 1 April 1901 in Claude Debussy, *Monsieur Croche et autres écrits*, rev. ed. (Paris: Gallimard, 1987), 23. For an English translation of this review, see Debussy, *Debussy on Music*, 13.

13. MR: See his review from 1 April 1901 in Debussy, *Monsieur Croche*, rev. ed., 24, and in Debussy, *Debussy on Music*, 13.

14. MR: See his review from 1 April 1901 in Debussy, *Monsieur Croche*, rev. ed., 23, and in Debussy, *Debussy on Music*, 13.

15. MR: Debussy's "L'archet" was edited by Denis Herlin and published in *Quatre nouvelles mélodies* (Paris: Durand, 2012), 2–5.

16. MR: See his review from 15 April 1901 in Debussy, *Monsieur Croche*, rev. ed., 30–31, and in Debussy, *Debussy on Music*, 22–23.

17. MR: See his review from 1 June 1901 in Debussy, *Monsieur Croche*, rev. ed., 47, and in Debussy, *Debussy on Music*, 41–42.

18. MR: See his review from 1 May 1901 in Debussy, *Monsieur Croche*, rev. ed., 35, and in Debussy, *Debussy on Music*, 28.

19. MR: See his review from 15 May 1901 in Debussy, *Monsieur Croche*, rev. ed., 42, and in Debussy, *Debussy on Music*, 37. The latter translates Carré's "prodiges" specifically as "marvelous scenery."

20. MR: See his review of Chevillard's performance of the third act of *Siegfried* in his review of 1 April 1901 in Debussy, *Monsieur Croche*, rev. ed., 25, and in Debussy, *Debussy on Music*, 14–15.

21. MR: See his review from 1 April 1901 in Debussy, *Monsieur Croche*, rev. ed., 25, and in Debussy, *Debussy on Music*, 14.

22. MR: Edmond Bailly, *Le son dans la nature* (Paris: Librairie de l'art indépendant, 1900), 42. This was basically a reprint of Bailly's earlier article, "Le monde sonore. Le son. Harmonie des sphères. Voix de la nature," which had appeared in *Le guide musical* 37, no. 8 (22 February 1891): 57–59, and had continued in subsequent issues of the same journal: 37, no. 9 (1 March 1891): 65–67; 37, no. 10 (8 March 1891): 73–75; and 37, no. 11 (15 March 1891): 81–82.

23. MR: The last two quotations are from Bailly, *Le son dans la nature*, 45.

24. MR: See his review from 1 June 1901 in Debussy, *Monsieur Croche*, rev. ed., 46, and in Debussy, *Debussy on Music*, 41.

25. MR: See his 1 June 1901 review in Debussy, *Monsieur Croche*, rev. ed., 47, and in Debussy, *Debussy on Music*, 41.

26. MR: See his review from 1 July 1901 in Debussy, *Monsieur Croche*, rev. ed., 49, and in Debussy, *Debussy on Music*, 45.

27. MR: See his review from 1 July 1901 in Debussy, *Monsieur Croche*, rev. ed., 51–52, and in Debussy, *Debussy on Music*, 47–48.

28. MR: See his review from 15 November 1901 in Debussy, *Monsieur Croche*, rev. ed., 55–56, and in Debussy, *Debussy on Music*, 52–53.

29. MR: See his review from 15 November 1901 in Debussy, *Monsieur Croche*, rev. ed., 57–58, and in Debussy, *Debussy on Music*, 54–55.

30. MR: See his review from 1 July 1901 in Debussy, *Monsieur Croche*, rev. ed., 48–53, and in Debussy, *Debussy on Music*, 44–49.

31. Edward Lockspeiser, *Debussy: His Life and Mind* (Cambridge: Cambridge University Press, 1978), 2:53. MR: Lockspeiser was referring specifically to Debussy's "Conversation with M. Croche" that was published in the 1 July 1901 issue of *La revue blanche*. This remark appears at the beginning of an entire chapter on "Monsieur Croche and Monsieur Teste" (2:52–70) in which Lockspeiser summarizes many of the ideas and traces the various lines of thinking that are present in Debussy's articles.

32. MR: See his review from 1 July 1901 in Debussy, *Monsieur Croche*, rev. ed., 51 and 52, and in Debussy, *Debussy on Music*, 46 and 48.

33. MR: Valéry had wanted to dedicate his story about Monsieur Teste to Degas, but the latter refused.

34. MR: Writers such as Paul Valéry, Henri de Régnier, Pierre Louÿs, André Lebey, and Jean de Tinan were active contributors to *Le centaure*. These authors' contributions are discussed in Anne Mairesse, "La revue du 'Centaure': Textes et contextes d'une œuvre esthétique et littéraire," *Nineteenth-Century French Studies* 32, no. 1–2 (fall–winter 2003–4): 104–20.

35. André Schaeffner, "M. Croche," in *Essais de musicologie et autres fantaisies* (Paris: Le Sycamore, 1980), 265–81; republished as *Variations sur la musique* (Paris: Librairie Arthème Fayard, 1998), 358–73. See also Lockspeiser [*Debussy: His Life and Mind*, 2:52–70]. MR: Valéry referred to M. Teste and M. Croche as "bonhommes."

36. [Paul Valéry,] *Introduction à la méthode de Léonard de Vinci (1894)* [Paris: Éditions Gallimard, 1957].

37. *Collection d'autographes littéraires: Lettres et manuscrits des XVIIe, XVIIIe, XIXe, XXe siècles*, deuxième partie, auction catalog (Paris, Drouot, 26 February 1969), item 146. [FL must have seen the actual letter because only excerpts are in the catalog description; see his notes in Fonds FL, BnF, carton I/6(3).] The original is not dated but is contemporaneous with the publication of the *Aventures du roi Pausole* in 1901.

38. MR: See Valéry's letter to Debussy in Paul Valéry, *Lettres à quelques-uns* (Paris: Gallimard, 1952), 63, where it is dated "Mardi [1900]." Lesure and Herlin establish the date as 15 January 1901 in *C*, 580.

39. See Valéry's letter from 15 January 1901 in Valéry, *Lettres a quelques-uns*, 63, and in *C*, 580.

40. MR: With respect to the Orpheus myth, Valéry points specifically to the "animation of everything by a spirit" (see his letter from 15 January 1901 in Valéry, *Lettres à quelques-uns*, 63, and in *C*, 580).

41. MR: Paul Valéry, *Pièces sur l'art* (Paris: Galllimard, 1934); see the chapter titled "Histoire d'Amphion," 87–102, especially 96–97. In the first paragraph of the

quotation, Valéry uses the word "moyens" (literally "means"), which I translate here as "elements."

42. Valéry, *Pièces sur l'art*, 98. In a letter to Gide, Valéry wrote sometime around 14 March 1913 [cited erroneously in FL 2003 as July 1918]: "I don't remember any more what I had written to Debussy. The main point was a curious division of the scenic space corresponding to the division of its elements. It was a ballet of categories." MR: See André Gide and Paul Valéry, *Correspondance, 1890–1942*, ed. Peter Fawcett (Paris: Éditions Gallimard, 2009), 715–16.

43. MR: Gide and Valéry, *Correspondance*, 99.

44. MR: See his letter to Fénéon from possibly 25 November 1901 in *C*, 626–27.

45. MR: See Debussy's letter to Fénéon from December 1901 in *C*, 628.

46. MR: This article was ultimately published in the 19 January 1903 issue of *Gil Blas*; see Debussy, *Monsieur Croche*, rev. ed., 76, and Debussy, *Debussy on Music*, 93–94.

47. MR: Further details are provided by François Lesure in Debussy, *Monsieur Croche*, rev. ed., 9 and 340, and in Debussy, *Debussy on Music*, xvii–xviii.

48. Debussy, *Debussy on Music*, 62–68.

49. MR: See Debussy's review "*L'étranger* de Vincent d'Indy," in *Gil Blas* (12 January 1903), reprinted in Debussy, *Monsieur Croche*, rev. ed., 69–73, and in Debussy, *Debussy on Music*, 87–91.

50. See d'Indy's letter of 14 January 1903 [in *C*, 714] and in Léon Vallas, *Vincent d'Indy* (Paris: Albin Michel, 1950), 2:320. MR: On 14 December of the same year, d'Indy wrote again to Debussy, telling him that his critique was more precious to him than thousandfold applause, and that he "loves and admires him for his art"; see Vallas, *Vincent d'Indy*, 321, and *C*, 806.

51. MR: See Debussy, "À la Schola Cantorum," in *Gil Blas* (2 February 1903), reprinted in Debussy, *Monsieur Croche*, rev. ed., 90, and in Debussy, *Debussy on Music*, 111.

52. MR: See Debussy's article on "L'orientation musicale," published in the October 1902 issue of *Musica*, in *Monsieur Croche*, rev. ed., 65–66, and in Debussy, *Debussy on Music*, 84–85.

53. MR: See Debussy, *Monsieur Croche*, rev. ed., 91, and Debussy, *Debussy on Music*, 112.

54. MR: See Debussy, *Monsieur Croche*, rev. ed., 91, and Debussy, *Debussy on Music*, 112.

55. MR: See Debussy, *Monsieur Croche*, rev. ed., 101, and Debussy, *Debussy on Music*, 124.

56. MR: See Debussy, *Monsieur Croche*, rev. ed., 101, and Debussy, *Debussy on Music*, 124.

57. MR: See Debussy, *Monsieur Croche*, rev. ed., 102, and Debussy, *Debussy on Music*, 125.

58. *La revue bleue* issued an inquiry on the theme: "Is there a French music?" Besides Debussy, Landormy solicited d'Indy, Alfred Bruneau, and Dukas. MR: He also received feedback from Henri Duparc, Hugo Riemann, and Romain Rolland; see Paul Landormy, "L'état actuel de la musique française," *Revue bleue* 5, no. 13 (26 March 1904): 394–97, and *Revue bleue* 5, no. 14 (2 April 1904): 421–26.

59. MR: See this excerpt from Landormy's interview, published on 2 April 1904, in Debussy, *Monsieur Croche*, rev. ed., 278.

60. MR: See Debussy, *Monsieur Croche*, rev. ed., 279.

61. MR: See Debussy's letter to Louis Laloy from 3 April 1904 in *C*, 834.

62. MR: Letter from Adolphe Boschot to M.-C. Poinsot and Georges Normandy, cited in Michel Décaudin, *La crise des valeurs symbolistes: Vingt ans de poésie française, 1895–1914* (Toulouse: Éditions Privat, 1960), 121.

63. MR: Charles Maurras was a conservative supporter of Classicism, a fervent French nationalist, and the primary philosopher of the Action française, a political movement that was monarchist, anti-Semitic, and counter-revolutionary.

64. MR: Adrien Mithouard was a cofounder of *L'occident* and president of the Paris Municipal Council from 1914 until his death in 1919.

65. On these transitional years, see Décaudin, *La crise des valeurs symbolistes*, 137.

66. MR: See Debussy's review, "Au concert Colonne: MM. Saint-Saëns, Alfred Bachelet.—Au concert Lamoureux," from the 16 March 1903 issue of *Gil Blas* in Debussy, *Monsieur Croche*, rev. ed., 122, and Debussy, *Debussy on Music*, 142.

67. MR: See Debussy's article on "Considérations sur le prix de Rome au point de vue musical," published in *Musica* in May 1903, in Debussy, *Monsieur Croche*, rev. ed., 175, and in Debussy, *Debussy on Music*, 198.

68. MR: See Debussy's review in *Gil Blas*, published in March 1903, in Debussy, *Monsieur Croche*, rev. ed., 137, and in Debussy, *Debussy on Music*, 159.

69. MR: See Debussy's review of 27 April 1903 in *Gil Blas*, reproduced in Debussy, *Monsieur Croche*, rev. ed., 161, and in Debussy, *Debussy on Music*, 184. Debussy alluded similarly to Massenet in his article in the 1 December 1901 issue of *La revue blanche*, reproduced in Debussy, *Monsieur Croche*, rev. ed., 59, and in Debussy, *Debussy on Music*, 56.

70. MR: See Debussy's review of 20 April 1903 in *Gil Blas*, reproduced in Debussy, *Monsieur Croche*, rev. ed., 155, and in Debussy, *Debussy on Music*, 179.

71. MR: See Debussy's review of 8 May 1903 in *Gil Blas*, reproduced in Debussy, *Monsieur Croche*, rev. ed., 163, and in Debussy, *Debussy on Music*, 193.

72. MR: See Debussy's review of the London performance of Wagner's tetralogy, published on 1 June 1903 in *Gil Blas*, in Debussy, *Monsieur Croche*, rev. ed., 182, and in Debussy, *Debussy on Music*, 205.

73. MR: See Debussy's review of 30 March 1903 in *Gil Blas*, reproduced in Debussy, *Monsieur Croche*, rev. ed., 139, and in Debussy, *Debussy on Music*, 160. In a later review, from the *S. I. M.* in December 1912, Debussy wrote that Strauss was "one of the most definitive geniuses of our time"; see Debussy, *Monsieur Croche*, rev. ed., 220, and Debussy, *Debussy on Music*, 271.

74. MR: See Debussy's "Le bilan musical en 1903," published in *Gil Blas* on 28 June 1903, in Debussy, *Monsieur Croche*, rev. ed., 196, and in Debussy, *Debussy on Music*, 184.

16. *Pelléas et Mélisande*: 1902

1. MR: See Constant Pierre, *Le Conservatoire national de musique et de déclamation* (Paris: Imprimerie nationale, 1900), 588.

2. MR: See Viñes's journal entry for 31 October 1901 in Ricardo Viñes, "Le journal inédit de Ricardo Viñes," trans. and ed. Nina Gubisch, *Revue internationale de musique française* 1, no. 2 (June 1980): 198.

3. MR: See Viñes's journal entry for 30 November 1901 in Viñes, "Le journal inédit," 198–99.

4. MR: See Viñes's journal entries for 14 December 1901 and for 5 January 1902 in Viñes, "Le journal inédit," 224.

5. See Viñes's journal entry for 11 January 1902 in Viñes, "Le journal inédit," 224.

6. MR: See the brief review of Viñes's performance of Debussy's "Toccata" several months later in "Chronique de la semaine," *Le guide musical* 48, no. 14 (6 April 1902): 323. A review immediately following the January 1902 concert was favorable, though no comparison to Chabrier was made; see Gustave Samazeuilh, "Chronique de la semaine: Paris—Société nationale de musique," *Le guide musical* 48, no. 3 (19 January 1902): 57.

7. MR: Pierre Lalo, "La musique," *Le temps* (28 January 1902): [2].

8. Samazeuilh, review in *Le guide musical* (19 January 1902): 57, cited in n6.

9. MR: See Dandelot's review in *Le monde musical* 14, no. 1 (15 January 1902): 10.

10. MR: See Debussy's letter to Georges Hartmann in *C*, 412.

11. [*C*, 618.]

12. René Peter, *Claude Debussy*, rev. ed. (Paris: Gallimard, 1944), 221. MR: Lesure and Herlin ascribe a date of March 1902 for this letter; see *C*, 642–43.

13. MR: Here Lesure is alluding to Debussy's letter from 25 October 1903, in which he complains that "the Opéra-Comique is taking up an absurd amount of my time. And this life in the theater disgusts me as much as it numbs me"; see *C*, 792.

14. MR: André Messager, "Les premières représentations de *Pelléas*," *La revue musicale* (1 May 1926): 110 (206), reprinted as a special issue in 1964.

15. Messager, "Les premières représentations," 110 (206).

16. MR: See Busser's entry for 2 December 1901 in Henri Busser, *De* Pelléas *aux* Indes galantes (Paris: Librairie Arthème Fayard, 1955), 106.

17. MR: See the notice under "Nouvelles diverses," *Le guide musical* 48, no. 5 (2 February 1902): 116.

18. [The announcement of Mary Garden in the role of Mélisande appeared in "Nouvelles diverses: Paris et départements," *Le ménestrel* 67, no. 52 (29 December 1901): 415.] Albert Carré, in *Souvenirs de théâtre* (Paris: Librairie Plon, 1950), 277–79, clearly writes that it was he who "extricated" Debussy from his involvement with Georgette Leblanc.

19. MR: Garden actually entered in act 3, opening with a performance of "Depuis le jour" that brought the house down.

20. Having learned of the reception of *Pelléas* at the Opéra-Comique, the publisher Choudens also indicated his interest and wrote to Debussy, on 13 May 1901: "Would you like me to publish your work being done at the Opéra-Comique? Give me your conditions. I have believed in you for a long time." [See *C*, 598.]

21. [*C*, 615 and 617, respectively.]

22. The copy dedicated to Albert Carré is dated "May 1902," while Henri Busser points out that Debussy dedicated his own score on 9 May (Busser, *De* Pelléas *aux* Indes galantes, 117).

23. "Notes et informations," *Le monde artiste* 42, no. 13 (30 March 1902), 204.

24. MR: Maeterlinck's letter to Carré is housed in the Harry Ransom Center of the University of Texas at Austin. I am grateful to David Grayson for informing me of this source.

25. MR: See Debussy's letter to Nicolas G. Coronio from 27 January 1902 in *C*, 637–38.

26. See transcriptions of the official reports of these three sessions (Archives of the Société des auteurs et compositeurs dramatiques) in François Lesure, *Debussy avant* Pelléas *ou les années symbolistes* (Paris: Klincksieck, 1992), 253–55. MR: Excerpts from the 14 February report, found in the archives of the SACD, are also given in *C*, 639n1, and copies of the actual reports of the meetings on 7 and 14 February are conserved among the Dietschy materials in DOSS-03.05 of the CDCD as well as in the Fonds FL, BnF, carton I/6(12), the latter written out by hand by Lesure.

27. MR: See "Notes et informations," *Le monde artiste* 42, no. 8 (23 February 1902): 124.

28. MR: See Georgette Leblanc, *Souvenirs (1895–1918)* (Paris: Éditions Bernard Grasset, 1931), 171–2, as well as Georgette Leblanc, "Debussy souvenirs (1895–1918)," *Silences* 4 (Paris: Éditions de la Différence, 1987): 85. FL 2003 adds that in 1906, when replying to Arthur Symons on the matter of a performance of his *Pelléas* in London, Maeterlinck suggested some incidental music that was "very good, they tell me, done by a German whose name I no longer remember [possibly Schönberg?]"; see *Autographes: Lettres – Documents – Photos*, catalog 25 (Geneva: L'autographe S.A., 20 May 1993), item 237. He swore that he had never heard Debussy's work; on 11 February 1912, he mentioned to the manager of the Nice production of *Pelléas* that "sort of inviolate vow" that prevented him from going to hear it [see Librairie du Casoar, Coetquidan, catalog 53 ([Nantes?], 1987), item 125; the page from the catalog on which this item is described may be viewed in the BnF, Fonds Lesure, carton I/6(12)]. But in June 1920, he confessed to Mary Garden: "Yesterday, I broke my oath, and I am a happy man." [See Mary Garden and Louis Biancolli, *Mary Garden's Story* (New York: Simon & Schuster, 1951), 116.] Georgette Leblanc would finally have an opportunity to perform the role of Mélisande in 1912, in Boston [see Leblanc, *Souvenirs (1895–1918)*, 176, and p. 181 in the English trans.]. (For details, see p. 293 in the present volume.)

29. MR: Maeterlinck's letter of 13 April appeared in "Courrier des théâtres," *Le Figaro* (14 April 1902): 4. FL 2003 reports that it was published on 13 April.

30. [*C*, 639.]

31. [Carré's immediate response appeared in the section titled "Courrier des théâtres" in *Le Figaro* (15 April 1902): 4, and was reprinted, following a copy of the text of Maeterlinck's letter in] *Le guide musical* 48, no. 16 (20 April 1902): 372.

32. MR: See "Notes et informations," *Le monde artiste* 42, no. 16 (20 April 1902): 252.

33. MR: See [Archives de l'Opéra-Comique,] 1 June 1901–14 July 1902 in the BnF, Bibliothèque-musée de l'opéra, Registres OC-46 (also available online at IFN-52506678).

34. These appointment books are housed in the BnF, département de la Musique, Rés. Vmf. Ms. 6. Fifty years later, Busser edited his souvenirs, *De* Pelléas *aux* Indes galantes (1955), taking quite a few liberties with the facts.

35. MR: The chronology that appears in FL 2003 has been expanded to include further details that are reported by Denis Herlin in annex 2 of "*Pelléas et Mélisande* aux Bouffes-Parisiens,*"* in Pelléas et Mélisande *cent ans après: Études et documents*, ed. Jean-Christophe Branger, Sylvie Douche, and Denis Herlin (Paris: Symétrie, 2012), 300–311.

36. MR: Landry (1867–99) had received a first prize in solfège in 1877, second prize in piano in 1879, second honorable mention in 1882 and second prize in 1883 in accompaniment, first honorable mention in organ in 1884 (the year in which Debussy won the Prix de Rome), first honorable mention in 1886 and second prize in 1887 in counterpoint and fugue, and he served as the Kapellmeister at St. Roch and chorus master at the Opéra-Comique; see Pierre, *Conservatoire national*, 788.

37. In his *Souvenirs de théâtre* (1950), 276 [cited as 270 in FL 2003], Carré simply wrote: "Our collaboration began even before his [Debussy's] work was completed. We would meet—Messager, him, and me—in the evenings at Weber's on the rue Royale, and we would urge him on to finish the last scenes. Before long, my scene-painters—Jusseaume, Ronsin, and Bianchini—joined us." MR: Michela Niccolai has studied sources such as Carré's manuscript notes and Durand's printed staging manual for a critical edition of the staging of *Pelléas*; see her *Debussy's* Pelléas et Mélisande*: The Staging by Albert Carré*, trans. Lesley Wright (Turnhout: Brepols, 2017).

38. MR: See Debussy's letter to Carré from 18 April 1902 in *C*, 646. In this letter, he also suggests that there be more light in the fifth scene, following Golaud's accident, which supposedly happens at noon. He makes the point that, given so many dark moments in the work, the audience will appreciate a bit more light on the relatively few occasions when it is appropriate to the story line.

39. MR: See n26.

40. MR: See n26.

41. MR: See n26.

42. [Reported in] Nicolet, "Courrier des spectacles," *Le gaulois* (19 March 1902): 3; reproduced in "Nouvelles diverses: Paris et departments," *Le ménestrel* 68, no. 12 (23 March 1902): 95, [and in *Le guide musical* 48, no. 13 (30 March 1902): 298]. FL 2003 cites the *Gaulois* and *Ménestrel* sources, with the date of 23 March.

43. MR: See the 19 March entry in Henri Busser, [4 agendas trimestriels], BnF Rés. Vmf. Ms. (2, I).

44. MR: This announcement appeared in Nicolet, *Le gaulois* (19 March 1902): 3, and its reproductions, cited in n42. FL 2003 references the notice that appeared in *Le guide musical* 48, no. 13 (30 March 1902): 299.

45. MR: See the 24 March entry in Henri Busser, [4 agendas trimestriels], BnF Rés. Vmf. Ms. (2, I).

46. See Debussy's letter to Paul-Jean Toulet [in *C*, 644]. Certain critics knew about the lengthening of these interludes at the time of the premiere. Hugues Imbert wrote in particular: "The orchestral pieces connecting the different scenes were considerably expanded by the composer, in order to facilitate the scene-changing" ([see p. 416 of] Hugues Imbert, "Pelléas et Mélisande," *Le guide musical* 48, no. 18 [4 May 1902]: 415–17), while Auguste Mangeot confirmed the matter, in his own way: "[The music] is not even aware that the curtain has fallen

and continues to unfold while the scene changes" (Auguste Mangeot, "Pelléas et Mélisande," *Le monde musical* 14, no. 9 [15 May 1902]: 154–56). These witnesses seem to settle definitively the debate, initiated by Busser and pursued further by André Schaeffner, regarding the possibility that the interludes were not added until the revival of *Pelléas* in September. MR: David Grayson's article on "The Interludes of *Pelléas et Mélisande*," *Cahiers Debussy*, nouv. sér. 12–13 (1988–89): 100–122, demonstrates that Debussy did indeed expand the interludes for the premiere, and also that he continued to revise them even beyond the first season. The complex evolution of the interludes, not to mention the various cuts and other modifications made during the opera's production, are nothing less than staggering. Grayson's critical edition of *Pelléas et Mélisande* in the *Œuvres complètes de Claude Debussy*, sér. VI, vol. 2 (Paris: Durand), offers the last version of the interludes but gives the version from the piano-vocal edition in an appendix. The piano-vocal score, volume 2 ter of the critical edition, was published in 2010. Volumes 1 and 2 bis, presenting the orchestral score and the critical notes, are forthcoming.

47. MR: See the 2 April entry in Henri Busser, [4 agendas trimestriels], BnF Rés. Vmf. Ms. (2, II).

48. MR: See the 7 April entry in Henri Busser, [4 agendas trimestriels], BnF Rés. Vmf. Ms. (2, II).

49. [See the entry for 7 and 9 April in Busser, *De* Pelléas *aux* Indes galantes, 112, as well as the 9 April entry in Henri Busser, [4 agendas trimestriels], BnF Rés. Vmf. Ms. (2, II).] Gustave Samazeuilh recalled, in "Claude Debussy tel que je l'ai connu," *Carrefour* (14 March 1962): 25, that "I had the good fortune to attend several of the final rehearsals, in the shadow of a favorable ground-floor box. I even remember the day when Debussy brought the wonderful orchestral page that follows Arkel's scene in the fourth act, and that he had composed in one evening to meet the needs of the scene-changes. Seeing my enthusiasm, he reminded me of our concerts at Mme Godard-Decrais's home, emphasizing his Parsifalian lineage. [...] He entrusted me with the piano transcription of the Interludes of *Pelléas*."

50. MR: Busser, *De* Pelléas *aux* Indes galantes, 112.

51. MR: See p. 422n29.

52. MR: See p. 422n31.

53. MR: See the 17 April entry in Henri Busser, [4 agendas trimestriels], BnF Rés. Vmf. Ms. (2, II).

54. MR: See n38. Carré replied on the same day, agreeing with Debussy and explaining that the lighting had not been finalized. He conveyed his plans to adjust the lighting at the rehearsal in the little theater that he was scheduling for 19 April; see *C*, 647.

55. MR: Busser, *De* Pelléas *aux* Indes galantes, 112–13.

56. MR: Octave Mirbeau, "Maurice Maeterlinck," *Le journal* (27 April 1902): [1]. Carré had invited Mirbeau to attend the rehearsal held on 19 April, in an effort to counter Maeterlinck's negative letter. I am grateful to David Grayson for providing this information.

57. However, it is in the course of this act that, according to Godet ["Weber and Debussy," *The Chesterian* 7, no. 55 (June 1926): 221], Xavier Leroux loudly joked: "Yes, old man, *smile Golaud!*" (unpublished lecture, Geneva, 1919). See also

Georges Ricou, "La générale de *Pelléas et Mélisande*," in *Histoire du théâtre lyrique en France depuis les origines jusqu'à nos jours* (Paris: Poste national Radio-Paris, n.d.), 3:69–81.

58. MR: See the 28 April entry in Henri Busser, [4 agendas trimestriels], BnF Rés. Vmf. Ms. (2, II).

59. See Debussy's letter [of 28 April 1902] to Gabriel Mourey [in *C*, 650–51].

60. MR: See the 30 April entry in Henri Busser, [4 agendas trimestriels], BnF Rés. Vmf. Ms. (2, II).

61. Louÿs invited five people "so as to fill the box with applause," informing Debussy and adding: "We've scarcely seen you since the nineteenth century, but that doesn't change my opinions of *Pelléas*." MR: See his letter from 27 April 1902 in *C*, 650.

62. MR: See her diary entry for 28 April 1902 in Marguerite de Saint-Marceaux, *Journal, 1894–1927*, ed. Myriam Chimènes et al. (Paris: Librairie Arthème Fayard, 2007), 270.

63. Godet, "Weber and Debussy," 222–26. Godet also alluded to this incident in his article, "En marge de la marge," in *La revue musicale* (1 May 1926): 84–85 (180–81). MR: In the former source, Godet's report of Debussy's thoughts on Weber is far more elaborate, while in the latter source, Godet describes a stop at Fromont's office, to mark the cut in the bedroom scene of the piano-vocal score and to dedicate a copy of the score to him, before heading back to Debussy's apartment.

64. Peter, *Claude Debussy*, rev. ed., 186. Godet noted the difference between his memories and those of Peter (see Godet's manuscript notes in a copy of Léon Vallas, *Claude Debussy et son temps* [Paris: Librairie Félix Alcan, 1932], fol. 9).

65. MR: See Debussy's letter to Jean Marnold, written from Bichain on 29 July 1902, where he would spend the remainder of the summer near his in-laws, in *C*, 680–81.

66. MR: Denis Herlin provides lists of performances of *Pelléas*—at the Opéra-Comique as well as in the provinces and outside of France—during Debussy's lifetime in annexes 3 and 4, respectively, of his article, "*Pelléas et Mélisande* aux Bouffes-Parisiens," 315–29. These appendixes are followed by a massive and invaluable anthology of the reaction of the press that supersedes several previous compilations; see pp. 333–569. Many of the reviews cited in this chapter are reprinted in Herlin's appendix.

67. Robert de Flers, "Critique des critiques," *Le Figaro* (16 May 1902): 4–5.

68. MR: Robert de Flers, "Critique des critiques," 4. The original article appeared in Catulle Mendès, "Premières représentations," *Le journal* (1 May 1902): 4.

69. MR: Robert de Flers, "Critique des critiques," 5. See also Henry Gauthier-Villars, "Les premières: Théâtre de l'Opéra-Comique—*Pelléas et Mélisande*," *Écho de Paris* (1 May 1902): 4.

70. MR: Robert de Flers, "Critique des critiques," *Le Figaro*, 5. See also p. 4 of Eugène d'Harcourt, "Les théâtres," *Le Figaro* (1 May 1902): 3–4.

71. MR: Often cited by Émile Vuillermoz, in his *Maurice Ravel par quelques-uns de ses familiers* (Paris: Éditions du tambourinaire, 1939), 12; in his *Histoire*

de la musique (Paris: Arthème Fayard, 1949), 355; in his *Claude Debussy* (Geneva: Éditions René Kister, 1957), 94; and in his *Claude Debussy* (Paris: Flammarion, 1962), 98.

72. MR: See p. 378 in Vincent d'Indy, "À propos de *Pelléas et Mélisande* (Essai de psychologie du critique d'art)," *L'occident* 1, no. 7 (June 1902): 374–81.

73. MR: See Debussy's letter to André Messager in *C*, 658.

74. MR: Pierre Lalo, "La musique," *Le temps* (20 May 1902): [1–2]. Lalo's extensive article extols the work's deep musicality, its sensitivity to the text, and its unique musical language that does not imitate Wagner or Massenet, although it also comments on the work's length and a mysterious lack of motivation behind the actions of the characters, who simply submit to their fate.

75. See Louÿs's letter to Debussy from sometime between 21 and 24 May 1902 in *C*, 661.

76. MR: Émile Vuillermoz described this "sacred battalion," or "avant-garde group," in his *Histoire de la musique*, 378–9: "The incomprehension and cynicism of the majority of the audience would have rendered the endurance of the work [*Pelléas*] impossible if this 'sacred battalion' had not come to each and every performance over a period of many months to maintain order in the hall and to sustain an atmosphere of infectious enthusiasm up until the moment when the opera could safely thrive on its own."

77. [*C*, 661.]

78. Edmond Maurat, *Souvenirs musicaux et littéraires* (Saint-Étienne: Centre interdisciplinaire d'études et de recherches sur l'expression contemporaine, 1977), 21.

79. MR: Émile Vuillermoz, "La musique," *La revue dorée* 3, no. 33 (November 1902): 180.

80. MR: Léon-Paul Fargue, *Refuges* (Paris: Gallimard, 1966), 147.

81. MR: This quote comes from Inghelbrecht's *Mouvement contraire* (Paris: Domat, 1947), 275.

82. MR: Vuillermoz, "La musique," 180, cited in n79.

83. MR: Peter, *Claude Debussy*, rev. ed., 194.

84. MR: See the entry for 11 May in Jules Renard, *Le journal de Jules Renard* (Paris: François Bernouard, 1927), 3:741–42.

85. MR: L'ouvreuse [Willy], "Lettres de l'ouvreuse," *L'écho de Paris* (23 June 1902): 4.

86. Max d'Ollone, *Henri Rabaud: Sa vie et son œuvre* (Paris: Heugel, 1948 [*recte* 1958]), 26.

87. Paul Locard, "La quinzaine," *Le courrier musical* 5, no. 11 (1 June 1902): 167.

88. Jean-Michel Nectoux, "Debussy et Fauré," *Cahiers Debussy*, nouv. sér. 3 (1979): 24.

89. MR: Letter of 6 August 1902, sent from Déodat de Séverac to René de Castéra, cited in Robert F. Waters, *Déodat de Séverac: Musical Identity in Fin de Siècle France* (London: Routledge, 2016), 33 and 33n67. Also cited by Blanche Selva, *Déodat de Séverac* (Paris: Librairie Delagrave, 1930), 38; and in Bibliothèque nationale, *Claude Debussy*, exhibition catalog (Paris: Les presses artistiques, 1962), 42.

90. MR: Jean Cocteau, "Fragments d'une conférence sur Eric Satie (1902)," *La revue musicale* 5, no. 5 (1 March 1924): 221.

91. MR: In his essay, "Des règles, du gout et du beau absolu," Charles Koechlin claimed that Ravel spoke to him of Debussy's genius in May 1902, after the premiere of *Pelléas*. See Charles Koechlin, *Écrits: Esthétique et langage musical*, ed. Michel Duchesneau (Sprimont, Belgium: Éditions Mardaga, 2006), 1:410. In addition, Pierre Lalo published, in his column "La musique" in *Le temps* (9 April 1907): [3], a letter from Ravel to Adrien Hébrard, the director of the paper; in it, Ravel called Debussy "an artistic genius." One might note that other contemporary writers, such as Émile Vuillermoz, in his essay on "Pelléas et Mélisande" in *La revue dorée* 3, no. 27 (May 1902): 25–29, made reference to Debussy's "genius" immediately following the premiere of his opera.

92. Claude Debussy, *Lettres à deux amis*, ed. Robert Godet and Georges Jean-Aubry (Paris: J. Corti, 1942), 84.

93. MR: See Debussy's letter to Lilly from 15 July 1902 in *C*, 675.

94. MR: Madame Virot was a milliner who sold fashionable hats at her shop on the rue de la Paix; see *C*, 350n8.

95. MR: See Debussy's letter to Lilly from 18 July 1902 in *C*, 678.

96. MR: See Debussy's letter to Lilly from 15 July 1902 in *C*, 675, and also 675n1.

97. MR: See *C*, 675n1. This passage is rendered as "I have never known anyone to lose himself so completely in the spectacle of great art" in Garden and Biancolli, *Mary Garden's Story*, 76.

98. MR: Percy Pitt did not become the director of Covent Garden until 1906, long after Debussy's trip to London to see Messager in 1902.

99. MR: In a letter to Messager from 22 July 1902, Debussy asked to be remembered to "the most illustrious M. Scotti"; see *C*, 680.

100. MR: FL 2003 cites a Robert Bunning, rather than Herbert Bunning, as the composer of the opera.

101. MR: Refer back to pp. 153–54 in the present volume.

102. Letter of 8 September 1902 [in *C*, 687].

103. [*C*, 668.]

104. MR: The date of 5 July 1902 is reported in Vallas, *Claude Debussy et son temps*, 256; in Marcel Dietschy, *La passion de Claude Debussy* (Neuchâtel: Éditions de la Baconnière, 1962), 136n5; and in English in Marcel Dietschy, *A Portrait of Claude Debussy*, trans. William Ashbrook and Margaret G. Cobb (Oxford: Oxford University Press, 1990), 108. All of these piano works, except for the *Marche écossaise* and the *Fantaisie*, are available in sér. I, vol. 1 of the *Œuvres complètes de Claude Debussy* (Paris: Durand, 2000). For further information on the complex publication history of these works, see the "Chronology" section of editor Roy Howat's foreword on pp. xi–xiv (in French) and pp. xix–xxii (in English).

105. MR: His precise words were that he felt like a "*citron pressé*." See his letter to Messager from 8 September 1902 in *C*, 687.

106. MR: See letter from Debussy to Nicolas Coronio, from the beginning of September 1902, in *C*, 684.

107. MR: In a letter to Jacques Durand from 14 August 1902, Debussy mentioned that the choral parts in the orchestral score of *La damoiselle élue* were not synchronous with those in the piano-vocal score, the latter of which was correct; see *C*, 682.

108. MR: *Les aventures du Capitaine Corcoran* was a book by Alfred Assollant that was adapted as a play in four acts with twenty-four scenes by Messieurs Paul Gavault, Georges Berr, and Adrien Vély, and was premiered at the Châtelet on 30 October 1902.

109. MR: Louis Delaquerrière sang the tenor role of Pierre in Messager's "comédie lyrique," *Madame Chrysanthème*, at its first performance on 21 January 1893 at the Théâtre de la Renaissance in Paris.

110. MR: Letter from Messager to Carré, dated 26 May 1902; see *C*, 664–65n1.

111. MR: See Debussy's letter to André Messager from 5 June 1902 in *C*, 664.

112. MR: See Debussy's letter to André Messager from 7 June 1902 in *C*, 665.

113. MR: See Debussy's letter to André Messager from 2 July 1902 in *C*, 673.

114. See Debussy's letter to André Messager from 2 July 1902 in *C*, 673.

115. MR: In 1898, the twenty-year-old Rigaux won a second prize in opera and received a first honorable mention in voice at the Conservatoire; see Pierre, *Conservatoire national*, 575, 658, and 841.

116. Letter from Debussy to Messager of 8 September 1902 [in *C*, 687].

117. "Nouvelles diverses," *Le guide musical* 48, nos. 31–32 (3 and 10 August 1902): 588. [A notice in "Nouvelles diverses," *Le guide musical* 48, nos. 35–36 (31 August and 7 September 1902): 630, reported that Leoncavallo's work would be performed in Rome during 1903. However, the news that Camille Erlanger had composed a five-act lyric drama, based on a libretto by Louis de Grammont, had already been announced by Serge Basset in "Courrier des théâtres," *Le Figaro* (23 July 1902): 5.] A few months later, Leoncavallo would go on to deny the news ("Ça et là," *La quinzaine musicale* 9, no. 8 [15 April 1903]: 116).

118. MR: Tonkin is in the north of Vietnam, east of north Laos and west of the Gulf of Tonkin. Following the Sino-French war (1884–85), it became a French protectorate and remained so until 1945.

119. MR: See Debussy's letter to Toulet from 21 October 1902 in *C*, 695. FL 2003 cites the date of 20 October.

120. MR: See Debussy's letter to Toulet from 25 October 1902 in *C*, 697.

121. MR: See the text of Debussy's communication from October 1902 in *C*, 690. This text is reproduced in Claude Debussy, *Monsieur Croche et autres écrits*, rev. ed. (Paris: Gallimard, 1987), 65–66; and in Claude Debussy, *Debussy on Music*, trans. Richard Langham Smith (New York: Alfred A. Knopf, 1977), 84–85.

122. [See p. 270 in] X.-Marcel Boulestin, "La quinzaine," *Le courrier musical* 5, no. 19 (15 November 1902): 269–70.

123. Boulestin, "La quinzaine," 270.

124. Henri de Curzon, "Chronique de la semaine: Paris—Les Théâtres," *Le guide musical* 48, no. 45 (9 November 1902): 804.

125. Boulestin, "La quinzaine," 270. [FL 2003 erroneously cites the 1 December 1902 issue of *Le courrier musical*.] As for Mme de Saint-Marceaux, her journal entry for 6 November notes: "Périer is replaced by a bad tenor. The child is replaced by a woman, who admirably renders, from a musical point of view, the scene at the window, and whose presence allows the very interesting atmosphere of the third act to

be restored. An exquisite evening. There are agitated and dissatisfied people in the audience next to the enthusiastic ones." [See Saint-Marceaux, *Journal*, 284.]

126. MR: See Jacques d'Offoël, "Chronique de la semaine: Paris—Concerts Lamoureux," *Le guide musical* 48, no. 46 (16 November 1902): 827.

127. MR: Debussy mentioned having the flu, as well as Colonne's visit, in a letter to Jacques Durand on 9 December 1902: see *C*, 702.

128. MR: As reported by Louis Laloy in *La musique retrouvée* (Paris: Librairie Plon, 1928), 130.

129. Laloy, *La musique retrouvée*, 132. Saint-Saëns had remained in Paris longer than usual in June "in order to speak badly of *Pelléas*."

130. MR: Recall that *La damoiselle élue* was first heard at the Société nationale in April 1893, with soloists Julia Robert and Thérèse Roger and an audience filled with friends such as the Chaussons (see pp. 107–8). It was also performed at the Libre Esthétique in Brussels, this time among sympathetic Ysaÿe followers, with Thérèse Roger again as soloist, in March 1894 (see pp. 119–20). And it received a third public hearing during the 1899 World's Fair (see pp. 165–66). In addition to these public performances, *La damoiselle élue* was played in salons such as those held by Meg de Saint-Marceaux and Mme Godard-Decrais (see pp. 118–19 and 141).

131. MR: See Charles Malherbe's program note in Edmond Stoullig, *Les annales du théâtre et de la musique* (Paris: Librairie Paul Ollendorff, 1902): 496.

132. MR: Jean d'Udine, "Les grands concerts," *Le courrier musical* 6, no. 1 (1 January 1903): 9.

133. Jacques d'Offoël, "Chronique de la semaine: Paris—Concerts Colonne," *Le guide musical* 48, no. 52 (28 December 1902): 971.

134. D'Udine, review in *Le courrier musical* (1 January 1903), cited in n132.

17. From the *Fêtes galantes* to *La mer*: 1903

1. René Peter, *Claude Debussy*, rev. ed. (Paris: Gallimard, 1944), 100–102. Among the others being honored in the same way were Combarieu, Tristan Bernard, and Henry Bataille, the future author of *La femme nue* [see pp. 455–56n3].

2. MR: Fernand Gregh, *L'age d'or* (Paris: Éditions Bernard Grasset, 1946), 312n1.

3. [See Gregh's article on "L'Humanisme in *Le Figaro* (12 December 1902): [1].] Michel Décaudin, *La crise des valeurs symbolistes: Vingt ans de poésie française, 1895–1914* (Toulouse: Éditions Privat, 1960), 123–24. The composer's relationship with Gregh would continue: on 21 February 1903, Viñes remarked on Gregh's presence at Debussy's home [see his journal entry in Ricardo Viñes, "Le journal inédit de Ricardo Viñes," trans. and ed. Nina Gubisch, *Revue internationale de musique française* 1, no. 2 (June 1980): 225].

4. In announcing the news, *La revue musicale* specified that Debussy had not applied for the honor.

5. MR: See Debussy's letter to Louis Laloy from 4 January 1903 in *C*, 712.

6. See pp. 47–49 and 57 in the present volume.

7. Letters from Debussy to Henriette Fuchs, dated [15 March and] 17 March 1903, [in *C*, 720 and 721, respectively].

8. See pp. 123–25 in the present volume.

9. [See Debussy's letter to Jeanne Chausson from] 17 May 1903 [in *C*, 731].

10. Robert Orledge, *Debussy and the Theatre* (Cambridge: Cambridge University Press, 1982), 266–68. MR: See also Debussy's letter to Victor-Émile Michelet from 28 December 1902 in *C*, 707.

11. MR: See Debussy's letter to Michelet from 31 December 1902 in *C*, 708.

12. [*C*, 712.]

13. Georges Servières, "Bibliographie," *Le guide musical* 49, nos. 28–29 (12 and 19 July 1903): 545.

14. MR: The *Ariettes oubliées* contained many musical changes from the former *Ariettes* as well; compare sér. II, vols. 2 and 4, edited by Marie Rolf and Denis Herlin, respectively, in the *Œuvres complètes de Claude Debussy* (Paris: Durand, 2016 and 2020). See also Marie Rolf, "Des *Ariettes* (1888) aux *Ariettes oubliées* (1903)," *Cahiers Debussy* 12–13 (1988–89): 29–47.

15. MR: Two manuscripts of "En sourdine," both dedicated to Catherine Stevens, are known; they are housed in the Robert Owen Lehman Collection at The Morgan Library & Museum in New York and at the Harry Ransom Center in Austin, Texas. A manuscript of "Clair de lune," dedicated "to Madame M. V. Peter," is in the former Honegger collection, now in a private collection in Paris.

16. Georges Servières, "Bibliographie," *Le guide musical* 49, no. 19 (10 May 1903): 430. MR: Although Servières may have been critical of Debussy's *Trois mélodies* (which included a "Romance" as well as "Paysage sentimental" and "La belle au bois dormant"), he praised the three *Fêtes Galantes* that had just been published.

17. On 6 February, at the Aeolian Hall, Debussy's String Quartet "unleashed a flood of enthusiasm" (see the notice, following the heading for Premier Concert Henri Sailler, by Jacques d'Offoël, "Chronique de la semaine: Paris," *Le guide musical* 49, no. 7 [15 February (1903)]: 145). MR: The String Quartet was also performed on 11 and 25 March; see the announcements in *Le courrier musical* 6, no. 5 (1 March 1903): 78, and in *Le courrier musical* 6, no. 6 (15 March 1903): 94.

18. MR: The concert was reviewed by M.-D. Calvocoressi in "La quinzaine: À la salle Erard," *Le courrier musical* 6, no. 8 (15 April 1903): 125; another review of the Salle Érard concert (*Le monde musical* 15, no. 7 [15 April 1903]: 107) simply reported that "those pages truly had a troubling charm."

19. MR: See the review of Bréval's 26 December 1909 recital in *Le monde musical* 21, no. 24 (30 December 1909): 355. FL 2003 contains a typographical error, citing the date of 30 December 1919 for this source.

20. MR: Vallas was reporting on Bréval's performance at the Concerts Colonne on 26 December 1909, and he added that her interpretation was "not in keeping with Debussy's art"; see Léon Vallas, *Claude Debussy et son temps* (Paris: Éditions Albin Michel, 1958), 194.

21. Today at the BnF; it has been reproduced in facsimile by François Lesure in Claude Debussy, *Esquisses de "Pelléas et Mélisande" (1893–1895)* (Geneva: Éditions Minkoff, 1977). Debussy also dedicated a score of the *Fêtes galantes* to the singer, with his "affectionate and customary devotion" (avec le dévouement affectueux et accoutumé) on 11 April 1903; see *C*, 2218.

22. See pp. 170–71 in the present volume, [and François Leisure, *Claude Debussy: Biographic critique* (Paris: Fayard, 2003), 527]. By contract on 17 April 1908, Ravel alone was subsequently charged with a new reduction of the *Nocturnes* for two pianos, which he premiered with Louis Aubert at the Société musicale indépendante on 24 April 1911.

23. Paul Landormy, *La musique française de Franck à Debussy*, 17th ed. (Paris: Gallimard, 1943), 226.

24. Michel Brenet, "Chronique de la semaine: Paris," *Le guide musical* 49, no. 17 (26 April 1903): 376.

25. MR: Jean de Muris, "Mois musical," *La tribune de Saint-Gervais* 9, no. 5 (May 1903): 190.

26. Jean Marnold, "Revue du mois: Musique," *Mercure de France* 46, no. 162 (June 1903): 808. MR: See also the positive review by M.-D. Calvocoressi in "La quinzaine: À la Scola Cantorum," *Le courrier musical* 6, no. 9 (1 May 1903): 140.

27. Henri de Vauplane, "Correspondances: Marseille," *Le courrier musical* 6, no. 2 (15 January 1903): 29.

28. Gabriel Rouchès, "Correspondances: Bordeaux," *Le courrier musical* 6, no. 4 (15 February 1903): 59.

29. MR: A notice for this concert appeared in "Le mouvement musical en Province," *Le courrier musical* 5, no. 21 (15 December 1902): 305. Brunel served as director of the Conservatoire in Nancy, and he helped found the Orchestre symphonique et lyrique de Nancy.

30. MR: A notice of the 11 December concert in Monte-Carlo, conducted by Léon Jehin, appeared in "Le mouvement musical en Province," *Le courrier musical* 5, no. 21 (15 December 1902): 305, and was reported by S. M. in "Concerts: Départements—Monte-Carlo," *Le monde musical* 15, no. 1 (15 January 1903): 14. The review of Paul Viardot's performance of the *Prélude à l'après-midi d'un faune* appeared in "Correspondances: Marseille," *Le courrier musical* 6, no. 2 (15 January 1903): 29.

31. J. P., "Correspondances: Vichy," *Le courrier musical* 6, no. 15 (1 August 1903): 220. MR: See also V. Y., "Province: Vichy," *Le monde artiste* 43, no. 32 (9 August 1903): 504. FL 2003 refers to the latter review (though he does not mention the journal), but reports that the concert took place on 7 August; this latter date is likely erroneous, because a review had already appeared in *Le courrier musical* on 1 August; no concert date was given in the brief notice from Vichy in *Le monde musical* 15, no. 16 (30 August 1903): 255.

32. His "chat" was published in *Le courrier musical* 6, no. 5 (1 March 1903): 65–67.

33. MR: X., "Correspondances: Lyon," *Le courrier musical* 5, no. 21 (15 December 1902): 302. See also Léon Vallas, "Correspondances: Lyon," *Le guide musical* 48, no. 51 (21 December 1902): 953.

34. MR: See the notice in "Échos et nouvelles diverses: France," *Le courrier musical* 6, no. 5 (1 March 1903): 78.

35. [See p. 133 of] Auguste Mangeot, "Notre portrait: M. Claude Debussy," *Le monde musical* 15, no. 9 (15 May 1903): 133–35.

36. MR: See Debussy's letter to Lilly from 28 April 1903 in *C*, 727.

37. MR: See Debussy's letter to Lilly from 27 April 1903 in *C*, 726.

38. MR: See his letter from 28 April 1903 in *C*, 727. He called this experience a "cure tétralogique," wittily alluding to a "full-body immersion in the *Ring*."

39. MR: See his letter to Lilly from 28 April 1903 in *C*, 727.

40. MR: See his letter to Lilly from 1 May 1903 in *C*, 728.

41. MR: See Debussy's review, "Impressions sur la Tétralogie à Londres," from the 1 June 1903 issue of *Gil Blas*, in Claude Debussy, *Monsieur Croche et autres écrits*, rev. ed. (Paris: Gallimard, 1987), 183; and in Claude Debussy, *Debussy on Music*, trans. Richard Langham Smith (New York: Alfred A. Knopf, 1977), 206.

42. MR: See Viñes's journal entry for 4 July 1903 in Viñes, "Le journal inédit," 226.

43. MR: See Debussy's letter to Messager from 6 May 1903 in *C*, 730.

44. Madame Gerard de Romilly, "Debussy professeur, par une de ses élèves (1898–1908)," *Cahiers Debussy*, nouv. sér. 2 (1978): 10.

45. MR: The partial manuscript of this work, housed at the New England Conservatory of Music in Boston, is titled a "Rapsodie mauresque." The manuscript from which the work was engraved, copied by Roger-Ducasse, was titled "Rapsodie pour orchestre et saxophone obligé" (with the descriptor "mauresque" crossed out); it is housed in the BnF, département de la Musique, Ms. 1001 (also accessible on microfilm; see Vm Bob-3840).

46. [*C*, 742.]

47. MR: See Debussy's letter to Lilly from 29 May 1903 in *C*, 733.

48. MR: See Debussy's letter to Lilly from 31 May 1903 in *C*, 736.

49. MR: See Viñes's entry for 13 June 1903 in Viñes, "Le journal inédit," 226. FL 2003 cites Viñes's description of the work as "une merveille" (a marvel), slightly different from Gubisch's translation ("de toute beauté").

50. This list was regularly repeated in the catalog of works added to the editions of Debussy that were published by Fromont during that period. *Le monde musical* indicated only that the *Suite* included "4 pieces."

51. MR: See Roy Howat, "En route for *L'isle joyeuse*: The Restoration of a Triptych," *Cahiers Debussy* 19 (1995): 37–52, and the avant-propos/foreword of his edition of piano works for the *Œuvres complètes de Claude Debussy*, sér. I, vol. 3 (Paris: Durand-Costallat, 1991): xi–xii and xvii–xviii. FL 2003 contends that "It is hard to believe that Debussy wavered between the three- and four-movement options, and we are inclined to think that Viñes (just like the aforementioned catalog) mixed up the new works that Debussy had discussed with him." Given the documentary evidence presented by Howat, it is unlikely that Viñes was confused, and it appears that this matter involved two different suites with the same title.

52. MR: See the contract in *C*, 748–49.

53. MR: The title of the final movement in the first set of piano *Images* was changed from "Mouvements" to simply "Mouvement."

54. MR: The "Gigue triste" became simply "Gigues" and the "Rondes" became "Rondes de printemps." In addition, the order of the movements was revised, now to begin with "Gigues," followed by "Ibéria" (itself in three parts), and concluding with the "Rondes de printemps."

55. MR: Gubisch, in Viñes, "Le journal inédit," 226, originally transcribed this passage as "ses dernièrs morceaux" (his latest pieces) instead of "ses nouvelles morceaux" (his new pieces). Roy Howat pointed out her self-correction to the adjective "nouvelles" in his "En route for *L'isle joyeuse*: The Restoration of a Triptych," 37n2.

56. MR: See Viñes's journal entry for 4 July 1903 in Viñes, "Le journal inédit," 226.

57. He was replaced by René Doire.

58. MR: Debussy's "Le bilan musical en 1903," from the 28 June 1903 issue of *Gil Blas*, is reprinted in Debussy, *Monsieur Croche*, rev. ed., 195, and in Debussy, *Debussy on Music*, 217.

59. MR: Laparra won the Prix de Rome with his cantata *Alyssa*, competing successfully against Maurice Ravel and Roger-Ducasse, among other candidates. FL 2003 does not include Laparra's surname in this quote.

60. MR: See Debussy's letter of 29 June 1903 to Messager in *C*, 745–46. In *C*, 746n1, Lesure and Herlin point out Debussy's comment that Leoncavallo's music feeds the audience's need to be bowled over by sensations; see his interview for *Musica* from 12 February 1910 in Debussy, *Monsieur Croche*, rev. ed., 299.

61. Roland-Manuel, *Maurice Ravel*, trans. Cynthia Jolly (New York: Dover Publications, 1972), 36. MR: Debussy wrote to Ravel on 4 March 1904, "In the name of all the gods and me [. . .] don't touch a thing"; see *C*, 830–31.

62. MR: See Debussy's letter to Lilly from 29 May in *C*, 733. As Lesure and Herlin point out in *C*, 733n5, Leprince was a fish shop located at 29 rue Boissy d'Anglas.

63. MR: Madame de Sévigné (1626–96) was renowned for her letter-writing. Most of her letters, full of wit and irony, were addressed to her daughter. They have been published in many different editions and are readily available in the original French as well as in English translation.

64. MR: See Debussy's letter to Lilly from 2 June 1903 in *C*, 738.

65. An announcement appeared in "Informations," *La revue musicale* 3, no. 6 (15 June 1903): 285: "Only a very small number of orchestral scores of *Pelléas et Mélisande* remain for subscribers."

66. See Debussy's letter to Messager from 7 September 1903 in *C*, 778.

67. Undated letter sent from Bichain. MR: Lesure and Herlin subsequently established the date of 18 September 1903 for this letter; see *C*, 785.

68 [*C*, 780.]

69. Marie Rolf, "Mauclair and Debussy: The Decade from 'Mer belle aux Îles sanguinaires' to *La Mer*," *Cahiers Debussy* 11 (1987): 9–23.

70. MR: See Debussy's letter to Louÿs in *C*, 753. As Lesure and Herlin point out in *C*, 753n5, Debussy was adapting a line from Verlaine's "Le son du cor s'afflige vers les bois," a poem that he had set in 1891. His phrase, "remplies d'été, de moustiques et d'un silence qu'on voudrait croire orphelin" comes from Verlaine's "Le son du cor s'afflige vers les bois d'une douleur on veut croire orpheline."

71. [*C*, 743–44.]

72. See his letter of 12 September in [*C*, 780].

73. [The notice appeared in] *Le guide musical* 49, nos. 26–27 (28 June and 5 July 1903): 518, and in "Nouvelles diverses: Un nouvel ouvrage de M. C. Debussy," *Le monde musical* 15, no. 13 (15 July 1903): 212.

74. [*C*, 788.]

75. [*C*, 788.]

76. [See Debussy's letter to Jacques Durand] from 12 September [in *C*, 779].

77. Léon Vallas, in his *Claude Debussy et son temps* (Paris: Éditions Albin Michel, 1958), 255–56, claimed that, for the summer of 1902, "He had just bought a little house in Bichain, on which he was making regular payments. The residents of Bichain [. . .] dreamed of making Debussy one of their municipal advisors, indeed their mayor!" On the other hand, Pasteur Vallery-Radot asserted that Debussy rented the house in Bichain for 200 francs a year. MR: See Pasteur Vallery-Radot, *Lettres de Claude Debussy à sa femme Emma* (Paris: Ernest Flammarion, 1957), 24.

78. MR: See Debussy's letter to Raoul Bardac from the end of August 1903 in *C*, 772–73.

79. MR: The dedicated score of Debussy's *Estampes* is conserved in the BnF, département de la Musique, Rés. Vma. 290. FL 2003 reports that this copy bears Debussy's final corrections; however, it is a clean score.

80. A few months later, Ravel would dedicate the third song of *Schéhérazade*, "L'indifférent," to Mme S. [not P., as given in FL 2003] Bardac.

81. MR: See Debussy's letter to Durand from 25 October 1903 in *C*, 792.

82. MR: See Debussy's contract with Durand, dated 14 October 1903, in *C*, 789–90, and the amendment to the contract, in which deadlines are stipulated, in *C*, 790–91.

83. MR: As reported by Edmond Stoullig in "Concerts," *Le monde artiste* 43, no. 47 (22 November 1903): 744.

84. Auguste Mercadier, "Concerts Colonne," *Le monde musical* 15, no. 23 (15 December 1903): 367.

85. MR: This remark, made by the German critic, M. Steuer, was reported by Lionel de la Laurencie in "Au pays de la critique musicale," *Le courrier musical* 7, no. 2 (15 January 1904): 80.

86. MR: While *D'un cahier d'esquisses* (1904) was the first piano work to utilize three staves throughout, Debussy had resorted to three staves already in the middle and at the end of "La soirée dans Grenade" (1903). In his *The Art of French Piano Music: Debussy, Ravel, Fauré, Chabrier* (New Haven: Yale University Press, 2009), 104, Roy Howat points out that in the latter passage Debussy was echoing Chabrier's "Habanera."

87. Maurice Ravel performed it in a concert of the Société musicale indépendante on 20 April 1910. MR: see p. 200 in the present volume for further context.

18. Debussyism; A New Life: 1904

1. See p. 55 in the present volume. MR: According to a notice in "Échos et nouvelles diverses: France," *Le courrier musical* 7, no. 1 (15 January 1904): 30, Xavier Leroux, Georges Marty, and Samuel Rousseau joined Debussy as supplemental jurors; those serving on the elected jury were Vincent d'Indy, Gabriel Fauré, André Messager, and Paul Vidal.

2. Auguste Mangeot, "Salles Érard: Société nationale," *Le monde musical* 16, no. 1 (15 January 1904): 10. MR: René Doire, "La quinzaine musicale: Société nationale," *Le courrier musical* 7, no. 4 (15 February 1904): 119, reported that Viñes "created so perfectly that warm atmosphere" of a "Soirée dans Grenade." The critic's reference to Liszt's *Rapsodies* may have been directed not only to his nineteen Hungarian works but also to his *Rapsodie espagnole*.

3. Jean Marnold, "Revue du mois: Musique—Deux concerts," *Mercure de France* 49, no. 170 (February 1904), 537.

4. MR: See the notice for the Concert Barat at the Salle Érard in *Le guide musical* 50, no. 6 (7 February 1904): 127; and a short but positive review in "Chronique de la semaine: Bruxelles," *Le guide musical* 50, no. 8 (21 February 1904): 175.

5. MR: See the review of Viñes's performance of Debussy's *Estampes* on a Parent Quartet concert in "La quinzaine musicale: Quatuor Parent," *Le courrier musical* 7, no. 8 (15 April 1904): 265.

6. MR: We know about this matinee performance from a journal entry for 16 January 1904 by Mme de Saint-Marceaux; see Marguerite de Saint-Marceaux, *Journal, 1894–1927*, ed. Myriam Chimènes et al. (Paris: Librairie Arthème Fayard, 2007), 329. Debussy also mentioned the event in a postscript of a letter to Louis Laloy from 17 January 1904; see *C*, 822. The Princesse de Cystria's salon concerts were called "Heures de musique"; see, for example, the notices in the "Échos et nouvelles diverses: France" sections of *Le courrier musical* 7, no. 4 (15 February 1904): 137, and in *Le courrier musical* 7, no. 6 (15 March 1904): 213. In letters to Louis Laloy from 17 December 1903, 3 January 1904, and 17 January 1904, Debussy alluded to the plans for performances of his music at her salon: see *C*, 806–7, 817, and 822.

7. MR: See her entry for 16 January 1904 in Saint-Marceaux, *Journal*, 329.

8. MR: See her entry for 16 January 1904 in Saint-Marceaux, *Journal*, 329.

9. MR: See pp. 121–25 in the present volume for information on Debussy's engagement to Thérèse Roger, and Mme de Saint-Marceaux's role in it.

10. MR: In addition to "Mes longs cheveux," Garden recorded three of the *Ariettes oubliées* with Debussy at the piano: "Il pleure dans mon cœur," "L'ombre des arbres," and "Green."

11. MR: See Debussy's letter to Clark from 21 February 1904 in *C*, 829.

12. MR: See the reports in "Le mouvement musical en province et à l'étranger: Bruxelles," *Le courrier musical* 7, no. 3 (1 February 1904): 100, and in L. D., "Chronique de la semaine: Bruxelles," *Le guide musical* 50, no. 2 (10 January 1904): 33. Her Berlin concert was mentioned in "Nouvelles diverses," *Le guide musical* 50, no. 7 (14 February 1904): 157. The London performance that included Debussy's *Danse* was reported in "Correspondances: Londres," *Le guide musical* 50, no. 14 (3 April 1904): 321.

13. MR: See the review of the Parent Quartet's performance of Debussy's quartet in "La quinzaine musicale: Quatuor Parent," *Le courrier musical* 7, no. 8 (15 April 1904): 264–65.

14. MR: See a review of the Enesco concert on 6 February in G. R., "Chronique de la semaine: Paris," *Le guide musical* 50, no. 7 (14 February 1904): 149.

15. MR: See a review of the 9 April concert by the Sechiari Quartet in "Chronique de la semaine: Paris," *Le guide musical* 50, no. 16 (17 April 1904): 361.

16. MR: In his review in *Le monde musical* 16, no. 5 (15 March 1904): 81, Em. F. specified that Billa played four works by Debussy: "Pagode [*sic*], Sarabande, Arabesque, Jardins sous la pluie." Billa performed Debussy's works in Nice, along with one of his own compositions, *Clarté grise*, that the critic claimed was "of a too flagrant Debussyism"; see Alfred Mortier, "Le mouvement musical en province et à l'étranger: Marseille," *Le courrier musical* 7, no. 8 (15 April 1904): 276.

17. MR: This was the first performance of *La damoiselle élue* by the orchestra and chorus of the Opéra-Comique, and it involved well-known singers other than Mary Garden, including Marguerite Carré and Yvette Guilbert, and Messieurs Périer, Dufranne, Vieuille, and Coquelin aîné, among others; the concert was announced in "Nouvelles diverses: Paris et départements," *Le ménestrel* 70, no. 5 (31 January 1904): 40, and mentioned only briefly in a review in "Nouvelles diverses: Paris et départements," *Le ménestrel* 70, no. 6 (7 February 1904): 48, and in a review by A. M. in *Le monde musical* 16, no. 3 (15 February 1904): 39. Recall that Garden had sung in a performance of *La damoiselle élue* only a few weeks earlier, at the Concerts Colonne on 21 December 1903 (see pp. 193–94 in the present volume).

18. MR: This concert was given a glowing review by J. Sauerwein in "Le mouvement musical en province et à l'étranger: Marseille," *Le courrier musical* 7, no. 6 (15 March 1904): 207–8.

19. MR: Performed at the ninth popular concert, the work was given a brief but favorable review by Eva, "Le mouvement musical en province et à l'étranger: Angers," *Le courrier musical* 7, no. 7 (1 April 1904): 238. The *Prélude à l'après-midi d'un faune* was also performed in Berlin, conducted by Vienna da Motta; see "Échos et nouvelles diverses: Étranger," *Le courrier musical* 7, no. 2 (15 January 1904): 66.

20. MR: A. Harentz, "Le mouvement musical en province et à l'étranger: Constantinople," *Le courrier musical* 7, no. 9 (1 May 1904): 313.

21. MR: FL 2003 is likely referring to a review by d'Udine, "Les grands concerts," in *Le courrier musical* 7, no. 10 (15 May 1904): 331.

22. MR: The concert of 24 January included all three *Nocturnes* and was mentioned in "Échos et nouvelles diverses: Belgique," *Le courrier musical* 7, no. 3 (1 February 1904): 103. The critic, N. L. [N. Liez?], in "Chronique de la semaine: Bruxelles," *Le guide musical* 50, no. 5 (31 January 1904): 99, assessed the first two *Nocturnes* as the most attractive, but found it difficult to judge the third, because it was "sung too poorly."

23. [*C*, 812.]

24. MR: Debussy's review of Grieg's music on 20 April 1903 is reprinted in Claude Debussy, *Monsieur Croche et autres écrits*, rev. ed. (Paris: Gallimard, 1987), 153–57; and in Claude Debussy, *Debussy on Music*, trans. Richard Langham Smith (New York: Alfred A. Knopf, 1977), 177–81. As for Grieg's reaction to Debussy's article, Calvocoressi reported a rather different response: "I am positively amazed at the tone which he, an artist, dares to adopt when speaking of a fellow artist. Of course, I likewise deplore his utter lack of comprehension of my art; but this is not the main point. The main point is his venomous and contemptuous tone. A genuine artist ought to strive to maintain a high level in all things of the mind, and to respect the point of view of other artists." See M.-D. Calvocoressi, *Musicians Gallery* (London: Faber & Faber, 1933), 91.

25. Victor Debay, "La quinzaine: À la Société nationale de musique," *Le courrier musical* 5, no. 110 (15 May 1902): 151. Present at the rehearsal, Debussy went to congratulate Séverac. As early as 1898, Willy considered Séverac to be "a very, very interesting Debussyist" (L'ouvreuse du Cirque d'été [Henry Gauthier-Villars], *La colle aux quintes* [Paris: H. Simonis Empis, 1899], 149).

26. Philippe Moreau, "Société nationale," *Le monde musical* 16, no. 6 (30 March 1904): 89.

27. MR: The quotation comes from RÉMI, "Le festival de Francfort-sur-le-Mein," *Le monde musical* 16, no. 12 (15 [*recte* 30] June 1904): 181. Paul de Stœcklin, in "Le mouvement musical en province et à l'étranger: Lettre de Munich à Lucie," *Le courrier musical* 7, no. 11 (1 June 1904): 366, notes more than "a kinship" between Debussy and Pfitzner; but, he writes, there is "an immense gulf between the races."

28. Auguste Mangeot, "Concerts Risler," *Le monde musical* 16, no. 9 (15 May 1904): 137. MR: Of course, Fauré's works pre-dated *Pelléas*; however, it is noteworthy that Mangeot attributed these novel harmonies to Debussy. Mangeot added the comment, crediting an American source, that "posterity would classify music as *before* and *after* Debussy." The reader will recall that Jean Marnold had made a similar remark in June of the previous year; see Jean Marnold, "Revue du mois: Musique," *Mercure de France* 46, no. 162 (June 1903): 808 (cited on p. 431n26).

29. Albert Diot, "La quinzaine musicale: Schumann et Debussy," *Le courrier musical* 7, no. 10 (15 May 1904): 336. [According to Diot, Debussy's "De soir" was also performed, though Laloy did not include it in his preconcert talk.] See also the notice in "Chronique de la semaine: Paris," *Le guide musical* 50, nos. 25–26 (19 and 26 June 1904): 504. Laloy's talk was not published, but was summarized by both of these journalists.

30. MR: Engel was an operatic tenor whose most famous pupil was Jane Bathori. They later married (in 1908) and together gave art-song recitals.

31. MR: La Bodinière served as a venue for a variety of attractions, such as musical performances, lectures, art exhibits, and shadow plays, from 1890 to 1902. Readers may be familiar with some of the posters by Théophile Alexandre Steinlen and Jules Cheret that advertised these events.

32. See the notice in "Chronique de la semaine: Paris," *Le guide musical* 50, nos. 21–22 (22 and 29 May 1904): 459–60; see also Jean Huré, "Salles diverses: Séances Engel-Bathori," *Le monde musical* 16, no. 11 (30 May [*recte* 15 June] 1904): 174.

33. Lionel de La Laurencie's article spanned two issues in *Le courrier musical*: that of 7, no. 5 (1 March 1904): 141–49, and that of 7, no. 6 (15 March): 181–85. The article was first published, with a catalog of Debussy's works, in *Durendal* (Brussels, October 1903): 614–30.

34. MR: See p. 416n78.

35. MR: De La Laurencie, "Notes sur l'art de Claude Debussy" (1 March 1904), 147.

36. MR: De La Laurencie, "Notes sur l'art de Claude Debussy" (15 March 1904), 183.

37. Jean Lorrain, *Lettres inédites à Gabriel Mourey et à quelques autres (1888–1905)*, ed. Jean-Marc Ramos (Lille: Presses universitaires de Lille, 1987), 13.

38. Lorrain, *Lettres inédites à Gabriel Mourey*, 7.

39. Lorrain, *Lettres inédites à Gabriel Mourey*, 8.

40. MR: Jean Lorrain, "Pelléastres," *Le journal* (22 January 1904): 3. A notice pointing out this newly adopted label appeared in "Pall-Mall quinzaine," *Le monde musical* 16, no. 2 (30 January 1904): 21.

41. MR: A reference to the opera by d'Indy.

42. MR: Lorrain, "Pelléastres," 3.

43. MR: See the letter from Louÿs to Debussy, with the date of 23 January 1904 ascribed by Lesure and Herlin, in *C*, 825.

44. Raymond Bouyer, "Petites notes sans portée," *Le ménestrel* 70, no. 13 (27 March 1904), 100.

45. MR: Debussy's comment dates from 8 January 1904 (not 3 January 1904, as posited by FL 2003); see *C*, 818.

46. "Échos et nouvelles diverses: France," *Le courrier musical* (1 January [*recte* February] 1904): 101.

47. Letter to Jean [not Édouard, as stated in FL 2003] Risler [in *C*, 804].

48. On 12 May 1905, Lacerda himself conducted the *Danse profane*, with Mme Ziélinska as soloist.

49. Albert Diot, ed., "Échos et nouvelles diverses: France," *Le courrier musical* 7, no. 13 (1 July 1904): 417; see also "Nouvelles diverses," *Le guide musical* 50, nos. 27–28 (3 and 10 July [1904]: 538). Perhaps so as not to reverse itself, the former journal announced in "Échos et nouvelles diverses: France," *Le courrier musical* 7, no. 17 (15 August [*recte* 1 September] 1904): 498, that Mme Caristie-Martel had "completely withdrawn" this score: "Poor Debussy! Poor Caristie!" it added. In February 1905, the press announced the performance of the play, with a score by Léon Moreau, at the Théâtre de l'Œuvre. MR: It was reviewed by Adolphe Brisson in "Chronique théâtrale," *Le temps* (27 February 1905): [2].

50. See the notice in "Chronique de la semaine: Paris," *Le guide musical* 50, no. 15 (10 April [1904]: 337). MR: NB that the original French cites *Le diable dans le clocher* rather than *Le diable dans le beffroi*.

51. [See Gustave Schlumberger, *Mes souvenirs, 1844–1928* (Paris: Librairie Plon, 1934), 1:323–24.] His collection of paintings, dispersed [at the Galerie Georges Petit in Paris on 10 and 11 May] in 1920, included canvases by Boucher, Chardin, Perronneau, Hubert Robert, and drawings by Fragonard and Watteau.

52. MR: Eugénie Vergin married the conductor Édouard Colonne in 1886. More information on Mme Colonne's background and professional activity may be found in Myriam Chimènes, *Mécènes et musiciens: Du salon au concert à Paris sous la IIIe République* (Paris: Librairie Arthème Fayard, 2004), 274–77.

53. Jean-Michel Nectoux, *Gabriel Fauré: Les voix du clair-obscur*, 2nd ed. (Paris: Librairie Arthème Fayard, 2008), 248. MR: See also Jean-Michel Nectoux, *Gabriel Fauré: A Musical Life*, trans. Roger Nichols (Cambridge: Cambridge University Press, 1991), 181.

54. MR: Robert Pitrou, *De Gounod à Debussy* (Paris: Éditions Albin Michel, 1957), 96.

55. However, on 31 May 1889, she had sung with other students of Mme Colonne, winning this praise from a columnist in *L'art musical*: "Mme Bardac, who very artfully delivered several songs, 'Vous souvenez-vous' by Gabriel Pierné,

among others." MR: See "Nouvelles diverses," *L'art musical* 28, no. 11 (15 June 1889): 86.

56. MR: Samain's collection of poems, *Au jardin de l'enfant*, published in 1893, had brought him notoriety.

57. Letter of 8 March 1896, Alfred Dupont collection, auction catalog (Paris: Hôtel Drouot, 3 June 1977), lot 171 [see Nectoux, *Fauré: Les voix du clair-obscur*, 260 and 260n48, and *Fauré: A Musical Life*, 189 and 573n52.] Around the same time Samain met Sigismond Bardac; he mentioned [in another letter to his sister, from 7 December 1897,] Bardac's "terribly thick eyebrows," although he appeared to have been charmed by him (Nectoux, *Fauré: Les voix du clair-obscur*, 247, and his *Fauré: A Musical Life*, 180).

58. Nectoux, *Fauré: Les voix du clair-obscur*, 260, and his *Fauré: A Musical Life*, 189.

59. L'ouvreuse du Cirque d'été [Henri Gauthier-Villars], in *La colle aux quintes*, 20–21, and in *Notes sans portées* (Paris: Ernest Flammarion, 1896). MR: See p. 248 in the latter source, where Mme Sigismond Bardac is mentioned in Willy's entry for 4 May 1896.

60. MR: According to Léon-Paul Fargue, Maurice Ravel was also called "Rara" by those close to him. See his article, "Autour de Ravel," in *Maurice Ravel par quelques-uns de ses familiers* (Paris: Éditions du Tambourinaire, 1939), 153.

61. MR: See letter of 18 March 1958 from Martin du Gard to Vallery-Radot in *Lettres et manuscrits autographes, documents historiques à Piasa*, auction catalog (Paris, 6 March 2007), lot 231.

62. *Les archives biographiques contemporaines* (Paris: Direction & Administration, 1911?), 4:247. In 1897, Mme Colonne sang his *Mélodies* in her salon (see "Nouvelles diverses; Paris et départements," *Le ménestrel* 63, no. 23 [6 June 1897]: 181). MR: The notice in vol. 4 of *Les archives biographique contemporaines* lists many songs and piano pieces, as well as works for the stage, including a "comédie lyrique" on Verlaine's *Les uns et les autres*, a setting of which Debussy had once contemplated.

63. See Koechlin's letter of 27 March 1918, in which he conveyed his condolences to Emma on Claude's death, and recalled their former performances together; see Librairie de l'Abbaye, catalog 281 (1985), item 153.

64. Marcel Marnat, *Maurice Ravel* (Paris: Fayard, 1986), 143–44, reprising Émile Vuillermoz, *Maurice Ravel par quelques-uns de ses familiers* (Paris: Éditions du Tambourinaire, 1939), 65–66. MR: The latter source discusses Ravel's "L'indifférent," without mentioning either Emma or Raoul.

65. MR: The French text from Klingsor's "L'indifférent" is "Ta lèvre chante sur le pas de ma porte [. . .] Mais non, tu passes, et de mon seuil, je te vois t'éloigner."

66. Letter of 15 July 1913 to Durand [in *C*, 1641].

67. MR: See Debussy's note to Emma from 6 June 1904 in *C*, 844–45.

68. Reminiscent of Rimbaud, for whom it rained "gently on the city" (inscribed in the second of [Debussy's] *Ariettes* [and the third of Verlaine's *Ariettes oubliées*]).

69. [*C*, 845.]

70. [*C*, 846.]

71. MR: "A. l. p. M." stands for "À la petite mienne," which may be translated as "To my little darling," a term of endearment that Debussy used to address Emma

throughout his life. Edward Lockspeiser, in *Debussy: His Life and Mind* (Cambridge: Cambridge University Press, 1978), 2:220n2, points out that this phrase was derived from Jules Laforgue's "Ô géraniums diaphanes," a poem from his collection of *Derniers vers*. The specific line from Laforgue is "Ô ma petite mienne, ô ma quotidienne."

72. MR: "Les mesures ci-jointes appartient à Mada[me] Bardac—p.m.—qui me les dicta un mardi de juin 1904. / la reconnaissance passionnée de son / Claude Debussy."

73. MR: Claude had been addressing Emma more formally, using "vous" rather than "tu"; see his letters from 6 and 9 June in *C*, 844–45 and 845, respectively.

74. MR: "À Mme Bardac. . . ces quatre cent neuf pages de timbres variés qui valent à peine l'ombre que fait ta petite main sur ce gros livre. . . Juillet 1904."

75. MR: This event was reported in "Échos et nouvelles diverses: France," *Le courrier musical* 7, no. 14 (15 July 1904): 438.

76. MR: While FL 2003 suggests that this letter was probably written in April, Lesure and Herlin subsequently date this postcard from 19 June 1904, based on its postage stamp; see *C*, 847.

77. MR: *C*, 849. FL 2003 gives the date of this letter as 23 June. However, Lesure and Herlin point out that Debussy dated it as "Wednesday, 23 June," and since the 23rd was a Thursday that year, they surmise that the actual date of the letter was 22 June 1904; see *C*, 848n2. In addition, the editors note that only Lilly went to the "country," as she left Paris for Bichain.

78. Louis Laloy, *La musique retrouvée* (Paris: Librairie Plon, 1928), 140. This month of June was decidedly very busy, for Mary Garden claimed in her memoirs that the Debussys stayed with her in Versailles for two weeks!

79. MR: See Debussy's letter to Lilly from 16 July 1904 in *C*, 852.

80. See Debussy's letter to Lilly from 16 July 1904 [in *C*, 852–53].

81. See Debussy's letter to Lilly from 19 July 1904 [in *C*, 853].

82. [See his letter from 19 July 1904 in *C*, 853.]

83. In her memoirs, Mary Garden mentions a quick stay with Debussy in London, where Sarah Bernhardt (Pelléas) and Mrs. Patrick Campbell (Mélisande) performed Maeterlinck's play in French at the Vaudeville Theater. Both were so disappointed by the production which, according to Lockspeiser, took place on 18 July, that they took the train back to Paris after the third act. It is rather doubtful that this trip even happened, since Debussy wrote the cited letter to Lilly from Paris on the 19th [see *C*, 853–54]. In an attempt to hoodwink Lilly, so that she would not suspect anything was amiss, the composer announced to her, on the following 11 August [see *C*, 861], another completely imaginary trip: "I will leave for London with Jacques-Émile Blanche, who is kindly offering [to cover] my travel and living [expenses]."

84. [Claude mentioned the surprise visit as well as the storm on the return to Paris in a letter to Lilly from 28 July 1904; see *C*, 856.] The timing of Claude and Emma's escapade to Arcachon remains difficult to establish. Marcel Dietschy (*La passion de Claude Debussy* [Neuchâtel: Editions de la Baconnière, 1962], 169; and *A Portrait of Claude Debussy*, trans. William Ashbrook and Margaret G. Cobb [Oxford: Oxford University Press, 1990], 132) fleetingly alludes to it, but Debussy mentions

it to Godet in a letter written in the middle of the [First World] War: "We had been to Arcachon before, about twelve years ago. I was already attending to my divorce. Life has some astounding 'encores.'" [See his letter from 6 October 1916 in *C*, 2033.]

85. [*C*, 858.]

86. MR: See Antoine Watteau's painting, *L'embarquement pour Cythère*. Léon Vallas, in both editions of his *Claude Debussy et son temps* ([Paris: Librairie Félix Alcan, 1932], 241, and [Paris: Éditions Albin Michel, 1958], 286), claimed that *L'isle joyeuse* was inspired by Watteau's *The Embarkation for Cythera*. Debussy himself alluded to this connection on 13 July 1914 in a letter to Désiré Walter; see *C*, 1835. Lesure, who had no knowledge of this letter when writing FL 2003, claimed that the comparison was specious. He likely was influenced by Dietschy, who pointed out the "uninhibited joy" of Debussy's *L'isle joyeuse*, in contrast to the elegant restraint depicted in Watteau's painting; see Dietschy, *Passion de Claude Debussy*, 171, and Dietschy, *Portrait of Claude Debussy*, 134.

87. MR: Lesure and Herlin ascribe a date of sometime between 31 July and 4 August 1904 to this letter; see *C*, 859.

88. MR: As early as June 1899, Debussy used the phrase "ma petite Mienne" in a letter to Lilly; see *C*, 499. In addition, the cryptic abbreviation of "p. F. A." appears in his dedication to Marie Vasnier on the manuscript of "Apparition" from 1884. It is possible that this abbreviation was a secretive reference to a "petite Femme Aimée."

89. MR: Debussy's request appeared as a postscript to his letter, already cited in n87, from the Grand Hotel in Jersey; see *C*, 859.

90. Maurice Dumesnil, "Coaching with Debussy," *The Piano Teacher* 5 (September–October 1962), 10–13, wrote in error [on p. 10] that the piano was purchased in Bournemouth. Dolly de Tinan corrected this information, stating that it was bought in Jersey, in "Memories of Debussy and his circle," *Recorded Sound* 50–51 (April–July 1973): 159. MR: However, Diane Enget Moore makes a compelling case for its purchase in Eastbourne; see "Debussy in Jersey by Diane Enget Moore, Page 4," http://www.litart.co.uk/bluthner.htm, accessed 16 January 2019. Debussy's Blüthner piano, inherited by Raoul Bardac, is now housed at the Musée Labenche in Brive-la-Gaillarde; several individuals, including Jean-Louis Haguenauer (see Claude Debussy, *Intégrale des mélodies*, Ligia LIDI 0201285–14), have recorded on this instrument. In 1909, the Bösendorfer piano company would extend the idea of the Aliquotflügel by manufacturing instruments that featured additional strings that resonated sympathetically, enhancing the depth of the sound.

91. [*C*, 861–62.]

92. MR: See Debussy's letter to Jacques Durand from 24 September 1904 in *C*, 868.

93. MR: See Debussy's letter to Lilly from 22 August, with the postage stamp of "Paris Av. Marceau," in *C*, 863.

94. MR: Lesure speculates that Lilly had returned by 13 September because Debussy's letter from 14 September, in which he writes about his return to Dieppe the previous day, was sent to her at the 58 rue Cardinet address in Paris; see *C*, 864.

95. [*C*, 864.]

96. MR: See Debussy's letter, with the date of 30 September 1904 ascribed by Lesure and Herlin, in *C*, 869.

97. Marcel Dietschy maintains that Debussy settled there alone, buying various furniture and art objects on credit. MR: A letter from Debussy to André Antoine, likely dating from 14 October 1904, gives the avenue Alphand address; see *C*, 870.

98. In a personal notebook, Debussy wrote: "Suicide attempt on 13 October with 4 warning letters—nothing in the papers until 3 November." MR: See BnF, département de la Musique, Rés. Vmf. Ms. 53, 3r.

99. MR: This information was reported on p. 4 of a letter by Lucien Monod to Marcel Dietschy, dated 2 May 1954; see Fonds FL, BnF, carton I/6(9).

100. Ricardo Viñes, "Le journal inédit de Ricardo Viñes," trans. and ed. Nina Gubisch, *Revue internationale de musique française* 1, no. 2 (June 1980): 228.

101. At the time of the polemic that pitted Prunières and Godet against Léon Vallas after the publication of the latter's book (1932), one of the anecdotes that circulated among Lilly's and Mary Garden's entourage was reported: Debussy, his father, or a relation, was said to have picked up a 200-franc note left on the nightstand after her transfer to the clinic (Henry Prunières, "Autour de Debussy," *La revue musicale* 15, no. 146 [May 1934]: 350).

102. MR: Lilly was a blonde, not a "beauté brune."

103. Debussy wrote in his personal notebook [BnF, département de la Musique, Rés. Vmf. Ms. 53, 2v]: "Mme D. has alleged that she would like to let herself starve to death; the maid, who did not leave her side, claims that every day she consumed four egg yolks in some tea."

104. MR: The correct address is rue Blomet.

105. "Faits divers: Le théâtre et la vie," *Le temps* (4 November 1904): [3]. The *New York Herald* repeated this information. MR: The same information appears, this time with more pointed references to "Mme D. . . ," "M. D. . . ," and "Mme B. . . ," in "Nouvelles diverses à Paris: Un drame parisien," *Le Figaro* (4 November 1904): 4.

106. MR: See Pierre Louÿs's letter to his half-brother Georges Louis, dated 8 November 1904, in Pierre Louÿs and George Louis, *Correspondance croisée, 1890–1917*, ed. Gordon Millan (Paris: Honoré Champion, 2015), 2:1218–19. See also the transcript of a passage from Louÿs's letter to his wife, written on 5 November 1904, in which he states that he will see Lilly the next day, and that "it goes without saying that I will not be approaching her husband in the same way"; see DOSS-03.02 ("Notes de la main d'un inconnu, rapportant des souvenirs de Pierre Louÿs sur Debussy"), 3, among the Dietschy materials in the CDCD.

107. MR: See René Peter, *Claude Debussy*, rev. ed. (Paris: Gallimard, 1944), 42.

108. Henri Busser, *De* Pelléas *aux* Indes galantes (Paris: Librairie Arthème Fayard, 1955), 138.

109. MR: A. de Sivry gave the work a very positive review in the section titled "Au Châtelet," *Le monde musical* 16, no. 21 (15 November 1904): 295.

110. MR: See the review by Musicien, "Les grands concerts," *La quinzaine musicale* 10, no. 22 (15 November 1904): 305.

111. MR: Recall that during the time he spent in Rome, Debussy considered composing a work based on Flaubert's *Salammbô*. While that idea never came to

fruition for Debussy, it was the subject of Ernest Reyer's final opera (composed in 1890). And of course, Salammbô herself has been the object of numerous portrayals in art, from Mucha to Rodin.

112. Hugues Imbert, "Chronique de la semaine: Concerts Colonne," *Le guide musical* 50, no. 45 (6 November 1904): 849–50.

113. De La Laurencie, "Notes sur l'art de Claude Debussy (Suite et fin)" (15 March 1904), 184. MR: On p. 359 of an article titled "Feuillets d'album," *Le courrier musical* 7, no. 11 (1 June 1904): 357–59, Camille Mauclair similarly linked the arts of Le Sidaner and Debussy. See also an article that Mauclair dedicated to Debussy, "Eaux-fortes d'après l'orchestre," *Le courrier musical* 7, no. 7 (1 April 1904): 217–20, in which he alluded to Carrière, among other artists, in the context of orchestral depictions.

114. Gabriel Fauré, "Les concerts," *Le Figaro* (7 November 1904): 5.

115. MR: Debussy elaborated on what he meant by this duplicity in his letter of 4 or 5 December 1904: she was "sad and sweet when near those whom she believes are truly my friends," but "using every means to harm me with the others" (see *C*, 877).

116. MR: See the same letter of 4 or 5 December (Lesure and Herlin point out that Debussy dated it "Dimanche, 5 Décembre/04," but that 5 December in 1904 was a Monday, so either his date or the day of the week was incorrect) in *C*, 876.

117. [*C*, 877.]

118. MR: Presumably, Mme Bardac. This quote is still from his December letter to Paul Robert; see *C*, 878.

119. [*C*, 877.]

19. *La mer*: 1905

1. MR: Louis Laloy, *La musique retrouvée* (Paris: Librairie Plon, 1928), 146.

2. MR: This is the phrase used by Debussy in a letter to Jacques Durand from 8 August 1905; see *C*, 913.

3. MR: Jean de Paris, "Une désespérée," *Le Figaro* (3 January 1905): 5.

4. MR: See his letter, ascribed by Lesure and Herlin from around 31 October 1904, in *C*, 872.

5. [*C*, 886.]

6. A respectable sum for a composer whose royalties amounted to 2,400 francs for the entire year of 1905. MR: His contract, dated 31 March 1905, is reprinted in *C*, 893–94.

7. MR: See the contract in *C*, 893.

8. MR: See his letter to Louis Laloy in *C*, 909.

9. BnF, Ms. 14517, [also available online at IFN-55007978. The musical excerpt contains six measures of seventh chords followed by three measures of ninths. The full text of Debussy's note to Emma from 4 June 1905 is transcribed in *C*, 911.]

10. MR: The contract for this annuity, along with other documents related to Debussy's divorce (including several from 1916 and 1918, as well as posthumous documents), may be found in Fonds FL, BnF, carton I/6(9).

11. MR: See *C*, 945–47 for an update (14 March 1906) to the Durand contract of 17 July 1905.

12. [*C*, 900–901.]

13. In his *Souvenirs*, Curne writes: "After his marriage, our interaction was less frequent. I will not say anything about his second marriage, other than that I had retained complete admiration for Lilly Texier." See Curnonsky [Maurice-Edmond Sailland], *Souvenirs littéraires et gastronomiques* (Paris: Éditions Albin Michel, 1958), 110.

14. MR: We know of no correspondence between Godet and Debussy between 13 June 1902 and 26 November 1910.

15. [See in particular pp. 71–72 of] François Lesure, "Raymond Bonheur: Un ermite, ami de Debussy (1861–1939)," *Cahiers Debussy* 17–18 (1993–94): 65–72.

16. MR: See his letter in *C*, 866.

17. MR: See BnF, département de la Musique, Rés. Vmf. Ms. 53.

18. MR: A *particelle* is the French term for a short score; it refers to a musical score, normally notated on three or four staves, of an orchestral work that contains most of the primary musical material, with notes on the orchestration in the margins or next to a particular line. A composer typically prepares the full orchestral score directly from the short score. The *particelle* of *La mer* is conserved in the Sibley Music Library at the Eastman School of Music (of the University of Rochester in Rochester, NY).

19. MR: See Debussy's letter to Jacques Durand in *C*, 880.

20. MR: This discussion may be found in his letter to Durand of 16 March 1905; see *C*, 889–90.

21. See p. 67 of Aloÿs Mooser, "Heurs et malheurs du *Prélude à l'Après-Midi d'un Faune* à Saint-Pétersbourg," *Cahiers Debussy* 16 (1992): 65–68.

22. Maurice Emmanuel, *Pelléas et Mélisande de Claude Debussy: Étude historique et critique, analyse musicale* (Paris: Paul Mellottée, Éditeur, [1926]); repr. as *Pelléas et Mélisande de Claude Debussy: Étude et analyse* (Paris: Éditions Mellottée, 1950), 71.

23. MR: This concert would be favorably reviewed by A. M. in *Le monde musical* 17, no. 3 (15 February 1905): 38.

24. [His journal entry for 10 February 1905 may be found in] Ricardo Viñes, "Le journal inédit de Ricardo Viñes," trans. and ed. Nina Gubisch, *Revue internationale de musique française* 1, no. 2 (June 1980), 228.

25. MR: Julien Torchet, "La semaine: Paris—Société nationale de musique," *Le guide musical* 51, no. 9 (26 February 1905): 167.

26. MR: Jean Chantavoine, "Chronique musicale: Publications et concerts," *La revue hebdomadaire* 14, no. 2 (10 December 1904): 194.

27. Torchet, review in *Le guide musical*, 167, cited in n25.

28. MR: Debussy's letters to these singers were all penned on 6 April 1905 and are available in *C*, 897.

29. MR: See Debussy's letter of 14 April in *C*, 900.

30. MR: An announcement of the Luquin concert at the Salle Érard appeared in "Concerts annoncés," *Le courrier musical* 8, no. 2 (15 January 1905): 63; and D'Jinn mentioned it very briefly in "Concerts divers: Sonatières et les alentours," *Le courrier musical* 8, no. 3 (1 February 1905): 87.

31. MR: This concert, given at the Schola Cantorum, also included a performance of some of Debussy's Verlaine songs by Camille Fourrier; see the review

by R. B. [Raymond Bouyer] in "La semaine: Paris," *Le guide musical* 51, no. 8 (19 February 1905): 149–50.

32. MR: See the reviews by Raymond Bouyer in the "La semaine: Paris" columns in *Le guide musical* 51, no. 8 (19 February 1905): 150, and in *Le guide musical* 51, no. 9 (26 February 1905): 168.

33. MR: Announcements about the Parent Quartet's plans to perform Debussy's work at the Salon d'Automne appeared in "Revue de la quinzaine: Échos," *Le mercure musical* 1, no. 1 (15 May 1905): 454; and in Hans Sachs, "Échos et nouvelles diverses: France," *Le courrier musical* 8, no. 21 (1 November 1905): 620. These announcements were followed by a brief review in "Échos et nouvelles diverses: France," *Le courrier musical* 8, no. 22 (15 November 1905): 652.

34. MR: See the brief reviews in "Échos et nouvelles diverses," *Le courrier musical* 8, no. 8 (15 April 1905): 262–63, and by P. M. in *Le monde musical* 17, no. 8 (30 April 1905): 109.

35. MR: See the review in "Concerts: Salles Pleyel," *Le monde musical* 17, no. 4 (28 February 1905): 50.

36. MR: Pierret played both "Jardins sous la pluie" and "Soirée dans Grenade" as an instrumental interlude within the second concert that was part of an "Exposition de la mélodie française," reviewed by Philippe Moreau in *Le monde musical* 17, no. 9 (15 May 1905): 124. Later in the year, Pierret performed Debussy's "Toccata" in Lille; see the review by Dr. G. B. in *Le monde musical* 17, no. 23 (15 December 1905): 308.

37. MR: See the review of her recital at the Salle Pleyel by T. in "La semaine: Paris," *Le guide musical* 51, no. 10 (14 May 1905): 401–2.

38. MR: See the review of her performance of Debussy's *Arabesques* at the Salle des Agriculteurs, written by Ch. C. [Charles Cornet?] in "La semaine: Paris," *Le guide musical* 51, no. 10 (14 May 1905): 403; see also the review by Jean Destaing in "Concerts: Salles diverses," *Le monde musical* 17, no. 9 (15 May 1905): 125.

39. MR: See the brief review of three concerts, given on 16, 24, and 30 May, in "La semaine: Paris," *Le guide musical* 51, no. 10 (14 May 1905): 404, see also Jean Destaing, "Concerts: Salles diverses," *Le monde musical* 17, no. 10 (30 May 1905): 135. After 1902, Magdeleine Boucherit was also known by her married name of Le Faure.

40. MR: A., "Correspondances: Grenoble," *Le guide musical* 51, no. 1 (1 January 1905): 13.

41. MR: FL 2003 mentions this recital as having taken place "at the end of January," but the *Guide musical* reported the date of 1 February. Julien Torchet wrote a short review of it in "La semaine: Bruxelles," *Le guide musical* 51, no. 6 (5 February 1905): 112, noting that the three *Chansons de Bilitis*, the *Fêtes galantes*, and four of the *Ariettes oubliées* were sung, in addition to two duets from *Pelléas et Mélisande*.

42. MR: At the "Soirées d'art" concert, Raunay sang "Le jet d'eau" and "Recueillement," which the reviewer A. M. claimed were "not among [Debussy's] best" songs; see *Le monde musical* 17, no. 23 (15 December 1905): 303.

43. MR: See the review by R. B. [Raymond Bouyer] in "La semaine: Paris," *Le guide musical* 51, no. 8 (19 February 1905): 149. Fourrier's recital in Brussels received a brief but positive review by D'Jinn, in "Concerts divers: Sonatières et les alentours," *Le courrier musical* 8, no. 4 (15 February 1905): 116. She also performed

Debussy's "Le balcon" and "Clair de lune" on 19 March; see the notice in "Échos et nouvelles diverses: France," *Le courrier musical* 8, no. 8 (15 April 1905): 262.

44. MR: A short but glowing review appeared in "Revue de la quinzaine: Chronique des concerts," *Le mercure musical* 1, no. 2 (1 June 1905): 91–92; apparently, Camille Fourrier and Auguste Delacroix had to repeat "La grotte" as an encore. A notice in "Théâtres," *Le temps* (15 May 1905): [3], reported that Camille Fourrier would be giving the premiere of Debussy's *Chansons de France*. The brief review by Jacques d'Offoël, in "La semaine: Paris," *Le guide musical* 51, no. 21 (21 May 1905): 421, mentioned only "several songs" by Debussy that were sung, without citing the specific repertoire. Similarly, no specific titles were identified in "Concerts: Salles diverses; Mme Camille Fourrier," *Le monde musical* 17, no. 10 (30 May 1905): 136. D'Jinn also alluded to this performance in "Concerts divers: Sonatières et les alentours," *Le courrier musical* 8, no. 11 (1 June 1905): 348.

45. MR: See the notice in "Échos et nouvelles diverses: France," *Le courrier musical* 8, no. 13 (1 July 1905): 415.

46. MR: For the performance in Biarritz, see the notice in "Concerts: La musique dans les casinos d'été," *Le monde musical* 17, no. 18 (30 September 1905): 230. According to J. P., "Le mouvement musical en province et a l'étranger: Vichy," *Le courrier musical* 8, no. 18 (15 September 1905): 522, the performance of Debussy's *Prélude à l'après-midi d'un faune* was the work's premiere in Vichy, but it received a lukewarm response from the local audience. Also performed in Pau, thanks to Paul Maufret, was Debussy's *Suite* for piano; see the notice in "Échos et nouvelles diverses: France," *Le courrier musical* 8, no. 8 (15 April 1905): 263.

47. Ch. C. [Charles Cornet?], "La semaine: Paris—Société nationale de musique," *Le guide musical* 51, no. 15 (9 April 1905): 294.

48. F. G. [Hippolyte Fierens-Gevaert?], "La semaine: Paris," *Le guide musical* 51, nos. 24–25 (11 and 18 June 1905): 464.

49. Jean Huré, "Salles Pleyel," *Le monde musical* 18, no. 10 (30 May 1906): 157.

50. Jean Huré, "Concerts Lamoureux," *Le monde musical* 18, no. 24 (30 December 1906): 342.

51. MR: The original German is "Debussyschule." This term appeared in "La Debussyte," an analysis of an article by Camille Mauclair that was published in the 27 September issue of the *Neue Zeitschrift*; see "Petite revue de la presse musicale allemande," *Le courrier musical* 8, no. 20 (15 October 1905): 581.

52. [See p. 56 of] Camile Mauclair, "La Debussyte," *Le courrier musical* 8, no. 18 (15 September 1905): 501–5.

53. Jean Huré, "C'est du Debussy," *Le monde musical* 17, no. 17 (15 September 1905): 210–11.

54. MR: See the letter from Debussy to Laloy in *C*, 907.

55. MR: See Debussy's letter to Laloy from 13 September 1905 in *C*, 921.

56. MR: In this context, the term "limpet" refers to a person who clings tenaciously to someone or something, just as the gastropod mollusk (also called a limpet) clings tightly to rocks when disturbed. For further information on Armande de Polignac, Jean Marnold, and Jean d'Udine, see *C*, 921n1, 2, 4.

57. Émile Vuillermoz, "Une tasse de thé," *Le mercure musical* 1, no. 13 (15 November 1905): 505–10.

58. MR: See Debussy's letter to Jacques Durand in *C*, 913. FL 2003 gives the date of 7 August, but Lesure and Herlin point out in *C*, 913n1, that 8 August is likely the correct date because Debussy also wrote "Mardi," and in 1905, 8 August fell on a Tuesday.

59. MR: See Debussy's comment about Chevillard in his letter to Jacques Durand from 18 or 19 August 1905 in *C*, 915.

60. MR: FL 2003 cites five years instead of four; the second edition of *La mer* was published by Durand in 1909.

61. MR: For a brief summary of early rehearsals, performances, and revisions of *La mer*, see Claude Debussy, *La mer*, in *Œuvres complètes de Claude Debussy*, sér. V, vol. 5, ed. Marie Rolf (Paris: Durand, 1997), xii and xvi.

62. MR: Presumably this is a reference to the grotesque character in Shakespeare's *The Tempest*.

63. MR: See Debussy's letter to Jacques Durand from 10 October 1905 in *C*, 925–26.

64. MR: A large selection of reviews of early performances of *La mer*, from 1905 to 1914, are available in appendix B of Marie Rolf, "Debussy's *La Mer*: A Critical Analysis in the Light of Early Sketches and Editions" (PhD diss., University of Rochester, 1976), 313–43.

65. MR: See Jean d'Udine, "Les grands concerts," *Le courrier musical* 8, no. 21 (1 November 1905): 611.

66. MR: J. Jemain, "Revue des grands concerts: Concerts Lamoureux," *Le ménestrel* 71, no. 44 (29 October 1905): 349.

67. MR: See Louis Vernon's review in *Le monde musical* 17, no. 20 (30 October 1905): 260.

68. MR: D'Udine, review in *Le courrier musical* (1 November 1905), cited in n65.

69. MR: Gaston Carraud, "Les concerts," *La liberté* (17 October 1905): 3, excerpted in *C*, 926n2. See also Debussy's letter to Laloy, from 17 October 1905, in which he cites this phrase from Carraud's article, in *C*, 926.

70. MR: See Debussy's letter to Lalo from 25 October 1905 in *C*, 928.

71. MR: See Durand, *"Concerts Durand" consacrés à la musique française moderne, 1910–1913: Programmes et notices analytiques* (Paris: A. Durand & fils, n.d.), 39. FL 2003 reports Malherbe's opinion that Debussy's work represented "musical Impressionism"; however, Malherbe wrote these words to describe Debussy's "Rondes de printemps," not *La mer*: see Durand, *"Concerts Durand,"* 31.

72. MR: Durand, *"Concerts Durand,"* 40.

73. MR: See Alfred Bruneau, "Musique: Les concerts," *Le matin* (16 October 1905): 4.

74. MR: Vernon noted the "exquisite charm" of the *Nocturne*s in his review of *La mer* in *Le monde musical*, cited in n67.

75. D'Udine, review in *Le courrier musical* (1 November 1905), 610–11 (cited in n65).

76. Michel-Dimitri Calvocoressi, "La semaine: Paris—Concerts Lamoureux," *Le guide musical* 51, no. 43 (22 October 1905): 672. MR: In the following issue of *Le guide musical* 51, no. 44 (29 October 1905): 690, Calvocoressi saw in *La mer* "the beginning of a new stage (*étape*)."

77. Jean Marnold, "Revue de la quinzaine: Musique," *Mercure de France* 58, no. 201 (1 November 1905): 134. Debussy thanked him for his understanding: "I'm trying to free music from its useless faded finery, to liberate it from everything that smothers it" [see his letter of 4 November 1905 in *C*, 930].

78. MR: See Dukas's review from November 1905 in Paul Dukas, *Les écrits de Paul Dukas sur la musique* (Paris: Société d'éditions françaises et internationales, 1948), 622.

79. MR: E. B., "La semaine: Bruxelles—Concerts populaires," *Le guide musical* 51, no. 50 (10 December 1905): 813.

80. E. B., "La semaine: Bruxelles—Concerts populaires," 813 (cited in n79). In two letters to Ernest Closson from 1907, Gilson tried to describe Debussy's technique of repetition. MR: See in particular p. 116 of Albert Vander Linden, "Claude Debussy, Octave Maus et Paul Gilson," *Revue belge de musicologie* 16 no. 1 (1962): 107–16.

81. MR: See especially p. 498 in Jean Chantavoine, "Chronique musicale," *La revue hebdomadaire* 14, no. 48 (28 October 1905): 496–99.

82. Edward Lockspeiser, *Debussy: His Life and Mind* (Cambridge: Cambridge University Press, 1978), 2:15–32 (the chapter on "Turner, Monet, and Hokusai").

83. MR: See Debussy's letter of 24–25 February 1906 to Raoul Bardac in *C*, 942.

84. Lockspeiser, *Debussy: His Life and Mind*, 2:17 and 29.

85. Roy Howat, *Debussy in Proportion: A Musical Analysis* (Cambridge: Cambridge University Press, 1983).

86. MR: Howat, *Debussy in Proportion*, 6–7; Howat explains the pun on "le divin nombre": as it applies to Plato, it refers to the golden section, but as applied to the *demi-mondaine* Liane de Pougy, it refers to the lovers left in her wake. Lesure and Herlin ascribe a date of 18 September 1903 to Debussy's letter, sent to Jacques Durand from Bichain; see *C*, 785.

87. MR: See Debussy's letter of 18 August 1913 to Igor Stravinsky in *C*, 1655.

88. MR: See Debussy's letter of 5 August 1915 to Jacques Durand in *C*, 1916.

89. MR: Debussy was likely referring to Thomas Young's and Augustin-Jean Fresnel's theories of "ondulations lumineuses"; for a brief explanation, see Helen Klus, "19th Century Wave Theories," chapter 5 in *How We Came to Know the Cosmos: Light and Matter* (UK: The Star Garden, 2017), available on Helen Klus's blog at http://www.thestargarden.co.uk/19th-Century-wave-theories.html, accessed 16 January 2019. Young (1773–1829) was an English physician and physicist—a true polymath—and Fresnel (1788–1827) was a French civil engineer and physicist.

90. MR: See Debussy's letter of 6 July 1898 to Georges Hartmann in *C*, 409.

91. MR: Edgar Allan Poe's essay on "The Philosophy of Composition" was published in 1846. In it, he offered his ideas on what good writing entails, covering aspects such as length, intuitive vs. methodical approaches, and a "unity of effect." It is unclear whether or not Poe followed this approach in his own writing. See also Debussy's citation of Poe as one of his favorite prose authors in response to a questionnaire from 16 February 1889 (in *C*, 67), and his allusion to it in a letter to Ernest Chausson from 3 September 1893 (in *C*, 154).

92. Jean Barraqué's most powerful analytical essay, "*La mer* de Debussy ou la naissance des formes ouvertes," was published in *Analyse musicale* 12 (June 1988): 15–62. MR: Apart from the Barraqué publication, numerous analyses of *La mer* have

appeared, including those by Marie Rolf ("Debussy's *La Mer*: A Critical Analysis in the Light of Early Sketches and Editions"); Wolfgang Dömling (*Claude Debussy: La Mer* [Munich: Fink, 1976]); Roy Howat (*Debussy in Proportion*, 64–135); Simon Trezise (*Debussy: La Mer* [Cambridge: Cambridge University Press, 1994]); Boyd Pomeroy ("Toward a New Tonal Practice: Chromaticism and Form in Debussy's Orchestral Music" [PhD diss., Cornell University, 2000], 138–222); and Mark de Voto (*Debussy and the Veil of Tonality* [Hillsdale, NY: Pendragon Press, 2004], 144–60).

93. MR: Debussy often referred to his compositional "chemistry." This descriptor may be found as early as 1893; see his letter to Chausson from 2 October 1893 in *C*, 160. See also *C*, 326n4.

94. MR: See Debussy's letter to Jacques Durand, with a date of 8 August 1905, ascribed by Lesure and Herlin, in *C*, 914.

95. MR: The date of 18 August 1905 is ascribed to Debussy's letter by Lesure and Herlin; see *C*, 914.

96. MR: See Debussy's letter of 13 September 1905 to Louis Laloy in *C*, 920.

97. The lease was issued in the name of Mme Emma Moyse.

98. MR: See Archives de la Ville de Paris, actes d'état civil, acte de naissance no. 1231; see also *C*, 929n2. Pierre Budin (the medical doctor who delivered the baby), Debussy, and Gaston van Brock presented Claude-Emma to the authorities.

99. MR: See Debussy's letter from 4 November 1905 in *C*, 929.

100. MR: See the review by Louis Laloy, "Revue de la quinzaine: Les concerts," *Le mercure musical* 1, no. 15 (15 December 1905): 630, in which he praised the artistry of Camille Fourrier and her pianist, Auguste Delacroix. In addition to "L'échelonnement des haïes," they performed "Fantoches" and "Le jet d'eau." G. R. reported in "La semaine: Paris," *Le guide musical* 51, no. 51 (17 December 1905): 833, simply that Fourrier sang "three songs by Debussy."

101. MR: This concert was reviewed by A. M. in *Le monde musical* 17, no. 24 (30 December 1905): 324.

102. This pianist later reported the advice that Debussy apparently gave to him for the performance of this work. See Maurice Dumesnil, "Coaching with Debussy," *The Piano Teacher* (September–October 1962): 10–13.

103. MR: Jacques d'Offoël, "La semaine: Paris—Au Conservatoire," *Le guide musical* 51, no. 52 (24 December 1905): 850. A. P., in "Revue des grands concerts," *Le ménestrel* 71, no. 52 (24 December 1905): 412, also noted that this was the first performance of Debussy's *Prélude à l'après-midi d'un faune* at the Conservatoire, and that the work was received with mild approval.

104. D'Offoël, review in *Le guide musical* (24 December 1905), cited in n103.

105. MR: See Debussy's letter of 28 June 1905 in *C*, 914.

20. Projects and Skirmishes: 1906–7

1. Lesure personal collection, confirmed by Denis Herlin.

2. This great benefactor, who died in February 1907, left money not only to erect a chapel in Lausanne to honor William Tell, but also for a prize for the gymnastic professors of the elementary schools in Paris and for the Society of Breastfeeding

and the Worker Shelters for Pregnant Women (Société de l'allaitement maternel et des refuges ouvriers pour les femmes enceintes).

3. MR: See Debussy's letter of 2 January 1906 to Louis Laloy in *C*, 934; Luigini had conducted a revival performance of *Pelléas et Mélisande* at the Opéra-Comique.

4. [See Debussy's letter of 8 February 1906 to Carré in *C*, 938.] Lacerda conducted the premiere of *La damoiselle élue* in Nantes on 1 March 1907.

5. MR: See Debussy's letter of 22 January 1906 to Lacerda in *C*, 936, as well as *C*, 936n1.

6. MR: See Debussy's letter of 23 June 1906 to Laloy in *C*, 959.

7. See p. 198 in the present volume.

8. Drouot catalog (3 July 1992), no. 104, presumably a letter or document involving Farrère and Segalen. [Unfortunately, this letter is not included in Victor Segalen, *Correspondance, vol. I: 1893–1912*, ed. Henry Bouillier et al. (Paris: Librairie Arthème Fayard, 2004). However, Lesure and Herlin include the contents of Farrère's letter to Louÿs in *C*, 953n2.] Did Segalen know that an announcement appeared in "Ça et là," *La quinzaine musicale* 9, no. 11 (1 June 1903): 167, about a forthcoming opera by Isidore de Lara, *Siddartha* (libretto by Paul Milliet), for the Théâtre des Arts in Rouen?

9. MR: Segalen followed up with a long letter to Debussy on 30 April 1906: see especially *C*, 953.

10. Max-Anély [Victor Segalen], "Voix mortes: Musiques maori," *Mercure musical et S. I. M.* (15 October 1907): 1001–27. Reissued with commentary by Annie Joly-Segalen and André Schaeffner [and including passages from the original essay that had been cut] in *Segalen et Debussy* (Monaco: Éditions du Rocher, 1962), 145–87.

11. [*C*, 954.]

12. MR: See the exchange of letters between Debussy and Toulet in *C*, 955–57; Toulet's first visit with Debussy was on 23 May, just a couple of weeks after they had a glimpse of each other at the Durand–Ruel gallery.

13. MR: Pierre Lalo gave a glowing report of this concert in "La musique," *Le temps* (21 February 1906): 3. See also a review by A. M. [Auguste Mangeot], "Concerts: Salles diverses; Œuvres de Claude Debussy," *Le monde musical* 18, no. 4 (28 February 1906): 62.

14. MR: FL 2003 reports that she sang two Baudelaire and three Verlaine songs, but an advertisement for the 6 February concert that appeared between pp. 128 and 129 in *Le mercure musical* 2, no. 3 (1 February 1906) lists "L'échelonnement des haïes" and "Le jet d'eau" as by Baudelaire; the text of the former song is of course by Verlaine. In addition, Fourrier sang "Clair de lune," "L'ombre des arbres," and "Chevaux de bois."

15. MR: While FL 2003 states that Bréval sang "two" of the *Chansons de Bilitis*, the glowing review of this concert, by Louis Laloy in "Revue de la quinzaine: Les concerts," *Le mercure musical* 2, no. 4 (15 February 1906): 166, reports not only that she sang all three songs but that the audience asked for an encore of the second, "La chevelure."

16. MR: See the advertisement that appeared in *Le mercure musical* (1 February 1906), cited in n14, as well as the review in *Le mercure musical* (15 February 1906), 165–66, cited in n15.

17. MR: See Viñes's journal entry for 6 February 1906 in Ricardo Viñes, "Le journal inédit de Ricardo Viñes," trans. and ed. Nina Gubisch, *Revue internationale de musique française* 1, no. 2 (June 1980): 229.

18. On 31 January 1908, Emma confided to Segalen that the version for four hands was not playable. MR: See *C*, 1062–63n6 for further context. The transcription for two pianos was premiered at the Cercle musical on 6 March 1908 by Marcel Chadeigne, Jean Roger-Ducasse, and Auguste Delacroix, and the score was published in 1909.

19. [*C*, 942.]

20. [*C*, 951.]

21. MR: See Debussy's letter to Jacques Durand in *C*, 957.

22. See Debussy's letter of 9 June 1906 to Jacques Durand [in *C*, 957].

23. MR: See Debussy's letter to Octavie Carrier-Belleuse from 8 March 1906 in *C*, 943.

24. MR: See Constant Pierre, *Le Conservatoire national de musique et de déclamation* (Paris: Imprimerie nationale, 1900), 715.

25. On 12 April, Debussy asked her to send a proof of the "Sérénade" [see *C*, 951].

26. MR: Debussy referred to the size of the table in his letter to Jacques Durand from 25 August 1906; see *C*, 965. Seventy-five centimeters is equivalent to just under thirty inches, a very minimal space on which to write a letter, much less a musical score.

27. MR: See Debussy's letter of 26 August 1906 to Paul-Jean Toulet in *C*, 965.

28. See Debussy's letter of 26 August 1906 to Paul-Jean Toulet in *C*, 965.

29. MR: See Debussy's letter of 8 August 1906 to Jacques Durand in *C*, 962.

30. MR: See *C*, 971 for Debussy's letter to Dukas.

31. MR: See Annie Joly-Segalen and André Schaeffner, eds., *Segalen et Debussy* (Monaco: Éditions du Rocher, 1961), 61.

32. MR: See Debussy's letter of 26 October 1906 to Hector Dufranne in *C*, 976.

33. MR: See Debussy's letter of 23 December 1906 to Albert Carré in *C*, 980.

34. MR: See "Échos: Une opinion," *Le mercure musical* 2, no. 17 (15 November 1906): 357.

35. MR: Mosco Carner, *Puccini: A Critical Biography*, 2nd ed. ([London]: Duckworth, 1974), 159.

36. MR: See Puccini's letter of 15 November 1906 to Giulio Ricordi in Giacomo Puccini, *Epistolario*, ed. Giuseppe Adami (Milan: A. Mondadori, 1928), 160; and in English translation in Giacomo Puccini, *Letters of Giacomo Puccini*, ed. Giuseppe Adami, trans. Ena Makin (Philadelphia: JB Lippincott Company, 1931), 164. Cited in Carner, *Puccini: A Critical Biography*, 2nd ed., 160. FL 2003 cites Giacomo Puccini, *Puccini* (Paris: J.-C. Lattès, 1984), 208–9. The Italian composer was curiously interested enough in Maeterlinck's *Pelléas* to attempt to obtain the poet's authorization to set it to music.

37. MR: Jacques Rivière, "Chronique: La musique à Paris," *Tanit* 1, no. 6 (1 July 1907): 219. FL 2003 cites a reprint of this article in *Bulletin des amis de Jacques Rivière et Alain-Fournier* 11, no. 38 (1985), 50.

38. MR: Lalo, *Le temps* (21 February 1906), cited in n13.

39. MR: Strauss's lunch meeting with Debussy was confirmed by Romain Rolland in his journal entry from 25 March 1906; see Romain Rolland, "Richard Strauss et Romain Rolland; correspondance, fragments de journal," *Cahiers Romain Rolland* 3 (Paris: Éditions Albin Michel, 1951): 147.

40. MR: This encounter was reported by Jacques Durand in his *Quelques souvenirs d'un éditeur de musique* (Paris: A. Durand & fils, 1925), 2:30.

41. MR: Debussy referred to Strauss in these terms in a letter to Jacques Durand from 24 March 1908; see *C*, 1077. Debussy's original French is "le domestique symphonique," a wordplay on the title of Strauss's tone poem, the *Symphonia domestica*.

42. [See Rolland's journal entry for 22 May 1907 in Rolland, "Richard Strauss et Romain Rolland," 159–60.] In his roman-fleuve titled *Jean-Christophe* (10 vols., 1904–12), Romain Rolland copied nearly verbatim part of these comments by Strauss [see in particular the discussion of *Pelléas* on pp. 92–96 in Romain Rolland, *Jean-Christophe à Paris* (Paris: Librairie Paul Ollendorff, 1912?)].

43. MR: Debussy mentioned the manuscript in his letter to Rolland from 19 April 1905; see *C*, 903.

44. MR: See "*Pelléas et Mélisande* de Claude Debussy" in Romain Rolland, *Musiciens d'aujourd'hui*, 2nd ed. (Paris: Librairie Hachette, 1908), 197–206; and in English translation in Romain Rolland, *Musicians of To-day*, trans. May Blaiklock (New York: H. Holt, 1915; repr. Freeport, NY: Books for Libraries Press, 1969), 234–45. According to Rolland, *Musiciens d'aujourd'hui*, 2nd ed., 279, the original article appeared in the 29 November 1907 issue of the Berlin journal titled *Morgen*.

45. MR: Rolland's summary appears in *Musiciens d'aujourd'hui*, 2nd ed., 206, and in *Musicians of To-day*, 244–45.

46. MR: See Rolland, *Musiciens d'aujourd'hui*, 2nd ed., 197n1, and Rolland, *Musicians of To-day*, 234.

47. Rimsky-Korsakov's and Arthur Nikisch's remarks were reported in "Nouvelles diverses: Quelques opinions sur *Pelléas et Mélisande*," *Le monde musical* 19, no. 10 (30 May 1907): 158.

48. [*C*, 986]. Debussy said nothing of Pelléas (Georges Petit) nor of Mélisande (Mary Garden, who did not care much for Petit). MR: More information about the singers cited may be found in *C*, 986n3–7.

49. [*C*, 993.]

50. MR: See Debussy's letter to Sylvain Dupuis from 8 January 1907 in *C*, 989.

51. MR: See Paul Gilson, "À la Monnaie—*Pelléas et Mélisande*. Drame lyrique de M. Cl. Debussy," *Le soir* (1 November 1907): 1–2. For a fascinating comparison between Gilson's and Debussy's works, see also Henri Lesbroussart, "Musiques maritimes: Aux Concerts populaires," *L'art moderne* 25, no. 50 (10 December 1905): 400–401.

52. MR: See Debussy's letter to Kufferath from 11 January 1907 in *C*, 990.

53. MR: On the other hand, a relatively favorable review was written by G. D. in "Concerts: Concerts Colonne," *Le monde musical* 19, no. 4 (28 February 1907): 57.

54. Debussy himself wrote to Durand, on 20 March 1906, to dissuade Colonne from playing "Cortège et Danse," adding: "I fear seeing myself accused of scraping from the bottom of the barrel." MR: See *C*, 948.

55. On the eve of the performance, Debussy specifically wrote a letter to Colonne in which he deplored the "coldness" with which this passage was being performed and the lack of volume in soloist Hélène Demellier's voice, and he asked that the harp and the trumpet lines be emphasized more [see *C*, 997]. MR: The beginning of the refrain from Baudelaire's poem, "Le jet d'eau," may be translated as "the spray of water that cradles its thousand flowers, through which the moon's pallors gleam."

56. MR: Émile Vuillermoz, "Les grands concerts," *La nouvelle presse* (3 March 1907): [1]. Lesure and Herlin reproduce this quoted text in *C*, 994n2, and it is also cited in "À travers la presse: Debussy et les debussystes," *Revue musicale de Lyon* 4, no. 23 (17 March 1907): 669–70.

57. MR: See Debussy's letter to Laloy from 25 July 1907 in *C*, 1019.

58. MR: See Louis Laloy, "Les écoliers," *Mercure musical et S. I. M.* (15 April 1907): 367–72.

59. MR: Laloy, "Les écoliers," 369.

60. Laloy, "Les écoliers," 371–72.

61. On 3 February 1906, Viñes [went to Debussy's home to play the *Images* for him; afterward, the composer called for Emma and they asked Viñes] to introduce them to Ravel's *Miroirs*. While Viñes recorded this encounter in his journal entry for 3 February, he said nothing of their reactions. MR: See Viñes, "Le journal inédit," 229.

62. MR: Sung by Jane Bathori, the *Histoires naturelles* were reviewed, for example, by Ch. C. in "La semaine: Paris—Société nationale de musique," *Le guide musical* 53, no. 3 (23 January 1907): 49.

63. MR: In his journal entry for 10 February 1905, Viñes added that he was playing *Masques* and *L'isle joyeuse* for the first time in public, and that they were met with "much success, but I did not play them very well for the simple reason that I didn't know them well enough"; see Viñes, "Le journal inédit," 204 and 228. The concert was reviewed by Michel-Dmitri Calvocoressi in "La quinzaine musicale: Le Quatuor Parent—Quatuors de Ravel et de Debussy," *Le courrier musical* 8, no. 5 (1 March 1905): 143–44, although the specific piano pieces were not identified.

64. Raymond Bouyer, "La semaine: Paris," *Le guide musical* 51, no. 9 (26 February 1905): 168. MR: The paintings of Adolphe Joseph Thomas Monticelli (1824–86) influenced Paul Cezanne and Vincent van Gogh. See information on an exhibit in Marseille, held from 16 September 2008 to 11 January 2009, that juxtaposed Monticelli's work with that of Van Gogh, "Van Gogh et Monticelli, Centre de la Vieille, Charité, Marseille," http://www.grandpalais.fr/fr/evenement/van-gogh-et-monticelli-centre-de-la-vieille-charite-marseille, accessed 16 January 2019.

65. [See especially pp. 513–14 in] M.-D. Calvocoressi, "Les 'Histoires naturelles' de Maurice Ravel et l'imitation Debussyste," [*La grande revue* 11, no. 9 (10 May 1907): 508–15]. MR: See also Calvocoressi's review in *Le courrier musical* (1 March 1905), cited in n63.

66. Letter of 30 December 1904 from Romain Rolland to André Suarès. MR: This letter was in the collection of Mme Suarès when Rolland's quote was cited by Marcel Dietschy in *La passion de Claude Debussy* (Neuchâtel: Éditions de la Baconnière, 1962), 194n6; see also William Ashbrook and Margaret G. Cobb's

English translation of Dietschy, *A Portrait of Claude Debussy* (Oxford: Oxford University Press, 1990), 145n5.

67. MR: Pierre Lalo, "La musique," *Le temps* (9 April 1907): [3]. FL 2003 gives the erroneous date of 16 April for this article.

68. MR: Louis Laloy, "Le mois: Concerts—Société nationale," *Mercure musical et S. I. M.* (15 February 1907): 156; Lesure and Herlin cite relevant excerpts from this review in *C*, 996n2.

69. MR: The text of Debussy's letter of 22 February 1907, as well as further information on Laloy's review in the *S. I. M.*, may be found in *C*, 996. It is helpful to know, as Lesure and Herlin point out in *C*, 996n4, that Calvocoressi was a friend of Ravel.

70. Letter of 25 February 1907 [in *C*, 997].

71. See letter of 8 March 1907 [in *C*, 999]. MR: As Lesure and Herlin point out in *C*, 999n2, Laloy defended Ravel as "un musicien humoriste" in an article titled "Musique nouvelle: Maurice Ravel," *Mercure musical et S. I. M.* (15 March 1908): 280.

72. Letter of 8 March 1907 [in *C*, 999].

73. It is discussed notably in the article by Léon Vallas, "L'affaire Ravel," *Revue musicale de Lyon* 4, no. 28 (1 May 1907): 793–97 [in which Vallas printed a letter from Jean Marnold, who passionately supported Ravel]; and in Vallas, *Claude Debussy et son temps* (Paris: Éditions Albin Michel, 1958), 276–77. See also François Lesure, "Ravel et Debussy," *Cahiers Maurice Ravel* 5 (1990–92): 27–33.

74. [On 8] January 1904, Mme de Saint-Marceaux was aware of it and wrote in her journal: "It seems that Debussy stole the main idea of the *Habanera*, a piece he [Ravel] had written ten years before." MR: See Marguerite de Saint-Marceaux, *Journal, 1894–1927*, ed. Myriam Chimènes et al. (Paris: Librairie Arthème Fayard, 2007), 326.

75. MR: See Debussy's letter to Astruc from 23 May 1907 in *C*, 1009.

76. Debussy's comment comes from an interview with Segalen on 8 October 1907 [see Joly-Segalen and Schaeffner, *Segalen et Debussy*, 75; reprinted in *C*, 2201].

77. Joseph Bédier's *Le roman de Tristan et Iseut* was published in 1900 by P. Sevin et E. Rey in Paris. MR: Bédier had been a student of Laloy at the École normale supérieure; see *C*, 1020n3.

78. MR: See letter of 26 July 1907 in *C*, 1020–21.

79. MR: See letter from Debussy to Victor Segalen of 26 July 1907 in *C*, 1021.

80. MR: See letter from Debussy to Louis Laloy of 25 July 1907 in *C*, 1019.

81. MR: See letter from Debussy to Jacques Durand of 23 August 1907 in *C*, 1025–26.

82. MR: See letter from Debussy to Paul-Jean Toulet from 27 August 1907 in *C*, 1029.

83. MR: Cited in a letter from Debussy to Jacques Durand, presumably from 6 August 1907; see *C*, 1024.

84. MR: A railroad abutted Debussy's home in Paris, at 80 square du Bois de Boulogne. Today, just beyond the rail tracks, is the Périphérique, which runs along the border of the Bois de Boulogne.

85. MR: See Debussy's letter to Jacques Durand from 23 August 1907 in *C*, 1026.

86. MR: See Debussy's letter to Jacques Durand from 3 September 1907 in *C*, 1030.

87. MR: An announcement—that Mourey's libretto for *L'histoire de Tristan* had been completed and that Debussy was writing the music for it—appeared already in *Le temps* on 30 May 1907, in the "Théâtres" section on p. [3] that was devoted to the Opéra-Comique.

88. MR: See Debussy's letter to Victor Segalen from 26 August 1907 in *C*, 1027.

89. MR: More information on Debussy's work with Segalen on a possible *Orphée-roi* may be found in Robert Orledge, *Debussy and the Theatre* (Cambridge: Cambridge University Press, 1982), 269–72.

90. MR: See Debussy's letter of 26 August 1907 to Segalen in *C*, 1027.

91. MR: See Debussy's letter to Gabriel Mourey from 19 September 1907 in *C*, 1031.

92. MR: See Debussy's letter to Louis Laloy from 29 September 1907 in *C*, 1033.

93. [*C*, 1032.]

94. The three scenes of the first act of *Tristan* are noted by Segalen and reproduced in Joly-Segalen and Schaeffner, *Segalen et Debussy*, 74. MR: The quotes by Debussy were made during his interview with Segalen on 8 October 1907; see *C*, 2201.

95. The Le Havre Circle concert took place on the following 22 May with Jane Bathori and Ricardo Viñes (J. B., "Concerts: Départements—Le Hâvre," *Le monde musical* 20, no. 8 [30 April 1908]: 130). Caplet had been director of the musical theater at the Porte Saint-Martin, and then at the Odéon.

96. [See entries for 29 October and 4 November in] Henri Busser, *De Pelléas aux Indes galantes* (Paris: Librairie Arthème Fayard, 1955), 171, who also reported that Debussy attended the dress rehearsal of Messager's *Fortunio* on 3 June, and that he was "thrilled" by it, as were Reynaldo Hahn and Gabriel Pierné [see Busser's entry for 3 June in *De Pelléas aux Indes galantes*, 168].

97. See p. 169 in the present volume.

98. [See the journal entry for 26 November 1907 in] Viñes, "Le journal inédit," 230.

99. Roman Rolland must have noticed the change of direction taken by the Schola toward dogmatism and traditionalism after Charles Bordes's manifesto in favor of a "free speech in music" (see the chapter titled "L'état présent de la musique française," in *Musiciens d'aujourd'hui*, 274–75). MR: To this day, the Schola Cantorum is located on the rue Saint-Jacques in the fifth arrondissement of Paris.

21. Orchestra Conductor: 1908

1. [*C*, 1036.]

2. MR: See Debussy's interview with Segalen from 8 October 1907 in Annie Joly-Segalen et André Schaeffner, eds., *Segalen et Debussy* (Monaco: Éditions du Rocher, 1962), 75, and in *C*, 2201.

3. The marriage agreement, whereby each spouse retained ownership of his/her property, was drawn up by Maître Duval, a lawyer on the rue Lafayette. In his

biography of Debussy, Victor Seroff granted importance to Henry Bataille's play, *La femme nue*, which premiered at the Théâtre de la Renaissance on 27 February 1908. In it, a young painter, poor and unknown, lives with a former model (Loulou) and suddenly enjoys success, thanks to his painting, *La femme nue*. Having become wealthy, he falls in love with a Jewish princess. Loulou overhears them and attempts to kill herself. Even though those hostile to him saw some of these situations as projections of the composer's life, Seroff inordinately exaggerated their impact, claiming that the play had "a disastrous psychological effect" which explained "the decline of Debussy's creative activity during the second part of his life." MR: See Victor I. Seroff, *Claude Debussy* (Paris: Éditions Buchet/Chastel, 1957), especially chapter 18 ("Le jour du jugement"), pp. 239–56. For a remark on the legitimization of Chouchou that was recorded in official documents, see Archives de la Ville de Paris, actes d'état civil, acte de naissance no. 1231.

4. In December 1902, he had refused to conduct *La damoiselle élue* at a Colonne concert; in August 1906, he had been invited to conduct the Philharmonic Society in London, and in July 1907, he planned to conduct not only in London but also in Rome and in Milan.

5. MR: See Debussy's letter of 15 January 1908 to Segalen in *C*, 1054.

6. See Debussy's letter of 15 January 1908 to Segalen [in *C*, 1055].

7. [*C*, 1061.]

8. Lettre de l'ouvreuse [Willy], "Les harmonies maritimes de Claude Debussy fanatisent le Châtelet," *Comœdia* (20 January 1908): 2. According to Luc Marvy, "M. Debussy's movement, at first a little cold, quickly took on the scope of a good conductor" ("Concerts Colonne," *Le monde musical* 20, no. 2 [30 January 1908]: 24).

9. Reported by Luc Marvy in "Concerts Colonne," 24 (cited in n8).

10. MR: Louis Laloy, "La nouvelle manière de Claude Debussy," *La grande revue* 47 (10 February 1908): 531.

11. Laloy, "La nouvelle manière de Claude Debussy," 534.

12. Laloy, "La nouvelle manière de Claude Debussy," 535.

13. MR: See *C*, 1026. FL 2003 mistakenly dates this letter to 1908; although it concerned the performance that would take place in Munich on 9 October 1908, the letter discussing personnel plans was written in 1907, according to Lesure and Herlin.

14. [See Debussy's letter to Jacques Durand from] 8 August 1906 [in *C*, 962]; the last two sentences were cut in the publication of the *Lettres de Claude Debussy à son editeur* (Paris: A. Durand & fils, 1927), 44. MR: Debussy's remarks were made upon his sending back the proofs of the score of *Pelléas* in German translation.

15. MR: Hugo Schlemüller, "Dur und Moll: Frankfurt am Main," *Signale für die musikalische Welt* 31/32 (24 April 1907): 526. The following year, *Pelléas et Mélisande* was reviewed by August Spanuth in *Signale für die musikalische Welt* 46 (11 November 1908): 1433–37. David G. W. Junker, "Le mouvement musical en province et à l'étranger: Lettre de Berlin," *Le courrier musical* 11, no. 22 (15 Nov. 1908): 648, reported that Debussy's opera was not well received but did not mention the review in *Signale*; however, N. D. L. D., "Le mouvement musical en province et à l'étranger: Lettre de Berlin," *Le courrier musical* 11, no. 23 (1 December 1908): 684, did refer to Spanuth's review. A notice in "Nouvelles," *Le guide musical* 54, no. 46 (15 November

1908): 740, reported on the performance of *Pelléas* at the Komische Oper in Berlin, remarking that "Debussy's magisterial work made a deep impression."

16. It was Paul Ottenheimer who conducted the German version of *Pelléas* in Prague on 28 September 1908, with "great success," as Debussy pointed out to his publisher [see Debussy's letter of 17 October to Jacques Durand in *C*, 1118].

17. J.-J. Nin, "La musique à Berlin," *Le monde musical* 20, no. 23 (15 December 1908): 350–51. MR: Léon Vallas, *Claude Debussy et son temps* (Paris: Éditions Albin Michel, 1958), 321, reports that a critic for the "*Allgemeine Muzik Zeitung* [sic]," P. Schwers, remarked that German composers could learn something from Debussy's treatment of the text setting, while Théodore Tagger wrote in 1909, "Hats off, sirs; Debussy is a genius!"

18. MR: Vallas, *Claude Debussy et son temps*, 320, reports eight performances.

19. MR: See p. 354 in particular of Ildebrando Pizzetti's extensive review of the Milan performance in "*Pelléas et Mélisande*," *Revista musicale italiana* 15 (June 1908): 350–63. A notice in "Nouvelles," *Le guide musical* 54, no. 14 (5 April 1908): 301, reported that "the audience seemed a bit hesitant at first, but gradually they were won over and so swept off their feet that the performance ended triumphantly."

20. MR: See Henry Wood, *My Life of Music* (London: Victor Gollancz, 1938), 208. See also Debussy's reference to Caruso in his letter to Jacques Durand from 15 July 1914 in *C*, 1837.

21. MR: Wood, *My Life of Music*, 209.

22. MR: Wood, *My Life of Music*, 297.

23. MR: See Segalen's letter to his wife from 30 January 1908 in Joly-Segalen and Schaeffner, *Segalen et Debussy*, 90–91.

24. In "Claude Debussy et la musique française moderne en Angleterre (1907–1908)," *S. I. M.* 5, no. 3 (March 1909): 262–85, Jean-Aubry would give details of the extensive timetable [of lectures, published writings, and performances that introduced Debussy's music to audiences in England].

25. MR: The former book was published under the name of Mrs. Franz Liebich, *Claude-Achille Debussy* (London: John Lane, The Bodley Head, 1907), and it concluded with a short chronological list of Debussy's works from 1880 to 1905. The biography by William H. Daly, *Debussy: A Study in Modern Music* (Edinburgh: Methven Simpson, 1908) was dedicated to Henry J. Wood and included a more extensive list of Debussy's compositions by genre.

26. The son of a cobbler, Charpentier, who had experienced years of extreme poverty with Forain, was a specialist in decorative art and had made the medallions of many actors at the Théâtre Libre. He had also worked on a mosaic grand piano [as well as on some of the sculptural interiors of the Chat Noir].

27. MR: See the entry for 21 February 1908 in Viñes's journal in Ricardo Viñes, "Le journal inédit de Ricardo Viñes," trans. and ed. Nina Gubisch, *Revue internationale de musique française* 1, no. 2 (June 1980), 231.

28. Marnold was "furious to see that Laloy was enthralled with Debussy" (see the journal entry for 22 January 1908 in Viñes, "Le journal inédit," 208).

29. While Golaud (Gaidan) was excellent, Geneviève and Arkel were quite poor; [the review appeared under] "Chronique lyonnaise: Grand-Théâtre," *Revue musicale de Lyon* 5, no. 25 (5 April 1908): 727–28, [and Vallas added further remarks

in "*Pelléas et Mélisande*," *Revue musicale de Lyon* 5, no. 26 (12 April 1908): 737–43]. The sets were sold to the Opéra in Nice, which used them in 1912 [see the notice under "Chronique lyonnaise: Grand-Théâtre," *Revue musical de Lyon* 5, no. 27 (19 April 1908): 778–79]. MR: The quotation in FL 2003 comes from a review of a performance early in 1909; see Léon Vallas, "Chronique lyonnaise: Grand-Théâtre—*Pelléas et Mélisande*," *Revue musicale de Lyon* 6, no. 14 (17 January 1909): 414.

30. MR: See p. 204 of the reprint of Debussy's article, "À propos d'*Hippolyte et Aricie*," *Le Figaro* (8 May 1908), in Claude Debussy, *Monsieur Croche et autres écrits*, rev. ed. (Paris: Gallimard, 1987), 202–5; and p. 230 in Claude Debussy, *Debussy on Music*, trans. Richard Langham Smith (New York: Alfred A. Knopf, 1977), 228–31.

31. MR: Debussy, *Monsieur Croche*, rev. ed., 205, and Debussy, *Debussy on Music*, 230.

32. MR: Joly-Segalen and Schaeffner, *Segalen et Debussy*, 99–100.

33. Joly-Segalen and Schaeffner, *Segalen et Debussy*, 100.

34. Camille Mauclair, "Les chapelles musicales en France," *La revue* 71 (15 November 1907): 179–93.

35. MR: Pierre Lalo, "La musique," *Le temps* (24 March 1908): [3].

36. MR: Lalo, "La musique," [3], cited in n35.

37. See Debussy's letter to Jacques Durand from 24 March 1908 [in *C*, 1077]. Four years later, on 25 February 1912, he would write to Vittorio Gui: "*Ariane et Barbe-bleue* is a masterpiece, but it's not a masterpiece of French music" [see *C*, 1494].

38. Jean Huré, "Salle Pleyel," *Le monde musical* 19, no. 5 (15 March 1907): 73.

39. MR: See Pierre Lalo, "La musique," *Le temps* (23 June 1908): [3].

40. MR: Lalo, "La musique," [3], cited in n39.

41. Marnold had written in *Le Mercure* that *Pelléas* was "visibly soaked like a sponge" in *Boris*. Mme de Saint-Marceaux had noted in her journal on 19 May 1908 that Debussy had "drawn shamelessly from it." MR: See Jean Marnold, "Revue de la quinzaine: Musique," *Mercure de France* 73, no. 264 (16 June 1908): 781; and Marguerite de Saint-Marceaux, *Journal, 1894–1927*, ed. Myriam Chimènes et al. (Paris: Librairie Arthème Fayard, 2007), 519.

42. MR: See Debussy's letter to Pierre Lalo from 23 June 1908 in *C*, 1098.

43. MR: Debussy conveyed this opinion to Jane Bathori-Engel in a letter, possibly from March 1908; see *C*, 1079.

44. Letter of 8 June 1908 from Debussy [to Jacques Durand in *C*, 1093].

45. [See Debussy's letter of 18 June 1908 to Jacques Durand in *C*, 1096.] "Her voice," wrote Auguste Mangeot, "is very weak in quality, primarily in the middle range" (see p. 168 of "Théâtres: Opéra-Comique," *Le monde musical* 20, no. 11 [15 June 1908]: 168–69). In her memoirs, Maggie Teyte claimed that she had worked on the role for nine months [see also Gillian Opstad, *Debussy's Mélisande: The Lives of Georgette Leblanc, Mary Garden and Maggie Teyte* (Woodbridge, Suffolk: Boydell Press, 2009), 179].

46. MR: See Ravel's letter to Ida Godebska in Arbie Orenstein, ed., *A Ravel Reader: Correspondence; Articles; Interviews* (New York: Columbia University Press, 1990), 98.

47. See Debussy's letter of 18 June 1908 to Jacques Durand [in *C*, 1097].

48. See Debussy's letter of 18 July 1908 to Jacques Durand [in *C*, 1102].

49. MR: See Debussy's letter of 5 July 1908 to Gatti-Casazza in *C*, 1100–1101.

50. MR: See Debussy's letter of 5 July 1908 to Gatti-Casazza in *C*, 1101.

51. Edward Lockspeiser, *Debussy et Edgar Poe: Manuscrits et documents inédits* (Monaco: Éditions du Rocher, 1962), 75. MR: This exchange is reported in English translation in Giulio Gatti-Casazza, *Memories of the Opera* (New York: Vienna House, 1973), 157.

52. MR: See Debussy's letter to Jacques Durand from 10 August 1908 in *C*, 1107.

53. The trip to Brittany, which Debussy mentioned to Edwin Evans on 28 August, seemed to be nothing more than an excuse for his tardy reply [see *C*, 1111].

54. MR: See Debussy's letter of 5 September 1908 to Francisco de Lacerda in *C*, 1113.

55. MR: The text of Debussy's February 1908 interview with Maurice Leclerq (for *L'éclair*) is published in full in Charles Francis Caillard and José de Bérys, *Le cas Debussy* (Paris: Bibliothèque du temps présent, [1910]), 3–6 (the citation is found on pp. 4–5), and in part in Debussy, *Monsieur Croche*, rev. ed., 280–81.

56. MR: See Debussy's interview with Emily Frances Bauer for the 29 August 1908 issue of *Harper's Weekly* in pp. 282–83 of Debussy, *Monsieur Croche*, rev. ed., 282–84, and on p. 233 of Debussy, *Debussy on Music*, 232–35.

57. MR: The text of Debussy's interview with Charles Henry Meltzer, likely from the November 1908 issue for *The American*, is available in Debussy, *Monsieur Croche*, rev. ed., 285–86; see p. 285 for this quote. FL 2003 identifies the author's last name as Meitzer instead of Meltzer.

58. MR: Debussy, *Monsieur Croche*, rev. ed., 286. For Debussy's specific thoughts on the length of *Pelléas*, see p. 235 in the present volume.

59. Robert Orledge, *Satie the Composer* [Cambridge: Cambridge University Press, 1990], 57, suggests that this might be referring to Satie's *Aperçues désagréables*. MR: For Debussy's letter to Lacerda, see *C*, 1112.

60. Debussy gave him a score of [the first edition of] *La mer* with corrections in his own hand. MR: This score is an important link between the first and second editions of the work, incorporating changes made by Debussy after his firsthand experience conducting the work in London in February 1908.

61. [*C*, 1094.]

62. See Debussy's letter to Jacques Durand [from 17 October 1908 in *C*, 1119].

63. MR: See Debussy's letter to Jacques Durand from 17 October 1908 in *C*, 1119.

64. MR: FL 2003 gives the date of 23 December in the text, but cites the correct date of 18 December in the catalog of Debussy's works on p. 542 of François Lesure, *Claude Debussy: Biographie critique* (Paris: Fayard, 2003).

65. MR: See Debussy's letter to Victor Segalen from 13 November 1908 in *C*, 1130.

66. MR: Years later, in an article published in the *New York Times* (21 December 1930), Bauer reminisced about the premiere at the Cercle musical: "He [Debussy] came to the concert, but stayed outside the auditorium, being, as I have ever since

believed, a little doubtful—shall I say, a little embarrassed?—regarding the outcome of his venture into a comical spirit. After the performance, I found him in the courtyard. 'Well, how was it?' he inquired laconically. 'They laughed,' I answered with equal brevity. He smiled broadly and shook my hand with great warmth."

67. Vallas, *Claude Debussy et son temps*, 314.

22. "The Procrastination Syndrome": 1909

1. MR: See Debussy's letter in *C*, 1145.
2. MR: See p. 201 in the present volume.
3. [Segalen's interview with Debussy is reproduced in] Annie Joly-Segalen et André Schaeffner, eds., *Segalen et Debussy* (Monaco: Éditions du Rocher, 1962), 107–8, [and in *C*, 2206–7].
4. MR: Maurice Leudet, "Que faire au Conservatoire? Conversation avec M. Claude Debussy," *Le Figaro* (14 February 1909): [3].
5. MR: Leudet, "Que faire au Conservatoire?" [4].
6. MR: Leudet, "Que faire au Conservatoire?" [4].
7. MR: See Debussy's letter to André Caplet from 28 February 1909 in *C*, 1159.
8. MR: See Debussy's letter to Jacques Durand from 26 August 1908 in *C*, 1110.
9. Henry J. Wood, *My Life of Music* (London: Victor Gollancz, 1938), 298–99. MR: Wood's account (on p. 298) goes so far as to report that "*The orchestra refused to stop.* [. . .] They obviously did not intend to stop: they knew that the audience would think the fault was theirs. Moreover, the work (which they liked immensely) was going beautifully and they meant to give it a first-rate performance; which they proceeded to do and succeeded in doing."
10. MR: See letter of 27 February 1909 in *C*, 1158–59. As explained in the next paragraph, this hemorrhaging was a sign of the cancer that would eventually take his life.
11. [See the interview conducted by M.-D. Calvocoressi, "An Appreciation of Contemporary Music: Claude Debussy," for *The Etude* 32, no. 6 (Philadelphia, June 1914), in Claude Debussy,] *Monsieur Croche et autres écrits*, rev. ed. (Paris: Gallimard, 1987), 335.
12. [*C*, 1162.]
13. MR: See Debussy's letter to André Caplet from 25 August 1909 in *C*, 1207.
14. MR: See Debussy's letter to Toulet from 9 March 1909 in *C*, 1163.
15. MR: This event was noted in "La semaine: Paris," *Le guide musical* 55, no. 14 (4 April 1909): 292.
16. MR: See "The New Music Cult in France and Its Leader: Claude Achille Debussy Tells of His Present and Future Works," *New York Times* (16 May 1909): Sunday Magazine, 9.
17. MR: As reported by André Lamette, "La semaine: Paris—Concerts Colonne," *Le guide musical* 55, no. 16 (18 April 1909): 332; and George Boulay, "Concerts Colonne," *Le monde musical* 21, no. 7 (15 April 1909): 108.
18. MR: Pierre Lalo, "Les grands concerts: Concerts Colonne et Lamoureux," *Le courrier musical* 12, no. 8 (15 April 1909): 268, described the songs as pastiches,

noting in particular that the first song, "Dieu! qu'il la fait bon regarder," took after Costeley; that the second, "Quand j'ai ouy le Tabourin," reminded listeners of Jannequin's *Bataille de Marignan*; and that the third, "Hyver, vous n'êtes qu'un villain," seemed to come from Roland de Lassus.

19. MR: The term "œuvrettes" was used by Pierre Lalo to refer to pieces written by composers who were imitating Debussy's style; Lalo used this term when reporting on a recent concert at the Société nationale in his column, "La musique," in *Le temps* (23 March 1909): [2], and again in *Le temps* (18 August 1909): [3]. He pointed out the tedium experienced by the audience when work after work, written in this same style and replete with compositional clichés such as harp glissandi, appeared on concert programs.

20. MR: See the review by H. in the section titled "Exécutions récentes," *La revue musicale* 9, no. 8 (15 April 1909): 208–9.

21. MR: See Lamette's review in *Le guide musical* (18 April 1909), cited in n17. Curiously, the critic of the *Revue musicale*, cited in n20, referred to Debussy's work as the *Princesse élue*.

22. MR: See Debussy's interview with Charles Henry Meltzer for *The American*, presumably from November 1908, in Debussy, *Monsieur Croche*, rev. ed., 286.

23. See Debussy's letter of 20 February 1909 in *C*, 1155. MR: The "mythological Elsa" refers to the character in the story of Wagner's *Lohengrin*.

24. MR: A chanson de geste is a lengthy, epic poem that combines some historical truth—primarily concerning events of the eighth and ninth centuries during the reigns of Charlemagne and his successors—with legends. The subject matter of these poems integrates battles and feudal allegiances with idealized courtly love and esoteric symbolism. The masterful *Chanson de Roland* is perhaps the best-known chanson de geste.

25. MR: See Debussy's letter to Gabriel Mourey from 29 March 1909 in *C*, 1165.

26. MR: See Debussy's letter of 29 April 1909 to Louis Laloy in *C*, 1173.

27. [In "Echos et nouvelles diverses: Que fait M. Debussy?"] *Le courrier musical* 13, no. 9 (1 May 1910): 380, appeared an announcement—thanks to whose indiscretions?—that *Orphée* "would begin with a part sung in the orchestra, which would most certainly be a novelty." MR: The beginning of the same announcement, on p. 379, stated that Debussy had completed two Poe works for the Opéra-Comique as well as a *Tristan*, on a text by Gabriel Mourey that was drawn from the adaptation by Bédier.

28. MR: See Segalen's interview with Debussy from 6 May 1908 in Joly-Segalen and Schaeffner, *Segalen et Debussy*, 96–97, and in *C*, 2205–6.

29. See Debussy's letter of 27 July [in *C*, 1198–99].

30. MR: See Debussy's letter of 18 April 1909 in *C*, 1170–71.

31. MR: See Debussy's letter to Jacques and Auguste Durand from 18 May 1909 in *C*, 1179.

32. MR: See Debussy's letter to Vanni Marcoux from 22 May 1909 in *C*, 1184.

33. MR: See Debussy's letter to the Durands from 18 May 1909 in *C*, 1179.

34. MR: See Debussy's letter to Paul-Jean Toulet, written on 21 May 1909 from the Royal Palace Hotel in Kensington, in *C*, 1183.

35. MR: As reported by Debussy to Jacques and Auguste Durand in his letter from 18 May 1909); see *C*, 1179.

36. MR: Debussy reported Campanini's remarks to Jacques Durand in a letter from 23 May 1909; see *C*, 1185.

37. Vittorio Gui, *Battute d'aspetto* (Florence: Casa Editrice Monsalvato, 1944), 210–17. The conductor was Giorgio Polacco. MR: In her review, "La musique française à Rome," *La revue musicale* 9, no. 9 (1 May 1909): 245, Hélène Barrère made the point that, given the disruptive demonstrations in the hall, the audience was unable to judge the music of the opera because it was impossible "to hear it under normal conditions."

38. MR: See Debussy's letter to Gabriel Astruc from 12 June 1909 in *C*, 1191.

39. MR: See Debussy's letter of 30 July 1909 to Laloy in *C*, 1199–1200.

40. See his letter of 23 October 1909 [in *C*, 1221].

41. MR: For a summary of the scenario, see Robert Orledge, *Debussy and the Theatre* (Cambridge: Cambridge University Press, 1982), 153–55.

42. MR: See the entry for 5 July 1909 in Henri Busser, *De Pelléas aux Indes galantes* (Paris: Librairie Arthème Fayard, 1955), 178. It was during this visit that Debussy asked Busser to orchestrate *Printemps*.

43. MR: See Debussy's letter to André Caplet from 24 July 1909 in *C*, 1197.

44. MR: Debussy reported that Novaes was only thirteen at the time (though she was actually all of fourteen!); see his letter to André Caplet from 25 November 1909 in *C*, 1224.

45. MR: See Debussy's letter of 26 June 1909 in *C*, 1193.

46. MR: As pointed out in Debussy, *Monsieur Croche*, rev. ed., 301n5 and 349 (see the note for 301), Laurence Sterne was an English novelist who became known as a sentimentalist. His best-known novels were *Tristram Shandy* and *A Sentimental Journey*.

47. [See Gino F. Zuccala, "En parlant avec Debussy," *Musica* (12 February 1910), reprinted in] Debussy, *Monsieur Croche*, rev. ed., 300–301.

48. MR: See Debussy's letter to Caplet from 24 July 1909 in *C*, 1197–98.

49. MR: See Debussy's letter to Caplet from 21 September 1909 in *C*, 1214.

50. MR: See Debussy's letter to Caplet from 30 June 1913 in *C*, 1626.

51. MR: See Debussy's letter to Caplet, likely from 14 February 1911, in *C*, 1391. In a letter to Caplet from 16 June 1908, Debussy already referred to Caplet's being guided by "pure instinct"; see *C*, 1094.

52. MR: See Louis Laloy, *Claude Debussy* (Paris: Les bibliophiles fantaisistes, 1909), 47.

53. MR: Laloy, *Claude Debussy*, 79.

54. MR: See Debussy's letter to Laloy from 27 July 1909 in *C*, 1199.

55. MR: See Debussy's letter to Laloy from 10 September 1909 in *C*, 1213.

56. Michel Arnauld (Marcel Drouin), "Concert Claude Debussy (Société des dilettantes, salle Mors.)," *La nouvelle revue française* 12 (1 January 1910), 554–55. The lecture preceded a concert in which Mme Raymonde Delaunois sang "La grotte," "Colloque sentimental," and the Bilitis songs, and M. Ennemond Trillat played *Children's Corner* [and "Les cloches à travers les feuilles"].

57. MR: The text of "M. Claude Debussy et le snobisme contemporain" is reprinted in Charles Francis Caillard and José de Bérys, *Le cas Debussy* (Paris: Bibliothèque du temps présent, [1910]), 7–47.

58. [Caillard and de Bérys, *Le cas Debussy*, 2.] In 1907, Jacques Rivière had expressed a radically opposite point of view: "Never was there a revolutionary less vocal and less despotic" ("Chronique: La musique à Paris," *Tanit* 1, no. 6 [1 July 1907]: 219).

59. MR: See Caillard and de Bérys, *Le cas Debussy*, 9.

60. MR: See Caillard and de Bérys, *Le cas Debussy*, 25.

61. MR: See Caillard and de Bérys, *Le cas Debussy*, 42.

62. MR: See Caillard and de Bérys, *Le cas Debussy*, 46. Caillard is quoting from Laloy's article in "Revue de la quinzaine: Les concerts," *Le mercure musical* 1, no. 12 (November 1905): 488.

63. MR: The survey is reproduced in Caillard and de Bérys, *Le cas Debussy*, 49–104.

64. MR: An exception is the comment by Yvonne Sarcey; see Caillard and de Bérys, *Le cas Debussy*, 97.

65. MR: See the entry for 20 December 1947 in Paul Léautaud, *Journal littéraire, vol. 17: Août 1946–Août 1949* (Paris: Mercure de France, 1964), 217–18.

66. MR: Caillard and de Bérys, *Le cas Debussy*, 89.

67. MR: Caillard and de Bérys, *Le cas Debussy*, 54–55.

68. MR: See Caillard and de Bérys, *Le cas Debussy*, 84–87, 91, and 102–3.

69. [See the letter of 23 January 1904 from Louÿs to Debussy in *C*, 825.] The 1910 publication of *Le cas Debussy* included an interview of the composer by Maurice Leclerq concerning Wagner's influence, a reprint of Cor's article, followed by the survey, [reprints of several other articles that referenced Cor's article,] and a conclusion titled "Le secret de M. Debussy."

70. MR: Debussy composed this piece for piano, based on the letters in Haydn's name, for a special issue of the *S. I. M.* (15 January 1910), published in honor of the centenary of Haydn's death.

71. See Debussy's letter of 20 January 1910 [to Jules Écorcheville, then director of the *S. I. M.*, in *C*, 1240].

72. See Debussy's letter from 18 January 1913 [in *C*, 1580].

73. See Debussy's letter from 11 September 1905 [in *C*, 919]. MR: Incidentally, Debussy wrote the phrase "as you like it," in English, referencing Shakespeare's play. He first contemplated an adaptation [of *As You Like It*] with Maurice Vaucaire in 1886; a second iteration, involving Paul-Jean Toulet, advanced to the level of a libretto in three acts and five scenes, but no music for it was ever begun (see Robert Orledge, *Debussy and the Theatre* [Cambridge: Cambridge University Press, 1982], 257–60 and 316).

74. Anne Bertrand, "Debussy et Jacques-Émile Blanche," *Cahiers Debussy* 17–18 (1993–94): 91.

75. See Segalen's interview of Debussy from 17 December 1908 [in Joly-Segalen and Schaeffner, *Segalen et Debussy*, 107, and in *C*, 2207].

76. See Debussy's letter from 12 July 1910 [in *C*, 1301]. In 1913, he promised an article on "color in piano music" for the American composer Daniel Gregory Mason, but he never wrote it.

77. See Debussy's letter of 1 September 1915 [to Jacques Durand in *C*, 1927].

78. MR: According to a notice in *The Etude* 27, no. 7 (July 1909): 497, Rudolph E. Reuter, an American pianist from Berlin, had "been appointed to teach piano in Tokyo, for the Japanese government."

79. Louis Laloy, *La musique retrouvée* (Paris: Librairie Plon, 1928), 120.

80. MR: See the transcript of Segalen's interview with Debussy on 14 November 1907 in Joly-Segalen and Schaeffner, *Segalen et Debussy*, 85, and in *C*, 2204.

81. MR: See George Copeland, "Debussy, the Man I Knew," *The Atlantic Monthly* (January 1955): 36.

82. See p. 217 in the present volume.

83. MR: See p. 10 of Maurice Dumesnil, "Coaching with Debussy," *The Piano Teacher* 5, no. 1 (September–October 1962): 10–13.

84. MR: De Tinan was the married name of Emma's daughter, Dolly Bardac, who married a cousin of Jean de Tinan.

85. MR: Mme Gaston de Tinan, "Memories of Debussy and his circle," *Recorded Sound* 50–51 (April–July 1973): 159.

86. MR: See "Debussy in Jersey by Diane Enget Moore, Page 4," http://www.litart.co.uk/bluthner.htm, accessed 16 January 2019.

87. MR: See Gino G. Zuccala, "Conversando con Debussy," *Musica* 4, no. 7 (12 February 1910): [1?]; a photocopy of the original article may be viewed in BnF, Fonds Lesure, carton V/2 (3). See also Gino F. Zuccala, "En parlant avec Debussy," *Musica* (12 February 1910), reprinted in Debussy, *Monsieur Croche*, rev. ed., 300–301.

88. MR: See Roy Howat, *The Art of French Piano Music* (New Haven: Yale University Press, 2009), 312, for further detail on Zuccala's and Casella's observations of the Bechsteins in Debussy's home.

89. MR: See Jacques Durand, *Lettres de Claude Debussy à son éditeur* (Paris: A. Durand & fils, 1927), 134. Of course, the "German piano" could also have referred to Debussy's Blüthner piano.

90. [See p. 72 of Raoul Bardac, "Dans l'intimité de Claude Debussy,"] *Terres latines* (March 1936): 71–74.

23. Orchestral *Images* and Piano *Préludes*: 1910

1. MR: A composition history of the *Images* is given in Matthew Brown, *Debussy's 'Ibéria'* (Oxford: Oxford University Press, 2003), 16–23.

2. MR: See Luc Marvy, "Concerts: Concerts Colonne," *Le monde musical* 22, no. 5 (15 March 1910): 73. Amédée Boutarel, "Revue des grands concerts: Concerts-Colonne," *Le ménestrel* 76, no. 9 (26 February 1910): 68, reported that one part of the audience demanded an encore, while the other part showed no interest in hearing the work again. André Lamette acknowledged the controversial reception of the work (despite his personal enjoyment of it) as well as its less than perfect performance in "La semaine: Paris: Concerts Colonne," *Le guide musical* 56, no. 9 (27 February 1910): 169.

3. In this same concert, Rhené-Baton conducted Ravel's *Rapsodie espagnole*, whose third movement, the "Habanera," recalled the controversy from 1907.

4. MR: See Debussy's letter to Jacques Durand in *C*, 1244.

5. MR: "Rive gauche" implies the Bohemian atmosphere of the "left bank" in Paris.
6. MR: See Debussy's letter of 25 February 1910 to André Caplet in *C*, 1252.
7. MR: This information came in the form of a postscript, dated on "Saturday morning," to Debussy's letter of 25 February 1909 to Caplet; see *C*, 1253.
8. [Luc Marvy reported on the performance of "Ibéria" at the Concerts Colonne in] *Le monde musical* 22, no. 5 (15 March 1910): 73.
9. MR: Jean Chantavoine, "Chronique musicale: Concerts Colonne," *La revue hebdomadaire* 19, no. 3 (5 March 1910): 278.
10. MR: Pierre Lalo, "La musique: Le concert du Châtelet—Première audition d'*Ibéria*," *Le temps* (26 February 1910): [3].
11. MR: Lalo, "La musique: Le concert du Châtelet—Première audition d'*Ibéria*," [3]. The shops and vendors along the rue du Caire at the 1889 World's Fair seemed straight out of Egypt.
12. Charles Koechlin, "Chronique musicale: Concert Colonne," *La chronique des arts et de la curiosité* 10 (5 March 1910): 76–77. MR: Of "Les parfums de la nuit," Koechlin wrote, "It's music that goes into the deepest parts of ourselves."
13. MR: See p. 3 of Gaston Carraud, "Les concerts," *La liberté* (1 March 1910): 2–3, in which he dwelled on the polarized audience reception of "Ibéria."
14. MR: See Jean Marnold, "Revue de la quinzaine: Musique," *Mercure de France* 84, no. 308 (16 April 1910): 718–23, reprinted as "Le rythme et la musique espagnole" in *Musique d'autrefois et d'aujourd'hui* (Paris: Dorbon-Ainé, [1912]): 353–62.
15. MR: Alfred Bruneau, "Musique: Le concerts," *Le matin* (21 February 1910): 2.
16. [See p. 517 of] Louis Laloy, "Claude Debussy et le debussysme," *S. I. M.* 6, nos. 8–9 (August–September 1910): 507–19 (FL 2003 reports a German translation in *Der Merker*, Vienna).
17. MR: Laloy, "Claude Debussy et le debussysme," 517–18.
18. MR: See "*Pelléas et Mélisande* de Claude Debussy" in Jacques Rivière, *Études* (Paris: Gallimard, 1944), 127.
19. [See especially pp. 479–80 of] Jacques Rivière, "Les poèmes d'orchestre de Claude Debussy," *Nouvelle revue française* 16 (1 April 1910): 476–82 [reprinted in Rivière, *Études*, 130–34]. See also Françoise Escal, "Le Debussysme de Jacques Rivière," *Revue d'histoire littéraire de la France* 87, no. 5 (September–October 1987): 837–57.
20. MR: This review appeared in "Mahler Features Debussy," *New-York Daily Tribune* (16 November 1916): 7.
21. MR: "The Philharmonic Concert," *New York Sun* (16 November 1910): 9.
22. MR: "The Philharmonic Concert," *New York Sun* (16 November 1910): 9.
23. MR: This quote actually came from a review of Mahler's performance of "Ibéria" on 3 January 1911, published in the *New York World* (4 January 1911): 11.
24. MR: See "The Philharmonic Concert," *New York Sun* (16 November 1910): 9.
25. MR: A notice in "Échos et nouvelles diverses: Une Société indépendante," *Le courrier musical* 13, no. 4 (15 February 1910): 168, reported that the initiative to establish the Société indépendante was led by Émile Vuillermoz. And another notice in "Échos et nouvelles diverses: Une Société indépendante," *Le courrier*

musical 13, no. 7 (1 April 1910): 288–89, reported the first official communication from the SMI, identifying Fauré as the president of the organization and announcing the first of five concerts planned for the season, to be given on 20 April 1910.

26. [Auguste Mangeot, "Concerts: Salle Gaveau; La Société Musicale Indépendante,"] *Le monde musical* 22, no. 8 (30 April 1910): 123–24. Ravel's work was *Ma mère l'oye*. MR: Also on the program was Fauré's *Chanson d'Ève*, performed by Jeanne Raunay with the composer himself at the piano, as well as three songs by Maurice Delage, sung by the baritone M. Stéphane Austin. The concert included other diverse works, such as the first movement of André Caplet's Septet for string quartet and voices, Roger-Ducasse's *Pastorale* for organ (performed by Alexandre Guilmant), and an extract from Liszt's *Prometheus*, titled "Chorus of the Reapers" and performed on piano by Messieurs Louis Aubert and Florent Schmitt.

27. Paul Landormy, *La musique française de Franck à Debussy*, 17th ed. (Paris: Gallimard, [1943]), 230–31.

28. [Auguste Mangeot, "Concerts: Société Musicale Indépendante,"] *Le monde musical* 22, no. 10 (31 May 1910): 153. MR: Mangeot believed the concert of 25 May to be the first in which Debussy performed his own *Préludes*, which included "four new" ones that were "remarkable": "Danseueses de Delphes," "Voiles," "La cathédrale engloutie," and "La danse de Puck."

29. MR: See the reviews by Camille Mauclair, "La quinzaine: Salle Pleyel," *Le courrier musical* 14, no. 10 (15 May 1911): 347; and by C., "La semaine: Paris; Salle Pleyel," *Le guide musical* 57, nos. 20–21 (14 and 21 May 1911): 393. Jean Marnold also mentioned this concert, the second of two given by Jane Mortier at the Salle Pleyel, in "Revue de la quinzaine: Musique," *Mercure de France* 92, no. 337 (1 July 1911): 178. A number of other works were performed on the concert of 3 May, including Ravel's "Le gibet" (from *Gaspard de la nuit*), two *Danses* by Granados, and Debussy's *Chansons de Bilitis*, sung by Lucienne Bréval.

30. Before the premieres, Maurice Ravel played and replayed these *Préludes*; on 7 May, he wrote to Jean Marnold that they were "admirable masterpieces." MR: See Ravel's letter to Jean Marnold from 7 May 1910 in René Chalupt and Marcelle Gerar, *Ravel au miroir de ses lettres* (Paris: Robert Laffont, 1956), 86; and in English translation in Arbie Orenstein, *A Ravel Reader: Correspondance, Articles, Interviews* (New York: Columbia University Press, 1990), 117. In his biography of Walter Morse Rummel, *Prince of Virtuosos* (Lanham, MD: Scarecrow Press, 2005), 45–57, Charles Timbrell devotes an entire chapter to the friendship between Debussy and Rummel.

31. MR: See Debussy's letter to Laloy from 16 June 1908 in *C*, 1095, in which he asked for the precise meaning of words such as *affray, m'acointeray, m'abutineray*, and *l'ay*.

32. MR: See Debussy's full response to the question posed by Fernand Divoire in the March 1911 issue of *Musica*: "Sous la musique que faut-il mettre: de beaux vers, de mauvais, des vers libres, de la prose?" (What sort of text should be set to music: beautiful or bad poetry, free verse or prose?), in Claude Debussy and Pierre Louÿs, *Correspondance de Claude Debussy et Pierre Louÿs* (1893–1904), ed. Henri Borgeaud (Paris: Librairie José Corti, 1945), 197–98; the quotation cited is on p. 198. The text is also reproduced in Claude Debussy, *Monsieur Croche et autres écrits*,

rev. ed. (Paris: Gallimard, 1987), 206–7; and in Claude Debussy, *Debussy on Music*, trans. Richard Langham Smith (New York: Alfred A. Knopf, 1977), 250–51.

33. MR: See Debussy's letter to Durand from 17 September 1910 in *C*, 1315.

34. MR: Debussy's medieval spelling of the adjective *jaulni*, instead of the contemporary form of the word *jauni*, reflects the medieval texts on which the songs are based.

35. MR: In a review, "Miss Maggie Teyte's Recital," published in *The Times* (19 November 1910): 15, the only Villon song mentioned was the "Ballade des femmes de Paris." Other Debussy songs performed by Teyte on this recital included "Fantoches," "La chevelure," and two of the *Ariettes oubliées*, including "Green."

36. MR: Blumenberg is mentioned in a letter from Debussy to Laloy, dated 13 May 1910; see *C*, 1276.

37. François Lesure, "Manuel de Falla, Paris et Claude Debussy," *Manuel de Falla tra la Spagna e l'Europa* (Florence: Leo S. Olschki Editore, 1989), 17.

38. MR: Alma Mahler, *Mahler*, French trans. Nathalie Godard (Paris: Éditions Jean-Claude Lattès, 1980), 151; and Alma Mahler, *Gustav Mahler: Memories and Letters*, English trans. Basil Creighton, 3rd ed. (Seattle: University of Washington Press, 1975), 169.

39. MR: Alma Mahler, *Mahler*, French trans., 151, and Alma Mahler, *Gustav Mahler*, English trans., 170.

40. MR: Reviews of the former concert in *New York Times* (18 February 1910): 7, and of the latter concert in *New York Sun* (11 March 1910): 9, are reproduced in Zoltan Roman, *Gustav Mahler's American Years, 1907–1911: A Documentary History* (Stuyvesant, NY: Pendragon, 1989), 343–44 and 355, respectively.

41. Alma Mahler, *Mahler*, French trans., 151, and Alma Mahler, *Gustav Mahler*, English trans., 170.

42. MR: This language appeared in an editorial note, "À nos lecteurs," in the "Französisches Musikfest in München: Festschrift und Programmbuch mit deutschem Text" section of *S. I. M.* 6, nos. 8–9 (August–September 1910): [iv].

43. MR: David Grayson, in "Claude Debussy Addresses the English-speaking World: Two Interviews, an Article, and *The Blessed Damozel*," *Cahiers Debussy* 16 (1992): 31, reminds us that the interview in *L'Ouest-artiste* predated the performance of Debussy's works in Munich.

44. MR: This article was reprinted in Debussy, *Monsieur Croche*, rev. ed., 305–6.

45. MR: For a reprint of the *Paris-Journal* article, see Debussy, *Monsieur Croche*, rev. ed., 305–6. See also the notice in "Échos et nouvelles diverses: M. Debussy et le festival français de Munich," *Le courrier musical* 13, no. 19 (1 October 1910): 641. The article was also reprinted in "Échos: M. Debussy et le festival français de Munich," *Revue musicale de Lyon* 8, no. 1 (16 October 1910): 36–37.

46. MR: According to *"Claude Debussy as I Knew Him" and Other Writings by Arthur Hartmann*, ed. Samuel Hsu, Sidney Grolnic, and Mark A. Peters (Rochester, NY: University of Rochester Press, 2003), 12–19, Hartmann met Debussy in 1908, and their friendship flourished during 1910, and then resumed again in 1914, when the Hartmanns returned to Paris from the United States. Hartmann was from a Hungarian Jewish family, rather than a Magyar (Hungarian Catholic) one.

47. Hartmann had already made a transcription of the second *Ariette*, "Il pleure dans mon cœur," for Fromont. MR: In a recital at the Salle des Agriculteurs on 5 February 1914, Debussy accompanied Hartmann in a recital that included transcriptions of "Il pleure dans mon cœur," "La fille aux cheveux de lin," and "Minstrels"; it was very well received, as reported by Louis Laloy in Émile Vuillermoz's column, "La musique au concert," in *Comœdia* (9 February 1914). The latter transcription was allegedly made by Hartmann but eventually published by Durand under Debussy's name; see Hartmann, "*Claude Debussy as I Knew Him*," 18. A manuscript of "Minstrels" for violin and piano, in Debussy's hand, is preserved in the Sibley Music Library at the Eastman School of Music (of the University of Rochester in Rochester, NY), where Hartmann served on the faculty until 1922.

48. MR: Hartmann, "*Claude Debussy as I Knew Him*," 78. According to Hartmann, Debussy described the Hungarian Gypsy band as "those gentlemen who wear red jackets!"

49. MR: See Debussy's letter to Arthur Hartmann from 3 August 1910 in *C*, 1307.

50. [See p. 156 of] Maurice Dumesnil, "Conferences with Claude Debussy, Part II," *The Etude* 51, no. 3 (March 1933): 155–56 and 204. MR: On p. 169 of this issue, *The Etude* published, with Emma's permission, the *Page d'album* for the first time, with editorial notes by Dumesnil.

51. MR: Scott is referred to as such, for example, in Jürgen Schaarwächter, *Two Centuries of British Symphonism* (Hildesheim: Georg Olms Verlag, 2015), 1:298.

52. MR: See the journal entry of 22 January 1904 in Marguerite de Saint-Marceaux, *Journal, 1894–1927*, ed. Myriam Chimènes et al. (Paris: Librairie Arthème Fayard, 2007), 331.

53. See letter of 18 September 1910 in *C*, 1315–16. See also [especially p. 102 of] Cyril Scott, *My Years of Indiscretion* (London: Mills & Boon, 1924), 100–105.

54. Grayson, "Claude Debussy Addresses the English-speaking World," 25–30.

55. MR: Cited in Grayson, "Claude Debussy Addresses the English-speaking World," 26.

56. MR: Cited in Grayson, "Claude Debussy Addresses the English-speaking World," 28.

57. MR: Cited in Grayson, "Claude Debussy Addresses the English-speaking World," 30.

58. See "Une renaissance de l'idéal classique?" from 20 May 1910 in the *Paris-Journal*, reprinted in Debussy, *Monsieur Croche*, rev. ed., 304.

59. MR: FL 2003 claims that Debussy and Toulet heard Mary Garden in Strauss's *Salome* on 2 July 1910, but in fact, performances of this opera were suspended during this time, while Mary Garden was on vacation; see Jean Prudhomme, "Paris: Opéra," *Comœdia* (26 June 1910): 3. Rather, as reported in the notice under "Paris: Théâtres," *Comœdia* (2 July 1910): 2, Stravinsky's *Firebird* ballet was being performed at the Opéra. The latter information is also mentioned in *C*, 1298n3.

60. MR: See Debussy's letter of 8 July 1910 in *C*, 1300.

61. MR: See Igor Stravinsky and Robert Craft, *Expositions and Developments* (London: Faber & Faber, 1962), 130–31.

62. MR: Stravinsky and Craft, *Expositions and Developments*, 131.

63. Marcel Dietschy comments as follows: "A final bedazzlement, secret, very sweet, but of no particular consequence." MR: See Marcel Dietschy, *La passion de Claude Debussy* (Neuchâtel: Éditions de la Baconnière, 1962), 204; Margaret G. Cobb and William Ashbrook translate this passage as "A final attachment, secret and very tender, but it led to no rupture," in *A Portrait of Claude Debussy* (Oxford: Oxford University Press, 1990), 160.

64. [*C*, 1259.]

65. [*C*, 1263.]

66. [*C*, 1299.]

67. [*C*, 1308–9.]

68. [*C*, 1316.]

69. There are no fewer than nine [*recte*, five] letters to Bertault for 1910 alone.

70. The letter is not dated, but the postmark clearly indicates 1910 [see *C*, 1366].

71. Interview by Alberto Gasco; see p. 7 of François Lesure, "Une interview romaine de Debussy (février 1914)," *Cahiers Debussy* 11 (1987): 3–8. Also note that Debussy stopped paying alimony to Lilly after July 1910.

72. The announcement mentioned the presence of other family members: M. and Mme Emmanuel Debussy and their children; Adèle Debussy; and M. and Mme Alfred Debussy and their daughter.

73. MR: See Debussy's letter of 4 November 1910 in *C*, 1327.

74. MR: A letter from Maud Allan to Debussy, dated on 30 September 1910, stated that she had received the contract from him and that she desired several emendations to it; see *C*, 1318–19.

75. Felix Cherniavsky, "Maud Allan, Part III: Two Years of Triumph, 1908–1909," *Dance Chronicle* 7, no. 2 (1984): 119–58.

76. MR: See *C*, 1344. Debussy's reference to Khamma (thoustra) was a play on words between the *Kama Sutra* and Richard Strauss's *Also sprach Zarathustra*. The former, written in India during the third century, is a classic guide to lovemaking. Debussy's comment was thus a sideways allusion to Allan's sexual allure as well as to Strauss's epic tone poem on philosophical ideas espoused by Nietzsche.

77. MR: See Debussy's letter from 21 November 1910 in *C*, 1332.

78. MR: Debussy used this phrase in a letter to Emma from Vienna on 30 November 1910; see *C*, 1338.

79. MR: See Debussy's letter to Emma from 30 November 1910 in *C*, 1338.

80. MR: See Debussy's letter to Jacques Durand, written from Budapest on 4 December 1910, in *C*, 1348.

81. MR: See Debussy's letter to Durand from 4 December 1910 in *C*, 1348.

82. MR: See Debussy's letter to Durand from 4 December 1910 in *C*, 1348.

83. MR: See Debussy's letter to Emma from 3 December 1910 in *C*, 1344.

84. MR: See pp. 321–22 of G. Linor's interview of Debussy, titled "Pour la décentralisation musicale," published in *Comœdia* on 26 January 1911, which is reproduced in Debussy, *Monsieur Croche*, rev. ed., 320–22.

85. MR: Debussy made this remark to Emma on 2 December 1910, the day of the performance in Vienna; see *C*, 1342.

86. According to Edward Lockspeiser, *Debussy: Sa vie et sa pensée*, trans. Léo Dilé (Paris: Fayard, 1980), 403n*, [and, in English, *Debussy: His Life and Mind* (Cambridge: Cambridge University Press, 1978), 2:129], the official Austrian was supposedly Ferdinand Löwe.

87. See Debussy's letter of 14 February 1911 to Caplet [in *C*, 1391].

88. MR: See his letter from 2 December 1910 in *C*, 1341–42.

89. MR: According to the report from Dr. Emeric Vadasz, "Le mouvement musical en province et à l'étranger: Lettre de Budapest," *Le courrier musical* 14, no. 8 (15 April 1911): 284, Debussy also performed "L'hommage à Rameau" and accompanied Rose Féart in four of the *Fêtes galantes*.

90. MR: See Debussy's letter to Emma from 4 December 1910 in *C*, 1346.

91. [Cited in] Vallas, *Claude Debussy et son temps* (1958), 354n1. MR: See Debussy's letter to Pierné from 9 November 1913 in *C*, 1686–87.

92. MR: See Debussy's letter to Robert Godet from 6 February 1911 in *C*, 1384.

93. MR: Debussy expressed this sentiment in a letter to Gusztáv Bárczy on 19 December 1910; see *C*, 1361.

94. MR: Zágon (born in Budapest with the name of Vilmos Zerkowitz, which he changed to Zágon in 1909) lived in Paris from 1912 to 1914, and his *Pierrot Lunaire* was premiered there on a concert of the Société musicale indépendante in December 1913. In the Géza Csáth, *Géza Vilmos Zágon in Paris, 1912–1914* exhibition (Budapest: National Széchényi Library, 26 March–31 May 2013), a copy of Zágon's *Pierrot lunaire* song cycle, based on six of the poems by Albert Giraud, was exhibited that had been "corrected" by Debussy; see the exhibition's website, http://www.museum.hu/exhibition/14188/Geza_Vilmos_Zagon_in_Paris_1912-1914, accessed 16 January 2019. Denis Herlin, in "Autour du *Pierrot lunaire* de Zágon: Debussy et la question de 'l'accent prosodique,'" paper given in Metz, France and in Budapest, Hungary in September 2018, discusses Debussy's corrections in each of the songs and provides context on Zágon as a composer, pianist, and critic; this paper will be published in *Debussy hier et aujourd'hui*, ed. Jean-Christophe Branger and Nicolas Moron (Paris: Société française de musicologie).

95. See p. 287 of Dénes Bartha, "L'influence de Debussy: Hongrie," in *Debussy et l'évolution de la musique au XXe siècle*, ed. Edith Weber (Paris: Éditions du Centre national de la recherche scientifique, 1965), 273–87. See also József Ujfalussy, "Debussy e Bartók," in *I consigli del vento che passa: Studi su Debussy*, ed. Paolo Petazzi (Milan: Edizioni Scolastiche Unicopli, 1989), 439–48.

96. MR: The source of this information is likely Virgil Thomson, *Music Right and Left* (New York: Henry Holt, 1951), 127. Even after Philipp's retort, Bartók still wanted to meet Debussy, although it seems he never did. NB that FL 2003 erroneously attributes this experience to Kodály rather than to Bartók.

97. See Debussy's letter to Bárczy from 19 December 1910 [in *C*, 1361]. MR: Debussy was pleading for valuing and preserving folk music in its natural state rather than adapting it in an artificial or scholarly way.

98. MR: FL 2003 states that Debussy's comment was made "two months" later, rather than "over a year" later.

99. MR: See Debussy's letter to Mme Bárczy from 12 February 1912 in *C*, 1492.

100. MR: See especially p. 214 of Debussy's article on the "Concerts Colonne" in the November 1912 issue of *S. I. M.*, reproduced in its entirety in Debussy, *Monsieur Croche*, rev. ed., 213–16, and on p. 265 in Debussy, *Debussy on Music*, 264–67.

101. MR: See the notice in "Auditions d'élèves," *Le monde musical* 22, no. 6 (30 March 1910): 107. FL 2003 cites the professor as "M. Chêne" rather than "Mme Chéné," who taught piano at the Conservatoire at the time, as reported in Anne Bongrain, *Le conservatoire national de musique et de declamation 1900–1930: Documents historiques et administratifs* (Paris: Vrin, 2012), 313.

24. *Le martyre de saint Sébastien*: 1911

1. Yet another project is revealed to us via an interview from January 1911: an "orchestration" of Rameau's *Pygmalion* for the Théâtre des Arts (Claude Debussy, *Monsieur Croche et autres écrits*, rev. ed. [Paris: Gallimard, 1987], 318; and Claude Debussy, *Debussy on Music*, trans. Richard Langham Smith (New York: Alfred A. Knopf, 1977), 245). A few months later, Saint-Pol-Roux approached Debussy for some incidental music for his *Dame à la faulx*, intended for a production by Jacques Rouché—another project that never came to fruition. MR: See the letter from Saint-Pol-Roux to Debussy, dated 28 February 1911, in *C*, 1397. FL 2003 erroneously cites the name of "Roulle" instead of "Rouché."

2. MR: For D'Annunzio's letter, see *C*, 1335.

3. MR: See Debussy's letter from 30 November 1910 in *C*, 1339.

4. MR: D'Annunzio was well known as a ladies' man. He worked his considerable charm on Emma, sending her an inscribed copy of his latest book and invoking the name of Robert de Montesquiou as a fervent admirer of Debussy who was interested in seeing a collaboration between him and D'Annunzio; see D'Annunzio's letter to Emma from 7 December 1910 in *C*, 1351.

5. MR: For Astruc's letter to Emma from 9 December 1910, see *C*, 1357.

6. MR: New Year's greetings between Debussy, D'Annunzio, and Emma all mention Chouchou in affectionate terms; see *C*, 1368. Astruc referred to Chouchou's eyes and her smile in his letter to Debussy from 23 January 1911; see *C*, 1378. Letters from D'Annunzio to Chouchou document the fact that he gave her gifts such as dolls and a bracelet; see, for example, his letters from 30 April or 1 May 1914 and from 23 July 1914 in *C*, 1805 and 1839, respectively.

7. A facsimile of this contract is in Eiko Kasaba, "*Le Martyre de Saint Sébastien*: Étude sur sa genèse," *Cahiers Debussy* 4–5 (1980–81): 20–21. MR: The text of the contract is also available in *C*, 1355–57.

8. MR: See *C*, 1357–58 for D'Annunzio's letter to Emma.

9. MR: Denis Herlin, in "*Le martyre de saint Sébastien*," in *Opéra et réligion*, ed. Jean-Christophe Branger and Alban Ramaut (Saint-Étienne: Presses de l'Université de Saint-Étienne, 2006), 201–6, reports that Jean Roger-Ducasse and Henry Février had refused, and that Florent Schmitt had accepted in principle. The replies of Roger-Ducasse and Florent Schmitt may be seen in Claude Debussy and Gabriele D'Annunzio, *Claude Debussy et Gabriele D'Annunzio: Correspondance inédite*, ed. Guy Tosi (Paris: Éditions Denoël, 1948), 114–15. Further details of the negotiations with

these individuals are provided in Jacques Depaulis, *Ida Rubinstein: Une inconnue jadis célèbre* (Paris: Éditions Honoré Champion, 1995), 109–12.

10. MR: See the letter dated 21 November 1908 in Gabriele D'Annunzio, *Le livre secret de Gabriele D'Annunzio et de Donatella Cross*, ed. Pierre Pascal (Venice: Edizioni letterarie "Il Pellicano," 1947), 1:22.

11. MR: This episode is mentioned in Depaulis, *Ida Rubinstein*, 90–91, based on a report by Piero Chiara in *Vita di Gabriele D'Annunzio* (Milan: Arnoldo Mondadori Editore, 1978), 219.

12. MR: See Annamaria Andreoli, *Il vivere inimitable: Vita de Gabriele d'Annunzio* (Milan: Arnoldo Mondadori Editore, 2000), 460. D'Annunzio told his personal secretary Tom Antongini that he had found his ideal Sébastien in Ida Rubinstein; see Depaulis, *Ida Rubinstein*, 92.

13. MR: See p. 31 of Gustave Cohen, "Gabriele d'Annunzio et *Le martyre de saint Sébastien*," *La revue musicale* 234 (1957): 29–39. Cohen's response was that, indeed, in earlier *mystères* there was nudity but that it was men who took on the roles of women. In this article, Cohen reminisced about his meeting and subsequent interactions with D'Annunzio, whereas in an earlier article, he had summarized D'Annunzio's *Martyre* in some detail; see Gustave Cohen, "Gabriele d'Annunzio et le *Martyre de saint Sébastien*," *Mercure de France* 91, no. 336 (16 June 1911): 688–709.

14. In addition to [pp. 22–23 and 114–15 of] Debussy and D'Annunzio, *Correspondance inédite*, see Guy Tosi, "La genèse musicale du *Martyre de saint Sébastien*," in *Il verri* 7–8 (Mantova: Edizioni del verri, September–December 1985): 7–34.

15. MR: See Georges Delaquys, "M. Claude Debussy nous confie ses projets et nous dit ses espoirs," *Excelsior* 64 (18 January 1911): 7; reprinted in Debussy, *Monsieur Croche*, rev. ed., 317, and in English translation in Debussy, *Debussy on Music*, 244.

16. In Louis Schneider, "La musique étrangère et les compositeurs français," *Le gaulois* (10 January 1911): 4, [where Debussy made the point that he composed music for artistic reasons, as opposed to financial ones, even though he acknowledged that programming decisions were often made for the latter reasons; hence *Carmen* and *Tosca*, written by foreign composers, might be performed more often than *Pelléas et Mélisande*]; in Delaquys, "M. Claude Debussy nous confie ses projets et nous dit ses espoirs," *Excelsior*, 7; and in G. Linor, "Pour la décentralisation musicale: L'opinion des compositeurs," *Comœdia* (26 January): 3, [where Debussy suggested a combination of public and private support for bringing more quality musical performances, especially theatrical ones, to the French provinces; he also discussed the difference between German and French musicians]. These three sources are reproduced in Debussy, *Monsieur Croche*, rev. ed., 314–22; the article from *Excelsior* is available in English translation in Debussy, *Debussy on Music*, 244–46.

17. MR: See Debussy's letter to Robert Godet from 18 January 1913 in *C*, 1579.

18. Louis Laloy, *La musique retrouvée* (Paris: Librairie Plon, 1928), 206.

19. MR: See Debussy's letter of 5 March 1911 in *C*, 1398.

20. Robert Orledge, *Satie the Composer* (Cambridge: Cambridge University Press, 1990), 59.

21. MR: See pp. 481–82 in Louis Schneider, "Festival Debussy," *Journal de l'Université des Annales* (15 October 1911): 480–88.

22. MR: Schneider, "Festival Debussy," 484.

23. Schneider, "Festival Debussy," [480]. MR: Jane Bathori-Engel also sang Debussy's settings of two of Verlaine's *Fêtes galantes*: "Colloque sentimental" followed by "Fantoches." Incidentally, Margaret G. Cobb, author of *The Poetic Debussy*, 2nd ed. (Rochester, NY: University of Rochester Press, 1994), studied piano with Henri Etlin.

24. MR: See the telegram that D'Annunzio sent to Debussy from Arcachon on 5 January 1911 in *C*, 1371.

25. MR: See D'Annunzio's letter to Debussy from 11 January in *C*, 1375.

26. MR: See D'Annunzio's letter to Debussy from 13 February in *C*, 1390.

27. MR: According to Tosi, *Debussy et D'Annunzio*, 26, the entire work was completed by D'Annunzio on 2 March 1911.

28. [See Debussy's letter to D'Annunzio] from 29 January [1909 in *C*, 1380–81].

29. See his letter from 20 February 1909 [in *C*, 1396].

30. MR: See his letter from March 1911 in *C*, 1406.

31. See Debussy's letter from 14 February 1911 [in *C*, 1392].

32. MR: This citation is cobbled together from Émile Vuillermoz, *Claude Debussy* (Paris: Flammarion, 1957), 147 and 144. FL 2003 references the whims of Gabriele D'Annunzio rather than those of Gabriel Astruc; of course, both Astruc and D'Annunzio strongly supported this collaboration with Ida Rubinstein.

33. MR: Vuillermoz, *Claude Debussy*, 148.

34. MR: Émile Vuillermoz, "Autour du *Martyre de Saint Sébastien*," *La revue musicale* 1, no. 2 (1 December 1920): 156. This passage is also cited in Germaine and D.-E. Inghelbrecht, *Claude Debussy* (Paris: Costard, 1953), 208, as well as in Tosi's introduction to *Claude Debussy et Gabriele d'Annunzio: Correspondance inédite*, 28.

35. MR: See Vuillermoz, "Autour du *Martyre de Saint Sébastien*," 157, as well as Tosi's introduction to *Claude Debussy et Gabriele d'Annunzio: Correspondance inédite*, 28.

36. [This quote is cited in many sources, including Vuillermoz, "Autour du *Martyre de Saint Sébastien*," 157; Vuillermoz, *Claude Debussy*, 149; Inghelbrecht, *Claude Debussy*, 208–9; and Tosi's introduction to *Claude Debussy et Gabriele d'Annunzio: Correspondance inédite*, 28.] Debussy confirmed this fact to Caplet, reminding him of those "precious moments of the first rehearsals—those when we were the masters—. [. . .] It is one of my best and strongest memories." See his letter from 15 August 1911 [in *C*, 1445].

37. MR: See Debussy's letter to Astruc from ca. 20 May 1911 in *C*, 1420.

38. MR: The archbishop's proclamation was reproduced in an article by René Bizet titled "M. Claude Debussy et la musique sacrée," *Comœdia* (18 May 1911): 3. The fact that the starring role of Sébastien was to be performed by a Jewish woman and that the production's impresario, Gabriel Astruc, was also Jewish only fueled the scandal further; see Depaulis, *Ida Rubinstein*, 124–25.

39. MR: See their letter from 17 May 1911 in *C*, 1418, which was also reproduced in Bizet, "M. Claude Debussy et la musique sacrée," 3 (cited in n38).

40. MR: See "M. Claude Debussy et *Le martyre de saint Sébastien*," *Excelsior* (11 February 1911); reprinted in Debussy, *Monsieur Croche*, rev. ed., 324, and in Debussy, *Debussy on Music*, 248.

41. MR: See Bizet, "M. Claude Debussy et la musique sacrée," 3 (cited in n38); reprinted in Debussy, *Monsieur Croche*, rev. ed., 327.

42. MR: Auguste Mangeot gave a rather extensive, and generally positive, report on the work in "*Le martyre de saint Sébastien*," *Le monde musical* 23, no. 10 (30 May 1911): 155–56. In contrast, Paul de Stœcklin panned both D'Annunzio's writing and the performance of Debussy's music in "Théâtre du Châtelet: *Le Martyre de Saint Sébastien*," *Le courrier musical* 14, no. 11 (1 June 1911): 408–10.

43. MR: See the entry for 23 May 1911 in Marguerite de Saint-Marceaux, *Journal, 1894–1927*, ed. Myriam Chimènes et al. (Paris: Librairie Arthème Fayard, 2007), 651.

44. Laloy, *La musique retrouvée*, 207–8.

45. Letter from Marcel Proust to Reynaldo Hahn from 23 May 1911, in Marcel Proust, *Correspondance*, ed. Philip Kolb (Paris: Plon, 1983), 10:289.

46. MR: Émile Vuillermoz, "Le mois: Paris—Les théâtres," *S. I. M.* 7, no. 6 (15 June 1911): 69.

47. MR: Vuillermoz, "Le mois: Paris—Les théâtres," 70 (cited in n46).

48. MR: See Louis Vuillemin, "Le martyre de Saint Sébastien," *Comœdia* (23 May 1911): 2.

49. MR: See "Revue de la presse quotidienne," *S. I. M.* 7, no. 6 (15 June 1911): 76 (see also n56).

50. MR: See Paul Stœcklin, "Théâtre du Châtelet: *Le martyre de Saint-Sébastien*," *Le courrier musical* 14, no. 11 (1 June 1911): 409; and "Revue de la presse quotidienne," *S. I. M.* (15 June 1911), 76 (cited in n49 and n56).

51. MR: Reynaldo Hahn, "Premières représentations," *Le journal* (23 May 1911): 4.

52. MR: Henri Ghéon, "M. D'Annunzio et l'art: À propos du *Martyre de St. Sébastien*," *La nouvelle revue française* 31 (1 July 1911): 9 and 13–14.

53. MR: Ghéon, "M. D'Annunzio et l'art," 15n1.

54. MR: See "Revue de la presse quotidienne," *S. I. M.* (15 June 1911): 76 (cited in n56). Debussy sent his thanks to Bruneau on 1 June 1911; see *C*, 1425–26.

55. MR: Pierre Lalo, "La musique: *Le martyre de saint Sébastien*," *Le temps* (30 May 1911): 3, as well as n56.

56. A small press file of excerpts from eight critiques of the *Martyre* is given in "Revue de la presse quotidienne," *S. I. M.* 7, no. 6 (15 June 1911): 75–76. MR: These include reviews by Félix Duquesnel for *Le gaulois*, Pierre Lalo for *Le temps*, Robert Brussel for *Le Figaro*, Reynaldo Hahn for *Le journal*, Alfred Bruneau for *Le matin*, Paul Souday for *L'éclair*, Gaston Carraud for *La liberté*, and Adolphe Jullien for the *Journal de débats politiques et littéraires*. A very short notice by François de Nion, extolling Debussy's music in *L'écho de Paris*, is also included. In addition, Émile Vuillermoz offered a brief review of the *Martyre* on pp. 69–70 of "Le mois: Paris—Les théâtres," *S. I. M.* 7, no. 6 (15 June 1911): 65–70.

57. MR: D'Annunzio referred to the legal trial in a telegram to Debussy on 14 October 1913; see *C*, 1671, and *C*, 1671n4. FL 2003 cites the year of 1911 as the fiftieth anniversary of the Risorgimento; however, as Italian unification was achieved in 1871, it would have been the fortieth anniversary in 1911.

58. MR: See Robert Orledge, *Debussy and the Theatre* (Cambridge: Cambridge University Press, 1982), 232–36, for this and other future plans for *Le martyre*.

59. MR: The cast for the performances in Chicago, given on 5 and 17 November and on 5 and 21 December 1910, and that for the performances in Vienna on 23, 26, and 29 May and on 6 and 13 June, are listed in annexe 4 of Denis Herlin, "*Pelléas et Mélisande* aux Bouffes-Parisiens," in Pelléas et Mélisande *cent ans après: Études et documents*, ed. Jean-Christophe Branger, Sylvie Douche, and Denis Herlin (Paris: Symétrie, 2012), 325 and 326, respectively.

60. Richard H. Stein, "Impressions parisiennes: Carnet de voyage d'un allemande en 1911," *S. I. M.* 8, no. 4 (15 April 1912): 31.

61. MR: Mahler's performance of "Ibéria" on 3 January 1911 was reviewed in the *New York World* (4 January 1911): 11. Excerpts from this review are reproduced in Zoltan Roman, *Gustav Mahler's American Years, 1907–1911: A Documentary History* (Stuyvesant, NY: Pendragon, 1989), 428.

62. MR: J. B. Trend, *Manuel de Falla and Spanish Music* (New York: Alfred A. Knopf), 65. Curiously, the review, "Concert of Spanish music," in *The Times* (26 May 1911): 10, mentioned both Liebich and Falla, stating that the latter studied with Debussy in Paris, but it focused primarily on other works performed, including compositions by Joaquín Turina and Falla himself. As pointed out by Chris Collins, in "Falla in Britain," *The Musical Times* 144, no. 1883 (Summer 2003): 35, the Falla–Liebich concert received so little attention because, that same evening, the premiere of Elgar's Second Symphony was taking place at Queen's Hall.

63. Vittorio Gui, *Battute d'aspetto: Meditazioni di un musicista militante* (Florence: Monsalvato, 1944), 222–34.

64. MR: See Debussy's letter to Durand from 25 June 1911 in *C*, 1432–33.

65. MR: See Leone Sinigaglia's letter to Debussy from 30 September 1911 in *C*, 1455. One wonders if Toscanini had already reorchestrated several passages in his score by that time and, if so, what Debussy thought of them. Toscanini's score of *La mer*, with its paste-overs especially at the end of the first movement, is presently conserved in the New York Public Library for the Performing Arts.

66. [*C*, 1436.]

67. MR: The letter is reproduced in *C*, 1445. A caravansary is an inn where caravans would rest for the night; the animals would stay in an interior courtyard. Debussy's use of this specific term thus alludes to the crowded and unpleasant conditions of his stay in Houlgate.

68. MR: See Debussy's letter to Caplet from 15 August 1911 in *C*, 1445. Joinville's text chronicles the Crusades. Debussy's interest in medieval literature had already been evident in his settings of Charles d'Orléans, François Villon, and Tristan l'Hermite.

69. MR: Debussy mentioned the proofs in his letter to André Caplet from 15 August 1911; see *C*, 1445.

70. MR: See his letter to Durand from 26 August 1911 in *C*, 1449.

71. [See Debussy's letter of 26 August 1911 in *C*, 1448.] This sentence was cut, as were many others, in the publication of Debussy's letters to Jacques Durand in 1927.

72. MR: See Debussy's letter to Durand from 6 September 1911 in *C,* 1451.

73. MR: See Debussy's letter to Durand from 6 September 1911 in *C,* 1452.

74. MR: FL 2003 inexplicably substitutes the word "and" instead of "if" in this sentence.

75. MR: See Debussy's letter to Caplet, written on 17 November 1911, in *C,* 1463.

76. MR: The term *trompe-oreille* literally translates as "fool-the-ear," a play on the well-known *trompe l'œil,* which means "fool the eye."

77. [*C,* 1471.]

78. MR: FL 2003 cites a "single" (*seule*) tradition, rather than a "tone-deaf" (*sourde*) one.

79. [*C,* 1472.]

80. Letter of 9 September 1911 from Satie to Roland Manuel [in Erik Satie, *Correspondance presque complète,* ed. Ornella Volta (Paris: Librairie Arthème Fayard, 2000), 157].

81. Cited in Pierre Boulez, "La corruption dans les encensoirs," *La nouvelle nouvelle revue française* année 4, no. 48 (1 December 1956): 1078–84. MR: Debussy's original comment was directed to Robert Godet; see his letter from 18 December 1911 in *C,* 1470.

82. Although the performance was announced for 30 November, it did not take place until 7 December 1911, at the Théâtre des Arts. MR: See Debussy's letter to Paul-Jean Toulet from 29 November 1911 in *C,* 1466; see also *C,* 1428n1.

83. MR: See Debussy's letter to André Caplet from 22 December 1911 in *C,* 1473.

84. MR: A copy of this Durand catalog may be viewed at the BnF, département de la Musique, 8-Vm-Pièce 4522.

85. MR: See the Durand catalog at the BnF, département de la Musique, 8-Vm-Pièce 4522.

86. [See pp. 138–40 of] Octave Séré [Jean Poueigh], *Musiciens français d'aujourd'hui* (Paris: Mercure de France, 1915), 130–47.

25. The Year of the Ballets: 1912

1. MR: This performance was reported by H. G. in "Le mouvement musical en province et à l'étranger: Nice," *Le courrier musical* 15, no. 4 (15 February 1912): 119.

2. MR: This production was announced in Franck Choisy, "Le mouvement musical en province et à l'étranger: Genève," *Le courrier musical* 15, no. 3 (1 February 1912): 87. FL 2003 cites a date of 8 March.

3. MR: This performance was announced in "Nouvelles," *Le guide musical* 58, no. 4 (28 January 1912): 79; and in "Échos et nouvelles diverses: Étranger," *Le courrier musical* 15, no. 3 (1 February 1912): 91. FL 2003 cites only the date of 30 March.

4. MR: A list of the productions of *Pelléas et Mélisande,* both within and outside of France, performed during Debussy's lifetime is provided in annexe 4 of Denis Herlin, "*Pelléas et Mélisande* aux Bouffes-Parisiens," in *Pelléas et Mélisande cent ans après: Études et documents,* ed. Jean-Christophe Branger, Sylvie Douche, and Denis

Herlin (Paris: Symétrie, 2012), 321–29. See pp. 326–27 for the performances cited here.

5. MR: See Debussy's letter from 6 February 1911 in *C*, 1384.

6. MR: According to Lesure and Herlin in *C*, 1487n2, this comment alluded to the strike by the female ballet chorus at the Opéra on 15 January.

7. MR: See Debussy's letter to Jacques Durand in *C*, 1491.

8. [See the journal entry for 23 January 1912 in] Ricardo Viñes, "Le journal inédit de Ricardo Viñes," trans. and ed. Nina Gubisch *Revue internationale de musique française* 1, no. 2 (June 1980): 232.

9. MR: See Debussy's note to Casella, from around 23 February, concerning their forthcoming meeting on 26 February 1912, in *C*, 1494.

10. MR: Five concerts were given on the Concerts Durand series: on 27 February, and on 5, 12, 19, and 26 March 1912.

11. MR: The third song was encored, according to H. D. [Henri Dupré?], "La semaine: Paris—Salle Érard," *Le guide musical* 58, no. 11 (17 March 1912): 212; see also François de Marsens, "La quinzaine: Salle Érard—Concerts Durand," *Le courrier musical* 15, no. 6 (15 March 1912): 180.

12. Luc Marvy, "Concerts de l'Édition Durand," *Le monde musical* 23, no. 7 (15 April 1911): 106.

13. MR: See his journal entry for 12 March 1912 in Viñes, "Le journal inédit," 232–33, in which he also wrote that he had not played "La soirée dans Grenade" since the first Concert Durand two weeks earlier.

14. MR: The program was advertised in *Le guide musical* 58, no. 10 (10 March 1912): 200, and a brief review was written by André-Lamette, "La semaine: Paris—Salle Érard," *Le guide musical* 58, no. 12 (24 March 1912): 235.

15. MR: The program was advertised in *Le guide musical* 58, no. 12 (24 March 1912): 244, and a favorable review by H. D. appeared in "La semaine: Paris—Salle Érard; Concerts Durand," *Le guide musical* 58, no. 14 (7 April 1912): 275.

16. MR: For the genesis of this work, see in particular p. 22 of Marie Rolf, "Debussy's Rites of Spring," in *Rethinking Debussy*, ed. Elliott Antokoletz and Marianne Wheeldon (Oxford: Oxford University Press, 2011), 3–30.

17. MR: FL 2003 mentions that Busser worked on the orchestration of *Printemps* for two years, rather than three; see n18.

18. Henri Busser, *De* Pelléas *aux* Indes galantes (Paris: Librairie Arthème Fayard, 1955), 178 [see the entry for 5 July 1909, when Debussy asked Busser to orchestrate *Printemps*] and 185 [see the entry for 31 March 1912, when Busser delivered his orchestration of the work, at which time Debussy played passages from *Le diable dans le beffroi* and Busser made the observations cited].

19. MR: The subtitle on the cover page of Morice's *Crimen amoris* was "Poème chanté et dansé d'après Verlaine."

20. MR: As Debussy himself pointed out in a letter to Charles Morice from 25 March 1912 (see *C*, 1499), *Crime d'amour* made him think of Paul Bourget's novel with the same title, published in 1886 by Alphonse Lemerre.

21. MR: FL 2003 cites "Pantomime" rather than "Clair de lune" at the beginning of this section. However, the printing of Morice's text, now in box 4, folder 19 of the Charles Morice papers in the Special Collections Research Center of the

Samuel L. Paley Library at Temple University in Philadelphia, clearly gives all three strophes of "Clair de lune." This fact is confirmed by a copy of *Crime d'amour* in the BnF, Fonds Lesure, carton I/7(12).

22. MR: Among the Morice papers at Temple University (see n21), there are five copies of Morice's publication, several with important annotations that Lesure likely never saw. The title of this section was changed from "Crimen amoris" to "Le Rêve," "Rêves," and "Rêve" in annotated versions of Morice's text.

23. MR: The seven deadly sins include Sloth (*la Paresse*), Wrath (*la Colère*), Greed (*l'Avarice*), Gluttony (*la Gourmandise*), Lust (*la Luxure*), Pride (*l'Orgueil*), and Envy (*l'Envie*).

24. MR: Specifically, Sloth becomes Courage (*la Force*), Wrath becomes Prudence (*la Prudence*), Greed becomes Justice (*la Justice*), Gluttony becomes Temperance (*la Tempérance*), Lust becomes Love (*la Charité*), Pride becomes Faith (*la Foi*), and Envy becomes Hope (*l'Espérance*).

25. MR: In the annotated copies of Morice's text at Temple University (see n22), the title of this section was changed from "Gaspard Hauser" to "Apaisement." In addition, other Verlaine poems were substituted for the passages from "Chevaux de bois" and "Gaspard Hauser"; this section now opened with passages from "Crimen amoris," followed by "O triste, triste était mon âme" (from the *Romances sans paroles*; NB the last four couplets are crossed out) and the first strophe of "Green" (from the *Aquarelles* collection within the *Romances sans paroles*), and ending with "Spleen" (also from the *Aquarelles* and also completely crossed out) and "En sourdine" (from the *Fêtes galantes*, the last three strophes of which are crossed out). Clearly, these changes were made following Debussy's letter of 25 March 1912 to Morice (see *C*, 1500), in which he expressed reservations about the inclusion of "Chevaux de bois" and "Gaspard Hauser," and suggested a return to the scene and characters from the first act; an alternative, he mentioned, would be to suppress the third act altogether.

26. MR: Morice gives this direction in the ballet portion of the second section of the work.

27. MR: These references come from the end of the "Sacrifice of Hell" within the second section.

28. François Lesure, "*Crime d'amour* ou *Fêtes galantes:* Un projet verlainien de Debussy (1912–1915)," *Cahiers Debussy*, nouv. sér. 10 (1986): 17–23. MR: See Debussy's letter to Charles Morice from 25 March 1912, in which he mentions Messager's enthusiasm for this project, in *C*, 1500.

29. MR: See the contract in *C*, 1508.

30. MR: See *C*, 1507. The entire contract is reproduced in *C*, 1507–9.

31. MR: Notices about Morice's *Crimen Amoris*, drawn from Verlaine and with music by Debussy, appeared in "Échos et Nouvelles diverses: France," *Le courrier musical* 15, no. 9 (1 May 1912): 283, and in "Échos," *Revue française de musique* 10, no. 5 (15 May 1912): 308.

32. See p. 56 of Maurice Ravel, "Les concerts: Les 'Tableaux symphoniques' de M. Fanelli," *Revue musicale S. I. M.* 8, no. 4 (15 April 1912): 55–56. In the following year, Debussy himself would devote a few lines to Fanelli in his article, "Du précurseur." MR: This article, published in *S. I. M.* (15 March 1913), is reproduced

in Claude Debussy, *Monsieur Croche et autres écrits*, rev. ed. (Paris: Gallimard, 1987), 232–37 (see in particular pp. 235–36), as well as in Claude Debussy, *Debussy on Music*, trans. Richard Langham Smith (New York: Alfred A. Knopf, 1977), 281–86 (see in particular pp. 284–85).

33. On the circumstances of the ballet, see in particular Jean-Michel Nectoux, *L'après-midi d'un faune*, Les Dossiers du Musée d'Orsay 29 (Paris: Éditions de la Réunion des musées nationaux, 1989), especially p. 22; and *Prélude à l'après-midi d'un faune: Mallarmé, Debussy, Nijinsky*, ed. Nectoux (Paris: Éditions Adam Biro, 1989). MR: The latter Nectoux source is also available in an English translation by Maximilian Vos (New York: Vendome Press, 1987). Romola Nijinsky, *Nijinsky* (London: Victor Gollancz, 1933), 149–50, translates Nijinsky's feeling about Debussy's music as being "too circular, too soft for the movement he had conceived. In everything, except its lack of angularity, it was the very thing he wanted."

34. François Lesure, "Une interview romaine de Debussy (février 1914)," *Cahiers Debussy*, nouv. sér. 11 (1987): 5. The interview by Alberto Gasco [appeared in "Claude Debussy à Roma. Un profilo e un colloquio," *La tribuna* (23 February 1914): 3].

35. See p. 66 of Émile Vuillermoz, "Le mois: Les théâtres—La grande saison de Paris," *Revue musicale S. I. M.* 8, no. 6 (15 June 1912): 65–66. This was also the opinion of dancer Miriam Ramberg, [also known as Marie Rambert,] who saw the ballet in Berlin, a little later: "The discrepancy between the impressionistic music of Debussy and Nijinsky's absolute austerity of style quite shocked me." MR: See Marie Rambert, *Quicksilver* (London: Macmillan, 1972), 54.

36. MR: This dedication is cited in item 233 of Georges Andrieux, *Catalogue de vente de livres précieux, anciens, romantiques, modernes, manuscrits, documents et lettres autographes, collections Jules Huret et Claude Debussy*, auction catalog (Abbeville: F. Paillart, 1933), 41. Stravinsky would dedicate his cantata *Le roi des étoiles*, published in 1913, to Debussy; see pp. 300–301 for Debussy's comments on this work. In 1920, two years after Debussy's death, Stravinsky dedicated his *Symphonies of Wind Instruments* to the memory of the French composer. Earlier, in 1915, Debussy had dedicated the third movement of his *En blanc et noir* for two pianos to the Russian.

37. MR: Stravinsky gives a more detailed account of this get-together in Igor Stravinsky and Robert Craft, *Expositions and Developments* (London: Faber & Faber, 1962), 138.

38. [This comment refers to] a passage in the first tableau where the charlatan playing the flute uncovers the three puppets (Petrushka, the Moor, and the ballerina), revealing them to the crowd (pp. 41–43 of the orchestral score).

39. [*C*, 1503.]

40. [*C*, 1462.]

41. Louis Laloy, *La musique retrouvée* (Paris: Librairie Plon, 1928), 213.

42. MR: See the entry for 20 June 1912 in Busser, *De* Pelléas *aux* Indes galantes, 186. If Busser's claim is true, what a change of heart it would be from Debussy's opinion of the opera twenty-five years previously; recall his description of *Tristan* as "the most beautiful thing I know" in a letter to Hébert from March 1887 (see *C*, 62).

43. The *Martyre* was given on the second part of the program on 14 and 17 June at the Salle Gaveau. The first part comprised works by Paul Ladmirault, Koechlin, Satie, and Jean Huré. MR: See an unenthusiastic review by Ch. Tenroc in "La semaine: Paris—Société Musicale indépendante," *Le guide musical* 58, nos. 25–26 (23 and 30 June 1912): 436–37. A more positive review was given by G. K. in "Les concerts," *S. I. M.* 8, no. 7 (July–August 1912): 67.

44. MR: See the lengthy description of *Le martyre* in the announcement of the performance by Richard Aldrich, "Schindler to Give Excerpts from Debussy's Music to d'Annunzio's Miracle Play," *New York Times* (11 February 1912): xii. See also the review of "The MacDowell Chorus" in the *New York Times* (13 February 1912): 9. Kurt Schindler founded the MacDowell Chorus in 1909 and changed its name to Schola Cantorum in 1912.

45. MR: *Le martyre de saint Sébastien* was performed in the afternoon, and *Pelléas et Mélisande* in the evening. See Philip Hale's review of both performances in "Season Closes at Opera House: Debussy's Pieces Produced Both in the Afternoon and Evening," *Sunday Herald* (31 March 1912): 5.

46. MR: This contract is reproduced in *C*, 1521.

47. MR: Richard Buckle, *Diaghilev* (New York: Atheneum, 1979), 234. This work was originally written in English, but FL 2003 cites the French translation by Tony Mayer (Paris: Lattès, 1980), 275.

48. To the three versions reported by Myriam Chimènes in her preface to *Jeux* in the *Œuvres complètes de Claude Debussy*, sér. V, vol. 8 (Paris: Durand, 1988), xii, Anne Bertrand adds a fourth: see her "Debussy et Jacques-Émile Blanche," *Cahiers Debussy* 17–18 (1993–94): 84–89.

49. Vaslav Nijinsky, *The Diary of Vaslav Nijinsky*, ed. Romola Nijinsky (New York: Simon & Schuster, 1936), 140–41. The intervention of an airplane was also suppressed.

50. MR: See the Ballets Russes program of Thursday, 15 May 1913, in the Collection Rondel, RO 12526, Bibliothèque de l'Arsenal, Paris (also available online at IFN-8415118).

51. MR: See Debussy's letter to Jacques Durand from 9 August 1912 in *C*, 1536.

52. Maud Allan's letter to Debussy, [written in English,] from 29 May 1912 [is reproduced in *C*, 1512–14].

53. MR: See Debussy's reply to Maud Allan from around 20 June 1912 in *C*, 1522.

54. Maud Allan's letter to Debussy from 26 June 1912, [again written in English, is reproduced in *C*, 1523–24].

55. MR: See his letter to Maud Allan in *C*, 1529.

56. [*C*, 1545.]

57. MR: Lesure's *sic* refers to the use of the word "reduction" for the piano score of *Khamma*, which preceded the orchestral version. In fact, as Myriam Chimènes points out in "Les vicissitudes de *Khamma*," *Cahiers Debussy*, nouv. sér. 2 (1978): 14, the piano score served as the draft for the orchestral score.

58. [For further details, see the complete article by] Chimènes, "Les vicissitudes de *Khamma*," 11–29.

59. [*C*, 1553.] The following references allow us to assess Debussy's royalties for the foreign productions of *Pelléas*: 1,438 francs for those in Frankfurt (April 1908);

1,000 francs for five performances in New York (January 1910); and 1,091 francs for two performances in Chicago, three in Covent Garden, and that in Vienna (1912). As for his account with Durand, at his death he would owe 66,000 francs. MR: Denis Herlin gives a detailed report of Debussy's financial state in "An Artist High and Low, or, Debussy and Money," in *Rethinking Debussy*, ed. Elliott Antokoletz and Marianne Wheeldon (Oxford: Oxford University Press, 2011), 149–202.

60. MR: Lesure and Herlin speculate that Debussy's letter to Laloy may be from January 1912; see *C*, 1491.

61. MR: Refer back to Debussy's letter to Durand from 30 October 1912 in *C*, 1553.

62. [See the announcement in "À nos lecteurs," *S. I. M.* 8, no. 12 (November 1912): ii.] To an American journalist, Debussy declared that the *S. I. M.* paid him 500 francs per article. MR: See Daniel Gregory Mason, *Music in My Time and Other Reminiscences* (New York: Macmillan, 1938), 256.

63. MR: See Debussy's letter to Godet from 18 January 1913 in *C*, 1580.

64. MR: See in particular p. 214 of Debussy's article on the "Concerts Colonne" in the November 1912 issue of *S. I. M.*, reproduced in its entirety in Debussy, *Monsieur Croche*, rev. ed., 213–16; see also p. 265 in Debussy, *Debussy on Music*, 264–67.

65. MR: See Debussy, *Monsieur Croche*, rev. ed., 215–16, and Debussy, *Debussy on Music*, 266–67.

66. MR: See pp. 217–18 of the article, reproduced in Debussy, *Monsieur Croche*, rev. ed., 217–22; see also p. 268 of Debussy, *Debussy on Music*, 268–72.

67. MR: For Dubois's letter to Debussy from 22 December 1912, see *C*, 1564. In his article, Debussy had argued that the venerable Dubois did not automatically deserve respect from the audience by virtue of his office as director of the Institut. Rather, respect was earned on the basis of the music itself.

68. MR: FL 2003 gives the date of 27 December 1912 for the hundredth performance of *Pelléas* at the Opéra-Comique. However, Debussy himself referred to the forthcoming celebration of this event (on 28 January 1913) in a letter to Émile Vuillermoz from 27 January 1913. According to Denis Herlin, the performance on 28 January 1913 was actually the 101st given at the Opéra-Comique; see annexe 3 of his article, "*Pelléas et Mélisande* aux Bouffes-Parisiens," 319.

69. Messager apologized to Carré for his absence, because he had to get up very early the next day. MR: According to an account of the celebratory dinner by P.-A. S. in "L'Opéra-Comique a fêté hier la centième de *Pelléas et Mélisande*," *Comœdia* (29 January 1913): 3, Pierné, the Laloys, Ruger-Ducasse, and Lalo were also among the invited guests.

70. MR: P.-A. S., "L'Opéra-Comique a fêté hier la centième de *Pelléas et Mélisande*," 3. FL 2003 states that the Under-secretary of State for the Fine Arts delivered "an inspirational speech"; however, the article in *Comœdia* specified that "no speeches were given." Perhaps FL 2003 was referencing Durand's memories of a toast made by a government official; see n71.

71. Jacques Durand, *Quelques souvenirs d'un éditeur de musique* (Paris: A. Durand & fils, 1924), 1:126. MR: A *chevalier* traditionally receives only a ribbon, whereas an *officier* would receive a rosette.

72. MR: See Debussy's letter to Godet from 18 January 1913 in *C*, 1579.

73. MR: It is well known that Proust subscribed to the théâtrophone service, whereby one could listen to opera performances via the telephone lines. See especially p. 77 in Danièle Laster, "Splendeurs et misères du théâtrophone," *Romantisme* 13, no. 41 (1983): 74–78.

74. See Proust's letter of 4 March 1911 to Reynaldo Hahn in Marcel Proust, *Correspondance*, ed. Philip Kolb (Paris: Plon, 1983), 10:256–57.

75. MR: The Boston performances occurred on 10, 13, 19, and 22 January, as well as on 30 March 1912. See annexe 4 of Herlin, "*Pelléas et Mélisande* aux Bouffes-Parisiens," 326. FL 2003 mentions a performance of *Pelléas* in Boston "a few months before" the end of January 1913 with performers Leblanc and Vanni-Marcoux; while Caplet did conduct *Pelléas* in Boston on 8 and 13 January 1913, Louise Edvina sang Mélisande and Vanni-Marcoux sang the role of Golaud (see annexe 4 of Herlin, "*Pelléas et Mélisande* aux Bouffes-Parisiens," 327). Thus, FL 2003 must be referencing the opera's production in Boston during January and March 1912.

76. MR: See H. T. P. (Henry Taylor Parker), "The New 'Pelléas': The Music-Drama at the Opera House," *Boston Evening Transcript* (11 January 1912): 14.

77. MR: See H. T. P. (Henry Taylor Parker), "The New 'Pelléas,'" 14.

78. MR: See Philip Hale, "*Pelléas* at the Opera House," *The Boston Herald* (11 January 1912): 2. FL 2003 states that this description was presented by "A. Darlos," but this name does not appear in any of the reviews I found.

79. See Debussy's letter to Paul-Jean Toulet from 18 January 1913 [in *C*, 1581].

26. *Jeux*, Travel to Russia: 1913

1. MR: Debussy's article, titled "Fin d'année" (End of the year), appeared in the 15 January 1913 issue of *S. I. M.* and is reproduced in Claude Debussy, *Monsieur Croche et autres écrits*, rev. ed. (Paris: Gallimard, 1987), 223–27 (the quote is found on p. 223); see also Claude Debussy, *Debussy on Music*, trans. Richard Langham Smith (New York: Alfred A. Knopf, 1977), 273–76 (the quote is on p. 273).

2. Aside from an article on Rameau, which Caplet had requested from him for an unidentified American publication; [this commentary, from November 1912, is available in] Debussy, *Monsieur Croche*, rev. ed., 210–12, [and in Debussy, *Debussy on Music*, 254–56].

3. MR: See Debussy, *Monsieur Croche*, rev. ed., 223–24, and Debussy, *Debussy on Music*, 273–74.

4. MR: See Debussy, *Monsieur Croche*, rev. ed., 225–26, and Debussy, *Debussy on Music*, 274–75.

5. MR: For example, see pp. 229–31 of his article titled "Du goût," from the 15 February 1913 issue of *S. I. M.*, in Debussy, *Monsieur Croche*, rev. ed., 228–31, and pp. 278–79 in Debussy, *Debussy on Music*, 277–80.

6. MR: See p. 239 of Debussy's review of the Concerts Colonne in the 15 May 1913 issue of *S. I. M.* in Debussy, *Monsieur Croche*, rev. ed., 238–40, and p. 288 in Debussy, *Debussy on Music*, 287–90.

7. MR: Lesure and Herlin report Kahn's memories of his time in Paris and with Debussy in *C*, 1599n1. See also Hazrat Inayat Khan, *Complete Works of Pir-O-Murshid*

Hazrat Inayat Khan: Original Texts (Suresnes: Nekbakht Foundation, 2010), 1:260, in which Khan comments on individuals of genius who do not possess practical skills for daily life. In this context, he reports that, among his travels, he met some great musicians, and then proceeds to tell the following story: Debussy's wife told him that she had "to see the publisher for him. [. . .] *He* is only capable of writing."

8. Letter of 29 April 1913 from Debussy to Rummel; see *C*, 1599. Inayat Khan gave a concert for the Fifth International Music Congress, which took place in Paris, and a "farewell" concert at the Continental Hotel in June 1914.

9. Roy Howat, "Debussy et les musiques de l'Inde," *Cahiers Debussy* 12–13 (1988–89): 141–52.

10. MR: See *C*, 1615n6, as well as a letter from Emma to D'Annunzio, dated by Lesure and Herlin as 10 June 1913, in *C*, 1620.

11. MR: See Debussy's letter to Paul-Jean Toulet from 20 February 1912 in *C*, 1493.

12. MR: Pratella wrote a *Manifesto of Future Musicians* in 1910 and a *Technical Manifesto of Futurist Music* in 1911, in which he called upon young composers to eschew the conservatories and study independently, thus liberating themselves from past musical traditions.

13. MR: See p. 240 of Debussy's review of the Concert Colonne in the 15 May 1913 issue of *S. I. M.* in Debussy, *Monsieur Croche*, rev. ed., 238–40, and p. 288 in Debussy, *Debussy on Music*, 287–90.

14. MR: See p. 248 of Debussy's review of the Concerts Colonne and the Société des nouveaux concerts in the 1 November 1913 issue of *S. I. M.* in Debussy, *Monsier Croche*, rev. ed., 245–49, and p. 298 in Debussy, *Debussy on Music*, 295–99.

15. MR: See *C*, 1532. As Lesure and Herlin point out in *C*, 1532n1, we do not know the precise nature of this "unfortunate accident," but it may have had something to do with the extreme heat at the time (about which Debussy complained) and/or the fact that his home was close to the railroad (to which he also alluded in this letter).

16. MR: See Debussy's letter to Jacques Durand from 7 December 1912 in *C*, 1559.

17. MR: See Debussy, "Du gout," in Debussy, *Monsieur Croche*, rev. ed., 231, and in Debussy, *Debussy on Music*, 280.

18. MR: See Gaston Carraud, "Les concerts," *La liberté* (28 January 1913): 3; and Joseph Jemain, "Revue des grands concerts: Concerts-Colonne," *Le ménestrel* 79, no. 5 (1 February 1913): 37.

19. MR: See André Lamette's review of the Concerts Colonne in the *Le guide musical* 59, no. 5 (2 February 1913): 89.

20. MR: Gustave Samazeuilh's review in *La république* is cited in Vallas, *Claude Debussy et son temps*, 344.

21. MR: Alfred Bruneau, "Les concerts," *Le matin* (27 January 1913): [4].

22. Maurice Ravel, "À propos des *Images* de Claude Debussy," *Les cahiers d'aujourd'hui* 3 (February 1913): 137, reissued in *Maurice Ravel* (Paris: SACEM, 1975), 27–28.

23. Vincent d'Indy, "Concerts Lamoureux; Le bon sens," *S. I. M.* 8, no. 11 (November 1912): 57.

24. André Gédalge, "M. V. d'Indy, critique musical et 'Le bon sens,' à propos d'un article de la *Revue S. I. M.*," *Le monde musicale* 25, no. 1 (15 January 1913): 2–4. MR: In this source, D'Indy's original article from the November 1912 issue of *S. I. M.* was reprinted along with Gédalge's response.

25. Alfredo Casella, "Les concerts: Le crépuscule du franckisme," *L'homme libre* 1, no. 99 (11 August 1913): 2. MR: Casella also lamented Franck's weak treatment of rhythm in his compositions.

26. Auguste Mangeot, "Les jeunes musiciens n'aiment-t-ils plus César Franck?" *Le monde musicale* 25, no. 17 (15 September 1913): 243–44.

27. MR: René Lenormand, *Étude sur l'harmonie moderne* (Paris: Éditions Max Eschig, 1971), 6; see also the English translation by Herbert Antcliffe, *A Study of Twentieth-Century Harmony* (London: Joseph Williams, 1915), 1:x.

28. MR: See Debussy's letter to Lenormand from 25 July 1912 in *C*, 1533.

29. MR: See Debussy's letter to Jacques Durand from 7 January 1913 in *C*, 1574.

30. Roy Howat, introduction to the *Préludes*, in *Œuvres complètes de Claude Debussy*, sér. I, vol. 5 (Paris: Durand-Costallat, 1985), xi and xv.

31. MR: Edmond Stoullig, "Concerts," *Le monde artiste* 53, no. 11 (15 March 1913): 166.

32. MR: See the section titled "L'édition musicale" in *S. I. M.* 9, no. 5 (15 May 1913): 73.

33. MR: For further information on Hellé, the circumstances surrounding his encounter with Debussy, and the story of the ballet, see Denis Herlin, "André Hellé et *La Boîte à joujoux*: Interview, conference et texte intégral de *L'Histoire d'une boîte à joujoux*," *Cahiers Debussy* 30 (2006): 96–120.

34. MR: See Debussy's letter to Jacques Durand from 25 July 1913 in *C*, 1646.

35. MR: "Poème dansé" is the subtitle of *Jeux*.

36. MR: FL 2003 refers to the Théâtre des Champs-Élysées as "the house of music" (*la maison de la musique*), but it actually was called the "the temple of music" (*le temple de la musique*) in its day. See, for example, the reference to it in a letter to the director of *Comœdia*, published in *Comœdia* (18 December 1913): 4.

37. MR: Debussy's remarks from the 15 May 1913 issue of *Le matin* are reprinted in Debussy, *Monsieur Croche*, rev. ed., 242–43, and in Debussy, *Debussy on Music*, 291.

38. MR: Debussy, *Monsieur Croche*, rev. ed., 242–43, and Debussy, *Debussy on Music*, 291.

39. MR: See Debussy's letter to André Caplet from 6 June 1913, several weeks after the premiere of *Jeux*, in *C*, 1614.

40. MR: See Georges-Paul Collet, *Jacques-Émile Blanche: Biographie* (Paris: Éditions Bartillat, 2006), 130, as well as n41.

41. MR: See Bibliothèque de l'Institut, Papiers Jacques-Émile Blanche, Ms. 7058 (Cahier 1913), notes for 14 and 25 May, 52v and 53r and v, cited in Anne Bertrand, "Debussy et Jacques-Émile Blanche," *Cahiers Debussy* 17–18 (1993–94): 86–87 and 87n59.

42. MR: See the review in "Théâtres: La saison russe au Théâtre des Champs-Élysées," *Le monde musical* 25, no. 10 (30 May 1913): 161.

43. MR: See pp. 51–52 of Émile Vuillermoz, "La saison russe au Théâtre des Champs Élysées," *S. I. M.* 9, no. 6 (15 June 1913): 49–56.

44. Letter of 9 June 1913 from Debussy to Godet [in *C*, 1619].

45. Letter to Laloy of 24 August 1910 [see *C*, 1308].

46. MR: Roland Manuel, "La musique: *Jeux*, ballet de M. Claude Debussy," *Montjoie!* 1, no. 8 (29 May 1913): 6.

47. MR: In the 1950s, the first important study of *Jeux*, by Herbert Eimert ("Debussy's *Jeux*," *Die Reihe* 5 [Vienna: Universal Edition, 1959; Bryn Mawr, PA: Theodore Press, 1961]: 3–20), appeared, and Pierre Boulez seized every opportunity to elevate the work's reputation. The 1960s and 1970s saw publications by various German authors, and it was not until the 1980s that analytical articles on *Jeux* were published in English. See in particular Lawrence Berman, "*Prelude to the Afternoon of a Faun*; *Jeux*: Debussy's Summer Rites," *19th Century Music* 3, no. 3 (March 1980): 225–38; and Jann Pasler, "Debussy, *Jeux*: Playing with Time and Form," *19th-Century Music* 6, no. 1 (Summer 1982): 60–75.

48. See Stravinsky's letter to Debussy [in *C*, 1561].

49. MR: See Debussy's letter to Stravinsky from 7 November 1912 [in *C*, 1554–55].

50. [*C*, 1609.]

51. MR: This score was displayed as item 99 in an exhibition catalog, *Igor Stravinsky: La carrière européenne*, for the Festival d'Automne on 14 October–30 November 1980 (Paris: Des presses de l'imprimerie union, 1980), 35.

52. [*C*, 1631.]

53. Georges Jean-Aubry, "Debussy et Strawinsky," *Revue de musicologie* 48, no. 125 (July–December 1962): 109.

54. Igor Stravinsky, *Avec Stravinsky: Textes d'Igor Stravinsky et al., lettres inédites de Claude Debussy et al., avec 14 photographies et un dessin d'Alberto Giacometti* (Monaco: Éditions du Rocher, 1958), 23. MR: Nevertheless, Stravinsky confessed that his *Sacre* "owe[d] more to Debussy than to anyone except myself"; see Igor Stravinsky and Robert Craft, *Expositions and Developments* (London: Faber & Faber, 1962), 142n1.

55. MR: FL 2003 states that Stravinsky's manuscript has been "lost." However, it has since surfaced and was sold at auction in 2019; see Aguettes, *Livres anciens & modernes—Manuscrits et autographes*, auction catalog (Paris: 22 February 2019), item 223.

56. MR: See the letter from Debussy to Stravinsky of 18 August 1913 in *C*, 1655.

57. See Debussy's letter to Godet from 14 October 1915 [in *C*, 1948].

58. MR: Louis Laloy, "Le gala de Claude Debussy," *La revue musicale* 9, no. 6 (15 June 1913): 68.

59. MR: Laloy, "Le gala de Claude Debussy," 68.

60. MR: See Debussy's letter of 23 June 1913 in *C*, 1630. The French here, "remuer de sourds cailloux," echoes Verlaine's line from "C'est l'extase": "les roulis sourds des cailloux."

61. MR: Gabriel Jules François Paulet was a tenor who received a first medal in solfège in 1907, and both a first prize in voice and a first honorable mention in opéra-comique in 1908 at the Conservatoire; see Anne Bongrain, *Le conservatoire national de musique et de declamation 1900–1930: Documents historiques et administratifs* (Paris: Vrin, 2012), 561.

62. MR: In act 4, scene 4 of *Pelléas*, the protagonist sings "Il y aurait plutôt de quoi pleurer" (Surely there's more reason now to weep).

63. MR: See Debussy's letter to André Caplet from 23 June 1913 in *C*, 1630.

64. MR: See Debussy's letter to Vuillermoz from 24 June 1913 in *C*, 1633.

65. MR: See Debussy's letter to André Caplet from 6 June 1913 in *C*, 1614.

66. MR: See Debussy's letter to Jacques Durand from 15 July 1913 in *C*, 1641. The spa resort at Vichy was celebrated for its thermal baths. NB that FL 2003 identifies the doctor as Crespel, not Crépel.

67. See Debussy's letter to Henry Russell from 4 July 1893 [in *C*, 1637, as well as a letter to Léon Bertault,] dated 9 November 1913, in which he mentions Monsieur Crevel, [in *C*, 1685].

68. See Debussy's letter [to Henry Russell] from 16 May 1913 [in *C*, 1605].

69. See Debussy's letter [to Henry Russell] from 4 July 1913 [in *C*, 1637].

70. [*C*, 1638.]

71. [*C*, 1638.]

72. MR: See Debussy's letter of 5 August 1913 in *C*, 1650. FL 2003 gives the erroneous date of 8 August.

73. MR: See Debussy's letter to Jacques Durand from 25 August 1913 in *C*, 1657.

74. See Debussy's letter of 30 August 1913 to Durand [in *C*, 1659].

75. MR: Ironically, Debussy had been accused of marrying Emma for her money and yet, not only was she not providing a substantial income to their household, but he was saddled with many expenses that he could not continue to support.

76. MR: See *C*, 1641–42, as well as Emma's remark (reported by Hazrat Inayat Khan) on p. 482n7.

77. MR: See Victor Segalen's letter of 5 September 1913 to his wife in Annie Joly-Segalen and André Schaeffner, eds., *Segalen et Debussy* (Monaco: Éditions du Rocher, 1961), 135; and in Victor Segalen, *Correspondance II (1912–1919)*, ed. Annie Joly-Segalen, Dominique Lelong, and Philippe Postel (Paris: Librairie Arthème Fayard, 2004), 214.

78. MR: See letter from 9 August 1912 in *C*, 1536.

79. MR: As pointed out by Lesure and Herlin in *C*, 1646n2, this reference to the rue Saint Jacques was a dig against the conservative Schola Cantorum.

80. MR: See Debussy's letter of 8 August 1913 in *C*, 1651.

81. MR: Letter of 7 August 1913 in *C*, 1650.

82. MR: See Ravel's letter in Arbie Orenstein, *A Ravel Reader: Correspondance, Articles, Interviews* (New York: Columbia University Press, 1990), 140.

83. MR: FL 2003 quotes the following sentence from Debussy's letter of 19 October 1913 to Gabriel Astruc: "On vous tombera certainement dessus à cause de cette <u>décision</u>." This is how it is transcribed in Claude Debussy, *Correspondance, 1884–1918*, ed. François Lesure (Paris: Hermann, 1993), 330. But the final word in this passage is transcribed as <u>désertion</u> in the later publication of *C*, 1673, and corroborated by the original letter, conserved at the BnF, département de le Musique, L. a. Debussy (C.) 53, and viewable on Gallica, IFN-53026080.

84. MR: See Debussy's letter to Astruc, dated 19 October 1913, in *C*, 1673–74. See also Lesure and Herlin's detailed discussion of the events and opinions with respect to Astruc's decision to abandon the Théâtre des Champs-Élysées in *C*, 1674n2.

85. MR: See p. 254 of Debussy's article on the "Concerts Colonne—Société des nouveaux concerts" in the 1 December 1913 issue of *S. I. M.*, printed in Debussy, *Monsieur Croche*, rev. ed., 250–54, as well as p. 303 in Debussy, *Debussy on Music*, 300–303. Debussy also used the adjective "admirable" to describe the performance of *Boris* in his letter of 9 November 1913 to Désiré-Émile Inghelbrecht; see *C*, 1686.

86. MR: See Émile Vuillermoz, "Le mois: Les théâtres," *S. I. M.* 9, no. 12 (1 December 1913): 40.

87. Mourey had just published an excerpt of his play in *La nouvelle revue française* 52 (1 April 1913): 542–48.

88. See Debussy's letter to Mourey [in *C*, 1679].

89. MR: See Debussy's letter to Mourey in *C*, 1696.

90. MR: For example, on 2 January 1910, the first two movements of the *Nocturnes* were performed by the Imperial Russian Musical Society at the Moscow Conservatory, and on 9 January, the *Marche écossaise* was played, in addition to "Nuages," at the Noble Assembly Building in Saint Petersburg. Emil Cooper conducted the former program, and Alexander Ziloti conducted the latter. I am grateful to Simon Morrison for providing this information.

91. MR: Between May and August 1911, the Imperial Russian Musical Society repeated a program of "foreign" music on Fridays outside of Saint Petersburg in Pavlovsk Vokzal (Vauxhall) that included the third movement of *La mer*. Cooper conducted ten of the concerts. See the chronicle of concert life in *Istoriia russkoi muzyki*, ed. Iurii Vsevolodovich Keldysh, 10 vols. (Moscow: Muzyka, 1983–97), 10B, 1:863. I am grateful to Simon Morrison for providing this reference, as well as those in n104 and n115.

92. See Debussy's letter to Durand from 8 December 1911 [in *C*, 1468].

93. MR: Cited in English (translated from the Russian) in Richard Taruskin, *Stravinsky and the Russian Traditions: A Biography of the Works through* Mavra (Berkeley: University of California Press, 1996), 55. Cited in French translation in Vladimir Fédorov, "Debussy vu par quelques Russes," in *Debussy et l'évolution de la musique au xxe siècle* (Paris: Éditions du Centre national de la recherche scientifique, 1965), 201–2. Recall that Rimsky-Korsakov called the *Prélude à l'après-midi d'un faune* "rubbish" and found *Pelléas* to be monotonous (see pp. 233 and 234 in the present volume).

94. Fédorov, "Debussy vu par quelques russes," 202.

95. Fédorov, "Debussy vu par quelques russes," 202.

96. Fédorov, "Debussy vu par quelques russes," 202.

97. MR: See the 4 December entry from Debussy's extended letter to Emma of 4–7 December 1913 in *C*, 1710.

98. MR: See the 4 December entry from Debussy's extended letter to Emma of 4–7 December 1913 in *C*, 1711.

99. MR: See the 5 December entry from Debussy's extended letter to Emma of 4–7 December 1913 in *C*, 1712. FL 2003 identifies him as Mr. Porter instead of Mr. Forter. The interpreter was most likely Lev Tseitlin, a soloist and concertmaster of Koussevitsky's orchestra in Moscow; see *The Great Soviet Encyclopedia*, 3rd ed. (1970–79), s.v. "Tseitlin, Lev Moiseevich," available on *The Free Dictionary by Farlex*, https://encyclopedia2.thefreedictionary.com/Lev+Tseitlin, accessed 16 January 2019.

100. MR: See the 5 December entry from Debussy's extended letter to Emma of 4–7 December 1913 in *C*, 1712–13.

101. MR: See the 6 December entry from Debussy's extended letter to Emma of 4–7 December 1913 in *C*, 1713.

102. MR: See the 7 December entry from Debussy's extended letter to Emma of 4–7 December 1913 in *C*, 1714.

103. Letter of 20 May 1917 [from Debussy to Diaghilev in *C*, 2113]. MR: In this letter, Debussy reminisced about the time they were together at the Hermitage, listening to the beautiful songs that had been sung there. On 6 December 1913, Debussy had written to Emma that he was dining with Diaghilev that evening (see *C*, 1713). The impresario noted on the verso of this letter, "The Hermitage, a restaurant in Moscow where the Gypsies sang their songs to Debussy and me all night long"; see *C*, 2113n4.

104. MR: See Prokofiev's essay, "Debussy in Moscow," referenced in V. A. Yuzefovich, *Sergey Kusevitskii: Russkie gody*, 2 vols. (Moscow: Iazyki slavianskoi kul'tury, 2004), 1:247. On 28 November, Prokofiev wrote about meeting Debussy during his visit to St. Petersburg; see *Sergey Prokofiev Diaries, 1907–1914*, trans. and annotated Anthony Phillips (Ithaca, NY: Cornell University Press, 2006), 552–53. However, he did not mention the incident with the blackbird in this diary entry.

105. François Lesure, "Deux documents," *Cahiers Debussy*, nouv. sér. 4–5 (1980–81): 63.

106. Lesure, "Deux documents," 63–64.

107. [*C*, 1722.]

108. [*C*, 1716.]

109. [*C*, 1717.]

110. MR: See Debussy's letter to Emma from 7 December 1913 in *C*, 1716.

111. MR: See Debussy's letter to Emma from 11 December 1913 in *C*, 1722.

112. Lazare Saminsky, "Russie: Debussy à Petrograd," *La revue musicale* (1 December 1920): 216.

113. MR: See Debussy's letter to Emma from 14 December 1913 in *C*, 1724.

114. Reproduced in Maurice Boucher, *Claude Debussy* (Paris: Éditions Rieder, 1930), plate 53.

115. MR: See "Skriabin v kontsertakh Ziloti," *Russkaia muzykal'naia gazeta* 47 (1911): 992.

116. Chennevière would soon emigrate to the United States, where he took the Hindu name of Dane Rudhyar, devoted himself to theosophy and astrology, and became a disciple of Scriabin.

117. MR: Daniel Chennevière, *Claude Debussy et son œuvre* (Paris: A. Durand & fils, 1913), 18.

118. MR: Chennevière, *Claude Debussy et son œuvre*, 15.

119. MR: Chennevière, *Claude Debussy et son œuvre*, 14.

120. MR: Chennevière, *Claude Debussy et son œuvre*, 25.

121. MR: Chennevière, *Claude Debussy et son œuvre*, 45.

122. Évelyne Hurard, "Aperçu sur le goût musical à Paris en 1913," in *L'année 1913: Les formes esthétiques de l'œuvre d'art à la veille de la première guerre mondiale*, ed. Liliane Brion-Guerry (Paris: Klincksieck, 1971), 521–22.

27. The Final Trips: 1914

1. MR: FL 2003 mistakenly identifies the year of publication as 1914, rather than 1913.

2. MR: The author was making a pun on the word *jeux*, or "games," which of course was the title of Debussy's ballet, composed in 1913.

3. "Nouvelles diverses: Fécondité," *Le monde musical* 25, no. 7 (15 April 1913): 122.

4. MR: See Debussy's letter of 5 June 1916 to Victor Segalen in *C*, 1999; Debussy went on to explain that Orphée will not sing "because he [himself] is song personified." As Lesure and Herlin point out in *C*, 1999n3, from the very beginning Debussy was thinking of having Orphée sing without words.

5. MR: The full text of the revised contract for the new title of *Fête galante* is available in *C*, 1753. Under the list of conditions, an original line—stating that Morice "wishes that his name not appear on the score"—was crossed out. The original contract for *Crimen amoris*, dated 21 May 1912, is given in *C*, 1507–9.

6. [See p. 18 of] François Lesure, "*Crime d'amour* ou *Fêtes galantes*: Un projet verlainien de Debussy (1912–1915)," *Cahiers Debussy*, nouv. sér. 10 (1986): 17–23. MR: This quote was taken from a notice at the beginning of Adrien Remacle, *Les Fêtes galantes: Drame-ballet en deux actes* (Paris: A. Messein, 1914). Remacle wrote the text of the play, based on poetry of Verlaine, as well as the music, and he dedicated the work "to the memory of Alfred Ernst, the one person who recognized most clearly and completely the reforms that Richard Wagner brought to our artistic theater, as well as those that will be conceived and put into practice in the future." The premiere of Remacle's work on 9 February 1914 was reviewed by J. B. in "Au Théâtre Idéaliste," *Comœdia* (17 February 1914): 2. Citing the event's moderate success, the critic found the drama "extremely odd" but the music "fascinating."

7. MR: Lesure, "*Crime d'amour* ou *Fêtes galantes*," 21. A letter from Charles Morice to Louis Laloy, dated 23 March, reports this permission from Georges Verlaine; see BnF, Fonds Lesure, carton I/7 (12) for a photocopy of this letter.

8. MR: A draft of the text for *Fêtes galantes, ballet en trois tableaux, d'après Paul Verlaine, par Claude Debussy* may be found in the BnF, département de la Musique, Rés. Vmb. 33.

9. MR: In a letter to Jacques Durand from 15 January 1913, Debussy referred to the "cauchemar Maud-Allan" [*sic*]; see *C*, 1576.

10. MR: See the extracts from Charles Koechlin's journal concerning the orchestration of *Khamma*, in DOSS-02.79 among the Dietschy materials in the CDCD.

11. MR: See Debussy's interview with Maurice Montabré in the 1 February 1914 issue of *Comœdia* in Claude Debussy, *Monsieur Croche et autres écrits*, rev. ed. (Paris: Gallimard, 1987), 330; and in English translation in Claude Debussy, *Debussy on Music*, ed. Richard Langham Smith (New York: Alfred A. Knopf, 1977), 311.

12. MR: See Debussy's letter to Jacques Durand from 16 January 1914 in *C*, 1744.

13. MR: See Debussy's letter to Durand, presumably from 19 May 1914, in *C*, 1812.

14. MR: See again Debussy's letter to Jacques Durand from 16 January 1914 in *C*, 1744.

15. MR: Debussy referred to this idea twice in letters to Godet from 3 December and 28 December 1916; see *C*, 2053 and 2065, respectively. In a letter to Jacques Durand from 1 November 1917, Debussy mentioned that he was working with Laloy to expand the *Martyre* into an operatic version; see *C*, 2160.

16. Debussy had already mentioned the idea of a significant expansion of the *Martyre* in a letter to Gaston Choisnel from 24 July 1913; see *C*, 1645.

17. D'Annunzio had also thought of Debussy for *Parisina*, a legend that he had proposed to Puccini in 1906, and then to Mascagni[, who ultimately completed an opera on D'Annunzio's libretto in 1913]. See Rubens Tedeschi, *D'Annunzio e la musica* (Florence: La Nuova Italia, 1988), 94–95. MR: For the veiled references to a film version of the *Martyre*, see D'Annunzio's letter to Emma Debussy, presumably from 4 June 1914, in *C*, 1820; see also Debussy's letter to D'Annunzio from 20 June 1914 in *C*, 1825.

18. See p. 390n24.

19. [*C*, 1742.]

20. MR: See, for example, Debussy's comment on Grieg's music in his review of the Concert Lamoureux in the 16 March 1903 issue of *Gil Blas*, reproduced in Debussy, *Monsieur Croche*, rev. ed., 127, and in Debussy, *Debussy on Music*, 147. See also his article on Edvard Hagerup Grieg in the 20 April 1903 issue of *Gil Blas*, reproduced in Debussy, *Monsieur Croche*, rev. ed., 153–57, and in Debussy, *Debussy on Music*, 177–81. FL 2003 references *La revue blanche* instead of *Gil Blas*.

21. Léon Vallas, *Claude Debussy et son temps* (Paris: Éditions Albin Michel, 1958), 395, reports that the idea to restore Grieg's reputation perhaps came from Laloy, who devoted an entire column to him in *Comœdia* that appeared on the same day as the concert [Louis Laloy, "La musique chez soi: Edvard Grieg (1843–1907)," *Comœdia* (5 February 1914): 2]. MR: Selva's book, *Quelques mots de la sonate: Évolution du genre* (Paris: Librairie Delaplane), was published in 1914.

22. MR: See in particular p. 263 of Debussy's review, "Pour la musique," in the 1 March 1914 issue of the *S. I. M.*, which is reproduced in Debussy, *Monsieur Croche*, rev. ed., 261–64; see also p. 315 in Debussy, *Debussy on Music*, 311–16.

23. Arthur Hartmann, "Claude Debussy as I Knew Him," *Musical Courier* 76, no. 21 (23 May 1918): 6–9. MR: See also Hartmann's *"Claude Debussy as I Knew Him" and Other Writings by Arthur Hartmann*, ed. Samuel Hsu, Sidney Grolnic, and Mark Peters (Rochester, NY: University of Rochester Press, 2003), 66. Debussy sent Hartmann a "Cappriccioso" theme for the work on 13 May 1910; see *C*, 1275. He referenced the "poëme pour violon et orchestre" again in a letter to Hartmann on 27 July 1910; see *C*, 1306. Still in September of that year, Debussy wrote to Hartmann that he was definitely going to write the piece; see Hartmann, *"Claude Debussy as I Knew Him" and Other Writings*, 119.

24. MR: See Debussy's letter to Laloy from 25 December 1906 in *C*, 982.

25. MR: FL 2003 phrases this reference to M. Croche as he "who decided to die" (qui a décidé de mourir) rather than "how M. Croche was going to be put to rest" (une heure pour décider comment mourra M. Croche), which is the phrase given in *C*, 1762.

26. MR: See Debussy's letter from 28 May 1914 in *C*, 1814.

27. MR: The volume of *Monsieur Croche* never appeared during Debussy's lifetime; it was published by the Librairie Dorbon Ainé only in 1921.

28. [*C*, 1729.]

29. [*C*, 1740.]

30. [*C*, 1748.]

31. [*C*, 1749.]

32. [*C*, 1750.]

33. [*C*, 1762.]

34. [*C*, 1785.]

35. MR: See Debussy's letter to Emma from 19 February 1914 in *C*, 1764.

36. MR: FL 2003 identifies him as Bernardo rather than Bernardino Molinari.

37. MR: FL 2003 reports the year of 1903, but in fact, the controversial performance of *Pelléas* at the Augusteo occurred in 1909, as noted by the author on p. 3 in François Lesure, "Une interview romaine de Debussy (février 1914)," *Cahiers Debussy*, nouv. sér. 11 (1987): 3–8.

38. Lesure, "Une interview romaine de Debussy," 4. Debussy's interview with Gasco was translated into French by Maria Manca.

39. MR: Lesure, "Une interview romaine de Debussy," 5.

40. MR: Lesure, "Une interview romaine de Debussy," 6.

41. Lesure, "Une interview romaine de Debussy," 6. MR: Goethe's alleged request for "mehr Licht" on his deathbed could be interpreted prosaically as his wish for more light in the room or, on the other hand, as an expression of his profound desire and lifelong quest for further enlightenment before dying.

42. MR: See Debussy's letter to Inghelbrecht from 24 February 1914 in *C*, 1770.

43. [René Lyr reported on the concert in the "Province: Belgique" section of] *S. I. M.* 10 (1 March 1914): [67].

44. MR: See Debussy's letter to Emma from 27 February 1914 in *C*, 1774.

45. [See his letter to Emma from 27 February in *C*, 1775.] Debussy had a score of the *Nocturnes*, with numerous corrections that he had made since 1900, sent to Doret; see his letter to Doret from 30 January 1914 in *C*, 1755.

46. MR: In addition, works by Saint-Saëns were performed on the first half of the concert; see Gustave Doret, *Temps et contretemps* (Freiburg: Éditions de la librairie de l'université, 1942), 190.

47. MR: See "Souvenirs de M. Rees," 1–2, a copy of which is in the BnF, Fonds Lesure, carton I/5(3). The contents of this unpublished memoir are also reproduced in *C*, 1778n3, and in English translation in Roger Nichols, *Debussy Remembered* (London: Faber & Faber, 1992), 231–34.

48. MR: See Debussy's letter to Emma from 1 March 1914 in *C*, 1778.

49. MR: See his letter of 1 March 1914 in *C*, 1778.

50. MR: See "Souvenirs de M. Rees," 3, copy in BnF, Fonds Lesure, carton I/5(3). Reproduced in *C*, 1778–79n1, and in Nichols, *Debussy Remembered*, 233.

51. MR: See letter from Doret to Godet, dated 31 March 1918 from Lausanne, 2, copy in BnF, Fonds Lesure, carton I/5(3). Reproduced in Nichols, *Debussy Remembered*, 234.

52. MR: Doret, *Temps et contretemps*, 192.

53. MR: Pierné's performance took place on 1 March 1914. It was reviewed by August Mangeot in "Concerts: Concerts Colonne; Debussy et Fanelli," *Le monde musical* 26, no. 5 (15 March 1914): 78; and by Amédée Boutarel in "Revue des grands concerts," *Le ménestrel* 80, no. 10 (7 March 1914): 76.

54. MR: FL 2003 states that the second performance was given by the Lamoureux orchestra, but it was still the Concerts Colonne and Pierné who performed *Jeux* on 8 March 1914; see, for example, the announcement of the program for the Concert Colonne for 8 March in *Le guide musical* 60, no. 10 (8 March 1914): 208. This performance was reviewed by J. Jemain in "Revue des grands concerts," *Le ménestrel* 80, no. 11 (14 March 1914): 76.

55. MR: See Debussy's letter to Pierné from 5 March 1914 in *C*, 1783.

56. MR: Roland Manuel, "La musique: *Jeux*, ballet de M. Claude Debussy," *Montjoie!* 1, no. 8 (29 May 1913): 6.

57. The program of this concert included a rather technical analysis by Paul Landormy, [which is excerpted in Mangeot's review, "Concerts: Concerts Colonne; Debussy et Fanelli," in *Le monde musical*, cited in n53.] MR: See Paul Le Flem, "Chronique musicale: La saison des Ballets Russes," *Le temps présent* 2, no. 2 (2 August 1913): 205.

58. Eiko Kasaba, "La musique de Debussy au Japon," *Cahiers Debussy*, nouv. sér. 10 (1986): 41. In "Salle Gaveau," *Le monde musical* 26, no. 7 (15 April 1914), 120, Auguste Mangeot complained about the tenuous quality of Debussy's accompaniment, which got lost in the Salle Gaveau.

59. MR: The "ainote" is a virtuosic instrumental interlude in shamisen music.

60. MR: Hippolyte-Jean's review of the 21 March 1914 concert in the Salle Gaveau appeared in *La critique musicale et "l'Information musicale*," the weekly appendix to the *Guide du concert*, sér. 2, no. 23 (24 March 1914): 183.

61. MR: See Debussy's letter to Doret from 10 March 1914 in *C*, 1787.

62. MR: See Debussy's letter to Bernardino Molinari from 18 October 1914 in *C*, 1853.

63. MR: See the account by X. X. in the section title "La semaine: Bruxelles," *Le guide musical* 60, nos. 19–20 (10 and 17 May 1914): 410.

64. MR: See her letters to various individuals from 23, 25, and 26 March 1914 in *C*, 1790–91. FL 2003 states that Debussy contracted shingles "a few days after the concert" rather than the month before.

65. MR: As Claude was ill, Emma responded to Fuller's repeated requests in letters from around 26 March and 1 May 1914; see *C*, 1791–92 and 1806. For a penetrating study of the early performance history of *La boîte à joujoux*, see Simon Morrison, "Debussy's Toy Stories," *Journal of Musicology* 30, no. 3 (Summer 2013): 424–59.

66. MR: See the brief review by O. Synave, "Concerts: Départements; Nice," *Le monde musical* 26, no. 5 (15 March 1914): 86. According to the critic, the performance of *Children's Corner* was a "triumph," and "Golliwog's Cake-Walk" had to be encored. On the same program, Fuller's class also danced to Debussy's *Nocturnes*.

67. MR: See the review by Auguste Mangeot, "École de danse de Loïe Fuller," *Le monde musical* 26, no. 10 (30 May 1914): 173.

68. MR: The sketches are discussed in Robert Orledge, *Debussy and the Theatre* (Cambridge: Cambridge University Press, 1982), 200–204.

69. MR: See Charles Koechlin, "Étude sur Charles Koechlin par lui-même" (1939, rev. 1947), in *La revue musicale* 340–341 (1981): 65. See also the English translation in Robert Orledge, *Charles Koechlin (1867–1950): His Life and Works* (Chur, Switzerland: Harwood Academic Publishers, 1989), 316; on p. 324n44 of the latter source, Orledge cautions that the authenticity of Debussy's remark cannot be guaranteed.

70. Orledge, *Debussy and the Theatre*, 186–205.

71. MR: See p. 407 of M.-D. Calvocaressi [sic], "An Appreciation of Contemporary Music, from an interview [. . .] with [. . .] Claude Debussy," *The Etude* (June 1914): 407–8. Reprinted on p. 333 of Debussy, *Monsieur Croche*, rev. ed., 332–35, and on p. 318 of Debussy, *Debussy on Music*, 317–21.

72. MR: Godet's remarks are reported by Henry Prunières in "Autour de Debussy," *La revue musicale* 15, no. 147 (June 1934): 25. It was Godet who was unsure about Debussy's knowledge of *Pierrot lunaire*.

73. François Lesure, "Debussy et Edgard Varèse," in *Claude Debussy et l'évolution de la musique au XXe siècle*, ed. Edith Weber (Paris: Éditions du Centre national de la recherché scientifique, 1965), 333–38. MR: See also Fernand Ouellette, *Edgard Varèse* (Paris: Éditions Seghers, 1966), 37, and the English translation of that volume by Derek Coltman (New York: Orion Press, 1968), 27.

74. MR: See *C*, 1948. As previously noted, Lesure suspected that Debussy was thinking of Stravinsky's *Le roi des étoiles* when he made this remark. However, Stravinsky himself later speculated that Debussy's comment "may have been prompted by his—Stravinsky's—enthusiasm for Schönberg's *Pierrot lunaire*"; see Pieter C. van den Toorn, *The Music of Igor Stravinsky* (New Haven: Yale University Press, 1983), 472n1.

75. MR: See Calvocaressi [sic], "An Appreciation of Contemporary Music," 408; reprinted on p. 334 of Debussy, *Monsieur Croche*, rev. ed., 332–35, and on p. 320 of Debussy, *Debussy on Music*, 317–21.

76. MR: See Calvocaressi [sic], "An Appreciation of Contemporary Music," 407; reprinted on p. 333 of Debussy, *Monsieur Croche*, rev. ed., 332–35, and on p. 319 of Debussy, *Debussy on Music*, 317–21.

77. MR: See Calvocaressi [sic], "An Appreciation of Contemporary Music," 407; reprinted on p. 333 of Debussy, *Monsieur Croche*, rev. ed., 332–35, and on p. 319 of Debussy, *Debussy on Music*, 317–21.

78. MR: See Calvocaressi [sic], "An Appreciation of Contemporary Music," 407; reprinted on pp. 333–34 of Debussy, *Monsieur Croche*, rev. ed., 332–35, and on p. 319 of Debussy, *Debussy on Music*, 317–21.

79. MR: The "generazione dell'Ottanta" (generation of '80, indicating composers who were born around 1880) included Italian composers such as Alfredo Casella, Gian Francesco Malipiero, and Ottorino Respighi, who focused on writing purely instrumental works, as opposed to the Puccini generation of operatic composers.

80. MR: See Calvocaressi [sic], "An Appreciation of Contemporary Music," 408; reprinted on p. 334 of Debussy, *Monsieur Croche*, rev. ed., 332–35, and on p. 320 of Debussy, *Debussy on Music*, 317–21.

81. MR: See Calvocaressi [sic], "An Appreciation of Contemporary Music," 408; reprinted on p. 334 of Debussy, *Monsieur Croche*, rev. ed., 332–35, and on p. 319 of Debussy, *Debussy on Music*, 317–21.

82. MR: Debussy referred to this performance in a letter to Louis Laly from 5 January 1914; see *C*, 1739.

83. MR: See Debussy's letter to D'Annunzio from 4 May 1914 in *C*, 1809.

84. MR: This quote is referenced in *C*, 1823n1, and may also be found in Lesure, "Debussy et Edgard Varèse," in *Debussy et l'évolution de la musique du XXe siècle*, 336.

85. MR: Debussy was not at all happy with Marguerite Carré in the role of Mélisande; see his letter to Pierre-Barthélemy Gheusi from 2 June 1914 in *C*, 1817, as well as Lesure and Herlin's comments in *C*, 1817n1 and 1817n3.

86. MR: See Debussy's letter of 4 June 1914 to Vanni Marcoux in *C*, 1818.

87. MR: See his letter of 4 June 1914 to Alfred Maguenat in *C*, 1818.

88. Henry Malherbe, "Deux maîtres que j'ai connus," *Candide* (9 December 1937): 19.

89. MR: This reference is to the assassination of Archduke Franz Ferdinand of Austria.

90. MR: See Debussy's letter to Rabani from 28 June 1914 in *C*, 1829.

91. See Debussy's letter of 29 July 1914 [in *C*, 1840].

92. MR: See Debussy's letter of congratulations to Widor from 23 July 1914 in *C*, 1839.

93. This seat was discussed in "Nouvelles diverses: M. Ch. M. Widor est nommé secrétaire perpétuel de l'Académie des beaux-arts," *Le monde musical* 26, nos. 13 and 14 (15 and 30 July 1914): 235. "It has been said that M. Widor intends to offer it to M. Claude Debussy and to support his candidacy. We believe we can affirm that this fact is not entirely accurate, as the new secretary has not yet made known his preference in the choice of his successor." MR: In an article by Charles Pons, "Pourquoi Claude Debussy ne fut pas de l'Institut," *Ordre* (3 June 1933): n.p., three unpublished letters (two of them written in Emma-Claude Debussy's hand) were printed that indicate Debussy's willingness to serve in this capacity even into March 1918, the month in which he died. It appears that Emma was constantly pushing for this appointment, as implied in several of her letters to Louis Laloy; see Fonds FL, BnF, carton I/10(2), and the letter she penned on behalf of Claude in *C*, 2189.

94. [*C*, 1836.]

28. The War; Pourville: 1914–15

1. [See Debussy's letter in *C*, 1841.] The bill was finally paid by Raoul Bardac, in 1921!

2. MR: See Debussy's letter to Jacques Durand from 8 August 1914 in *C*, 1843.

3. MR: See his letter to Durand from 8 August 1914 in *C*, 1843.

4. From his perspective, d'Indy wrote [on 8 September 1914, in a letter to René de Castéra,] that Paris was "finally rid of the political and cowardly clique" (Léon Vallas, *Vincent d'Indy* [Paris: Éditions Albin Michel, 1950], 2:94).

5. See Debussy's letter to Désiré-Émile Inghelbrecht from 18 August 1914 in *C*, 1844.

6. MR: Here Debussy was alluding to the Franco-Prussian war, during which time his father fought for the Commune and was captured and imprisoned.

7. MR: See Debussy's letter to Inghelbrecht from 18 August 1914 in *C*, 1845.

8. MR: See Debussy's letter of 31 August in *C*, 1846.

9. MR: Angers is roughly 165 miles southwest of Paris. A memo from the railway, facilitating "the trip of M. Debussy and four people," from Paris to Angers on 5 September 1914 is found in a dossier titled [Papiers officiels et archives] at the BnF, département de la Musique, NLA 32-bis. See also *C*, 1846n5.

10. [Facsimiles of Debussy's sketches were] reproduced by Maurice Dumesnil in "Conferences with Claude Debussy: Part II," *The Etude* 51, no. 3 (March 1933): 156.

11. MR: See Debussy's letter to Paul Dukas from 5 October 1914 in *C*, 1851.

12. MR: See Debussy's letter to Jacques Durand from 21 September 1914 in *C*, 1847.

13. MR: See Debussy's letter from the end of September 1914 in *C*, 1849–50. See also *C*, 1849n1–2 for further details on Debussy's thoughts regarding Strauss and Schönberg, respectively, and *C*, 1850n1–2 for further context on Debussy's remarks about Beethoven and Wagner, respectively.

14. See his letter to Bernardino Molinari from 18 October 1914 [in *C*, 1854].

15. MR: Debussy alluded to this specific editorial problem in a letter to Jacques Durand from 24 February 1915; see *C*, 1877.

16. MR: *La Brabançonne* is the national anthem of Belgium.

17. MR: See his letter to Robert Godet from 1 January 1915 in *C*, 1863.

18. MR: See his letter to Godet from 1 January 1915 in *C*, 1862.

19. MR: See this letter in *C*, 1866; in *C*, 1866n1, Lesure and Herlin summarize the effect of the war on the numbers of concerts given and the composers whose works were performed.

20. [See Debussy's letter to Inghelbrecht] from 10 January 1915 [in *C*, 1867].

21. MR: Hence the clever conflation of Chevillard's and Pierné's last names in Debussy's letter to Inghelbrecht, cited in n20.

22. MR: In a letter to Jacques Durand from 18 February 1915, Debussy reported that he had the flu; see *C*, 1874.

23. MR: See Dukas's original letter to Brussel in the BnF, département de la Musique, N.L.a. 26 (315).

24. MR: These letters are given in *C*, 1882–89.

25. MR: Emma Debussy was a member of the committee for the "Clothing of the Wounded," and a benefit was being planned to provide aid to the soldiers and their families. Debussy's *Pièce pour l'œuvre du "Vêtement du blessé"* has since become known as the *Page d'album*.

26. MR: See Debussy's letter to Pierre-Barthelémy Gheusi from 7 April 1915 in *C*, 1892.

27. MR: See Debussy's letter to Inghelbrecht from 3 June 1915 in *C*, 1899.

28. MR: See Debussy's letters from 3 June 1915 to Pierre Chéreau and to Claire Croiza in *C*, 1898 and 1899, respectively.

29. MR: See p. 266 in Claude Debussy, *Monsieur Croche et autres écrits*, rev. ed. (Paris: Gallimard, 1987), 265–66; and p. 323 in Claude Debussy, *Debussy on Music*, trans. Richard Langhan Smith (New York: Alfred A. Knopf, 1977), 322–23.

30. This is what Vallas repeated, following Godet: "A certain article, signed by Debussy and published twice in 1915, had been written entirely not by the signer

but by one of his disciples and friends" (see "Réponse de M. Léon Vallas," *La revue musicale* 15, no. 147 [June 1934]: 31, written in reaction to the publication by Henry Prunières, "Autour de Debussy," *La revue musicale* 15, no. 146 [May 1934]: 349–58). One should not be surprised that Vuillermoz was not around more at Debussy's home on the avenue du Bois de Boulogne; he hated Emma. MR: See *C*, 1881 for Debussy's letter of 12 March 1915 to Vuillermoz concerning this article, and *C*, 1881n1 for more detail on its authorship.

31. MR: See Debussy's letter in *C*, 1904.

32. MR: See Debussy's letter to Jacques Durand from 7 July 1915 in *C*, 1906.

33. MR: Debussy mentioned Chouchou's condition in his letter to Durand from 7 July 1915; see *C*, 1906.

34. The BnF, département de la Musique, L.a. Debussy (C.) 4, preserves notes taken by Debussy on the applicants: "useless. . . ! / lovely voice – / knows nothing – [. . .] theatrical qualities – / continues to know nothing. / sings out of tune and from the throat – / operatic temperament – / nice."

35. MR: With this phrase, "j'ai d'autres livrets à fouetter," Debussy was punning on the idiom "j'ai d'autre chats à fouetter," (I have other fish to fry); see his letter in *C*, 1939.

36. MR: See Debussy's letter to Jacques Durand from 27 September 1915 in *C*, 1938.

37. MR: See Debussy's letter to Jacques Durand from 14 July 1915 in *C*, 1909.

38. MR: Debussy used this phrase in his letter to Durand on 14 July, implying that he lightened the texture of the score, which was too dark and "as tragic as a Goya *Caprice*"; see *C*, 1909. Francisco Goya's *Caprices* had clearly inspired the two-piano work, *Caprices en blanc et noir* (his original title for *En blanc et noir*). Most likely the composer was thinking of the "emphatic caprices" (*caprichos enfáricos*) from Goya's *The Disasters of War* (*Los desastres de la guerra*) series of etchings, which had been published posthumously in 1863, rather than the earlier *Los caprichos* (published in 1799), which vividly condemned the foibles of the society experienced by Goya.

39. MR: See Debussy's letter to Jacques Durand from 22 July 1915 in *C*, 1912.

40. MR: See *C*, 1910. In an obvious gesture of anti-German innuendo, Debussy wove Martin Luther's "Ein feste Burg" chorale melody into the musical fabric of the second movement.

41. MR: See the end of Debussy's letter to Jacques Durand from 22 July 1915 in *C*, 1912; see also *C*, 1912n1.

42. Jacques Durand, *Quelques souvenirs d'un éditeur de musique* (Paris: A. Durand & fils, 1925), 2:78. Debussy's *Rapsodie* for clarinet had been played by Louis-Jean-Baptiste Cahuzac and Philipp Jarnach at that concert.

43. MR: See Debussy's letter of 16 November 1913 in *C*, 1694.

44. MR: See Debussy's letter to Bernardino Molinari from 6 October 1915 in *C*, 1943.

45. [See Debussy's letter to Robert Godet] from 14 October 1915 [in *C*, 1947. In *C*, 1947n3, Lesure and Herlin provide context for d'Indy's support for the French classics as well as his Wagnerism.]

46. [*C*, 1916.]

47. MR: See Debussy's letter of 7 August to Durand in *C*, 1917.

48. MR: See Debussy's letter of 14 July to Durand in *C*, 1909.

49. MR: Debussy referenced a tendency toward the "black" in his second *Caprice*, comparing it to Goya's *Caprice* (in *C*, 1909), but mentioned the "gray" of Diego Velázquez in a letter to Godet from 4 February 1916 (see *C*, 1972).

50. MR: See Debussy's letter to Durand from 24 July 1915 in *C*, 1913.

51. MR: See Debussy's letter to Durand from 5 August in *C*, 1916.

52. MR: See Debussy's letter to Durand from 1 November 1915 in *C*, 1955.

53. MR: See Debussy's letter to Durand from 5 August in *C*, 1916.

54. [This calendar is conserved at the] BnF, département de la Musique, W. 54 (3). The sketches for the *Études* have been reproduced in facsimile in Claude Debussy, *Études*, ed. Roy Howat (Geneva: Éditions Minkoff, 1989).

55. MR: See Debussy's letter to Durand from 19 August 1915 in *C*, 1922–23, as well as his letter from 28 August in *C*, 1925.

56. MR: See Debussy's note to Emma from 22 August 1915 in *C*, 1923. The composer's dedications to Emma are reported in Howat's facsimile edition of Debussy, *Études*, 12n17.

57. MR: See Debussy's letter to Durand from 28 August 1915 in *C*, 1925.

58. MR: See Debussy's letter to Durand from 12 August 1915 in *C*, 1920.

59. [Refer back to Debussy's letter to Durand from] 28 August 1915 [in *C*, 1925].

60. MR: See Debussy's letter to Durand from 1 September 1915 in *C*, 1926.

61. [See Debussy's letter to Durand from] 7 September 1915 [in *C*, 1931].

62. MR: See Debussy's letter to Durand from 27 September 1915 in *C*, 1939.

63. See Debussy's letter to Robert Godet from 4 September 1916 [in *C*, 2023].

64. MR: See the attached page to his letter of 16 September 1915, sent to Jacques Durand, in which he crossed out the word "oboe" and replaced it with "viola"; see *C*, 1933n2.

65. MR: See Debussy's letter to Durand from 30 September 1915 in *C*, 1940.

66. MR: See Debussy's letter to Godet from 14 October 1915 in *C*, 1947.

67. MR: See Debussy's letter to Durand from 9 October 1915 in *C*, 1944. Debussy repeated this idea in quite similar terms in a letter written on the same day to Inghelbrecht; see *C*, 1945. Chénier was one of the last political prisoners to be guillotined by Robespierre, in July 1794. He had continued to write poetry during his 140-day imprisonment. His reputation as a poet is based mainly on his posthumously published work, and his life and fate have been immortalized in many genres, notably the opera *Andrea Chénier* by Umberto Giordano.

68. MR: Debussy referred to this concert in a letter to Jacques Durand from 1 September 1915; see *C*, 1927.

69. MR: Debussy remarked on seeing Baron in a letter to Durand from 4 October 1915; see *C*, 1941.

70. MR: See Debussy's letter to Durand of 30 September 1914 in *C*, 1848.

71. MR: See Debussy's letter to Godet of 1 January 1915 in *C*, 1862.

72. MR: See Debussy's letter to Igor Stravinsky from 24 October 1915 in *C*, 1953.

73. MR: See his letter to Stravinsky from 24 October 1915 in *C*, 1952.

74. See Satie's letter to Dukas from 18 August 1915 [in Erik Satie, *Correspondance presque complète*, ed. Ornella Volta (Paris: Librairie Arthème Fayard, 2000), 212].

75. [*C*, 1952.]

76. MR: See Debussy's letter to Jacques Durand from 25 October 1915 in *C,* 1954. FL 2003 states erroneously that the premiere of the *Berceuse héroïque* occurred two days after 24 October.

77. MR: Debussy cited Karatygin in his letter to Durand of 23 November 1915; see *C,* 1955–56, as well as other citations from him in *C,* 1956n1. Karatygin was a critic and composer who favored the works of Mussorgsky, Prokofiev, Stravinsky, and Scriabin, as well as those of Debussy and Ravel and even Schönberg.

78. MR: According to Charles Koechlin, *Debussy* (Paris: Henri Laurens, 1927), 55, Debussy's exclamation was made in response to a remark made by the disrespectful horn player. Alfredo Casella was conducting, and unfortunately Koechlin did not report his reaction to this incident.

79. MR: See his letter from 28 November 1915 in *C,* 1957.

80. [*C,* 1960.]

81. MR: See Debussy's letter to Fauré from 9 January 1916 in *C,* 1966.

82. MR: FL 2003 adds a sentence here that is not in the published version of this letter (see n83): "The disease has spread." It is conceivable that this sentence was in the original letter, shared by Jean-Paul Goujon with Lesure, and that it was excised in the publication.

83. MR: Pierre Louÿs and Georges Louis, *Correspondance croisée, 1890–1917* (Paris: Honoré Champion, 2015), 4:2209. Louÿs began this letter by (falsely) reporting Debussy's death, and then proceeded to gossip about personal details concerning his romantic life and illness.

84. MR: This letter dates from the beginning of April 1917; see *C,* 2093.

85. [See the letter of 27 December 1915 from Saint-Saëns to Fauré in] Camille Saint-Saëns and Gabriel Fauré, *Correspondance: Soixante ans d'amitié,* ed. Jean-Michel Nectoux (Paris: Heugel, 1973), 108. MR: This letter was published again in *Camille Saint-Saëns and Gabriel Fauré, Correspondance (1862–1920),* ed. Jean-Michel Nectoux (Paris: Publications de la Société française de musicologie/Éditions Klincksieck, 1994), 115; and it appeared in English translation in *The Correspondance of Camille Saint-Saëns and Gabriel Fauré: Sixty Years of Friendship,* ed. Jean-Michel Nectoux, trans. J. Barrie Jones (Aldershot: Ashgate, 2004), 108.

29. "The Factories of Nothingness": 1916–18

1. MR: See Debussy's letters to Robert Godet from 4 February 1916 in *C,* 1972, and from 6 October 1916 in *C,* 2033, as well as his letter to Paul Dukas from 19 May 1917 in *C,* 2110. He used the expression of "les usines du Néant," adapted from a line in Jules Laforgue's *Dragées grises,* as early as 1906; see his letter to Jacques Durand from 18 April 1906 in *C,* 951. Debussy's oft-repeated phrase no doubt emanates from the following line in Laforgue's "Les Dragées grises," published in *Entretiens politiques et littéraires* 2, no. 11 (1 January 1911): 9: "Je croupis dans les Usines du Négatif" (I have been stagnating in Factories of Nothingness).

2. MR: See Debussy's letter to Jacques Durand from 13 January 1916 in *C,* 1967. This comment is in reference to Debussy's colostomy procedure.

3. MR: See Debussy's letter to Emma from 8 January 1916 in *C,* 1965.

4. MR: The pertinent letter for this comment involves Debussy's note to Lemercier from 15 January 1916 in *C*, 1968. It is referenced as a "n2" in FL 2003, but not attached to any text. Furthermore, the "n1" in FL 2003, attached to the present comment, is an error; it references Debussy's letter to Gabriel Fauré from 9 January 1915 [*recte* 1916], in the BnF, département de la Musique, N.L. a-3 (75). However, this letter (in *C*, 1966) is cited more appropriately in n81 of the previous chapter.

5. MR: See letter of 31 January 1916 from Emma Debussy to Louis-Pasteur Vallery-Radot in *C*, 1970. Emma added that her husband was facing a long convalescence.

6. MR: See Debussy's letter to Louis-Pasteur Vallery-Radot from 15 February 1916 in *C*, 1976.

7. See Debussy's letter to Martenot from 4 February [in *C*, 1973].

8. MR: A brief notice for this concert appeared in "London Concerts," *The Musical Times* 57, no. 878 (1 April 1916): 202. The author commented that the work "did not prove especially interesting, although it was finely played."

9. MR: See "Spectacles et concerts: Concerts annoncés," *Journal de Genève* (9 March 1916): 6.

10. MR: According to the brief review in "Les concerts," *Journal de Genève* (17 March 1916): 8, Mme Rolland-Maugé (NB the different spelling of her name, compared to the notice cited in n9) sang Debussy's three Mallarmé songs in addition to the "Noël des enfants qui n'ont plus de maison," which was encored. The reviewer also noted that M. Vianna da Motta filled in for the absent Mme Panthès; he accompanied the cellist Allard and also performed Debussy's "La cathédrale engloutie."

11. Gaston G. [*sic*], "Mots sur. . . Claude Debussy," *L'intransigeant* (24 February 1929): 2; Gaston Courty, "Dernières années de Debussy: Lettres inédites," *La revue des deux mondes* (15 May 1958): 313. MR: See Debussy's letter of 18 June 1916 to Gaston Courty in *C*, 2002.

12. MR: See Segalen's letter of 4 May 1916 in Victor Segalen, *Correspondance II (1912–1919)*, ed. Annie Joly-Segalen, Dominique Lelong, and Philippe Postel (Paris: Librairie Arthème Fayard, 2004), 743.

13. MR: See Debussy's letter to Paul Dukas from 17 May 1916 in *C*, 1992.

14. MR: See Debussy's letter to Jacques Durand from 4 May 1916 in *C*, 1988.

15. MR: See Debussy's letter to Jacques Durand from 6 May 1916 in *C*, 1990.

16. See Debussy's letter of 15 June 1916 to Robert Godet [in *C*, 2002].

17. MR: This letter was written to Miguel Salvador on 18 April 1916; see *C*, 1987.

18. MR: This letter dates from 22 May 1916; see *C*, 1994–95.

19. MR: See Debussy's letter to Jacques Durand from 8 June 1916 in *C*, 2000.

20. MR: See Debussy's letter to Jacques Durand from 3 July 1916 in *C*, 2006.

21. *C*, 2006. MR: Debussy refers to Planté's performance in his letter to Jacques Durand from 3 July 1916 in *C*, 2006. As Lesure and Herlin point out in *C*, 2006n2, Planté's idea was to focus on wartime repertoire, performing near the altars in churches, hidden by plants, so the audience would be able to experience the full evocative power of the music.

22. MR: See Debussy's letter from 21 July 2016 to his lawyer in *C*, 2008.

23. MR: Lesure cites the date of 28 July 1916 for this response to Maud Allan. In fact, the quote is from a letter to Allan dated 30 July; see *C*, 2013. However, Debussy

did write to Maud Allan, and also separately to her conductor, Ernest Bloch, on 28 July, to suggest that Bloch revise the score of *Khamma*; see *C*, 2011–12 for his letter to Allan, and *C*, 2012–13 for his letter to Bloch, as well as n24 below for details.

24. MR: See *C*, 2013. As Lesure and Herlin point out in *C*, 2013n1, Bloch viewed the proposal that he reduce *Khamma* for forty musicians to be "incredibly nervy"; he was not about to spend months of his time revising a project for which Debussy had already been paid.

25. MR: The bugler school trained military musicians, and Debussy mentioned the raging sounds they created, noting that they were improving while his health was not, in a letter of 10 August to Paul Dukas; see *C*, 2016.

26. MR: See Debussy's letter of 4 September 1916 to Robert Godet in *C*, 2022; in *C*, 2022n3, Lesure and Herlin explain the fascinating and complex connection of Debussy's allusion to Weber's *La dernière pensée* (known as his "Last Waltz" in English).

27. MR: See Dukas's letter to Poujaud from 31 July 1916, now conserved at Yale University, Music Library Special Collections, Misc. Ms. 288. An excerpt from this letter is cited in *C*, 2016n1.

28. [See Dukas's letter to Poujaud from 11 March 1915, now conserved at Yale University, Music Library Special Collections, Misc. Ms. 288. An excerpt from this letter is cited in *C*, 1879n2.] Poujaud had not remained very fond of Debussy. On 10 April 1913, he wrote to his mother: "Debussy has become an upstart, a pontiff, a hedonist," in contrast to the simplicity of d'Indy.

29. MR: See Debussy's letter of 4 September 1916 to Robert Godet in *C*, 2021.

30. See Debussy's letter of 5 September 1916 [in *C*, 2024].

31. MR: See Debussy's letter of 19 September 1916 to Dukas in *C*, 2028.

32. MR: See Debussy's letter of 15 September 1916 to Inghelbrecht in *C*, 2027.

33. MR: See Debussy's letter of 19 September 1916 to Dukas in *C*, 2028. FL 2003 adds that Debussy was responding to a letter that Dukas had recently sent in which he announced his marriage.

34. MR: See Debussy's of 30 September 1916 to Rummel in *C*, 2031. One wonders if Debussy heard some of Duparc's works for piano, less known today, as opposed to some of the seventeen exquisite songs on which his musical legacy is based.

35. MR: See Debussy's letter of 14 September 1916 in *C*, 2026.

36. MR: See Debussy's letter of 6 October 1916 in *C*, 2034.

37. In his programs, Rosoor claimed, in addition, to have heard these comments from the composer himself; for example: "Pierrot wakes with a start, and shakes off his sleepiness. He rushes off, serenades his lady friend, who, in spite of his entreaties, remains unreceptive; he consoles himself by singing a song of freedom." MR: One of Rosoor's grandchildren, Antoine Pery, has written about the origin of this performance indication; see his "Louis Rosoor et l'interprétation de la *Sonate pour violoncelle et piano* de Debussy," *Cahiers Debussy* 39 (2015): 30–45. Facsimiles of two of Rosoor's concert programs (from 20 November 1922 and 5 June 1923, reproduced on pp. 36 and 38) print virtually the same language. Rosoor's annotated copy of Debussy's score (see p. 35) reveals yet another variant of this comment, handwritten at the top of the first page of music.

38. [See his letter of 12 October 1916 in *C*, 2036.] This lack of understanding would unexpectedly persist; it is still evident in nearly all of the biographies and studies on Debussy.

39. [*C*, 2037.]

40. MR: FL 2003 reports that Debussy "desired" (*envie*) rather than that he "was troubled" (*ennui*) by Busser's proposal to orchestrate the "Noël." *C*, 2040 clearly reports the latter text.

41. [*C*, 2040.]

42. [*C*, 2040.] In his memoirs, as in several other places, Busser's memory was faulty; according to him, Debussy supposedly said: "No, no, I've already rejected that idea with André Caplet. I want this piece to be sung with the most discreet piano accompaniment" (Henri Busser, *De* Pelléas *aux* Indes galantes [Paris: Librairie Arthème Fayard, 1955], 204).

43. Darius Milhaud, who was twenty-four years old at the time, described how he paid a visit to Debussy, who played the sonata for him twice, hands trembling, on the piano (*Essays on Music: An Anthology from "The Listener*," ed. Felix Aprahamian [London: Cassell, 1967], 79–80).

44. MR: See Debussy's letter of 14 December 1916 to Jacques Durand in *C*, 2059. The premiere took place on 10 December 2016; see Debussy's letter to Robert Godet in *C*, 2056 as well as *C*, 2056n5.

45. MR: This concert took place on 14 December 1916; see *C*, 2050n1. Debussy referred to the event in his letter to Rummel from 26 November 1916; see *C*, 2050.

46. MR: In addition to playing with Roger-Ducasse, Debussy accompanied Jane Bathori in several songs, including the "Noël des enfants qui n'ont plus de maison"; see *C*, 2060n2 for details.

47. [*C*, 2076–77.]

48. MR: See Gabriel Fauré, "Appel aux musiciens français," *Le courrier musical* 19 (15 March 1917): 133. Fauré's original manuscript is housed in The Morgan Library & Museum.

49. MR: Literally "white ballet," which is a term that describes the pure classical form of ballet in which the female dancers wear white tutus.

50. See p. 376 in Henry Prunières, "Portraits et médaillons de musiciens," part of chapter 12 in *Cinquante ans de musique française de 1874 à 1925*, ed. Ladislas Rohozinski (Paris: Les Éditions musicales de la Librairie de France, 1926), 2:371–76.

51. Debussy gave her a signed photo of himself that had been taken by Otto [Wegener, a Swedish-born photographer who worked in Paris and was linked with figures such as Marcel Proust and Countess Greffuhle.]

52. MR: See Debussy's letter to Croiza from 27 February 2017, in which he invited her to visit the following afternoon, in *C*, 2079.

53. See his letter of 10 March 1917 to Joseph Schurmann [in *C*, 2084].

54. MR: See Manuel de Falla, "Prólogo de la Música francesca contemporánea," *Revista musical Hispano-Americana* (July 1916): 3; and Manuel de Falla, *Écrits sur la musique et sur les musiciens*, trans. Jean-Dominique Krynen (Arles: Actes Sud, 1992), 57.

55. MR: See *C*, 2085n1 for details on this premiere of Debussy's *Sonate en trio*, performed by Albert Manouvrier (flute), Sigismond Jarecki (viola), and Pierre

Jamet (harp). Many other works were presented on the same program: Rose Féart and Debussy performed the *Trois ballades de François Villon*, the first series of *Fêtes galantes*, and the "Noël des enfants qui n'ont plus de maison"; Walter Morse Rummel played the second series of *Images* as well as "Danseuses de Delphes" and "La danse de Puck" from the first book of *Préludes*, and he began the concert with his own transcription of three chorale preludes and a fugue in C Major by J. S. Bach.

56. MR: Debussy referred to this rehearsal in a brief letter to Gaston Poulet on 14 March 1917; see *C*, 2085.

57. MR: Debussy asked Claire Croiza to sing at the last minute, as Rose Féart was indisposed; see his letter to Croiza, written on 17 March 1917 in *C*, 2087. Works performed on this concert included *Le promenoir des deux amants*, two of the *Proses lyriques* ("De grève" and "De soir"), the "Noël des enfants qui n'ont plus de maison," as well as the *Six épigraphes antiques* for piano, four hands (performed by Walter Rummel and Thérèse Chaigneau) and the String Quartet (played by the Gaston Poulet Quartet).

58. MR: This concert was announced in "L'organisation des secours," *Le temps* (20 March 1917): 2, although some of the performers changed. FL 2003 and the announcement in *Le temps* state that Rose Féart was to sing, but it appears that Claire Croiza replaced her yet again (see n57); see Debussy's letter to Jacques Durand from 22 March 2017 in *C*, 2090. Further details of this event are given in *C*, 2088n1. On this same concert, Jeanne Dalliès performed the *Deux danses* for harp as well as the *Sonate pour flûte, alto et harpe* (with Sigismond Jarecki on harp and Albert Manouvrier on flute).

59. Robert Orledge, *Debussy and the Theatre* (Cambridge: Cambridge University Press, 1982), 175. MR: See Debussy's letter to Jacques Durand from 14 April 1917 in *C*, 2098.

60. [*C*, 2099.]

61. MR: See Jean d'Udine, "Les grands concerts," *Le courrier musical* 8, no. 21 (1 November 1905): 610–11.

62. MR: See Jean d'Udine, "Les grands concerts: Concerts Colonne et Lamoureux," *Le courrier musical* 13, no. 5 (1 March 1910): 194.

63. MR: See Jean d'Udine's letter of 27 April 1917 in *C*, 2103.

64. MR: Cocteau's tribute was in the form of a poem and printed in the program; see Robert Orledge, *Satie the Composer* (Cambridge: Cambridge University Press, 1990), 222 and 361n46.

65. [*C*, 2083]. Robert Godet ("En marge de la marge," *La revue musicale* [May 1926]: 84 [180]) remembered that Satie "then bore the title of Precursor with some pride, like a relic, that he had taken on from his own lofty initiative" since 1902, while emphasizing that Debussy's article "Du précurseur" (On the precursor) in *S. I. M.* (15 March 1913) was doubtless written in part with Satie in mind. [Debussy's article is reprinted in Claude Debussy, *Monsieur Croche et autres écrits*, rev. ed. (Paris: Gallimard, 1987), 232–37; and in Claude Debussy, *Debussy on Music*, trans. Richard Langham Smith (New York: Alfred A. Knopf, 1977), 281–86.] In 1920, while dedicating his *Quatre petites mélodies* to Debussy's memory, Satie wanted to remember only "an admiring and dear friendship of thirty years" (en souvenir d'une admirative et douce amitié de trente ans). MR: Ornella Volta, in Erik Satie,

Écrits (Paris: Éditions Champ Libre, 1977), 263, points out that this dedication was for the "Élégie," the first of the four songs.

66. Debussy wrote to Dandelot [see his letter of 18 May 1917 in *C*, 2109] that he was at the theater the day before (on the 17th, when there were no performances, but no doubt there was a rehearsal); in his letter to Diaghilev from 20 May [see *C*, 2113], he wrote that he had been there "last Wednesday"—in other words, 16 May.

67. MR: See Debussy's letter of 26 May 1917 to Diaghilev in *C*, 2116.

68. [*C*, 2092.]

69. MR: Francis Poulenc, *J'écris ce qui me chante*, ed. Nicolas Southon (Paris: Librairie Arthème Fayard, 2011), 306.

70. MR: See Debussy's letter to Fauré from 18 May 1917 in *C*, 2110.

71. MR: See Debussy's letter to Paul-Jean Toulet from 7 June 1917 in *C*, 2117. Firmin Gémier (whose real name was Firmin Tonerre) was a French actor and theatrical director whose most famous roles included, among others, Shylock in Shakespeare's *The Merchant of Venice* and Ubu in Alfred Jarry's *Ubu roi*. He created the latter role with Lugné-Poe in 1896 and the former role for the Société Shakespeare in 1917. See Firmin Gémier, *Firmin Gémier, le démocrate du théâtre*, ed. Nathalie Coutelet (Montpellier: Éditions l'Entretemps, 2008).

72. MR: In a letter to Paul Baudry, written from Guéthary in spring 1918, Toulet mentioned Debussy's passing, and reminisced about their collaboration on *As You Like It* while the composer was at Saint-Jean-de-Luz in 1917; see *Les Autographes: Autographes, lettres et manuscrits, documents et souvenirs* catalog 140 (Paris, July 2015), item 280.

73. MR: See Debussy's letter of 20 June 1917 to Paul-Jean Toulet in *C*, 2123.

74. André Schaeffner, "Ses projets Shakespeariens" in *Essais de musicologie et autres fantaisies* (Paris: Le Sycomore, 1980), 216; republished in *Variations sur la musique* (Paris: Librairie Arthème Fayard, 1998), 309.

75. Élisabeth de Gramont, *Mémoires* (Paris: Éditions Bernard Grasset, 1932), 3:172. At the end of 1914, she had organized a gala for the refugees of the Aisne, with a performance by Ninon Vallin and Debussy; given the success of "Mandoline," Debussy muttered angrily, in her presence: "They always prefer the bad pieces." MR: See in Gramont's *Mémoires*, 3:102.

76. MR: See Debussy's letter of 28 June 1917 to Jacques Durand in *C*, 2125. FL 2003 calls the conductor Bernardo instead of Bernardino, and lists only one concert, when three were actually given.

77. R. D., "Concerts Franco-Italiens." *Le courrier musical* 19 (July–August 1917): 285–86. MR: The critic also mentioned a work by Mussorgsky, which surely was closer to Debussy's aesthetic. It is likely that the Elgar work was performed, along with the Beethoven Violin Concerto in D Major, op. 61, and some works by Gaspare Spontini, Niccolò Paganini, and Chopin, on an earlier concert within the series of three that were reviewed.

78. Debussy's letter to Jacques Durand of 22 July 1917 [is available in *C*, 2131; as Lesure and Herlin point out in *C*, 2131n5, the Maeterlinck quotation comes from Pelléas's words to Mélisande at the beginning of act 2, scene 1].

79. The impression one gets from reading Marguerite Long (*Au piano avec Claude Debussy* [Paris: René Julliard, 1960]; and *At the Piano with Debussy*, English

trans. Olive Senior-Ellis [London: Dent, 1972]) is that during his visit to the Chalet Habas, Debussy was especially busy working with her. The 169 pages of her original book could only have been written by mixing all sorts of other accounts with the few sessions that the composer was able to grant her.

80. Debussy's letter to Inghelbrecht from [around 20] August 1917 [in *C*, 2141].

81. Debussy's letter to Jacques Durand [from the end of August 1917; see *C*, 2146–47].

82. Debussy's letter to Jacques Durand from [12] September 1917 [in *C*, 2149; in *C*, 2149n2, Lesure and Herlin reveal details of the concerts, gleaned from a letter written by Emma to Arthur Hartmann in September 1924].

83. Writing to Debussy on 16 August, Godet directed this questionable entreaty to him, as a form of encouragement: "Let the inspiration of little children come to you, at the appropriate time; be very sure—whatever you do—to rob from Ravel, in one fell swoop, the glory of immortalizing his homeland (as he seems to want to do, for, wasn't he born near the village of Habas?). But his articulated Pickwick marionette will only be able to move with the help of strings." MR: See Godet's letter in *C*, 2140.

84. MR: See Debussy's letter of 27 September 1917 to Jacques Durand in *C*, 2151.

85. MR: See Debussy's letter to Jacques Durand from 12 September 1917 in *C*, 2148.

86. MR: See Debussy's letter to Jacques Durand from 27 September 1917 in *C*, 2152. The treaty of Brest-Litovsk was signed on 3 March 1918 and ended Russia's participation in World War I. It also gave independence to a number of eastern European nations (such as the Balkan states of Estonia, Latvia, and Lithuania, as well as Belarus, the Ukraine, and Finland) that had been under Russian rule.

87. MR: See Debussy's letter to Robert Godet, ascribed the date of 31 October 1917 by Lesure and Herlin, in *C*, 2158.

88. MR: See Debussy's letter to Robert Godet, ascribed the date of 31 October 1917 by Lesure and Herlin, in *C*, 2158.

89. MR: See Debussy's letter to Gaston Poulet from 18 October 1917 in *C*, 2155.

90. MR: See Debussy's letter to Alfred Bruneau from 21 October 1917 in *C*, 2156.

91. MR: See Debussy's letter of 24 October 1917 in *C*, 2156–57.

92. MR: See Debussy's letter, presumably from 31 October 1917, to Robert Godet in *C*, 2159.

93. MR: See Debussy's letter, presumably from 31 October 1917, to Robert Godet in *C*, 2158–59.

94. [*C*, 2160.]

95. MR: The *Ode à la France* was completed, at Emma's behest, by Marius-François Gaillard and published by Choudens in 1928. For details, see especially pp. 64–65 in Caroline Rae, "Debussyist, Modernist, Exoticist: Marius-François Gaillard Rediscovered," *The Musical Times* 152, no. 1916 (Autumn 2011): 59–80.

96. MR: See Godet's letter to Debussy in *C*, 2176.

97. MR: Godet's letter is reproduced in *C*, 2176–82.

98. MR: See Emma's letter to Marie Toulet in *C*, 2173.

99. MR: In *C*, 2183n3, Lesure and Herlin cite more details as well as the sources for this exchange of letters between Toulet and Pasteur Vallery-Radot.

100. [*C*, 2183n3.]

101. MR: Although FL 2003 gives a date of 31 December for Debussy's message, Lesure and Herlin ascribe the date of 1 January 1918 to this incomplete note; see *C*, 2168. According to Lesure and Herlin, the composer wrote yet another note to Emma on 8 January 1918; see *C*, 2172.

102. MR: Laloy described the dress rehearsal as having taken place during the afternoon of 21 March, so as to avoid the aerial bombardment of the city during the evenings; see Louis Laloy, *La musique retrouvée* (Paris: Librairie Plon, 1928), 238–39.

103. MR: Debussy had written a glowing review for the 2 February 1903 issue of *Gil Blas*; see Debussy, *Monsieur Croche et autres écrits*, rev. ed., 89–93, and Debussy, *Debussy on Music*, 110–13.

104. Jacques Durand, *Quelques souvenirs d'un éditeur de musique* (Paris: A. Durand & fils, 1925), 2:90–91.

105. On 24 March, with the consent of Widor and Marcel Baschet, Emma did her best to forge Debussy's signature at the bottom of a letter of application to the Institut for the position of Widor, whose vacancy had been declared the previous day [see *C*, 2189]. Some days after Rodin's death, on 18 November 1917, a similar ploy had been attempted by the sculptor's inner circle.

106. MR: See the letter of 8 April 1918 from Chouchou Debussy to Raoul Bardac in *C*, 2195–96.

107. Laloy, *La musique retrouvée*, 229. MR: Laloy added that both Camille Chevillard and Gabriel Pierné made the trek to the cemetery on foot.

108. MR: The French is "union sacrée," a phrase that was first used by Raymond Poincaré, the president of the Republic, in a speech that he gave on 4 August 1914, but was also employed by Debussy in a letter to Xavier Leroux on 30 November 1916; see *C*, 2051 as well as *C*, 2051n2 for further context.

109. Camille Bellaigue, "Revue musicale: Claude Debussy—*Castor et Pollux* à l'Opéra," *Revue des deux mondes* 88, no. 45 (1 May 1918), 458.

110. MR: See Henri Quittard, "Claude Debussy," *Le Figaro* (27 March 1918): 3.

111. MR: See Pierre Lalo, "La musique: Claude Debussy," *Le temps* (27 May 1918): 3.

112. MR: Lalo, "La musique: Claude Debussy," 3. FL 2003 cites only the first phrase of this comment.

113. MR: Julien Tiersot, in "Claude Debussy," *Le courrier musical* 20 (15 April 1918): 171, described Debussy's music as "infinitely subtle and rare." The 1 and 15 April issues of *Le courrier musical* contained articles by several different authors, all of whom commented on the musical legacy left by the recently deceased composer.

114. MR: FL 2003 attributes this remark to Carraud's writing in his column in *La liberté*; while Carraud did pen a brief obituary in "Claude Debussy," *La liberté* (1 April 1918): [2], this particular citation comes from his more elaborate remarks in "Les concerts: Association Colonne–Lamoureux (Concerts du 24 et du 31 mars)," published in *Le courrier musical* 20 (15 April 1918): 179.

Index of Works

"Apparition," 50, 91, 441n88
"L'archet," 80, 172
Ariettes, 56, 61, 65–66, 72, 74, 77, 80–81, 97, 410n66, 430n14
Ariettes oubliées, 196, 208–9, 215, 286, 310, 317, 439n68, 445n41, 450n14, 467n35, 468n47, 478n25
Axël, 78, 146

"Ballade à la lune," 28
Ballade slave, 88, 95, 191, 196
"Beau soir," 95
"La belle au bois dormant," 92, 116, 430n16
"Berceuse," 152
Berceuse héroïque, 321, 324, 336
La boîte à joujoux, 297–98, 310, 315

"Caprice," 36
Chansons de Bilitis, 131, 141, 144, 150–51, 158, 164–65, 191, 197–98, 209, 232, 276, 315, 445n41, 466n29, 467n35
Chansons de Bilitis (incidental music), 166, 170, 318
Chansons de Charles d'Orléans, 141, 247, 252, 263, 276, 301
"Chanson espagnole," 45
Children's Corner, 232, 247, 249, 270, 276, 285, 314–15, 317, 492n66
La chute de la maison Usher, 97, 190, 247, 255, 267, 309, 329, 405n34
Cinq poèmes de Baudelaire, 75, 78, 80–81, 84–86, 90, 92–94, 101, 103, 120, 144, 191, 209, 214, 235–36, 389n112, 445n41, 446n43, 449n100, 450n14
"Clair de lune," 144, 196, 285, 446n43, 450n14

"Les cloches," 370n45
"Coquetterie posthume," 45
Crimen amoris, 285–86, 309–10, 322

La damoiselle élue, 73, 75–77, 81, 86, 92, 97, 100, 103, 105, 107–9, 111, 118–20, 128, 130, 134, 141, 146, 154, 165–66, 191, 193, 196, 208, 249, 252, 257, 303, 395n64, 450n4, 456n4
Daniel, 42
Danse bohémienne, 32
Deux arabesques, 141, 208, 224
Deux danses, 219, 317, 332
Le diable dans le beffroi, 199, 204–5, 212, 232, 247–48, 255, 285, 309
Diane au bois, 45, 64
D'un cahier d'esquisses, 200, 206, 262, 434n86

Élégie, 325
"Les elfes," 40
En blanc et noir, 228, 322–23, 325, 331, 479n36
"En sourdine," 44, 196, 478n25
L'enfant prodigue, 52, 55–56, 75, 81, 239, 272, 367n9
Épigraphes antiques, 318, 502n57
Estampes, 202–5, 207–9, 224, 228, 232, 238, 258, 270–71, 285, 305, 315, 328
Études, 1, 319, 323–24, 328, 330–31

Fantaisie pour piano et orchestra, 82, 84, 86–87, 95, 105, 114, 133, 145, 191
"Fantoches," 40, 66, 449n100, 467n35, 473n23
"Fête galante," 40
Fêtes galantes: Series I, 285; Series II, 285, 462n56

"La fille aux cheveux de lin," (piano prelude), 258, 263, 265, 310, 313
"La fille aux cheveux de lin," (song), 36
"Fleur des blés," 95
"Flots, palmes, sables," 42

Le gladiateur, 45, 52

Hélène, 36, 38, 55
Hommage à Haydn, 258
Hymnis, 42

Images oubliées, 395n64
Images pour piano, 116, 199, 315, 453n61; Series I, 229, 232, 259, 285, 335, 432n53, 470n89; Series II, 240, 244, 462n56, 502n55
Images pour orchestre, 1, 199, 203, 232–33, 239, 250, 255, 258, 260–62, 269, 272–73, 280, 282, 290, 295–96, 301, 303, 312, 332, 337, 447n71
Intermezzo, 42
Invocation, 45
L'isle joyeuse, 200, 215–16, 218, 223–24, 228, 237, 271, 285, 312, 433n55

"Jane," 36
Jeux, 289–90, 294–95, 298–300, 309, 314, 332, 354n2

Khamma, 268–69, 284, 290, 310, 315, 328–29

"Le lilas," 360n1
Lindaraja, 170

"Madrid," 28
"Mandoline," 44, 66, 79, 208, 272, 503n75
Marche écossaise, 95, 110, 125–26, 144, 191, 196, 303, 305, 307, 312–13
Le martyre de saint Sébastien, 273, 276–81, 284, 289, 301, 304, 310, 336, 342n8
Masques, 200, 217, 223, 237
Masques et bergamasques, 254, 268

Mazurka, 95, 191
La mer, 202–3, 208, 211, 218, 223, 226–29, 232, 235, 241–43, 245, 257, 262, 269, 272, 280, 282, 305, 307, 312, 332, 334, 354n2, 388n91, 459n60

Nocturne, 103
Nocturne et scherzo, 40, 42
Nocturnes, 103, 126–27, 149, 155, 161–64, 166–71, 173, 179, 197–98, 203, 208–10, 223, 227, 231, 236–37, 240, 251, 257, 264–65, 269, 272, 298, 305–7, 313, 315, 321, 324–25, 336, 402n48
"Noël des enfants qui n'ont plus de maison," 325, 327, 331, 336, 501n46, 502n55, 502n57
No-Ja-Li. See *Le palais du silence*
Nuits blanches, 153, 190
"Nuit d'étoiles," 40

Ode à la France, 336
Ouverture Diane, 38–39

Page d'album, 468n50, 495n25
Le palais du silence, 310, 391
"Pantomime," 477n21
"Paysage sentimental," 46, 61, 69, 72, 116, 430n16
Pelléas et Mélisande, 2, 84, 88, 97, 113–16, 118, 125–28, 130, 133, 135, 138, 141–49, 157–59, 161–64, 167–68, 170–72, 174–77, 179–82, 184–97, 199, 202–5, 208–11, 215, 221, 223–24, 226–27, 233–36, 242–47, 249–50, 253–54, 256–58, 262, 275–76, 279–81, 283–84, 292–93, 298, 300–301, 312–14, 317, 321, 324, 329, 334, 339, 383n41, 390n21, 407n16
Petite suite, 81, 224, 240, 269, 317
La plus que lente, 265
Pour le piano, 141, 150, 170–71, 179, 184, 197–98, 201, 237, 259, 335
Prélude à l'après-midi d'un faune, 94, 104, 120, 127–30, 132–34, 138, 144, 150, 170, 193, 198, 206, 208, 223–24, 229,

235, 243, 251–52, 257, 264, 269, 271–72, 280, 283, 287, 298, 305, 307, 312–13, 317, 335, 357n41, 408n28, 410n51
Préludes, 273, 275–76, 279, 301, 309, 313, 315; Book One, 258, 262–63, 285, 310; Book Two, 258, 282, 297
Printemps, 75, 81, 285, 303, 306, 315, 378n66, 462n42, 477nn17–18
Le printemps, ("L'aimable printemps"), 52, 68, 372n71
Le printemps, ("Salut printemps"), 42, 360n2
Le promenoir des deux amants, 275, 285, 301, 502n57
Proses lyriques, 103, 118–20, 153–54, 197–98, 208, 214, 252, 270, 301, 315, 502n57, 437n29

Rapsodie pour clarinette, 275, 281, 305, 307, 396n42
Rapsodie pour orchestre et saxophone, 432n45
"Regret," 57
Rêverie, 95
Rodrigue et Chimène, 79, 86–89, 97, 100, 108, 114
Le roi Lear, 211, 218, 235
"Romance" ("L'âme évaporée"), 370n45
"Romance" ("Voici que le printemps"), 50
"La romance d'Ariel," 50
"Rondeau," 359n64
"Rondel chinois," 40
"Les roses," 40

Salammbô, 64, 220, 226
La saulaie, 137–38, 148, 161
Scènes au crépuscule, 103, 105, 162
"Séguidille," 45, 403n54
Sonate pour flûte, alto et harpe, 323–24, 327, 331–32, 334
Sonate pour violon et piano, 323, 330, 333
Sonate pour violoncelle et piano, 323, 325, 327, 330
"Souhait," 38
String Quartet, 86, 103, 116–17, 120, 127–28, 130, 165, 197, 208, 218, 224, 237, 270–71, 314–15, 502n57
Suite bergamasque, 95, 191, 200–201
Symphony in B Minor, 37
Syrinx, 304

Tarentelle styrienne, 88, 95, 164, 191, 208
Trio, 32
"Triolet à Phillis" ("Zéphyr"), 38
Le triomphe de Bacchus, 42
Trois ballades de François Villon, 263, 275–76, 302, 322, 475n68
Trois chansons de Charles d'Orléans, 141, 247, 252, 263, 276, 301, 384n48, 475n68
Trois chansons de France, 212, 214, 224, 232, 247, 252, 276
Trois mélodies de Verlaine, 86, 171, 208–9, 229, 389n113, 433n70
Trois poèmes de Stéphane Mallarmé, 303, 314

Valse romantique, 88–89, 95–96, 191, 196

Zuleima, 64

Subject Index

Académie des Beaux-Arts, 52–53, 314, 317, 362n25, 372n72, 374n24
Adam, Paul, 97
Aicard, Jean, 253
Albéniz, Isaac, 15, 137, 261, 264, 316
Allais, Alphonse, 96
Allan, Maud, 268–69, 284, 290–91, 310, 329
Allard, Léonce, 327, 349n42
Almanz, Fernand, 253
Alvarez, Albert, 193
Andersen, Hans Christian, 258
André, Jeanne, 72
Anély, Max. *See* Segalen, Victor
Annunzio, Gabriele D'. *See* D'Annunzio, Gabriele
Ansermet, Ernest, 257, 336
Antoine, André, 146–47, 211, 218
Apaches, 171, 188–89, 214
Arnaud, Edmond, 224
Arosa, Achille, 4–5, 17
Arosa, Gustave, 5
Artus, Henri, 235
Artus, Louis, 252
Astruc, Gabriel, 238, 271, 273–74, 277, 298, 302–4, 309, 321, 387n81, 406n51, 462n38
Auber, Daniel, 13, 181, 187
Aubert, Louis, 325, 431n22, 466n26
Aubry, Marie, 113
Auer, Leopold, 358n58
Axilette, Alexis, 66, 68
Azéma, Louis, 249

Babaïan, Marguerite, 275
Bach, Johann Sebastian, 10, 14, 17, 48, 65, 128, 205, 263, 322, 332, 334, 362n35, 362n37, 379n86, 411n73

Bachelet, Alfred, 56, 75, 177
Bagès, Maurice, 75, 80, 83, 208
Baillot, René-Paul, 21, 350n58
Bailly, Edmond, 90–92, 100, 103, 105, 125, 130, 173, 196, 207, 231, 394n49
Bakst, Léon, 254, 277, 289, 299
Balakirev, Mily, 43, 74, 128, 141, 193, 286
Baldensperger, Fernand, 198
Ballets Russes, 254, 268, 274, 286, 288, 298, 301, 402n41, 480n50
Balmont, Constantin, 300
Banès, Antoine, 23
Banville, Théodore de, 25, 36–38, 42, 45, 64–65, 138, 359n64, 360n1
Barat, Joseph Édouard, 208
Barbier, Jules, 52, 87
Barbotin, William, 61, 68
Bárczy, Gustáv, 270, 470n93, 470n97
Bardac, Emma, 205, 213–18, 222, 229–31, 241, 248, 251, 254, 266–70, 273–75, 280–82, 302, 305–6, 312–13, 319, 321–23, 325, 327, 329–30, 333, 336–37, 341n1, 451n18, 453n61, 464n84, 468n50, 483n10, 490n17, 492n65
Bardac, Raoul, 168, 171, 197, 205, 212–13, 215, 230, 232, 259, 319, 337, 404n8, 441n90, 448n83
Bardac, Sigismond, 205, 212–13, 215, 222, 302
Baron, Émile, 67, 91
Baron, 324
Barrère, Georges, 129
Barrie, James Matthew, 297
Bartók, Béla, 228, 270, 316
Baschet, Marcel, 68, 505n105
Bataille, Henry, 429n1, 456n3

SUBJECT INDEX

Bathori, Jane, 209, 224, 252, 272, 275–76, 324, 332, 453n62, 455n95, 458n43
Baudelaire, Charles, 47, 75, 78, 81, 84–86, 89–90, 94, 96, 101, 120, 125, 144, 177, 179, 190–91, 198, 210, 214, 235–36, 258, 301, 389n112, 450n14
Baudoux, Émile, 128
Baudry, Paul, 35, 63, 373n4, 503n72
Bauer, Emily Frances, 248
Bauer, Harold, 249
Bazille, Auguste, 29
Bazin, François, 16
Beardsley, Aubrey, 79, 120
Beauclair, Henri. *See* Floupette, Adoré
Bédier, Joseph, 239, 252
Beethoven, Ludwig van, 20–21, 25, 40, 59, 115, 131, 168, 173, 226, 292, 320, 503n77
Bellaigue, Camille, 14–15, 17–18, 20–22, 24, 80, 154, 257, 338
Bellon, Jean, 128
Bennigsen, Alexandra, 38
Benois, Alexandre, 254
Benoit, Camille, 27, 77, 86, 93, 108, 127
Bérard, Léon, 292
Berlioz, Hector, 176–77, 226, 292, 346n51
Bernhardt, Sarah, 440n83
Bertault, Léon, 267, 302, 311
Bertrand, Eugène, 109
Bérys, José de, 257, 459n55
Besnard, Albert, 116, 406n46
Billa, René, 208
Bizet, Georges, 15, 22, 31, 33, 35, 60, 87, 127, 180, 219, 382n18, 403n54
Blanche, Jacques-Émile, 35, 71, 113, 199–200, 204, 259, 289, 299, 369n34, 440n83
Blitz, David, 224
Bloch, Ernest, 329
Blumenberg, M., 263
Bobeuf, George Alexis. *See* Ghasne
Boidin-Puisais, Mme, 55, 372n75
Boieldieu, François-Adrien, 187
Bois, Jules, 91, 100, 210

Bonaparte, Charlotte, 56
Bongard, Mme, 332
Bonheur, Raymond, 14, 17, 24–25, 39, 76–79, 82, 99, 104, 108, 110–11, 113–14, 116, 124, 132, 139–40, 144–45, 220, 223, 385n57
Bonis, Mélanie, 39
Bonnard, Pierre, 249
Bonniot, Edmond, 303
Bordes, Charles, 108, 116, 126, 189, 334–35, 455n99
Borodin, Alexander, 74, 120, 333
Botticelli, Sandro, 68
Bouchenez, Louis. *See* Baron
Boucherit, Magdeleine, 224
Bouchor, Maurice, 40, 77
Bouilhet, Louis, 40
Boulanger, Ernest, 16
Boulanger, Lili, 331
Boulez, Pierre, 476n81, 485n47
Boulogne, R., 293
Bour, Armand, 277
Bourbon, Jean, 235, 253
Bourdeau, Eugène, 160
Bourgault-Ducoudray, Louis-Albert, 34, 363n38
Bourgeat, General, 190–91, 200
Bourgeois, Jeanne, 235
Bourget, Paul, 46–47, 50, 56, 60–61, 64, 95, 477n20
Boyer, Georges, 64, 99
Brahms, Johannes, 66, 358n58
Brahy, Édouard, 208
Brayer, Jules de, 75, 77, 79, 112–13, 116
Bréval, Lucienne, 109, 197, 232, 466n29
Bréville, Pierre de, 75, 80, 83, 108, 121, 126, 148, 154, 166, 172, 189
Bruch, Max, 98
Bruneau, Alfred, 33, 43, 72, 120, 127, 134, 165, 167, 177, 187, 227, 261, 264, 279, 296, 321, 335, 349n50, 366n82
Brunel, Édouard, 198
Brussel, Robert, 321, 373n14, 373n15, 374n19, 378n62, 474n56
Bulla, Émile, 41

Busoni, Ferrucio, 206, 223, 269, 306
Busser, Henri, 81, 92, 172, 180–81, 184–87, 191, 219, 240, 255, 285, 289, 303, 315, 330, 501n40, 501n42
Bussy, Clémentine de. *See* Debussy, Clémentine

Cabat, Louis, 58
Caccini, Giulio, 243
Caillard, Charles Francis, 257, 459n55
Cain, Georges, 253
Callias, Nina de, 10, 346n46, 377n53
Calvé, Emma, 390n22
Calvocoressi, Michel-Dimitri, 227, 237–38, 316, 430n18, 431n26, 436n24, 460n11
Campanini, Cleofonte, 243, 253–54
Campbell, Mrs. Patrick, 440n83
Canudo, Ricciotto, 300
Caplet, André, 13, 240, 245, 255–56, 258, 260–62, 266–67, 269–70, 276–77, 280–82, 289, 293, 295, 300–301, 335, 341nn1–2, 359n66, 403n54, 460n7, 460n13, 482n2, 486n63, 486n65, 501n42
Cardonnel, Louis Le. *See* Le Cardonnel, Louis
Caristie-Martel, Mme, 212
Carnegie, Andrew, 105
Carnot, Marie François Sadi, 104
Carolus-Duran, 26
Caron, Rose, 52–53, 55, 109, 373n11
Carraud, Gaston, 167, 257, 261, 279, 296, 339, 447n69
Carré, Albert, 149, 163, 167, 172, 176, 180–87, 191, 210, 224, 231, 292, 450n4, 451n33
Carré, Marguerite, 233, 275, 293, 436n17, 494n85
Carrier-Belleuse, Octavie, 232, 249
Carrière, Eugène, 120, 140, 220
Carriès, Jean, 80, 89
Caruso, Enrico, 243
Casella, Alfredo, 259, 285, 296, 322, 493n79, 498n78
Castro, Guilhen de, 87

Cerutti, Jean, 7
Cevruti, Mme, 289
Chabrier, Emmanuel, 64, 76, 79, 83, 88, 108, 118–19, 134, 140, 146, 172, 179, 206, 225, 243, 261, 280, 303, 389n5
Chadeigne, Marcel, 224, 245, 277, 451n18
Chaigneau, Thérèse, 331, 502n57
Chaliapin, Feodor, 246, 254
Chansarel, René, 25, 52–53, 75, 77, 81–82, 85–86, 88, 93
Chantavoine, Jean, 223, 227, 261
Charlot, André, 315, 320
Charpentier, Alexandre, 200, 244, 284
Charpentier, Gustave, 72, 99, 163–64, 180–81, 215, 292, 356n34, 362n27, 394n46
Chat Noir, 80, 92–93, 100, 151, 457n26
Chausson, Ernest, 31, 74, 77, 80–81, 83, 85–86, 91, 93, 107–19, 121–27, 139–42, 144, 148, 155, 160, 162, 172, 196–97, 294, 388n103, 405n20, 429n130, 448n91, 449n93
Chénier, André, 125, 324
Chennevière, Daniel, 305, 307
Chevillard, Camille, 21, 77, 155, 164, 166, 168–69, 172, 193, 206, 223, 226–27, 240, 242, 257, 259, 269, 282, 295, 324, 495n21
Choisnel, Gaston, 85, 226, 320, 490n16
Chopin, Frédéric, 9, 15–17, 25, 49, 53, 141, 173, 225, 259, 263, 320–23, 334, 351n66, 503n77
Choudens, 86, 95, 200, 504n95
Cinti-Damoreau, Laure, 35
Clark, Charles William, 275
Clark, Alfred, 208
Claudel, Camille, 96, 120
Claudel, Paul, 96, 261
Clément, Edmond, 321
Clermont-Tonnere, Marquise de, 334
Clèves, Paul, 53
Coates, Albert, 317
Cocteau, Jean, 102, 299, 332, 427n90
Cohen, Gustave, 274
Cohen, Jules, 17

Colette, Gabrielle Sidonie, 132, 155, 167, 175, 381n7, 404n12
Collin, Raphaël, 80
Colonne, Édouard, 31, 73, 109, 126–27, 132–33, 138, 164, 189, 193, 205, 223, 235–36, 241, 315, 372n74, 438n52
Colonne, Mme Eugénie, 212, 215, 235
Combarieu, Jules, 195, 429n1
Concerts Colonne, 129, 133, 145, 206, 213, 219, 252, 260, 271, 291, 296, 314–15, 321, 324–25, 358n58, 412n2, 420n66, 429n133, 430n20, 436n17, 443n112, 452n53, 456n4, 456nn8–9
Concerts Durand, 260, 285, 323, 447nn71–72
Concerts Lamoureux, 69, 77, 94, 98, 112, 164, 166, 168, 206, 226, 291, 321, 324–25, 420n66, 429n126, 446n50
Concerts Sechiari, 252, 271, 275, 336
Concordia, 47–49, 54, 57, 64, 196
Cooper, Emil, 305
Copeland, George, 259
Coppola, Piero, 248
Coquard, Arthur, 181, 257
Cor, Raphaël, 256–57
Corneau, André, 171
Corneille, Pierre, 87
Coronio, Nicolas, 170, 183, 219, 320, 427n106
Cortot, Alfred, 79, 181, 320, 381n12
Couperin, François, 176, 282, 294, 323
Courty, Gaston, 328
Crépel, Dr., 302, 325
Crevel, M., 302
Croche, Monsieur, 2, 52, 152, 169, 172–74, 177, 192–93, 225, 311, 490n25
Croiza, Claire, 321, 331–32
Cros, Charles, 40, 80, 172, 345n42
Cuignache, Georges, 34, 37
Cumont, M. de, 16
Curnonsky, 142, 168, 186, 191, 200, 222, 239, 381n7, 398n44
Cystria, Princesse de, 208, 305

Dalcroze, Émile-Jaques, 299, 332
Dallier, Henri, 35
Halliès, Jeanne, 331, 502n58
Daly, William H., 244
Damrosch, Walter, 105
Danbé, Jules, 198
Dandelot, Arthur, 166, 179, 333, 413n33, 416n71, 416n76
Danhauser, Adolphe, 16
Danilchenko, Peter, 32–33
D'Annunzio, Gabriele, 273–76, 278–80, 294–96, 310, 317, 400n6, 480n44
Dansaert, Jean-Baptiste Florimond, 144, 410n52
Dansaert, Régine, 152, 341n5, 405n30, 410n52
Darcours, Charles, 53, 108, 129, 391n29
Dargomyzhsky, Alexander, 83
Das, Marguerite, 235
Daudet, Léon, 14, 142
Daudet, Lucien, 121
David, Félicien, 11
Debay, Victor, 198, 209, 381n2
Debussy, Adèle, 4–5, 343n17, 343n21, 347n11, 383n41, 469n72
Debussy, Alfred, 6, 72, 469n72
Debussy, Claude-Alexandre, 3
Debussy, Claude-Emma (Chouchou), 229
Debussy, Clémentine, 4–6, 72
Debussy, Emma Bardac. See Bardac, Emma
Debussy, Emmanuel, 5–6, 469n72
Debussy, Eugène, 22
Debussy, Jules-Alexandre, 5
Debussy, Lilly. See Texier, Lilly
Debussy, Manuel-Achille, 3–11, 16, 22, 25, 72, 79, 231
Debussy, Pierre, 3
Debussy, Victorine. See Manoury, Victorine
Degas, Edgar, 90, 94, 116, 173, 369n34
Deglane, Henri, 61, 65
Deguingand, Mme, 95
Delaborde, Henri, 56

SUBJECT INDEX 515

Delacroix, Auguste, 232, 245, 446n44, 449n100
Delacroix, Eugène, 15, 89
Delage, Maurice, 189, 466n26
Delaquerrière, Louis, 191, 428n109
Delaunois, Raymonde, 462n56
Delhaye, Angéline, 120
Delibes, Léo, 29, 33, 35, 50–51, 53, 76, 380n92
Delmet, Paul, 92
Demellier, Hélène, 235
Denis, Maurice, 103, 116, 120, 127, 140, 171, 177, 249
Dépaquit, Jules, 102
Depecker, Rose, 88
Derain, André, 249
Desboutin, Marcellin, 101, 310
Desjardins, Abel, 160, 216, 218, 325
Destefani, César, 17
Destranges, Étienne, 83, 115, 119
Diaghilev, Sergei, 246, 253–54, 266, 271, 289–90, 298–99, 306, 332–33, 402n41
Dickens, Charles, 297
Diémer, Louis-Joseph, 15, 20
Dietschy, Marcel, 2, 59, 63, 342n5, 344n28, 345n37, 346n43, 358n45, 363n44, 363n45, 369n41, 373n5, 374n25, 393n38, 404n17, 405nn19–20, 409n46, 413n30, 422n26, 441n86, 442n106, 489n10
Dillard, Marius, 40
d'Indy, Vincent, 27, 75, 77, 83–84, 86, 97, 108–9, 114, 117, 120, 126–27, 144, 148–49, 172, 175–77, 187, 189, 206–7, 211, 223, 226, 231, 238, 248, 280, 291–92, 296, 298, 308, 313, 320, 323, 365n78, 378n62, 389n3, 494n4, 500n28
Domergue, Charles, 244, 271, 276, 320
Donizetti, Gaetano, 4, 18, 367n15
Donnay, Maurice, 93, 137, 386n68
Doret, Gustave, 128, 151, 313–14
Dorian, Tola, 146–47, 394n43
d'Orléans, Charles. *See* Orléans, Charles d'

Dreyfus Affair, 171, 345n35
Dreyfus González, Édouard, 164
Dron, Marthe, 238
Dubois, Théodore, 35, 38, 42, 51, 129, 165, 292, 354n9, 361n17
Dufranne, Hector, 181, 224, 233, 243, 436n17
Dujardin, Édouard, 72–73, 75, 90, 109, 152, 374n20
Dukas, Paul, 73–74, 77, 81–84, 93, 108, 113–14, 116–17, 125–26, 141, 152, 167, 170, 172–73, 177, 187–88, 222, 227, 233, 245–46, 257, 264, 268, 280, 289, 292, 298, 320–21, 324–25, 327, 329–30, 333
Dumas *fils*, Alexandre, 67, 89, 351n68
Dumesnil, Maurice, 217, 229, 259, 468n50, 495n10
Dumesnil, Suzanne, 193
Duncan, Isadora, 269
Duparc, Henri, 330, 500n34
Dupin, Étienne, 74–75, 83, 85, 89–90, 93, 111, 124, 144–45
Dupont, Gabriel, 257
Dupont, Gaby, 35, 87, 89, 104, 111, 115, 121–22, 125, 130, 132–33, 142–44, 154–57, 302
Dupont, Paul, 5–6, 8, 103, 116, 197
Dupuis, Sylvain, 235
Durand, Auguste, 81
Durand, Émile, 23–25, 29, 34, 39, 50, 52, 139
Durand, Jacques, 6, 52–53, 81–82, 84–86, 125, 180, 201, 203, 205, 216–17, 221–23, 226, 229–30, 231–35, 238–39, 242–43, 247, 251, 254, 259, 264–67, 269, 271, 280–81, 283, 286, 290–92, 295, 297, 302–3, 305, 309–10, 315, 317, 319, 320–23, 325, 328, 330–32, 335, 337, 423n37, 481n70
Duvernoy, Alphonse, 14, 21–22

Elgar, Edward, 280, 334
Emmanuel, Maurice, 23, 29, 50–51, 84, 163, 349n50, 357n40, 371n64, 444n22, 469n72

Enesco Quartet, 208
Engel, Émile, 209, 224, 252, 272, 324, 377n53, 458n43, 473n23
Erlanger, Camille, 76, 137, 187, 319, 428n117
Ernst, Alfred, 73, 134, 171, 489n6
Ernst, Heinrich Wilhelm, 40
Escudier, Mme Philippe, 118, 141
Espouy, Hector d', 68
Etlin, Henri, 276
Evans, C. Warwick, 327
Evans, Edwin, 253, 459n53

Falla, Manuel de, 248, 264, 280, 297, 316, 331
Fanelli, Ernest, 286, 492n53, 492n57
Fantin-Latour, Henri, 353n103, 375n35
Fargue, Léon-Paul, 132, 186, 188, 439n60
Farrère, Claude, 231
Faure, Jean-Baptiste, 35
Fauré, Gabriel, 71, 75, 80, 86, 108, 115, 117–19, 121, 126, 149, 171, 189, 197, 202, 209, 213–14, 220, 229, 238, 251, 256, 262, 264, 285, 296, 298, 305, 308, 320–22, 325, 331, 333, 346n4, 434n86, 434n1, 499n4
Féart, Rose, 269–70, 502n55, 502nn57–58
Fénéon, Félix, 175, 389n10
Ferrary, Désiré Maurice, 68
Ferronnière, Octavie de la. *See* Debussy, Clémentine
Feuillet, Octave, 139
Feure, Georges de, 102, 310, 315
Février, Henry, 274, 295
Feydeau, Georges, 74
Fissot, Alexis-Henry, 17, 20–22, 24
Fitelberg, Grzegorz, 324
Flaubert, Gustave, 26, 64, 97, 442n111
Flers, Robert de, 187
Fleury, Louis, 18, 304, 400n4
Flon, Philippe, 245

Floupette, Adoré, 65, 92
Fokine, Michel, 277
Fontaine, Arthur, 125, 127, 140–41, 144, 160–61, 196, 222, 319
Fontaine, Mme Lucien, 141
Fontaine, Lucien, 141, 160, 196, 216
Fontaine, Mme Arthur, 141, 144
Foottit, 141
Forain, Jean-Louis, 142, 151
Fort, Paul, 94, 100, 146
Fourrier, Camille, 209, 224, 229, 232, 381n2
Franck, César, 33–34, 73–74, 77, 81, 86, 117, 127–28, 225–26, 296, 330, 431n23, 466n27, 476n2
Frères en art, 2, 152, 377n52
Fromont, Eugène, 127, 158, 181, 191, 196, 200–202, 221, 425n63, 468n47
Fuchs, Edmond, 47, 57, 64, 414n41
Fuchs, Henriette, 47–49, 54, 57–58, 196, 359n63, 364n50, 364n61, 370n46, 375n33, 414n41
Fugère, Lucien, 181
Fuller, Loïe, 298, 315

Gandillot, Léon, 74
Garban, Lucien, 171, 179, 197, 214
Gard, Roger Martin du. *See* Martin du Gard, Roger
Garden, Mary, 137, 181–83, 190, 194, 196, 208, 210, 219–20, 243, 246, 415n62, 440n78, 440n83, 452n48
Gardet, Joseph-Antoine, 68
Gasco, Alberto, 312, 469n71, 479n34
Gatti-Casazza, Giulio, 247
Gauguin, Paul, 5, 80, 94, 120, 261
Gauthier-Villars, Henri. *See* Willy
Gautier, Judith, 344n30, 376n38
Gautier, Théophile, 36, 45, 138, 264
Gedalge, André, 202, 214, 296
Gémier, Firmin, 333
George, Georges, 315
Gevaert, François-Auguste, 87, 120
Ghasne, 249
Gheusi, Pierre-Barthélemy, 310, 321, 494n85

Gide, André, 91, 125, 131, 138, 140, 150, 171, 279, 292, 299, 389n110, 401n19, 419nn42–43
Gilson, Paul, 227, 235
Ginisty, Paul, 196
Girod, Mme Étienne, 74, 95, 196
Glazunov, Alexander, 83, 305
Glinka, Mikhail, 33, 37, 83
Gluck, Christoph Willibald, 49, 176–77
Godard, Benjamin, 33, 77
Godard-Decrais, Mme Maurice, 141, 398n33, 424n49, 429n130
Godet, Robert, 75, 77, 79–80, 82–84, 86, 94, 96–97, 100, 102, 108, 112–13, 138, 161, 182, 184, 186, 196, 222, 247, 258, 282, 284, 292, 297, 316–17, 321, 330, 336, 341n3, 383n30, 385n65, 427n92, 441n84, 442n101, 470n92, 472n17, 485n44, 485n57, 490n15, 491n51, 496n45, 497n49, 497n63, 497n66, 497n71, 498n1, 499n16, 501n44, 502n65
Goethe, Johann Wolfgang von, 80, 312
Goncourt, Edmond de, 78, 90, 93, 96, 377n53, 379n84
González, Édouard Dreyfus. *See* Dreyfus González, Édouard
Gounod, Charles, 34, 42–43, 46–49, 53, 55, 60, 77, 82, 87, 180, 387n82, 396n4, 438n54
Goya, Francisco de, 323
Gramont, Elisabeth de. *See* Clermont-Tonnere, Marquise de
Granados, Enrique, 328, 332, 466n29
Grand, Ernest Le. *See* Le Grand, Ernest
Grand-Jany, Anatole-Léon, 20
Greffulhe, Countess, 71, 126
Gregh, Fernand, 189, 195
Gregor, Hans, 280
Grévy, Jules, 26
Grieg, Edvard, 120, 128, 209–10, 310–11, 370n46
Groux, Henry de, 102, 182, 258, 282
Grovlez, Gabriel, 224, 257, 282
Gueritte, Tony Jules, 251

Gui, Vittorio, 280, 458n37, 462n37
Guiard, Mme Georges, 331
Guidé, Guillaume, 234
Guilbert, Yvette, 137, 377n53, 436n17
Guilmant, Alexandre, 189, 466n26
Guinand, Édouard, 52
Guiraud, Ernest, 17, 22, 27, 33, 37, 39, 42, 44–46, 50–53, 55, 64–65, 75, 81, 83–84, 88, 92, 100, 128, 354n9, 403n54
Guitry, Lucien, 22

Habans, Jean-Paul. *See* Paulus
Hahn, Reynaldo, 118, 193, 257, 279, 286, 293, 377n53, 455n96
Halévy, Fromental, 18
Halévy, Geneviève, 22
Hall, Élise, 200
Halvorsen, Johan, 209
Hamelle, 95
Hartmann, Arthur, 265, 310–11, 504n82
Hartmann, Georges, 127–28, 132–33, 136, 138, 140, 145–49, 154–55, 158, 160, 162–64, 180–81, 190–91, 383n41, 407n2, 407n7, 448n90
Hawkins, Louis Welden, 78, 80
Haydn, Franz Joseph, 18–19, 226, 463n70
Hayot Quartet, 165, 314
Hébert, Ernest, 60–66, 69, 71, 479n42
Hébert, Gabrielle, 59–66, 68, 70
Héler, A., 53, 364n68, 365n69, 365n81
Hellé, André, 297
Heller, Stephen, 20, 40, 49
Herbécourt, Jeanne d', 224
Heredia, José-Maria de, 138, 150, 157, 400n6
Heredia, Louise de, 157, 398n37
Herman, Émile, 198
Hermite, Tristan l', 177, 212, 475n68
Herold, André-Ferdinand, 4, 83, 85, 90–91, 93–94, 130, 135, 139, 171, 388n110
Herz, Henri, 20
Hettich, Amédée Louis. *See* Héler, A.

Heugel, Henri, 109, 351n69, 389n5, 392n16
Higgins, H. V., 253
Hillemacher, Lucien and Paul, 39
Hirsch, Charles-Henry, 134
Hobday, Mrs. Alfred, 327
Hochon, Louise, 64–66, 406n46
Hocquet, Vital, 92–93
Hokusai, Katsushika, 96, 227
Holmès, Augusta, 27
Honegger, Arthur, 175, 406n44, 430n15
Hottinguer, Mme Philippe. *See* Wustemberg, Nelly de
Hubay, Jenö, 263
Hüe, Georges, 83, 180, 187, 389n3
Hugo, Victor, 102, 125, 138–39, 345n36, 373n16
Huré, Jean, 97, 187, 224–25, 246, 437n32, 480n43
Huret, Jules, 97, 479n36
Huysmans, Joris-Karl, 67, 81, 179, 379n84
Hyspa, Vincent, 92

Ibsen, Henrik, 113, 153
Imbert, Hugues, 134, 164, 220, 423n46
Imperial Russian Musical Society, 305
Inghelbrecht, Désiré-Émile, 188, 277, 289, 298, 301, 303, 319, 321, 328, 487n85, 491n42, 497n67, 500n32, 504n80
Ingres, Jean-Auguste-Dominique, 249, 370n52
Injalbert, Jean Antoine, 80
Institut de France, 11, 35, 46, 53, 55–56, 68, 75–76, 171, 256, 292, 317, 326, 338
Isle-Adam, Villiers de l'. *See* Villiers de l'Isle-Adam
Isnardon, Jacques, 322

Jaëll, Alfred, 22
Jamet, Pierre, 501n55
Jammes, Francis, 140, 161
Jarecki, Sigismond, 501n55, 502n58
Jarry, Alfred, 132, 503n71

Jean-Aubry, Georges, 28, 189, 240, 251, 300, 375n35, 379n76, 385n65, 386n69, 391n34, 395n55, 398n27, 457n24
Jeannin, Paul, 39
Jéhin, Léon, 148, 189, 198
Jemain, Joseph, 198, 296, 226n66, 492n54
Jimenez, José, 22, 26
Joachim, Joseph, 223
Joly, Charles, 379n86, 416n75
Jouy, Jules, 92
Jullien, Adolphe, 165, 261, 474n56
Jusseaume, Lucien, 181, 210, 317, 423n37

Kaiser, Henri-Charles, 29, 52
Kajanus, Robert, 280
Karatygin, Viacheslav Gavrilovich, 324
Karsavina, Tamara, 254, 298–99
Kelly, Edmond, 72
Khan, Inayat, 294, 482n7, 486n76
Kipling, Rudyard, 297
Kleeberg-Samuel, Clotilde, 208
Klingsor, Tristan, 214
Kodály, Zoltan, 262, 270, 316
Koechlin, Charles, 128, 189, 213–14, 261–62, 310, 315, 325, 406n51, 480n43, 493n69
Koussevitsky, Serge, 305–7
Krauss, Gabrielle, 46, 52, 55
Kufferath, Maurice, 120, 234–35, 315

La Laurencie, Lionel de, 209, 220, 434n85
Labatut, Jean, 60
Lacerda, Francisco de, 212, 231, 248–49
Lacroix, Eugène, 225
Laforgue, Jules, 79, 97, 153, 217, 327, 440n71
Lalo, Édouard, 39, 127, 141, 166, 181, 187, 226, 303
Lalo, Pierre, 166, 169, 173, 179, 188, 226, 233, 236–37, 245–46, 261, 279, 296, 427n91, 460n18, 461n19, 481n69

SUBJECT INDEX 519

Laloy, Louis, 7, 9, 21, 26, 28, 61, 94, 169, 177, 193, 195, 207–9, 215, 221–22, 225, 229, 231–32, 234–36, 238, 240–42, 244, 253–54, 256–57, 259, 261–64, 266–67, 275, 278, 282, 284, 288, 291, 301, 309, 311, 322, 327, 336, 338–89, 346n44, 359n65, 393n38, 394n40, 395n63, 481n60, 481n69, 494n93
Lamartine, Alphonse de, 45
Lamette, André, 296, 460n17, 461n21, 464n2, 477n14
Lamotte, Antony, 224
Lamoureux, Charles, 75, 77, 128, 373n11
Lamy, Fernand, 301
Landormy, Paul, 176, 197–98, 263, 412n2, 492n57
Landry, Louis, 181, 184–85
Laparra, Raoul, 202
Lapuchin, Jean-Louis Frédéric, 80
Larochelle, Paul, 146–47
Lascoux, Antoine, 27, 83, 375n35
Laurencie, Lionel de La. *See* La Laurencie, Lionel de
Lavignac, Albert, 14–17, 19–20, 34, 83, 353n103
Lazzari, Sylvio, 148, 196
Le Cardonnel, Louis, 80
Le Grand, Ernest, 127–28
Le Sidaner, Henri, 220
Lebeau, Narcisse. *See* Hocquet, Vital
Lebey, André, 125, 130, 132, 186, 389n110, 404n13, 418n34
Leblanc, Georgette, 167, 182–83, 293, 458n45
Leclerq, Maurice, 248, 463n69
Lecocq, Charles, 292
Leconte de Lisle, 36, 40, 55, 198, 258
Legrand, Marthe, 208
Lejeune, Émile, 332
Lekeu, Guillaume, 119, 142, 378n2, 407n1
Lemoine, Léon-Lucien-Henri, 17
Lenepveu, Charles, 49, 363n38
Lenormand, René, 35, 296–97

Leoncavallo, Ruggero, 137, 192, 202
Leoni, 265
Lépine, Jean, 14, 160, 343n23
Lerolle, Christine, 140, 144
Lerolle, Henry, 110–11, 113–16, 119–27, 140, 144–45, 162, 200, 264
Lerolle, Yvonne, 140, 144, 396n65, 416n4
Leroux, Xavier, 45, 52–53, 59, 65, 69, 207, 292, 424n57, 505n108
Librairie de l'art indépendant, 90–92, 131, 417n22
Liebich, Franz, 263, 280
Liebich, Louise, 244
Limet, Henri-Edmond. *See* Bailly, Edmond
Lisle, Leconte de. *See* Leconte de Lisle
Liszt, Franz, 30, 48–49, 60, 64, 98, 208, 225, 335, 466n26
Lockspeiser, Edward, 152–53, 173, 227–28, 440n83
Loewenstein, Marguerite, 144
Loewenstein, Régina, 144
Lombard, Henri-Édouard, 68
Long, Marguerite, 334
Longy, Georges, 200
Lorin, Georges, 79
Lorrain, Jean, 210, 258
Louÿs, Pierre, 76, 91, 93–95, 98, 104, 113, 115, 121, 123, 125, 129–40, 142–43, 150–52, 154–55, 157–58, 160–61, 164–68, 170–72, 174, 180, 186, 188, 191, 203–4, 207, 211, 215, 219, 231, 233, 258, 311, 315, 325, 379n88, 383n41, 406n35, 466n32
Löwe, Ferdinand, 269, 470n86
Lucca, Pauline, 44
Lugné-Poe, Aurélien-Marie, 113–14, 146–48, 210, 381n7, 386n71, 390nn11–12, 503n71
Luigini, Alexandre, 224, 231
Luquin Quartet, 224
Lyon, Gustave, 212
Lyre et palette society, 332

Mac-Nab, Maurice, 385n64

Maeterlinck, Maurice, 97, 111, 113–15, 146–47, 149, 167, 182–85, 221, 234, 248, 274, 293, 331, 334, 386n71, 440n83
Magnard, Albéric, 109, 117, 119, 126, 220
Maguenat, Alfred, 317
Mahler, Alma, 264
Mahler, Gustav, 262, 264, 280
Malherbe, Charles, 226, 264, 283, 429n131
Mallarmé, Stéphane, 50, 72–73, 77, 80, 85–87, 89–91, 93–97, 103–4, 113, 115–16, 119–20, 129–30, 134, 138, 150–53, 244, 303, 314, 346n48, 479n33, 499n10
Manet, Édouard, 68, 89, 345n42
Mangeot, Auguste, 199, 209, 262–63, 296, 423n46, 435n2, 450n13, 458n45, 474n42, 492n53, 492nn57–58, 492n67
Manoury, Victorine, 4–8, 16, 25
Manouvrier, Albert, 331
Mansart, M., 19, 349n42
Manuel, Roland. *See* Roland-Manuel
Marcoux, Vanni, 253, 293, 317
Marie, Gabriel, 108, 208
Marmontel, Antoine, 14–26, 29–30, 33, 50–51, 53, 66, 80
Marnold, Jean, 169, 198, 208, 210, 225, 227, 245, 261, 291, 425n65, 454n73, 466nn29–30
Marot, Blanche, 154, 164–65
Marquet, Georges-Eugène, 42
Martenot, Raphaël, 327
Martin du Gard, Roger, 171, 213
Marty, Georges, 24, 33, 58, 65, 76, 99, 207, 229
Marvy, Luc, 285, 456nn8–9, 464n2, 465n8
Mascheroni, Edoardo, 59
Masselon, Bernard, 317
Massenet, Jules, 17, 20, 28, 31–33, 39, 52–53, 73–74, 76–77, 87, 107, 118, 125, 127–29, 131, 136, 167, 175–77, 180, 184–85, 187, 189, 202, 212, 308

Mathias, Georges, 22
Mathilde, Princess, 56–57, 61
Matisse, Henri, 249, 332
Mauclair, Camille, 94, 113, 125, 146–47, 200, 203, 220, 225, 245, 257, 296, 395n56, 412n4, 443n113, 466n29
Maurat, Edmond, 188
Maurras, Charles, 177
Maus, Octave, 117, 120–21, 388n106, 448n80
Mauté de Fleurville, Antoinette-Flore, 9–11, 15
Mauvernay, Mme, 198
Meck, Alexander von, 38, 43
Meck, Julia von, 30, 39
Meck, Karl von, 30
Meck, Nadezhda von, 28, 30–33, 37–39, 43–44, 47, 270, 306, 350n58
Meck, Nicolas von, 38–39
Meck, Sonia von, 39, 306
Meck, Vladimir von, 30
Meissonier, Jean-Louis-Ernest, 18
Mel-Bonis, Mélanie. *See* Bonis, Mélanie
Melchissédec, Pierre Léon, 322
Mélicourt-Lefebvre, Armand Constant, 71, 369n34
Mellor, Mme Paul Alexandre, 325
Meltzer, Charles Henry, 248, 461n22
Mendelssohn, Felix, 47, 49, 70, 360n76
Mendès, Catulle, 78–79, 86–88, 94–96, 100, 103, 108–9, 113–14, 187, 193, 206, 344n30
Mendès, Léontine, 18–19, 22
Mengelberg, Willem, 313
Mercier, Henri, 79, 89
Merrill, Stuart, 132, 177
Meshcherskaya, Princess. *See* Dorian, Tola
Messager, André, 75, 88, 118, 127, 149, 163, 180–82, 184–87, 190–91, 199–200, 202–4, 208, 220, 223–24, 238, 243, 286, 322, 455n96, 481n69
Meuris, Mlle, 113
Michelet, Victor-Émile, 91–92, 196
Milhaud, Darius, 331
Milton, Mlle, 170

SUBJECT INDEX   521

Mimart, Prosper, 275
Mirbeau, Octave, 97, 186
Missa, Edmond, 28, 42, 45, 177, 193
Mithouard, Adrien, 177
Molinari, Bernardino, 312, 321, 334, 492n62, 495n14, 496n44
Monet, Claude, 153, 448n82
Montesquiou, Robert de, 274–75, 278, 347n12, 377n59, 383n32, 406n46
Monteux, Pierre, 271, 298, 300
Moréas, Jean, 67, 73, 80, 177
Moreau, Émile, 45
Moreau, Gustave, 138, 210
Moreau-Sainti, Victorine, 34–36, 40, 49, 95
Moreno, Henri. *See* Heugel, Henri
Moreno, Marguerite, 212
Morice, Charles, 67, 94, 285–86, 309–10, 322
Morrell, Lady Ottoline, 289
Mortier, Jane, 263
Moscheles, Ignaz, 11, 14
Motte Fouqué, Friedrich de la, 297
Mottl, Felix, 75, 243, 257
Mounet-Sully, 70, 135
Mourey, Gabriel, 79, 97, 210, 239–40, 250, 252–53, 304, 425n59, 487nn87–89
Moyse, Emma. *See* Bardac, Emma
Mozart, Wolfgang Amadeus, 49, 61, 226, 237, 250
Muratet, Antoine, 46
Musset, Alfred de, 28, 45, 90
Mussorgsky, Modest, 79, 110, 112–13, 172, 238, 286, 298, 306, 334, 498n77

Nadar, 258
Natanson brothers, 125, 171
Naudé, Henri, 60
Neitzel, Otto, 243
Nijinsky, Vaslav, 254, 286–87, 289–90, 298–99
Nin, Joaquin, 243, 334

Oberlé, Clémence, 224
Ochsé, Fernand, 298

Offenbach, Jacques, 18, 68, 138, 142, 324
Offoël, Jacques d', 193–94, 229, 416n71, 416n77, 430n17, 446n44
O'Kelly, Henri-Joseph, 20, 352n83
Orléans, Charles d', 177, 212, 384n48, 475n68
Orlowska, Countess, 331
Osiris, Daniel Iffla, 230, 321
Ottenheimer, Paul, 457n16

Pachulsky, Ladislas, 32, 37
Paladilhe, Émile, 17, 361n17
Palestrina, Giovanni Pierluigi da, 49, 73, 94, 100–101, 276, 279
Panthès, Marie, 327
Parent Quartet, 197, 224, 237, 271, 435n5, 435n13
Pasdeloup, Jules, 27, 73, 271, 372n74
Passama, Jeanne, 193
Passérieu, François-Henri-Alexandre, 28, 354n4
Paulet, Gabriel, 301
Paulus, 188
Péladan, Joséphin, 75, 101–2, 387n82
Péladan, Sâr. *See* Péladan, Joséphin
Pelouze, Marguerite, 26–27, 47, 83
Pennequin, M., 198
Père-Lachaise, 90, 338
Périer, Jean, 172, 181, 186, 188, 191, 193, 224, 232, 243, 246, 275–76, 293, 321, 436n17
Pessard, Émile, 28, 359n64, 382n18
Peter, Alice, 144, 196, 341n5, 407n15, 410n52
Peter, Michel, 74, 81
Peter, René, 66, 74, 140, 142–44, 152, 156, 180, 183, 186, 191, 219, 222, 341n5, 342n4, 370n52, 383n31, 410n52, 429n1
Petit, Armand, 232
Pfitzner, Hans, 209
Philipp, Isidore, 134, 270, 351n66
Pierné, Gabriel, 14, 17, 21–22, 24, 28, 59, 65, 69, 72, 88, 99, 181, 206, 260,

264, 270, 280, 282, 295, 314–15, 321, 337, 360n2, 439n55, 455n96, 481n69
Pierret, Auguste, 224
Piffaretti, Florentin, 39
Pinelli, Ettore, 59
Pinta, Henri, 68
Pitt, Percy, 190, 253
Planquette, Robert, 38
Planté, Francis, 15, 328, 335
Poe, Edgar Allan, 79, 90, 97, 148, 173, 179, 190, 204, 211–12, 228, 247–48, 253, 255–56, 273, 282, 312, 378n68, 402n48, 405n34, 415n64
Poiret, Paul, 315
Polignac, Princesse de, 118, 331–32
Poliziano, Angelo, 261
Ponchon, Raoul, 79
Poniatowski, André, 92–94, 104–5, 107, 389n4
Popelin, Claudius, 57, 61–62, 72
Popelin, Gustave, 61–62, 71, 90
Pougy, Liane de, 228
Poujaud, Paul, 75, 83, 127, 182, 187, 329, 353n105
Poulet, Gaston, 332, 335, 502n57
Pourtalès, Mélanie de, 68
Pratella, Francesco, 295
Primoli, Giuseppe (Gégé), 56–57, 60–62, 65, 374n20
Prix de Rome, 31, 42–45, 53–54, 56–57, 59, 62, 66, 72, 74–75, 78–79, 84, 88, 93, 99, 109, 171, 173, 202, 207, 240, 251, 368n21, 370n46, 371n64, 372nn65–66, 372n68, 372n70, 420n67, 423n36
Prokofiev, Sergei, 305–6, 498n77
Proust, Marcel, 22, 56, 80, 118, 142, 278, 293, 370n52, 397n24, 401n19, 501n51
Prunières, Henry, 342n9, 361n20, 362n30, 366n1, 367n11, 381n5, 442n101, 493n72, 496n30, 501n50
Puccini, Giacomo, 233, 280, 490n17, 493n79
Pugno, Raoul, 109, 145, 351n66

Quillard, Pierre, 91, 130, 171

Rabaud, Henri, 137, 189, 365n74
Rabeau, Eugène-Ferdinand, 17
Rackham, Arthur, 297
Radics, 270
Rameau, Jean-Philippe, 176–78, 201, 207, 231, 245, 276, 294, 321, 337, 387n73, 471n1
Raunay, Jeanne, 191, 224, 381n2, 466n26
Ravel, Maurice, 155, 171, 179, 189, 197, 202, 209, 213–14, 224, 237–38, 245, 247, 262, 286, 296, 300, 303, 308, 316, 332, 335, 402n41, 425n71, 434n80, 434nn86–87, 464n3, 498n77
Read, General Meredith, 95
Redon, Gaston, 372n66
Redon, Odilon, 59, 64, 68, 91, 94, 108, 120, 140, 179, 210, 293
Régnier, Henri de, 14, 91, 94, 103, 109, 113–15, 125, 130, 171, 186, 194, 388n110, 411n73, 418n34
Remacle, Adrien, 309–10
Renard, Jules, 96, 188, 376n47
Renaud, Armand, 42
René, Charles, 45–46, 52–53, 57, 72, 99
Renoir, Pierre-Auguste, 116, 120
Respighi, Ottorino, 334, 493n79
Réty, Charles, 11, 53, 129
Reuter, Rudolph E., 259
Reyer, Ernest, 46, 51, 53, 69, 131, 211, 251, 354n9, 443n111
Rhené-Baton, 225, 265, 303, 464n3
Richter, Hans, 44, 75, 199
Rigaux, Lucien, 191, 193
Rimbaud, Arthur, 11, 79, 439n68
Rimsky-Korsakov, Nicolai, 83, 155, 223, 234, 254, 286, 298, 305, 393n27, 452n47
Rioton, Marthe, 181
Risler, Édouard, 119, 172, 209, 285, 414n58, 438n47
Ritter, Théodore, 20, 363n44
Rivière, Henri, 92

Rivière, Jacques, 233, 262, 463n58
Robert, Julia, 108, 146, 151, 429n130
Robert, Paul, 93, 125, 142, 151, 220
Rochefort, Henry de, 9
Rochefoucauld, Antoine de la, 101
Rodenbach, Georges, 94
Rodin, Auguste, 96, 153, 287, 443n111, 505n105
Roger, Thérèse, 108, 119–22, 124, 133, 172, 208, 429n130
Roger-Ducasse, Jean, 213, 245, 262, 274, 280, 331, 337, 355n18, 432n45, 433n59, 451n18
Roland-Manuel, 300, 303, 433n61, 476n80, 492n56
Rollan-Mauger, Mme, 327, 499n10
Rolland, Romain, 97, 234, 237, 257, 264, 365n71, 368n30, 419n58, 455n99
Rollinat, Maurice, 79–80, 153, 385n61
Romilly, Madame Gerard de. *See* Worms de Romilly, Mlle
Ronsin, Eugène, 317, 423n37
Ropartz, Guy, 83, 117, 119, 154, 320, 399n46
Rops, Félicien, 91
Rose+Croix, 101–2
Rosoor, Louis, 330
Rossetti, Dante Gabriel, 72–73, 75, 97, 137–38, 244, 414n34
Rossini, Gioachino, 18, 49
Rostand, Alexis, 66, 68
Rouart, Mme Eugène. *See* Lerolle, Yvonne
Rouault, Georges, 249
Rouché, Jacques, 271, 321, 337
Roustan, Alfred, 5
Rouvière, Marie de la, 208
Rubinstein, Anton, 30, 32, 49
Rubinstein, Ida, 175, 274, 277–78
Rubinstein, Nicolas, 31–32
Ruhlmann, Franz, 233
Rummel, Walter, 263, 294, 330–32, 334, 336, 483n8
Russell, Henry, 279, 281, 291, 302, 317
Russolo, Luigi, 295

Sailland, Maurice. *See* Curnonsky
Saint-Marceaux, Marguerite de, 80, 118–19, 121, 123, 166, 186, 208, 212, 265, 278, 368n30, 428n125, 429n130, 454n74, 458n41
Saint-Pol-Roux, 471n1
Saint-Saëns, Camille, 20, 49, 56, 66, 73, 77, 82, 84, 87, 112, 127–28, 137, 173, 177, 193, 212, 226, 231, 262, 264, 298, 308, 320, 323, 326, 334, 360n5, 367n15, 491n46
Sainte-Croix, Camille de, 80
Saléza, Luc Albert, 332
Salis, Rodolphe, 92
Samain, Albert, 76, 78, 146, 213, 373n16
Samary, M., 18–19
Samazeuilh, Gustave, 141, 179, 296, 424n49
Sarrazin, Gabriel, 76
Sassoferrato, Giovanni Battista Salvi de, 371n64
Satie, Erik, 92, 101–2, 111, 140, 151, 160, 166, 186, 189, 248, 276, 282, 286, 288, 298, 319, 321, 324, 332–33, 348n31, 351n66
Savard, Augustin, 68, 173, 375n28
Sayn-Wittgenstein, Princess, 60, 64
Schaeffner, André, 2, 113, 356n21
Schindler, Kurt, 289
Schmitt, Florent, 127–28, 171, 224–25, 262, 275, 292, 471n9
Schönberg, Arnold, 301, 316, 320, 422n28, 498n77
Schopenhauer, Arthur, 80
Schubert, Franz, 64, 172, 228, 264
Schumann, Robert, 22, 141, 173, 209, 259, 363n38, 363n44
Schwob, Marcel, 94, 132
Scilla, Princess, 60
Scott, Cyril, 265, 379n86
Scotti, Antonio, 190
Scriabin, Alexander, 307, 498n77
Sechiari Quartet, 208
Segalen, Victor, 10, 231, 233, 239–41, 244, 247, 250, 253, 259, 302, 309, 328, 343n22, 450n10

524 ❧ SUBJECT INDEX

Ségur, Anatole de, 42
Seidl, Anton, 104–5
Selva, Blanche, 208–9, 311, 320, 334, 426n89
Senart, Maurice, 320
Seroff, Victor, 358n45, 370n52, 387n91, 404n16, 405n20, 456n3
Servières, Georges, 85, 119, 197
Séverac, Déodat de, 172, 189, 209, 224–25, 247
Shakespeare, William, 65–66, 80, 97, 139, 192, 205, 211, 258, 372n76, 447n62, 503n71
Signorelli, Luca, 371n64
Siloti, Alexander I., 305, 488n115
Sinibaldi, Paul Jean Raphael, 74
Sivry, Charles-Erhard de, 9–10, 78–79, 92–93, 151, 344n30
Sizes, Eugène Gabriel, 322
Speyer, Edgar, 243, 301, 317
Steinlen, Théophile, 328, 437n31
Stevens, Alfred, 74, 89, 108, 142
Stevens, Catherine, 90, 108, 142, 144, 196
Stevens, Léopold, 89–90, 108, 142
Strauss, Richard, 178, 233–34, 244, 250, 254, 264, 266, 289, 306, 308, 319–20
Stravinsky, Igor, 228, 266, 287–89, 297–98, 300–301, 316, 323–24, 331, 333, 487n93
Suarès, André, 36, 53, 97, 453n66
Sulzbach, Mme Maurice, 115
Swedenborg, Emanuel, 91
Swinburne, Algernon Charles, 97, 146, 400n6
Symons, Arthur, 244, 422n28
Szántó, Theodor, 263

Tailhade, Laurent, 102
Taskin, Alexandre, 46, 52, 55
Tchaikovsky, Pyotr Ilyich, 30–33, 37–38, 43–44, 330
Ternusse, Aubert, 20, 51
Teste, Monsieur, 173–74
Texier, Lilly, 35, 153, 156–61, 165, 186, 190–91, 199–200, 202, 204–5,

214–23, 230, 248, 264, 302, 328, 383n41, 469n71
Teyte, Maggie, 244, 246, 263, 272, 285, 302, 306
Thaulow, Frits, 96, 200
Thibaud, Alphonse, 20–21
Thieberg, Maurice, 40
Thomas, Ambroise, 13, 16, 18, 22, 43, 49, 87
Tiersot, Julien, 14, 81, 387n82, 392n7, 505n113
Tinan, Jean de, 91, 118, 125, 130, 132, 142, 150, 275, 381n7, 389n110, 418n34
Tinan, Mme Gaston Pochet le Barbier de (Dolly), 259, 275, 441n90
Toché, Charles, 26–27
Tonerre, Firmin. See Gémier, Firmin
Toscanini, Arturo, 243, 280
Toulet, Paul-Jean, 168, 186, 191–92, 200, 205, 231–32, 242, 252, 266, 286, 289, 295, 334, 336–37, 381n7, 423n46, 454n82, 463n73, 476n82, 482n79
Toulouse-Lautrec, Henri de, 141
Trillat, Ennemond, 462n56
Turner, Joseph Mallord William, 199, 201, 227–28

Udine, Jean d', 166, 194, 208, 225, 227, 257, 332

Valéry, Paul, 125, 130–32, 150, 173–74, 186, 389n110
Vallas, Léon, 2, 59, 197, 245, 249, 342n3, 408n24, 442n101
Vallery-Radot, Pasteur, 327, 337, 398n35, 416n5, 434n77, 439n61
Vallette, Alfred, 133
Vallin, Ninon, 198, 301, 314–15, 321, 503n75
Van Dyck, Ernest, 52–53, 55, 75–76, 109, 382n19
Van Rees, Richard, 313
Varèse, Edgard, 248, 259, 269, 316, 321

Vasnier, Henri-A., 35, 43, 45, 50, 58–59, 61–65, 67, 71, 380nn97–99
Vasnier, Marguerite, 43, 45, 47, 71, 350n64, 368n33
Vasnier, Marie, 15, 18, 35–37, 39–41, 43–47, 49–50, 54, 56–58, 61–63, 65–66, 71–72, 95, 144, 153, 215, 217
Vaucaire, Maurice, 66, 74, 93, 463n73
Velázquez, Diego, 323
Verdi, Giuseppe, 35, 69, 193, 280, 317, 349n42
Verlaine, Mathilde, 9
Verlaine, Paul, 11, 40, 45–46, 56, 65, 79–81, 94–95, 97–98, 101, 150–51, 158, 171, 177, 196, 213, 224, 244, 256, 285–86, 309–10, 322, 344n34, 433n70, 450n14, 473n23, 485n60
Viardot, Paul, 198
Viardot, Pauline, 88
Vicaire, Bariel. *See* Floupette, Adoré
Vidal, Paul, 14, 22, 24–25, 27–28, 33–34, 37–39, 45–48, 50, 52, 54–55, 57–60, 64–66, 69, 86, 108, 126, 207, 245, 346n50, 361n13, 375n33
Viélé-Griffin, Francis, 91, 94, 103, 150, 177
Vieuille, Félix, 181, 224, 246, 436n17
Villiers de l'Isle Adam, 72, 78, 285
Villon, François, 276, 467n35, 475n68
Viñes, Ricardo, 155, 164, 166, 171, 179, 197, 200–201, 207–8, 218, 223–24, 232, 237–38, 240, 244–45, 252, 259, 264, 275, 284–85, 297, 301, 332, 334, 429n3
Vlaminck, Maurice de, 249
Vorska, Suzanne, 303
Vuillermoz, Émile, 167, 187–88, 225, 236, 245, 262, 277, 279, 287, 291, 299, 301, 304, 322, 409n42, 427n91, 439n64, 468n47, 487n85

Wagner, Cosima, 83
Wagner, Richard, 26–27, 34, 44, 50, 52, 59–60, 70, 73, 77–79, 84–85, 108–9, 114, 120, 131, 134, 138, 149, 164, 178, 181–82, 199, 225, 239, 248, 250, 256–57, 266, 271, 319–20, 370n46, 386n73, 392n35, 393n38, 426n74, 461n23, 489n6
Wagner, Siegfried, 258
Waldbauer Quartet, 270
Warnery, Edmond, 253
Watteau, Jean-Antoine, 201, 294, 438n51, 441n86
Weber, Carl Maria von, 24, 141, 186, 226, 329, 347n23, 349n44, 423n37
Whistler, James Abbott McNeill, 89, 94, 113, 127, 162, 237, 406n46
Widor, Charles-Marie, 47–48, 248, 317, 505n105
Wilder, Victor, 109
Willette, Adolphe, 79
Willy, 86, 98, 108, 117–18, 129, 132, 134, 167–68, 171, 175, 187–89, 213, 242, 397n10, 437n25
Wilson, Daniel, 26–27
Wilson, Marguerite, 26, 350n58
Witkowski, Georges-Martin, 198
Wittouck, Frantz, 315
Wolff, Auguste, 20
Wood, Henry, 244, 251
Woollett, Henry, 224
Worms de Romilly, Mlle, 140–41, 160, 186, 343n23, 415n61, 416n4, 432n44
Wurmser, Lucien, 164
Wurmser-Delcourt, Mme, 220
Wustemberg, Nelly de, 88

Ysaÿe, Eugène, 109–10, 115–17, 120, 125–26, 138, 142, 148–49, 162, 208, 214, 429n130
Ysaÿe Quartet, 116–17

Zágon, Géza Vilmos, 270
Zamoïska, Countess, 119
Zeitlin Quartet, 208
Zola, Émile, 101, 134

Eastman Studies in Music

Ralph P. Locke, Senior Editor
Eastman School of Music

Additional Titles of Interest

Berlioz: Scenes from the Life and Work
Edited by Peter Bloom

"Claude Debussy As I Knew Him" and Other Writings of Arthur Hartmann
Edited by Samuel Hsu, Sidney Grolnic, and Mark Peters
Foreword by David Grayson

Debussy's Letters to Inghelbrecht: The Story of a Musical Friendship
Annotated by Margaret G. Cobb
Translations by Richard Miller

French Music, Culture, and National Identity, 1870–1939
Edited by Barbara L. Kelly

Maurice Duruflé: The Man and His Music
James E. Frazier

Musical Encounters at the 1889 Paris World's Fair
Annegret Fauser

Pentatonicism from the Eighteenth Century to Debussy
Jeremy Day-O'Connell

The Poetic Debussy: A Collection of His Song Texts and Selected Letters
Edited by Margaret G. Cobb
Translations by Richard Miller

The Sea on Fire: Jean Barraqué
Paul Griffiths

Widor: A Life beyond the Toccata
John R. Near

A complete list of titles in the Eastman Studies in Music series
may be found on our website, www.urpress.com

François Lesure's "critical biography" of Claude Debussy (Fayard, 2003) is widely recognized by scholars as the most comprehensive and reliable account of that composer's life and career as well as of the artistic milieu in which he worked. This encyclopedic volume draws extensively on Debussy's complete correspondence (at that time unpublished), a painstaking tracking of contemporary reviews and comments in the press, and an examination of other primary documents—including private diaries—that had not been available to previous biographers. As such, Lesure's book presents a wealth of new information while debunking a number of myths that had developed over the years since the composer's death in 1918.

The present English translation and revised edition, by Debussy authority Marie Rolf, augments Lesure's numerous notes with several thousand new ones by Rolf, providing more precise information on crucial and sometimes contentious points. It also reflects Debussy scholarship that has appeared since 2003, updating Lesure's seminal work. Rolf's translation—the first ever—will make Lesure's findings accessible to scholars, musicians, and music lovers in English-speaking lands and around the world.

FRANÇOIS LESURE (1923–2001) was the director of the music division of the Bibliothèque nationale de France, professor of musicology at the Université libre de Bruxelles, and chair of musicology at the École pratique des Hautes Études.

MARIE ROLF is senior associate dean of graduate studies and professor of music theory at the Eastman School of Music and a member of the editorial board for the *Œuvres complètes de Claude Debussy*.

"This book is an outstanding event in Debussy scholarship and literature. François Lesure was at the center of international Debussy scholarship over several decades, devoting much of his career at the Bibliothèque nationale de France to collecting the material that lies at the core of this richly detailed biography. Marie Rolf has similarly dedicated the major part of a distinguished career to Debussy, having worked closely with François Lesure from the early 1980s on the *Œuvres complètes de Claude Debussy*. She is perfectly placed to have realized the present edited and updated English translation, making a wealth of vital information available in English for the first time."

—Roy Howat, Royal Academy of Music, London, and
Royal Conservatoire of Scotland

"In Marie Rolf's new English edition of François Lesure's classic biography, *Claude Debussy*, Anglophones will discover Debussy's personality, his large network of friends and collaborators, and his impassioned relationships with women, all animating a rich chronology of his compositional life. A beautifully written, fluid translation incorporating new sources and over two thousand new footnotes, it is a welcome contribution to the burgeoning interest in the composer."

—Jann Pasler, University of California–San Diego